www.wadsworth.com

wadsworth.com is the World Wide Web site for Wadsworth and is your direct source to dozens of online resources.

At *wadsworth.com* you can find out about supplements, demonstration software, and student resources. You can also send email to many of our authors and preview new publications and exciting new technologies.

wadsworth.com
Changing the way the world learns®

The Criminal Justice System

The Criminal Justice System

Politics and Policies

Eighth Edition

GEORGE F. COLE
University of Connecticut

MARC G. GERTZ
Florida State University

AMY BUNGER
Florida State University

WADSWORTH

™

THOMSON LEARNING

Australia • Canada • Mexico • Singapore • Spain • United Kingdom • United States

WADSWORTH
™
THOMSON LEARNING

Criminal Justice Editor: Shelley Murphy
Executive Editor, Criminal Justice: Sabra Horne
Assistant Editor: Dawn Mesa
Editorial Assistant: Lee McCracken
Marketing Manager: Jennifer Somerville
Marketing Assistant: Neena Chandra
Project Manager, Editorial Production:
  Erica Silverstein

Print/Media Buyer: Robert King
Permissions Editor: Joohee Lee
Copy Editor: Adrienne Armstrong
Cover Designer: Stephen Rapley
Cover Image: PhotoDisc
Text and Cover Printer: The Maple-Vail Book
  Manufacturing Group
Compositor: Buuji, Inc.

For more information about our products,
contact us at:
Thomson Learning Academic Resource Center
1-800-423-0563
For permission to use material from this text,
contact us by:
Phone: 1-800-730-2214
Fax: 1-800-730-2215
Web: http://www.thomsonrights.com

Wadsworth/Thomson Learning
10 Davis Drive
Belmont, CA 94002-3098
USA

Asia
Thomson Learning
60 Albert Street, #15-01
Albert Complex
Singapore 189969

Australia
Nelson Thomson Learning
102 Dodds Street
South Melbourne, Victoria 3205
Australia

Canada
Nelson Thomson Learning
1120 Birchmount Road
Toronto, Ontario M1K 5G4
Canada

Europe/Middle East/Africa
Thomson Learning
Berkshire House
168-173 High Holborn
London WC1V 7AA
United Kingdom

Latin America
Thomson Learning
Seneca, 53
Colonia Polanco
11560 Mexico D.F.
Mexico

Spain
Paraninfo Thomson Learning
Calle/Magallanes, 25
28015 Madrid, Spain

Library of Congress Cataloging-in-Publication Data
Cole, George F.
    The criminal justice system: politics and policies / George F. Cole, Marc G. Gertz,
Amy Bunger —8th ed.
    p. cm.
    ISBN 0-534-59472-7
    1. Criminal justice, Administration of—United States. I. Gertz, Marc G. II. Bunger,
Amy. III. Title.

KF9223 .C648 2001
364.973—dc21   2001045342

Contents

Preface

Since the first edition of *The Criminal Justice System: Politics and Policies* was published in 1972, there have been many changes in the American system of criminal justice. The links between law, politics, and public policy are increasingly obvious, particularly with the growth of media attention to crime. The public continues to express high levels of fear and worry about crime, reacting strongly to events like school shootings, irrespective of a declining crime rate. Citizens also rank crime as an important public problem, relative to other social problems. Politicians respond with "tough on crime" campaigns and legislation. Policy questions about the death penalty, community policing, sex offender registration, trying juveniles as adults, plea bargaining, mandatory sentencing, and the impact of race are enduring issues that are being addressed.

Scholarly thinking about crime and justice has changed over the past thirty years. In 1972 social scientists had very little understanding of the operations of the police, prosecution, defense, courts, and corrections. The heavy funding of criminal justice research since that time has enabled scholars to describe ongoing practices systematically, to use the tools of empirical methodologies, and to contribute to the formation of criminal justice policies. As a result, much of the conventional wisdom has been challenged. Research has also led to new theoretical perspectives, to interdisciplinary studies, and to an expanded research community, so that in addition to academic studies, investigations are conducted by members of government agencies, nonprofit organizations, and private research companies.

As editors of this book we are pleased that it has received such wide and continuing use in criminal justice, political science, and sociology courses. Because we are aware of the responsibility of maintaining a collection that is current, academically sound, and readable, we have included articles that reflect the developments noted above. We have written the introductory sections so that they are up to date and serve to integrate the individual articles; as a result, the book is more than an assemblage of readings. The changes in this edition were made to continue the emphasis that the criminal justice system can be understood as a relationship between politics and policy, as well as between citizen and state.

We wish to extend our gratitude to Jeremy Gordon, whose helpful insights, hard work, and dedication to the completion of this project were vitally important and greatly appreciated. Special thanks are also extended to Sabra Horne, executive editor, criminal justice, at Wadsworth, who continues to be an important source of encouragement.

George F. Cole
Marc G. Gertz
Amy Bunger

The Criminal Justice System

✪

PART I

Politics and the Administration of Justice

The close relationship between law, policy, and politics has been recognized since ancient times. Yet it has taken the social conflicts of the past quarter century to make us aware that the way criminal justice is allocated reflects the values of the individuals and groups that hold the power in the political system. Consider the changes over the past decade. Policies toward crime and justice, formulated in a more liberal political era, have changed along with the attitudes of the American public. Consequently, the government and legislators are reacting to what they think the public wants, and in effect have increased the power that the state has over individuals.

In a democracy such as the United States, a tension exists between the need (1) to maintain public order, (2) to ensure public safety, and (3) to protect such precious values as individual liberties, the rule of law, and democratic government. One might hope that citizens in the "land of the free" could live without having to devote great physical and psychological energies, let alone resources, to personal protection, but for many Americans the possibility of being victimized by criminals is ever present. When in 1973 the National Advisory Commission on Criminal Justice Standards and Goals set as a target the reduction of crime over the ensuing ten years, it stated that a time would come in the immediate future when:

- A couple can walk in the evening in their neighborhood without fear of assault and robbery.

- A family can go away for the weekend without fear of returning to a house ransacked by burglars.
- A woman can take a night job without fear of being raped on her way to or from work.
- Every citizen can live without fear of being brutalized by unknown assailants.

Although crime levels have been cut dramatically in recent years, these goals are still elusive. Indeed, the number of crimes committed by strangers has grown.

Public opinion polls indicate that Americans remain steadfast in identifying crime as one of the top five public problems to be addressed by government. Criminality and fear of crime are not new phenomena; they have always been part of the American experience. Yet the founders structured a society juxtaposing crime control with primacy for due process protections for the individual, later asserting that if the "constable blundered" the criminal should go free. Worry about crime in all its forms—violence as well as robberies, thefts, and assaults—has always been present in the United States, but is balanced by fear of an omnipresent or intrusive government. Incidents of extreme, large-scale violence threatened the social order. For example, farmers and others openly rebelled in the earliest years of the country. Military policies produced significant draft riots during the Civil War. In the early twentieth century, mobs of whites set upon and murdered African Americans in cities throughout the United States, including St. Louis, Kansas City, and Chicago. In other decades, police officers battled labor union organizers, veterans seeking payment of benefits, war protesters, and civil rights advocates. Thus, when riots erupted in Los Angeles in 1992 in the aftermath of the acquittal of police officers who were videotaped beating African-American motorist Rodney King, the country was not witnessing a new kind of event. Americans tolerate crime as the unacceptable end of the continuum of freedom. Until triggering events—real or media driven—force the issue into public consciousness, most citizens are either desensitized or immune to its effects.

Experts agree that, contrary to public opinion and the claims of politicians, crime rates have not been steadily rising. Rates for most crimes have dropped since the early 1980s.

The National Crime Victimization Surveys show that the victimization rate peaked in 1981 and has declined since then. The greatest declines are in property crimes, but crimes of violence have also dropped, especially since 1993. The *Uniform Crime Reports* show similar results. They reveal a rapid rise in crime rates beginning in 1964 and continuing until 1980, when the rates began to level off or decline. The overall crime rate has declined each year since 1991.

The most surprising trend has been the 34 percent decline in violent crimes from 50 to 53 victimizations per 1,000 persons age 12 or older between 1993 and 1999. During the 1993–1999 period, significant decreases were evident in every major type of violent and property crime, and every demographic group experienced substantial drops in violent victimization. For example, between 1993 and 1999 violent victimizations against males fell 38 percent and against females 34 percent. Victimizations against African Americans decreased

38 percent. Thus, perceptions and fears about the "crime problem" respond not only to the actual number of people committing illegal acts but also to government decisions about which problems should be criminalized, and which deserve full enforcement.

CRIME AND JUSTICE
AS PUBLIC POLICY ISSUES

Crime and justice are crucial public policy issues. In a democracy, striking a balance between maintaining public order and protecting individual freedom is a struggle. Policies could be imposed that make citizens feel safe from crime, such as placing a police officer on every street corner and executing suspected criminals. Such severe practices have been used elsewhere in the world. Although they may reduce crime, they also fly in the fact of democratic values. If law enforcement officers were given a free hand to work their will on the public, citizens in a democracy would be giving up individual freedom, due process, and their conception of justice.

Some critics of criminal justice, such as Jeffrey Reiman, argue that the U.S. system is designed "not to reduce crime or to achieve justice but to project to the American people a visible image of the threat of crime." This is done by maintaining a sizable population of criminals while at the same time failing to reduce crime. Reiman argues that a move needs to be made away from a system of **criminal** justice to one of criminal **justice**. He urges policies that:

- end crime-producing poverty
- criminalize the dangerous acts of the affluent and white-collar offenders
- create a correctional system that promotes human dignity
- make the exercise of police, prosecution, and judicial power more just
- establish economic and social justice

If adopted, Reiman's thought-provoking critical perspective would revolutionize the criminal justice system as well as many of the attitudes and customs of American society.

Dealing with the crime problem concerns not only the arrest, conviction, and punishment of offenders. Policies must also be developed to deal with a host of issues such as gun control, stalking, hate crimes, cybertheft, drugs, child abuse, and global criminal organizations. Many of these issues are controversial. Policies must be hammered out in the political arenas of state legislatures and Congress.

Crime Control and American Ideals

The way we control crime represents a basic test of our ideals. The administration of justice in a democracy can be distinguished from that in an authoritarian state by the extent and form of protections provided for the accused as guilt is determined and punishment is imposed.

Our laws begin with the premise that all people have rights, the guilty as well as the innocent. Moreover, unlike in some other countries, our laws reflect our concern to avoid unnecessarily depriving people of liberty, either by permitting police to search people at will or by mistakenly punishing an innocent person for a crime that he or she did not commit. Our greatest challenge may be to find ways to remain true to these principles of fair treatment and justice while also operating a system that can effectively protect, investigate, and punish. Significant divisions exist, especially between liberals and conservatives, in respect to policies about how to deal with crime within our democratic framework.

Conservatives believe that the answer lies in stricter enforcement of the law through the expansion of police forces and the enactment of punitive measures that will result in the swift and certain punishment of criminals. The holders of this conservative view have remained politically dominant since the early 1980s. They argue that we must strengthen crime control, which they assert has been hurt by decisions of the U.S. Supreme Court and by liberal programs that have weakened traditional values of responsibility and family.

In contrast, liberals argue that the strengthening of crime control has endangered our cherished values of due process and justice. They claim that strict approaches are ineffective in reducing crime because the answer lies in reshaping the lives of individual offenders and changing the social and economic conditions from which, they believe, criminal behavior springs.

As you encounter these arguments, think about how they relate to actual crime trends. Crime increased in the 1960s when we were trying the liberal approach of rehabilitating offenders. Does this mean that the approach does not work? Perhaps the liberal approach was merely overwhelmed by the number of people in their crime-prone years at that time. Perhaps there would have been even more crime if not for the efforts to rehabilitate. On the other hand, crime rates diminished when tough policies were implemented in the 1980s. But was that because of the conservative policies or because of the shrinking size of the crime-prone age group? If conservative policies are effective, then why did violent crime rates move upward in the early 1990s when tough policies were still in force? Why has there been such a decrease in crime during the past decade? Obviously, there are no easy answers, yet we cannot avoid making choices about how to use our police, our courts, and corrections system most effectively.

The Politics of Crime and Justice

As we examine alternative criminal justice policies, we need to remember that such policies are developed in national, state, and local political arenas. Because the public is so deeply concerned about crime, there is always a risk that politicians will simply say what they believe the voters want to hear rather than think seriously about whether the policies will achieve their goals.

The crime bill passed by Congress in 1994 expanded the death penalty to sixty additional crimes, including murder of members of Congress, the Supreme Court, and the president's staff. These are tough provisions, but do they actually accomplish anything relevant to crime in America or to people's fear of crime?

Politicians may claim that they "got tough on crime," but the public has little knowledge of the specific provisions of most legislation.

The most visible connection between politics and criminal justice is in the arguments and posturing by Republicans and Democrats who attempt to outdo each other in showing the voters how tough they can be. Equally important are the more "routine" linkages between politics and the justice system. Penal codes and the budgets of criminal justice agencies are passed by legislators who are responsive to the voters. Congress appropriates millions of dollars to assist states and cities in waging the War on Drugs but prohibits any expenditures for legal counsel for poor defendants. At the state and local level, many criminal justice authorities, including sheriffs, prosecutors, and judges, are also elected officials. Thus, their decisions will be influenced by the community's concerns and values.

As you learn about each part of the criminal justice system, keep in mind the ways in which decision makers and institutions are connected to politics and government. Criminal justice is intimately connected to society and its institutions, and to fully understand it we must recognize those connections.

CRIMINAL JUSTICE AS A SYSTEM

To achieve the goals of criminal justice, many organizational subunits—police, prosecution, courts, corrections—have been developed. Each of these organizations has its own personnel, functions, and responsibilities. If we were to construct an organizational chart, we might assume that criminal justice is an orderly process in which a variety of professionals act on the accused's case in the interests of society. To understand how the system really works, however, we must look beyond the formal organizational chart. To assist in this task, we can use the social science concept of system: a complex whole consisting of interdependent parts whose operations are directed toward goals and are influenced by the environment within which they function. This system operates in a market model context, where economic assumptions about free will and efficiency fashion an assembly line response to be carried out by seemingly autonomous rational individuals.

Criminal Justice from a System Perspective

Criminal justice is a system made up of a number of parts or subsystems—police, courts, corrections. The subsystems have their own goals and needs but are also interdependent. When one unit changes its policies, practices, or resources, other units will be affected. An increase in the number of people arrested by the police on felony charges, for example, will affect the work not only of the judicial subsystem but also of the probation and correctional subsystems. For criminal justice to achieve its goals, each part must make its own distinctive contribution; each part must also have at least minimal contact with at least one other component of the system.

Although it is important to understand the characteristics and operations of the entire criminal justice system and its individual subsystems, we must also see how individual actors play their roles. The criminal justice system is made up of a great many persons performing specific tasks. Some, such as police officers and judges, are well known to the public. Other important actors, such as bail bond agents and probation officers, are less visible and less well known.

A key concept for analysis of the relationships among individual decision makers is *exchange*. In this context, exchange refers to a mutual transfer of resources among individual decision makers, each of whom has interests and goals that he or she cannot readily accomplish alone. Therefore, each needs to gain cooperation and assistance from other actors by contributing to their interests and goals. The concept of exchange allows us to see interpersonal behavior as the result of individual decisions about the values and costs of alternative courses of action.

A variety of exchange relationships characterize the criminal justice system, some of which are more visible than others. Probably the most obvious example of an exchange relationship is plea bargaining. In this situation, a defendant's fate is determined not through a trial but rather through an agreement between the defense attorney and the prosecutor whereby the defendant agrees to plead guilty in exchange for a reduction of charges or a specific sentence recommendation. As a result of the exchange, the defendant achieves a shorter sentence; the prosecutor secures a quick, sure conviction; and the defense attorney can move on to the next case. Thus, the cooperation underlying the exchange promotes the goals of each participant.

The concept of exchange reminds us that decisions are the products of interactions among individuals and that the major subsystems—police, courts, and corrections—are tied together by the actions of individual decision makers.

The concepts of system and exchange are closely linked, and their value as tools for the analysis of criminal justice cannot be overemphasized. These concepts can be used as the basis for an organizing framework to describe individual subsystems and actors and to help us understand how the justice process really works. However, several additional characteristics of the criminal justice system shape its composition and functioning.

Characteristics of the Criminal Justice System

Four important attributes characterize the workings of the criminal justice system: (1) discretion, (2) resource dependence, (3) sequential tasks, and (4) filtering.

Discretion   At all levels of the justice process, officials exercise a high degree of discretion—the ability to act according to one's own judgment and conscience. For example, police officers decide how to handle a crime situation, prosecutors decide what charges to file against the accused, judges decide how long a sentence will be, and parole boards decide when an offender should be released from prison.

The fact that discretion exists throughout the criminal justice system may seem odd given that our country is ruled by law and has created procedures to ensure that decisions are made in accordance with that law. However, instead of a mechanical system in which law preempts human decision making, criminal justice is a system in which the participants may consider a wide variety of circumstances and exercise many options as they dispose of a case.

Two primary arguments are frequently used to justify discretion in the criminal justice system. First, discretion is needed because the system lacks the resources to treat every case in the same fashion. If every violation of the law were pursued through trial, the costs would be staggering. Second, many officials in the system believe that their discretionary authority permits them to achieve greater justice than rigid rules would produce.

Resource Dependence Criminal justice agencies generally do not generate their own resources—operating funds, staff, and equipment—but depend on others for them. Therefore, criminal justice actors (police chiefs, prosecutors, judges) frequently must cultivate and maintain good relationships with people responsible for the allocation of resources—that is, the political decision makers (legislators, mayors, city council members, and so on).

Because the budgetary decision makers are elected officials who seek to please the public, criminal justice officials must also maintain a positive image and good relations with the voters. If the police enjoy strong public support, for example, then the mayor will be reluctant to reduce the law enforcement budget. In maintaining positive public relations, criminal justice officials inevitably seek favorable coverage from local news media. Because the media often provide a crucial link between government agencies and the public, criminal justice officials may publicize notable achievements while simultaneously seeking to limit or control publicity about controversial cases and decisions.

Sequential Tasks Decisions in the criminal justice system are made in a particular sequence. The police must make an arrest before defendants are passed to the prosecutor, whose decisions ultimately determine the nature of the workload for courts and corrections. Officials cannot achieve their objectives by acting out of sequence. For example, prosecutors and judges cannot bypass the police by making arrests on their own, and corrections officials cannot punish anyone who has not already passed through the decision-making stages administered by the police, prosecution, and courts. Obviously, the sequential nature of the system is a key element in the exchange relationships that characterize the interactions of decision makers who depend on each other to achieve their respective goals. Thus, the system is highly interdependent.

Filtering The criminal justice system may be viewed as a filtering process through which cases are screened. At each stage, some defendants are sent on to the next stage of decision making while others are either released or processed under changed conditions. It should be noted that very few suspects arrested by the police are prosecuted, tried, and convicted. Some go free because the police decide that a crime has not been committed or that the evidence is not sound. The prosecutor may drop charges by deciding that justice would be better served by diverting the suspect to a substance abuse clinic. Large numbers of defendants will plead guilty, the judge may dismiss charges against others, and the jury may acquit a few defendants. Most of the offenders who are actually tried, however, will be convicted. Thus, the criminal justice system is often described as a "funnel" into which many cases enter but only a few result in conviction and punishment.

The administration of criminal justice may be viewed as having goals that are antagonistic to due process. Decisions concerning the disposition of cases are influenced by the selective nature of the filtering process in which administrative discretion and interpersonal exchange relationships are extremely important. At each decision-making level, actors in the judicial system are able to determine which types of crime will come to official notice, which kinds of offenders will be processed, and how enthusiastically a conviction will be sought. It is in these day-to-day practices and policies of criminal justice agencies that the law is put into effect, and it is out of this activity that organizations and individuals shape the law.

SUGGESTIONS FOR FURTHER READING

Cole, David, *No Equal Justice*. New York: New Press, 1999. Argues that a double standard compromises the legitimacy of criminal justice and exacerbates racial divisions.

Friedman, Lawrence M. *Crime and Punishment in American History*. New York: Basic Books, 1993. A historical overview of criminal justice from colonial times. Argues that the evolution of criminal justice reflects transformations in American character.

Hall, Jerome. *General Principles of Criminal Law*, 2d ed. Indianapolis: Bobbs-Merrill, 1947. One of the clearest texts outlining the foundations of criminal law and the defenses that may be used.

Reiman, Jeffrey. *The Rich Get Richer and the Poor Get Prision: Economic Bias in American Criminal Justice*. Boston: Allyn & Bacon, 1996. A stinging critique of the system. Argues that the criminal justice system serves the powerful by its failure to reduce crime.

Roberts, J. V., and A. N. Doob. *Public Opinion, Crime and Criminal Justice*. Boulder, Colo.: Westview Press, 1997. Details areas in criminal justice policy that are influenced by public opinion or politicians' response to it, such as "three strikes you're out" laws, drugs, and gun control.

Scheingold, Stuart A. *The Politics of Law and Order: Street Crime and Public Policy*. New York: Longman, 1984. Broad overview of the political context of the criminal justice system arguing the importance of considering the symbolic nature of crime policy, and the simultaneous complexity of the phenomenon of crime.

Tonry, Michael, ed. *The Handbook of Crime and Punishment*. New York: Oxford University Press, 1998. This encyclopedia volume provides current literature reviews in criminal justice and its context.

Walker, Samuel. *Sense and Nonsense About Crime and Drug Policy*, 5th ed. Belmont, Calif.: Wadsworth, 2001. A provocative look at crime policies.

1

❂

Two Models of the Criminal Process

HERBERT L. PACKER

In one of the most important contributions to systematic thought about the administration of criminal justice, Herbert Packer articulates the values supporting two models of the justice process. He notes the gulf existing between the "Due Process Model" of criminal administration, with its emphasis on the rights of the individual, and the "Crime Control Model," which sees the regulation of criminal conduct as the most important function of the judicial system.

Two models of the criminal process will let us perceive the normative antinomy at the heart of the criminal law. These models are not labeled Is and Ought, nor are they to be taken in that sense. Rather, they represent an attempt to abstract two separate value systems that compete for priority in the operation of the criminal process. Neither is presented as either corresponding to reality or representing the ideal to the exclusion of the other. The two models merely afford a convenient way to talk about the operation of a process whose day-to-day functioning involves a constant series of minute adjustments between the competing demands of two value systems and whose normative future likewise involves a series of resolutions of the tensions between competing claims.

I call these two models the Due Process Model and the Crime Control Model. . . . As we examine the way the models operate in each successive stage, we will raise two further inquiries: first, where on a spectrum between

Source: Reprinted from *The Limits of the Criminal Sanction* by Herbert L. Packer, with the permission of the publisher, Stanford University Press. © 1968 by Herbert L. Packer.

the extremes represented by the two models do our present practices seem approximately to fall; second, what appears to be the direction and thrust of current and foreseeable trends along each such spectrum?

There is a risk in an enterprise of this sort that is latent in any attempt to polarize. It is, simply, that values are too various to be pinned down to yes-or-no answers. The models are distortions of reality. And, since they are normative in character, there is a danger of seeing one or the other as Good or Bad. The reader will have his preferences, as I do, but we should not be so rigid as to demand consistently polarized answers to the range of questions posed in the criminal process. The weighty questions of public policy that inhere in any attempt to discern where on the spectrum of normative choice the "right" answer lies are beyond the scope of the present inquiry. The attempt here is primarily to clarify the terms of discussion by isolating the assumptions that underlie competing policy claims, and examining the conclusions that those claims, if fully accepted, would lead to.

VALUES UNDERLYING THE MODELS

Each of the two models we are about to examine is an attempt to give operational content to a complex of values underlying the criminal law. As I have suggested earlier, it is possible to identify two competing systems of values, the tension between which accounts for the intense activity now observable in the development of the criminal process. The actors in this development—lawmakers, judges, police, prosecutors, defense lawyers—do not often pause to articulate the values that underlie the positions that they take on any given issue. Indeed, it would be a gross oversimplification to ascribe a coherent and consistent set of values to any of these actors. Each of the two competing schemes of values we will be developing in this section contains components that are demonstrably present some of the time in some of the actors' preferences regarding the criminal process. No one person has ever identified himself as holding all of the values that underlie these two models. The models are polarities, and so are the schemes of values that underlie them. A person who subscribed to all of the values underlying the other would be rightly viewed as a fanatic. The values are presented here as an aid to analysis, not as a program for action.

Some Common Ground

However, the polarity of the two models is not absolute. Although it would be possible to construct models that exist in an institutional vacuum, it would not serve our purposes to do so. We are postulating, not a criminal process that operates in any kind of society at all, but rather one that operates within the framework of contemporary American society. This leaves plenty of room for polarization, but it does require the observance of some limits. A model of the criminal process that left out of account relatively stable and enduring features of the American legal system would not have much relevance to our central inquiry. For convenience, these elements of stability and continuity can be roughly equated with minimal agreed limits expressed in the Constitution of the United States and, more importantly, with unarticulated assumptions that can be perceived to underlie those limits. Of course, it is true that the Constitution is constantly appealed to by proponents and opponents of many measures that affect the criminal process. And only the naive would deny that there are few conclusive positions that can be reached by appeal to the Constitution. Yet there are assumptions about the criminal process that are widely shared and that may be viewed as common ground for the operation of any model of the criminal process. Our first task is to clarify these assumptions.

First, there is the assumption, implicit in the ex post facto clause of the Constitution, that the function of defining conduct that may be treated as criminal is separate from and prior to the process of identifying and dealing with persons as criminals. How wide or narrow the definition of criminal conduct must be is an important question of policy that yields highly variable results depending on the values held by those making the relevant decisions. But that there must be a means of definition that is in some sense separate from and prior to the operation of the process is clear. If this were not so, our efforts to deal with the phenomenon of organized crime would appear ludicrous indeed (which is not to say that we have by any means exhausted the possibilities for dealing with that problem within the limits of this basic assumption).

A related assumption that limits the area of controversy is that the criminal process ordinarily ought to be invoked by those charged with the responsibility for doing so when it appears that a crime has been committed and that there is a reasonable prospect of apprehending and convicting its perpetrator. Although police and prosecutors are allowed broad discretion for deciding not to invoke the criminal process, it is commonly agreed that these officials have no general dispensing power. If the legislature has decided that certain conduct is to be treated as criminal, the decision makers at every level of the criminal process are expected to accept that basic decision as a premise for action. The controversial nature of the occasional case in which the relevant decision makers appear not to have played their appointed role only serves to highlight the strength with which the premise holds. This assumption may be viewed as the other side of the ex post facto coin. Just as conduct that is not proscribed as criminal may not be dealt with in the criminal process, so conduct that has been denominated as criminal must be treated as such by the participants in the criminal process acting within their respective competences.

Next, there is the assumption that there are limits to the powers of government to investigate and apprehend persons suspected of committing crimes. I do not refer to the controversy (settled recently, at least in broad outline) as to whether the Fourth Amendment's prohibition against unreasonable searches and seizures applies to the states with the same force with which it applies to the federal government. Rather, I am talking about the general assumption that a degree of scrutiny and control must be exercised with respect to the activities of law-enforcement officers, that the security and privacy of the individual may not be invaded at will. It is possible to imagine a society in which even lip service is not paid to this assumption. Nazi Germany approached but never quite reached this position. But no one in our society would maintain that any individual may be taken into custody at any time and held without any limitation of time during the process of investigating his possible commission of crimes, or would argue that there should be no form of redress for violation of at least some standards for official investigative conduct. Although this assumption may not appear to have much in the way of positive content, its absence would render moot some of our most hotly controverted problems. If there were not general agreement that there must be some limits on police power to detain and investigate, the highly controversial provisions of the Uniform Arrest Act, permitting the police to detain a person for questioning for a short period even though they do not have grounds for making an arrest, would be a magnanimous concession by the all-powerful state rather than, as it is now perceived, a substantial expansion of police power.

Finally, there is a complex of assumptions embraced by terms such as "the adversary system," "procedural due process," "notice and an opportunity to be heard," and "day in court." Common to them all is the notion that the alleged criminal is not merely an object to be acted upon but an independent entity in the process who may, if he so desires, force the operators of the process to demonstrate to an independent authority (judge and jury) that he is guilty of the charges against him. It is a minimal assumption. It speaks in terms of "may" rather than "must." It permits but does not require the accused, acting by himself or through his own agent, to play an active role in the process. By virtue of that fact the process becomes or has the capacity to become a contest between, if not equals, at least independent actors. As we shall see, much of the space between the two models is occupied by stronger or weaker notions of how this contest is to be arranged, in what cases it is to be played, and by what rules. The Crime Control Model tends to de-emphasize this adversary aspect of the process; the Due Process Model tends to make it central. The common ground, and it is important, is the agreement that the process has, for everyone subjected to it, at least the potentiality of becoming to some extent an adversary struggle.

So much for common ground. There is a good deal of it, even in the narrowest view. Its existence should not be overlooked, because it is, by definition, what permits partial resolutions of the tension between the two models to take place. The rhetoric of the criminal process consists largely of claims that disputed territory is "really" common ground: that, for example, the premise of an adversary system "necessarily" embraces the appointment of counsel for everyone accused of crime, or conversely, that the obligation to pursue persons suspected of committing crimes "necessarily" embraces interrogation of suspects without the intervention of counsel. We may smile indulgently at such claims; they are rhetoric, and no more. But the form in which they are made suggests an important truth: that there *is* a common ground of value assumption about the criminal process that makes continued discourse about its problems possible.

Crime Control Values

The value system that underlies the Crime Control Model is based on the proposition that the repression of criminal conduct is by far the most important function to be performed by the criminal process. The failure of law enforcement to bring criminal conduct under tight control is viewed as leading to the breakdown of public order and thence to the disappearance of an important condition of human freedom. If the laws go unenforced—which is to say, if it is perceived that there is a high percentage of failure to apprehend and convict in the criminal process—a general disregard for legal controls tends to develop. The law-abiding citizen then becomes the victim of all sorts of unjustifiable invasions of his interests. His security of person and property is sharply diminished, and, therefore, so is his liberty to function as a member of society. The claim ultimately is that the criminal process is a positive guarantor of social freedom. In order to achieve this high purpose, the Crime Control Model requires that primary attention be paid to the efficiency with which the criminal process operates to screen suspects, determine guilt, and secure appropriate dispositions of persons convicted of crime.

Efficiency of operation is not, of course, a criterion that can be applied in a vacuum. By "efficiency" we mean the system's capacity to apprehend, try, convict, and dispose of a high proportion of criminal offenders whose offenses become known. In a society in which only the grossest forms of antisocial behavior were made criminal and in which the crime rate was exceedingly low, the criminal process might require the devotion of many more man-hours of police, prosecutorial, and judicial time per case than ours does, and still operate with tolerable efficiency. A society that was prepared to increase even further the resources devoted to the suppression of crime might cope with a rising crime rate without sacrifice of efficiency while continuing to maintain an elaborate and time-consuming set of criminal processes. However, neither of these possible characteristics corresponds with social reality in this country. We use the criminal sanction to cover an increasingly wide spectrum of behavior thought to be antisocial, and the amount of crime is very high indeed, although both level and trend are hard to assess. At the same time, although precise measures are not available, it does not appear that we are disposed in the public sector of the economy to increase very drastically the quantity, much less the quality, of the resources devoted to the suppression of criminal activity through the operation of the criminal process. These factors have an important bearing on the criterion of efficiency, and therefore on the nature of the Crime Control Model.

The model, in order to operate successfully, must produce a high rate of apprehension and conviction, and must do so in a context where the magnitudes being dealt with are very large and the resources for dealing with them are very limited. There must then be a premium on speed and finality. Speed, in turn, depends on informality and on uniformity; finality depends on minimizing the occasions for challenge. The process must not be cluttered up with ceremonious rituals that do not advance the progress of a case. Facts can be established more quickly through interrogation in a police station than through the formal process of examination and cross-examination in a court. It follows that extrajudicial processes should be preferred to judicial processes, informal operations to formal ones. But informality is not enough; there must also be uniformity. Routine, stereotyped procedures are essential if large numbers are being handled. The model that will operate successfully on these presuppositions must be an administrative, almost a managerial, model. The image that comes to mind is an assembly-line conveyor belt down which moves an endless stream of cases, never stopping, carrying the cases to workers who stand at fixed stations and who perform on each case as it comes by the same small but essential operation that brings it one step closer to being a finished product, or, to exchange the metaphor for the reality, a closed file. The criminal process, in this model, is seen as a screening process in which each successive state—prearrest investigation, arrest, postarrest investigation, preparation for trial, trial or entry of plea, conviction, disposition—involves a series of routinized operations whose success is gauged primarily by their tendency to pass the case along to a successful conclusion.

What is a successful conclusion? One that throws off at an early stage those cases in which it appears unlikely that the person apprehended is an offender and then secures, as expeditiously as possible, the conviction of the rest, with a minimum of occasions for challenge, let alone post-audit. By the application of administrative expertness, primarily that of the police and prosecutors, an early determination of the probability of innocence or guilt emerges. Those who are probably innocent are screened out. Those who are probably guilty are passed quickly through the remaining stages of the process. The key to the operation of the model regarding those who are not screened out is what I shall call a presumption of guilt. The concept requires some explanation, since it may appear startling to assert that what appears to be the precise converse of our generally accepted ideology of a presumption of innocence can be an essential element of a model that does correspond in some respects to the actual operation of the criminal process.

The presumption of guilt is what makes it possible for the system to deal efficiently with large numbers, as the Crime Control Model demands. The supposition is that the screening processes operated by police and prosecutors are reliable indicators of probable guilt. Once a man has been arrested and investigated without being found to be probably innocent, or, to put it differently, once a determination has been made that there is enough evidence of guilt to permit holding him for further action, then all subsequent activity directed toward him is based on the view that he is probably guilty. The precise point at which this occurs will vary from case to case; in many cases it will occur as soon as the suspect is arrested, or even before, if the evidence of probable guilt that has come to the attention of the authorities is sufficiently strong. But in any case the presumption of guilt will begin to operate well before the "suspect" becomes a "defendant."

The presumption of guilt is not, of course, a thing. Nor is it even a rule of law in the usual sense. It simply is the consequence of a complex of attitudes, a mood. If there is confidence in the reliability of informal administrative fact-finding activities that take place in the early stages of the criminal process, the remaining stages of the process can be relatively perfunctory without any loss in operating efficiency. The presumption of guilt, as it operates in the Crime Control Model, is the operational expression of that confidence.

It would be a mistake to think of the presumption of guilt as the opposite of the presumption of innocence that we are so used to thinking of as the polestar of the criminal process and that, as we shall see, occupies an important position in the Due Process Model. The presumption of innocence is not its opposite; it is irrelevant to the presumption of guilt; the two concepts are different rather than opposite ideas. The difference can perhaps be epitomized by an example. A murderer, for reasons best known to himself, chooses to shoot his victim in plain view of a large number of people. When the police arrive, he hands them his gun and says, "I did it and I'm glad." His account of what happened is corroborated by several eyewitnesses. He is placed under arrest and led off to jail. Under these circumstances, which may seem extreme but which in fact characterize with rough accuracy the evidentiary situation in a large proportion of criminal cases, it would be plainly absurd to maintain that more probably than not the suspect did not commit the killing. But that is not what the presumption of innocence means. It means that until there has been an adjudication of guilt by an authority legally competent to make such an adjudication, the suspect is to be treated, for reasons that have nothing whatever to do with the probable outcome of the case, as if his guilt is an open question.

The presumption of innocence is a direction to officials about how they are to proceed, not a prediction of outcome. The presumption of guilt, however, is purely and simply a prediction of outcome. The presumption of innocence is, then, a direction to the authorities to ignore the presumption of guilt in their treatment of the suspect. It tells them, in effect, to close their eyes to what will frequently seem to be factual probabilities. The reasons why it tells them this are among the animating presuppositions of the Due Process Model, and we will come to them shortly. It is enough to note at this point that the presumption of guilt is descriptive and factual; the presumption of innocence is normative and legal. The pure Crime Control Model has no truck with the presumption of innocence, although its real-life emanations are, as we shall see, brought into uneasy compromise with the dictates of this dominant ideological position. In the presumption of guilt this model finds a factual predicate for the position that the dominant goal of repressing crime can be achieved through highly summary processes without any great loss of efficiency (as previously defined), because of the probability that, in the run of cases, the preliminary screening process operated by the police and the prosecuting officials contains adequate guarantees of reliable fact-finding. Indeed, the model takes an even stronger position. It is that subsequent processes, particularly those of a formal adjudicatory nature, are unlikely to produce as reliable fact-finding as the expert administrative process that precedes them is capable of. The criminal process thus must put special weight on the quality of administrative fact-finding. It becomes important, then, to place as few restrictions as possible on the character of the administrative fact-finding processes and to limit restrictions to such as enhance reliability, excluding those designed for other purposes. As we shall see, this view of restrictions on administrative fact-finding is a consistent theme in the development of the Crime Control Model.

In this model, as I have suggested, the center of gravity of the process lies in the early, administrative fact-finding stages. The complementary proposition is that the subsequent stages are relatively unimportant and should be truncated as much as possible. This, too, produces tensions with presently dominant ideology. The pure Crime Control Model has very little use for many conspicuous features of the adjudicative process, and in real life works out a number of ingenious compromises with them. Even in the pure model, however, there have to be devices for dealing with the suspect after the preliminary screening process has resulted in a determination of probable guilt. The focal device, as we shall see, is the plea of guilty; through its use, adjudicative fact-finding is reduced to its barest essentials and operating at its most successful pitch, it offers two possibilities: an administrative fact-finding process leading (1) to exoneration of the suspect, or (2) to the entry of a plea of guilty.

Due Process Values

If the Crime Control Model resembles an assembly line, the Due Process Model looks very much like an obstacle course. Each of its successive stages is designed to present formidable impediments to carrying the accused any further along in the process. Its ideology is not the converse of that underlying the Crime Control Model. It does not rest on the idea that it is not socially desirable to repress crime, although critics of its application have been known to claim so. Its ideology is composed of a complex of ideas, some of them based on judgments about the efficacy of crime control devices, others having to do with quite different considerations. The ideology of due process is far more deeply impressed on the formal structure of the law than is the ideology of crime control; yet an accurate tracing of the strands that make it up is strangely difficult. What follows is only an attempt at an approximation.

The Due Process Model encounters its rival on the Crime Control Model's own ground in respect to the reliability of fact-finding processes. The Crime Control Model, as we have suggested, places heavy reliance on the ability of investigative and prosecutorial officers, acting in an informal setting in which their distinctive skills are given full sway, to elicit and reconstruct a tolerably accurate account of what actually took place in an alleged criminal event. The Due Process Model rejects this premise and substitutes for it a view of informal, nonadjudicative fact-finding that stresses the possibility of error. People are notoriously poor observers of disturbing events—the more emotion-arousing the context, the greater the possibility that recollection will be incorrect; confessions and admissions by persons in police custody may be induced by physical or psychological coercion so that the police end up hearing what the suspect thinks they want to hear rather than the truth; witnesses may be animated by bias or interest that no one would trouble to discover except one specially charged with protecting the interests of the accused (as the police are not). Considerations of this kind all lead to a rejection of informal fact-finding processes as definitive of factual guilt and to an insistence on formal, adjudicative, adversary fact-finding processes in which the factual case against the accused is publicly heard by an impartial tribunal and is evaluated only after the accused has had a full opportunity to discredit the case against him. Even then, the distrust of fact-finding processes that animates the Due Process Model is not dissipated. The possibilities of human error being what they are, further scrutiny is necessary, or at least must be available, in case facts have been overlooked or suppressed in the heat of battle. How far this subsequent scrutiny must be available is a hotly controverted issue today. In the pure Due Process Model the answer would be: at least as long as there is an allegation of factual error that has not received an adjudicative hearing in a fact-finding context. The demand for finality is thus very low in the Due Process Model.

This strand of due process ideology is not enough to sustain the model. If all that were at issue between the two models was a series of questions about the reliability of fact-finding processes, we would have but one model of the criminal process, the nature of whose constituent elements would pose questions of fact not of value. Even if the discussion is confined, for the moment, to the question of reliability, it is apparent that more is at stake than simply an evaluation of what kinds of fact-finding processes, alone or in combination, are likely to produce the most nearly reliable results. The stumbling block is this: How much reliability is compatible with efficiency? Granted that informal fact-finding will make some mistakes that can be remedied if backed up by adjudicative fact-finding, the desirability of providing this backup is not affirmed or negated by factual demonstrations or predictions that the increase in reliability will be x percent or x plus n percent. It still remains to ask how much weight is to be given to the competing demands of reliability (a high degree of probability in each case that factual guilt has been accurately determined) and efficiency (expeditious handling of the large numbers of cases that the process ingests). The Crime Control Model is more optimistic about the improbability of error in a significant number of cases: but it is also, though only in part therefore, more tolerant about the amount of error that it will put up with. The Due Process Model insists on the prevention and elimination of mistakes to the extent possible; the Crime Control Model accepts the probability of mistakes up to the level at which they interfere with the goal of repressing crime, either because too many guilty people are escaping or, more subtly, because general awareness of the unreliability of the process leads to a decrease in the deterrent efficacy of the criminal law. In this view, reliability and efficiency are not polar opposites but rather complementary characteristics. The system is reliable *because* efficient; reliability becomes a matter of independent concern only when it becomes so attenuated as to impair efficiency. All of this the Due Process Model rejects. If efficiency demands shortcuts around reliability, then absolute efficiency must be rejected. The aim of the process is at least as much to protect the factually innocent as it is to convict the factually guilty. It is a little like quality control in industrial technology; tolerable deviation from standard varies with the importance of conformity to standard in the destined uses of the product. The Due Process Model resembles a factory that has to devote a substantial part of its input to quality control. This necessarily cuts down on quantitative output.

All of this is only the beginning of the ideological difference between the two models. The Due Process Model could disclaim any attempt to provide enhanced reliability for the fact-finding process and still produce a set of institutions and processes that would differ sharply from those demanded by the Crime Control Model. Indeed, it may not be too great an oversimplification to assert that in point of historical development the doctrinal pressures emanating from the demands of the Due Process Model have tended to evolve from an original matrix of concern for the maximization of reliability into values quite different and more far-reaching. These values can be expressed in, although not adequately described by, the concept of the primacy of the individual and the complementary concept of limitation on official power.

The combination of stigma and loss of liberty that is embodied in the end result of the criminal process is viewed as being the heaviest deprivation that government can inflict on the individual. Furthermore, the processes that culminate in these highly afflictive sanctions are seen as in themselves coercive, restricting, and demeaning. Power is always subject to abuse—sometimes subtle, other times, as in the criminal process, open and ugly. Precisely because of its potency in subjecting the individual to the coercive power of the state, the criminal process must, in this model, be subjected to controls that prevent it from operating with maximal efficiency. According to this ideology, maximal efficiency means maximal tyranny. And, although no one would assert that minimal efficiency means minimal tyranny, the proponents of the Due Process Model would accept with considerable equanimity a substantial diminution in the efficiency with which the criminal process operates in the interest of preventing official oppression of the individual.

The most modest-seeming but potentially far-reaching mechanism by which the Due Process Model implements these antiauthoritarian values is the doctrine of legal guilt. According to this doctrine, a person is not to be held guilty of a crime merely on a showing that in all probability, based upon reliable evidence, he did factually what he is said to have done. Instead, he is to be held guilty if and only if these factual determinations are made in procedurally regular fashion and by authorities acting within competences duly allocated to them. Furthermore, he is not to be held guilty, even though the factual determination is or might be adverse to him, if various rules designed to protect him and to safeguard the integrity of the process are not given effect: the tribunal that convicts him must have the power to deal with his kind of case ("jurisdiction") and must be geographically appropriate ("venue"); too long a time must not have elapsed since the offense was committed ("statute of limitations"); he must not have been previously convicted or acquitted of the same or a substantially similar offense ("double jeopardy"); he must not fall within a category of persons, such as children or the insane, who are legally immune to conviction ("criminal responsibility"); and so on. None of these requirements has anything to do with the factual question of whether the person did or did not engage in the conduct that is charged as the offense against him; yet favorable answers to any of them will mean that he is legally innocent. Wherever the competence to make adequate factual determination lies, it is apparent that only a tribunal that is aware of these guilt-defeating doctrines and is willing to apply them can be viewed as competent to make determinations of legal guilt. The police and the prosecutors are ruled out by lack of competence, in the first instance, and by lack of assurance of willingness, in the second. Only an impartial tribunal can be trusted to make determinations of legal as opposed to factual guilt.

In this concept of legal guilt lies the explanation for the apparently quixotic presumption of innocence of which we spoke earlier. A man who, after police investigation, is charged with having committed a crime can hardly be said to be presumptively innocent, if what we mean is factual innocence. But if what we mean is that it has yet to be determined if any of the myriad legal doctrines that serve in one way or another the end of limiting official power through the observance of certain substantive and procedural regularities may be appropriately invoked to exculpate the accused man, it is apparent that as a matter of prediction it cannot be said with confidence that more probably than not he will be found guilty.

Beyond the question of predictability this model posits a functional reason for observing the presumption of innocence: by forcing the state to prove its case against the accused in an adjudicative context, the presumption of innocence serves to force into play all the qualifying and disabling doctrines that limit the use of the criminal sanction against the individual, thereby enhancing his opportunity to secure a favorable outcome. In this sense, the presumption of innocence may be seen to operate as a kind of self-fulfilling prophecy. By opening up a procedural situation that permits the successful assertion of defenses having nothing to do with factual guilt, it vindicates the proposition that the factually guilty may nonetheless be legally innocent and should therefore be given a chance to qualify for that kind of treatment.

The possibility of legal innocence is expanded enormously when the criminal process is viewed as the appropriate forum for correcting its own abuses. This notion may well account for a greater amount of the distance between the two models than any other. In theory the Crime Control Model can tolerate rules that forbid illegal arrests, unreasonable searches, coercive interrogations, and the like. What it cannot tolerate is the vindication of those rules in the criminal process itself through the exclusion of evidence illegally obtained or through the reversal of convictions in cases where the criminal process has breached the rules laid down for its observance. And the Due Process Model, although it may in the first instance be addressed to the maintenance of reliable fact-finding techniques, comes eventually to incorporate prophylactic and deterrent rules that result in the release of the factually guilty even in cases in which blotting out the illegality would still leave an adjudicative fact-finder convinced of the accused person's guilt. Only by penalizing errant police and prosecutors within the criminal process itself can adequate pressure be maintained, so the argument runs, to induce conformity with the Due Process Model.

Another strand in the complex of attitudes underlying the Due Process Model is the idea—itself a shorthand statement for a complex of attitudes—of equality. This notion has only recently emerged as an explicit basis for pressing the demands of the Due Process Model, but it appears to represent, at least in its potential, a most powerful norm for influencing official conduct. Stated most starkly, the ideal of equality holds that "there can be no equal justice where the kind of trial a man gets depends on the amount of money he has." The factual predicate underlying this assertion is that there are gross inequalities in the financial means of criminal defendants as a class, that in an adversary system of criminal justice an effective defense is largely a function of the resources that can be mustered on behalf of the accused, and that the very large proportion of criminal defendants who are, operationally speaking, "indigent" will thus be denied an effective defense. This factual premise has been strongly reinforced by recent studies that in turn have been both a cause and an effect of an increasing emphasis upon norms for the criminal process based on the premise.

The norms derived from the premise do not take the form of an insistence upon governmental responsibility to provide literally equal opportunities for all criminal defendants to challenge the process. Rather, they take as their point of departure the notion that the criminal process, initiated as it is by the government and containing as it does the likelihood of severe deprivations at the hands of government, imposes some kind of public obligation to ensure that financial inability does not destroy the capacity of an accused to assert what may be meritorious challenges to the processes being invoked against him. At its most gross, the norm of equality would act to prevent situations in which financial inability forms an absolute barrier to the assertion of a right that is in theory generally available, as where there is a right to appeal that is, however, effectively conditional upon the filing of a trial transcript obtained at the defendant's expense. Beyond this, it may provide the basis for a claim whenever the system theoretically makes some kind of challenge available to an accused who has the means to press it. If, for example, a defendant who is adequately represented has the opportunity to prevent the case against him from coming to the trial stage by forcing the state to its proof in a preliminary hearing, the norm of equality may be invoked to assert that the same kind of opportunity must be available to others as well. In a sense the system, as it functions for the small minority whose resources permit them to exploit all its defensive possibilities, provides a benchmark by which its functioning in all other cases is to be tested: not, perhaps, to guarantee literal identity but rather to provide a measure of whether the process as a whole is recognizably of the same general order. The demands made by a norm of this kind are likely by their very nature to be quite sweeping. Although the norm's imperatives may be initially limited to determining whether in a particular case the accused was injured or prejudiced by his relative inability to make an appropriate challenge, the norm of equality very quickly moves to another level on which the demand is that the process in general be adapted to minimize discriminations rather than that a mere series of post hoc determinations of discriminations be made or makeable.

It should be observed that the impact of the equality norm will vary greatly depending upon the point in time at which it is introduced into a model of the criminal process. If one were starting from scratch to decide how the process ought to work, the norm of equality would have nothing very important to say on such questions as, for example, whether an accused should have the effective assistance of counsel in deciding whether to enter a plea of guilty. One could decide, on quite independent considerations, that it is or is not a good thing to afford that facility to the generality of persons accused of crime. But the impact of the equality norm becomes far greater when it is brought to bear on a process whose contours have already been shaped. If our model of the criminal process affords defendants who are in a financial position to do so the right to consult a lawyer before entering a plea, then the equality norm exerts powerful pressure to provide such an opportunity to all defendants and to regard the failure to do so as a malfunctioning of the process of whose consequences the accused is entitled to be relieved. In a sense, this has been the role of the equality norm in affecting the real-world criminal process. It has made its appearance on the scene comparatively late and has therefore encountered a system in which the relative financial inability of most persons accused of crime results in treatment very different from that accorded the small minority of the financially capable. For this reason, its impact has already been substantial and may be expected to be even more so in the future.

There is a final strand of thought in the Due Process Model that is often ignored but that needs to be candidly faced if thought on the subject is not to be obscured. This is a mood of skepticism about the morality and utility of the criminal sanction, taken either as a whole or in some of its applications. The subject is a large and complicated one, comprehending as it does much of the intellectual history of our times. It is properly the subject of another essay altogether. To put the matter briefly, one cannot improve upon the statement by Professor Paul Bator:

> In summary we are told that the criminal law's notion of just condemnation and punishment is a cruel hypocrisy visited by a smug society on the psychologically and economically crippled; that its premise of a morally autonomous will with at least some measure of choice whether to comply with the values expressed in a penal code is unscientific and outmoded; that its reliance on punishment as an educational and deterrent agent is misplaced, particularly in the case of the very members of society most likely to engage in criminal conduct; and that its failure to provide for individualized and humane rehabilitation of offenders is inhuman and wasteful.[1]

This skepticism, which may be fairly said to be widespread among the most influential and articulate contemporary leaders of informed opinion, leads to an attitude toward the processes of the criminal law that, to quote Mr. Bator again, engenders "a peculiar receptivity toward claims of injustice which arise within the traditional structure of the system itself; fundamental disagreement and unease about the very bases of the criminal law has, inevitably, created acute pressure at least to expand and liberalize those of its processes and doctrines which serve to make more tentative its judgments or limit its power." In short, doubts about the ends for which power is being exercised create pressure to limit the discretion with which that power is exercised.

The point need not be pressed to the extreme of doubts about or rejection of the premises upon which the criminal sanction in general rests. Unease may be stirred simply by reflection on the variety of uses to which the criminal sanction is put and by a judgment that an increasingly large proportion of those uses may represent an unwise invocation of so extreme a sanction. It would be an interesting irony if doubts about the propriety of certain uses of the criminal sanction prove to contribute to a restrictive trend in the criminal process that in the end requires a choice among uses and finally an abandonment of some of the very uses that stirred the original doubts, but for a reason quite unrelated to those doubts.

There are two kinds of problems that need to be dealt with in any model of the criminal process. One is what the rules shall be. The other is how the rules shall be implemented. The second is at least as important as the first, as we shall see time and again in our detailed development of the models. The distinctive difference between the two models is not only in the rules of conduct that they lay down but also in the sanctions that are to be invoked when a claim is presented that the rules have been breached and, no less importantly, in the timing that is permitted or required for the invocation of those sanctions.

As I have already suggested, the Due Process Model locates at least some of the sanctions for breach of the operative rules in the criminal process itself. The relation between these two aspects of the process—the rules and the sanctions for their breach—is a purely formal one unless there is some mechanism for bringing them into play with each other. The hinge between them in the Due Process Model is the availability of legal counsel. This has a double aspect. Many of the rules that the model requires are couched in terms of the availability of counsel to do various things at various stages of the process—this is the conventionally recognized aspect; beyond it, there is a pervasive assumption that counsel is necessary in order to invoke sanctions for breach of any of the rules. The more freely available these sanctions are, the more important is the role of counsel in seeing to it that the sanctions are appropriately invoked. If the process is seen as a series of occasions for checking its own operation, the role of counsel is a much more nearly central one than is the case in a process that is seen as primarily concerned with expeditious determination of factual guilt. And if equality of operation is a governing norm, the availability of counsel is seen as requiring it for all. Of all the controverted aspects of the criminal process, the right to counsel, including the role of government in its provision, is the most dependent on what one's model of the process looks like, and the least susceptible of resolution unless one has confronted the antinomies of the two models.

I do not mean to suggest that questions about the right to counsel disappear if one adopts a model of the process that conforms more or less closely to the Crime Control Model, but only that such questions become absolutely central if one's model moves very far down the spectrum of possibilities toward the pure Due Process Model. The reason for this centrality is to be found in the assumption underlying both models that the process is an adversary one in which the initiative in invoking relevant rules rests primarily on the parties concerned, the state, and the accused. One could construct models that placed central responsibility on adjudicative agents such as committing magistrates and trial judges. And there are, as we shall see, marginal but nonetheless important adjustments in the role of the adjudicative agents that enter into the models with which we are concerned. For present purposes it is enough to say that these adjustments are marginal, that the animating presuppositions that under-lie both models in the context of the American criminal system relegate the ad-judicative agents to a relatively passive role, and therefore place central importance on the role of counsel.

One last introductory note: . . . What assumptions do we make about the sources of authority to shape the real-world operations of the criminal process? Recognizing that our models are only models, what agencies of government have the power to pick and choose between their competing demands? Once again, the limiting features of the American context come into play. Ours is not a system of legislative supremacy. The distinctively American institution of judi-cial review exercises a limiting and ultimately a shaping influence on the crimi-nal process. Because the Crime Control Model is basically an affirmative model, emphasizing at every turn the existence and exercise of official power, its vali-dating authority is ultimately legislative (although proximately administrative). Because the Due Process Model is basically a negative model, asserting limits on the nature of official power and on the modes of its exercise, its validating au-thority is judicial and requires an appeal to supralegislative law, to the law of the Constitution. To the extent that tensions between the two models are resolved by deference to the Due Process Model, the authoritative force at work is the judicial power, working in the distinctively judicial mode of invoking the sanc-tion of nullity. That is at once the strength and the weakness of the Due Process Model: its strength because in our system the appeal to the Constitution pro-vides the last and overriding word; its weakness because saying no in specific cases is an exercise in futility unless there is a general willingness on the part of the officials who operate the process to apply negative prescriptions across the board. It is no accident that statements reinforcing the Due Process Model come from the courts, while at the same time facts denying it are established by the police and prosecutors.

NOTE

1. Paul Bator, "Finality in Criminal Law and Federal Habeas Corpus for State Pris-oners," *Harvard Law Review* 76 (1963): 441–442.

2

✪

Toward a Theory of
Street-Level Bureaucracy

MICHAEL LIPSKY

Most people employed by criminal justice organizations can be described as street-level bureaucrats. They are public employees who interact constantly with nonvoluntary clients and have a considerable amount of discretion about how to deal with them. Michael Lipsky argues that street-level bureaucrats must do their jobs in spite of inadequate resources and in an environment where their authority is regularly challenged and where expectations about how they should be doing their job are contradictory and/or ambiguous.

STREET-LEVEL BUREAUCRACY
AND THE STRUCTURE OF WORK

This essay is an attempt to develop a theory of the political behavior of street-level bureaucrats and their interactions with clients. Street-level bureaucrats, defined below, are those men and women who, in their face-to-face encounters with citizens, "represent" government to the people. The essay is also an effort to inquire into aspects of organizational life common to various urban bureaucracies, so that we may begin to develop generalizations about

Source: Reprinted from Michael Lipsky, "Street-Level Bureaucracy and the Analysis of Urban Reform," *Urban Affairs Quarterly,* Vol. 6 (June 1971), pp. 391–409. Copyright © 1971 by Sage Publications. Reprinted by permission of Sage Publications, Inc. Footnotes and references deleted.

urban bureaucratic behavior that transcend discussions of individual bureaucratic contexts. We seek answers to the general question: What behavioral and psychological factors are common to such bureaucratic roles as teacher, policeman, welfare worker, lower-court judge? To identify such common elements would be to make a start toward theory in the study of urban bureaucracy.

Concentrating on the reactions of some urban bureaucrats to conditions of stress, this essay also draws attention to various structural factors that may contribute to the inherent inability of some urban bureaucracies to provide objective, nondiscriminatory service, to recognize the existence of biased behavior, and to respond to pressures from some client groups. These assertions are matters of public urgency at a time when police departments, school systems, welfare offices, and urban legal systems increasingly have come under severe criticism.

The discussion is focused upon two types of urban public-service employees currently experiencing considerable pressure from many groups: policemen and teachers. The example provided by lower-court judges is also utilized considerably, and other urban bureaucracies are referred to when relevant.

While we concentrate on the relationship of some urban bureaucrats to conditions of stress, the term *street-level bureaucrat* is used throughout to draw attention to individuals in organizational roles requiring frequent and significant contacts with citizens. Specifically, a "street-level bureaucrat" is defined as a public employee whose work is characterized by the following three conditions:

1. He is called upon to interact constantly with citizens in the regular course of his job.

2. Although he works within a bureaucratic structure, his independence on the job is fairly extensive. One component of this independence is discretion in making decisions; but independence is not limited to discretion. The attitude and general approach of the street-level bureaucrat toward the citizen may affect the individual significantly. These considerations are broader than the term *discretion* suggests.

3. The potential impact on citizens with whom he deals is fairly extensive.

This paper will concentrate on the interaction of street-level bureaucrats and the nonvoluntary clients with whom they deal in the course of their jobs.

In American cities today, their work environments frequently require street-level bureaucrats to confront problems stemming from lack of organizational and personal resources, physical and psychological threat, and conflicting and/or ambiguous role expectations. People in these bureaucratic roles both deliberately and unconsciously develop mechanisms to cope with these problems. Street-level bureaucrats are also receptive to and supportive of organizational structural mechanisms that simplify and reduce the burdens of office. We will attempt to describe and assess the impact of selected bureaucratic resolutions of these problems on job performance and community relations.

A few other job conditions common to street-level bureaucrats should be mentioned here. They perform their jobs with nonvoluntary clients, and, no doubt related, these clienteles for the most part do not serve as primary bureaucratic reference groups. These points may be illustrated by considering the nature of police interactions with offenders and suspects, teachers' interactions with pupils, and lower-court judges' interactions with individuals charged with criminal or deviant behavior.

Another condition commonly characterizing street-level bureaucrats is that they have limited control—although extensive influence—over clientele performance, accompanied in part by high expectations and demands concerning that performance. Police and lower-court judges are charged with controlling behavior that has profound social roots. Teachers are asked to compensate for aspects of children's upbringing for which they are not responsible.

Still another condition characterizing street-level bureaucracies is the difficulty in measuring job performance in terms of ultimate bureaucratic objectives. Work standards may be established and attempts made to determine if those standards are being achieved. For example, when policemen are asked to make a certain number of arrests per month, or social workers are asked to maintain a certain size caseload, they are being asked to measure up to work standards. But these measures are only problematically related to public safety or clients' ability to cope with problems, which are the ultimate objectives in police–citizen or social worker–client interactions. The practical impossibility of accurately measuring job performance, in combination with wide discretion, contributes to substantial problems in controlling or shaping these organizations from above.

Although the theoretical aspects of this essay to some degree are generally applicable to interactions between street-level bureaucrats and citizens, they are most applicable to interactions with low-income and minority-group clients. Poor people and minority-group members tend to command fewer personal resources than more favored individuals and thus are more dependent upon governmental bureaucratic structures for fair treatment or provision of basic services.

In this brief essay I will not be able to provide a comprehensive analysis of street-level bureaucratic groups. Nor can the jobs or professions be described in monolithic fashion; they encompass a wide range of variation. In attempting to develop a parsimonious theory of governmental organizational behavior and client interaction, I am interested rather in making more understandable certain problems of these bureaucratic structures and in initiating critical analysis of certain aspects of governmental organizational behavior at the point of consumption.

The discussion will apply to aspects of street-level bureaucracy when the following conditions are relatively salient in the job environment:

1. Available resources are inadequate.

2. Work proceeds in circumstances where there exists clear physical and/or psychological threat and/or the bureaucrat's authority is regularly challenged.

3. Expectations about job performance are ambiguous and/or contradictory and include unattainable idealized dimensions.

Although to some extent these conditions prevail in most bureaucratic contexts, they are *relatively salient* in street-level bureaucracies in the contemporary American urban setting. They are the result of (and I will suggest they are in some ways the causes of) what is known as the urban "crisis." Evidence of the existence of these conditions may be found in contemporary discussions of these professions and to some degree in general analyses of organizational behavior. The conditions do not invariably obtain, and they are less salient in some bureaucratic contexts than in others. In some settings street-level bureaucrats are relatively free from these conditions. This fact does not invalidate the argument. It only suggests that at times the inferences drawn here are not applicable and that it would be useful to specify those conditions under which they *are* applicable. Although the analysis is concentrated to some extent on police, teachers, and lower-court judges, it is intended to be relevant in other bureaucratic contexts when the characteristics and qualifications discussed above obtain.

The remainder of this section extends and amplifies the discussion of conditions of stress under which street-level bureaucrats often must work.

Inadequate Resources

Almost all bureaucratic decision-making contexts are characterized by limited time and information. Street-level bureaucrats, however, work in a relatively high degree of uncertainty relative to the complexity of individuals about whom they must make decisions, although they are required to act as if certainty were achievable and were regularly achieved.

Resources necessary to function adequately as street-level bureaucrats may be classified as organizational resources and personal resources. Organizationally, street-level bureaucrats must be provided with adequate technical assistance and tools and with settings conducive to client compliance. Perhaps most important, the manpower/client ratio must be such that service may be provided with a relatively low degree of stress consistent with expectations of service provision.

Typical personal resources necessary for adequate job performance are sufficient time to make decisions (and act upon them), access to information, and information itself. For the policeman in many encounters with citizens, scarce personal resources frequently make it difficult to collect relevant information or process information adequately. When breaking up a fight in a bar, a policeman may not have time to determine the initiating party and so must make a double arrest. The need to mobilize information quickly in an uncertain bureaucratic environment may account for police practices of collecting or hoarding as much information as possible on individuals and situations in which policemen may be called to intervene, even if this information is inadmissible in court. It is not only that guidelines governing police behavior are inadequate but that inadequacy of personal and organizational resources contributes to the "improvisational" ways in which law enforcement is carried out.

In big cities, lower-court judges who process tens of thousands of cases each year and have great difficulty bringing cases to trial in timely fashion hardly have time to obtain a comprehensive picture of every case on which they sit. One might attribute this pressure to lack of manpower, since more judges would permit each case to be heard more fully. But whether one attributes it to lack of time or to inadequate staffing, lower-court judges lack the resources to do their job adequately. Many big-city teachers must perform in overcrowded classrooms with inadequate materials and with clients requiring intense personal attention.

Threats and Challenges to Authority

The conditions under which street-level bureaucrats are asked to do their jobs often include distinct physical and psychological threats. This component is most clearly relevant to the police role. Police constantly work under the threat of violence that may come from any direction at any time. Threat may exist independent of the actual incidence of threat materialization. The fact that policemen spend most of their time in nonthreatening tasks does not reduce the threat affecting their job orientations.

Teachers in inner-city schools under some circumstances also appear to work under threat of physical harm. But more common may be the threat that chaos poses for a teacher attempting to perform his job. The potential for chaos, or a chaotic classroom, implies the elimination of the conditions under which teaching can take place. The threat of chaos is present whether or not teachers commonly experience chaos and regardless of whether chaotic classroom conduct is caused by students or inspired by the teacher.

Although the institutional setting in which lower-court judges conduct cases reduces the potential for threat, judges are harried by the enormous case backlogs that confront them and by the knowledge that individuals who cannot make bail spend long periods in jail without trial. They are under constant pressure from administrative judicial superiors to reduce this backlog. The imperative to "keep the calendar moving," reinforced by the (often unrealized) judicial goal of a minimum wait from arrest to trial, is distinctly dissonant with the component of the ideal judicial image, which stresses hearing each case on its merits.

Threat and authority seem reciprocally related for street-level bureaucrats. The greater the degree of personal or role authority, the less the threat. One might also hypothesize that the greater the threat, the less bureaucrats feel that authority is respected, and the more they feel the need to invoke it. These hypotheses are supported by invocations to teachers to establish classroom control as a precondition to teaching. They also tend to be confirmed by studies of police behavior. Danger and authority have been identified as the principal variables of the police role. The authority vested in the role of policeman is seen by police as an instrument of control, without which they are endangered. Hence comes the often reported tendency to be lenient with offenders whose attitude and demeanor are penitent, but harsh and punitive to those offenders who show signs of disrespect. Indeed, policemen often appear to "test" the extent to which an offender is respectful in order to determine whether he is a "wise guy" and thus has an improper attitude.

Expectations about Job Performance

Street-level bureaucrats often must perform their jobs in response to ambiguous and contradictory expectations. These expectations in part may be unattainable. Some goal orientations may be unrealistic, mutually exclusive, or unrealized because of lack of control over the client's background and performance, as discussed above.

Role theorists generally have attempted to locate the origin of role expectations in three "places": in peers and others who occupy complementary role positions; in reference groups, in terms of whom expectations are defined, although they are not literally present; and in public expectations generally, where consensus about role expectations can sometimes be found. While we cannot specify here how role expectations are generated for various street-level bureaucrats, we can make a few points concerning conflict in urban areas over these bureaucracies.

Conflicting and ambiguous role expectations stemming from divided community sentiments are the source of considerable bureaucratic strain. As public officials, street-level bureaucrats are subject to expectations that they will treat individuals fairly and impartially. To some degree they are also subject, as public officials, to expectations that individuals and individual cases will be treated on their unique merits. Provision of services in terms of the ideal is constantly challenged by "realists," who stress the legitimacy of adjustments to working conditions and the unavailability of resources.

Apparently in direct conflict with expectations concerning equal treatment are expectations from more parochial community interests, to which street-level bureaucrats are also subject as public officials. In a real sense, street-level bureaucrats are expected by some reference groups to recognize the desirability of providing *unequal* treatment. Invocations to "clean up" certain sections of town, to harass undesirables through heavy surveillance (prostitutes, motorcycle or juvenile gangs, civil rights workers, hippies), to prosecute vigorously community "parasites" (junkies, slumlords), and even to practice reverse discrimination (for minority groups)—all such instances represent calls for unequal bureaucratic treatment. They illustrate the efforts of some community segments to use street-level bureaucracies to gain relative advantages.

Conflicts stemming from divisive, parochial community expectations will be exacerbated in circumstances of attitudinal polarization. As relative consensus or indifference concerning role expectations diminishes, street-level bureaucrats may respond by choosing among conflicting expectations rather than attempting to satisfy more than one of them. In discussing police administrative discretion, James Q. Wilson suggests that there is a "zone of indifference" in the prevailing political culture within which administrators are free to act. When values are polarized, the zone may become wider. But indifference and, as a result, discretion may be diminished as bureaucratic performance is increasingly scrutinized and practices formerly ignored assume new meaning for aroused publics.

The police role is significantly affected by conflicting role expectations. In part stemming from public ambivalence about the police, policemen must perform their duties somewhere between the demands for strict law enforcement, the necessity of discretion in enforcement, and various community mores. They must accommodate the constraints of constitutional protection and demands for efficiency in maintenance of order and crime control. They must enforce laws they did not make in communities where demands for law enforcement vary with the laws and with the various strata of the population, and where police may perceive the public as hostile yet dependent. Police role behavior may conflict significantly with their own value preferences as individuals and with the behavior and outlook of judges. They are expected to be scrupulously objective and impartial, protective of all segments of society. Speaking generally, we may expect lack of clarity in role expectations in these cases to be no less dysfunctional than in other circumstances where lack of role clarity has been observed.

In discussing the generation of role expectations in street-level bureaucracies, we should note the relative unimportance of nonvoluntary clients. This is not to say that children are unimportant to teachers, or that litigants and defendants are unimportant to judges. But they do not primarily, or even secondarily, determine bureaucratic role expectations. Some contemporary political movements that appear to be particularly upsetting to some street-level bureaucrats, such as demands for community control and community health planning, may be understood as demands for inclusion in the constellation of bureaucratic reference groups by nonvoluntary clients. It may not be that street-level bureaucracies are *generally* unresponsive, as is sometimes claimed. Rather, they have been responsive in the past to constellations of reference groups that have excluded a significant portion of the population with whom they regularly deal.

Public bureaucracies are somewhat vulnerable to the articulated demands of any organized segment of society because they partially share the ethos of public responsiveness and fairness. But street-level bureaucracies seem particularly incapable of responding positively to the new groups because of the ways in which their role expectations are currently framed. Demands for bureaucratic changes are most likely to be responded to when they are articulated by primary reference groups. When they are articulated by client groups outside the regular reference group arena, probabilities of responsiveness in ways consistent with client demands are likely to be significantly lower.

ADAPTATIONS TO THE WORK SITUATION

In order to make decisions when confronted with a complex problem and an uncertain environment, individuals who play organizational roles will develop bureaucratic mechanisms to make the tasks easier. To the extent that street-level bureaucrats are threatened by the three kinds of problems described in the first section, they will develop coping mechanisms specifically related to these concerns. In this discussion we will focus on the ways in which simplifications, routines, and various coping mechanisms or strategies for dealing with the bureaucratic problems described earlier are integrated into the behavior of street-level bureaucrats and their organizational lives.

By simplifications, we refer to those symbolic constructs in terms of which individuals order their perceptions so as to make the perceived environment easier to manage. They may do this for reasons of instrumental efficiency and/or reasons of anxiety reduction. By routines, we mean the establishment of habitual or regularized patterns in terms of which tasks are performed. For this essay we will concentrate on routines for the purpose of, or with the effect of, alleviating bureaucratic difficulties arising from resource inadequacy, threat perception, and unclear role expectations. This essay may be said to focus on the trade-offs incurred in, and the unintended consequences of, developing such mechanisms.

Having discussed three conditions under which street-level bureaucrats frequently must work, we now examine some of the ways in which they attempt to accommodate these conditions and some of the implications of the mechanisms developed in the coping process.

Accommodations to Inadequate Resources

The development of simplifications and routines permits street-level bureaucrats to make quick decisions and thereby accomplish their jobs with less difficulty (perhaps freeing scarce resources through time saving), while at the same time partly reducing tensions with clients or personal anxiety over the adequacy of decisions made. "Shortcuts" developed by these bureaucracies are often made because of inadequate resources. Police limit enforcement because of inability to enforce constantly all laws (even if the community wanted total enforcement). Routinization of judicial activities in the lower courts is pervasive. Decisions on bail and sentencing are made without knowledge of the defendant's background or an adequate hearing of the individual cases, as judges "become preoccupied simply with moving the cases. Clearing the dockets becomes a primary objective of all concerned, and cases are dismissed, guilty pleas are entered, and bargains are struck with that end as the dominant consideration."

Not only does performance on a case basis suffer with routinization but critical decisions may effectively be made by bureaucrats not ultimately responsible for the decisions. Thus, for example, judges in juvenile courts have effectively transferred decision making to the police or probationary officers whose undigested reports form the basis of judicial action. Both in schools and in the streets, the record of an individual is likely to mark him for special notice by teachers and policemen who, to avoid trouble or find guilty parties, look first among the pool of known "troublemakers." Certain types of crimes, and certain types of individuals, receive special attention from street-level bureaucrats who develop categorical attitudes toward offenses and offenders.

Additionally, routines may become ends in themselves. Special wrath is often reserved for clients who fail to appreciate the bureaucratic necessity of routine. Clients are denied rights as individuals because to encourage exercise of individual rights would jeopardize processing of caseloads on a mass basis.

Accommodations to Threat

Routines and simplifications are developed by street-level bureaucrats who must confront physical and psychological threat. Inner-city schoolteachers, for example, consider maintaining discipline one of their primary problems. It is a particularly critical problem in "slum" schools, where "keeping them in line" and avoiding physical confrontations consume a major portion of teachers' time, detracting from available educational opportunities. Even under threatening circumstances, elementary schoolteachers are urged to "routinize as much as possible" in order to succeed.

"You gotta be tough, kid, or you'll never last" appears to be typical of the greeting most frequently exchanged by veteran officers in socializing rookies into the force. Because a policeman's job continually exposes him to potential for violence, he develops simplifications to identify people who might pose danger. Skolnick has called individuals so identified "potential assailants." Police may find clues to the identity of a potential assailant in the way he walks, his clothing, his race, previous experiences with police, or other "nonnormal" qualities. The moral worthiness of clients also appears to have an impact on judicial judgment. In this regard, the police experience may be summed as the development of faculties for suspicion.

Mechanisms may be developed to reduce threat potential by minimizing bureaucratic involvement. Thus policemen are tutored in how to distinguish cases that should be settled on the spot with minimal police intervention. Ploys are developed to disclaim personal involvement or to disclaim discretion within the situation. "It's the law," or "Those are the rules" may be empirically accurate assertions, but they are without substance when weighed with the relationship between discretion and law enforcement. Street-level bureaucrats may totally evade involvement through avoidance strategies. Thus, according to one account, failure to report incidents in ghetto neighborhoods are "rationalize[d] . . . with theories that the victim would refuse to prosecute because violence has become the accepted way of life for his community, and that any other course would result in a great loss of time in court, which would reduce the efficiency of other police functions."

Routines also serve to provide more information about potential difficulties and to protect an image of authority. "Potential assailants" are frequently approached by police in a brusque, imperious manner in order to determine if they respect police authority. Early teacher identification of "troublemakers," and the sensitivity of policemen to sudden movements on the part of a suspect (anticipating the reaching for a weapon), further illustrate the development of simplifications for the purposes of reducing the possibility of physical threat.

Threats to the systems of which street-level bureaucrats are a part also contribute to the sense of threat personally perceived. Thus street-level bureaucrats attempt to provide an atmosphere in which their authority will be unquestioned and conformity to their system of operation will be enhanced. The courtroom setting of bench, bar, and robes, as well as courtroom ritual, all function to establish such an environment. Uniforms also support the authoritative image, as do institutional rules governing conduct and dress. Imposition of symbols of authority function to permit street-level bureaucrats to test the general compliance of the client to the system. Thus the salute to the uniform, not the man; thus a policeman's concern that disrespect for him is disrespect for the law.

We suggest the following hypotheses about these mechanisms for threat reduction. The mechanisms will be employed more frequently than objective conditions might seem to warrant because for them to be effective they must be employed in all instances of possible threat. The consequences of failure to guard against physical threat are so severe that the tendency will develop to employ safety mechanisms as often, rather than as little, as possible. This pattern contrasts significantly with routines invoked for efficiency. Traffic law enforcement, for example, may be ensured by sporadic enforcement; occasional intervention serves as a sufficient deterrent for the police department. But in threatening circumstances, the risks are too great for *individual* bureaucrats to depend upon sporadic invocation.

Threat-reduction mechanisms also are more likely to be invoked in circumstances where the penalties for employing them are nonexistent, rarely imposed, or not severe. Penalties for using threat-reducing mechanisms are least likely to be invoked in street-level bureaucracies where employees are most exposed to threat, because for these bureaucracies ability to reduce threat and thus reduce personnel anxiety are organizational maintenance requisites.

Additionally, street-level bureaucrats may have a stake in exaggerating the potential for danger or job-oriented difficulties. The reasoning is similar. If the threat is exaggerated, then the threat-reduction mechanisms will be employed more often, presumably decreasing the likelihood of actual physical danger. However, as suggested below, increased invocation of threat-reducing routines may evoke the very actions that are feared.

Exaggerating the threat publicly will also reduce the likelihood of imposition of official sanctions, since bureaucrats' superiors will have greater confidence that knowledge of the dangers accompanying job performance will be widely disseminated. Thus street-level bureaucrats paradoxically have a stake in continuing to promote information about the difficulties of their jobs at the same time that they seek to publicize their professional competence. This is analogous to the paradox of police administrators who thrive simultaneously on public anxiety over crime waves and on the recognition of victories over crime.

One function of professional associations of policemen and teachers has been to publicize information about the lack of adequate resources with which they must work. This public relations effort permits the street-level bureaucrat to say (to himself and publicly) with greater confidence that his position will be appreciated by others: "Any failures attributed to me can be understood as failures to give me the tools to do the job."

The psychological reality of the threat may bear little relationship to the statistical probabilities. One teacher knifed in a hallway will evoke concern among teachers for order, even though statistically the incident might be insignificant. Policemen may imagine an incipient assault and shoot to kill, not because of the probabilities that the putative assailant will have a knife, but perhaps because once, some years ago, a policeman failed to draw a gun on an assailant and was stabbed to death. Such incidents may also be affected by tendencies to perceive some sets of people as hostile and potentially dangerous. In such circumstances the threat would be heightened by the conjunction of both threatening event and actor.

Accommodations to Role Expectations

Role expectations that are ambiguous, contradictory, and in some ways unrealizable represent additional job difficulties with which street-level bureaucrats must cope. Here we will discuss two coping processes with which street-level bureaucrats may effectively reduce the pressures generated by lack of clarity and unattainability of role expectations.

Changing Role Expectations Street-level bureaucrats may attempt to alter expectations about job performance. They may try to influence the expectations of people who help give their role definition. They may try to create a definition of their roles that includes a heroic component recognizing the quality of job performance as a function of the difficulties encountered. Teachers may see themselves and try to get others to see them as the unsung heroes of the city. They may seek an image of themselves as people who work without public recognition or reward, under terrific tension, and who, whatever their shortcomings, are making the greatest contribution to the education of minority groups. Similarly, policemen appear interested in projecting an image of themselves as soldiers of pacification, keeping the streets safe despite community hostility and general lack of recognition. Judges, too, rationalize their job performance by stressing the physical strain under which they work and the extraordinary caseloads they must process.

One of the implications of role redefining may be the disclaiming of responsibility over the results of work. It is surely difficult to demand improvement in job performance if workers are not responsible for the product. Furthermore, the claim of lack of responsibility is often not falsifiable unless illustrations are available of significantly more successful performances under similar constraints.

Another facet of role redefinition may be efforts to perform jobs *in some way* in accordance with perceived role expectations. Such efforts are manifested in greater teacher interest in some children who are considered bright ("If I can't teach them all, I can at least try to teach the few who have something on the ball"); in the extraordinary time some judges will take with a few cases while many people wait for their turn for a hearing; and in the time policemen spend investigating certain crimes. In these cases, street-level bureaucrats may be responding to role expectations that emphasize individual attention and personal concern for community welfare. The judge who takes the time to hear a case fully is hardly blameworthy. But these tendencies, which partially fulfill role expectations, deflect pressures for adequate routine treatment of clienteles. They also marginally divert resources from the large bulk of cases and clients, although not so many resources as to make a perceptible dent in public impressions of agency performance. Like the public agency that creates a staff to ensure a quick response to "crisis" cases, these developments may be described as routines to deal with public expectations on a selective case basis, reducing pressures to develop routines conforming to idealized role expectations on a *general* basis.

Changing Definition of the Clientele A second set of strategies by which street-level bureaucrats can attempt to alter expectations about job performance is to alter assumptions about the clientele to be served. This approach may take the form either of attributing responsibility for all actions to the client or of perceiving the client as so victimized by social forces that he cannot really be helped by service. Goffman explains well the function of the first mode of perception:

> Although there is a psychiatric view of mental disorder and an environmental view of crime and counterrevolutionary activity, both freeing the offender from moral responsibility for his offense, total institutions can little afford this particular kind of determinism. Inmates must be caused to *self-direct* themselves in a manageable way, and, for this to be promoted, both desired and undesired conduct must be defined as springing from the personal will and character of the individual inmate himself, and defined as something he himself can do something about.

Police tendencies to attribute riots to the riffraff of the ghettos (criminals, transients, and agitators) may also be explained in this way. Instances of teachers beating children who clearly display signs of mental disturbance provide particularly brutal illustrations of the apparent need of at least some street-level bureaucrats to attribute self-direction to noncompliant clients.

The second perceptual mode also functions to absolve street-level bureaucrats from responsibility by attributing clients' performance difficulties to cultural or societal factors. If children are perceived to be primitive, racially inferior, or "culturally deprived," a teacher can hardly fault himself if his charges fail to progress. Just as policemen respond to calls in different ways depending on the victim's "legitimacy," teachers often respond to children in terms of their "moral acceptability." According to Howard Becker, children may be morally unacceptable to teachers in terms of values centered around health and cleanliness, sex and aggression, ambition and work, and age-group relations. These considerations are particularly related to class discrepancies between teacher and pupil.

Undeniably there are cultural and social factors that affect client performance. Similarly, there is a sense in which people are responsible for their actions and activities. What is important to note, however, is that these explanations function as cognitive shields between the client and street-level bureaucrat, reducing what responsibility and accountability may exist in the role expectations of street-level bureaucrats. These explanations may also contribute to hostility between clients and bureaucrats.

The street-level bureaucrat can conform to role expectations by redefining the clientele in terms of which expectations are framed. This may be called "segmenting the population to be served." In police work the tendency to segment the population may be manifested in justifications for differential rates of law enforcement between white and black communities. It is also noticeable in police harassment of hippies, motorcycle gangs, and college students where long hair has come to symbolize the not-quite-human quality that a black skin has long played in some aspects of law enforcement. The police riots during the Democratic National Convention of 1968, and since then in various university communities, may be more explicable if one recognizes that long-haired white college students are considered by police in some respects to be "outside" of the community that can expect to be protected by norms of due process. Segmenting the population to be served reinforces police and judicial practices that condone failure to investigate crimes involving black against black or encourage particular vigilance in attempting to control black crime against whites. In New York City, the landlord orientations of public officials and judges concerned with landlord-tenant disputes are reinforced by diffuse but widely accepted assumptions that low-income blacks and Puerto Ricans are insensitive to property and property damage.

As coping behavior these strategies are similar to defense mechanisms, in that they involve reappraisal and distortion of the conditions of threat and work-related stresses. For street-level bureaucrats segmentation functions psychologically to permit bureaucrats to make some of their clienteles even more remote in their hierarchies of reference groups. At the same time, it allows bureaucrats to perform without the need to confront their manifest failure. They can think of themselves as having performed adequately in situations where raw materials were weak or the resources necessary to deploy their technical skills were insufficient.

We conclude this section by noting some of the institutional mechanisms developed in street-level bureaucracies that are conducive to greater bureaucratic control over the work environment and thus responsive to the needs of street-level bureaucrats. These relationships obtain regardless of the reasons for introducing the structural arrangements discussed here. The tracking system, whereby early in a pupil's career schools institutionally structure teacher expectations about him, represents one such institutional mechanism. Thus the educational "system" becomes responsible for pupils' progress and direction, and teachers are free to make only marginal decisions about their students (to decide in rare cases whether a student should leave a given track). In addition to reducing the decision-making burden, the tracking system, as many have argued, largely determines its own predicted stability.

Another institutional mechanism that results in reducing client-related difficulties in street-level bureaucracies is the development of procedures for effectively limiting clientele demands by making systems financially or psychologically costly or irritating to use. For lower courts this kind of development results in inducing people to plead guilty in exchange for lighter sentences. Welfare procedures and eligibility requirements have been credited with limiting the number of actual recipients. Inability to solve burglary cases results in peremptory investigations by police departments, resulting further in reduced citizen burglary reports. The Gothic quality of civilian review board procedures effectively limits complaints. The unfathomable procedures for filing housing violation complaints in New York City provides yet another illustration of effective limitation of demand.

Still another institutional mechanism resulting in reduced pressures on the general system is the "special unit" designed to respond to particularly intense client complaints. Illustrations may be found in the establishment of police review boards, human relations units of public agencies, and public agency emergency services. The establishment of such units, whether or not they perform their manifest functions, also works to take bureaucracies off the hook by making it appear that something is being done about problems. However, usually in these cases the problems about which clients want something done (police brutality, equitable treatment for minority groups, housing inspections and repairs) are related to *general* street-level bureaucratic behavior. Thus they can only be ameliorated through *general* attacks on bureaucratic performance. These units permit street-level bureaucrats to allege that problems are being handled and provide a "place" in the bureaucracy where particularly vociferous and persistent complainants can be referred. At the same time, the existence of the units deflects pressures for general reorientations.

THE ROLE OF STEREOTYPES

Routines, simplifications, and other mechanisms utilized by street-level bureaucrats in interactions with their nonvoluntary clients are not made in a social vacuum. The ways in which these mechanisms are structured will be highly significant. Some simplifications will have a greater impact on people's lives than others, and the ways they are structured will affect some groups more than others. The simplifications by which park department employees choose which trees to trim will have much less impact on people's lives than the simplifications in terms of which policemen make judgments about potential suspects.

In urban bureaucracies, stereotyping and other forms of racial and class biases significantly inform the ways in which simplifications and routines are structured. This simple conclusion is inescapable for anyone familiar with studies of police, teachers, and judges.

Stereotypes affect simplifications and routines, but they are not equivalent. In the absence of stereotypes, simplifying and routinizing would go on anyhow. Categorization is a necessary part of the bureaucratic process. But in American urban life, easily available stereotypes affect bureaucratic decision making in ways which independently exacerbate urban conflict.

First, in a society that already stigmatizes certain racial and income groups the bureaucratic needs to simplify and routinize become colored by the available stereotypes, resulting in *institutionalization* of the stereotyping tendencies.

Second, as will be discussed below, street-level bureaucratic behavior is perceived as bigoted and discriminatory, probably to a greater degree than the sum of individual discriminatory actions.

Third, and perhaps most interesting, the results of the interaction between simplifications, routines, and biases are masked from both bureaucrats and clients. Clients primarily perceive bias, while street-level bureaucrats primarily perceive their own responses to bureaucratic necessities as neutral, fair, and rational (that is, based upon empirical probabilities). The bureaucratic mode becomes a defense against allegations of unfairness or lack of service. By stressing the need for simplifying and routinizing, street-level bureaucrats can effectively deflect confrontations concerning inadequate client servicing by the mechanisms mentioned earlier. And when confrontations do occur, street-level bureaucrats may effectively diminish the claims of organized client groups by insisting that clients are unappreciative of service, ignorant of bureaucratic necessity, and unfair in attributing racial motives to ordinary bureaucratic behavior.

The conflict over the tracking systems in Washington, D.C., and other cities illustrates this point. The school bureaucracy defended tracking as an inherently neutral mechanism for segregating students into ability groupings for more effective teaching. Rigidities in the system were denied; reports that tracking decisions were made on racial bases were ignored; and evidence of abuse of the tracking system was attributed to correctable malfunctioning of an otherwise useful instrument. Missing from the school bureaucracy's side of the debate was recognition that in the District school system, tracking would inevitably be permeated by stereotypic and biased decision making.

In addition to the interaction between stereotyping and simplifications, three developments may be mentioned briefly that tend to reinforce bureaucratic biases: (1) playing out of self-fulfilling prophecies; (2) street-level bureaucrats' acceptance of partial empirical validation; and (3) their acceptance of illustrative validation.

In categorizing students as low or high achievers, in a sense predicting their capacity to achieve, teachers appear to create validity for the very simplifications in which they engage. Evidence has been presented that suggests that on the whole students will perform better in class if teachers think pupils are bright, regardless of whether or not they are. Policemen ensure the validity of their suspicions in many ways. They provoke "symbolic assailants" through baiting them or through oversurveillance tactics. They also concentrate patrol among certain segments of the population, thereby ensuring that there will be more police confrontations with that group. In this context there is triple danger in being young, black, and noticed by the law. Not only may arrests be more frequent, but employers' concerns for clean arrest records and the ways in which American penal institutions function as schools for criminals rather than rehabilitative institutions increase the probabilities that the arrested alleged petty offender will become the hardened criminal that he was assumed to be turning into. Hospital staffs, to illustrate from somewhat different sets of bureaucrats, appear to "teach" people how to be mentally and physically ill by subtly rewarding conforming behavior. Value judgments may intrude into supposedly neutral contexts to ensure that the antipathies of some bureaucrats will be carried over in subsequent encounters, for instance, in the creating of client "records" that follow them throughout their dealings with bureaucracies.

Partial empirical validation of the legitimacy of simplifications informed by stereotypes may occur through selective attention to information. Statistics can be marshaled to demonstrate that black crime has increased. A policeman may screen out information that places the statistical increase in perspective, never recognizing that his own perceptions of the world have contributed to the very increases he deplores. He also "thinks" he knows that black crime is worse than it was, although some studies have suggested that he overestimates its extent. Similarly, it is unquestionable that children from minority groups with language difficulties have greater problems in school than those without difficulties. Obviously there is something about lack of facility in English in an English-speaking school system that will affect achievement, although it may not be related to potential.

Illustrative validation may confirm simplifications by illustration. The common practice of "proving" the legitimacy of stereotypes, and thus the legitimacy of biased simplifications, by example may be a logical horror but it is also a significant social fact that influences the behavior of street-level bureaucracies. Illustrative validity not only confirms the legitimacy of simplifications but also affects the extent to which simplifications are invoked. The policeman killed in the course of duty because he neglected to shoot his assailant provides the basis for illustrative validity not only about the group of which the assailant is a part but also about the importance of invoking simplifications in the first place.

STREET-LEVEL BUREAUCRACY
AND URBAN CONFLICT

To better understand the interaction between government and citizens at the "place" where government meets people, I have attempted to demonstrate common factors in the behavior of street-level bureaucrats. I have suggested that there are patterns to this interaction, that continuities may be observed that transcend individual bureaucracies, and that certain conditions in the work environment of these bureaucracies appear to be relatively salient in structuring the bureaucrat–citizen interaction.

This analysis may help to explain some aspects of citizen antagonism to contemporary urban bureaucracies. Clients may conclude that service is prejudiced, dehumanizing, and discriminatory in greater degree than is warranted by the incidence of such behavior. Just as it may take only one example of a policeman killed by an assailant to reinforce police tendencies to overreact to potential assailants, so it only takes a few examples of bigoted teachers or prejudiced policemen to reinforce widespread conviction on the part of clients that the system is prejudiced. As Herman Goldstein has put it in discussing police–client relations:

A person who is unnecessarily aggrieved is not only critical of the procedure which was particularly offensive to him. He tends to broaden his interest and attack the whole range of police procedures which suddenly appear to him to be unusually oppressive.

To refer again to propositions concerning threat, citizen stereotyping of bureaucracies may be greater in direct relation to the extent of control and impact that these bureaucracies have on their lives. Thus these tendencies will be relatively salient in institutional settings with considerable impact on citizens, such as schools, in courts, and in police relations. And they will be relatively salient to low-income clients, whose resource alternatives are minimal. Furthermore, such clients may recognize the sense in which the bureaucracies "create" them and the circumstances in which they live.

Just as street-level bureaucrats develop conceptions of nonvoluntary clients that deflect responsibility away from themselves, so citizens may also respond to bureaucracies by attributing to bureaucracies qualities that deflect attention away from their own shortcomings. This may result in citizens' developing conceptions of bureaucrats and bureaucracies as more potent than they actually are. On the other hand, because of predicted neglect or negative experiences in the past, citizens may withdraw from bureaucratic interaction or act with hostility toward street-level bureaucrats, evoking the very reactions *they* have "predicted." Minority groups particularly may have negative experiences with these bureaucracies, since they may be the citizens most likely to be challenged by street-level bureaucrats and most likely to be unable to accept gracefully challenges to self-respect.

Citizens will also share to some extent the role expectations of street-level bureaucrats, although they may have had little influence in shaping them. This may be another source of tension, since citizens may expect personal, individualized consideration or may demand it in spite of bureaucratic needs to provide impersonal treatment in a routinized fashion.

This analysis may help place in perspective the apparent paradox that some community groups insist that street-level bureaucracies are biased and discriminatory, while at the same time, members of these bureaucracies insist in good faith that their members do not engage in discriminatory and biased practices. Regardless of whatever dissemblance may be involved here, we can partially explain the paradox by noting: (1) the ways in which relatively little discriminatory behavior can result in client ascription of a great deal of bureaucratic behavior to discriminatory attitudes; (2) the ways in which mechanisms developed by street-level bureaucrats to cope with problems in job performance are informed and colored by discriminatory stereotypes; and (3) the ways in which street-level bureaucrats institutionalize bias without necessarily recognizing the implications of their actions.

If this analysis has been at all persuasive, it suggests that in significant respects street-level bureaucracies as currently structured may be inherently incapable of responding favorably to contemporary demands for improved and more sympathetic service to some clients. Street-level bureaucrats respond to work-related pressures in ways that, however understandable or well-intentioned, may have invidious effects on citizen impressions of governmental responsiveness and equity in performance. If, indeed, government may be most salient to citizens where there is frequent interaction with its "representatives" and where the interactions may have important consequences for their lives, then these conclusions should evoke sympathy for current proposals for urban decentralization of authority. Whatever their other merits or difficulties, these proposals commend themselves at least for their concentration on fundamental alterations of the work environment of street-level bureaucrats.

3

Racial Politics, Racial Disparities, and the War on Crime

MICHAEL TONRY

African Americans make up more than 50 percent of the prison population but only 12 percent of all U.S. residents. When all punishments—probation, intermediate sanctions, incarceration—are taken into account, one in three African-American men in their twenties are currently under correctional supervision. Michael Tonry believes that racial disparities are a reflection of racial politics, especially the War on Drugs.

Racial disparities in arrests, jailing, and imprisonment steadily worsened after 1980 for reasons that have little to do with changes in crime patterns and almost everything to do with two political developments. First, conservative Republicans in national elections "played the race card" by using anticrime slogans (remember Willie Horton?) as a way to appeal to anti–Black sentiments of White voters. Second, conservative politicians of both parties promoted and voted for harsh crime control and drug policies that exacerbated existing racial disparities.

The worsened disparities might have been ethically defensible if they had been based on good faith beliefs that some greater policy good would thereby have been achieved. Sometimes unwanted side effects of social policy are inevitable. Traffic accidents and fatalities are a price we pay for the convenience of automobiles. Occupational injuries are a price we pay for engaging in the industries in which they occur.

Source: Michael Tonry, "Racial Politics, Racial Disparities, and the War on Crime," *Crime and Delinquency* 40 (1994): 475–497. Copyright © 1994. Reprinted by permission of Sage Publications, Inc.

The principal causes of worse racial disparities have been the War on Drugs launched by the Bush and Reagan administrations, characterized by vast increases in arrests and imprisonment of street-level drug dealers, and the continuing movement toward harsher penalties. Policies toward drug offenders are a primary cause of recent increases in jail and prison admissions and populations. Racial disparities among drug offenders are worse than among other offenders.

It should go without saying in the late 20th century that governments detest racial injustice and desire racial justice, and that racial disparities are tolerable only if they are unavoidable or are outweighed by even more important social gains. There are no offsetting gains that can justify the harms done to Black Americans by recent drug and crime control policies.

This article presents data on racial trends in arrests, jailing, and imprisonment; examines the rationales for the policies that have produced those trends; and considers whether the adoption of policies known to have disparate adverse effects on Blacks can be ethically justified. First, the evidence concerning the effectiveness of recent drug and crime control policies that have exacerbated racial disparities is examined. Next, data on arrests, jail, and imprisonment trends are presented and demonstrate that racial disparities have worsened, but not because Blacks are committing larger proportions of the serious offenses (homicide, rape, robbery, aggravated assault) for which offenders were traditionally sent to prison. Finally, the reasons why recent policies were adopted and whether they can be ethically justified are considered.

CRIME REDUCTION EFFECTS
OF CRIME CONTROL POLICY

There is no basis for a claim that recent harsh crime control policies or the enforcement strategies of the War on Drugs were based on good faith beliefs that they would achieve their ostensible purposes. In this and other countries, practitioners and scholars have long known that manipulation of penalties has few, if any, effects on crime rates.

Commissions and expert advisory bodies have been commissioned by the federal government repeatedly over the last 30 years to survey knowledge of the effects of crime control policies, and consistently they have concluded that there is little reason to believe that harsher penalties significantly enhance public safety. In 1967, the President's Commission on Law Enforcement and Administration of Justice observed that crime control efforts can have little effect on crime rates without much larger efforts being directed at crime's underlying social and economic causes. "The Commission . . . has no doubt whatever that the most significant action that can be taken against crime is action designed to eliminate slums and ghettos, to improve education, to provide jobs. . . . We shall not have dealt effectively with crime until we have alleviated the conditions that stimulate it."

In 1978, the National Academy of Sciences Panel on Research on Deterrent and Incapacitative Effects, funded by President Ford's department of justice and asked to examine the available evidence on the crime-reductive effects of sanctions, concluded: "In summary, we cannot assert that the evidence warrants an affirmative conclusion regarding deterrence" (Blumstein, Cohen, and Nagin 1978). Fifteen years later, the National Academy of Sciences Panel on the Understanding and Control of Violent Behavior, created and paid for with funds from the Reagan and Bush administration departments of justice, surveyed knowledge of the effects of harsher penalties on violent crime (Reiss and Roth 1993). A rhetorical question and answer in the panel's final report says it all: "What effect has increasing the prison population had on violent crime? Apparently very little. . . . If tripling the average length of sentence of incarceration per crime [between 1976 and 1989] had a strong preventive effect," reasoned the panel, "then violent crime rates should have declined" (p. 7). They had not.

I mention that the two National Academy of Sciences panels were created and supported by national Republican administrations to demonstrate that skepticism about the crime-preventive effects of harsher punishments is not a fantasy of liberal Democrats. Anyone who has spent much time talking with judges or corrections officials knows that most, whatever their political affiliations, do not believe that harsher penalties significantly enhance public safety.

Likewise, outside the United States, conservative governments in other English-speaking countries have repudiated claims that harsher penalties significantly improve public safety. In Margaret Thatcher's England, for example, a 1990 White Paper (an official policy statement of the government), based on a 3-year study, expressed its skepticism about the preventive effects of sanctions:

> Deterrence is a principle with much immediate appeal. . . . But much crime is committed on impulse, given the opportunity presented by an open window or an unlocked door, and it is committed by offenders who live from moment to moment: their crimes are as impulsive as the rest of their feckless, sad, or pathetic lives. It is unrealistic to construct sentencing arrangements on the assumption that most offenders will weigh up the possibilities in advance and base their conduct on rational calculation. (Home Office 1990)

Canada is the other English-speaking country that has recently had a conservative government. In Brian Mulroney's Canada, the Committee on Justice and the Solicitor General (in American terms, the judiciary committee) proposed in 1993 that Canada shift from an American-style crime control system to a European-style preventive approach. In arguing for the shift in emphasis, the committee observed that "the United States affords a glaring example of the limited effect that criminal justice responses may have on crime. . . . If locking up those who violate the law contributed to safer societies then the United States should be the safest country in the world" (Standing Committee on Justice and the Solicitor General 1993). Six years earlier, the Canadian Sentencing Commission (1987) had reached similar conclusions: "Deterrence cannot be used, with empirical justification, to guide the imposition of sanctions."

There is no better evidentiary base to justify recent drug control policies. Because no other western country has adopted drug policies as harsh as those of the

United States, a bit of background may be useful before I show why there was no reasonable basis for believing recent policies would achieve their ostensible goals. In drug policy jargon, the United States has adopted a prohibitionistic rather than a harm-reduction strategy and has emphasized supply-side over demand-side tactics (Wilson 1990). This strategic choice implies a preference for legal threats and moral denunciation of drug use and users instead of a preference for minimizing net costs and social harms to the general public, the law enforcement system, and drug users. The tactical choice is between a law enforcement emphasis on arrest and punishment of dealers, distributors, and importers, interdiction, and source-country programs or a prevention emphasis on drug treatment, drug-abuse education in schools, and mass media programs aimed at public education. The supply-side bias in recent American policies was exemplified throughout the Bush administration by its insistence that 70% of federal antidrug funds be devoted to law enforcement and only 30% to treatment and education (Office of National Drug Control Policy 1990).

It has been a long time since most researchers and practitioners believed that current knowledge justifies recent American drug control policies. Because the potential income from drug dealing means that willing aspirants are nearly always available to replace arrested street-level dealers, large-scale arrests have repeatedly been shown to have little or no effect on the volume of drug trafficking or on the retail prices of drugs (e.g., Chaiken 1988; Sviridoff, Sadd, Curtis, and Grinc 1992). Because the United States has long and porous borders, and because an unachievably large proportion of attempted smuggling would have to be stopped to affect drug prices significantly, interdiction has repeatedly been shown to have little or no effect on volume or prices (Reuter 1988). Because cocaine, heroin, and marijuana can be grown in many parts of the world in which government controls are weak and peasant farmers' incentives are strong, source-country programs have seldom been shown to have significant influence on drug availability or price in the United States (Moore 1990).

The evidence in support of demand-side strategies is far stronger. In December 1993, the President's Commission on Model State Drug Laws, appointed by President Bush, categorically concluded, "Treatment works." That conclusion is echoed by more authoritative surveys of drug treatment evaluations by the U.S. General Accounting Office (1990), the National Institute of Medicine (Gerstein and Jarwood 1990), and in *Crime and Justice* by Anglin and Hser (1990). Because drug use and offending tend to coincide in the lives of drug-using offenders, the most effective and cost-effective way to deal with such offenders is to get and keep them in well-run treatment programs.

A sizable literature now also documents the effectiveness of school-based drug education in reducing drug experimentation and use among young people (e.g., Botvin 1990; Ellickson and Bell 1990). Although there is no credible literature that documents the effects of mass media campaigns on drug use, a judge could take judicial notice of their ubiquity. It is not unreasonable to believe that such campaigns have influenced across-the-board declines in drug use in the United States since 1980 (a date, incidentally, that precedes the launch of the War on Drugs by nearly 8 years).

That the preceding summary of our knowledge of the effectiveness of drug control methods is balanced and accurate is shown by the support it receives from leading conservative scholars. Senator-scholar Daniel Patrick Moynihan (1993) has written, "Interdiction and 'drug busts' are probably necessary symbolic acts, but nothing more." James Q. Wilson (1990), for two decades America's leading conservative crime control scholar, observed that "significant reductions in drug abuse will come only from reducing demand for those drugs. . . . The marginal product of further investment in supply reduction is likely to be small" (p. 534). He reports that "I know of no serious law-enforcement official who disagrees with this conclusion. Typically, police officials tell interviewers that they are fighting either a losing war or, at best, a holding action" (p. 534).

Thus a fair-minded survey of existing knowledge provides no grounds for believing that the War on Drugs or the harsh policies exemplified by "three strikes and you're out" laws and evidenced by a tripling in America's prison population since 1980 could achieve their ostensible purposes. If such policies cannot be explained in instrumental terms, how can they be explained? The last section answers that question, but first a summary of recent data on racial trends in arrests, jailing, and incarceration.

RACIAL DISPARITIES
IN ARRESTS, JAIL, AND PRISON

Racial disparities, especially affecting Blacks, have long bedeviled the criminal justice system. Many hundreds of studies of disparities have been conducted and there is now widespread agreement among researchers about causes. Racial bias and stereotyping no doubt play some role, but they are not the major cause. In the longer term, disparities in jail and prison are mainly the result of racial differences in offending patterns. In the shorter term, the worsening disparities since 1980 are not primarily the result of racial differences in offending but were foreseeable effects of the War on Drugs and the movement toward increased use of incarceration. These patterns can best be seen by approaching the recent increases in racial disparities in imprisonment as a mystery to be solved. (Because of space limitations, jail data are not discussed here at length, but the trends parallel those for prisons. Between 1980 and 1991, e.g., the percentage of jail inmates who were Black increased from 40% to 48%.)

Figure 1, showing the percentages of prison inmates who were Black or White from 1960 to 1991, reveals two trends. First, for as long as prison population data have been compiled, the percentage of inmates who are Black has by several times exceeded the percentage of Americans who are Black (10% to 13% during the relevant period). Second, since 1980 the Black percentage among prisoners has increased sharply.

Racial disproportions among prison inmates are inherently undesirable, and considerable energy has been expended on efforts to understand them. In 1982,

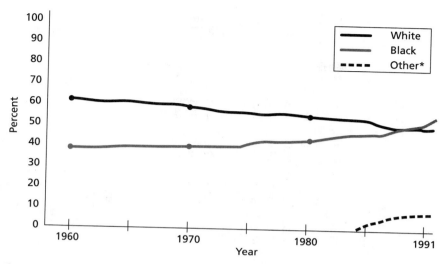

Figure 1 Prisoners in State and Federal Prisons on Census Date by Race, 1960–1991

* = Hispanics in many states, Asians, Native Americans.

SOURCES: For 1960, 1970, 1980: Cahalan 1986, table 3.31; for 1985–1991: Bureau of Justice Statistics 1993, 1991a, 1991b, 1989a, 1989b, 1987.

Blumstein showed that around 80% of the disproportion could be explained on the basis of racial differences in arrest patterns. Of the unexplained 20%, Blumstein argued, some might represent bias and some might reflect racial differences in criminal history or arguably valid case-processing differences. Some years earlier, Hindelang (1976, 1978) had demonstrated that racial patterns in victims' identifications of their assailants closely resembled racial differences in arrests. Some years later, Langan (1985) skipped over the arrest stage altogether and showed that racial patterns in victims' identifications of their assailants explained about 80% of disparities in prison admissions. In 1990, Klein, Petersilia, and Turner showed that, after criminal history and other legitimate differences between cases were taken into account, the offender's race had no independent predictive effect in California on whether he was sent to prison or for how long. There the matter rests. Blumstein (1993a) updated his analysis and reached similar conclusions (with one important exception that is discussed below).

Although racial crime patterns explain a large part of racial imprisonment patterns, they do not explain why the Black percentage rose so rapidly after 1980. Table 1 shows Black and White percentages among people arrested for the eight serious FBI Index Crimes at 3-year intervals from 1976 to 1991 and for 1992. Within narrow bands of fluctuation, racial arrest percentages have been stable since 1976. Comparing 1976 with 1992, for example, Black percentages among people arrested for murder, robbery, and burglary were slightly up and Black percentages among those arrested for rape, aggravated assault, and theft

Table 1 Percentage Black and White Arrests for Index 1 Offenses, 1976–1991 (3-year intervals)*

	1976		1979		1982		1985		1988		1991		1992	
	White	Black	White	Black	White	Black	White	Black	White	Black	White	Black	White	Black
Murder and nonnegligent manslaughter	45.0	53.5	49.4	47.7	48.8	49.7	50.1	48.4	45.0	53.5	43.4	54.8	43.5	55.1
Forcible rape	51.2	46.6	50.2	47.7	48.7	49.7	52.2	46.5	52.7	45.8	54.8	43.5	55.5	42.8
Robbery	38.9	59.2	41.0	56.9	38.2	60.7	37.4	61.7	36.3	62.6	37.6	61.1	37.7	60.9
Aggravated assault	56.8	41.0	60.9	37.0	59.8	38.8	58.0	40.4	57.6	40.7	60.0	38.3	59.5	38.8
Burglary	69.0	29.2	69.5	28.7	67.0	31.7	69.7	28.9	67.0	31.3	68.8	29.3	67.8	30.4
Larceny-theft	65.7	32.1	67.2	30.2	64.7	33.4	67.2	30.6	65.6	32.2	66.6	30.9	66.2	31.4
Motor vehicle theft	71.1	26.2	70.0	27.2	66.9	31.4	65.8	32.4	58.7	39.5	58.5	39.3	58.4	39.4
Arson	—	—	78.9	19.2	74.0	24.7	75.7	22.8	73.5	25.0	76.7	21.5	76.4	21.9
Violent crime†	50.4	47.5	53.7	44.1	51.9	46.7	51.5	47.1	51.7	46.8	53.6	44.8	53.6	44.8
Property crime‡	67.0	30.9	68.2	29.4	65.5	32.7	67.7	30.3	65.3	32.6	66.4	31.3	65.8	31.8
Total crime index	64.1	33.8	65.3	32.4	62.7	35.6	64.5	33.7	62.4	35.7	63.2	34.6	62.7	35.2

*Because of rounding, the percentages may not add to total.

†Violent crimes are offenses of murder, forcible rape, robbery, and aggravated assault.

‡Property crimes are offenses of burglary, larceny-theft, motor vehicle theft, and arson.

SOURCES: *Sourcebook of Criminal Justice Statistics.* Various years. Washington, DC: U.S. Department of Justice, Bureau of Justice Statistics; FBI 1993, Table 43.

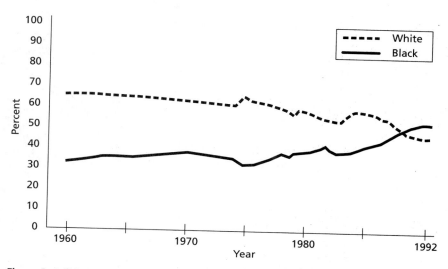

Figure 2 Admissions to Federal and State Prisons by Race, 1960–1992

NOTE: Hispanics are included in Black and White populations.

SOURCES: Langan 1991; Gilliard 1992; Perkins 1992, 1993; Perkins and Gilliard 1992.

were slightly down. Overall, the percentage among those arrested for violent crimes who were Black fell from 47.5% to 44.8%. Because prison sentences have traditionally been imposed on people convicted of violent crimes, Blumstein's and the other analyses suggest that the Black percentage among inmates should be flat or declining. That, however, is not what Figure 1 shows. Why not?

Part of the answer can be found in prison admissions. Figure 2 shows racial percentages among prison admissions from 1960 to 1992. Arrests of Blacks for violent crimes may not have increased since 1980, but the percentage of Blacks among those sent to prison has increased starkly, reaching 54% in 1991 and 1992. Why? The main explanation concerns the War on Drugs.

Table 2 shows racial percentages among persons arrested for drug crimes between 1976 and 1992. Blacks today make up about 13% of the U.S. population and, according to National Institute on Drug Abuse (1991) surveys of Americans' drug use, are no more likely than Whites ever to have used most drugs of abuse. Nonetheless, the percentages of Blacks among drug arrestees were in the low 20% range in the late 1970s, climbing to around 30% in the early 1980s and peaking at 42% in 1989. The number of drug arrests of Blacks more than doubled between 1985 and 1989, whereas White drug arrests increased only by 27%. Figure 3 shows the stark differences in drug arrest trends by race from 1976 to 1991.

Drug control policies are a major cause of worsening racial disparities in prison. In the federal prisons, for example, 22% of new admissions and 25% of the resident population were drug offenders in 1980. By 1990, 42% of new admissions were drug offenders and in 1992 were 58% of the resident population. In state prisons, 5.7% of inmates in 1979 were drug offenders, a figure that by

Table 2 U.S. Drug Arrests by Race, 1976–1992

Year	Total Violations	White	White %	Black	Black %
1976	475,209	366,081	77	103,615	22
1977	565,371	434,471	77	122,594	22
1978	592,168	462,728	78	127,277	21
1979	516,142	396,065	77	112,748	22
1980	531,953	401,979	76	125,607	24
1981	584,776	432,556	74	146,858	25
1982	562,390	400,683	71	156,369	28
1983	615,081	423,151	69	185,601	30
1984	560,729	392,904	70	162,979	29
1985	700,009	482,486	69	210,298	30
1986	688,815	463,457	67	219,159	32
1987	809,157	511,278	63	291,177	36
1988	844,300	503,125	60	334,015	40
1989	1,074,345	613,800	57	452,574	42
1990	860,016	503,315	59	349,965	41
1991	763,340	443,596	58	312,997	41
1992	919,561	546,430	59	364,546	40

SOURCES: FBI 1993, Table 43; *Sourcebook of Criminal Justice Statistics*—1978–1992. Various tables. Washington, DC: U.S. Department of Justice, Bureau of Justice Statistics.

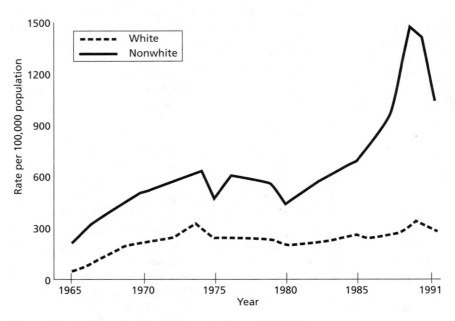

Figure 3 Arrest Rates for Drug Offenses by Race, 1965–1991

SOURCE: Blumstein 1993b.

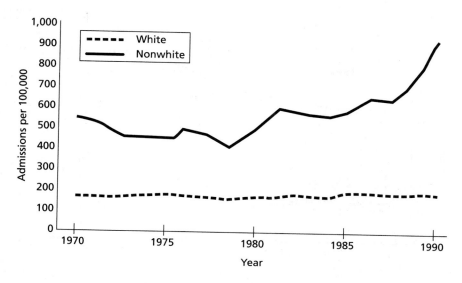

Figure 4 Prison Admissions per 100,000 General Population, North Carolina, by Race, 1970–1990

SOURCE: Clarke 1992.

1991 had climbed to 21.3% to become the single largest category of prisoners (robbers, burglars, and murderers were next at 14.8%, 12.4%, and 10.6%, respectively) (Beck et al. 1993).

The effect of drug policies can be seen in prison data from a number of states. Figure 4 shows Black and White prison admissions in North Carolina from 1970 to 1990. White rates held steady; Black rates doubled between 1980 and 1990, rising most rapidly after 1987. Figure 5 shows prison admissions for drug crimes in Virginia from 1983 to 1989; the racial balance flipped from two-thirds White, one-third non-White in 1983 to the reverse in 1989. Similarly, in Pennsylvania, Clark (1992) reports, Black male prison admissions for drug crimes grew four times faster (up 1,613%) between 1980 and 1990 than did White male admissions (up 477%). In California, according to Zimring and Hawkins (1994), the number of males in prison for drug crimes grew 15 fold between 1980 and 1990 and "there were more people in prison in California for drug offences in 1991 than there were for *all* offences in California at the end of 1979" (p. 89; emphasis in original).

Why, if Blacks in their lives are no more likely than Whites to use illicit drugs, are Blacks so much more likely to be arrested and imprisoned? One possible answer, which is almost certainly wrong, is that Blacks are proportionately more likely to sell drugs. We have no representative surveys of drug dealers and so cannot with confidence paint demographic pictures. However, there is little reason to suspect that drug crimes are more interracial than are most other crimes. In addition, the considerations that make arrests of Black dealers relatively easy make arrests of White dealers relatively hard.

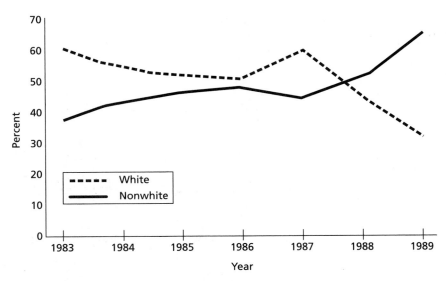

Figure 5 Percentage of New Drug Commitments by Race,
Virginia, Fiscal Years 1983–1989

SOURCE: Austin and McVey 1989.

Drug arrests are easier to make in socially disorganized inner-city minority areas than in working- or middle-class urban or suburban areas for a number of reasons. First, although drug sales in working- or middle-class areas are likely to take place indoors and in private spaces where they are difficult to observe, drug sales in poor minority areas are likely to take place outdoors in streets, alleys, or abandoned buildings, or indoors in public places like bars. Second, although working- or middle-class drug dealers in stable areas are unlikely to sell drugs to undercover strangers, dealers in disorganized areas have little choice but to sell to strangers and new acquaintances. These differences mean that it is easier for police to make arrests and undercover purchases in urban minority areas than elsewhere. Because arrests are fungible for purposes of both the individual officer's personnel file and the department's year-to-year statistical comparisons, more easy arrests look better than fewer hard ones. And because, as ethnographic studies of drug trafficking make clear (Fagan 1993; Padilla 1992), arrested drug dealers in disadvantaged urban minority communities are generally replaced within days, there is a nearly inexhaustible potential supply of young minority Americans to be arrested.

There is another reason why the War on Drugs worsened racial disparities in the justice system. Penalties for drug crimes were steadily made harsher since the mid-1980s. In particular, purveyors of crack cocaine, a drug used primarily by poor urban Blacks and Hispanics, are punished far more severely than are purveyors of powder cocaine, a pharmacologically indistinguishable drug used primarily by middle-class Whites. The most notorious disparity occurs under federal law, which equates 1 gram of crack with 100 grams of powder. As a result, the average prison sentence served by Black federal prisoners is 40% longer than the average sentence for Whites (McDonald and Carlson 1993). Although the Minnesota Supreme Court and two federal district courts have struck down the 100-to-1 rule as a denial of constitutional equal protection to Blacks, at the time of writing, every federal court of appeals that had considered the question had upheld the provision.

The people who launched the drug wars knew all these things—that the enemy troops would mostly be young minority males, that an emphasis on supply-side antidrug strategies, particularly use of mass arrests, would disproportionately ensnare young minority males, that the 100-to-1 rule would disproportionately affect Blacks, and that there was no valid basis for believing that any of these things would reduce drug availability or prices.

Likewise, as the first section showed, there was no basis for a good faith belief that the harsher crime control policies of recent years—more and longer mandatory minimum sentences, tougher and more rigid sentencing guidelines, and three-strikes-and-you're-out laws—would reduce crime rates, and there was a good basis for predicting that they would disproportionately damage Blacks. If Blacks are more likely than Whites to be arrested, especially for drug crimes, the greater harshness of toughened penalties will disproportionately be borne by Blacks. Because much crime is intraracial, concern for Black victims might justify harsher treatment of Black offenders if there were any reason to believe that harsher penalties would reduce crime rates. Unfortunately, as the conservative national governments of Margaret Thatcher and Brian Mulroney and reports of National Academy of Sciences Panels funded by the administrations of Republican Presidents Ford, Reagan, and Bush all agree, there is no reason to believe that harsher penalties significantly reduce crime rates.

JUSTIFYING THE UNJUSTIFIABLE

There is no valid policy justification for the harsh drug and crime control policies of the Reagan and Bush administrations, and for their adverse differential effect on Blacks. The justification, such as it is, is entirely political. Crime is an emotional subject and visceral appeals by politicians to people's fears and resentments are difficult to counter.

It is easy to seize the low ground in political debates about crime policy. When one candidate campaigns with pictures of clanging prison gates and grief-stricken relatives of a rape or murder victim, and with disingenuous promises that newer, tougher policies will work, it is difficult for an opponent to explain that crime is a complicated problem, that real solutions must be long term, and that simplistic toughness does not reduce crime rates. This is why, as a result, candidates often compete to establish which is tougher in his views about crime. It is also why less conservative candidates often try to preempt their more conservative opponents by adopting a tough stance early in the campaign. Finally, it is why political pundits congratulate President Clinton on his acumen in proposing federal crime legislation as or more harsh than his opponents. He has, it is commonly said, "taken the crime issue away from the Republicans."

Conservative Republican politicians have, since the late 1960s, used welfare, especially Aid to Families with Dependent Children, and crime as symbolic issues to appeal to anti-Black sentiments and resentments of White voters, as Thomas and Mary Edsall's *Chain Reaction: The Impact of Race, Rights, and Taxes on American Politics* (1991) makes clear. The Edsalls provide a history, since the mid-1960s, of "a conservative politics that had the effect of polarizing the electorate along racial lines." Anyone who observed Ronald Reagan's portrayal in several campaigns of Linda Evans, a Black Chicago woman, as the "welfare queen" or George Bush's use of Black murderer Willie Horton to caricature Michael Dukakis's criminal justice policies knows of what the Edsalls write.

The story of Willie Horton is the better known and makes the Edsalls' point. Horton, who in 1975 had been convicted of the murder of a 17-year-old boy, failed to return from a June 12, 1986, furlough. The following April, he broke into a home in Oxon Hill, Maryland, where he raped a woman and stabbed her companion.

Lee Atwater, Bush's campaign strategist, after testing the visceral effects of Willie Horton's picture and story on participants in focus groups, decided a year later to make Horton a wedge issue for Republicans. Atwater reportedly told a group of Republican activists that Bush would win the presidency "if I can make Willie Horton a household name." He later told a Republican gathering in Atlanta, "there's a story about a fellow named Willie Horton who, for all I know, may end up being Dukakis's running mate." Atwater for a time denied making both remarks but in 1991, dying of cancer, recanted: "In 1988, fighting Dukakis, I said that I would . . . make Willie Horton his running mate. I am sorry."

The sad reality is that tragedies like the crimes of Willie Horton are inevitable. So are airplane crashes, 40,000 to 50,000 traffic fatalities per year, and defense department cost overruns. Every person convicted of a violent crime cannot be held forever. Furloughs are used in most corrections systems as a way to ease offenders back into the community and to test their suitability for eventual release on parole or commutation. Horton had successfully completed nine previous furloughs, from each of which he had returned without incident, under a program established in 1972 not by Michael Dukakis but by Governor Francis Sargent, a Republican.

Public discourse about criminal justice issues has been debased by the cynicism that made Willie Horton a major participant in the 1988 presidential election. That cynicism has made it difficult to discuss or develop sensible public policies, and that cynicism explains why conservative politicians have been able year after year successfully to propose ever harsher penalties and crime control and drug policies that no informed person believes can achieve their ostensible goals.

Three final points, arguments that apologists for current policies sometimes make, warrant mention. First, it is sometimes said to be unfair to blame national Republican administrations for the failures and disparate impacts of recent crime control policies. This ignores the efforts of the Reagan and Bush administrations to encourage and, through federal mandates and funding restrictions, to coerce states to follow the federal lead. Attorney General William Barr (e.g., 1992) made the most aggressive efforts to compel state adoption of tougher criminal justice policies, and the Bush administration's final proposed crime bills restricted eligibility for federal funds to states that, like the federal government, abolished parole release and adopted sentencing standards no less severe than those in the federal sentencing guidelines. In any case, as the Edsalls' book makes clear, the use of crime control issues (among others including welfare reform and affirmative action) to elicit anti-Black sentiments from White voters has long been a stratagem of both state and federal Republican politicians.

Second, sometimes it is argued that political leaders have merely followed the public will; voters are outraged by crime and want tougher policies (DiIulio 1991). This is a half-truth that gets the causal order backwards. Various measures of public sentiment, including both representative surveys like Gallup and Harris polls and work with focus groups, have for many years consistently shown that the public is of two minds about crime (Roberts 1992). First, people are frustrated and want offenders to be punished. Second, people believe that social adversity, poverty, and a troubled home life are the principal causes of crime, and they believe government should work to rehabilitate offenders. A number of surveys have found that respondents who would oppose a tax increase to pay for more prisons would support a tax increase to pay for rehabilitative programs. These findings of voter ambivalence about crime should not be surprising. Most people have complicated views about complicated problems. For example, most judges and corrections officials have the same ambivalent feelings about offenders that the general public has. Conservative politicians have seized upon public support of punishment and ignored public support of rehabilitation and public recognition that crime presents complex, not easy, challenges. By presenting crime control issues only in emotional, stereotyped ways, conservative politicians have raised [crime's] salience as a political issue but made it impossible for their opponents to respond other than in the same stereotyped ways.

Third, sometimes it is argued that disparate impacts on Black offenders are no problem and that, because much crime is intraracial, failure to adopt tough policies would disserve the interests of Black victims. As former Attorney General Barr (1992) put it, perhaps in ill-chosen words, "the benefits of increased incarceration would be enjoyed disproportionately by Black Americans" (p. 17). This argument also is based on a half-truth. No one wants to live in unsafe neighborhoods or to be victimized by crime, and in a crisis, people who need help will seek it from the police, the public agency of last resort. Requesting help in a crisis and supporting harsh policies with racially disparate effects are not the same thing. The relevant distinction is between acute and chronic problems. A substantial body of public opinion research (e.g., National Opinion Research Center surveys conducted throughout the 1980s summarized in Wood 1990) shows that Blacks far more than Whites support establishment of more generous social welfare policies, full employment programs, and increased social spending. The congressional Black and Hispanic caucuses have consistently opposed bills calling for tougher sanctions and supported bills calling for increased spending on social programs aimed at improving conditions that cause crime. Thus, in claiming to be concerned about Black victims, conservative politicians are responding to natural human calls for help in a crisis while ignoring evidence that Black citizens would rather have government support efforts to ameliorate the chronic social conditions that cause crime and thereby make calls for help in a crisis less necessary.

The evidence on the effectiveness of recent crime control and drug abuse policies, as the first section demonstrated, cannot justify their racially disparate effects on Blacks, nor, as this section demonstrates, can the claims that such policies merely manifest the peoples' will or respect the interests of Black victims. All that is left is politics of the ugliest kind. The War on Drugs and the set of harsh crime control policies in which it was enmeshed were adopted to achieve political, not policy, objectives, and it is the adoption for political purposes of policies with foreseeable disparate impacts, the use of disadvantaged Black Americans as means to the achievement of White politicians' electoral ends, that must in the end be justified. It cannot.

REFERENCES

Anglin, M. Douglas, and Yih-Ing Hser (1990). "Treatment of Drug Abuse." In M. Tonry and J. Q. Wilson (eds.), *Drugs and Crime*. Chicago: University of Chicago Press.

Austin, James, and Aaron David McVey (1989). *The Impact of the War on Drugs*. San Francisco: National Council on Crime and Delinquency.

Barr, William P. (1992). "The Case for More Incarceration." Washington, D.C.: U.S. Department of Justice, Office of Policy Development.

Blumstein, Alfred (1982). "On the Racial Disproportionality of United States' Prison Populations." *Journal of Criminal Law and Criminology* 73:1259–81.

——— (1993a). "Racial Disproportionality of U.S. Prison Populations Revisited." *University of Colorado Law Review* 64:743–60.

——— (1993b). "Making Rationality Relevant—The American Society of Criminology 1992 Presidential Address." *Criminology* 31:1–16.

Blumstein, Alfred, Jacqueline Cohen, and Daniel Nagin (1978). *Deterrence and Incapacitation*. Report of the National Academy of Sciences Panel on Research on Deterrent and Incapacitative Effects. Washington, D.C.: National Academy Press.

Botvin, Gilbert J. (1990). "Substance Abuse Prevention: Theory, Practice, and Effectiveness." In M. Tonry and J. Q. Wilson (eds.), *Drugs and Crime*. Chicago: University of Chicago Press.

Bureau of Justice Statistics (1987). *Correctional Populations in the United States, 1985*. Washington, D.C.: U.S. Department of Justice, Bureau of Justice Statistics.

——— (1989a). *Correctional Populations in the United States, 1987*. Washington, D.C.: U.S. Department of Justice, Bureau of Justice Statistics.

——— (1989b). *Correctional Populations in the United States, 1986*. Washington, D.C.: U.S. Department of Justice, Bureau of Justice Statistics.

——— (1991a). *Correctional Populations in the United States, 1989*. Washington, D.C.: U.S. Department of Justice, Bureau of Justice Statistics.

———— (1991b). *Correctional Populations in the United States, 1988.* Washington, D.C.: U.S. Department of Justice, Bureau of Justice Statistics.

———— (1993). *Correctional Populations in the United States, 1991.* Washington, D.C.: U.S. Department of Justice, Bureau of Justice Statistics.

Cahalan, Margaret Werner (1986). *Historical Corrections Statistics in the United States, 1850–1984.* Washington, D.C.: U.S. Department of Justice, Bureau of Justice Statistics.

Canadian Sentencing Commission (1987). *Sentencing Reform: A Canadian Approach.* Ottawa: Canadian Government Publishing Centre.

Chaiken, Marcia, ed. (1988). *Street Level Enforcement: Examining the Issues.* Washington, D.C.: U.S. Government Printing Office.

Clark, Stover (1992). "Pennsylvania Corrections in Context." *Overcrowded Times* 3:4–5.

Clarke, Stevens H. (1992). "North Carolina Prisons Growing." *Overcrowded Times* 3:1, 11–13.

DiIulio, John J. (1991). *No Escape: The Future of American Corrections.* New York: Basic Books.

Edsall, Thomas, and Mary Edsall (1991). *Chain Reaction: The Impact of Race, Rights, and Taxes on American Politics.* New York: Norton.

Ellickson, Phyllis L., and Robert M. Bell (1990). *Prospects for Preventing Drug Use Among Young Adolescents.* Santa Monica, Calif.: RAND.

Fagan, Jeffrey (1993). "The Political Economy of Drug Dealing Among Urban Gangs." In R. C. Davis, A. J. Lurigio, and D. P. Rosenbaum (eds.), *Drugs and the Community.* Springfield, Ill.: Charles C. Thomas.

Federal Bureau of Investigation (1993). *Uniform Crime Reports for the United States—1992.* Washington, D.C.: U.S. Government Printing Office.

Gerstein, Dean R., and Henrik J. Jarwood, eds. (1990). *Treating Drug Problems.*

Report of the Committee for Substance Abuse Coverage Study, Division of Health Care Services, National Institute of Medicine. Washington, D.C.: National Academy Press.

Gilliard, Darrell K. (1992). *National Corrections Reporting Program, 1987.* Washington, D.C.: U.S. Department of Justice, Bureau of Justice Statistics.

Hindelang, Michael. (1976). *Criminal Victimization in Eight American Cities: A Descriptive Analysis of Common Theft and Assault.* Washington, D.C.: Law Enforcement Assistance Administration.

———— (1978). "Race and Involvement in Common Law Personal Crimes." *American Sociological Review* 43:93–108.

Home Office (1990). *Protecting the Public.* London: H. M. Stationery Office.

Klein, Stephen, Joan Petersilia, and Susan Turner (1990). "Race and Imprisonment Decisions in California." *Science* 247:812–16.

Langan, Patrick A. (1985). "Racism on Trial: New Evidence to Explain the Racial Composition of Prisons in the United States." *Journal of Criminal Law and Criminology* 76:666–83.

———— (1991). *Race of Persons Admitted to State and Federal Institutions, 1926–86.* Washington, D.C.: U.S. Department of Justice, Bureau of Justice Statistics.

McDonald, Douglas, and Ken Carlson (1993). *Sentencing in the Federal Courts: Does Race Matter?* Washington, D.C.: U.S. Department of Justice, Bureau of Justice Statistics.

Moore, Mark H. (1990). "Supply Reduction and Drug Law Enforcement." In M. Tonry and J. Q. Wilson (eds.), *Drugs and Crime.* Chicago: University of Chicago Press.

Moynihan, Daniel Patrick (1993). "Iatrogenic Government—Social Policy and Drug Research." *American Scholar* 62:351–62.

National Institute on Drug Abuse (1991). *National Household Survey on Drug Abuse: Population Estimates 1990.* Washington, D.C.: U.S. Government Printing Office.

Office of National Drug Control Policy (1990). *National Drug Control Strategy—January 1990.* Washington, D.C.: Author.

Padilla, Felix (1992). *The Gang as an American Enterprise.* New Brunswick, N.J.: Rutgers University Press.

Perkins, Craig (1992). *National Corrections Reporting Program, 1989.* Washington, D.C.: U.S. Department of Justice, Bureau of Justice Statistics.

Perkins, Craig, and Darrell K. Gilliard (1992). *National Corrections Reporting Program, 1988.* Washington, D.C.: U.S. Department of Justice, Bureau of Justice Statistics.

Reiss, Albert J., Jr., and Jeffrey Roth (1993). *Understanding and Controlling Violence, Report of the National Academy of Sciences Panel on the Understanding and Control of Violence.* Washington, D.C.: National Academy Press.

Reuter, Peter (1988). "Can the Borders Be Sealed?" *Public Interest* 92:51–65.

Roberts, Julian V. (1992). "Public Opinion, Crime, and Criminal Justice." In M. Tonry (ed.), *Crime and Justice: A Review of Research,* vol. 16. Chicago: University of Chicago Press.

Sourcebook of Criminal Justice Statistics (1978–1992). Washington, D.C.: Department of Justice, Bureau of Justice Statistics.

Standing Committee on Justice and the Solicitor General (1993). *Crime Prevention in Canada: Toward a National Strategy.* Ottawa: Canada Communication Group.

Sviridoff, Michele, Susan Sadd, Richard Curtis, and Randolph Grinc (1992). *The Neighborhood Effects of Street-Level Drug Enforcement.* New York: Vera Institute of Justice.

U.S. General Accounting Office (1990). *Drug Abuse: Research on Treatment May Not Address Current Needs.* Washington, D.C.: U.S. General Accounting Office.

Wilson, James Q. (1990). "Drugs and Crime." In M. Tonry and J. Q. Wilson (eds.)., *Drugs and Crime.* Chicago: University of Chicago Press.

Wood, Floris W. (1990). *An American Profile: Opinions and Behavior, 1972–1989.* New York: Gale Research.

Zimring, Franklin E., and Gordon Hawkins (1994). "The Growth of Imprisonment in California." *British Journal of Criminology* 34:83–95.

4

✪

The Media, Moral Panics
and the Politics
of Crime Control

TED CHIRICOS

Criminologists use the concept of the "moral panic" to try to understand why the public becomes almost hysterical over some perceived threat to societal values and interests. In recent years moral panics about serial killers, drug dealers, and child sexual abuse have dominated the headlines. Public pressures have been directed at political leaders to "do something!" Ted Chiricos argues that moral panics are used by political leaders to justify expansion of the power of the state.

In the summer and fall of 1993, violent crime captured popular consciousness in the United States with a speed and intensity seldom seen. Searing images of "random" violence—tourists in Florida, a truck driver in Los Angeles, passengers on a train—competed with natural disasters to hold a nation in awe.

By January 1994, television networks had run week-long series on *Kids and Crime* (CNN) and *America the Violent* (NBC) or had featured specials on *Florida, the State of Fear* (ABC) and *"Monster" Kody Scott* (CBS), the notorious gang-banger from Los Angeles. Newsmagazines ran cover stories on "Growing Up Scared" (*Newsweek*), "Lock 'Em Up and Throw Away the Key" (*Time*) and "Florida: The State of Rage" (*U.S. News and World Report*).

In the wake of the media feeding frenzy, Americans ranking crime/violence as the nation's foremost problem jumped from 9 percent to 49 percent between January 1993 and January 1994 (Gallup 1994:6). Not surprising was the response

Source: Written specifically for this book.

of politicians and moral entrepreneurs who swam furiously to stay atop the wave of public anxiety. Proposals to deal with the "epidemic" of violence escalated demands for "getting tough"—more police, more prison beds, longer mandatory sentences, "hard time" for kids, more and faster executions, "three strikes, you're out."

In April of 1999, the tragedy of Columbine High School captured the nation's attention, becoming the focal point of public, media and congressional attention. The importance of Columbine was elevated, in part, by several prior school shootings, especially since 1996, none of which reached the level of devastation witnessed in Littleton, Colorado. Columbine served as a focusing event for youth violence. Indeed, the massacre of Columbine became the most covered news story of 1999 (Pew Research Center 2000). Coverage of juvenile crime included school shootings, club drugs and "raves."

When asked about watching the continuing coverage of the aftermath of the violence at Columbine, 50 percent of respondents indicated they followed it "very closely," while 32 percent watched "fairly closely" (Henry J. Kaiser Family Foundation 1999). Events in Littleton, Colorado, had significant influence on the public's perception of safety in schools. When asked, "How much, if at all, did the Columbine shooting last year change your views about how safe your child is at school?" 44 percent of those surveyed reported, "a lot," while 27 percent indicated "some" (Pew Research Center 2000). News and polling organizations began surveying the public on the sources of this seeming rise in youth violence, asking questions about parenting, Internet access and monitoring for weapons and bomb making information, the availability of guns to youth, the Goth culture and the influence of the entertainment industry.

In response to this widespread attention, the White House convened a summit within a few weeks of events at Columbine. The violence in Colorado seemingly prompted the most intense period of legislative activity on school violence in the 106th Congress. During this time, 35 percent of all bills addressing school violence were introduced in April and May of 1999 whereas no other month of the year for the legislative session contained more than 9 percent of bills on juvenile crime (Lawrence and Birkland 2000).

THE CONCEPT OF MORAL PANIC

Hysteria over violent crime is a classic example of "moral panic." This concept was developed by Cohen, who noted that at certain times a "condition, episode, person or group of persons emerges to become defined as a threat to societal values and interests" (Cohen 1972:9). He notes that typically the threat is presented in the media in a simplistic fashion; spokespersons such as editors, the clergy, and politicians man the moral barricades; and experts pronounce their diagnoses of the problem and present solutions. As he emphasizes, the point of moral panic is "not that there's nothing there" but that societal responses are fundamentally inappropriate (Cohen 1972:204).

Cohen studied a moral panic involving British teenagers—"Mods" and "Rockers"—in the 1960s. Though substantially peaceful, large gatherings of these youths at several beaches provoked massive popular concern. A flood of media reports were used to justify an emergent "control culture" that included everything from local "action groups" to a largely symbolic "malicious damage" bill passed by Parliament. "Mods" and "Rockers" were typified as "folk devils" whose "premature affluent and aggressive" ways were the consequence of "permissiveness" and—at a time of rapid social change—a threat to established values of "sobriety and hard work." The beaches involved had already lost prosperous and even working-class clientele. Desperate to shore up declining status, they adopted what Cohen described as "the rhetoric of moral panics— 'We won't allow our seafront/area/town/country to be taken over by hooligans/hippies/blacks/Pakistanis'" (1972:177–198).

Stuart Hall (1978:140–147) and his colleagues studied a British "mugging" panic during which the media helped mobilize popular support for commands to get tougher on crime. That the typical "mugger" was portrayed as a young black man simplified the process of defining the problem of crime as a reflection of the "erosion of 'traditional' working-class neighborhoods and communities." In a number of English cities, black youth were increasingly unemployed, militant, and at odds with the police. Concerns were expressed about the apparent decline of "core values" such as respectability, work, discipline, family—England. As the authors note, a consequence of changes in society is the "emergence of a predisposition to the use of 'scapegoats' into which *all* the disturbing experiences are condensed and then symbolically rejected or 'cast out'" (1978:157).

Moral panics can be understood as having an ideological dimension in that they initiate *partisan* calls to "do something" and there is a *distortion of reality* in pursuit of that objective. Gouldner (1976:23–66) argues that ideology is discourse that "seeks to gather, assemble, husband, defer and control the *discharge* of political energies." Popular support for "public projects" is mobilized without reference to tradition, authority, or faith. Instead, *reports* are made about the world that justify *commands* to do something of a public nature. Moreover, the core of ideology—a relationship between reports and commands—is rooted in partisanship, yet mobilization of broad public support generally requires the misrepresentation of partisan interests. Thus, the function of ideology is not merely to report and to reveal but also to blur and conceal.

Specifically, the moral panic over violence is used to justify expanding the punitive apparatus of the state—even as crime rates are falling. In addition, the panic diverts attention from contradictions of the nation's political economy that have promoted an extraordinary growth of economic inequality and expansion of the urban underclass. It is precisely this underclass that has become an increasingly "privileged target group" for incarceration.

In short, these moral panics not only provide the "vocabularies of punitive motive" to justify an explosive growth of prison populations, but they obscure the declining condition of those most victimized by a changing political economy and by crime—even as they are incarcerated in unprecedented numbers.

Over the past fifteen years, the United States has had an *expanding* underclass, a *declining* crime rate and an *exploding* prison population. An expanding underclass has not led to an increase in crime, but members of that underclass are being incarcerated in unprecedented numbers. Something is missing in the chain linking political economy and punishment. Melossi (1985) has suggested that an important link in this chain may be provided by *discourse* that justifies repression.

The central point of this paper is that moral panics provide one part of that discursive link. They provide a "vocabulary of punitive motive" (Melossi 1985) that justifies a massive increase in prison population—even in the face of declining crime rates. At the same time, they divert attention from the consequences of investment decisions that include a rapid expansion in the number of people who either have nothing to lose from crime or who may actually derive value from the use of drugs or involvement in violence.

THE RECENT MORAL PANICS:
DRUGS AND VIOLENCE

The United States has experienced two major moral panics in the past decade. The first, involving crack cocaine, began in the summer and peaked in the fall of 1986; the second, involving violent crime, began in the summer of 1993 and peaked early in 1994.

The two panics share several key features that underscore their common ideological substance and significance. The first was an explosion in the *volume* of media *reports*—increasing in each case more than 400 percent during a six-month period. Moreover, these panics had several common *thematic emphases*. Both reported (1) that behaviors thought characteristic of urban ghettos were spreading to previously "safe" places and (2) that "carriers" of the spreading menace were increasingly children. In both instances the panics promoted a critical *misunderstanding* of the underlying behaviors which helped to justify *commands* for a radical expansion of *punitive controls*. At the same time, these panics *displaced* attention from the coercive consequences of investment decisions that diminished the value of work for so many and devastated the circumstances of America's urban ghettos.

Volume of Media Reports:
Crack Cocaine and Violent Crime

Figure 1 shows media coverage of drug issues from January 1985 through March 1987. In the early 1980s, drugs accounted for about 1 percent of total news coverage tracked by the Conference on Issues and Media (CIM). At the beginning of 1986 the CIM index was still below 1 percent after a brief surge in 1985 (Merriam 1989:22–24).

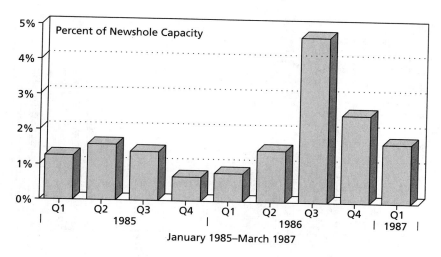

Figure 1 Media Coverage of Drug Issues*

*Adapted from: Merriam, 1989:23.

Spurred by the death of basketball star Len Bias (June 19) media coverage of drugs shot up to 6 percent of all news in the two weeks ending August 10. Ironically, the White House declared a renewed "war" on drugs in August and coverage began to fall. By the first quarter of 1987 the CIM index was back down to 1.1 percent (Merriam 1989:24–25).

The explosion of media coverage was punctuated by key reports in both print and television media. The *New York Times* assigned a full-time reporter to cover illegal drugs in November 1985 and ran its first front-page story on crack during that month. On March 17, 1986, a *Newsweek* cover story reported on the "Coke Plague" and the "almost instant addiction" of "crack" that moved a Los Angeles detective to conclude "we have lost the cocaine battle." By May 23, NBC News anchor Tom Brokaw declared that "crack" was "flooding America" and had become the nation's "drug of choice." In June, *Newsweek* proclaimed crack the biggest story since Vietnam and Watergate. On September 2, Dan Rather of CBS News hosted *48 Hours on Crack Street*—the most widely watched documentary in five years. NBC followed three days later with a prime-time special: *Cocaine Country*. This was just one of four hundred crack or cocaine stories—fifteen hours of air time—that NBC ran between April and November of 1986 (Reinarman and Levine 1989:118). By September, *Time* had recognized crack as "the issue of the year." Between March 30 and December 31, 1986, the *New York Times* carried 139 cocaine stories and the *Washington Post* carried 60 more (Danielian and Reese 1989:49).

The pattern of media coverage during the panic over violent crime was remarkably similar. Figure 2 shows the combined frequency of television and newspaper stories involving violent crime and juvenile violence between January 1992

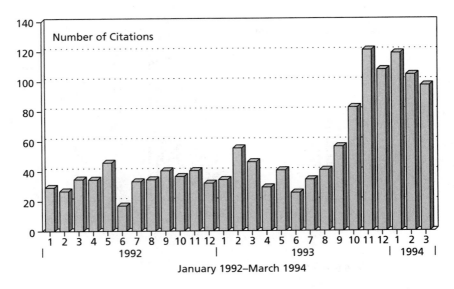

Figure 2 Media Coverage of Violent Crime and Juvenile Violence

and March 1994. By these measures, media attention varied within narrow parameters until the middle of 1993. Monthly newspaper citations rose from a low of eighteen in June to a high of ninety-five in November, dropping only slightly thereafter. Network television stories rose from a low of four in April to a high of thirty-four in January 1994.

Noting that Los Angeles "has the equivalent of a St. Valentine's Day massacre every day," a May 31 editorial in *U.S. News & World Report* ascribed a mood of "panic" to the citizens of that city. That mood seemed to escalate nationally after the July rape and murder of two teenage girls by six Houston gang members to whom "life means nothing" (*Newsweek* 1993a:16). Two weeks later (August 2) each of the national newsmagazines ran cover stories on violent crime and the panic was on.

The images of violence escalated further with the murder of a German tourist in Miami (September 11) and a British tourist at a highway rest stop in North Florida. *Newsweek* headlined its coverage a "State of Terror" and noted that the incident "sends shock waves overseas and reminds Americans of the epidemic violence in our streets." Two weeks later, *U.S. News* headlined Florida as "The State of Rage" where "nine foreign visitors [had] been murdered since last October," and *Time's* report on "Taming the Killers" asked if young murderers can be reformed or if "they are fated to repeat their crimes." On October 1, twelve-year-old Polly Klaas was kidnaped from her California home—a story that galvanized all media outlets until her body was found two months later.

The media blitz continued through the end of the year with a major *U.S. News* report (November 8) on "Violence in Schools" followed the next week

with "The Voters Cry for Help" in dealing with "the wave of crime fear grip-
ping Americans." *Newsweek* headlined "Death at an Early Age" on November 8
(1993) and three weeks later ran an eight-page cover story on "Gangsta Rap and
the Culture of Violence." On December 8, CBS aired a one-hour special on
Florida—"State of Fear."

The mid-December "Massacre on the Long Island Railroad," which left five
dead and nineteen wounded, pushed the panic to its greatest heights. Most major
media outlets gave the story front-page and lead coverage. *U.S. News* carried the
headline "Violence and Its Terrifying Randomness" and asked, "Is no place in
America safe from violence?" Shortly thereafter NBC News and CNN ran
week-long series on *America the Violent* and *Kids and Crime,* respectively.

Reports: Qualitatively Different Dangers

In addition to the escalating volume of media attention, the moral panics over
crack, violence, and youth crime were characterized by reports emphasizing new
and greater dangers. Both drugs and violence were common to the American
experience, and the warrant for panic included, in both cases, reports of a menace that was qualitatively different and more terrifying.

Out of the Ghetto—Out of Control A key element in both panics was a
presumption that dangerous behaviors thought common to inner-city neighborhoods were suddenly spreading out of the ghetto into middle America. By
the early 1980s, freebasing—the precursor to "crack" as a form of cocaine use—
was common to inner-city after-hours clubs (base houses) in Los Angeles and
New York. Cocaine freebase, packaged in retail form as "crack" or "rock," appeared in 1984. Its low price encouraged widespread use in the poor neighborhoods of many cities by 1986.

The March 17 *Newsweek*—which some consider pivotal for the emerging
"panic"—sounded the alarm on its cover: "An Epidemic Strikes Middle America." The seven-page story included these descriptions of crack's expanding
menace:

> Crack . . . is already creating social havoc in the ghettos of Los Angeles,
> New York and other large cities, and it is rapidly spreading into the sub-
> urbs on both coasts.

> And in Camden County NJ . . . prosecutor Samuel Asbell is convinced
> that the city's contagion has already spread to suburbia.

> There is simply no question that cocaine in all its forms is seeping into the
> nation's schools.

Subsequent issues of *Newsweek* in the summer of 1986 repeated the message
of a spreading contagion:

> Crack has captured the ghetto and is inching its way into the suburbs.
> (1986b:16)

There are ominous signs that crack and rock dealers are expanding well beyond the inner city. (1986b:20)

In part, the change in the public mood has a racist tinge: drugs simply have moved from the black and Hispanic underclass to the middle-class mainstream and are being felt as a problem there. (1986c:15)

One analysis of television reporting on the "crack epidemic" compared it with coverage given to "Black Tar"—an especially potent form of heroin—that NBC News (March 28, 1986) identified as responsible "for a growing number of addicts and corpses." Why did crack become a major story in 1986 when Black Tar did not? Writing in *T.V. Guide,* Diamond, Acosta, and Thornton suggest:

One reason has to do with those who are being affected and where those victims live. Black Tar stays in the ghetto, while crack is depicted as moving into "our"—that is the comfortable TV viewers—neighborhoods. (1987:7)

Extraordinary violence has been a fact of life in many inner-city neighborhoods for more than twenty years, drive-by shootings, gang-banging and narco-warfare have plagued many inner-city neighborhoods—terrifying their residents, and shortening their lives. Yet through all of this, from July 1980 to January 1993 no more than 9 percent of Americans considered crime to be the nation's most important problem (U.S. Justice Department 1993a:162). Suddenly in January of 1994 this measure jumped to 49 percent (Gallup 1994:6).

A central issue in the moral panic of 1993 was the presumption that violence was spreading from the inner city into places once considered safe. *Time* (1993b:45) was especially active in developing this theme. First, a carjacking feature—"Hell on Wheels"—noted that "the generation that fled the cities to escape violent crime finds that crime commutes too." A week later *Time* (1993c:29) featured "Danger in the Safety Zone," which chronicled violence "in virtually all public places once regarded as safe havens," such as schools, hospitals, libraries, and homes.

Reports about the spread of violence to places like Omaha, Nebraska, and Kenosha, Wisconsin, or Tomball, Texas—"the sort of safe town where many residents leave their front doors unlocked at night" (*Time,* 1993c:31)—established the premise that no place is safe. Quoting a Texas sociologist, *Newsweek* (1993b:40) observed that "We can be followed home from the supermarket, followed when we rent a car"—possibilities that "reinforce the sense that there is no protection, there is nothing you can do."

Littleton, Colorado, was a "safe" upper middle class suburb of Denver, Colorado, where massacres like this "didn't happen." In the case of Columbine and other school shootings the previous year, these random acts of violence occurred in small-town America, or the prototypical bedroom community, suburbs of larger cities.

The vehicle by which youth violence "spread" is a different one from crack cocaine, and represents a different avenue for threat to enter. What is more frightening here is the failure of geography to limit this dissemination of information—all roads lead to home, when the destination is a personal computer. The Internet has proven to be a steady source of information for school shooters. There are now Web sites on "how to build a bomb." Email has proven to be a source of communication to coordinate attacks. Computers are now regularly confiscated in the wake of school shootings. Schools across the country are now requiring consent forms from parents for their children to be allowed to access the Internet, the entrepreneurial techniques involving blocking access to certain sites, and restricting particular search engines, have emerged.

The presumed *randomness* of violence elevates its threat to people who had learned to avoid "dangerous" places. After the Long Island Railroad murders, *U.S. News* (1993e:6) decried "Violence and its Terrifying Randomness" and *Newsweek* (1993g:27) reported that Americans are "sick at heart about the recurrent episodes of random violence which mock our pretensions to order and civility." *U.S. News* (1993f:49) concluded that "it's the randomness and viciousness of crime in the 1990s, not just its extent, that elevates it as an issue," and *Time* (1993c:29) noted "the fear is getting worse because there is no pattern . . . it is random, spontaneous and episodic."

Reports: It's Spreading to Our Children The panics over crack cocaine and violent crime both drew heavily from reports emphasizing the escalating involvement of young people in drugs and violence. Menace, both to and from youth, is a common theme in the anxiety of moral panics. Among the reasons may be that youngsters are presumably (1) more vulnerable, (2) less predictable, (3) less remorseful, and (4) physically closer to the rest of us, because they still live in our homes. Moreover, as Hall et al. observed, fears and panics about youth center on the "indiscipline" of the young (1978:145)—an episodic if not perennial threat to social order. Spread of the "ghetto pathologies" of crack and violence to and through children clearly escalated the moral purchase for urgent punitive *commands* to deal with the behavior.

As noted above, the crack "epidemic" was touched off by a *Newsweek* cover story—"Kids and Cocaine"—that emphasized the availability of crack to young people due to its low cost. The story offered the following observations:

> An epidemic of cheap, deadly "crack" exposes a generation of American children to the nightmare of cocaine addiction. (1986a:58)

> In New York, eager buyers queue up outside crack houses . . . and the lines according to one drug agent "are loaded with kids." There are white kids, black kids, Hispanic kids—kids from the ghetto and kids from the suburbs. (1986a:59–60)

> "There are two trends in cocaine use" says Frank LaVecchia, a former high-school guidance counselor who runs a drug-treatment center in suburban Miami: "*Younger and younger and more and more.*" (1986a:58)

Television, too, reported that cocaine was claiming younger and younger victims as it spread from college campuses to maternity wards. Tom Brokaw, on NBC *Nightly News* (July 7), reported that cocaine "is becoming the college drug of the eighties" and ABC's *World News Tonight* (July 11) reported on babies born with a cocaine addiction ". . . the newest victims of the American cocaine epidemic" (Diamond, Acosta, and Thornton 1987:8).

At the height of the panic, President and Nancy Reagan appeared on television from the White House. He emphasized that "Drugs . . . [are] killing our children," and she warned that drug use was so pervasive that "no one is safe from it—not you, not me and certainly not our children because this epidemic has *their* name on it" (*Time* 1986:25).

The involvement of youth in violence—as both assailant and victim—is a major theme of the recent panic. In April of 1993, the *New York Times* ran a ten-part series entitled "Children of the Shadows" that chronicled the violence-filled world of ten kids from New York, Memphis, and Oakland. On November 1, the *Washington Post* presented a front-page story titled: "Getting Ready to Die Young: Children in Violent D.C. Neighborhoods Plan Their Own Funerals" (Brown, 1993). On November 7, "Monster" Kody Scott—who began gang-banging at age 11—was featured on *60 Minutes*.

In the six months between July 19, 1993, and January 10, 1994, the three major weekly newsmagazines ran the following headlines either on stories or covers:

> "Life Means Nothing: In Houston six teenagers are accused of mindlessly killing two young girls and seem not to care. Is adolescent brutality on the rise?" (*Newsweek* 1993a:16)

> "Teen Violence: Wild in the Streets." (*Newsweek* 1993f: Cover)

> "A Boy and His Gun: Even in a town like Omaha, Nebraska, the young are packing weapons in a deadly battle against fear and boredom." (*Time* 1993e:20–21)

> "Taming the Killers: Can young murderers be reformed?" (*Time* 1993a:58)

> "Death at an Early Age." (*Newsweek* 1993c:69)

> "Violence in the Schools: When Killers Come to Class." (*U.S. News* 1993c: Cover)

> "When is Rap 2 Violent?" (*Newsweek* 1993d: Cover)

> "Growing Up Scared." (*Newsweek* 1994a: Cover)

U.S. News called attention to a "chilling shift in adolescent attitudes: a sharp drop in respect for life" (1993c:31), and *Time* led a story with this:

> The names of the teenagers in this story aren't real, but the kids are—and they are all killers. They have murdered, some more than once, and are serving time. And they will still be young when they come up for parole. (1993a:58)

A sixteen-year-old was quoted as saying: "If you have a gun you have power. . . . Guns are just a part of growing up these days" (*Time* 1993b:21). In the same article Attorney General Janet Reno noted that violence is devastating this generation as surely as polio cut down young people forty years ago, and concluded that youth violence is "the single greatest crime problem in America today" (*Time* 1993b:43).

THE RECENT PANICS: MISUNDERSTANDING DRUGS AND VIOLENCE

Like other moral panics, those concerning crack cocaine and violence involved key ideological distortions—"misunderstandings"—with important conse-quence for the commands developed to deal with them. In particular, while drug abuse and violence have been *substantial* and *enduring* problems in many inner-city neighborhoods for decades, moral panic created the impression of a *sudden* and *escalating* firestorm spreading through society. The result is a polit-ical response that is—in Cohen's (1972) terms—*fundamentally inappropriate.*

In fact, in the United States, cocaine use *declined* during 1986 and violent crime rates *declined* during 1993—the years of spreading moral panic. What did *not* decline in those years of panic were the dissolution, despair, and nihilism (West 1994) increasingly characteristic of inner-city neighborhoods, where the choice of drugs or violence has become, for many, as reasonable and available as the choice of work. The consequence of treating the substantial and enduring problems of drugs and violence as if they are a sudden and escalating firestorm is that commands to deal with them seek *sudden* solutions that are *fundamentally in-appropriate*. In an atmosphere of panic, building walls and stacking people behind them is faster and easier than doing the difficult work of restoring work and community to neighborhoods devastated by disinvestment and de-skilling.

In showing how moral panic has misunderstood drug abuse and violence, I am *not* suggesting that these are somehow inconsequential problems. Rather, I argue that panic disguises the fact that drugs and violence have been *extraordinary* problems for several decades—problems borne disproportionately by the resi-dents of inner-city neighborhoods. Indeed, these inner-city residents have been doubly victimized—first, by the profound changes in the political economy of cities and then by the drugs and violence that long ago began taking the place of work and community in many of those neighborhoods.

The principal misunderstanding helping to fuel the panic about cocaine in 1986 was that its use was increasing and spreading—especially among youth out-side of the urban underclass. The spread was presumably a function of the low unit cost of the "rock" or crack form of the drug.

Most important, whatever was happening to the *forms* of cocaine, there is lit-tle evidence that cocaine use *per se* was increasing—particularly in the general population. In fact, the annual survey of high school seniors conducted by the University of Michigan showed that reported use of cocaine *dropped* during 1986—and has continued to drop—after reaching a ten-year high in 1985 (U.S. Justice Department 1993a:329). Among college students, reported use of cocaine

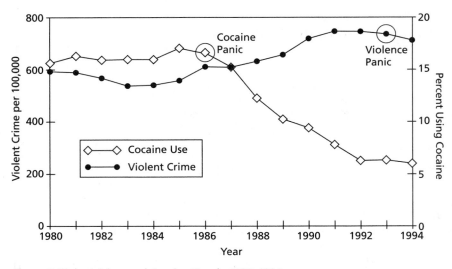

Figure 3 Violent Crime and Cocaine Trends: 1980–1994

SOURCES: U.S. Justice Dept. 1994a; U.S. Justice Dept., 1995b; and Johnston, 1994;
High School Survey.

"in the last year" was also *lower* in 1986 than in 1985 (U.S. Justice Department 1993a:330–331). And with regard to the general population, the Justice Department reports that

> Trend data from the national Household Survey on Drug Abuse indicates that current use of most drugs [including cocaine] rose from the early to late 1970s, peaked between 1979 and 1982 and has since declined. The increase in cocaine use was especially sharp in the late 1970s. (U.S. Justice Department 1992:30)

The limits of survey data as a measure of behavior are well known, but there is little reason to conclude that reports of declining drug use after 1985 (or increasing drug use before 1985) reflect variation in the validity of self-reports more than variation in drug-using behavior. And while there *is* evidence from hospital data that "emergency room mentions" of cocaine and "drug-related deaths" increased between 1985 and 1986, the Drug Enforcement Administration issued a report at the height of the "crack" panic that concluded that crack was a "secondary, not a primary drug problem in most cities" and that "its prevalence has been exaggerated by heavy news media attention" (*Washington Post* 1986:A18).

Even within the underclass, the *spread* of cocaine use during the crack "epidemic" was likely exaggerated. In a major review essay on "Drug Abuse in the Inner City," Bruce Johnson and his colleagues concluded that "the number of cocaine users has not increased substantially because of crack. Rather, the relatively few regular cocaine users appear to have increased the frequency of their consumption"—presumably due to the addictiveness of crack (Johnson, Williams, Dei, and Sanabria 1990:16–17).

While it is clear and widely acknowledged that the panic over crack cocaine greatly exaggerated its spreading menace, it is not as clear *why* the panic assumed the proportions it did *when* it did. Several hypotheses have been suggested. These include (1) competition among the various news media to stay on top of an issue that had so captured the attention of the agenda-setting *New York Times* and *Washington Post* and (2) preelection competition between congressional Democrats and Republicans to—in the words of presidential spokesman Marlin Fitzwater—"outdrug each other in terms of political rhetoric" (Reinarman and Levine 1989:129). Whatever the reason, the ideological consequence of the cocaine panic was realized in repressive measures of uncommon proportions.

The recent moral panic over violence has involved a similar pattern of exaggeration, distortion, or "misunderstanding." Specifically, during 1993, when media coverage of violent crime increased by more than 400 percent and Americans ranking crime/violence as the nation's foremost problem also increased by more than 400 percent, the rate of violent crime, as measured by the *Uniform Crime Reports,* showed a *decrease* of 1.5 percent from the previous year (see Fig. 3). The National Crime Victimization Survey showed similar though not identical patterns for 1993. Overall, the rate of violent victimizations—including attempts—increased slightly (5.6 percent) from the previous year. However, rates of *completed* violence actually *decreased* (3.2 percent) (U.S. Justice Department 1995a:2).

So if crime and violence were declining in 1993, what accounts for the 400 percent increase in media coverage for these issues in the last six months of 1993 and the more than 400 percent increase in concern about crime and violence in the twelve months ending in January 1994? One possibility is that there was little competing news, and as Sabato has noted, media "feeding frenzies are more likely to develop in slow news periods such as the doldrums of summer" (1991:79).

It is also possible that in the summer of 1993, several highly publicized violent attacks so captured public consciousness that they came to define for many the essence of the crime problem. Because of saturation news coverage, there are few Americans who could not recount at least some details of the Reginald Denny beating in South Central Los Angeles, or the Monticello, Florida, rest area murder, or the Fort Lauderdale tourist murders, or the Long Island Railroad killings, in which a gunman walked the aisles of a speeding train and emptied his gun several times. And as noted above, all three national news magazines did lengthy features on violence two weeks after the gang-rape and murder of two teenage girls who took a short-cut through the woods to their homes in Houston.

One common theme to these crimes is that each involved *white* victims and allegedly *black male* assailants who were unknown to the victims. Except for the Houston murders, each involved *adult* victims and except for the Long Island Railroad "massacre" each of the assailants was *young.* Yet far from typical criminal violence these are tragic exceptions to the norm of victimization that occurs overwhelmingly *within* age and race bounds. Departures from the norm are often considered newsworthy. They may become more so when they resonate criminal stereotypes and tap into deeply held racial anxieties.

It is almost as if the recent panic emerged precisely when the violence that has devastated inner-city neighborhoods for decades threatened—even if by stunning exception—to leap the boundaries and defy the norms of violent victimization. And as we have noted above, this is precisely what the reports of the moral panic tried to convey.

RECENT PANICS: COMMANDS

The bottom line of all ideological discourse is the use of reports—whether they distort reality or not—to mobilize popular support to *do* something in the public arena. Because moral panics have such relentless energy and because they employ rhetoric like "epidemic," "firestorm," "rising tide," and "plague," the *urgency* of swift and serious action is explicitly justified. The character of decision making in the context of frenzied media attention is well captured by presidential adviser George Stephanopolous (1993), appearing on the ABC *Nightline* special concerning the media's coverage of violence:

> What happens when a picture that powerful, even if incomplete, is presented on television? The only governing virtue is decisiveness. The question is: "What are you going to do?" It doesn't really matter what the answer is. It's just "Do something!" [The media] starts the drumbeat . . . "What are you going to do?" "What are you going to do?" "What are you going to do?"

Indeed, the command implications of moral panic over drugs and violence have been decisive, if nothing else. The response to the crack cocaine panic has been well documented elsewhere (Belenko et al. 1991) and is briefly summarized here. In Washington, drug politics were rapidly transformed in the summer of 1986 by several factors, none more significant than the explosion of media reports. According to members of Congress and their aides "when the media started talking about it, it lit a fire" (Kerr 1986:B6).

Commands—Drugs

On July 23, House Speaker "Tip" O'Neill announced plans for comprehensive drug legislation to be voted on by September. The extraordinary pace of action was justified by House Democratic leader Jim Wright, who commented that "his most pressing concern was that Congress act before television lost interest in the drug story." And Republican leader Robert Michel expressed fears that "unless House Republicans joined in quickly, the Democrats could grab the issue as their own in time for the [November] election" (Kerr 1986:B6). In September, President and Nancy Reagan went on television to call for a new "crusade" against drugs and on October 17, 1986 Congress passed the Anti-Drug Abuse Act of 1986—called by some "the most far-reaching drug law ever passed" (Kerr 1986:B6).

Even as the panic quickly subsided in Washington (Kerr 1986), enthusiasm for getting tough on drugs—particularly crack cocaine offenders—mushroomed in the states. The "no lose" proposition of moving swiftly and severely against marginalized segments of the urban underclass, who were seen as responsible for the spreading menace of crack—among other things—became a centerpiece of state and local social policy in the last half of the 1980s.

Nationwide, drug arrests increased more than 65 percent between 1986 and 1989 (U.S. Justice Department, 1993b:9), and state prison admissions for drug crimes mushroomed 214 percent (33,100 to 103,800) between 1986 and 1990 (U.S. Justice Department, 1994b:10). As a proportion of all state prison admissions in the United States, those for drug offenses increased 372 percent during the 1980s—rising from 6.8 percent in 1980 to 32.1 percent in 1990 (U.S. Justice Department, 1994b:10).

The most celebrated feature of this newest war on drugs was the extraordinary set of penalties applied to the possession, sale, or trafficking of *crack* as opposed to powder cocaine. Under federal law, 1 gram of crack counts as much as 100 grams of powder. Possession of 50 grams of crack brings a ten-year sentence; to get ten years for powder cocaine one would need 5,000 grams. Though patterns vary among the states, at least eight have adopted sentences for crack cocaine that are much more severe than for other drugs. Moreover, in federal law, only crack has mandatory minimum sentences for simple possession. All other drugs require possession with intent to sell.

A direct consequence of this panic-inspired legislation has been a substantial increase in the flow of African Americans into prison. Specifically, because almost 92 percent of federal crack defendants are black (as opposed to 27 percent for powder cocaine) harsher penalties for crack weigh most heavily against African-American drug users. As a result, the rate of incarceration (per 100,000) increased 48 percent for blacks between 1986 and 1991 as compared to 34 percent for whites (U.S. Justice Department 1994b:9). Looked at another way, African Americans accounted for 38.2 percent of those in state prisons for drugs in 1986 and 53.2 percent by 1991. More remarkably, blacks incarcerated for drugs made up 3.3 percent of all state prisoners in 1986 and 11.3 percent—a 242 percent increase—in 1991 (U.S. Justice Department 1993b:623). By 1992, the rate of incarceration for African-American males (2,678 per 100,000) was almost eight times as great as for the total population (344) (U.S. Justice Department 1994b:9). If those in jail, on probation, or on parole are included, almost *one of every ten* adult black males in America was in the punitive custody of the state by 1991 (U.S. Justice Department 1993b, 1994c).

Commands—Violent Crime

Commands "justified" by the panic over violent crime in late 1993 are still being realized, and their full consequence can only be known in years to come. However, the variety of measures proposed, if not always implemented, has given freer rein to repressive imaginations than even the drug panic did. Proposals in one state—"Florida, the State of Fear"—have included fingerprinting and uniforms for all school children, curfews, caning and castration. While these have yet to gain legislative approval, more traditional measures such as boot camps and easier transfer to adult court for juveniles as well as a massive increase in prison capacity, certainly have. In fact, Florida, which doubled its prison population (19,700 to 39,991) between 1980 and 1990, will see it doubled again to more than 80,000 by June, 1996. Early in 1994, at the peak of the panic over violence, Florida legislators appropriated almost as many *new* prison beds—17,000—as existed in 1980.

At the federal level, the "Violent Crime Control and Law Enforcement Act of 1994" was passed in August of that year. Touted by the Justice Department as "the largest crime bill in the history of the country," it "will provide for 100,000 new police officers, $9.7 billion in funding for prisons and $6.1 billion in funding for prevention programs" (U.S. Justice Department, 1994c:1). Beyond that, it expands the death penalty to cover sixty additional federal offenses; authorizes adult prosecution for thirteen year olds charged with serious violent crimes; provides "stiffer penalties for violent and drug trafficking crimes committed by gang members"; has its own version of a "three strikes" provision; doubles the maximum term for repeat Federal sex offenders, creates new crimes and enhances penalties for others.

Several states, including California, have implemented "three strikes" provisions mandating sentences between twenty-five years and life for persons convicted of a third felony. Many states have extended the reach of mandatory minimum sentencing, and many are greatly expanding their prison capacities. In state after state, during the 1994 political campaigns, candidates fired competing "get tough" salvos in efforts to cash in on the wave of crime fear sweeping the nation.

Almost immediately following the shooting in Littleton, Colorado, the White House called a meeting of politically odd bedfellows—Hollywood and media executives, gun industry officials, religious leaders and crime and mental health experts.

Coverage of Columbine was omnipresent, but the type of coverage varied between print and broadcast media (Lawrence and Birkland 2000). Common themes included: school violence and shootings; school safety and design; guns (safety, lobbying and gun control); media, pop culture, the Internet and movie violence; American sociocultural context, including Goth; mental health, the culture of teenage life, including alienation and peer pressure; and parenting and parental liability (Lawrence and Birkland 2000). In ways previously described by Iyengar (1991), television coverage was mostly detailing the chaos in Littleton, while stories in the *Los Angeles Times* and the *New York Times* were more thematic and explored the range of themes. The amount of media attention is less important than the lack of congruence between the media's definition of school shootings and the congressional definition of the problem.

While the media fueled attention to the problem, it did not define how the problem was addressed. Press coverage did elevate youth violence above other competing social problems, but it did not influence competing definitions within the problem (Lawrence and Birkland 2000). The media and public opinion polls helped "tell" Congress that school shootings were a problem, but the debates in

Congress did not track the debates in the press. What was notably absent from print and broadcast coverage, with respect to Columbine, but was front and center in congressional debate, was illicit drug use. An analysis of 675 news stories about Columbine reveal only two stories about illicit drug use, while nine of the fifty-six bills in Congress were about drugs, particularly as related to the Safe and Drug-Free Schools acts (Lawrence and Birkland 2000). It is also important what *wasn't* focused on in Congress. A Gallup report shows that 62 percent of Americans supported more mental health counseling for teenagers, the same number of respondents who supported stricter gun control laws (Newport 1999).

Congress is motivated to create avenues to their ideological or parochial initiatives. Indeed, contrary to the idea that the media is defining the problem for Congress, it may alternatively be possible that media attention simply serves as a resource—a moral panic as resource—for partisan initiative. While Gusfield (1981) developed the idea of public problems, in his discussion of drunk driving in the United States, whereby the problem is constructed as one of individual responsibility, Lawrence and Birkland conceptualize "institutions like the media and Congress as public arenas for the social construction of public problems" (2000:3). Congress, in recognizing certain problems officially, tells us how the federal government is defining problems. The case of school shootings illustrates more than competition among social problems, it tells about "alternative ways of framing the problem" (Hilgartner and Bosk 1988:70).

The tragedy in Littleton, Colorado, combines things with symbolic relevance—violence, children and suburban America. Hilgartner and Bosk argue that the more innately dramatic certain events are, the more likely they are to tap "broad cultural preoccupations" (1988:71). These are likely to be the types of problems that are championed by commanding political and economic coalitions (Lawrence and Birkland 2000). The grand-scale public reaction builds on the collective fear begun with crack and cocaine and violent crime: "It's spreading to our children."

Columbine was a "free pass" for Congress and Washington officialdom. It demonstrates responsiveness by convening White House summits, and showing live C-SPAN coverage on the House and Senate floors. Ultimately, however, the amount of attention criminal justice receives is disproportionate to the ability to truly do something about crime. Most real change in criminal justice stems from local authorities and how they mold or implement federal monies or guidelines (Scheingold 1991). This allows Congress to demonstrate action without ultimate accountability.

CONCLUSION: MORAL PANIC
AS IDEOLOGICAL DISPLACEMENT

And so it's off to war again—if not the metaphorical war on drugs, then the literal war in the streets. And prisoners *will* be taken. The "success" of moral panic as an ideological phenomenon could be no more aptly demonstrated. It not only mobilizes a massive expansion of the state's repressive apparatus—even as drug use and crime *decline*—but it diverts attention from the consequences of a one-sided class war that has involved not only disinvestment and de-skilling, but regressive taxation, the pillaging of pension funds and the social safety net, and assaults on the well-being of both the workplace and the environment (Barlett and Steele 1992; Lind 1995).

These actions, which have made American capital more competitive in the "global marketplace," have also assisted in the dismantling of the middle class, the growth of an isolated underclass, and a more unequal distribution of wealth and opportunity than at any time since the onset of the last Great Depression (Batra 1987; Lind 1995). The same conditions that have made enormous fortunes for a handful of investors have made most Americans work harder for less and have consigned so many others—particularly in the urban underclass—to a superfluous present and a hopeless future.

But instead of waging war on the inhuman conditions fostered by policies of disinvestment and de-skilling that have hollowed our inner-city neighborhoods, we wage war on those individuals dehumanized by the lack of reasonable choices. Instead of waging war on unemployment, inadequate schools, and the loss of hope we wage war on individuals destroyed by those very conditions. Instead of waging war on the factors contributing to an increasingly isolated underclass—for whom life has less and less meaning—we wage war against individuals who seek meaning in drugs and violence.

Instead of seeing the world as it is—one in which investment decisions by the owners of capital have caused the devastation of inner-city neighborhoods, communities, and families and the economic stagnation of almost all others—these moral panics force us to see as "in all ideology, men and their circumstances . . . upside-down as in a *camera obscura*" (Marx and Engels 1846/1970:47). The greatest victims of private and public policies that have literally determined that people will count less than profits are demonized by moral panics and herded behind ever-widening walls of exclusion.

As noted above, the real danger of the recent moral panics is that they treat problems that have been *substantial* and *enduring* for several decades in many inner-city neighborhoods as if they are a *sudden* firestorm. An atmosphere of panic mobilizes demands for immediate repression and causes us to ignore the root problems of urban America, which have grown and festered for decades. The same media frenzy that raises *decisiveness* to the cardinal virtue of public policy lowers the chance that meaningful response to enduring problems will be undertaken.

Put behind walls another hundred thousand or five hundred thousand or a million young men for whom drugs and violence have become meaningful choices—and what will happen? If nothing is done to restore work, family, and community to our central city neighborhoods, then successive waves of children will have and will make those same choices.

The triumph of moral panic as ideology is realized in the promotion of "solutions" to the contradictions of capitalism that literally misrepresent and conceal their existence while mobilizing support to repress their most disadvantaged and visible victims. At the same time, and perhaps most important, moral panic keeps the vast majority of Americans—who are "doing with less so that big business can have more"—focused on ostensible dangers from the underclass instead of the policies and profits of the investors of capital, who are responsible not only for the growth of that underclass but the frustrations and anxieties plaguing so many Americans.

REFERENCES

Barlett, Donald L., and James B. Steele (1992). *America: What Went Wrong?* Kansas City: Andrews & McMeel.

Batra, Ravi (1987). *The Great Depression of 1990.* New York: Simon & Schuster.

Belenko, Steven, Jeffrey Fagan, and Ko-Lin Chin (1991). "Criminal justice responses to crack." *Journal of Research in Crime & Delinquency* 28:55–74.

Brown, DeNeen L. (1993). Getting ready to die young: Children in violent D.C. neighborhoods plan their own funerals. *Washington Post 1* November: A1.

Cohen, Stan (1972). *Folk Devils and Moral Panics: The Creation of the Mods and Rockers.* Oxford: Blackwell.

Danielian, Lucig H., and Stephen D. Reese (1989). "A closer look at intermedia influences on agenda setting: The cocaine issue of 1986." In *Communication Campaigns About Drugs,* ed. Pamela J. Shoemaker, 47–66. Hillsdale, N.J.: Lawrence Erlbaum Associates.

Diamond, Edwin, Frank Acosta, and Leslie-Jean Thornton (1987). "Is TV news hyping America's cocaine problem?" *T.V. Guide* (7 February): 4–10.

Gallup, George Jr. (1994). *The Gallup Poll, No. 341* (February). Wilmington, Del.: Scholarly Resources, Inc.

Gouldner, Alvin (1976). *The Dialectic of Ideology and Technology.* New York: Oxford University Press.

Gusfield, Joseph (1981). *The Culture of Public Problems.* Chicago: University of Chicago Press.

Hall, Stuart, Chas Critcher, Tony Jefferson, John Clarke, and Brian Roberts (1978). *Policing the Crisis: Mugging, the State and Law and Order.* London: MacMillan.

Henry J. Kaiser Family Foundation, Harvard School of Public Health, Health News Interest Index Poll (June 18, 1999).

Hilgartner, S., and James Bosk (1988). "The rise and fall of social problems: A public arena's model." *American Journal of Sociology* 94(1):53–78.

Iyengar, Shanto (1991). *Is Anyone Responsible?* Chicago: University of Chicago Press.

Johnson, Bruce D., Terry Willliams, Kojo A. Dei, and Harry Sanabria (1990). "Drug Abuse in the Inner City: Impact on Hard-Drug Users and the Community." In Michael Tonry and James Q. Wilson (eds.), *Drugs and Crime.* Chicago: University of Chicago Press, pp. 9–67.

Johnston, Lloyd D. (1994). "Drug use continues to climb among American teenagers." Press Release by the University of Michigan News and Information Services (8 December).

Kerr, Peter (1986). "Anatomy of the Drug Issue: How, After Years, It Erupted." *New York Times* November 17: A1, B6.

Lawrence, Regina G., and Thomas A. Birkland (2000). "Guns, Hollywood and Criminal Justice: Defining the School Shootings Problem Across Public Arenas." American Political Science Association Meeting (August).

Lind, Michael (1995). "To Have and to Have Not: Notes on the Progress of the American Class War." *Harpers Magazine* (June) pp. 35–47.

Marx, Karl, and Frederick Engels (1846/1970). *The German Ideology.* New York: International Publishers.

Melossi, Dario (1985). "Punishment and Social Action: Changing Vocabularies of Punitive Motive within a Political Business Cycle." *Current Perspectives in Social Theory* 6:169–197.

Merriam, John E. (1989). "National Media Coverage of Drug Issues, 1983–1987." In Pamela J. Shoemaker (ed.), *Communication Campaigns About Drugs: Government, Media and the Public.* Hillsdale, N.J.: Lawrence Erlbaum, pp. 21–28.

Newport, Frank (1999). Media Portrayals of Violence Seen by Many as Causes of Real-Life Violence. Gallup News Services. http://www.gallup.com/poll/release/pr990510.asp.

Pew Research Center, News Interest Index Poll (April 19, 2000).

Newsweek (1986a). "Kids and Cocaine." March 17: 58–65.

———— (1986b). "Crack and Crime." June 16: 15–22.

———— (1986c). "Trying to Say No." August 11: 14–19.

———— (1993a). "Life Means Nothing." July 19: 16–17.

———— (1993b). "In a State of Terror." September 27: 40–41.

———— (1993c). "Death at an Early Age." November 8: 69.

———— (1993d). "Criminal Records: Gangsta Rap and the Culture of Violence." November 29: 60–64.

———— (1993e). "Death Ride: Massacre on the LIRR." December 20: 26–31.

———— (1993f). "Wild in the Streets." August 2: 40–47.

———— (1993g). "Brutality as a Teen Fashion Statement." August 23: 61.

———— (1993h). "Growing Up Fast and Frightened." November 22: 52.

———— (1994a). "Kids Growing Up Scared." January 10: 43–50.

Reinarman, Craig, and Harry G. Levine (1989). "The Crack Attack: Politics and Media in America's Latest Drug Scare." In Joel Best (ed.), *Images of Issues: Typifying Contemporary Social Problems.* New York: Aldine de Gruyter, pp. 115–137.

Sabato, Larry J. (1991). *Feeding Frenzy: How Attack Journalism Has Transformed American Politics.* New York: Free Press.

Scheingold, Stuart (1991). *The Politics of Street Crime.* Philadelphia: Temple University Press.

Stephanopolous, George (1993). Comments recorded in appearance on "Crime, violence and T.V. news," an ABC News *Nightline* special (December 10).

Time (1986). "Bringing Out the Big Guns: The First Couple and Congress Press the Attack on Drugs." September 22: 25–26.

———— (1993a). "Taming the Killers." October 11: 58–59.

———— (1993b). "Hell on Wheels." August 16: 44–48.

———— (1993c). "Danger in the Safety Zone." August 23: 29–32.

———— (1993d). "Up in Arms." December 20: 18–26.

———— (1993e). "A Boy and His Gun." August 2: 20–27.

U.S. Justice Department (1992). Drugs, Crime, and the Justice System. Washington, D.C: U.S. Government Printing Office.

———— (1993a). Sourcebook of Criminal Justice Statistics—1992. Washington, D.C.: U.S. Government Printing Office.

———— (1993b). Drugs and Crime Facts, 1992. Washington, D.C.: Bureau of Justice Statistics.

———— (1994a). Crime in the United States—1993. Washington, D.C.: U.S. Government Printing Office.

———— (1994b). Prisoners in 1993. Washington, D.C.: Bureau of Justice Statistics.

———— (1994c). Fact Sheet: Violent Crime Control and Law Enforcement Act of 1994. Washington, D.C. (24, October).

———— (1995a). Criminal Victimization 1993. Washington, D.C.: Bureau of Justice Statistics.

———— (1995b). Uniform Crime Reports: 1994 Preliminary Annual Release. Washington, D.C. (21, May).

U.S. News & World Report (1993a). "Los Angeles under the Gun." May 31: 82.

———— (1993b). "Florida: The State of Rage." October 11: 40–44.

———— (1993c). "Violence in the Schools." November 8: 31–36.

———— (1993d). "The Voters Cry for Help." November 15: 26–30.

———— (1993e). "Violence and Its Terrifying Randomness." December 20: 6.

———— (1993f). "A New Attack on Crime." October 18: 49.

Washington Post (1986). New York leads in "crack" use: DEA says prevalence elsewhere overstated. 25 September: A18.

West, Cornel (1994). *Race Matters.* New York: Vintage Books.

5

Criminal Justice, Legal Values and the Rehabilitative Ideal

FRANCIS A. ALLEN

In this classic article written in 1959 Francis A. Allen notes the rise during the twentieth century of the rehabilitative ideal. He asserts that the rhetorical influence of the "rehabilitative ideal" compromised its real meaning. He describes the ways that this more scientific approach to an understanding of criminality and its correction had a number of unintended consequences for the criminal justice system, allowing it to effectively be used as a justification for net-widening.

Although one is sometimes inclined to despair of any constructive changes in the administration of criminal justice, a glance at the history of the past half-century reveals a succession of the most significant developments. Thus, the last fifty years have seen the widespread acceptance of three legal inventions of great importance: the juvenile court, systems of probation, and systems of parole. During the same period, under the inspiration of Continental research and writing, scientific criminology has become an established field of instruction and inquiry in American universities and in other research agencies. At the same time, psychiatry has made its remarkable contributions to the theory of human behavior and, more specifically, to that form of human behavior described as criminal. These developments have been accompanied by nothing less than a

Source: Francis A. Allen, *The Borderland of Criminal Justice* (Chicago: University of Chicago Press, 1964), pp. 25–41. First delivered as a lecture at the Institute for Juvenile Research, Chicago, Illinois, on March 17, 1959. Some footnotes deleted, one renumbered. Reprinted with permission.

revolution in public conceptions of the nature of crime and the criminal and in public attitudes toward the proper treatment of the convicted offender.

This history with its complex developments of thought, institutional behavior, and public attitudes must be approached gingerly; for in dealing with it we are in peril of committing the sin of oversimplification. Nevertheless, despite the presence of contradictions and paradox, it seems possible to detect one common element or theme I shall describe, for want of a better phrase, as the rise of the rehabilitative ideal.

The rehabilitative ideal is itself a complex of ideas which, perhaps, defies an exact definition. The essential points, however, can be identified. It is assumed, first, that human behavior is the product of antecedent causes. These causes can be identified as part of the physical universe, and it is the obligation of the scientist to discover and to describe them with all possible exactitude. Knowledge of the antecedents of human behavior makes possible an approach to the scientific control of human behavior. Finally, and of primary significance for the purposes at hand, it is assumed that measures employed to treat the convicted offender should serve a therapeutic function; that such measures should be designed to effect changes in the behavior of the convicted person in the interests of his own happiness, health, and satisfactions and in the interest of social defense.

Although these ideas are capable of quite simple statement, they have provoked some of the modern world's most acrimonious controversies. And the disagreements among those who adhere in general to these propositions have been hardly less intense than those prompted by the dissenters. This is true, in part, because these ideas possess a delusive simplicity. No idea is more pervaded with ambiguity than the notion of reform or rehabilitation. Assuming, for example, that we have the techniques to accomplish our ends of rehabilitation, are we striving to produce in the convicted offender something called "adjustment" to his social environment or is our objective something different from or more than this? By what scale of values do we determine the ends of therapy?

These are intriguing questions, well worth extended consideration. But it is not my purpose to pursue them here. Rather, I am concerned with describing some of the dilemmas and conflicts of values that have resulted from efforts to impose the rehabilitative ideal on the system of criminal justice. There is no area in which a more effective demonstration can be made of the necessity for greater mutual understanding between the law and the behavioral disciplines.

There is, of course, nothing new in the notion of reform or rehabilitation of the offender as being one objective of the penal process. This idea is given important emphasis, for example, in the thought of the medieval churchmen. The church's position, as described by Sir Francis Palgrave, was that punishment was not to be "thundered in vengeance for the satisfaction of the state, but imposed for the good of the offender: in order to afford the means of amendment and to lead the transgressor to repentance, and to mercy." Even Jeremy Bentham, whose views modern criminologists have often scorned and more often ignored, is found saying: "It is a great merit in a punishment to contribute to the *reformation of the offender*, not only through fear of being punished again, but by a change in his character and habits." But this is far from saying that the modern expression of the rehabilitative ideal is not to be sharply distinguished form earlier expressions. The most important differences, I believe, are two. First, the modern statement of the rehabilitative ideal is accompanied by, and largely stems from, the development of scientific disciplines concerned with human behavior, a development not remotely approximated in earlier periods when notions of reform of the offender were advanced. Second, and of equal importance for the purposes at hand, in no other period has the rehabilitative ideal so completely dominated theoretical and scholarly inquiry, to such an extent that in some quarters it is almost assumed that matters of treatment and reform of the offender are the only questions worthy of serious attention in the whole field of criminal justice and correction.

THE NARROWING
OF SCIENTIFIC INTERESTS

This narrowing of interests prompted by the rise of the rehabilitative ideal during the past half-century should put us on our guard. No social institutions as complex as those involved in the administration of criminal justice serve a single function or purpose. Social institutions are multivalued and multipurposed. Values and purposes are likely on occasion to prove inconsistent and to produce internal conflict and tension. A theoretical orientation that evinces concern for only one or a limited number of the purposes served by the institution must inevitably prove partial and unsatisfactory. In certain situations it may prove positively dangerous. This stress on the unfortunate consequences of the rise of the rehabilitative ideal need not involve failure to recognize the substantial benefits that have also accompanied its emergence. Its emphasis on the fundamental problems of human behavior, its numerous contributions to the decency of the criminal-law processes are of vital importance. But the limitations and dangers of modern trends of thought need to be clearly identified in the interest, among others, of the rehabilitative ideal itself.

My first proposition is that the rise of the rehabilitative ideal has dictated what questions are to be investigated, with the result that many matters of equal or even greater importance have been ignored or insufficiently examined. This tendency can be abundantly illustrated. Thus, the concentration of interest on the nature and needs of the criminal has resulted in a remarkable absence of interest in the nature of crime. This is, indeed, surprising, for on reflection it must be apparent that the question of what is a crime is logically the prior issue: how crime is defined determines in large measure who the criminal is who becomes eligible for treatment and therapy. A related observation was made some years ago by the late Karl Llewellyn: "When I was younger I used to hear smuggish assertions among my sociological friends, such as: 'I take the sociological, *not* the legal, approach to crime'; and I suspect an inquiring reporter could still hear much the same (perhaps with 'psychiatric' often substituted for 'sociological')— though it is surely somewhat obvious that when you take 'the legal' out, you also take out 'crime.'" This disinterest in the definition of criminal behavior has afflicted the lawyers quite as much as the behavioral scientists. Even the criminal law scholar has tended, until recently, to assume that problems of procedure and treatment are the things that "really matter." Only the issue of criminal responsibility as affected by mental disorder has attracted the consistent attention of the non-lawyer, and the literature reflecting this interest is not remarkable for its cogency or its wisdom. In general, the behavioral sciences have left other issues relevant to crime definition largely in default. There are a few exceptions. Dr. Hermann Mannheim, of the London School of Economics has manifested intelligent interest in these matters. The late Professor Edwin Sutherland's studies of "white-collar crime" may also be mentioned, although, in my judgment, Professor Sutherland's efforts in this field are among the least perceptive and satisfactory of his many valuable contributions.

The absence of widespread interest in these areas is not to be explained by any lack of challenging questions. Thus, what may be said of the relationships between legislative efforts to subject certain sorts of human behavior to penal regulation and the persistence of police corruption and abuse of power? Studies of public attitudes toward other sorts of criminal legislation might provide valuable clues as to whether given regulatory objectives are more likely to be attained by the provision of criminal penalties or by other kinds of legal sanctions. It ought to be re-emphasized that the question, What sorts of behavior should be declared criminal? is one to which the behavioral sciences might contribute vital insights. This they have largely failed to do, and we are the poorer for it.

Another example of the narrowing of interests that has accompanied the rise of the rehabilitative ideal is the lack of concern with the idea of deterrence—indeed, many modern criminologists are hostile toward it. This, again, is a most surprising development. It must surely be apparent that the criminal law has a general preventive function to perform in the interests of public order and of security of life, limb, and possessions. Indeed, there is reason to assert that the influence of criminal sanctions on the millions who never engage in serious criminality is of greater social importance than their impact on the hundreds of thousands who do. Certainly, the assumptions of those who make our laws is that the denouncing of certain kinds of conduct as criminal and providing the means for the enforcement of legislative prohibitions will generally prevent or minimize such behavior. Just what the precise mechanisms of deterrence are is not well understood. Perhaps it results, on occasion, from the naked threat of punishment. Perhaps, more frequently, it derives from a more subtle process wherein the mores and moral sense of the community are recruited to advance the attainment of the criminal law's objectives. The point is that we know very little about these vital matters, and the resources of the behavioral sciences have rarely been employed to contribute knowledge and insight in their investigation. Not only have the criminologists displayed little interest in these matters, some have suggested that the whole idea of general prevention is invalid or worse. Thus, speaking of the deterrent theory of punishment, the authors of a leading textbook in criminology assert: "This is simply a derived rationalization of revenge. Though social revenge is the actual psychological basis of punishment today, the apologists for the punitive regime are likely to bring forward in their defense the more sophisticated, but equally futile, contention that punishment deters from [sic] crime." We are thus confronted by a situation in which the dominance of the rehabilitative ideal not only diverts attention from many serious issues but leads to a denial that these issues even exist.

DEBASEMENT OF THE
REHABILITATIVE IDEAL

I now turn to another kind of difficulty that has accompanied the rise of the rehabilitative ideal in the areas of corrections and criminal justice. It is a familiar observation that an idea once propagated and introduced into the active affairs of life undergoes change. The real significance of an idea as it evolves in actual practice may be quite different from that intended by those who conceived it and gave it initial support. An idea tends to lead a life of its own; and modern history is full of the unintended consequences of seminal ideas. The application of the rehabilitative ideal to the institutions of criminal justice presents a striking example of such a development. My second proposition, then, is that the rehabilitative ideal has been debased in practice and that the consequences resulting from this debasement are serious and, at times, dangerous.

This proposition may be supported, first, by the observation that, under the dominance of the rehabilitative ideal, the language of therapy is frequently employed, wittingly or unwittingly, to disguise the true state of affairs that prevails in our custodial institutions and at other points in the correctional process. Certain measures, like the sexual psychopath laws, have been advanced and supported as therapeutic in nature when, in fact, such a characterization seems highly dubious. Too often the vocabulary of therapy has been exploited to serve a public-relations function. Recently, I visited an institution devoted to the diagnosis and treatment of disturbed children. The institution had been established with high hopes and, for once, with the enthusiastic support of the state legislature. Nevertheless, fifty minutes of an hour's lecture, delivered by a supervising psychiatrist before we toured the building, were devoted to custodial problems. This fixation on problems of custody was reflected in the institutional arrangements which included, under a properly euphemistic label, a cell for solitary confinement.[1] Even more disturbing was the tendency of the staff to justify these custodial measures in therapeutic terms. Perhaps on occasion the requirements of institutional security and treatment coincide. But the inducements to self-deception in such situations are strong and all too apparent. In short, the language of therapy has frequently provided a formidable obstacle to a realistic analysis of the conditions that confront us. And realism in considering these problems is the one quality that we require above all others.

There is a second kind of unintended consequence that results from the application of the rehabilitative ideal to the practical administration of criminal justice. Surprisingly enough, the rehabilitative ideal has often led to increased severity of penal measures. This tendency may be seen in the operation of the juvenile court. Although frequently condemned by the popular press as a device for leniency, the juvenile court is authorized to intervene punitively in many situations in which the conduct, were it committed by an adult, would be wholly ignored by the law or would subject the adult to the mildest of sanctions. The tendency of proposals for wholly indeterminate sentences, a clearly identifiable fruit of the rehabilitative ideal, is unmistakably in the direction of lengthened periods of imprisonment. A large variety of statutes authorizing what is called "evil" commitment of persons, but which, except for the reduced protections afforded the parties proceeded against, are essentially criminal in nature, provide for absolutely indeterminate periods of confinement. Experience has demonstrated that, in practice, there is a strong tendency for the rehabilitative ideal to serve purposes that are essentially incapacitative rather than therapeutic in character.

THE REHABILITATIVE IDEAL AND INDIVIDUAL LIBERTY

This reference to the tendency of the rehabilitative ideal to encourage increasingly long periods of incarceration brings me to my final proposition. It is that the rise of the rehabilitative ideal has often been accompanied by attitudes and measures that conflict, sometimes seriously, with the values of individual liberty and volition. As I have already observed, the role of the behavioral sciences in the administration of criminal justice and in the area of public policy lying on the borderland of the criminal law is one of obvious importance. But I suggest that, if the function of criminal justice is considered in its proper dimensions, it will be discovered that the most fundamental problems in these areas are not those of psychiatry, sociology, social case work, or social psychology. On the contrary, the most fundamental problems are those of political philosophy and political science. The administration of the criminal law presents to any community the most extreme issues of the proper relations of the individual citizen to state power. We are concerned here with the perennial issue of political authority: Under what circumstances is the state justified in bringing its force to bear on the individual human being? These issues, of course, are not confined to the criminal law, but it is in the area of penal regulation that they are most dramatically manifested. The criminal law, then, is located somewhere near the center of the political problem, as the history of the twentieth century abundantly reveals. It is no accident, after all, that the agencies of criminal justice and law enforcement are those first seized by an emerging totalitarian regime. In short, a study of criminal justice is fundamentally a study in the exercise of political power. No such study can properly avoid the problem of the abuse of power.

The obligation of containing power within the limits suggested by a community's political values has been considerably complicated by the rise of the rehabilitative ideal. For the problem today is one of regulating the exercise of power by men of good will, whose motivations are to help not to injure, and whose ambitions are quite different from those of the political adventurer so familiar to history. There is a tendency for such persons to claim immunity from the usual forms of restraint and to insist that professionalism and a devotion to science provide sufficient protection against unwarranted invasion of individual rights.

• • •

There is one proposition which, if generally understood, would contribute more to clear thinking on these matters than any other. It is not a new insight. Garofalo asserted: "The mere deprivation of liberty, however benign the administration of the place of confinement, is undeniably punishment." This proposition may be rephrased as follows: Measures which subject individuals to the substantial and involuntary deprivation of their liberty contain an inescapable punitive element, and this reality is not altered by the facts that the motivations that prompt incarceration are to provide therapy or otherwise contribute to the person's well-being or reform. As such, these measures must be closely scrutinized to insure that power is being applied consistently with those values of the community that justify interference with liberty for only the most clear and compelling reasons.

But the point I am making requires more specific and concrete application to be entirely meaningful. It should be pointed out, first, that the values of individual liberty may be imperiled by claims to knowledge and therapeutic technique that we, in fact, do not possess and by our failure to concede candidly what we do not know. At times, practitioners of the behavioral sciences have been guilty of these faults. At other times, such errors have supplied the assumptions on which legislators, lawyers, and lay people generally have proceeded. An illustration of these dangers is provided by the sexual psychopath laws, to which I return, for they epitomize admirably some of the worst tendencies of modern practice. Doubts almost as serious can be raised as to a whole range of other measures. The laws providing for the commitment of persons displaying the classic symptoms of psychosis and advanced mental disorder have proved a seductive analogy for other proposals. But does our knowledge of human behavior really justify the extension of these measures to provide for the indefinite commitment of persons otherwise afflicted?

There are other ways in which the modern tendencies of thought accompanying the rise of the rehabilitative ideal have imperiled basic political values. The most important of these is the encouragement of procedural laxness and irregularity. It is my impression that there is a greater awareness of these dangers today than at some other times in the past. Nevertheless, in our courts of so-called socialized justice one may still observe, on occasion, a tendency to assume that, since the purpose of the proceeding is to "help" rather than to "punish," some lack of concern in establishing the charges against the person before the court may be justified. Thus, in some courts the judge is supplied with a report on the offender by the psychiatric clinic before the judgment of guilt or acquittal is announced. Such reports, while they may be relevant to the defendant's need for therapy or confinement, are ordinarily wholly irrelevant to the issue of his guilt of the particular offense charged. Yet it asks too much of human nature to assume that the judge is never influenced on the issue of guilt or innocence by a strongly adverse psychiatric report.

Let me give one final illustration of the problems that have accompanied the rise of the rehabilitative ideal. Some time ago we encountered a man in his eighties incarcerated in a state institution. He had been confined for some thirty years under a statute calling for the automatic commitment of defendants acquitted on grounds of insanity in criminal trials. It was generally agreed by the institution's personnel that he was not then psychotic and probably had never been psychotic. The fact seemed to be that he had killed his wife while drunk. An elderly sister of the old man was able and willing to provide him with a home, and he was understandably eager to leave the institution. When we asked the director of the institution why the old man was not released, he gave two significant answers. In the first place, he said, the statute requires me to find that this inmate is no longer a danger to the community; this I cannot do, for he may kill again. And of course the director was right. However unlikely commission of homicide by such a man in his eighties might appear, the director could not be certain. But, as far as that goes, he could not be certain also about himself or about you or me. The second answer was equally interesting. The old man, he said, is better off here. To understand the full significance of this reply it is necessary to know something about the place of confinement. Although called a hospital, it was in fact a prison, and not at all a progressive prison. Nothing worthy of the name of therapy was provided and very little even by way of recreational facilities.

This case points several morals. It illustrates, first, a failure of the law to deal adequately with the new requirements which are being placed upon it. The statute, as a condition of the release of the inmate, required the director of the institution virtually to warrant the future good behavior of the inmate, and, in so doing, made unrealistic and impossible demands on expert judgment. This might be remedied by the formulation of release criteria more consonant with actuality. Provisions for conditional release to test the inmate's reaction to the free community would considerably reduce the strain on administrative decision-making. But there is more here. Perhaps the case reflects that arrogance and insensitivity to human values to which men who have no reason to doubt their own motives appear peculiarly susceptible.

I have attempted to describe some of the continuing problems and difficulties associated with, what I have called, the rise of the rehabilitative ideal. In so doing, I have not sought to cast doubt on the substantial benefits associated with that movement. It has exposed some of the most intractable problems of our time to the solvent properties of human intelligence. Moreover, the devotion to the ideal of empirical investigation provides the movement with a self-correcting mechanism of great importance and justifies hopes for constructive future development.

Nevertheless, no intellectual movement produces only unmixed blessings. I have suggested that the ascendancy of the rehabilitative ideal has, as one of its unfortunate consequences, diverted attention from other questions of great criminological importance. This has operated unfavorably to the full development of criminological science. Not only is this true, but the failure of many students and practitioners in the relevant areas to concern themselves with the full context of criminal justice has produced measures dangerous to basic political values and has, on occasion, encouraged the debasement of the rehabilitative ideal to produce results which are unsupportable whether measured by the objectives of therapy or of correction. The worst manifestations of these tendencies are undoubtedly deplored as sincerely by competent therapists as by others. But the occurrences are neither so infrequent nor so trivial that they can be safely ignored.

NOTE

1. As I recall, it was referred to as the "quiet room." In another institution the boy was required to stand before a wall while a seventy pound fire hose was played on his back. This procedure went under the name of "hydrotherapy."

6

❋

Congress, Symbolic Politics and the Evolution of the 1994 "Violence against Women Act"

BARBARA ANN STOLZ*

Only recently has domestic violence been placed on the public policy agenda. Beginning in 1990 Congress considered legislation to provide a federal criminal justice response to domestic violence. These efforts culminated in 1994 with enactment of the "Violence against Women Act." The law sent a message to the public that domestic violence is not just a "family problem," or a "women's issue," to be handled through social services, but it is a national crime problem.

G enerally, congressional anti-crime initiatives have resulted in the federalization of more crimes, increased federal anti-crime dollars, and federally sponsored criminal justice research. The social science literature has, however, characterized much of the proposed and enacted criminal justice legislation as symbolic. . . . That is, such legislation is directed toward the general public and may perform one or more symbolic functions—educative, reassurance/threat, moral educative, and model for the states—in response to the concerns of that

*The opinions expressed are solely those of the author, not the U.S. General Accounting Office.
Source: *Criminal Justice Policy Review,* Vol. 10, No. 3/99, pp. 401–428. Reprinted by permission of Sage Publications, Inc. Notes and references deleted.

audience. Moreover, it appears that much federal criminal justice legislation has been introduced or enacted primarily in response to public outcries of concern about a crime problem and not in reaction to interest group lobbying, narrow constituency politics, or changes in the composition of Congress.

• • •

This article will examine the evolution of the "Violence against Women Act". . . from the perspective of symbolic politics. Viewing criminal justice legislation as symbolic acts does not mean that this legislation has no meaning, but focuses legislative analysis on how policy makers react to concerns of the general public or how the policy makers may direct the policy-making process toward the public in order to evoke a desired public reaction. Determining definitively why the "Violence against Women Act" was enacted in 1994 is not possible, because it was passed as one provision of an omnibus crime bill. Examining the evolution of the act from the perspective of symbolic politics, while not considering the full spectrum of influences that impacted the course of legislation, does provide insight into the Congressional criminal justice policy-making process, particularly from the perspective of Congress as an institution. It suggests an explanation as to why Congress, collectively, was galvanized to act on this issue in 1994 and a rationale for Congress' enactment of this and other criminal justice legislation seemingly in response to public outcries.

SYMBOLIC POLITICS AND CRIMINAL
JUSTICE POLICY: THE LITERATURE

Traditionally, the legislative research has been presented as the study of who gets what, where, and how. The who is usually interest groups; the what is most often tangible rewards; and the how describes the methods used to influence legislators to respond in a particular way to the who to provide the desired what. In recent years, however, political scientists and sociologists have come to recognize that the policy making process cannot always or simply be explained using this approach. This is, examining interest group behavior or requests from defined constituencies may not explain why certain legislation was introduced, enacted, or contained certain provisions. In the criminal justice field, interest groups, generally, and nonprofessional groups, in particular, have been found to play a limited role in the legislative process. . . . Tangible rewards are often not provided; and federal criminal justice legislative initiatives have often been introduced in reaction to highly publicized incidents rather than traditional lobbying by interest groups. Accordingly, in order to shed light on the criminal justice policy-making, it is imperative that that process and the resultant legislation be examined from a variety of political science perspectives.

Among the alternative approaches used by political scientists and sociologists to analyze legislation and the legislative process is symbolic politics. . . . From this perspective, political acts are viewed as symbols. These acts are directed toward an audience—usually the general public. The substance of the act is less important than the audience's perception of and/or reaction to the act. Moreover, at times whether or not the legislation is enacted, is not as important as the fact that the legislation has been introduced.

In general, political acts, as symbol, are said to serve to reassure or to threaten the onlooker. . . . Each political act also reinforces the impression that the political system is to translate individual wants into public policy and, accordingly, symbolization instills a feeling of well being. Criminal justice legislation performs such a reassurance function—communicating to the law-abiding that something is being done about a crime problem. . . . Such legislation also communicates a threat to the potential lawbreaker.

Two other symbolic functions of federal criminal law are identified in the literature—moral educative and model for the states. Criminal justice legislation fulfills a moral educative function for the lawbreaker and the law-abiding by communicating the line between right and wrong behavior. It also praises the law abiding, and by praising teaches law abidingness. . . . Federal criminal justice legislation may also provide a model for the states. . . . For example, one purpose of federal death penalty legislation may be to provide for the states a model of "rational criteria" for imposing the death penalty. Or, the practices of the Federal Bureau of Prisons may be presented to the states as a model of enlightened correctional policies.

• • •

In applying the symbolic politics approach to the study of legislative policy making, scholars have varied somewhat in their specific emphasis. Some authors have focused on the audience reaction to symbols. . . . Others have studied the symbol manipulators, their perceptions of the symbolic functions of law and how they use law as symbol to promote public responses. . . . Since the rationale behind much federal criminal justice legislation has tended to confound criminologists, . . . it is important to attempt to understand relationship between symbolism and criminal law as perceived by those [who] create the communicate through those symbols.

• • •

It should be noted that symbolic politics is not the tool of either liberals or conservatives, Democrats or Republicans, but may be used by political actors of all persuasions. An analysis of recent federal criminal justice legislation indicates, however, that substantively different policies may be directed toward fulfilling the same symbolic function. For example, the 1988 anti-drug legislation included diverse provisions to reassure the public that something was being done about the drug problem. This legislation included provisions to institute grant programs to promote drug education and treatment programs at the state and local levels, as well as provisions to impose more punitive sanctions against drug traffickers. The former may be characterized as a liberal response, while the latter as a conservative response. With respect to the three symbolic functions of criminal law—reassurance, moral educative, and model for the states, a "liberal" approach is usually associated with provisions that reassure by providing funds for services, draw a line using a mental health model, and promote model approaches by providing federal funding for desired state activities (carrot approach). A "conservative" approach tends to support policies that reassure or threaten by providing criminal penalties, draw a distinct line between the law-abiding and law breaker, and promote model approaches by threatening to withhold funds if states fail to follow certain policies (sick approach). Characterizing federal criminal justice provisions as conservative or liberal has often been difficult in recent years because of a blurring of ideologies; however, such a contrast is relevant to the discussion of the domestic violence, because the legislation includes ideologically diverse policies that serve the same symbolic function.

THE VIOLENCE AGAINST WOMEN ACT OF 1994: THE PROVISIONS

As enacted in 1994, the "Violence against Women Act" included more than a dozen provisions. These provisions can be organized into 3 categories—revision and expansion of federal law, grant programs to the states, and additional federal programs.

Federal Law

The provisions of the act that established or amended federal law

- Revised and expanded protections for women against violent crime,
- Directed the U.S. Sentencing commission to promulgate revised sentencing guidelines for ex-crime offenders and mandated financial restitution to victims by offenders,
- Amended the Federal Rules of Evidence pertaining to sexual assault cases,
- Established criminal penalties for crossing state lines to commit domestic violence or violate protection orders,
- Established a civil rights cause of action for civil suits against persons who commit sexual assault and other "gender-motivated" crimes, and
- Amended the Immigration and Nationality Act to authorize certain aliens suffering spousal abuse to petition for change in immigration status.

Grant Programs to the States Authorized

The act also created several grant programs for the states. Specifically, the legislation

- Authorized Department of Justice (DOJ) grants to state and local governments for law enforcement, prosecution, and victim services in violent crimes against women;
- Authorized Department of Transportation (DOT) grants for capital improvements to prevent crimes in public transit systems and other grants to reduce crime in public parks;

- Amended the Public Health and Human Services Act to authorize State use of certain funds for rape prevention and education programs;
- Amended the Runaway and Homeless Youth Act to authorize grants for runaways, homeless, and street youth who have been subjected to or are at risk of being subjected to sexual abuse;
- Authorized appropriations for grants for battered women's shelters, community programs on domestic violence, and rural domestic violence and child abuse enforcement; and
- Authorized State Justice Institute grants for education and training for Federal and state judges and court personnel on topics pertaining to violent crimes against women.

Other Federal Programs Authorized

In addition, the act established several other federal programs. The Act

- Authorized various programs under the Victims of Child Abuse Act of 1990 and
- Amended the Family Violence Prevention and Services Act to authorize a Department of Health and Human Services national domestic violence telephone hotline.

CASE STUDY

Congressional efforts leading to the enactment of the 1994 "Violence against Woman Act" began in 1990. Legislation was introduced in both Houses during the 101st (1989–1990), 102nd (1991–1992), and 103rd (1993–1994). Nine hearings were held. The Senate Judiciary Committee also issued a number of investigative reports.

During the 101st Congress, Senate Judiciary Committee Chairman Joseph Biden (Democrat) introduced the "Violence against Women Act of 1990." Representative Barbara Boxer (Democrat) introduced companion legislation in the House.

• • •

Chairman Biden held hearings on violence against women legislation in 1990. The message communicated during these hearings through the statements of Committee members and witnesses was that the acts of domestic violence are crimes. Moreover, these crimes of violence against women are not limited to the sensational newspaper stories, but occur every day, every hour, every minute. Witnesses testified to their personal tragedies and the failures of the criminal justice system's response. Representatives of organizations, such as the National Organization for Women (NOW), made recommendations that were incorporated into later versions of the bill. . . . Democratic Senators Dennis DeConcini and Howard Metzenbaum joined Senator Biden in introducing the legislation, but by the end of the 101st Congress, twenty-six senators, primarily Democrats but including Republicans William Cohen and Bob Packwood, had signed on as legislative cosponsors.

During the 102nd Congress, Senator Biden reintroduced violence against women legislation and held hearings. These hearings addressed the provisions of the legislation. In his opening statement at the April 1991 hearings, the Senator says that he suspects that the most controversial provisions of the proposed legislation are those declaring that "gender-motivated" crimes are a violation of a woman's civil rights. While acknowledging that none of the bill's provisions alone or together would solve the crisis, he asserts that they were a start. . . .

Furthermore, in a 1992 Committee Print, Senator Biden describes his efforts to enact the legislation. In these remarks he not only asserts the importance of the legislation, but the need for the public to recognize the seriousness of the problem before a change could occur. He states that:

> For some time now, I have shared the view of others that the Nation does not fully comprehend the magnitude and severity of the problem of violence against women. Two years ago, I began a series of hearings held during 1990 and 1991 on the topics of rape, domestic violence, and existing legal protections. In tandem with those hearings, I introduced the Violence against Women Act—the first comprehensive legislation attacking the problem. Through this process, I have come to believe more firmly than ever before that this Nation will be powerless to change the course of violence against women, unless and until its citizens fully realize the devastation this violence yields.

This same report discusses the seriousness of the problem . . . ; reports on 200 episodes of violence that occurred between Sept 1 and Sept 7, a small fraction of incidents that occurred during that time period . . . ; attempts to shatter the myths about abuse . . . ; and indicates the failure of laws, policies, and attitudes that remained inadequate to the task of fighting the epidemic of violence. . . .

In 1991, Representative Barbara Boxer and Constance Morella, a Democrat and Republican, respectively, introduced H.R. 1502, a companion to Senator Biden's bill. By 1992 the House bill had 178 cosponsors. The House Subcommittee on Crime and Criminal Justice held hearings on violence against women on February 6, 1992. These were general hearings, although the Boxer/Morella legislation might have provided the focus for the hearing. In his opening remarks, subcommittee Chairman Charles Schumer (Democrat) explains that his philosophy regarding the federal government's role in preventing crime, generally, and in relation to domestic violence, is to make sure

> that local law enforcement officers have the wherewithal and equipment they need to do their jobs. It should act as a facilitator to help good ideas that are successful in one area spread across the country. It can lead by example. The Federal Government has a loud voice that can send a message that violence against women is not accepted behavior in today's society, and I hope today's hearing will be the first step to doing just that. . . .

Representative James Sensenbrenner, the Ranking Republican, asserts it is important to "have this hearing today dealing with the general subject to at least get the ball rolling to see what type of legislation would be possible to draft and pass before the 102nd Congress adjourns sine die" (p.3). Representative Boxer includes with her testimony a list of organizations supporting her bill, H.R. 1502. On September 22, 1992, the subcommittee favorably reported H.R. 1502 to the full Judiciary Committee. The legislation, however, did not reach the House floor that year.

During the 103rd Congress, Senator Biden again introduced violence against women legislation. The Senate Judiciary Committee held field hearings that session in the states of both Democratic and Republican, Committee members. . . . Local witnesses testified and the hearings provided the opportunity to discuss what might be done about the problem at the federal level. During the 103rd Congress, 67 Senators signed on as cosponsors of the Senate violence against women legislation.

In the House, Representatives Pat Schroeder (Democrat), Charles Schumer, Louise Slaughter (Democrat), and Constance Morella introduced violence against women legislation, during the 103rd Congress. Two hundred twenty five Members signed on as cosponsors of this legislation. Hearings were held before the House Judiciary Subcommittee on Civil and Constitutional Rights, not the Subcommittee on Crime and Criminal Justice, as in 1992. At a November 16, 1993 hearing, chaired by Representative Don Edwards (Democrat), Members heard from witnesses from civil liberties and women's organizations, including NOW; the Fund for the Feminist Majority; and the American Civil Liberties Union (ACLU); as well as the Acting U.S. Assistant Attorney General, Civil Rights Division, James P. Turner.

The hearing focused on the provisions of the legislation. Acting Assistant Attorney General Turner testified that the proposed bill was based on the power of Congress to enforce the Fourth Amendment and to regulate the interstate commerce clause. . . . A NOW witness emphasized that

> . . . the impact of this legislation will not be purely symbolic. Many victims who are currently denied access to justice under State criminal and civil laws would for the first time have the opportunity to seek legal redress. The Congress has a historic opportunity to play a crucial role in the effort to combat crime and to redress discrimination against women.

NOW supported the civil rights provisions of the proposed violence against women bills, H.R. 1133 and S. 11, further asserting that the legislation contained certain important limitations that curtailed the scope of the new federal remedy. For example, the legislation did not confer jurisdiction over divorce and domestic relations to the federal courts and would not provide that all crimes against women qualify for relief under the civil rights provisions. . . . There were, however, differences of opinion among the organization witnesses. The hearing record indicates a conflict between NOW and ACLU over the provisions of the bill providing a civil rights remedy. NOW supported the provisions and the ACLU opposed them. . . .

The House Subcommittee on Crime and Criminal Justice met on November 16, 1993, to consider H.R. 1133. The Subcommittee adopted an amendment in the nature of a substitute, dropping certain titles that did not fall within its jurisdiction. The House Judiciary Committee met the next day and, with some changes, favorable reported out the bill.

Prior to 1994, both House and Senate Judiciary Committees reported out violence against women legislation—the Senate, three times and the House, once. The Senate legislation was even placed on the Calendar for consideration on the floor, but not put to a vote. During the four years, the Senate Judiciary Committee issued numerous legislative committee reports, based on its hearings, as well as several investigative reports. In November 1993, the House passed the legislation 421 to 0. Not until 1994, however, was the legislation passed and agreed to by both Houses.

In 1994, the Senate and House considered the violent crime against women bill, as part of an omnibus anti-crime package (H.R. 3355). The *Congressional Records* of June and July 1994 include statements by a number of House and Senate Members in support of the proposed violence against women legislation. These statements advocate enactment of the act, inclusion of the act in the crime package, and/or support for funding for the act. The statements also link the O. J. Simpson case with the need for the violence against women legislation. For example, in their record statements, Democrats, including Representatives Pat Schroeder and James Traficant and Senators Paul Simon and Patrick Leahy acknowledge the forgotten or hidden victims. Representative Schroeder asserts that the "Simpson" case (although stating he was innocent of the murder charge until proven guilty) showed how spouse abuse and domestic violence were ignored even by the best police departments and that the House and Senate conference committee (see below) should support "tough" legislation that "finally focuses the Federal government on this critical issue." . . . Representative Susan Molinari, a Republican, asks "What about other stories?" She asserts, "It is time we opened our eyes to the secret shame in homes across this country." "Let this be a lesson to us all. The O. J. Simpson case is focusing attention on domestic violence like never before, but the laws in our country are inadequate and so is society's attitude—still—toward domestic violence." . . .

Both Houses passed the omnibus crime legislation, that included the violence against women provisions. Because there were differences between the House and Senate versions, the legislation was sent to conference. One of the differences was in the provisions dealing with violence against women. The Senate bill, as passed, included a provision to create a new federal civil rights violation for crimes "motivated by gender," but the House version did not. Reportedly, Senate advocates saw the provision as an important and symbolic step because many state justice systems did not take attacks on women seriously. House opponents, in contrast, thought the provision to be an unwarranted and unwieldy burden on the federal courts. In the end, the Senate proponents prevailed. The first conference report failed, but a second conference report was agreed to in August 1994 and by so doing Congress enacted the omnibus crime legislation.

• • •

The President signed the omnibus crime legislation into law on September 13, 1994. . . .

Subsequently, at a 1994 hearing on the implementation of the "Violence against Women Act," Senator Biden reflected on its legislative history. The Senator said:

> It has been a long, hard fight. It has gotten wide bipartisan support. It started off 4 1/2 years ago with some of the women in this room being the only allies I had in the drafting of this legislation. In the beginning, even many of the women's groups were not enthusiastic about this.
>
> It is a testament to, I hope, sound judgement and perseverance that not only have we passed the bill, but with overwhelming support. Senator Hatch, the ranking Republican, being a prime cosponsor of the legislation, as well as the vast majority of Republicans and Democrats supporting it.
>
> As a law, the "Violence against Women Act," puts everyone on notice that we will no longer tolerate the violence in the home and the assaults on the street that continue to push the crime rate against women up and up and up, even as the overall crime rate has dropped. . . .

The Senator also noted the commitment of federal resources, stating that the resources were to meet the three goals of the legislation, which were:

1. To turn the justice system into a mechanism that works for women, not against women, a user-friendly system. . . .

2. To take practical steps that will make women actually safer on the streets, in the workplace, and in their homes; and

3. To reform attitudes, attitudes that have allowed violence against women to flourish in this country. . . .

SYMBOLIC FUNCTIONS AND THE 1994 "VIOLENCE AGAINST WOMEN ACT": FINDINGS AND ANALYSIS

Although analysis of the evolution of the 1994 "Violence against Woman Act" is confounded by its having been enacted as part of omnibus anti-crime legislation, the case study provides evidence of the four symbolic functions discussed in the social science literature—educative, reassurance, moral educative and model for the states. Moreover, examining the evolution of the legislation in terms of these four functions offers some insight into legislative process and Congressional behavior that affected the course of the legislation.

Educative

The initial hearings on the violence against women legislation, particularly those held in the Senate, focused on communicating to the public, and also seemingly to Members of Congress, that domestic violence is a crime. These hearings sought to perform an educative function. In statements during the hearings and in committee reports, Chairman Biden not only argues that domestic violence is a crime, but asserts that the public must be made aware of this relationship. The testimony of victims and advocates describes the nature of the violence, the common occurrence of domestic violence, and the failures of the criminal justice system to deal with the problem. The field hearings further illustrate that the problem occurs in different states, in different parts of the country. The 1992 House hearings had a similar educative focus.

• • •

The purpose of the early Senate and House . . . hearings was to establish an educational record regarding the nature and extent of the crime of domestic violence, the inadequacies of current laws and the responses of the criminal justice system, as well as alternative approaches for dealing with the problem.

It might be argued that the growth in the number of cosponsors over the three Congresses during which the legislation was considered suggests increased Member awareness of the problem of domestic violence as a crime. Typically, the number of cosponsors is a rough indicator of Member support for legislation. This is not to attribute this increased awareness solely to the hearings. The media, events focusing attention on women's issues, books and television programs about the victims of domestic violence may also have contributed to an overall societal awareness of the problem. . . . In 1994, one event, however, seems to have clearly contributed [to] the process of educating the public and Members of Congress that domestic violence is a crime. It would appear that Nicole Brown Simpson's murder and its link to past domestic violence may have provided a moral eye-opener to the effect that domestic violence is a crime.

• • •

Although some Members and informed publics were aware that domestic violence was a crime, the requisite support to enact the legislation was not present. The O. J. Simpson case would seem to have provided the needed impetus to move the process toward enactment of the legislation. Members of Congress spoke of the case "opening our eyes" to the problem of domestic violence and the inadequacies of current law. Subsequent to the Simpson weekend, domestic violence was no longer a subject for public education; Congressional action to enact the legislation was necessary.

Reassurance and Threat

A second symbolic function of criminal law, identified in the literature, is reassurance/threat. From the beginning of its legislative history, the violence against women legislation communicated a reassurance message to the victims of domestic violence and a threat to the violators. Just the introduction of the legislation may serve that function. Here again, however, the Simpson case seems to have impacted the legislative process. Subsequent to this event, simply introducing the legislation was no longer sufficient to reassure the public or threaten the violator.

In response to the concerns raised by the Simpson case, Congress needed to respond to reassure the general public that such behavior was not accepted and that domestic violence, as it is a crime, would not be tolerated. Moreover, there was a need to reassure the victims of domestic violence that the federal government was in their corner. After "the O. J. Simpson weekend," it appears that Congress had to enact legislation to communicate that message.

Scholars may view Congress' seeming precipitous enactment of criminal justice legislation in response to events as irrational. . . . Such a description of Congressional behavior fails to point out that in many cases Congress has been considering legislation on the issue, but has not reached the consensus necessary to enact it.

Examining the legislative history of recent crime legislation from the perspective of the reassurance/threat symbolic function suggests, however, that events, rather than being the sole cause of Congressional action, may precipitate Congressional action on issues already under review, in response to the need to reassure the public that Congress is addressing the problem. For example, the "Anti-drug Abuse Act of 1986" was, at least in part, a Congressional response to public concerns raised by the cocaine-related death of University of Maryland basketball star Len Bias. . . . Newspaper accounts in June 1994 reported that the Simpson case broke a legislative logjam over the domestic violence. Congress could not not react to the problem. . . . In both instances, however, Congress had relevant legislative proposals under consideration. While appearing to respond to events, Congress, as an institution, is translating the wants of individuals into public policy, thereby instilling a feeling of well being, and supporting the legitimacy of the institution as the representative of the people.

While the very enactment of the legislation can serve the symbolic function of reassurance/threat, the specific provisions of the legislation also perform this function. By providing programmatic resources and enhanced penalties, the provisions of the violence against women legislation performed the reassurance/threat function of criminal law.

• • •

Moral Educative Function

Throughout the legislative history of the "Violence against Women Act," one finds discussions of the content of the legislation and in those discussions specific evidence of the symbolic functions of moral education. For example, focusing on the civil rights provisions of the proposed legislation during the 1993 Housek hearings highlighted the moral educative symbolic function of the legislation. These provisions send (1) a message as to what behavior would no longer be tolerated, (2) a threat to the lawbreaker, and (3) a message to the victim that the federal government was concerned. They sent a message that "gender-based" violence was to be considered a violation of civil rights, just as racism was. The society would no longer tolerate that behavior and the victims of that behavior were considered in need of and were to receive the support of the federal government.

In addition to the civil rights provisions, federal punitive measures were included in the act. The legislation directed the U.S. Sentencing commission to promulgate revised sentencing guidelines for "ex-crime offenders" and mandated financial restitution to victims by offenders. It also established criminal penalties for crossing state lines to commit domestic violence or violate protection orders. In so doing, the legislation communicated a threat to the offender.

Moreover, the line was drawn. The law served as a moral educator for the lawbreaker and the law-abiding.

• • •

Model for the States

The violence against women legislation also included provisions that served the symbolic function of model for the states. By providing assistance to the states through a number of grant programs, Congress identified what it viewed as "good policies." Through these grants programs, the federal government would provide resources to the states to support training and education of law enforcers, education programs, and other supports to the victims of violence. Moreover, such programs were to support state efforts to address the legislative goal "to reform attitudes, attitudes that have allowed violence against women to flourish in this country." . . . Such a "carrot" approach is more indicative of a liberal than a conservative approach to the function of model for the states. . . . Whether or not the states actually implement these policies does not affect the symbolic argument. The purpose of the legislation is to show that Congress and the federal government know what should be done; they are at the forefront of addressing the problem.

The 1994 domestic violence legislation also provided support for research programs to develop information about the problem. Better statistics would provide better information on the nature and extent of the problem. Evaluation of arrest policies would support improvements in state and local systems, in support of the goal of making the criminal justice system "a mechanism that works for women, not against women, a user-friendly system." . . . Support for research programs has also tended to be associated with a liberal approach to the model function.

SUMMARY, CONCLUSION
AND IMPLICATIONS

This article has sought to analyze the legislative development of the 1993 "Violence against Women Act" from the perspective of the symbolic functions of criminal justice legislation—educative, reassurance and threat, moral educative, and model for the states. As noted earlier, the term symbolic, as used in this article, does not mean that legislation is meaningless, but focuses the analysis on the policy makers and the audience to whom they direct the legislation. The analysis is, however, confounded by the fact that the 1994 "Violence against Women Act" was enacted as part of omnibus crime legislation. Whether or not the act would have been enacted in 1994 without the omnibus vehicle is a matter of speculation. Despite this limitation, the analysis of the history of the "Violence against Women Act," enacted in 1994, contributes to our understanding of the role of symbolic politics in several respects.

First, the analysis illustrates the role of the educative function of legislation and legislative hearings, at a time when public and congressional consensus may not be sufficient to enact legislation. Initially, the proposed violence against Women legislation and the hearing process served primarily as a means to educate public and Congress that violence against women is a crime.

Second, this case study demonstrates how Congressional emphasis on the various specific symbolic functions may vary over time. Although the other symbolic functions were evident during the early history of the legislation, the educative function, as suggested by the statements of the Members, dominated. Once Congress was focused on enacting the legislation, the functions of reassurance/threat, moral educative, and model for the states were more prominent. Although simply introducing the legislation initially provided reassurance and a threat, events seemed to make it necessary for Congress to enact the legislation in order to perform that function.

Third, the analysis provides insight into the role that events may play in the federal criminal justice legislative process. As in the case of other crime legislation during the last three decades, events seem to have affected the content and dynamic of the legislative debate regarding violence against women legislation, as it relates to the symbolic functions. After the "O. J. Simpson weekend," public awareness was aroused. Whether he was, in fact, guilty or innocent, the O.J. Simpson case put human faces on the problem of domestic violence. Subsequently, the Congress seemed to focus more on the need to reassure the public and to send a threat to the potential offender that Congress was concerned about domestic violence. Because the "Violence against Women Act" was part of an omnibus bill, it is not possible to assess the direct impact of the O. J. Simpson case on its ultimate passage. One can postulate, however, that after the O. J. Simpson allegations, it would have been difficult for most Members of Congress to oppose the legislation. The Simpson case appears to have provided the basis for Congressional consensus. The consensus reached was that domestic violence is a crime with national dimensions, and, therefore, the federal government had a responsibility to address the problem.

Fourth, the provisions of this legislation reflected both conservative and liberal criminal justice policies. This observation supports the assertion made at the beginning of the article that symbolic politics is not the tool of either liberals or conservatives or Democrats or Republicans, but any of the above. Moreover, ideologically different policies may perform the same symbolic function. Providing program grants or punitive penalties both seek to reassure the law-abiding. In its ideological complexity, the violence against women legislation is similar to other federal anti-crime and anti-drug legislation enacted during the last three decades.

In short, although symbolic politics is only one aspect of the analysis of a piece of legislation, its application to the study of the 1994 "Violence against Women Act" provides insight into evolutionary history of this legislation. Moreover, analyzing federal criminal justice legislation from the perspective of symbolic politics sheds light on how our criminal laws are actually enacted and some of the considerations that affect federal criminal justice policy making. . . .

✷

PART II

Police

A key question in a democratic society is, "For what purpose do the police exist?" History gives us little help in providing an answer, because
police agencies have often played many different and contradictory roles.
Are the police to be concerned primarily with crime fighting or peace keeping?
Should they be social workers with guns or gun-toters in social work? Should
they be instruments of social change or defenders of the faith?

THREE ERAS OF AMERICAN POLICING

American policing is often described in terms of three historical periods: the Political Era (1840–1920), the Professional Era (1920–1970), and the Community
Era (1970–present). This division of history has been criticized as describing
policing only in the urban areas of the Northeast without taking into account
the very different development of the police in rural areas of the South and West.
Even so, it is useful as a framework through which we can note differences in
the organization of the police, the primary tasks they are charged with, and the
specific policies and strategies that they are instructed to follow.

The Political Era: 1840–1920

The early history of policing in the United States has been characterized as the
Political Era because of the close ties that developed between the police and
urban political leaders. In many cities, the police appeared to work for the mayor
or the political party in power rather than for the citizens in general. In some
places, guns and badges were issued to white males who supported the mayor or
the ruling political machine. These police officers would then help their political patrons stay in power by working to get out the vote on election day. Ranks

in the force were often for sale to the highest bidder, and many police officers were "on the take."

During this era the police focused on crime prevention and order maintenance by foot patrol. The officer on the beat dealt with crime, disorder, and other problems as they arose. In addition, the police in urban areas carried out service functions such as caring for derelicts, operating soup kitchens, regulating public health, and handling medical and social emergencies. Through their closeness to the communities they served, the police became both city servants and crime control officers. Because of this, the police enjoyed citizen support.

The twentieth century brought increasing urbanization to all parts of the country. There was growing criticism of the influence of politics on the police. This resulted in efforts to reform the nature and organization of the police. Reformers sought to make police into law enforcement professionals and reduce their connection to local politics.

The Professional Era: 1920–1970

Policing was greatly influenced by the Progressive reform movement in the early twentieth century. The Progressives were mostly upper-middle-class, educated Americans interested in two primary goals: efficient government and the provision of government services to improve the conditions of the less fortunate. Belief in the importance of expertise was high, and the growth in an expert-driven administrative state provided impetus for professionalization and bureaucratization at all levels of government. A related goal was the removal of political influences, such as party politics and patronage, on government. When the Progressives applied these goals to the police, they envisioned professional law enforcement officials who would use modern technology to benefit the entire society, not just the local politicians.

August Vollmer, chief of police of Berkeley, California, from 1909 to 1932, was one of the leading advocates of professional policing. He and other reformers argued that the police should be a professional force, a nonpartisan agency of government committed to the highest ideals of public service. Six essential elements comprise this model of professional policing:

1. The force should stay out of politics.
2. Members should be well trained, disciplined, and tightly organized.
3. Laws should be equally enforced.
4. The force should take advantage of technological developments.
5. Personnel procedures should be based on merit.
6. The crime-fighting role should be prominent.

The refocusing of police attention on crime control and away from maintaining order probably did more than anything else to change the nature of American policing. This narrow focus on crime fighting severed many of the ties that the police had developed with the communities they served. Instead, for the most part, cops became crime fighters.

By the 1930s, with their new orientation toward fighting crime, the police were adopting modern technologies and methods in order to combat serious crimes. Effectiveness in fighting serious crimes like murder, rape, and robbery was especially important for gaining citizen support. By contrast, efforts to control victimless offenses and to strictly maintain order often aroused citizen opposition. The clean, professionalized model of policing put forth by the reformers could be sustained only if the scope of police responsibility was narrowed to crime fighting.

In the 1960s, the civil rights and antiwar movements, urban riots, and rising crime rates challenged many assumptions of the professional model. With American cities increasingly populated by low-income members of racial minorities, the professional style isolated officers from the communities they served. In the eyes of many inner-city residents, the police were an occupying army keeping them at the bottom of society rather than public servants providing help to all citizens.

Although the police continued to portray themselves to the public as crime fighters, citizens became increasingly aware that the police were often ineffective in this role. Crime rates rose for many offenses, and the police were unable to change the perception that the quality of urban life was diminishing.

Community Policing Era: 1970–Present

Beginning in the 1970s, there were calls for movement away from the overriding crime-fighting focus and toward greater emphasis on maintaining order and providing services to the community. Major research studies were published showing the complexities of police work and the extent to which day-to-day practices deviated from the ideals of the professional model. The research also questioned the effectiveness of the police in catching and deterring criminals.

Three findings of the research are especially noteworthy:

1. Increasing the number of patrol officers in a neighborhood was found to have little effect on the crime rate.

2. Rapid response to calls for service did not greatly increase the arrest rate.

3. Improving the percentage of crimes solved is difficult.

These findings undermined the principles of the professional crime-fighter model.

Critics argue that the professional style isolated the police from the community and reduced their knowledge about and accountability to the neighborhoods they served. Motorized patrols encapsulated officers inside their patrol cars so that they have few personal contacts with citizens. As an alternative, it is argued that officers should get out of their cars and spend more time directly meeting and assisting citizens.

Advocates of the community policing approach urge greater use of foot patrols so that officers will become known to citizens, who in turn will cooperate with the police. They believe that through attention to little problems, the police may not only reduce disorder and fear but also improve public attitudes toward policing. Through a problem-oriented approach to policing, officers should identify the underlying causes of such problems as noisy teenagers, spouse batterers, and abandoned buildings used as drug houses. By addressing various problems, small or large, within neighborhoods, the police can reduce disorder and the fear of crime.

Questions still remain about community policing and whether it can or should be implemented throughout the nation. The populations in some cities, especially in the West, are too dispersed to permit a switch from motorized to foot patrols. In addition, some critics of community policing question whether the professional model really disconnected police from community residents and whether Americans actually want their police to be something other than crime fighters.

POLICE CULTURE

The position of "police officer" is more than a cluster of formally prescribed duties and role expectations held jointly by criminal justice officials and members of the political community. In addition to the formal administrative language that specifies duties and responsibilities, there is a cultural dimension to the position that has a profound influence on the operational code of the police, both as a unit and as individuals behaving within a bureaucratic framework. There remains an inherent tension between an officer's role conception and the mandate required by the law.

Social scientists have demonstrated that there is a definite relationship between one's occupational environment and the way one interprets events; an occupation may be seen as a major badge of identity that an individual acts to protect as a facet of his or her self-esteem and person. Thus, entry requirements, training, and professional socialization produce a homogeneity of attitudes that guides the police in their daily work.

National studies of occupational status have shown that the public ascribes more prestige to the police now than in prior decades, even though police officers do not believe the public regards their calling as honorable. Publications of police organizations repeatedly take up the theme that the public does not appreciate law enforcement agents. In a Denver survey, 98 percent of police officers reported that they had experienced verbal or physical abuse and that these incidents tended to occur in neighborhoods of minority and underprivileged groups. Part of the burden of the police is that they have doubts about their professional status. Yet opinion polls consistently indicate that the overwhelming majority of citizens, even those in the ghetto, see the police as protectors of persons and property.

Discretion is a characteristic of bureaucracy. Unlike most organizations, however, the discretion the police have increases as one moves down the hierarchy. Thus the patrol officer, the most numerous and lowest-ranking of officers, has the greatest amount of discretion. He or she deals with clients alone and is almost solely in charge of enforcing the most ambiguous laws—conflicts among citizens in which the definition of offensive behavior is most often open to dispute. The police officer's perception of the situation, as shaped by his or her personal values and norms, is crucial in determining what action the officer will take and what charges will be filed.

The police officer's world is circumscribed by the all-encompassing demands of the job. Not only are the police socialized to norms that accentuate loyalty to fellow officers, a professional esprit de corps, and the symbolism of authority, but the situational context of their position limits their freedom to isolate their vocational role from other aspects of their lives. From the time they are first given their badges and guns, they must always carry these reminders of their position—the tools of the trade—and be prepared to use them. Thus, the requirements that the police maintain vigilance against crime even when off duty and that they work at "odd hours," along with the limited opportunities for social contact with persons other than fellow officers, reinforce the values of the police subculture.

THE "IMPOSSIBLE" MANDATE

In a thoughtful essay Peter Manning wrote that the police agree with their audiences, their professional interpreters—the American family, criminals, and politicians—in at least one respect: they have an "impossible" mandate. In society, various occupational groups are given license to carry out certain activities that others are not. Indeed, groups achieving professional status have formal rules and codes of ethics that not only set their own standards but also define their occupational mandate. Medical doctors, for example, have the right to prescribe drugs and perform operations, but they are also able to set the boundaries of their mandate. Because over time the practice of medicine has become a secure profession, there is little disagreement in society about the tasks, attitudes, and values that set its practitioners apart.

The police in contemporary society are in trouble largely because they have been unable to define their mandate; it has been defined for them by those they serve. As a result, citizens have a distorted notion of police work. People are aware of the excitement of a small portion of police work, but then mistakenly broaden this notion to include all police activities. For much of the public, the police are viewed as always ready to respond to citizen demands—as highly organized crime fighters able to keep society from falling apart.

Sociopolitical changes in the United States have added to the tensions between the mandate of the police and their ability to fulfill it. In the past hundred years there have been massive shifts of population from rural areas to the cities. Criminal law has been called upon to serve a variety of purposes that are only tangentially related to law enforcement and order maintenance. Affluence has brought the criminal justice system new problems—such as the ease of communication and the abundance of property. Police have been assigned the tasks of crime prevention, crime detection, and the apprehension of criminals. Because they have a monopoly on legal violence, they have a mandate that claims to include efficient, apolitical, and professional enforcement of the law. All this is to be accomplished within the bounds dictated by a democratic society that values due process of law.

The mandate given the police is indeed "impossible." This will be true so long as there are misunderstandings, on the part of the police and the public, about the nature of law enforcement work, the potential for success in controlling crime, and the role of law in a democratic society.

SUGGESTIONS FOR FURTHER READING

Bayley, David H. *Police for the Future*. New York: Oxford University Press, 1994. A thoughtful examination of police work with a blueprint for the future.

Goldstein, Herman. *Problem-Oriented Policing*. New York: McGraw-Hill, 1990. Basic examination of the move toward problem-oriented, or community, policing.

Lawrence, Regina. *The Politics of Force: Media and the Construction of Police Brutality*. Berkeley: University of California Press, 2000. Emphasizes the interplay between the criminal justice system and the media, using coverage of use of force incidents. Shows how coverage influences public perception of crime, and may shape political reaction.

Skolnick, Jerome H., and James J. Fyfe. *Above the Law: Police and the Excessive Use of Force*. New York: Free Press, 1993. Written in light of the Rodney King beating and the riots that followed. The authors believe that only by recruiting and supporting police chiefs who will uphold a policy of strict accountability can brutality be eliminated.

Tonry, Michael, and Norval Morris, eds. *Modern Policing*. Chicago: University of Chicago Press, 1992. An outstanding collection of essays by leading scholars examining the history, organization, and operational tactics of the police.

Wilson, James Q. *Varieties of Police Behavior*. Cambridge, Mass.: Harvard University Press, 1968. A classic study of the styles of policing in different types of communities. Shows the impact of politics on the operations of the force.

7

Police Discretion Not to Invoke the Criminal Process

Low-Visibility Decisions in the Administration of Justice

JOSEPH GOLDSTEIN

Legislatures write the criminal laws as if they were commands to be enforced by the police, but officers have wide latitude in determining how the laws will be enforced. Professor Joseph Goldstein of the Yale Law School notes that decisions not to invoke the law are shielded from the public's view. Of particular interest is his development of the concepts of "total," "full," and "actual" enforcement. The extent to which the police pursue a policy approaching "full" enforcement for all offenses depends upon the values of the community.

Police decisions not to invoke the criminal process largely determine the outer limit of law enforcement. By such decisions, the police define the ambit of discretion throughout the process of other decision makers—prosecutor, grand and petit jury judge, probation officer, correction authority, and parole and pardon boards. These police decisions, unlike their decisions to invoke the law, are generally of extremely low visibility and consequently are seldom the subject of review. Yet an opportunity for review and appraisal of nonenforcement decisions is essential to the functioning of the rule of law in our system of criminal justice. This article will therefore be an attempt to determine how the visibility of such police decisions may be increased and what procedures should be established to evaluate them on a continuing basis in the light of the

Source: Reprinted by permission of the Yale Law Journal Company and Fred B. Rothman & Company from *The Yale Law Journal,* Vol. 69, pp. 543–594. Footnotes omitted.

complex of objectives of the criminal law and of the paradoxes toward which the administration of criminal justice inclines.

I. The criminal law is one of many intertwined mechanisms for the social control of human behavior. It defines behavior which is deemed intolerably disturbing to or destructive of community values and prescribes sanctions which the state is authorized to impose upon persons convicted or suspected of engaging in prohibited conduct. Following a plea or verdict of guilty, the state deprives offenders of life, liberty, dignity, or property through convictions, fines, imprisonments, killings, and supervised releases, and thus seeks to punish, restrain, and rehabilitate them, as well as to deter others from engaging in proscribed activity. Before a verdict, and despite the presumption of innocence which halos every person, the state deprives the suspect of life, liberty, dignity, or property through the imposition of deadly force, search and seizure of persons and possessions, accusation, imprisonment, and bail, and thus seeks to facilitate the enforcement of the criminal law.

These authorized sanctions reflect the multiple and often conflicting purposes which now surround and confuse criminal law administration at and between key decision points in the process. The stigma which accompanies conviction, for example, while serving a deterrent, and possibly retributive, function, becomes operative upon the offender's release and thus impedes the rehabilitation objective of probation and parole. Similarly, the restraint function of imprisonment involves the application of rules and procedures which, while minimizing escape opportunities, contributes to the deterioration of offenders confined for reformation. Since police decisions not to invoke the criminal process may likewise further some objectives while hindering others, or, indeed, run counter to all, any meaningful appraisal of these decisions should include an evaluation of their impact throughout the process on the various objectives reflected in authorized sanctions and in the decisions of other administrators of criminal justice.

Under the rule of law, the criminal law has both a fair-warning function for the public and a power-restricting function for officials. Both post- and preverdict sanctions, therefore, may be imposed only in accord with authorized procedures. No sanctions are to be inflicted other than those which have been prospectively prescribed by the Constitution, legislation, or judicial decision for a particular crime or a particular kind of offender. These concepts, of course, do not preclude differential disposition, within the authorized limits, of persons suspected or convicted of the same or similar offenses. In an ideal system differential handling, individualized justice, would result, but only from an equal application of officially approved criteria designed to implement officially approved objectives. And finally a system which presumes innocence requires that preconviction sanctions be kept at a minimum consistent with assuring an opportunity for the process to run its course.

A regularized system of review is a requisite for ensuring substantial compliance by the administrators of criminal justice with these rule-of-law principles. Implicit in the word "review" and obviously essential to the operation of any review procedure is the visibility of the decisions and conduct to be scrutinized.

Pretrial hearings on motions, the trial, appeal, and the writ of habeas corpus constitute a formal system for evaluating the actions of officials invoking the criminal process. The public hearing, the record of proceedings, and the publication of court opinions—all features of the formal system—preserve and increase the visibility of official enforcement activity and facilitate and encourage the development of an informal system of appraisal. These proceedings and documents are widely reported and subjected to analysis and comment by legislative, professional, and other interested groups and individuals.

But police decisions not to invoke the criminal process, except when reflected in gross failures of service, are not visible to the community. Nor are they likely to be visible to official state reviewing agencies, even those within the police department. Failure to tag illegally parked cars is an example of gross failure of service, open to public view and recognized for what it is. An officer's decision, however, not to investigate or report adequately a disturbing event which he has reason to believe constitutes a violation of the criminal law does not ordinarily carry with it consequences sufficiently visible to make the community, the legislature, the prosecutor, or the courts aware of a possible failure of service. The police officer, the suspect, the police department, and frequently even the victim, when directly concerned with a decision not to invoke, unlike the same parties when responsible for or subject to a decision to invoke, generally have neither the incentive nor the opportunity to obtain review of that decision or the police conduct associated with it. Furthermore, official police records are usually too incomplete to permit evaluations of nonenforcement decisions in the light of the purposes of the criminal law. Consequently, such decisions, unlike decisions to enforce, are generally not subject to the control which would follow from administrative, judicial, legislative, or community review and appraisal.

Confidential reports detailing the day-to-day decisions and activities of a large municipal police force have been made available to the author by the American Bar Foundation. These reports give limited visibility to a wide variety of police decisions not to invoke the criminal process. Three groups of such decisions will be described and analyzed. Each constitutes a police "program" of nonenforcement either based on affirmative departmental policy or condoned by default. All of the decisions, to the extent that the officers concerned thought about them at all, represent well-intentioned, honest judgments, which seem to reflect the police officer's conception of his job. None of the decisions involve bribery or corruption, nor do they concern "obsolete," though unrepealed, criminal laws. Specifically, these programs involve police decisions (1) not to enforce the narcotics laws against certain violators, who inform against other "more serious" violators; (2) not to enforce the felonious assault laws against an assailant whose victim does not sign a complaint; and (3) not to enforce gambling laws against persons engaged in the numbers racket, but instead to harass them. Each of these decisions is made even though the police "know" a crime has been committed and even though they may "know" who the offender is and may, in fact, have apprehended him. But before describing and evaluating these nonenforcement programs, as an agency of review might do, it is necessary to determine what discretion, if any, the police, as invoking agents, have, and conceptually to locate the police in relation to other principal decision makers in the criminal law process.

II. The police have a duty not to enforce the substantive law of crimes unless invocation of the process can be achieved within bounds set by constitution, statute, court decision, and possibly official pronouncements of the prosecutor. *Total enforcement,* were it possible, is thus precluded, by generally applicable due process restrictions on such police procedures as arrest, search, seizure, and interrogation. *Total enforcement* is further precluded by such specific procedural restrictions as prohibitions on invoking an adultery statute unless the spouse of one of the parties complains, or an unlawful-possession-of-firearms statute if the offender surrenders his dangerous weapons during a statutory period of amnesty. Such restrictions of general and specific application mark the bounds, often ambiguously, of an area of *full enforcement* in which the police are not only authorized but expected to enforce fully the law of crimes. An area of *no enforcement* lies, therefore, between the perimeter of *total enforcement* and the outer limits of *full enforcement.* In this *no-enforcement* area, the police have no authority to invoke the criminal process.

Within the area of *full enforcement,* the police have not been delegated discretion not to invoke the criminal process. On the contrary, those state statutes providing for municipal police departments which define the responsibility of police provide:

> It shall be the duty of the police . . . under the direction of the mayor and chief of police and in conformity with the ordinances of the city, and the laws of the state, . . . to pursue and arrest any persons fleeing from justice . . . to apprehend any and all persons in the act of committing any offense against the laws of the state . . . and to take the offender forthwith before the proper court or magistrate, to be dealt with for the offense; to make complaints to the proper officers and magistrates of any person known or believed by them to be guilty of the violation of the ordinances of the city or the penal laws of the state; and at all times diligently and faithfully to enforce all such laws. . . .

Even in jurisdictions without such a specific statutory definition, declarations of the *full enforcement* mandate generally appear in municipal charters, ordinances, or police manuals. Police manuals, for example, commonly provide, in sections detailing the duties at each level of the police hierarchy, that the captain, superintendent, lieutenant, or patrolman shall be responsible, so far as is in his power, for the prevention and detection of crime and the enforcement of all criminal laws and ordinances. Illustrative of the spirit and policy of *full enforcement* is this protestation from the introduction to the Rules and Regulations of the Atlanta, Georgia, Police Department:

> Enforcement of all Criminal Laws and City Ordinances, is my obligation. There are no specialties under the Law. My eyes must be open to traffic problems and disorders, though I move on other assignments, to slinking vice in back streets and dives though I have been directed elsewhere, to the suspicious appearance of evil wherever it is encountered. . . . I must

be impartial because the Law surrounds, protects, and applies to all alike, rich and poor, low and high, black and white. . . .

Minimally, then, *full enforcement,* so far as the police are concerned, means (1) the investigation of every disturbing event which is reported to or observed by them and which they have reason to suspect may be a violation of the criminal law; (2) following a determination that some crime has been committed, an effort to discover its perpetrators; and (3) the presentation of all information collected by them to the prosecutor for his determination of the appropriateness of further invoking the criminal process.

Full enforcement, however, is not a realistic expectation. In addition to ambiguities in the definitions of both substantive offenses and due process boundaries, countless limitations and pressures preclude the possibility of the police seeking or achieving *full enforcement.* Limitations of time, personnel, and investigative devices—all in part but not entirely functions of budget—force the development, by plan or default, of priorities of enforcement. Even if there were "enough police" adequately equipped and trained, pressures from within and without the department, which is after all a human institution, may force the police to invoke the criminal process selectively. By decisions not to invoke within the area of *full enforcement,* the police largely determine the outer limits of *actual enforcement* throughout the criminal process. This relationship of the police to the total administration of criminal justice can be seen in the diagram [Figure 1]. They may reinforce, or they may undermine, the legislature's objectives in designating certain conduct "criminal" and in authorizing the imposition of certain sanctions following conviction. A police decision to ignore a felonious assault "because the

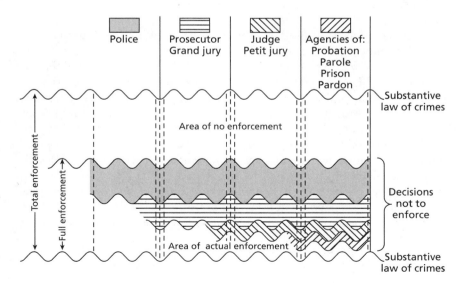

Figure 1 The Police in Relation to Other Decision Makers in the Criminal Process

victim will not sign a complaint" usually precludes the prosecutor or grand jury from deciding whether to accuse, judge or jury from determining guilt or innocence, judge from imposing the most "appropriate" sentence, probation or correctional authorities from instituting the most "appropriate" restraint and rehabilitation programs, and finally parole or pardon authorities from determining the offender's readiness for release to the community. This example is drawn from one of the three programs of nonenforcement about to be discussed.

III. Trading enforcement against a narcotics suspect for information about another narcotics offense or offender may involve two types of police decisions not to invoke fully the criminal process. First, there may be a decision to ask for the dismissal or reduction of the charge for which the informant is held; second, there may be a decision to overlook future violations while the suspect serves as an informer. The second type is an example of a relatively pure police decision not to invoke the criminal process while the first requires, at a minimum, tacit approval by prosecutor or judge. But examination of only the pure types of decisions would oversimplify the problem. They fail to illustrate the extent to which police nonenforcement decisions may permeate the process as well as influence, and be influenced by, prosecutor and court action in settings which fail to prompt appraisal of such decisions in light of the purposes of the criminal law. Both types of decision, pure and conglomerate, are nonetheless primarily police decisions. They are distinguishable from a prosecutor's or court's decision to trade information for enforcement under an immunity statute, and from such parliamentary decisions as the now-repealed seventeenth- and eighteenth-century English statutes which gave a convicted offender who secured the conviction of his accomplice an absolute right to pardon. Such prosecutor and parliamentary decisions to trade information for enforcement, unlike the police decisions to be described, have not only been authorized by a legislative body but have also been made sufficiently visible to permit review.

In the municipality studied, regular uniformed officers, with general law enforcement duties on precinct assignments, and a special narcotics squad of detectives, with citywide jurisdiction, are responsible for enforcement of the state narcotics laws. The existence of the special squad acts as a pressure on the uniformed officer to be the first to discover any sale, possession, or use of narcotics in his precinct. Careful preparation of a case for prosecution may thus become secondary to this objective. Indeed, approximately 80 percent of those apprehended for narcotics violations during one year were discharged. In the opinion of the special squad, which processes each arrested narcotics suspect, either the search was illegal or the evidence obtained inadequate. The precinct officer's lack of interest in carefully developing a narcotics case for prosecution often amounts in effect to a police decision not to enforce but rather to harass.

But we are concerned here primarily with the decisions of the narcotics squad, which, like the Federal Narcotics Bureau, has established a policy of concentrating enforcement efforts against the "big supplier." The chief of the squad claimed that informers must be utilized to implement that policy, and that in order to get informants it is necessary to trade "little ones for big ones." Informers are used to arrange and make purchases of narcotics, to elicit information from suspects, including persons in custody, and to recruit additional informants.

Following arrest, a suspect will generally offer to serve as an informer to "do himself some good." If an arrestee fails to initiate such negotiations, the interrogating officer will suggest that something may be gained by disclosing sources of supply and by serving as an informer. A high mandatory minimum sentence for selling, a high maximum sentence for possession, and, where users are involved, a strong desire on their part to avoid the agonies of withdrawal, combine to place the police in an excellent bargaining position to recruit informers. To assure performance, each informer is charged with a narcotics violation, and final disposition is postponed until the defendant has fulfilled his part of the bargain. To protect the informer, the special squad seeks to camouflage him in the large body of releasees by not disclosing his identity even to the arresting precinct officer, who is given no explanation for release. Thus persons encountered on the street by a uniformed patrolman the day after their arrest may have been discharged, or they may have been officially charged and then released on bail or personal recognizance to await trial or to serve as informers.

While serving as informers, suspects are allowed to engage in illegal activity. Continued use of narcotics is condoned; the narcotics detective generally is not concerned with the problem of informants who make buys and use some of the evidence themselves. Though informers are usually warned that their status does not give them a "license to peddle," possession of a substantial amount of narcotics may be excused. In one case, a defendant found guilty of possession of marijuana argued that she was entitled to be placed on probation since she had cooperated with the police by testifying against three persons charged with the sale of narcotics. The sentencing judge denied her request because he discovered that her cooperation was related to the possession of a substantial amount of heroin, an offense for which she was arrested (but never charged) while on bail for the marijuana violation. A narcotics squad inspector, in response to an inquiry from the judge, revealed that the defendant had not been charged with possession of heroin because she had been cooperative with the police on that offense.

In addition to granting such outright immunity for some violations, the police will recommend to the prosecutor either that an informer's case be *nolle prossed* or, more frequently, that the charge be reduced to a lesser offense. And, if the latter course is followed, the police usually recommend to the judge, either in response to his request for information or in the presentence report, that informers be placed on probation or given relatively light sentences. Both the prosecutor and judge willingly respond to police requests for reducing a charge of sale to a lesser offense because they consider the mandatory minimum too severe. As a result, during a four-year period in this jurisdiction, less than 2.5 percent of all persons charged with the sale of narcotics were convicted of that offense.

The narcotics squad's policy of trading *full enforcement* for information is justified on the grounds that apprehension and prosecution of the "big supplier" is facilitated. The absence of any such individual is attributed to this policy. As one member of the squad said, "[The city] is too hot. There are too many informants." A basic, though untested, assumption of the policy is that ridding the city of the "big supplier" is the key to solving its narcotics problem. Even if this assumption were empirically validated, the desirability of continuing such a policy cannot be established without taking into account its total impact on the administration of criminal justice in the city, the state, and the nation. Yet no procedure has been designed to enable the police and other key administrators of criminal justice to obtain such an appraisal. The extent and nature of the need for such a procedure can be illustrated, despite the limitations of available data, by presenting in the form of a mock report some of the questions, some of the answers, and some of the proposals a policy appraisal and review board might consider.

Following a description of the informer program, a report might ask: *To what extent, if at all, has the legislature delegated to the police the authority to grant, or obtain a grant of, complete or partial immunity from prosecution, in exchange for information about narcotics suppliers?* No provisions of the general immunity or narcotics statutes authorize the police to exercise such discretion. The general immunity statute requires a high degree of visibility by providing that immunity be allowed only on a written motion by the prosecuting attorney to the court and that the information given be reduced to writing under the direction of the judge to preclude future prosecution for the traded offense or offenses. The narcotics statutes, unlike comparable legislation concerning other specific crimes, make no provision for obtaining information by awarding immunity from prosecution. Nor is there any indication, other than possibly in the maximum sentences authorized, that the legislature intended that certain narcotics offenses be given high priority or be enforced at the expense of other offenses. What evidence there is of legislative intent suggests the contrary; this fact is recognized by the local police manual. And nothing in the statute providing for the establishment of local police departments can be construed to authorize the policy of trading enforcement for information. That statute makes *full enforcement* a duty of the police. The narcotics squad has ignored this mandate and adopted an informer policy which appears to constitute a usurpation of legislative function. It does not follow that the police must discontinue employing informers, but they ought to discontinue trading enforcement for information until the legislature, the court, or the prosecutor explicitly initiates such a program. Whether the police policy of trading enforcement for information should be proposed for legislative consideration would depend upon the answers to some of the questions which follow.

Does trading enforcement for information fulfill the retributive, restraining, and reformative functions of the state's narcotics laws? By in effect licensing the user–informer to satisfy his addiction and assuring the peddler–informer, who may also be a user, that he will obtain dismissal or reduction of the pending charge to a lesser offense, the police undermine, if not negate, the retributive and restraining functions of the narcotics laws. In addition, the community is deprived of an opportunity to subject these offenders, particularly the addicts, to treatment aimed at reformation. In fact, the police ironically acknowledge the inconsistency of their program with the goal of treatment: "cured" addicts are not used as informers for fear that exposure to narcotics might cause their relapse. A comparison of the addict-release policies of the police, sentencing judge, and probation and parole authorities demonstrates the extent to which the administration of criminal justice can be set awry by a police nonenforcement program. At one point on the continuum, the police release the addict to informer status so that he can maintain his association with peddlers and users. The addict accepts such status on the tacit condition that continued use will be condoned. At other points on the continuum, the judge and probation and parole authorities make treatment a condition of an addict's release and continued use or even association with narcotics users the basis for revoking probation or parole. Thus the inherent conflict between basic purposes of the criminal law is compounded by conflicts among key decision points in the process.

Does trading enforcement for information implement the deterrent function of criminal law administration? If deterrence depends—and little if anything is really known about the deterrent impact of the criminal law—in part at least, upon the potential offender's perception of law enforcement, the informer policy can have only a negative effect. In addition to the chance of nondetection which accompanies the commission of all crimes in varying degrees, the narcotics suspect has four-to-one odds that he will not be charged following detection and arrest. And he has a high expectation, even if charged, of obtaining a reduction or dismissal of an accurate charge. These figures reflect and reinforce the offender's view of the administration of criminal justice as a bargaining process initiated either by offering information "to do himself some good" or by a member of the narcotics squad advising the uninformed suspect, the "new offender," of the advantages of disclosing his narcotics "connections." Such law enforcement can have little, if any, deterrent impact.

That the "big supplier," an undefined entity, has been discouraged from using the city as a headquarters was confirmed by a local federal agent and a U.S. attorney in testimony before a Senate committee investigating illicit narcotics traffic. They attributed the result, however, to the state's high mandatory minimum sentence for selling, not to the informer policy. In fact, that municipal police policy was not made visible at the hearings. It was mentioned neither in their testimony nor in the testimony of the chief of police and the head of the narcotics squad. These local authorities may have reasoned that since the mandatory sentence facilitates the recruitment of informers who, in turn, are essential to keeping the "big supplier" outside city limits, the legislature's sentencing policy could be credited with the "achievement."

Whether the police informer program, the legislature's sentencing policy, both, or neither, caused the "big supplier" to locate elsewhere is not too significant; the traffic and use of narcotics in the city remain major problems. Since user demand is maintained, if not increased, by trading enforcement for information, potential and actual peddlers are encouraged to supply the city's addicts. Testimony before the Senate committee indicates that although the "big suppliers" have moved their headquarters to other cities, there are now in the city a large number of small peddlers serving a minimum of 1,500 and in all probability a total of 2,500 users, and that the annual expenditure for illicit narcotics in the city is estimated at not lower than $10 million and probably as high as $18 million. Evaluated in terms of deterrent effect, the program of trading enforcement for information to reach the "big supplier" has failed to implement locally the ultimate objective of the narcotics laws—reducing addiction. Furthermore, the business of the "big supplier" has not been effectively deterred. At best suppliers have been discouraged from basing their operations in the city, which continues to be a lucrative market. Thus by maintaining the market, local policy, although a copy of national policy, may very well hinder the efforts of the Federal Narcotics Bureau.

A report of a policy appraisal and review board might find: "Trading little ones for big ones" is outside the ambit of municipal police discretion and should continue to remain so because it conflicts with the basic objectives of the criminal law. Retribution, restraint, and reformation are subverted by a policy which condones the use and possession of narcotics. And deterrence cannot be enhanced by a police program which provides potential and actual suppliers and users with more illustrations of nonenforcement than enforcement.

A report might conclude by exploring and suggesting alternative programs for coping with the narcotics problem. No attempt will be made here to exhaust or detail all possible alternatives. An obvious one would be a rigorous program of *full enforcement* designed to dry up, or at least drastically reduce, local consumer and peddler demand for illicit narcotics. If information currently obtained from suspects is essential and worth a price, compensation might be given to informers, with payments deferred until a suspect's final release. Such a program would neither undermine the retributive and restraining objectives of the criminal law nor deprive the community of an opportunity to impose rehabilitation regimes on the offender. Funds provided by deferred payments might enhance an offender's chances of getting off to a good start upon release. Moreover, changing the picture presently perceived by potential violators from nonenforcement to enforcement would at least not preclude the possibility of deterrence. Such a program might even facilitate the apprehension of "big suppliers" who, faced with decreasing demand, might either be forced to discontinue serving the city because sales would no longer be profitable or to adopt bolder sales methods which would expose them to easier detection.

Full enforcement will place the legislature in a position to evaluate its narcotics laws by providing a basis for answering such questions as: Will *full enforcement* increase the price of narcotics to the user? Will such inflation increase the frequency of crimes committed to finance narcotics purchases? Or will *full enforcement* reduce the number of users and the frequency of connected crimes? Will too great or too costly an administrative burden be placed on the prosecutor's office and the courts by *full enforcemen*? Will correctional institutions be filled beyond "effective" capacity? The answers to these questions are now buried or obscured by decisions not to invoke the criminal process.

Failure of a *full enforcement* program might prompt a board recommendation to increase treatment or correctional personnel and facilities. Or a board, recognizing that *full enforcement* would be either too costly or inherently ineffective, might propose the repeal of statutes prohibiting the use and sale of narcotics and/or the enactment, as part of a treatment program, of legislation authorizing sales to users at a low price. Such legislative action would be designed to reduce use and connected offenses to a minimum. By taking profits out of sales it would lessen peddler incentive to create new addicts and eliminate the need to support the habit by the commission of crimes.

These then are the kinds of questions, answers, and proposals a policy appraisal and review board might explore in its report examining this particular type of police decision not to invoke the criminal process.

IV. Another low-visibility situation which an appraisal and review board might uncover in this municipality stems from police decisions not to invoke the felonious assault laws unless the victim signs a complaint. Like the addict–informer, the potential complainant in an assault case is both the victim of an offense and a key source of information. But unlike him, the complainant, who is not a suspect, and whose initial contact with the police is generally self-imposed, is not placed under pressure to bargain. And in contrast with the informer program, the police assault program was clearly not designed, if designed at all, to effectuate an identifiable policy.

During one month under the nonenforcement program of a single precinct, thirty-eight out of forty-three felonious assault cases, the great majority involving stabbings and cuttings, were cleared "because the victim refused to prosecute." This program, which is coupled with a practice of not encouraging victims to sign complaints, reduces the pressure of work by eliminating such tasks as apprehending and detaining suspects, writing detailed reports, applying for warrants to prefer charges, and appearing in court at inconvenient times for long periods without adequate compensation. As one officer explained, "run-of-the-mill" felonious assaults are so common in his precinct that prosecution of each case would force patrolmen to spend too much time in court and leave too little time for investigating other offenses. This rationalization exposes the private value system of individual officers as another policy-shaping factor. Some policemen feel, for example, that assault is an acceptable means of settling disputes among Negroes, and that when both assailant and victim are Negro, there is no immediate discernible harm to the public which justifies a decision to invoke the criminal process. Anticipation of dismissal by judge and district attorney of cases in which the victim is an uncooperative witness, the police claim, has been another operative factor in the development of the assault policy. A policy appraisal and review board, whose investigators had been specifically directed to examine the assault policy, should be able to identify these or other policy-shaping factors more precisely. Yet on the basis of the data available, a board could tentatively conclude that court and prosecutor responses do not explain why the police have failed to adopt a policy of encouraging assault victims to sign complaints, and, therefore, that the private value system of department members, as reflected in their attitude toward work load and in a stereotypical view of the Negro, is of primary significance.

Once some of the major policy-shaping factors have been identified, an appraisal and review board might formulate and attempt to answer the following or similar questions: Would it be consistent with any of the purposes of the criminal law to authorize police discretion in cases of felonious assaults as well as other specified offenses? Assuming that it would be consistent or at least more realistic to authorize police discretion in some cases, what limitations and guides, if any, should the legislature provide? Should legislation provide that factors such as work load, willingness of victims or certain victims to sign a complaint, the degree of violence, and attitude of prosecutor and judge be taken into account in the exercise of police discretion? If work load is to be recognized, should the legislature establish priorities of enforcement designed to assist the police in deciding which offenses among equally pressing ones are to be ignored or enforced? If assaults are made criminal in order to reduce threats to community peace and individual security, should a victim's willingness to prosecute, if he happens to live, be relevant to the exercise of police discretion? Does resting prosecution in the hands of the victim encourage him to "get even" with the assailant through retaliatory lawlessness? Or does such a policy place the decision in the hands of the assailant whose use of force has already demonstrated an ability and willingness to fulfill a threat?

Can the individual police officer, despite his own value system, sufficiently respond to officially articulated community values to be delegated broad powers of discretion? If not, can or should procedures be designed to enable the police department to translate these values into rules and regulations for individual policemen? Can police officers or the department be trained to evaluate the extent to which current practice undermines a major criminal law objective of imposing upon all persons officially recognized minimum standards of human behavior? For example, can the individual officer of the department be trained to evaluate the effect of decisions in cases of felonious assault among Negroes on local programs for implementing national or state policies of integration in school, employment, and housing, and to determine the extent to which current policy weakens or reinforces stereotypes which are used to justify not only police policy but, more importantly, opposition to desegregation programs? Or should legislation provide that the police invoke the process in all felonious assault cases unless the prosecutor or court publicly provides them in recorded documents with authority and guides for exercising discretion, and thus make visible both the policy of nonenforcement and the agency or agencies responsible for it?

Some of these issues were considered and resolved by the Oakland, California, Police Department in 1957 when, after consultation with prosecutors and judges, it decided to abandon a similar assault policy and seek *full enforcement*. Chief of Police W. W. Vernon, describing Oakland's new program, wrote:

> In our assault cases for years we had followed this policy of releasing the defendant if the complainant did not feel aggrieved to the point of being willing to testify. . . . [Since] World War II . . . our assault cases increased tremendously to the point where we decided to do something about the increase.

Training materials prepared by the Oakland Police Academy disclose that between 1952 and 1956, while the decision to prosecute was vested in the victim, the rate of reported felonious assaults rose from 93 to 161 per 100,000 population and the annual number of misdemeanor assaults rose from 618 to 2,630. The materials emphasize that these statistics mean a work load of "nearly ten assault reports a day every day of the year." But they stress:

> The important point about these figures is not so much that they represent a substantial police workload, which they do, but more important, that they indicate an increasing lack of respect for the laws of society by a measurable segment of our population, and a corresponding threat to the rest of the citizens of our city. The police have a clear responsibility to develop respect for the law among those who disregard it in order to ensure the physical safety and well-being of those who do. . . .
>
> We recognize that the problem exists mainly because the injured person has refused to sign a complaint against the perpetrator. The injured person has usually refused to sign for two reasons: first, because of threats of future bodily harm or other action by the perpetrator and, secondly, because it has been a way of life among some people to adjust grievances by physical assaults and not by the recognized laws of society which are available to them.
>
> We, the police, have condoned these practices to some extent by not taking advantage of the means at our disposal: that is, by not gathering sufficient evidence and signing complaints on information and belief in those cases where the complainant refuses to prosecute. The policy and procedure of gathering sufficient evidence and signing complaints on information and belief should instill in these groups the realization that the laws of society must be resorted to in settling disputes. When it is realized by many of these people that we will sign complaints ourselves and will not condone fighting and cuttings, many of them will stop such practices.

Following conferences with the police, the local prosecutors and judges pledged their support for the new assault program. The district attorney's office will deny a complainant's request that a case be dropped and suggest that it be addressed to the judge in open court. The judge, in turn, will advise the complainant that the case cannot be dismissed, and that a perjury, contempt, or false-report complaint will be issued in "appropriate cases" against the victim who denies facts originally alleged. The police have been advised that the court and prosecutor will actively cooperate in the implementation of the new program, but that every case will not result in a complaint since it is the "job [of the police] to turn in the evidence and it's the prosecuting attorney's job to determine when a complaint will be issued." Thus the role of each of the key decision-making agencies with pre-conviction invoking authority is clearly delineated and integrated.

With the inauguration of a new assault policy, an appraisal and review board might establish procedures for determining how effectively the objectives of the policy are fulfilled in practice. A board might design intelligence-retrieving devices which would provide more complete data than the following termed by Chief Vernon "the best evidence that our program is accomplishing the purpose for which it was developed." Prior to the adoption of the new policy, 80 percent

of the felonious assault cases "cleared" were cleared because "complainant re-
fuses to prosecute," while only 32.2 percent of the clearances made during the
first three months in 1958 were for that reason, even though the overall clear-
ance rate rose during that period. And "during the first quarter of this year
Felony Assaults dropped 11.1 percent below the same period last year, and in
March they were 35.6 percent below March of last year. Battery cases were
down 19.0 percent for the first three months of 1958." An appraisal and review
board might attempt to determine the extent to which the police in cases formerly dropped because "complainant refused to testify" have consciously or otherwise substituted another reason for "case cleared." And it might estimate the
extent to which the decrease in assaults *reported* reflects, if it does, a decrease in
the *actual* number of assaults or only a decrease in the number of victims willing
to report assaults. Such follow-up investigations and what actually took place in
Oakland on an informal basis between police, prosecutor, and judge illustrate
some of the functions an appraisal and review board might regularly perform.

V. Police decisions to harass, though generally perceived as overzealous enforcement, constitute another body of nonenforcement activities meriting investigation by an appraisal and review board. Harassment is the imposition by the
police, acting under color of law, of sanctions prior to conviction as a means of
ultimate punishment, rather than as a device for the invocation of criminal proceedings. Characteristic of harassment are efforts to annoy certain "offenders"
both by temporarily detaining or arresting them without intention to seek prosecution and by destroying or illegally seizing their property without any intention to use it as evidence. Like other police decisions not to invoke the criminal
process, harassment is generally of extremely low visibility, probably because the
police ordinarily restrict such activity to persons who are unable to afford the
costs of litigation, who would, or think they would, command little respect even
if they were to complain, or who wish to keep themselves out of public view in
order to continue their illicit activities. Like the informer program, harassment
is conducted by the police in an atmosphere of cooperation with other administrators of criminal justice. Since harassment, by definition, is outside the rule of
law, any benefits attributed to such police activity cannot justify its continuation.
An appraisal and review board, however, would not limit its investigations to
making such a finding. It would be expected to identify and analyze factors underlying harassment and to formulate proposals for replacing harassment—lawless nonenforcement—with enforcement of the criminal law.

Investigators for an appraisal and review board in this jurisdiction would discover, for example, a mixture of enforcement and harassment in a police program designed to regulate the gambling operations of mutual-numbers
syndicates. The enforcement phase is conducted by a highly trained unit of less
than a dozen men who diligently gather evidence in order to prosecute and convict syndicate operators of conspiracy to violate the gambling laws. This specialized unit, which operates independently of and without the knowledge of other
officers, conducts all its work within the due process boundaries of *full enforcement*. Consequently, the conviction rate is high for charges based upon its investigations. The harassment phase is conducted by approximately sixty officers

who tour the city and search on sight, because of prior information, or such tell-tale actions as carrying a paper bag, a symbol of the trade, persons who they suspect are collecting bets. They question the "suspect" and proceed to search him, his car, or home without first making a valid arrest to legalize the search. If gambling paraphernalia are found, the police, fully aware that the exclusionary rule prohibits its use as evidence in this jurisdiction, confiscate the "contraband" and arrest the individual without any intention of seeking application of the criminal law.

Gambling operators treat the harassment program as a cost of doing business, "a risk of the trade." Each syndicate retains a bonding firm and an attorney to service members who are arrested. When a "runner" or "bagman" is absent from his scheduled rounds, routine release procedures are initiated. The bondsman, sometimes prematurely, checks with the police to determine if a syndicate man has been detained. If the missing man is in custody, the syndicate's attorney files an application for a writ of habeas corpus and appears before a magistrate who usually sets bail at a nominal amount and adjourns hearing the writ, at the request of the police, until the following day. Prior to the scheduled hearing, the police usually advise the court that they have no intention of proceeding, and the case is closed. Despite the harassee's release, the police retain the money and gambling paraphernalia. If the items seized are found in a car, the car is confiscated, with the cooperation of the prosecutor, under a nuisance abatement statute. Cars are returned, however, after the harassee signs a "consent decree" and pursuant to it, pays "court costs"—a fee which is based on the car's value and which the prosecutor calls "the real meat of the harassment program." The "decree," entered under a procedure devised by the court and prosecutor's office, enjoins the defendant from engaging in illegal activity and, on paper, frees the police from any tort liability by an acknowledgment that seizure of the vehicle was lawful and justified—even though one prosecutor has estimated that approximately 80 percent of the searches and seizures were illegal. A prosecuting attorney responsible for car confiscation initially felt that such procedures "in the ordinary practice of law would be unethical, revolting, and shameful," but explained that he now understands why he acted as he did:

> To begin with . . . laws in . . . [this state] with respect to gambling are most inadequate. This is equally true of the punishment feature of the law. To illustrate . . . a well-organized and productive gambling house or numbers racket would take in one-quarter of a million dollars each week. If, after a long and vigorous period of investigation and observation, the defendant was charged with violating the gambling laws and convicted therefor, the resulting punishment is so obviously weak and unprohibitive that the defendants are willing to shell out a relatively small fine or serve a relatively short time in prison. The . . . [city's] gamblers and numbers men confidently feel that the odds are in their favor. If they operate for six months or a year, and accumulate untold thousands of dollars from the illegal activity, then the meager punishment imposed upon them if they are caught is well worth it. Then, too, because of the search and seizure laws in . . . [this

state], especially in regard to gambling and the numbers rackets, the hands of the police are tied. Unless a search can be made prior to an arrest so that the defendant can be caught in the act of violating the gambling laws, or a search warrant issued, there is no other earthly way of apprehending such people along with evidence sufficient to convict them that is admissible in court.

Because of these two inadequacies of the law (slight punishment and conservative search and seizure laws with regard to gambling) the prosecutor's office and the police department are forced to find other means of punishing, harassing, and generally making life uneasy for gamblers.

This position, fantastic as it is to be that of a law-trained official, a guardian of the rule of law, illustrates how extensively only one of many police harassment programs in this jurisdiction can permeate the process and be tolerated by other decision makers in a system of criminal administration where decisions not to enforce are of extremely low visibility.

Having uncovered such a gambling-control program, an appraisal and review board should recommend that the police abandon such harassment activities because they are antagonistic to the rule of law. In addition, the board might advance secondary reasons for eliminating harassment by exposing the inconsistencies between this program and departmental justifications for its narcotics and assault policies. While unnecessary to the condemnation of what is fundamentally lawless nonenforcement, such exposure might cause the police to question the wisdom of actions based on a personal or departmental belief that the legislature has authorized excessively lenient sanctions and restrictive enforcement procedures. The comparison might emphasize the inconsistencies of police policy toward organized crime by exposing the clash between an informer program designed to rid the city of the "big supplier" and a harassment program which tends to consolidate control of the numbers racket in a few syndicates "big" enough to sustain the legal, bonding, and other "business" costs of continued interruptions and the confiscation of property. More importantly, it should cause a reexamination and redefinition of "work load" which was so significant in the rationalization of the assault policy. A cost accounting would no doubt reveal that a significant part of "work load," as presently defined by the police, includes expenditures of public funds for personnel and equipment employed in unlawful activities. Once harassment is perceived by municipal officials concerned with budgets as an unauthorized expenditure of public funds, consideration for increased awards to the police department might be conditioned upon a showing that existing resources are now deployed for authorized purposes. Such action should stimulate police cooperation in implementing the board's proposal for curtailing harassment.

Further, to effectuate its recommendation, the board might attempt to clarify and redefine the duties of the police by a reclassification of crimes which would emphasize the mandate that no more than *full enforcement* of the existing criminal law as defined by the legislature is expected. For many crimes, this may mean little or no *actual enforcement* because the values protected by procedural limitations are more important than the values which may be infringed by a particular offense. A board might propose, for example, that crimes be classified not only as felonies and misdemeanors, but in terms of active and passive police enforcement. An *active enforcement* designation for an offense would mean that individual police officers or specialized squads are to be assigned the task of ferreting out and even triggering violations. *Passive enforcement* would mean that the police are to assume a sit-back-and-wait posture, that is, that they invoke the criminal process only when the disturbing event is brought to their attention by personal observation during a routine tour of duty or by someone outside the police force registering a complaint. Designation of gambling, for example, as a *passive enforcement* offense would officially apprise the police that substantial expenditures of personnel and equipment for enforcement are not contemplated unless the local community expresses a low tolerance for such disturbing events by constantly bringing them to police attention. The adoption of this or a similar classification scheme might not only aid in training the police to understand that harassment is unlawful, but it may also provide the legislature with a device for officially allowing local differences in attitude toward certain offenses to be reflected in police practice and for testing the desirability of removing criminal sanctions from certain kinds of currently proscribed behavior.

VI. The mandate of *full enforcement*, under circumstances which compel selective enforcement, has placed the municipal police in an intolerable position. As a result, nonenforcement programs have developed undercover, in a hit-or-miss fashion, and without regard to impact on the overall administration of justice or the basic objectives of the criminal law. Legislatures, therefore, ought to reconsider what discretion, if any, the police must or should have in invoking the criminal process, and what devices, if any, should be designed to increase visibility and hence reviewability of these police decisions.

The ultimate answer is that the police should not be delegated discretion not to invoke the criminal law. It is recognized, of course, that the exercise of discretion cannot be completely eliminated where human beings are involved. The frailties of human language and human perception will always admit of borderline cases (although none of the situations analyzed in this article are "borderline"). But nonetheless, outside this margin of ambiguity, the police should operate in an atmosphere which exhorts and commands them to invoke impartially all criminal laws within the bounds of *full enforcement*. If a criminal law is ill advised, poorly defined, or too costly to enforce, efforts by the police to achieve *full enforcement* should generate pressures for legislative action. Responsibility for the enactment, amendment, and repeal of the criminal laws will not, then, be abandoned to the whim of each police officer or department, but retained where it belongs in a democracy—with elected representatives.

Equating *actual enforcement* with *full enforcement*, however, would be neither workable nor humane nor humanly possible under present conditions in most, if not all, jurisdictions. Even if there were "enough police" (and there are not) to enforce all of the criminal laws, too many people have come to rely on the nonenforcement of too many "obsolete" laws to justify the embarrassment, discomfort, and misery which would follow implementation of *full enforcement* programs for every crime. *Full enforcement* is a program for the future, a program which could be initiated with the least hardship when the states, perhaps stimulated by the work of the American Law Institute, enact new criminal codes clearing the books of obsolete offenses.

In the interim, legislatures should establish policy appraisal and review boards not only to facilitate coordination of municipal police policies with those of other key criminal law administrators, but also to assist commissions drafting new codes in reappraising basic objectives of the criminal law and in identifying laws which have become obsolete. To ensure that board appraisals and recommendations facilitate the integration of police policies with overall state policies and to ensure the cooperation of local authorities, board membership might include the state's attorney general, the chief justice of the supreme court, the chairman of the department of correction, the chairman of the board of parole and the chief of parole supervision, the chairman of the department of probation, the chairman of the judiciary committees of the legislature, the chief of the state police, the local chief of police, the local prosecutor, and the chief judge of each of the local trial courts. In order regularly and systematically to cull and retrieve information, the board should be assisted by a full-time director who has a staff of investigators well trained in social science research techniques. It should be given power to subpoena persons and records and to assign investigators to observe all phases of police activity including routine patrols, bookings, raids, and contacts with both the courts and the prosecutor's office. To clarify its functions, develop procedures, determine personnel requirements, and test the idea itself, the board's jurisdiction should initially be restricted to one or two major municipalities in the state. The board would review, appraise, and make recommendations concerning municipal police nonenforcement policies as well as follow up and review the consequences of implemented proposals. In order to make its job both manageable and less subject to attack by those who cherish local autonomy and who may see the establishment of a board as a step toward centralization, it would have solely an advisory function and limit its investigations to the enforcement of state laws, not municipal ordinances. And to ensure that board activity will not compromise current enforcement campaigns or place offenders on notice of new techniques of detection or sources of information, boards should be authorized, with court approval, to withhold specified reports from general publication for a limited and fixed time.

Like other administrative agencies, a policy appraisal and review board will in time no doubt suffer from marasmus and outlive its usefulness. But while viable, such a board has an enormous potential for uncovering in a very dramatic fashion basic inadequacies in the administration of criminal justice and for prompting a thorough community reexamination of the why of a law of crimes.

8

❁

Broken Windows

The Police
and Neighborhood Safety

JAMES Q. WILSON
GEORGE L. KELLING

The role of the police in the United States today is being reexamined. After almost a half-century of emphasis on professionalism, crime control, and efficiency, James Q. Wilson and George L. Kelling argue that there should be a shift in patrol strategy toward a focus on order maintenance and community accountability.

In the mid-1970s, the state of New Jersey announced a "Safe and Clean Neighborhoods Program," designed to improve the quality of community life in twenty-eight cities. As part of that program, the state provided money to help cities take police officers out of their patrol cars and assign them to walking beats. The governor and other state officials were enthusiastic about using foot patrol as a way of cutting crime, but many police chiefs were skeptical. Foot patrol, in their eyes, had been pretty much discredited. It reduced the mobility of the police, who thus had difficulty responding to citizen calls for service, and it weakened headquarters control over patrol officers.

Many police officers also disliked foot patrol, but for different reasons: it was hard work, it kept them outside on cold, rainy nights, and it reduced their chances for making a "good pinch." In some departments, assigning officers to foot patrol had been used as a form of punishment. And academic experts on policing doubted that foot patrol would have any impact on crime rates; it was, in the opinion of most, little more than a sop to public opinion. But since the state was paying for it, the local authorities were willing to go along.

Source: Atlantic Monthly 249 (March 1982): 29–38. By permission of James Q. Wilson.

Five years after the program started, the Police Foundation, in Washington, D.C., published an evaluation of the foot-patrol project. Based on its analysis of a carefully controlled experiment carried out chiefly in Newark, the foundation concluded, to the surprise of hardly anyone, that foot patrol had not reduced crime rates. But residents of the foot-patrolled neighborhoods seemed to feel more secure than persons in other areas, tended to believe that crime had been reduced, and seemed to take fewer steps to protect themselves from crime (staying at home with the doors locked, for example). Moreover, citizens in the foot-patrol areas had a more favorable opinion of the police than did those living elsewhere. And officers walking beats had higher morale, greater job satisfaction, and a more favorable attitude toward citizens in their neighborhoods than did officers assigned to patrol cars.

These findings may be taken as evidence that the skeptics were right—foot patrol has no effect on crime; it merely fools the citizens into thinking that they are safer. But in our view, and in the view of the authors of the Police Foundation study (of whom Kelling was one), the citizens of Newark were not fooled at all. They knew what the foot-patrol officers were doing, they knew it was different from what motorized officers do, and they knew that having officers walk beats did in fact make their neighborhoods safer.

But how can a neighborhood be "safer" when the crime rate has not gone down—in fact, may have gone up? Finding the answer requires first that we understand what most often frightens people in public places. Many citizens, of course, are primarily frightened by crime, especially crime involving a sudden, violent attack by a stranger. This risk is very real, in Newark as in many large cities. But we tend to overlook or forget another source of fear: the fear of being bothered by disorderly people—not violent people, nor, necessarily, criminals, but disreputable or obstreperous or unpredictable people: panhandlers, drunks, addicts, rowdy teenagers, prostitutes, loiterers, the mentally disturbed.

What foot-patrol officers did was to elevate, to the extent they could, the level of public order in these neighborhoods. Though the neighborhoods were predominantly black and the foot patrolmen were mostly white, this "order-maintenance" function of the police was performed to the general satisfaction of both parties.

One of us (Kelling) spent many hours walking with Newark foot-patrol officers to see how they defined "order" and what they did to maintain it. One beat was typical: a busy but dilapidated area in the heart of Newark, with many abandoned buildings, marginal shops (several of which prominently displayed knives and straight-edged razors in their windows), one large department store, and, most important, a train station and several major bus stops. Though the area was run-down, its streets were filled with people, because it was a major transportation center. The good order of this area was important not only to those who lived and worked there but also to many others who had to move through it on their way home, to supermarkets, or to factories.

The people on the street were primarily black; the officers who walked the street were white. The people made up of "regulars" and "strangers." Regulars included both "decent folk" and some drunks and derelicts who were always there but who "knew their place." Strangers were, well, strangers, and viewed suspiciously, sometimes apprehensively. The officer—call him Kelly—knew who the regulars were, and they knew him. As he saw his job, he was to keep an eye on strangers, and make certain that the disreputable regulars observed some informal but widely understood rules. Drunks and addicts could sit on the stoops, but could not lie down. People could drink on the side streets, but not on the main intersection. Bottles had to be in paper bags. Talking to, bothering, or begging from people waiting at the bus stop was strictly forbidden. If a dispute erupted between a businessman and a customer, the businessman was assumed to be right, especially if the customer was a stranger. If a stranger loitered, Kelly would ask him if he had any means of support and what his business was; if he gave unsatisfactory answers, he was sent on his way. Persons who broke the informal rules, especially those who bothered people waiting at bus stops, were arrested for vagrancy. Noisy teenagers were told to keep quiet.

These rules were defined and enforced in collaboration with the "regulars" on the street. Another neighborhood might have different rules, but these, everybody understood, were the rules for *this* neighborhood. If someone violated them, the regulars not only turned to Kelly for help but also ridiculed the violator. Sometimes what Kelly did could be described as "enforcing the law," but just as often it involved taking informal or extralegal steps to help protect what the neighborhood had decided was the appropriate level of public order. Some of the things he did probably would not withstand a legal challenge.

A determined skeptic might acknowledge that a skilled foot-patrol officer can maintain order but still insist that this sort of "order" has little to do with the real sources of community fear—that is, with violent crime. To a degree, that is true. But two things must be borne in mind. First, outside observers should not assume that they know how much of the anxiety now endemic in many big-city neighborhoods stems from a fear of "real" crime and how much from a sense that the street is disorderly, a source of distasteful, worrisome encounters. The people of Newark, to judge from their behavior and their remarks to interviewers, apparently assign a high value to public order, and feel relieved and reassured when the police help them maintain that order.

Second, at the community level, disorder and crime are usually inextricably linked, in a kind of developmental sequence. Social psychologists and police officers tend to agree that if a window in a building is broken *and is left unrepaired,* all the rest of the windows will soon be broken. This is as true in nice neighborhoods as in run-down ones. Window breaking does not necessarily occur on a large scale because some areas are inhabited by determined window breakers whereas others are populated by window lovers; rather, one unrepaired broken window is a signal that no one cares, and so breaking more windows costs nothing. (It has always been fun.)

Philip Zimbardo, a Stanford psychologist, reported in 1969 on some experiments testing the broken-window theory. He arranged to have an automobile without license plates parked with its hood up on a street in the Bronx and a comparable automobile on a street in Palo Alto, California. The car in the Bronx was attacked by "vandals" within ten minutes of its "abandonment." The first to arrive were a family—father, mother, and young son—who removed the radiator and battery. Within twenty-four hours, virtually everything of value had been removed. Then random destruction began—windows were smashed, parts torn off, upholstery ripped. Children began to use the car as a playground. Most of the adult "vandals" were well-dressed, apparently clean-cut whites. The car in Palo Alto sat untouched for more than a week. Then Zimbardo smashed part of it with a sledgehammer. Soon, passersby were joining in. Within a few hours, the car had been turned upside down and utterly destroyed. Again, the "vandals" appeared to be primarily respectable whites.

Untended property becomes fair game for people out for fun or plunder, and even for people who ordinarily would not dream of doing such things and who probably consider themselves law-abiding. Because of the nature of community life in the Bronx—its anonymity, the frequency with which cars are abandoned and things are stolen or broken, the past experience of "no one caring"—vandalism begins much more quickly than it does in staid Palo Alto, where people have come to believe that private possessions are cared for, and that mischievous behavior is costly. But vandalism can occur anywhere once communal barriers—the sense of mutual regard and the obligations of civility—are lowered by actions that seem to signal that "no one cares."

We suggest that "untended" behavior also leads to the breakdown of community controls. A stable neighborhood of families who care for their homes, mind each other's children, and confidently frown on unwanted intruders can change, in a few years or even a few months, to an inhospitable and frightening jungle. A piece of property is abandoned, weeds grow up, a window is smashed. Adults stop scolding rowdy children; the children, emboldened, become more rowdy. Families move out, unattached adults move in. Teenagers gather in front of the corner store. The merchant asks them to move; they refuse. Fights occur. Litter accumulates. People start drinking in front of the grocery; in time, an inebriate slumps to the sidewalk and is allowed to sleep it off. Pedestrians are approached by panhandlers.

At this point it is not inevitable that serious crime will flourish or violent attacks on strangers will occur. But many residents will think that crime, especially violent crime is on the rise, and they will modify their behavior accordingly. They will use the streets less often, and when on the streets will stay apart from their fellows, moving with averted eyes, silent lips, and hurried steps. "Don't get involved." For some residents, this growing atomization will matter little, because the neighborhood is not their "home" but "the place where they live." Their interests are elsewhere; they are cosmopolitans. But it will matter greatly to other people, whose lives derive meaning and satisfaction from local attachments rather than worldly involvement; for them, the neighborhood will cease to exist except for a few reliable friends whom they arrange to meet.

Such an area is vulnerable to criminal invasion. Though it is not inevitable, it is more likely that here, rather than in places where people are confident they can regulate public behavior by informal controls, drugs will change hands, prostitutes will solicit, and cars will be stripped. That the drunks will be robbed by boys who do it as a lark, and the prostitutes' customers will be robbed by men who do it purposefully and perhaps violently. That muggings will occur.

Among those who often find it difficult to move away from this are the elderly. Surveys of citizens suggest that the elderly are much less likely to be the victims of crime than younger persons, and some have inferred from this that the well-known fear of crime voiced by the elderly is an exaggeration: perhaps we ought not to design special programs to protect older persons; perhaps we should even try to talk them out of their mistaken fears. This argument misses the point. The prospect of a confrontation with an obstreperous teenager or a drunken panhandler can be as fear-inducing for defenseless persons as the prospect of meeting an actual robber; indeed, to a defenseless person, the two kinds of confrontation are often indistinguishable. Moreover, the lower rate at which the elderly are victimized is a measure of the steps they have already taken—chiefly, staying behind locked doors—to minimize the risks they face. Young men are more frequently attacked than older women, not because they are easier or more lucrative targets but because they are on the streets more.

Nor is the connection between disorderliness and fear made only by the elderly. Susan Estrich, of the Harvard Law School, has recently gathered together a number of surveys on the sources of public fear. One, done in Portland, Oregon, indicates that three-fourths of the adults interviewed cross to the other side of a street when they see a gang of teenagers; another survey, in Baltimore, discovered that nearly half would cross the street to avoid even a single strange youth. When an interviewer asked people in a housing project where the most dangerous spot was, they mentioned a place where young persons gathered to drink and play music, despite the fact that not a single crime had occurred there. In Boston public housing projects, the greatest fear was expressed by persons living in the buildings where disorderliness and incivility, not crime, were the greatest. Knowing this helps one understand the significance of such otherwise harmless displays as subway graffiti. As Nathan Glazer has written, the proliferation of graffiti, even when not obscene, confronts the subway rider with the "inescapable knowledge that the environment he must endure for an hour or more a day is uncontrolled and uncontrollable, and that anyone can invade it to do whatever damage and mischief the mind suggests."

In response to fear, people avoid one another, weakening controls. Sometimes they call the police. Patrol cars arrive, an occasional arrest occurs, but crime continues and disorder is not abated. Citizens complain to the police chief, but he explains that his department is low on personnel and that the courts do not punish petty or first-time offenders. To the residents, the police who arrive in squad cars are either ineffective or uncaring; to the police, the residents are animals who deserve each other. The citizens may soon stop calling the police, because "they can't do anything."

The process we call urban decay has occurred for centuries in every city. But what is happening today is different in at least two important respects. First, in the period before, say, World War II, city dwellers—because of money costs, transportation difficulties, familial and church connections—could rarely move away from neighborhood problems. When movement did occur, it tended to be along public-transit routes. Now mobility has become exceptionally easy for all but the poorest or those who are blocked by racial prejudice. Earlier crime waves had a kind of built-in self-correcting mechanism: the determination of a neighborhood or community to reassert control over its turf. Areas in Chicago, New York, and Boston would experience crime and gang wars, and then normalcy would return, as the families for whom no alternative residences were possible reclaimed their authority over the streets.

Second, the police in this earlier period assisted in that reassertion of authority by acting, sometimes violently, on behalf of the community. Young toughs were roughed up, people were arrested "on suspicion" or for vagrancy, and prostitutes and petty thieves were routed. "Rights" were something enjoyed by decent folk, and perhaps also by the serious professional criminal, who avoided violence and could afford a lawyer.

This pattern of policing was not an aberration or the result of occasional excess. From the earliest days of the nation, the police function was seen primarily as that of a night watchman: to maintain order against the chief threats to order—fire, wild animals, and disreputable behavior. Solving crimes was viewed not as a police responsibility but as a private one. In the March 1969 *Atlantic,* one of us (Wilson) wrote a brief account of how the police role had slowly changed from maintaining order to fighting crimes. The change began with the creation of private detectives (often ex-criminals), who worked on a contingency-fee basis for individuals who had suffered losses. In time, the detectives were absorbed into municipal police agencies and paid a regular salary; simultaneously, the responsibility for prosecuting thieves was shifted from the aggrieved private citizen to the professional prosecutor. The process was not complete in most places until the twentieth century.

In the 1960s, when urban riots were a major problem, social scientists began to explore carefully the order-maintenance function of the police, and to suggest ways of improving it—not to make streets safer (its original function) but to reduce the incidence of mass violence. Order maintenance became, to a degree, co-terminous with "community relations." But, as the crime wave that began in the early 1960s continued without abatement throughout the decade and into the 1970s, attention shifted to the role of the police as crime fighters. Studies of police behavior ceased, by and large, to be accounts of the order-maintenance function and became, instead, efforts to propose and test ways whereby the police could solve more crimes, make more arrests, and gather better evidence. If these things could be done, social scientists assumed, citizens would be less fearful.

A great deal was accomplished during this transition, as both police chiefs and outside experts emphasized the crime-fighting function in their plans, in the allocation of resources, and in deployment of personnel. The police may well have become better crime fighters as a result. And doubtless they remained aware of their responsibility for order. But the link between order maintenance and crime prevention, so obvious to earlier generations, was forgotten.

That link is similar to the process whereby one broken window becomes many. The citizen who fears the ill-smelling drunk, the rowdy teenager, or the importuning beggar is not merely expressing his distaste for unseemly behavior, he is also giving voice to a bit of folk wisdom that happens to be a correct generalization—namely, that serious street crime flourishes in areas in which disorderly behavior goes unchecked. The unchecked panhandler is, in effect, the first broken window. Muggers and robbers, whether opportunistic or professional, believe they reduce their chances of being caught or even identified if they operate on streets where potential victims are already intimidated by prevailing conditions. If the neighborhood cannot keep a bothersome panhandler from annoying passersby, the thief may reason, it is even less likely to call the police to identify a potential mugger or to interfere if the mugging actually takes place.

Some police administrators concede that this process occurs, but argue that motorized patrol officers can deal with it as effectively as foot patrol officers. We are not so sure. In theory, an officer in a squad car can observe as much as an officer on foot; in theory, the former can talk to as many people as the latter. But the reality of police–citizen encounters is powerfully altered by the automobile. An officer on foot cannot separate himself from the street people; if he is approached, only his uniform and his personality can help him manage whatever is about to happen. And he can never be certain what that will be—a request for directions, a plea for help, an angry denunciation, a teasing remark, a confused babble, a threatening gesture.

In a car, an officer is more likely to deal with street people by rolling down the window and looking at them. The door and the window exclude the approaching citizen; they are a barrier. Some officers take advantage of this barrier, perhaps unconsciously, by acting differently if in the car than they would on foot. We have seen this countless times. The police car pulls up to a corner where teenagers are gathered. The window is rolled down. The officer stares at the youths. They stare back. The officer says to one, "C'mere." He saunters over, conveying to his friends by his elaborate casual style the idea that he is not intimidated by authority. "What's your name?" "Chuck." "Chuck who?" "Chuck Jones." "What'ya doing, Chuck?" "Nothin'." "Got a P.O. [parole officer]?" "Nah." "Sure?" "Yeah." "Stay out of trouble, Chuckie." Meanwhile, the other boys laugh and exchange comments among themselves, probably at the officer's expense. The officer stares harder. He cannot be certain what is being said, nor can he join in and, by displaying his own skill at street banter, prove that he cannot be "put down." In the process, the officer has learned almost nothing, and the boys have decided the officer is an alien force who can safely be disregarded, even mocked.

Our experience is that most citizens like to talk to a police officer. Such exchanges give them a sense of importance, provide them with the basis for gossip, and allow them to explain to the authorities what is worrying them (whereby they gain a modest but significant sense of having "done something" about the problem). You approach a person on foot more easily, and talk to him more readily, than you do a person in a car. Moreover, you can more easily retain some anonymity if you draw an officer aside for a private chat. Suppose you want to pass on a tip about who is stealing handbags, or who offered to sell you a stolen TV. In the inner city, the culprit, in all likelihood, lives nearby. To walk up to a marked patrol car and lean in the window is to convey a visible signal that you are a "fink."

The essence of the police role in maintaining order is to reinforce the informal control mechanisms of the community itself. The police cannot, without committing extraordinary resources, provide a substitute for that informal control. On the other hand, to reinforce those natural forces the police must accommodate them. And therein lies the problem.

Should police activity on the street be shaped, in important ways, by the standards of the neighborhood rather than by the rules of the state? Over the past two decades, the shift of police from order maintenance to law enforcement has brought them increasingly under the influence of legal restrictions, provoked by media complaints and enforced by court decisions and departmental orders. As a consequence, the order-maintenance functions of the police are now governed by rules developed to control police relations with suspected criminals. This is, we think, an entirely new development. For centuries, the role of the police as watchmen was judged primarily not in terms of its compliance with appropriate procedures but rather in terms of its attaining a desired objective. The objective was order, an inherently ambiguous term but a condition that people in a given community recognized when they saw it. The means were the same as those the community itself would employ, if its members were sufficiently determined, courageous, and authoritative. Detecting and apprehending criminals, by contrast, was a means to an end, not an end in itself; a judicial determination of guilt or innocence was the hoped-for result of the law-enforcement mode. From the first, the police were expected to follow rules defining that process, though states differed in how stringent the rules should be. The criminal-apprehension process was always understood to involve individual rights, the violation of which was unacceptable because it meant that the violating officer would be acting as a judge and jury—and that was not his job. Guilt or innocence was to be determined by universal standards under special procedures.

Ordinarily, no judge or jury ever sees the persons caught up in a dispute over the appropriate level of neighborhood order. That is true not only because most cases are handled informally on the street but also because no universal standards are available to settle arguments over disorder, and thus a judge may not be any wiser or more effective than a police officer. Until quite recently in many states, and even today in some places, the police make arrests on such charges as "suspicious person" or "vagrancy" or "public drunkenness"—charges with scarcely any legal meaning. These charges exist not because society wants judges to punish vagrants or drunks but because it wants an officer to have the legal tools to remove undesirable persons from a neighborhood when informal efforts to preserve order in the streets have failed.

Once we begin to think of all aspects of police work as involving the application of universal rules under special procedures, we inevitably ask what constitutes an "undesirable person" and why we should "criminalize" vagrancy or drunkenness. A strong and commendable desire to see that people are treated fairly makes us worry about allowing the police to rout persons who are undesirable by some vague or parochial standard. A growing and not-so-commendable utilitarianism leads us to doubt that any behavior that does not "hurt" another person should be made illegal. And thus many of us who watch over the police are reluctant to allow them to perform, in the only way they can, a function that every neighborhood desperately wants them to perform.

This wish to "decriminalize" disreputable behavior that "harms no one"—and thus remove the ultimate sanction the police can employ to maintain neighborhood order—is, we think, a mistake. Arresting a single drunk or a single vagrant who has harmed no identifiable person seems unjust, and in a sense it is. But failing to do anything about a score of drunks or a hundred vagrants may destroy an entire community. A particular rule that seems to make sense in the individual case makes no sense when it is made a universal rule and applied to all cases. It makes no sense because it fails to take into account the connection between one broken window left untended and a thousand broken windows. Of course, agencies other than the police could attend to the problems posed by drunks or the mentally ill, but in most communities—especially where the "de-institutionalization" movement has been strong—they do not.

The concern about equity is more serious. We might agree that certain behavior makes one person more undesirable than another, but how do we ensure that age or skin color or natural origin or harmless mannerisms will not also become the basis for distinguishing the undesirable from the desirable? How do we ensure, in short, that the police do not become the agents of neighborhood bigotry?

We can offer no wholly satisfactory answer to this important question. We are not confident that there *is* a satisfactory answer, except to hope that by their selection, training, and supervision the police will be inculcated with a clear sense of the outer limit of their discretionary authority. That limit, roughly, is this—the police exist to help regulate behavior, not to maintain the racial or ethnic purity of a neighborhood.

Consider the case of the Robert Taylor Homes in Chicago, one of the largest public housing projects in the country. It is home for nearly 20,000 people, all black, and extends over ninety-two acres along South State Street. It was named after a distinguished black who had been, during the 1940s, chairman of the Chicago Housing Authority. Not long after it opened, in 1962, relations between project residents and the police deteriorated badly. The citizens felt that the police were insensitive or brutal; the police, in turn, complained of unprovoked attacks on them. Some Chicago officers tell of times when they were afraid to enter the Homes. Crime rates soared.

Today, the atmosphere has changed. Police–citizen relations have improved—apparently, both sides learned something from the earlier experience. Recently, a boy stole a purse and ran off. Several young persons who saw the theft voluntarily passed along to the police information on the identity and residence of the thief, and they did this publicly, with friends and neighbors looking on. But problems persist, chief among them the presence of youth gangs that terrorize residents and recruit members in the project. The people expect the police to "do something" about this, and the police are determined to do just that.

But do what? Though the police can obviously make arrests whenever a gang member breaks the law, a gang can form, recruit, and congregate without breaking the law. And only a tiny fraction of gang-related crimes can be solved by an arrest; thus, if an arrest is the only recourse for the police, the residents' fears will go unassuaged. The police will soon feel helpless, and the residents will again believe that the police "do nothing." What the police in fact do is to chase known gang members out of the project. In the words of one officer, "We kick ass." Project residents both know and approve of this. The tacit police-citizen alliance in the project is reinforced by the police view that the cops and the gangs are the two rival sources of power in the area, and that the gangs are not going to win.

None of this is easily reconciled with any conception of due process or fair treatment. Since both residents and gang members are black, race is not a factor. But it could be. Suppose a white project gang confronted a black gang, or vice versa. We would be apprehensive about the police taking sides. But the substantive problem remains the same: How can the police strengthen the informal social-control mechanisms of natural communities in order to minimize fear in public places? Law enforcement, per se, is no answer. A gang can weaken or destroy a community by standing about in a menacing fashion and speaking rudely to passersby without breaking the law.

We have difficulty thinking about such matters, not simply because the ethical and legal issues are so complex but because we have become accustomed to thinking of the law in essentially individualistic terms. The law defines *my* rights, punishes *his* behavior, and is applied by *that* officer because of *this* harm. We assume, in thinking this way, that what is good for the individual will be good for the community, and what doesn't matter when it happens to one person won't matter when it happens to many. Ordinarily, those are plausible assumptions. But in cases where behavior that is tolerable to one person is intolerable to many others, the reactions of the others—fear, withdrawal, flight—may ultimately make matters worse for everyone, including the individual who first professed his indifference.

It may be their greater sensitivity to communal as opposed to individual needs that helps explain why the residents of small communities are more satisfied with their police than are the residents of similar neighborhoods in big cities. Elinor Ostrom and her co-workers at Indiana University compared the perception of police services in two poor, all-black Illinois towns—Phoenix and East Chicago Heights—with those of three comparable all-black neighborhoods in Chicago. The level of criminal victimization and the quality of police-community relations appeared to be about the same in the towns and the Chicago neighborhoods. But the citizens living in their own villages were much more likely than those living in the Chicago neighborhoods to say that they do not stay at home for fear of crime, to agree that the local police have "the right to take any action necessary" to deal with problems, and to agree that the police "look out for the needs of the average citizen." It is possible that the residents and the police of the small towns saw themselves as engaged in a collaborative effort to maintain a certain standard of communal life, whereas those of the big city felt themselves to be simply requesting and supplying particular services on an individual basis.

If this is true, how should a wise police chief deploy his meager forces? The first answer is that nobody knows for certain, and the most prudent course of action would be to try further variations on the Newark experiment, to see more precisely what works in what kinds of neighborhoods. The second answer is also a hedge—many aspects of order maintenance in neighborhoods can probably best be handled in ways that involve the police minimally, if at all. A busy, bustling shopping center and a quiet, well-tended suburb may need almost no visible police presence. In both cases, the ratio of respectable to disreputable people is ordinarily so high as to make informal social control effective.

Even in areas that are in jeopardy from disorderly elements, citizen action without substantial police involvement may be sufficient. Meetings between teenagers who like to hang out on a particular corner and adults who want to use that corner might well lead to an amicable agreement on a set of rules about how many people can be allowed to congregate, where, and when.

Where no understanding is possible—or, if possible, not observed—citizen patrols may be a sufficient response. There are two traditions of communal involvement in maintaining order. One, that of the "community watchmen," is as old as the first settlement of the New World. Until well into the nineteenth century, volunteer watchmen, not policemen, patrolled their communities to keep order. They did so, by and large, without taking the law into their own hands—without, that is, punishing persons or using force. Their presence deterred disorder or alerted the community to disorder that could not be deterred. There are hundreds of such efforts today in communities all across the nation. Perhaps the best known is that of the Guardian Angels, a group of unarmed young persons in distinctive berets and T-shirts, who first came to public attention when they began patrolling the New York City subways but who claim now to have chapters in more than thirty American cities. Unfortunately, we have little information about the effect of these groups on crime. It is possible, however, that whatever their effect on crime, citizens find their presence reassuring, and that they thus contribute to maintaining a sense of order and civility.

The second tradition is that of the "vigilante." Rarely a feature of the settled communities of the East, it was primarily to be found in those frontier towns that grew up in advance of the reach of government. More than 350 vigilante groups are known to have existed; their distinctive feature was that their members did take the law into their own hands, by acting as judge, jury, and often executioner as well as policeman. Today, the vigilante movement is conspicuous by its rarity, despite the great fear expressed by citizens that the older cities are becoming "urban frontiers." But some community watchmen groups have skirted the line, and others may cross it in the future. An ambiguous case, reported in the *Wall Street Journal,* involved a citizens' patrol in the Silver Lake area of Belleville, New Jersey. A leader told the reporter, "We look for outsiders." If a few teenagers from outside the neighborhood enter it, "we ask them their business," he said. "If they say they're going down the street to see Mrs. Jones, fine, we let them pass. But then we follow them down the block to make sure they're really going to see Mrs. Jones."

Though citizens can do a great deal, the police are plainly the key to order maintenance. For one thing, many communities, such as the Robert Taylor Homes, cannot do the job by themselves. For another, no citizen in a neighborhood, even an organized one, is likely to feel the sense of responsibility that wearing a badge confers. Psychologists have done many studies on why people fail to go to the aid of persons being attacked or seeking help, and they have learned that the cause is not "apathy" or "selfishness" but the absence of some plausible grounds for feeling that one must personally accept responsibility. Ironically, avoiding responsibility is easier when a lot of people are standing about. On streets and in public places, where order is so important, many people are likely to be "around," a fact that reduces the chance of any one person acting as the agent of the community. The police officer's uniform singles him out as a person who must accept responsibility if asked. In addition, officers, more easily than their fellow citizens, can be expected to distinguish between what is necessary to protect the safety of the street and what merely protects its ethnic purity.

But the police forces of America are losing, not gaining, members. Some cities have suffered substantial cuts in the number of officers available for duty. These cuts are not likely to be reversed in the near future. Therefore, each department must assign its existing officers with great care. Some neighborhoods are so demoralized and crime-ridden as to make foot patrol useless; the best the police can do with limited resources is respond to the enormous number of calls for service. Other neighborhoods are so stable and serene as to make foot patrol unnecessary. The key is to identify neighborhoods at the tipping point—where the public order is deteriorating but not unreclaimable, where the streets are used frequently but by apprehensive people, where a window is likely to be broken at any time, and must quickly be fixed if all are not to be shattered.

Most police departments do not have ways of systematically identifying such areas and assigning officers to them. Officers are assigned on the basis of crime rates (meaning that marginally threatened areas are often stripped so that police can investigate crimes in areas where the situation is hopeless) or on the basis of calls for service (despite the fact that most citizens do not call the police when they are merely frightened or annoyed). To allocate patrol wisely, the department must look at the neighborhoods and decide, from firsthand evidence, where an additional officer will make the greatest difference in promoting a sense of safety.

One way to stretch limited police resources is being tried in some public housing projects. Tenant organizations hire off-duty police officers for patrol work in their buildings. The costs are not high (at least not per resident), the officer likes the additional income, and the residents feel safer. Such arrangements are probably more successful than hiring private watchmen, and the Newark experiment helps us understand why. A private security guard may deter crime or misconduct by his presence, and he may go to the aid of persons needing help, but he may well not intervene—that is, control or drive away—someone challenging community standards. Being a sworn officer—a "real cop"—seems to give one the confidence, the sense of duty, and the aura of authority necessary to perform this difficult task.

Patrol officers might be encouraged to go to and from duty stations on public transportation and, while on the bus or subway car, enforce rules about smoking, drinking, disorderly conduct, and the like. The enforcement need involve nothing more than ejecting the offender (the offense, after all, is not one with which a booking officer or a judge wishes to be bothered). Perhaps the random but relentless maintenance of standards on buses would lead to conditions on buses that approximate the level of civility we now take for granted on airplanes.

But the most important requirement is to think that to maintain order in precarious situations is a vital job. The police know this is one of their functions, and they also believe, correctly, that it cannot be done to the exclusion of criminal investigation and responding to calls. We may have encouraged them to suppose, however, on the basis of our oft-repeated concerns about serious, violent crime, that they will be judged exclusively on their capacity as crime fighters. To the extent that this is the case, police administrators will continue to concentrate police personnel in the highest-crime areas (though not necessarily in the areas most vulnerable to criminal invasion), emphasize their training in the law and criminal apprehension (and not their training in managing street life), and join too quickly in campaigns to decriminalize "harmless" behavior (though public drunkenness, street prostitution, and pornographic displays can destroy a community more quickly than any team of professional burglars).

Above all, we must return to our long-abandoned view that the police ought to protect communities as well as individuals. Our crime statistics and victimization surveys measure individual losses, but they do not measure communal losses. Just as physicians now recognize the importance of fostering health rather than simply treating illness, so the police—and the rest of us—ought to recognize the importance of maintaining, intact, communities without broken windows.

9

✦

A Sketch of the Policeman's "Working Personality"

JEROME H. SKOLNICK

Each of us views the real world through cognitive lenses that influence our perception and interpretation of events. Because their role contains the two important variables of danger and authority, police officers develop a distinctive view of the world. Sociologist Jerome Skolnick explores this view and shows how the "working personality" affects the actions of the police.

A recurrent theme of the sociology of occupations is the effect of a man's work on his outlook on the world.[1] Doctors, janitors, lawyers, and industrial workers develop distinctive ways of perceiving and responding to their environment. Here we shall concentrate on analyzing certain outstanding elements in the police milieu, danger, authority, and efficiency, as they combine to generate distinctive cognitive and behavioral responses in police: a "working personality." Such an analysis does not suggest that all police are alike in "working personality," but that there are distinctive cognitive tendencies in police as an occupational grouping. Some of these may be found in other occupations sharing similar problems. So far as exposure to danger is concerned, the policeman may be likened to the soldier. His problems as an authority bear a certain similarity to those of the schoolteacher, and the pressures he feels to prove himself efficient are not unlike those felt by the industrial worker. The

Source: From *Justice without Trial: Law Enforcement in a Democratic Society* by Jerome H. Skolnick (New York: John Wiley & Sons, 1966), pp. 42–62. Reprinted by permission of the author and publisher.

combination of these elements, however, is unique to the policeman. Thus, the police, as a result of combined features of their social situation, tend to develop ways of looking at the world distinctive to themselves, cognitive lenses through which to see situations and events. The strength of the lenses may be weaker or stronger depending on certain conditions, but they are ground on a similar axis.

Analysis of the policeman's cognitive propensities is necessary to understand the practical dilemma faced by police required to maintain order under a democratic rule of law. . . . A conception of order is [essential] to the resolution of this dilemma. [We suggest] that the paramilitary character of police organization naturally leads to a high evaluation of similarity, routine, and predictability. Our intention is to emphasize features of the policeman's environment interacting with the paramilitary police organization to generate a "working personality." Such an intervening concept should aid in explaining how the social environment of police affects their capacity to respond to the rule of law.

[Emphasis] will be placed on the division of labor in the police department . . . ; "operational law enforcement" [cannot] be understood outside these special work assignments. It is therefore important to explain how the hypothesis emphasizing the generalizability of the policeman's "working personality" is compatible with the idea that police division of labor is an important analytic dimension for understanding "operational law enforcement." Compatibility is evident when one considers the different levels of analysis at which the hypotheses are being developed. Janowitz states, for example, that the military profession is more than an occupation; it is a "style of life" because the occupational claims over one's daily existence extend well beyond official duties. He is quick to point out that any profession performing a crucial "life and death" task, such as medicine, the ministry, or the police, develops such claims.[2] A conception like "working personality" of police should be understood to suggest an analytic breadth similar to that of "style of life." That is, just as the professional behavior of military officers with similar "styles of life" may differ drastically depending upon whether they command an infantry battalion or participate in the work of an intelligence unit, so too does the professional behavior of police officers with similar "working personalities" vary with their assignments.

The policeman's "working personality" is most highly developed in his constabulary role of the man on the beat. For analytical purposes that role is sometimes regarded as an enforcement specialty, but in this general discussion of policemen as they comport themselves while working, the uniformed "cop" is seen as the foundation for the policeman's "working personality." There is a sound organizational basis for making this assumption. The police, unlike the military, draw no caste distinction in socialization, even though their order of ranked titles approximates the military's. Thus, one cannot join a local police department as, for instance, a lieutenant, as a West Point graduate joins the army. Every officer of rank must serve an apprenticeship as a patrolman. This feature of police organization means that the constabulary role is the primary one for all police officers, and that whatever the special requirements of roles in enforcement specialties, they are carried out with a common background of constabulary experience.

The process by which this "personality" is developed may be summarized: the policeman's role contains two principal variables, danger and authority, which should be interpreted in the light of a "constant" pressure to appear efficient.[3] The element of danger seems to make the policeman especially attentive to signs indicating a potential for violence and lawbreaking. As a result, the policeman is generally a "suspicious" person. Furthermore, the character of the policeman's work makes him less desirable as a friend, since norms of friendship implicate others in his work. Accordingly, the element of danger isolates the policeman socially from that segment of the citizenry which he regards as symbolically dangerous and also from the conventional citizenry with whom he identifies.

The element of authority reinforces the element of danger in isolating the policeman. Typically, the policeman is required to enforce laws representing puritanical morality, such as those prohibiting drunkenness, and also laws regulating the flow of public activity, such as traffic laws. In these situations the policeman directs the citizenry, whose typical response denies recognition of his authority and stresses his obligation to respond to danger. The kind of man who responds well to danger, however, does not normally subscribe to codes of puritanical morality. As a result, the policeman is unusually liable to the charge of hypocrisy. That the whole civilian world is an audience for the policeman further promotes police isolation and, in consequence, solidarity. Finally, danger undermines the judicious use of authority. Where danger, as in Britain, is relatively less, the judicious application of authority is facilitated. Hence, British police may appear to be somewhat more attached to the rule of law, when, in fact, they may appear so because they face less danger, and they are as a rule better skilled than American police in creating the appearance of conformity to procedural regulations.

THE SYMBOLIC ASSAILANT
AND POLICE CULTURE

In attempting to understand the policeman's view of the world, it is useful to raise a more general question: What are the conditions under which police, as authorities, may be threatened?[4] To answer this, we must look to the situation of the policeman in the community. One attribute of many characterizing the policeman's role stands out: the policeman is required to respond to assaults against persons and property. When a radio call reports an armed robbery and gives a description of the man involved, every policeman, regardless of assignment, is responsible for the criminal's apprehension. The raison d'être of the policeman and the criminal law, the underlying collectively held moral sentiments which justify penal sanctions, arises ultimately and most clearly from the threat of violence and the possibility of danger to the community. Police who "lobby" for severe narcotics laws, for instance, justify their position on grounds that the addict is a harbinger of danger since, it is maintained, he requires $100 a day to support his habit, and he must steal to get it. Even though the addict is not typically a violent criminal, criminal penalties for addiction are supported on grounds that he may become one.

The policeman, because his work requires him to be occupied continually with potential violence, develops a perceptual shorthand to identify certain kinds of people as symbolic assailants, that is, as persons who use gesture, language, and attire that the policeman has come to recognize as a prelude to violence. This does not mean that violence by the symbolic assailant is necessarily predictable. On the contrary, the policeman responds to the vague indication of danger suggested by appearance.[5] Like the animals of the experimental psychologist, the policeman finds the threat of random damage more compelling than a predetermined and inevitable punishment.

Nor, to qualify for the status of symbolic assailant, need an individual ever have used violence. A man backing out of a jewelry store with a gun in one hand and jewelry in the other would qualify even if the gun were a toy and he had never in his life fired a real pistol. To the policeman in the situation, the man's personal history is momentarily immaterial. There is only one relevant sign: a gun signifying danger. Similarly, a young man may suggest the threat of violence to the policeman by his manner of walking or "strutting," the insolence in the demeanor being registered by the policeman as a possible preamble to later attack.[6] Signs vary from area to area, but a youth dressed in a black leather jacket and motorcycle boots is sure to draw at least a suspicious glance from a policeman.

Policemen themselves do not necessarily emphasize the peril associated with their work when questioned directly, and may even have well-developed strategies of denial. The element of danger is so integral to the policeman's work that explicit recognition might induce emotional barriers to work performance. Thus, one patrol officer observed that more police have been killed and injured in automobile accidents in the past ten years than from gunfire. Although his assertion is true, he neglected to mention that police are the only peacetime occupational group with a systematic record of death and injury from gunfire and other weaponry. Along these lines, it is interesting that of the 224 working Westville policemen (not including the sixteen juvenile policemen) responding to a question about which assignment they would like most to have in the police department,[7] 50 percent selected the job of detective, an assignment combining elements of apparent danger and initiative. The next category was adult street work, that is, patrol and traffic (37 percent). Eight percent selected the juvenile squad,[8] and only 4 percent selected administrative work. Not a single policeman chose the job of jail guard. Although these findings do not control for such factors as prestige, they suggest that confining and routine jobs are rated low on the hierarchy of police preferences, even though such jobs are least dangerous. Thus, the policeman may well, as a personality, enjoy the possibility of danger, especially its associated excitement, even though he may at the same time be fearful of it. Such "inconsistency" is easily understood. Freud has by now made it an axiom of personality theory that logical and emotional consistency are by no means the same phenomenon.

However complex the motives aroused by the element of danger, its consequences for sustaining police culture are unambiguous. This element requires him, like the combat soldier, the European Jew, the South African (white or black), to live in a world straining toward duality, and suggesting danger when "they" are perceived. Consequently, it is in the nature of the policeman's situation that his conception of order emphasizes regularity and predictability. It is, therefore, a conception shaped by persistent *suspicion*. The English "copper," often portrayed as a courteous, easygoing, rather jolly sort of chap, on the one hand, or as a devil-may-care adventurer, on the other, is differently described by Colin MacInnes:

> The true copper's dominant characteristic, if the truth be known, is neither those daring nor vicious qualities that are sometimes attributed to him by friend or enemy, but an ingrained conservatism, and almost desperate love of the conventional. It is untidiness, disorder, the unusual, that a copper disapproves of most of all: far more, even than of crime which is merely a professional matter. Hence his profound dislike of people loitering in streets, dressing extravagantly, speaking with exotic accents, being strange, weak, eccentric, or simply any rare minority—of their doing, in fact, anything that cannot be safely predicted.[9]

Policemen are indeed specifically *trained* to be suspicious, to perceive events or changes in the physical surroundings that indicate the occurrence or probability of disorder. A former student who worked as a patrolman in a suburban New York police department describes this aspect of the policeman's assessment of the unusual:

> The time spent cruising one's sector or walking one's beat is not wasted time, though it can become quite routine. During this time, the most important thing for the officer to do is notice the *normal*. He must come to know the people in his area, their habits, their automobiles and their friends. He must learn what time the various shops close, how much money is kept on hand on different nights, what lights are usually left on, which houses are vacant . . . only then can he decide what persons or cars under what circumstances warrant the appellation "suspicious."[10]

The individual policeman's "suspiciousness" does not hang on whether he has personally undergone an experience that could objectively be described as hazardous. Personal experience of this sort is not the key to the psychological importance of exceptionality. Each, as he routinely carries out his work, will experience situations that threaten to become dangerous. Like the American Jew who contributes to the "defense" organizations such as the Anti-Defamation League in response to Nazi brutalities he has never experienced personally, the policeman identifies with his fellow cop who has been beaten, perhaps fatally, by a gang of young thugs.

SOCIAL ISOLATION

The patrolman in Westville, and probably in most communities, has come to identify the black man with danger. James Baldwin vividly expresses the isolation of the ghetto policeman:

The only way to police a ghetto is to be oppressive. None of the police commissioner's men, even with the best will in the world, have any way of understanding the lives led by the people they swagger about in twos and threes controlling. Their very presence is an insult, and it would be, even if they spent their entire day feeding gumdrops to children. They represent the force of the white world, and that world's criminal profit and ease, to keep the black man corralled up here, in his place. The badge, the gun in the holster, and the swinging club make vivid what will happen should his rebellion become overt. . . .

It is hard, on the other hand, to blame the policeman, blank, good-natured, thoughtless, and insuperably innocent, for being such a perfect representative of the people he serves. He, too, believes in good intentions and is astounded and offended when they are not taken for the deed. He has never, himself, done anything for which to be hated—which of us has?—and yet he is facing, daily and nightly, people who would gladly see him dead, and he knows it. There is no way for him not to know it; there are few things under heaven more unnerving than the silent, accumulating contempt and hatred of a people. He moves through Harlem, therefore, like an occupying soldier in a bitterly hostile country; which is precisely what, and where he is, and is the reason he walks in twos and threes.[11]

While Baldwin's observations on police–black relations cannot be disputed seriously, there is greater social distance between police and "civilians" in general regardless of their color than Baldwin considers. Thus, Colin MacInnes has his English hero, Mr. Justice, explaining:

The story is all coppers are just civilians like anyone else, living among them not in barracks like on the Continent, but you and I know that's just a legend for mugs. We *are* cut off: we're *not* like everyone else. Some civilians fear us and play up to us, some dislike us and keep out of our way but no one—well, very few indeed—accepts us as just ordinary like them. In one sense, dear, we're just like hostile troops occupying an enemy country. And say what you like, at times that makes us lonely.[12]

MacInnes' observation suggests that by not introducing a white control group, Baldwin has failed to see that the policeman may not get on well with anybody regardless (to use the hackneyed phrase) of race, creed, or national origin. Policemen whom one knows well often express their sense of isolation from the public as a whole, not just from those who fail to share their color. Westville police were asked, for example, to rank the most serious problems police have. The category most frequently selected was not racial problems, but some form of public relations: lack of respect for the police, lack of cooperation in enforcement of law, lack of understanding of the requirements of police work.[13] One respondent answered:

As a policeman my most serious problem is impressing on the general public just how difficult and necessary police service is to all. There seems to be an attitude of "law is important, but it applies to my neigh-bor—not to me."

Of the 282 Westville policemen who rated the prestige police work receives from others, 70 percent ranked it as only fair or poor, while less than 2 percent ranked it as "excellent" and another 29 percent as "good." Similarly, in Britain, two-thirds of a sample of policemen interviewed by a royal commission stated difficulties in making friends outside the force; of those interviewed 58 percent thought members of the public to be reserved, suspicious, and constrained in conversation; and 12 percent attributed such difficulties to the requirements that policemen be selective in associations and behave circumspectly.[14]

A Westville policeman related the following incident:

Several months after I joined the force, my wife and I used to be socially active with a crowd of young people, mostly married, who gave a lot of parties where there was drinking and dancing, and we enjoyed it. I've never forgotten, though, an incident that happened on one Fourth of July party. Everybody had been drinking, there was a lot of talking, people were feeling boisterous, and some kid there—he must have been twenty or twenty-two—threw a firecracker that hit my wife in the leg and burned her. I didn't know exactly what to do—punch the guy in the nose, bawl him out, just forget it. Anyway, I couldn't let it pass, so I walked over to him and told him he ought to be careful. He began to rise up at me, and when he did, somebody yelled, "Better watch out, he's a cop." I saw everybody standing there, and I could feel they were all against me and for the kid, even though he had thrown the firecracker at my wife. I went over to the host and said it was probably better if my wife and I left because a fight would put a damper on the party. Actually, I'd hoped he would ask the kid to leave, since the kid had thrown the firecracker. But he didn't, so we left. After that incident, my wife and I stopped going around with that crowd, and decided that if we were going to parties where there was to be drinking and boisterousness, we weren't going to be the only police people there.

Another reported that he seeks to overcome his feelings of isolation by conceal-ing his police identity:

I try not to bring my work home with me, and that includes my social life. I like the men I work with, but I think it's better that my family doesn't become a police family. I try to put my police work into the background, and try not to let people know I'm a policeman. Once you do, you can't have normal relations with them.[15]

Although the policeman serves a people who are, as Baldwin says, the es-tablished society, the white society, these people do not make him feel ac-cepted. As a result, he develops resources within his own world to combat social rejection.

POLICE SOLIDARITY

All occupational groups share a measure of inclusiveness and identification. People are brought together simply by doing the same work and having similar career and salary problems. As several writers have noted, however, police show an unusually high degree of occupational solidarity.[16] It is true that the police have a common employer and wear a uniform at work, but so do doctors, milkmen, and bus drivers. Yet it is doubtful that these workers have so close knit an occupation or so similar an outlook on the world as do police. Set apart from the conventional world, the policeman experiences an exceptionally strong tendency to find his social identity within his occupational milieu.

Compare the police with another skilled craft. In a study of the International Typographical Union, the authors asked printers the first names and jobs of their three closest friends. Of the 1,236 friends named by the 412 men in their sample, 35 percent were printers.[17] Similarly, among the Westville police, of 700 friends listed by 250 respondents, 35 percent were policemen. The policemen, however, were far more active than printers in occupational social activities. Of the printers, more than half (54 percent) had never participated in any union clubs, benefit societies, teams, or organizations composed mostly of printers, or attended any printers' social affairs in the past five years. Of the Westville police, only 16 percent had failed to attend a single police banquet or dinner in the past *year* (as contrasted with the printers' *five years*); and of the 234 men answering this question, 54 percent had attended three or more such affairs *during the past year.*

These findings are striking in light of the interpretation made of the data on printers. Lipset, Trow, and Coleman do not, as a result of their findings, see printers as an unintegrated occupational group. On the contrary, they ascribe the democratic character of the union in good part to the active social and political participation of the membership. The point is not to question their interpretation, since it is doubtless correct when printers are held up against other manual workers. However, when seen in comparison to police, printers appear a minimally participating group; put positively, police emerge as an exceptionally socially active occupational group.

POLICE SOLIDARITY AND DANGER

There is still a question, however, as to the process through which danger and authority influence police solidarity. The effect of danger on police solidarity is revealed when we examine a chief complaint of police: lack of public support and public apathy. The complaint may have several referents including police pay, police prestige, and support from the legislature. But the repeatedly voiced broader meaning of the complaint is resentment at being taken for granted. The policeman does not believe that his status as civil servant should relieve the public of responsibility for law enforcement. He feels, however, that payment out of public coffers somehow obscures his humanity and, therefore, his need for help.[18] As one put it:

> Jerry, a cop, can get into a fight with three or four tough kids, and there will be citizens passing by, and maybe they'll look, but they'll never lend a hand. It's their country too, but you'd never know it the way some of them act. They forget that we're made of flesh and blood too. They don't care what happens to the cop so long as they don't get a little dirty.

Although the policeman sees himself as a specialist in dealing with violence, he does not want to fight alone. He does not believe that his specialization relieves the general public of citizenship duties. Indeed, if possible, he would prefer to be the foreman rather than the workingman in the battle against criminals.

The general public, of course, does withdraw from the workday world of the policeman. The policeman's responsibility for controlling dangerous and sometimes violent persons alienates the average citizen perhaps as much as does his authority over the average citizen. If the policeman's job is to ensure that public order is maintained, the citizen's inclination is to shrink from the dangers of maintaining it. The citizen prefers to see the policeman as an automaton, because once the policeman's humanity is recognized, the citizen necessarily becomes implicated in the policeman's work, which is, after all, sometimes dirty and dangerous. What the policeman typically fails to realize is the extent he becomes tainted by the character of the work he performs. The dangers of their work not only draw policemen together as a group but separate them from the rest of the population. Banton, for instance, comments:

> Patrolmen may support their fellows over what they regard as minor infractions in order to demonstrate to them that they will be loyal in situations that make the greatest demands upon their fidelity. . . .
>
> In the American departments I visited it seemed as if the supervisors shared many of the patrolmen's sentiments about solidarity. They too wanted their colleagues to back them up in an emergency, and they shared similar frustrations with the public.[19]

Thus, the element of danger contains seeds of isolation which may grow in two directions. In one, a stereotyping perceptual shorthand is formed through which the police come to see certain signs as symbols of potential violence. The police probably differ in this respect from the general middle-class white population only in degree. This difference, however, may take on enormous significance in practice. Thus, the policeman works at identifying and possibly apprehending the symbolic assailant; the ordinary citizen does not. As a result, the ordinary citizen does not assume the responsibility to implicate himself in the policeman's required response to danger. The element of danger in the policeman's role alienates him not only from populations with a potential for crime but also from the conventionally respectable (white) citizenry, in short, from that segment of the population from which friends would ordinarily be drawn. As Janowitz has noted in a paragraph suggesting similarities between the police and the military, ". . . any profession which is continually preoccupied with the threat of danger requires a strong sense of solidarity if it is to operate effectively. Detailed regulation of the military style of life is expected to enhance group cohesion, professional loyalty, and maintain the martial spirit."[20]

SOCIAL ISOLATION AND AUTHORITY

The element of authority also helps to account for the policeman's social isolation. Policemen themselves are aware of their isolation from the community, and are apt to weight authority heavily as a causal factor. When considering how authority influences rejection, the policeman typically singles out his responsibility for enforcement of traffic violations.[21] Resentment, even hostility, is generated in those receiving citations, in part because such contact is often the only one citizens have with police, and in part because municipal administrations and courts have been known to utilize police authority primarily to meet budgetary requirements, rather than those of public order. Thus, when a municipality engages in "speed trapping" by changing limits so quickly that drivers cannot realistically slow down to the prescribed speed or, while keeping the limits reasonable, charging high fines primarily to generate revenue, the policeman carries the brunt of public resentment.

That the policeman dislikes writing traffic tickets is suggested by the quota system police departments typically employ. In Westville, each traffic policeman has what is euphemistically described as a working "norm." A motorcyclist is supposed to write two tickets an hour for moving violations. It is doubtful that "norms" are needed because policemen are lazy. Rather, employment of quotas most likely springs from the reluctance of policemen to expose themselves to what they know to be public hostility. As a result, as one traffic policeman said:

> You learn to sniff out the places where you can catch violators when
> you're running behind. Of course, the department gets to know that you
> hang around one place, and they sometimes try to repair the situation
> there. But a lot of the time it would be too expensive to fix up the engi-
> neering fault, so we keep making our norm.

When meeting "production" pressures, the policeman inadvertently gives a false impression of patrolling ability to the average citizen. The traffic cyclist waits in hiding for moving violators near a tricky intersection, and is reasonably sure that such violations will occur with regularity. The violator believes he has observed a policeman displaying exceptional detection capacities and may have two thoughts, each apt to generate hostility toward the policeman: "I have been trapped," or "They can catch me; why can't they catch crooks as easily?" The answer, of course, lies in the different behavior patterns of motorists and "crooks." The latter do not act with either the frequency or predictability of motorists at poorly engineered intersections.

While traffic patrol plays a major role in separating the policeman from the respectable community, other of his tasks also have this consequence. Traffic patrol is only the most obvious illustration of the policeman's general responsibility for maintaining public order, which also includes keeping order at public accidents, sporting events, and political rallies. These activities share one feature: the policeman is called upon to *direct* ordinary citizens and therefore to restrain their freedom of action. Resenting the restraint, the average citizen in such a situation typically thinks something along the lines of "He is supposed to catch crooks; why is he bothering me?" Thus, the citizen stresses the "dangerous" portion of the policeman's role while belittling his authority.

Closely related to the policeman's authority-based problems as *director* of the citizenry are difficulties associated with his injunction to *regulate public morality*. For instance, the policeman is obliged to investigate "lovers' lanes" and to enforce laws pertaining to gambling, prostitution, and drunkenness. His responsibility in these matters allows him much administrative discretion since he may not actually enforce the law by making an arrest, but instead merely interfere with continuation of the objectionable activity.[22] Thus, he may put the drunk in a taxi, tell the lovers to remove themselves from the backseat, and advise a man soliciting a prostitute to leave the area.

Such admonitions are in the interest of maintaining the proprieties of public order. At the same time, the policeman invites the hostility of the citizen so directed in two respects: he is likely to encourage the sort of response mentioned earlier (that is, an antagonistic reformulation of the policeman's role) and the policeman is apt to cause resentment because of the suspicion that policemen do not themselves strictly conform to the moral norms they are enforcing. Thus, the policeman, faced with enforcing a law against fornication, drunkenness, or gambling, is easily liable to a charge of hypocrisy. Even when the policeman is called on to enforce the laws relating to overt homosexuality, a form of sexual activity for which police are not especially noted, he may encounter the charge of hypocrisy on grounds that he does not adhere strictly to prescribed heterosexual codes. The policeman's difficulty in this respect is shared by all authorities responsible for maintenance of disciplined activity, including industrial foremen, political leaders, elementary schoolteachers, and college professors. All are expected to conform rigidly to the entire range of norms they espouse.[23] The policeman, however, as a result of the unique combination of the elements of danger and authority, experiences a special predicament. It is difficult to develop qualities enabling him to stand up to danger and to conform to standards of puritanical morality. The element of danger demands that the policeman be able to carry out efforts that are in their nature overtly masculine. Police work, like soldiering, requires an exceptional caliber of physical fitness, agility, toughness, and the like. The man who ranks high on these masculine characteristics is, again like the soldier, not usually disposed to be puritanical about sex, drinking, and gambling.

On the basis of observations, policemen do not subscribe to moralistic standards for conduct. For example, the morals squad of the police department, when questioned, was unanimously against the statutory rape age limit, on grounds that as late teenagers they themselves might not have refused an attractive offer from a seventeen-year-old girl.[24] Neither, from observations, are policemen by any means total abstainers from the use of alcoholic beverages. The policeman who is arresting a drunk has probably been drunk himself; he knows it and the drunk knows it.

More than that, a portion of the social isolation of the policeman can be attributed to the discrepancy between moral regulation and the norms and behavior of policemen in these areas. We have presented data indicating that police engage in a comparatively active occupational social life. One interpretation might attribute this attendance to a basic interest in such affairs; another might explain the policeman's occupational social activity as a measure of restraint in publicly violating norms he enforces. The interest in attending police affairs may grow as much out of security in "letting oneself go" in the presence of police, and a corresponding feeling of insecurity with civilians, as an authentic preference for police social affairs. Much alcohol is usually consumed at police banquets with all the melancholy and boisterousness accompanying such occasions. As Horace Cayton reports on his experience as a policeman:

> Deputy sheriffs and policemen don't know much about organized recreation: all they usually do when celebrating is get drunk and pound each other on the back, exchanging loud insults which under ordinary circumstances would result in a fight.[25]

To some degree the reason for the behavior exhibited on these occasions is the company, since the policeman would feel uncomfortable exhibiting insobriety before civilians. The policeman may be likened to other authorities who prefer to violate moralistic norms away from onlookers for whom they are routinely supposed to appear as normative models. College professors, for instance, also get drunk on occasion, but prefer to do so where students are not present. Unfortunately for the policeman, such settings are harder for him to come by than they are for the college professor. The whole civilian world watches the policeman. As a result, he tends to be limited to the company of other policemen for whom his police identity is not a stimulus to carping normative criticism.

CORRELATES OF SOCIAL ISOLATION

The element of authority, like the element of danger, is thus seen to contribute to the solidarity of policemen. To the extent that policemen share the experience of receiving hostility from the public, they are also drawn together and become dependent upon one another. Trends in the degree to which police may exercise authority are also important considerations in understanding the dynamics of the relation between authority and solidarity. It is not simply a question of how much absolute authority police are given, but how much authority they have relative to what they had, or think they had, before. If, as Westley concludes, police violence is frequently a response to a challenge to the police-man's authority, so too may a perceived reduction in authority result in greater solidarity. Whitaker comments on the British police as follows:

> As they feel their authority decline, internal solidarity has become increas-ingly important to the police. Despite the individual responsibility of each police officer to pursue justice, there is sometimes a tendency to close ranks and to form a square when they themselves are concerned.[26]

These inclinations may have positive consequences for the effectiveness of po-lice work, since notions of professional courtesy or colleagueship seem unusually high among police.[27] When the nature of the policing enterprise requires much joint activity, as in robbery and narcotics enforcement, the impression is received that cooperation is high and genuine. Policemen do not appear to cooperate with one another merely because such is the policy of the chief, but because they sin-cerely attach a high value to teamwork. For instance, there is a norm among de-tectives that two who work together will protect each other when a dangerous situation arises. During one investigation, a detective stepped out of a car to ques-tion a suspect who became belligerent. The second detective, who had remained overly long in the backseat of the police car, apologized indirectly to his partner by explaining how wrong it had been of him to permit his partner to encounter a suspect alone on the street. He later repeated this explanation privately, in genuine consternation at having committed the breach (and possibly at having been cul-pable in the presence of an observer). Strong feelings of empathy and cooperation, indeed almost of "clannishness," a term several policemen themselves used to de-scribe the attitude of police toward one another, may be seen in the daily activi-ties of police. Analytically, these feelings can be traced to the elements of danger and shared experiences of hostility in the policeman's role.

Finally, to round out the sketch, policemen are notably conservative, emo-tionally and politically. If the element of danger in the policeman's role tends to make the policeman suspicious, and therefore emotionally attached to the status quo, a similar consequence may be attributed to the element of authority. The fact that a man is engaged in enforcing a set of rules implies that he also becomes implicated in *affirming* them. Labor disputes provide the commonest example of conditions inclining the policeman to support the status quo. In these situations, the police are necessarily pushed on the side of the defense of property. Their re-sponsibilities thus lead them to see the striking and sometimes angry workers as their enemy and, therefore, to be cool, if not antagonistic, toward the whole conception of labor militancy.[28] If a policeman did not believe in the system of laws he was responsible for enforcing, he would have to go on living in a state of conflicting cognitions, a condition which a number of social psychologists agree is painful.[29]

This hypothetical issue of not believing in the laws they are enforcing sim-ply does not arise for most policemen. In the course of the research, however, there was one example. A Negro civil rights advocate (member of CORE) be-came a policeman with the conviction that by so doing he would be aiding the cause of impartial administration of laws for Negroes. For him, however, this outside rationale was not enough to sustain him in administering a system of laws that depends for its impartiality upon a reasonable measure of social and economic equality among the citizenry. Because this recruit identified so much with the Negro community as to be unable to meet the enforcement requirements of the Westville Police Department, his efficiency was impaired, and he resigned in his rookie year.

Police are understandably reluctant to appear to be anything but impartial politically. The police are forbidden from publicly campaigning for political candidates. The London police are similarly prohibited, and before 1887 were not allowed to vote in parliamentary elections or in local ones until 1893.[30] It was not surprising that the Westville chief of police forbade questions on the questionnaire that would have measured political attitudes.[31] One policeman, however, explained the chief's refusal on grounds that "A couple of jerks here would probably cut up, and come out looking like Commies."

During the course of administering the questionnaire over a three-day period, I talked with approximately fifteen officers and sergeants in the Westville department, discussing political attitudes of police. In addition, during the course of the research itself, approximately fifty were interviewed for varying periods of time. Of these, at least twenty were interviewed more than once, some over time periods of several weeks. Furthermore, twenty police were interviewed in Eastville, several for periods ranging from several hours to several days. Most of the time was *not* spent on investigating political attitudes, but I made a point of raising the question, if possible, making it part of a discussion centered around the contents of a right-wing newsletter to which one of the detectives subscribed. One discussion included a group of eight detectives. From these observations, interviews, and discussions, it was clear that a Goldwater type of conservatism was the dominant political and emotional persuasion of police. I encountered only three policemen who claimed to be politically "liberal," at the same time asserting that they were decidedly exceptional.

Whether or not the policeman is an "authoritarian personality" is a related issue, beyond the scope of this discussion partly because of the many questions raised about this concept. Thus, in the course of discussing the concept of "normality" in mental health, two psychologists make the point that many conventional people were high scorers on the California F scale and similar tests. The great mass of the people, according to these authors, is not much further along the scale of ego development than the typical adolescent who, as they describe him, is "rigid, prone to think in stereotypes, intolerant of deviations, punitive and anti-psychological—in short, what has been called an authoritarian personality."[32] Therefore it is preferable to call the policeman's a conventional personality.

Writing about the New York police force, Thomas R. Brooks suggests a similar interpretation. He writes:

> Cops are conventional people. . . . All a cop can swing in a milieu of marijuana smokers, interracial dates, and homosexuals is the night stick. A policeman who passed a Lower East Side art gallery filled with paintings

of what appeared to be female genitalia could think of doing only one thing—step in and make an arrest.[33]

Despite his fundamental identification with conservative conventionality, however, the policeman may be familiar, unlike most conventional people, with the argot of the hipster and the underworld. (The policeman tends to resent the quietly respectable liberal who comes to the defense of such people on principle but who has rarely met them in practice.) Indeed, the policeman will use his knowledge of the argot to advantage in talking to a suspect. In this manner, the policeman *puts on* the suspect by pretending to share his moral conception of the world through the use of "hip" expressions. The suspect may put on a parallel show for the policeman by using only conventional language to indicate his respectability. (In my opinion, neither fools the other.)

NOTES

1. For previous contributions in this area, see the following: Ely Chinoy, *Automobile Workers and the American Dream* (Garden City: Doubleday and Company, Inc., 1955); Charles R. Walker and Robert H. Guest, *The Man on the Assembly Line* (Cambridge: Harvard University Press, 1952); Everett C. Hughes, "Work and the Self," in his *Men and Their Work* (Glencoe, Ill.: The Free Press, 1958), pp. 42–55; Harold L. Wilensky, *Intellectuals in Labor Unions: Organizational Pressures on Professional Roles* (Glencoe, Ill.: The Free Press, 1956); Wilensky, "Varieties of Work Experience," in Henry Borow, ed., *Man in a World at Work* (Boston: Houghton Mifflin Company, 1964), pp. 125–154; Louis Kriesberg, "The Retail Furrier: Concepts of Security and Success," *American Journal of Sociology* 57 (March 1952): 478–485; Waldo Burchard, "Role Conflicts of Military Chaplains," *American Sociological Review* 19 (October 1954): 528–535; Howard S. Becker and Blanche Geer, "The Fate of Idealism in Medical School," *American Sociological Review* 23 (1958): 50–56; and Howard S. Becker and Anselm L. Strauss, "Careers, Personality, and Adult Socialization," *American Journal of Sociology* 62 (November 1956): 253–363.

2. Morris Janowitz, *The Professional Soldier: A Social and Political Portrait* (New York: The Free Press of Glencoe, 1964), p. 175.

3. By no means does such an analysis suggest there are no individual or group differences among police. On the contrary, most of this study emphasizes differences, endeavoring to relate these to occupational specialties in police departments. This [section], however, explores similarities rather than differences, attempting to account for the policeman's general disposition to perceive and to behave in certain ways.

4. William Westley was the first to raise such questions about the police, when he inquired into the conditions under which police are violent. Whatever merit this analysis has, it owes much to his prior insights, as all subsequent sociological studies of the police must. See his "Violence and the Police," *American Journal of Sociology* 59 (July 1953): 34–41; also his unpublished Ph.D. dissertation "The Police: A Sociological Study of Law, Custom, and Morality," University of Chicago, Department of Sociology, 1951.

5. Something of the flavor of the policeman's attitude toward the symbolic assailant comes across in a recent article by a police expert. In discussing the problem of selecting subjects for field interrogation, the author writes:
A. Be suspicious. This is a healthy police attitude, but it should be controlled and not too obvious.
B. Look for the unusual.

1. Persons who do not "belong" where they are observed.

2. Automobiles which do not "look right."

3. Businesses opened at odd hours, or not according to routine or custom.

C. Subjects who should be subjected to field interrogations.

1. Suspicious persons known to the officer from previous arrests, field interrogations, and observations.

2. Emaciated appearing alcoholics and narcotics users who invariably turn to crime to pay for cost of habit.

3. Person who fits description of wanted suspect as described by radio, teletype, daily bulletins.

4. Any person observed in the immediate vicinity of a crime very recently committed or reported as "in progress."

5. Known troublemakers near large gatherings.

6. Persons who attempt to avoid or evade the officer.

7. Exaggerated unconcern over contact with the officer.

8. Visibly "rattled" when near the policeman.

9. Unescorted women or young girls in public places, particularly at night in such places as cafés, bars, bus and train depots, or streetcorners.

10. "Lovers" in an industrial area (make good lookouts).

11. Persons who loiter about places where children play.

12. Solicitors or peddlers in a residential neighborhood.

13. Loiterers around public rest rooms.

14. Lone male sitting in car adjacent to schoolground with newspaper or book in his lap.

15. Lone male sitting in car near shopping center who pays unusual amount of attention to women, sometimes continuously manipulating rearview mirror to avoid direct eye contact.

16. Hitchhikers.

17. Person wearing coat on hot days.

18. Car with mismatched hub caps, or dirty car with clean license plate (or vice versa).

19. Uniformed "deliverymen" with no merchandise or truck.

20. Many others. How about your own personal experiences?
From Thomas F. Adams, "Field Interrogation," *Police* (March–April 1963): 28.

6. See Irving Piliavin and Scott Briar, "Police Encounters with Juveniles," *American Journal of Sociology* 70 (September 1964): 206–214.

7. A questionnaire was given to all policemen in operating divisions of the police force: patrol, traffic, vice control, and all detectives. The questionnaire was administered at police lineups over a period of three days, mainly by the author but also by some of the police personnel themselves. Before the questionnaire was administered, it was circulated to and approved by the policemen's welfare association.

8. Indeed, the journalist Paul Jacobs, who has ridden with the Westville juvenile police as part of his own work in poverty, observed in a personal communication that juvenile police appear curiously drawn to seek out dangerous situations, as if juvenile work without danger is degrading.

9. Colin MacInnes, *Mister Love and Justice* (London: New English Library, 1962), p. 74.

10. Peter J. Connell, "Handling of Complaints by Police," unpublished paper for course in criminal procedure, Yale Law School, Fall 1961.

11. James Baldwin, *Nobody Knows My Name* (New York: Dell Publishing Company, 1962), pp. 65–67.

12. MacInnes, op. cit., p. 20.

13. Respondents were asked, "Anybody who knows anything about police work knows that police face a number of problems. Would you please state—in order—what you consider to be the most serious problems police have." On the basis of a number of answers, the writer and J. Richard Woodworth devised a set of categories. Then Woodworth classified each response into one of the categories (see table, p. 156). When a response did not seem clear, he consulted with the writer. No attempt was made to independently check Woodworth's classifications because the results are used impressionistically, and do not test a hypothesis. It may be, for instance,

Westville Police Ranking of Number-One Problem Faced by Police

	Number	Percent
Relations with public	74	26
Racial problems and demonstrations	66	23
Juvenile delinquents and delinquency	23	8
Unpleasant police tasks	23	8
Lack of cooperation from authorities (DA, legislature, courts)	20	7
Internal departmental problems	17	6
Irregular life of policeman	5	2
No answer or other answer	56	20
	284	100

that "relations with public" is sometimes used to indicate racial problems, and vice versa. "Racial problems" include only those answers having specific reference to race.

14. Royal Commission on the Police, 1962. Appendix IV to *Minutes of Evidence,* cited in Michael Banton, *The Policeman in the Community* (London: Tavistock Publications, 1964), p. 198.

15. Similarly, Banton found Scottish police officers attempting to conceal their occupation when on holiday. He quotes one as saying: "If someone asks my wife 'What does your husband do?', I've told her to say, 'He's a clerk,' and that's the way it went because she found that being a policeman's wife—well, it wasn't quite a stigma, she didn't feel cut off, but that sort of invisible wall was up for conversation purposes when a policeman was there" (p. 198).

16. In addition to Banton, William Westley and James Q. Wilson have noted this characteristic of police. See Westley, op. cit., p. 294; Wilson, "The Police and Their Problems: A Theory," *Public Policy* 12 (1963): 189–216.

17. S. M. Lipset, Martin H. Trow, and James S. Coleman, *Union Democracy* (New York: Anchor Books, 1962), p. 123.

18. On this issue there was no variation. The statement "the policeman feels" means that there was no instance of a negative opinion expressed by the police studies.

19. Banton, op. cit., p. 114.

20. Janowitz, op. cit.

21. O. W. Wilson, for example, mentions this factor as a primary source of antagonism toward police. See his "Police Authority in a Free Society," *Journal of Criminal Law, Criminology, and Police Science* 54 (June 1964): 175–177. In the current study, in addition to the police themselves, other people interviewed, such as attorneys in the system, also attribute the isolation of police to their authority. Similarly, Arthur L. Stinchcorabe, in "The Control of Citizen Resentment in Police Work," provides a stimulating analysis, to which I am indebted, of the ways police authority generates resentment.

22. See Wayne R. La Fave, "The Police and Nonenforcement of the Law," *Wisconsin Law Review* (1962): 104–137, 179–239.

23. For a theoretical discussion of the problems of leadership, see George Homans, *The Human Group* (New York: Harcourt, Brace and Company, 1950), especially the chapter on "The Job of the Leader," pp. 415–440.

24. The work of the Westville morals squad is analyzed in detail in an unpublished master's thesis by J. Richard Woodworth, "The Administration of Statutory Rape Complaints: A Sociological Study" (University of California, 1964).

25. Horace R. Cayton, *Long Old Road* (New York: Trident Press, 1965), p. 154.

26. Ben Whitaker, *The Police* (Middlesex, England: Penguin Books, 1964), p. 137.

Closest Friends of Printers and Police, by Occupation

	Printers N = 1.236 (%)	Police N = 700 (%)
Same occupation	35	35
Professionals, business executives, and independent business owners	21	30
White-collar or sales employees	20	12
Manual workers	25	22

27. It would be difficult to compare this factor across occupations, since the indicators could hardly be controlled. Nevertheless, I felt that the sense of responsibility to policemen in other departments was on the whole quite strong.

28. In light of this, the most carefully drawn lesson plan in the "professionalized" Westville police department, according to the officer in charge of training, is the one dealing with the policeman's demeanor in labor disputes. A comparable concern is now being evidenced in teaching policemen appropriate demeanor in civil rights demonstrations. See, e.g., Juby E. Towler, *The Police Role in Racial Conflicts* (Springfield, Ill.: Charles C Thomas, 1964).

29. Indeed, one school of social psychology asserts that there is a basic "drive," a fundamental tendency of human nature, to reduce the degree of discrepancy between conflicting cognitions. For the policeman, this tenet implies that he would have to do something to reduce the discrepancy between his beliefs and his behavior. He would have to modify his behavior, his beliefs, or introduce some outside factor to justify the discrepancy. If he were to modify his behavior, so as not to enforce the law in which he disbelieves, he would not hold his position for long. Practically, then, his alternatives are to introduce some outside factor, or to modify his beliefs. How-

ever, the outside factor would have to be compelling in order to reduce the pain resulting from the dissonance between his cognitions. For example, he would have to be able to convince himself that the only way he could possibly make a living was by being a policeman. Or he would have to modify his beliefs. See Leon Festinger, *A Theory of Cognitive Dissonance* (Evanston, Ill.: Row-Peterson, 1957). A brief explanation of Festinger's theory is reprinted in Edward E. Sampson, ed., *Approaches, Contexts, and Problems of Social Psychology* (Englewood Cliffs, N.J.: Prentice-Hall, 1964), pp. 9–15.

30. Whitaker, op. cit., p. 26.

31. The questions submitted to the chief of police were directly analogous to those asked of printers in the study of the I.T.U. See Lipset et al., op. cit., "Appendix II– Interview Schedule," pp. 493–503.

32. Jane Loevinger and Abel Ossorio, "Evaluations of Therapy by Self-Report: A Paradox," *Journal of Abnormal and Social Psychology* 58 (May 1959): 392; see also Edward A. Shils, "Authoritarianism: 'Right' and 'Left'," in R. Christie and M. Jahoda, eds., *Studies in Scope and Method of "The Authoritarian Personality"* (Glencoe, Ill.: The Free Press, 1954), pp. 24–49.

33. Thomas R. Brooks, "New York's Finest," *Commentary* 40 (August 1965): 29–30.

1 0

✵

General Deterrent Effects of Police Patrol in Crime "Hot Spots"

A Randomized, Controlled Trial

LAWRENCE W. SHERMAN
DAVID WEISBURD

Many criminal justice specialists doubt that the number of police officers on patrol in an area causes any measurable difference in crime. The authors challenge this view and report on their one-year randomized deployment of officers to crime "hot spots" in Minneapolis. They conclude that substantial increases in police patrol presence can cause modest reductions in crime and more impressive reductions in disorder within high crime locations. This requires that police "resources" be applied unequally, and focus not just on police presence, but their task.

In 1974 the Kansas City Preventive Patrol Experiment (Kelling et al. 1974a) shook the theoretical foundations of American policing. The year-long study found that experimentally manipulated variations in the dosage of police patrol across 15 patrol beats had virtually no statistically significant effects on street crime. Then-Kansas City Police Chief Joseph McNamara concluded that

Source: Lawrence W. Sherman and David Weisburd, "General Deterrent Effects of Police Patrol in Crime 'Hot Spots': A Randomized, Controlled Trial," *Justice Quarterly* 12 (December 1995), pp. 625–648. Reprinted with permission of the Academy of Criminal Justice Sciences. Some footnotes deleted, others renumbered.

"routine preventive patrol in marked police cars has little value in preventing crime or making citizens feel safe."

This finding has dominatd police thinking about patrol strategies for more than two decades. Despite contradictory evidence from studies employing equally rigorous research designs (Chaiken 1978; Press 1971; Schnelle et al. 1977; Sherman 1990), the Kansas City finding remains the most influential test of the general deterrent effects of patrol on crime. It has convinced many distinguished scholars that no matter how it is deployed, police presence does not deter. Klockars (1983:130), for example, concludes that "it makes about as much sense to have police patrol routinely in cars to fight crime as it does to have firemen patrol routinely in fire trucks to fight fire." Skolnick and Bayley (1986:4) conclude that "random motor patrolling neither reduces crime nor improves chances of catching suspects." Gottfredson and Hirschi (1990:270) conclude that "no evidence exists that augmentation of police forces or equipment, differential patrol strategies, or differential intensities of surveillance have an effect on crime rates." Even Felson (1994:10–11), a rational choice theorist, interprets the Kansas City findings as evidence that "patrol has no impact on crime rates" because the low density of modern metropolitan areas makes police presence a "drop in the bucket."

The Kansas City experiment does not justify such strong conclusions. Years of debate have revealed substantial statistical, measurement, and conceptual problems in its design. The *statistical* problem is the bias, found in most area-level designs, toward the null hypothesis; the weak statistical power of such designs makes it very difficult to find an effect of patrol (or any other intervention) even when such an effect may be present (Fienberg et al. 1976). The *measurement* problem lies in determining exactly how much dosage was delivered in each of the experimental conditions, which the Kansas City study did not do. Both of these issues point up Felson's conceptual problem of dosage levels: the premise that large patrol beats or neighborhoods are the appropriate unit for allocating and testing the impact of patrol, which dilutes available dosage too much to make a reasonable impact likely (Farrington 1982).

In this article we explore those problems and a research solution: the use of very small clusters of high-crime addresses ("hot spots") as the unit of analysis instead of patrol beats or neighborhoods. We then present the research design and the results of a test of the general deterrent effects of patrol in hot spots.

RESEARCH DESIGN ISSUES
IN PATROL AND CRIME

Statistical Bias Toward the Null Hypothesis

The major statistical limitation in all experiments in patrol beat or neighborhood-level crime reduction is lack of power (Freiman et al. 1978; Sherman 1986:362–64; Zimring 1978:162–63). This problem has three dimensions, each of which creates a bias against demonstrating any impact of policing (or other interventions) on crime. One statistical power issue is the low frequency of *crimes* in most neighborhoods. A second is the number of *citizens* who must be interviewed in each community to permit reliable estimates of changes in the victimization rate of that community. The third is the number of *communities* included in community-level tests of policing strategies.

Most patrol beat-sized neighborhoods in most cities suffer relatively few serious crimes each year. To provide a reliable estimate of the prevalence of most types of crime through victimization surveys, large samples must be drawn for each area. The expense entailed in drawing these samples is so great that it limits the number of areas which can be studied at reasonable cost. Measures of reported crime are less expensive to collect, but they also provide low base rates. One robbery (or less) per month, for example, is a common rate for many patrol beats, as it was in the San Diego Field Interrogation Experiment in beats of 7,000 to 14,000 residents (Boydstun 1975:16, 32). That rarity creates a bias toward the null hypothesis for any crime-specific statistical tests of the impact of interventions. Kelling et al. (1974b:96), for example, found that a 300 percent increase in reported robberies in the less heavily patrolled areas was not statistically significant because the large relative difference reflected an absolute difference of less than one outside robbery per month. The observed difference in Kansas City might have been significant with a sample size of hundreds of patrol beats. Few cities of over 250,000, however, have even 50 patrol beats, let alone hundreds.

Measuring and Varying Patrol Dosage Levels

A substantive bias toward the null hypothesis in the Kansas City design may have been created by insufficient differences in patrol dosage. Larson (1975) argued that five factors created as much visible patrol presence in the unpatrolled beats as would normal patrol dosage (but see Pate and Kelling 1975): (1) travel into and out of the beats to answer calls for service, (2) the operation of other (non-patrol) units in marked cars, (3) greater use of sirens and lights, (4) more frequent responses by two units, and (5) more police-initiated contacts. This does not necessarily discount the failure of the areas with increased dosage to show more crime reduction than those with normal dosage (Zimring 1978:143). Yet it raises a key question: How certain can we be of the exact dosage of visible police presence delivered in any of the 15 beats?

If we assume that the dosage levels in Kansas City actually may have varied very little, that point alone may explain why the Kansas City results differ from those of most other quasi-experimental patrol deterrence studies. In the 1966 study of New York City police, a reported 40 percent increase in patrol car presence reduced target crimes (Press 1971). In the New York City subway study, an increase of almost 300 percent in police staffing apparently caused an initial deterrent effect (Chaiken 1978). In Nashville, a 400 percent increase in police-recorded patrol time in four target areas was associated with significant reductions in total crime (Schnelle et al. 1977). Large increases in dosage thus may be essential if any effect on crime is to be observed. The Kansas City design called for substantial increases, but could not measure the dosage reliably. In the absence of carefully measured levels of patrol dosage, it is almost impossible to interpret the Kansas City preventive patrol experiment.

The measurement and the control of dosage are closely related. Where dosage levels cannot be measured, it is difficult to advise police supervisors on whether proper levels are being delivered. It is also impossible to develop a precise dosage-response curve from multiple experiments, an essential condition for building theory. Thus the basic issues in measuring police patrol dosage must be carefully considered.

Patrol dosage can be measured from the perspective of either the police or the criminal. The police perspective on their own whereabouts can be measured through police logs or notes of independent observers riding in patrol cars. The potential criminal's perspective on police whereabouts can be measured by independent observers stationed in public places. To estimate with any precision the odds that police will pass any particular location, one would require repeated observations from a large sample of all possible observation posts within patrol car beats. The need to sample both space and time could make the gathering of such estimates even more costly per unit of analysis than personal victimization surveys—as long as the unit of analysis remained the entire low-density patrol beat rather than the small parts of each beat where crime is concentrated.

Moreover, spreading observations over entire patrol beats would dilute the power of the observation sample to produce a reliable estimate of police presence in any given place—just as spreading patrol itself dilutes the potential deterrent threat of police presence in any one place. This point raises the more general question of the appropriate unit of analysis for patrol experiments and operations, which should guide the methods of measurement.

The Unit of Analysis: Patrol Beats or Hot Spots

The premise of organizing patrol by beats is that crime could happen anywhere and that the entire beat must be patrolled. Computer-age data, however, have given new support to Henry Fielding's ([1751] 1977) eighteenth century proposal that police pay special attention to a small number of locations at high risk of crime. If only 3 percent of the addresses in a city produce more than half of all the requests for police response, if no police cars are dispatched to 40 percent of the addresses and intersections in a city over one year, and, if among the 60 percent with any requests, the majority (31%) register only one request per year (Sherman, Gartin, and Buerger 1989), then concentrating police in a few locations makes more sense than spreading them evenly throughout a beat (Sherman and Weisburd 1995).

The main argument against directing extra resources to the hot spots is that it would simply displace crime problems from one address to another without achieving any overall or lasting reduction in crime. The premise of this argument is that a fixed supply of criminals is seeking outlets for the fixed number of crimes they are predestined to commit. Although that argument may fit some public drug markets (Sherman 1990; but see Green 1995; Weisburd and Green 1995), it does not fit all crime or even all vice. One carefully studied prostitution market was closed by a police crackdown (and road closing) with no apparent displacement

(Matthews 1986). There is no evidence that displacement is certain across all crime categories (Cornish and Clarke 1987); the most thorough study of displacement from increased patrol (Press 1971) found that the estimate of displaced crime was less than the reduction of crime in the experimental precinct (see also Barr and Pease 1990).

In any case, displacement is merely a rival theory explaining *why* crime declines at a specific hot spot, *if* it declines. The first step is to see whether crime can be reduced at those spots at all, with a research design capable of giving a fair answer to that question.

The geographic concentration of many crimes and many calls to police about crime provides a solution to all three dimensions of the statistical power problem discussed above. First, each "hot spot" cluster of visually connected addresses offers ample numbers of calls and crimes for statistical analysis of changes at that location. Second, any city contains far more hot spots than patrol beats, so there is no difficulty in constructing a large sample of hot spot locations. Third, concentrating patrol dosage in a hot spot could create a substantial increase in patrol dosage in a very small world, and would make systematic observation an economically viable way of measuring patrol dosage levels. Although this solution does not make victimization interviews more economical, it makes feasible an even more direct measure of the most frequent kinds of crime: systematic observation, which also can measure patrol presence. The design presented below demonstrates how this solution can be operationalized, and shows the resulting statistical power.

EXPERIMENTAL DESIGN

Selection of City

We designed the experiment in collaboration with the Minneapolis Police Department, where the pattern of hot spots across all offenses had first been demonstrated (Sherman et al. 1989). The experiment was endorsed by a vote of the City Council upon the Mayor's recommendation, despite the predicted effect of minimizing patrols in outlying Council members' areas and concentrating police presence in the inner core of the city, where hot spots of crime were more prevalent. The experiment also required the cooperation of the entire patrol force; this was facilitated by a recent change in case law, which gave the Chief of Police more control over the four patrol precinct commanders. Police cooperation was also pursued through briefings, pizza parties, and t-shirts bearing the project's logo ("Minneapolis Hot Spot City").

Selection of Hot Spots

We defined hot spots operationally as small clusters of addresses with frequent "hard" crime calls as well as substantial "soft" crime calls for service (Reiss 1985).[1] We then limited the boundaries of each spot conceptually as easily visible from an epicenter (Sherman et al. 1989). This definition failed to solve the problem of crimes occurring at rear entrances to addresses listed in the dispatch data, but the "noise" from this problem should not threaten an internally valid comparison between two randomized groups of hot spots, both of which suffer that noise problem to roughly the same extent.

The selection procedure began with a data file on all dispatched calls for police service citywide for the most recent year before the beginning of the selection analysis (June 6, 1987 through June 5, 1988; this is described below as the "selection year," as distinct from the "baseline" year preceding the starting date of the experiment). In the selection year we identified 5,538 addresses and intersections with more than three calls to police about incidents that we defined as "hard crime." We then employed a computer mapping program, MAPINFO, to locate most of the addresses, so that inspection of the computer printouts for each map grid could reveal what appeared to be visually connected clusters of these addresses.[2] Using this technique, we identified and mapped 420 address clusters with 20 or more hard crime calls (see Buerger, Cohn, and Petrosino 1995).

All 420 of these clusters were visually inspected by field staff members. The inspections had three principal goals. One goal was to reconfigure the boundaries suggested by the computer map to make them consistent with the definition based on visual contact. The second was to determine whether the type of premises at each address was eligible. To limit the sample to places where crime occurred in public and could reasonably be deterred by police presence, we excluded all residential and most commercial buildings of more than four stories (including two hotels), almost all parking garages and department stores, indoor malls, public schools, office buildings, residential social service institutions (such as homeless shelters), hospitals, police stations, and fire stations. We also excluded parks because almost all were too large to meet the visual contact criterion. Finally, we excluded a few known "magnet phone" locations, at which events occurring elsewhere were routinely reported.

The third goal of the inspection was to determine the visual proximity *between* the cluster and the possible contamination of each site by patrol car presence in the closest neighboring site. The two independent field workers, Michael E. Buerger and Ellen G. Cohn, examined each site and drew what appeared to be logical boundaries. Their separate versions of boundaries for the final hot spots initially randomized achieved 75 percent agreement. Their reconfigurations followed these general principles:

1. No hot spot is larger than one standard linear street block (although a few exceptions were allowed on the basis of visual sightings on very short blocks).

2. No hot spot extends for more than one half block from either side of an intersection.

3. No hot spot is within one standard linear block of another hot spot (again we made a few exceptions).

The site visits produced a provisional list of 321 maps, with some overlap which we narrowed to a final list of 268 reconfigured clusters (with the ineligible locations excluded). We marked the 268 on a map to make final eliminations based on proximity. Using memoranda about the layout of each site and its proximity to nearby clusters, the principal investigators created a new list of eligible clusters, all of which were required to generate at least 20 hard crime calls in the selection year. This list was also informed by the "soft crime" totals for the selection year (with a minimum of 20), and by an element crucial to the statistical power of the analysis: the percentage change (positive or negative) in the total calls for hard and soft crime from the year ending May 1987 to the year ending May 1988. High variance from year to year could have attenuated the treatment effects, so clusters with greater than 150 percent increases or 75 percent decreases in hard crime calls from one year to the next were excluded from the possible sample. The greatest decrease included in the final sample was 66 percent.

After we made exclusions for variance and the most severe cases of proximity, only 155 hot spots were left. We eliminated four more on the grounds of new data on proximity; one was eliminated because it had become dormant in recent months. At our request, the surviving 150 were randomized by an independent statistician into three treatment groups, which we presented to a planning committee of the Minneapolis Police Department. The committee concluded that the department could not handle 100 target hot spots with adequate dosage to provide a reliable test of the theory, and asked us to reduce the experimental group to 50. The final agreement called for 55 hot spots assigned to extra patrol; thus 110 sites had to be selected for randomization.

We derived the final selection of the 110 sites from the 150 previously identified sites, primarily by taking the top-ranked hot spots in order of volume of hard crime calls. The final 110 were rerandomized by University of Minnesota statistician Kinley Larntz, despite concerns that about 10 of the clusters would not appear "hot" enough to patrol officers. In the final 110 clusters, the mean number of hard and soft crime calls for service at the active addresses was 182.9 in the selection year, with a minimum of 56 and a maximum of 628.

Characteristics of Hot Spots

The typical hot spot in the final sample of 110 was a group of attached two- and three-story buildings clustered around an epicenter, usually a street corner. Addresses included in the cluster extended in all four directions but only as far as the eye could see from sidewalk corners. These intersections often consisted of a mix of commercial services, usually including food and drink, generally open until late at night. Exceptions to this pattern included low-rise multifamily housing developments and convenience stores. Bus stops and pay telephones were common features of hot spots, as was intensive street lighting.

"Hot" Times

The calls at the 110 spots were concentrated between 7:00 p.m. and 3:00 a.m. We determined this by summing the calls over the selection year by each hour of the day, for both the experimental and the control group. The 7-to-3 window for the experimental group accounted for 51.9 percent of the crime calls;

for the control group, this window accounted for 50.5 percent. The 11:00 a.m. to 7:00 p.m. period registered the next highest concentrations, with 32 percent of the experimental group's calls and 33.6 percent of those for the control group. The 3:00 a.m. to 11:00 a.m. period, with the exception of a few sites, registered the fewest calls, with only 16.3 percent of the experimental group's calls and 15.8 percent of the control group's. Thus the experiment was restricted to the period from 11 a.m. to 3 a.m.

Hot Spot Sample Sizes

The sample sizes include several dimensions: the numbers of hot spot clusters, the addresses used to select the clusters, the total number of addresses within those boundaries, numbers of calls for all reasons at those addresses, and the numbers of calls about hard and soft crimes dispatched to those addresses.

The experiment randomly assigned 110 address clusters to treatment and control groups. These clusters contained a total of 677 specific "selection" addresses and intersections (320 experimental group addresses and 357 control), with a mean of six addresses per site. When all of the addresses included within the boundaries of each hot spot are considered (not only those addresses with three or more calls, as in the selection data cited above), the total was 1,663 (a mean of 15 addresses per spot): 832 addresses in the experimental group and 831 in the control.

During the *baseline* year before the experiment began, these "all-inclusive" clusters produced a total of 19,322 calls for all reasons in the experimental group and 19,693 in the control, or a mean of 355 calls per hot spot. This total constituted 10.8 percent of the 364,365 calls dispatched for all reasons citywide in the one-year baseline period, December 1, 1987 to November 30, 1988. Adjustment for nontraffic calls produced virtually identical proportions.

Treatments

This experiment tests a theory of intensified but intermittent patrol, not a theory of constant, security guard-style presence. The experimental patrol treatment approximates a crackdown-backoff pattern; a police car was not present at the target address clusters at all times. Cars left to answer calls and then returned unexpectedly. They stayed at one spot for as long as an hour or more, or for only a few minutes. Both one-officer and two-officer units were used; foot patrol presence was measured separately. Both officers and observers were given maps of the hot spot boundaries; the addresses generating the most police calls were highlighted in red.

What the officers did while present at the sites varied widely by officer. During an inspection visit at our invitation, George Kelling (1990, personal communication) observed that some were reading newspapers or sunning themselves while sitting on the patrol car, while others were engaging citizens in friendly interaction in community-policing style. The experiment was clearly no test of the content of police presence, only of the amount. To gain police cooperation in achieving the dosage goals, we did not presume to restrict the officers' discretion in *how* to police a hot spot, but only in *how much*.

Random Assignment

The final sample of 110 address clusters was assigned randomly to two groups of 55 by the independent statistician, who used a computerized pseudo-random number generator to allocate the clusters equally to two groups. The allocation was performed in five statistical "blocks," based on natural cutting points within the distribution of hard crime call frequencies. This decision was intended to increase statistical power by minimizing the differences in variance between the groups. Although blocking results in a loss of degrees of freedom in analysis of experimental effects, it products a gain over simple randomization by maximizing the equivalence of the groups. Further, a comparison of randomization by pairs with randomization in five blocks showed little difference in statistical power.

Dosage

After extensive debate, the police department committed itself to (but never fully achieved) a goal of three hours a day of patrol presence at each of the 55 target hot spots. The dosage, based on the above analysis of "hot times," was to be divided evenly between the 11–7 and the 7–3 time periods, and was to be provided seven days a week. To enhance the power of the experiment (Weisburd 1993), our goal (which was largely achieved) was to keep dosage levels as consistent as possible. We encouraged this by giving patrol managers weekly reports on the dosage levels reported by officers in their official logs. These reports were supplemented by a monthly report on the amount of dosage recorded by our field observers. When some spots appeared in the logs to be receiving more dosage than others, we asked patrol supervisors to assign less time at those spots and to order more time at the locations receiving less logged dosage.

The independent observations by our field staff of 16 observers and three supervisors were limited to the 100 most active control and experimental spots; the five "coolest" spots in each treatment group were eliminated from the observations to maximize measurement of the places producing the largest volume of crime. The observations covered a total of 75 hours per hot spot over the course of the year. All observations were made between 7:00 p.m. and 3:00 a.m. The 7,542-hour sample thus constituted 2.6 percent of all hours on that period over 365 days times 100 locations (292,000 hours).

The observation sample was divided equally into 13 periods of 28 days each for each hot spot. Observations were conducted in a total of 6,465 blocks of 70 minutes each. Each of the 13 28-day periods contained 497 observation blocks, or about five per hot spot. A total of 3,232 observation blocks were conducted for the 50 experimental hot spots, and 3,233 for the 50 observed controls.

Observers were trained to use a systematic observation instrument that employed separate sections for observations of uniformed officers and of crime and disorder. Both sections were structured chronologically so that each entry had a start and a finish time, as did the entire observation period. Entries registering official presence included "drive-throughs" and longer stays of police in cars and on foot, private security guards, fire truck and ambulance personnel, and whether and how long police left their cars or entered buildings. Observations of crime and disorder included an array [of] both criminal offenses and offenses against conventional civility, as noted below.

Outcome Measures

We collected two primary outcome measures: calls about crime and observed disorders. The hot spots were selected on the basis of telephone calls about criminal activity reported by the public—as distinct form dispatchers' records of events reported by police officers over the radio, which also can generate a "call" record. Therefore citizen calls should be treated as the primary outcome measure. Calls about "soft" and "hard" crime were counted for the full 24–hour day, not only the 16 hours in which the experiment was operational, for two reasons. One was theoretical, based on our conception of general deterrence as including "residual" effects even when police patrols are not present (Sherman 1990). The other reason was statistical: we concluded the full 24 hours in order to increase the power of the test by using higher base rates of crime calls in each hot spot.

The other outcome measure was a more direct measure of crime than citizen calls, although it necessarily lacked baseline data for sample selection. Systematic observation data on crime and disorder in the evening observation hours coded each incident of fights, drug sales, apparent solicitation for prostitution, playing of loud music or shouting, rummaging through garbage cans, urinating, and other offensive "signs of crime" (Skogan 1990). The data even included two minor assaults on an observer sitting in a parked car.

We planned to analyze the police call data by comparing Time 1/ Time 2 differences between the two groups, and to analyze the observations at Time 2 only. Time 1 is the 12 months preceding the experiment; Time 2 is the 12 months of the experiment (December 1, 1988 through November 30, 1989).

Analysis of Statistical Power

The statistical power of a test "is the probability that it will lead to a rejection of the null hypothesis" (Cohen 1977:4), or the odds of detecting a statistically significant result in an experiment (at each significance level) given a true difference between experimental and control groups. We computed the power of our incidence measure using the selection-year data for the final 100 hot spots with a one–tailed 10 percent test. We used a one–tailed test because of our strong hypothesis that patrol presence reduces crime. We chose a 10 percent significance level because police executives are more interested in size of an effect than in the exact odds that the effect is due to chance. On the basis of tables provided by Cohen (1977), and assuming a standard deviation of 33.5 percent for total crime and a 10 percent significance level, we estimated that we had an 85 percent chance of gaining a significant finding in our experiment if the true impact of the treatment was about 15 percent. This level of power exceeds the .80 threshold suggested by Cohen (1977) for powerful experimental designs.

Summary of the Design

We designed this experiment to test the hypothesis that substantial increases in police patrol in high-crime hot spots could reduce crime reported and observed in those spots. We selected the hot spots on the basis of calls for service and visual proximity. The independent variable was assigned at random to half of a group of 110 hot spots constituting a universe of all address clusters meeting certain minimal levels of "hard" and "soft" crimes, as well as stability over two years in calls for police service for those types of incidents. We measured the independent variable by police logs and by independent observation of the 50 most active hot spots in each group of 55. The dependent variable was measured by police calls for service and by independently observed incidents of crime and disorder.

For 6½ months, the design was implemented as planned. What happened then to modify the design produced results generally consistent with the hypothesis, even while it reduced the intended statistical power by cutting the anticipated experimental period almost in half.

RESULTS

Independent Variable: Observed Differences in Dosage

From December 1, 1988 to November 30, 1989, the observers counted 34,416 police unit-minutes in the 50 observed experimental hot spots and 14,765 unit-minutes in the 50 observed control hot spots, a pooled ratio of 2.3 to 1. The difference in mean police presence per hot spot was slightly lower at 1.99 to 1, with $\overline{X} = .149$ police unit-minutes per minute of observation in the 50 observed experimental hot spots and $\overline{X} = .0748$ police unit-minutes per minute of observation in the 50 control hot spots. A "unit-minute" refers to the number of minutes each police unit spent in each location; "units" include one-officer marked cars, two-officer marked cars, and one- or two-officer foot patrols. Whenever a police unit entered the boundaries of the hot spot, the observer started the clock counting for the minutes of that unit's presence. The count ended when either the unit or the observer left the hot spot. The minutes present for each unit sometimes overlapped, so that unit-minutes divided by observation minutes cannot be taken as a prevalence measure of any police presence at all.

Compliance with the experimental protocol can be estimated by analyzing the ratio of unit-minutes to all observed minutes in each of the 100 observed hot spots. Using a criterion of one unit-minute of observed police presence for every 10 minutes of observations as threshold for defining an "experimental" case, we

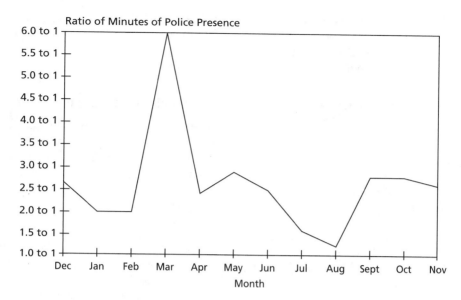

Figure 1 Ratio of Experimental to Control Minutes of Observed Police Presence, by Month

find five hot spots assigned to the experimental group which failed to receive that level of dosage and four hot spots assigned to the control group which did receive that amount. Thus the "misassignment" or "crossover" rate in traditional experimental terms is 9 percent, or 9 out of the 100 observed cases. This rate is moderate for randomized trials generally, and better than the rate in most police experiments (see Dennis 1988; Weinstein and Levin 1989). Otherwise the hot spots received highly similar within-group dosage levels: 46 of the 50 experimental hot spots received 1.3 to 1.7 minutes of patrol per 10 minutes of observation, and 40 of the controls received either .7 or .8 police minutes per 10 observed minutes.

The Summer Design Breakdown Although the mean unit-minutes across hot spots within treatment groups were relatively homogeneous, the pooled ratio between experimental and control unit-minutes varied widely by calendar month. The ratio began at 2.6 to 1 in December and fall in January to 2 to 1, where it remained until March. At that time it rose to 6 to 1 and then fell to about 2.5 to 1 in April through June. The ratio then plummeted to 1.2 to 1 in August, and rose in September to a plateau of 2.8 to 1, and remained at that level for the rest of the experiment (see Figure 1). The police logs reflect the same pattern, declining from an average of just under three hours per day in the experimental hot spots from February through May to only two hours in July and August, and rising again in the autumn. Although the observed police unit-minutes ratio exceeded 2 to 1 for every month except

August, the disruption of the experiment during the summer peak in call load (and vacation time) for police complicates the interpretation of any differences in outcomes over the entire one-year period, leaving only 6.5 months of a fully implemented design.

Dependent Variable 1: Differences in Calls about Crime

The virtual disappearance of a difference in patrol dosage between experimental and control groups in the summer months raises several options for analysis. These options are further complicated by an outcome measurement problem caused by the introduction of a new computer-aided dispatch (CAD) system from October through November 10, 1989. During that period, errors and missing data made the calls about crime an unreliable indicator. One option—perhaps the simplest—is to analyze the period from December 1 through June 15, when the police logs show the most consistent and most uninterrupted implementation of the experiment throughout the 16-hour target zone. Another option is to cut off analysis at July 31, before the only month in which observational data show virtually no difference in dosage (a period in which the overall ratio is 2.5 to 1). A third option is to analyze the full year, despite the six weeks of CAD measurement problems in October and November. A fourth option is to analyze the full year minus the period of suspect CAD data.

We find the July 31 cutoff to be the most appropriate test of the hypothesis because that date is the last date on which the experiment was minimally implemented as planned. Because others may disagree, however, we present the data for all four of the time periods defined above.

Table 1 presents the raw data for differences in hard, soft, and total citizen calls about crime for each of the four periods, as well as the significance levels for the mean Time 1 to Time 2 differences per hot spot between treatment and control groups as calculated from a mixed model ANOVA test taking randomization block into account. It shows that total crime calls and calls about soft crime increased from the baseline to the experimental year in both treatment and control groups, while calls about hard crime decreased in both groups from the baseline to the experimental year. Thus the analysis centers on the *differences of differences* between the baseline and the experimental years, comparing experimental with control hot spots.

Figure 2 shows that the predicted effect, on total crime calls, of the reduced difference in patrol dosage appears in August, on schedule. At that time the experimental group fails for the first time to show a more favorable absolute difference, in calls from the same period in the prior year, than the control group. In every month before August, when the experimental group received far more police presence than the control group, the Time-1-to-Time-2 change in total calls had been more favorable for the experimental group. The August violation of that pattern disappeared in September but returned in October, when the data on calls became questionable. The violation of the predicted difference disap-

Table 1 Crime Calls by Time Period and Treatment Group

Time Period	Hard Crime		Soft Crime		Total Crime	
	Experimental	Control	Experimental	Control	Experimental	Control
June 15						
Baseline year	1,469	1,394	3,544	3,590	5,013	4,984
Experimental year	1,377	1,374	3,919	4,542	5,296	5,916
Absolute change	−92	−20	375	952	283	932
1-Tailed P Value	.27		.047*		.054*	
July 31						
Baseline year	1,893	1,798	4,638	4,693	6,531	6,491
Experimental year	1,776	1,793	5,155	5,909	6,931	7,702
Absolute change	−117	−5	517	1,216	400	1,211
1-Tailed P Value	.20		.046*		.049*	
November 30[a]						
Baseline year	2,533	2,432	6,523	6,644	9,056	9,076
Experimental year	2,455	2,419	7,116	8,049	9,571	10,468
Absolute change	−78	−13	593	1,405	515	1,392
1-Tailed P Value	.33		0.46*		.058*	
November 30[b]						
Baseline year	2,873	2,741	7,396	7,664	10,269	10,405
Experimental year	2,754	2,700	8,163	9,016	10,917	11,716
Absolute change	−119	−41	767	1,352	648	1,311
1-Tailed P Value	.31		.155		.159	

* $p < .10$

[a]Excludes period from 10/1 to 11/10.

[b]Includes period from 10/1 to 11/10/89.

peared again in November, when the new CAD system was thought to be reliably established.

Table 2 presents the absolute baseline–experimental percentage differences and the difference of those differences between experimental and control hot spots as computed by a mixed–model analysis of variance using the five-block design. The effect of increasing patrol is greater on total and soft crime calls than on hard crime. Soft crime effects are strong in every period except the full year including the CAD changeover errors; they range in magnitude of relative percentage differences (experimental group baseline to experimental year percentage change minus control group baseline to experimental year percentage change) from 7 percent for the full year to 16 percent for the period ending June 15. The effects for total crime calls are similar but attenuated because the soft crime calls account for most of the total crime calls.

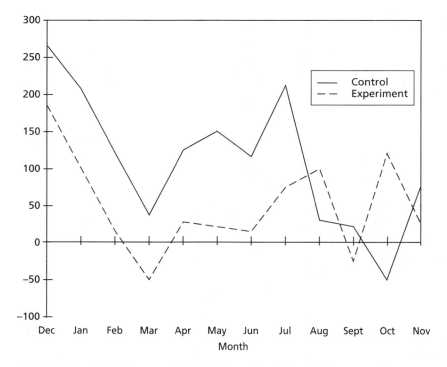

Figure 2 Absolute Differences from Baseline to Experimental Year in Total Crime Calls by Month and Treatment Group

Table 2 Percentage Changes of Crime Calls from Baseline to Experimental Year, by Time Period, Treatment Group, and Significance Levels of Mixed-Model ANOVA Tests

Time Period	Hard Crime			Soft Crime			Total Crime		
	Exp.	Control	Difference	Exp.	Control	Difference	Exp.	Control	Difference
June 15 Percent change	−6.3	−1.4	−4.9	10.6	26.5	−15.9	5.6	18.7	−13.1
July 31 Percent change	−6.2	−.3	−5.9	11.1	25.9	−14.8	6.1	18.7	−12.6
November 30[a] Percent change	−3.1	−.5	−2.6	9.1	21.1	−12.0	5.7	15.3	−9.6
November 30[b] Percent change	−4.1	−1.5	−2.6	10.4	17.6	−7.2	6.3	12.6	−6.3

[a]Excludes period from 10/1 to 11/10.
[b]Includes period from 10/1 to 11/10.

The concept of percentage difference is presented conservatively; we compare absolute percentage changes rather than the percentage difference of percentage differences. That is, even for the full year we could say that the increase

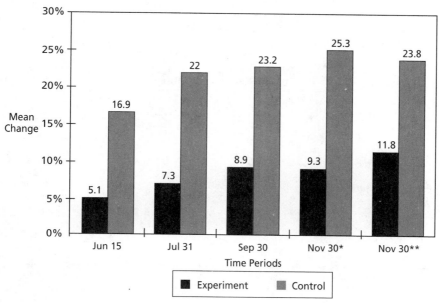

* Excludes period from 10/01/89 – 11/10/89
** Includes period from 10/01/89 – 11/10/89

Figure 3 Percentage Change from Baseline to Experimental Year in Total Crime Calls Per Hot Spot by Treatment Group and Period

in soft crime calls was 75 percent greater in the control group than in the experimental group (17.6 percent divided by 10.4 percent). By subtracting the percentage differences rather than dividing them, we focus the analysis on the magnitude of crime differences associated with more patrol rather than on its proportionate effect.

Figure 3 reports and illustrates the mean Time 1/ Time 2 differences in calls for the experimental and the control groups, using different cutoff dates for the experiment. It is clear that no matter what cutoff date is selected, the increase in citizen calls in the 55 control hot spots is substantially greater than in the 55 experimental hot spots. The absolute size of the difference at any one hot spot is quite modest, however—about one fewer crime call per month.

Dependent Variable 2: Differences
in Observed Crime and Disorder

The disorder analysis shows the most striking differences between the experimental and the control groups of any analyses. Table 3 displays the percentage of minutes of observations in different time periods in which disorderly public conduct was observed, by treatment group. For the entire experimental period, we find a significant relative difference of 25 percent less disorder in the

Table 3 Minutes of Disorder Observed in Experimental and Control Groups Compared with ANOVA Tests Controlled for Blocking

Period and Group	Minutes of Disorder	Minutes of Observations	Mean Ratio Per Hot Spot
Entire Year			
Experimental	5,855	225,991	.026
Control	8,623	226,295	.038
1-Tailed P Value			.022*
Until 6/15/89			
Experimental	2,267	121,363	.019
Control	4,493	122,736	.037
1-Tailed P Value			.006*
Until 7/31/89			
Experimental	3,545	148,617	.024
Control	5,915	149,889	.040
1-Tailed P Value			.007*

* $p < .10$

experimental than in the control group. For the two periods in which the experiment had the greatest integrity (ending June 15 or July 31), the effect was even stronger: half as much disorder was observed in the experimental group as in the control. The absolute difference of only 2 percent of all observed minutes versus 4 percent reflects a difference, in odds of encountering a disorder, between 1 in 50 and 1 [in] 25. For a resident or user of any cluster of addresses, this difference is noticeable and substantial.

This large relative difference is not due simply to a deterrent effect on disorder while police are present. Only 6 percent (209 of 3,513) of observed disorder events began while police were present across the entire observed sample. Koper (1995) reports significant differences in observed disorders between experimental and control groups when police are *not* present—up to 65 percent less criminal disorder in the experimentals.

An analysis of 13 specific types of disorder for the entire year shows that the greatest effects (in which ratios of control disorder incidents to experimental disorder incidents exceeded 1.5 to 1) were on the categories of person down (on the ground), drug activity, vandalism, solicitation for prostitution, and assault. We found no difference, however, in observations of persons apparently drunk or drugged, the largest single category of disorder (but perhaps the one theoretically least deterrable by police presence).

Table 3 displays the difference between experimental and control groups in observed disorder ratios. One-tailed P values are derived from ANOVA tests taking into account the five blocks used for the original random assignment of all 110 hot spots, only 100 of which were observed. All ten unobserved spots (five experimentals and five controls) were in the same randomization block because the blocks were stratified by volume of hard crime calls. That block is fortunately the largest, with 58 hot spots. Of which observations on ten (17%) are missing. The analysis simply treats those cases as missing data. No matter what time period we examine, these experimental year treatment group differences in observed disorder ratios are highly unlikely to be due to chance sampling fluctuations.

CONCLUSIONS

These results show clear, if modest, general deterrent effects of substantial increases in police presence in crime hot spots. Just as police strikes reveal major increases in crime due to major reductions in police presence (Makinen and Takala 1980; Russell 1975), our findings show that the difference in crime is proportionate to the difference in police. If urban police agencies decided to assign even higher priority to hot spot patrols, the magnitude of the crime reductions might be even greater.

This conclusion, however, presents two problems. One is that the effects of police on crime in hot spots may be attenuated by displacement of that crime to other locations. Absent any test of that interpretation, we cannot rule out the claim that more police will push crime around rather than preventing it. Yet in light of the strong conclusions drawn about the Kansas City Preventive Patrol Experiment (Kelling et al. 1974), even these results falsify the claim that patrol has no effect on crime at all.

Although we cannot conclude that these findings show a general deterrent effect of police presence throughout the community, we can claim evidence of place-specific "micro-deterrence." Even if police patrol pushes the crime elsewhere, it has been generally deterred by police presence in that location. The concept of deterrence is based on a rational calculation of risks and benefits. The prevention of crime and disorder in experimental hot spots, even when police are not there, is consistent with the hypotheses of apprehension and punishment in that place. This may be the same mechanism that causes displacement to a location where the fear of punishment is less, but it also fits the micro-general deterrence model precisely.

A second, different problem in recommending more hot spot patrols is that police may find directed patrol distasteful. The deterrent findings suggest that the more time police stay in a hot spot, the less opportunity they will have to exercise police powers. This is good for the community but can be boring for the police. Rather than preventing crime by keeping hot spots cool, most police would prefer to catch criminals after crime has already occurred and the harm has been done. Prevention lacks glamour; apprehensions offer the excitement of the chase. A substantial change to a community policing philosophy could make hot spot patrols more interesting, especially if police leave their cars and talk to frequent users of the hot spots. But historically the resistance to such a change has been formidable.

More detailed analysis suggests how to minimize police resistance without a major philosophical change. The greatest deterrent effect may be produced not by police staying in the same hot spot for extended periods, but by police roving from hot spot to hot spot, staying in each for only a limited time. In this issue, Koper (1995) reports a curvilinear effect of the duration of police presence in hot spots on the amount of time that elapses until the first disorder or crime event is observed after police leave. The optimal length of a hot spot patrol appears to be about 12 minutes. This should be well within the police boredom threshold, allowing them to move on to the next hot spot to see who might be causing trouble upon their arrival.

This experiment remains unreplicated, and may be limited in external validity to the time and place where it was conducted. We urge caution in generalizing its results to other settings. At the same time, we conclude that the experiment offers a more powerful and more externally valid test of the patrol deterrence hypothesis than the Kansas City experiment. At the very least, it is time for criminologists to stop saying "there is no evidence" that police patrol can affect crime.

NOTES

1. Examples of "hard crime" calls are holdup alarms, burglary, shooting, stabbing, auto theft, theft from autos, assault, and rape. Examples of "soft crime" calls are audible break-in alarms, disturbances, drunks, noise, unwanted persons at businesses, vandalism, prowlers, fights, and person down.

2. Some difficulty developed in this process because different definitions of places were used by the City of Minneapolis and by MAPINFO. We were able to reconcile most of these differences, usually by hand-plotting addresses on the computer map, but some 5 percent of the "hot' addresses were left out of our mapping analysis.

REFERENCES

Barr, R. and K. Pease (1990) "Crime Placement, Displacement, and Deflection." In M. Tonry and N. Morris (eds.), *Crime and Justice,* Vol. 12, pp. 227–318. Chicago: University of Chicago Press.

Boydstun, J. (1975) *San Diego Field Interrogation: Final Report.* Washington, DC: Police Foundation.

Buerger, M. E., E. G. Cohn, and A. J. Petrosino (1995) "Defining the Hot Spots of Crime: Operationalizing Theoretical Concepts for Field Research." In D. A. Weisburd and J. E. Eck (eds.), *Crime and Place: Crime Prevention Studies,* Vol. 4. [1995.] Monsey, NY: Criminal Justice Press.

Chaiken, J. (1978) "What is Known About Deterrent Effects of Police Activities," pp. 109–36. In J. Cromer, ed., *Preventing Crime.* Beverly Hills, CA: Sage.

Cohen, J. (1977) *Statistical Power Analysis for the Behavioral Sciences.* NY: Academic Press.

——— (1987) "Understanding Crime Displacement: An Application of Rational Choice Theory." *Criminology* 25: 933–47.

Dennis, M. L. (1988) "Implementing Randomized Field Experiments: An Analysis of Criminal and Civil Justice Research." Doctoral dissertation, Northwestern University, Department of Psychology.

Farrington, D. P. (1982) "Randomized Experiments on Crime and Justice." In M. Tonry and N. Morris (eds.), *Crime and Justice: An Annual Review of Research*, Vol. 4, pp. 257–308. Chicago: University of Chicago Press.

Felson, M. (1994) *Crime and Everyday Life*. Thousand Oaks, CA: Pine Forge Press.

Fielding, H. ([1751] 1977) *An Enquiry into the Causes of the Late Increase of Robbers*. Montclair, NJ: Patterson-Smith.

Fienberg, S., K. Larntz, and A. J. Reiss Jr. (1976) "Redesigning the Kansas City Preventive Patrol Experiment." *Evaluation* 3:124–31.

Freiman, J. A., T. C. Chalmers, H. Smith Jr., and R. R. Kuebler (1978) "The Importance of Beta, the Type II Error and Sample Size in the Design and Interpretation of the Randomized Controlled Trial: A Survey of 71 'Negative' Trials." *New England Journal of Medicine* 299:690–4.

Gottfredson, M. and T. Hirschi (1990) *A General Theory of Crime*. Stanford: Stanford University Press.

Green, L. (1995) "Cleaning Up Drug Hot Spots in Oakland, California: The Displacement and Diffusion Effects." *Justice Quarterly* [12:737–54].

Kelling, G., A. M. Pate, D. Dieckman, and C. Brown (1974a) *The Kansas City Preventive Patrol Experiment: Technical Report*. Washington, DC: Police Foundation.

——— (1974b) *The Kansas City Preventive Patrol Experiment: Technical Report*. Washington, DC: Police Foundation.

Klockars, C., ed. (1983) *Thinking about Police*. New York: McGraw-Hill.

Koper, C. (1995) "Just Enough Police Presence: Reducing Crime and Disorderly Behavior by Optimizing Patrol Time in Crime Hot Spots." *Justice Quarterly* [12:649–72].

Larson, R. C. (1975) "What Happened to Patrol Operations in Kansas City?" *Journal of Criminal Justice* 3:267–97.

Makinen, T. and H. Talaka (1980) "The 1976 Police Strike in Finland." *Scandinavian Studies in Criminology* 7:87–106.

Matthews, R. (1986) *Policing Prostitution: A Multi-Agency Approach*. London: Middlesex Polytechnic Centre for Criminology.

Pate, A. M. and G. L. Kelling (1975) "A Response to 'What Happened to Patrol Operations in Kansas City?'" *Journal of Criminal Justice* 3:299–30.

Press, S. J. (1971) *Some Effects of an Increase in Police Manpower in the 20th Precinct of New York*. New York: New York City RAND Institute.

Reiss, A. J., Jr. (1985) *Policing a City's Central District: The Oakland Story*. Washington, DC: National Institute of Justice.

Russell, F. (1975) *A City in Terror: 1919—The Boston Police Strike*. New York: Viking.

Schnelle, J. F., R. E. Kirchner Jr., J. D. Casey, P. H. Uselton Jr., and M. P. McNees (1977) "Patrol Evaluation Research: A Multiple-Baseline Analysis of Saturation Police Patrolling during Day and Night Hours." *Journal of Applied Behavior Analysis*, 10:33–40.

Sherman, L. W. (1986) "Policing Communities: What Works?" In A. J. Reiss Jr. and M. Tonry (eds.), *Communities and Crime*, pp. 343–86. Chicago: University of Chicago Press.

——— (1990) "Police Crackdowns: Initial and Residual Deterrence." In M. Tonry and N. Morris (eds.), *Crime and Justice*, Vol. 12, pp. 1–48. Chicago: University of Chicago Press.

Sherman, L. W., P. R. Gartin, and M. E. Buerger (1989) "Hot Spots of Predatory Crime: Routine Activities and the Criminology of Place." *Criminology* 27:27–55.

Sherman, L. W. and D. Weisburd (1995) "Does Patrol Prevent Crime? The Minneapolis Hot Spots Experiment." In Koicki Miyazawa and Setsuo Miyazawa (eds.), *Crime Presentation in the Urban Community*. Boston: Kluwer.

Skogan, W. (1990) *Disorder and Decline*. New York: Free Press.

Skolnick, J. and D. Bayley (1986) *The New Blue Line*. New York: Free Press.

Weinstein, G. S. and B. Levin (1989) "Effect of Crossover on the Statistical Power of Randomized Studies." *Annals of Thoracic Surgery* 48:490–5.

Weisburd, D. A., with Anthony Petrosino and Gail Mason (1993) "Design Sensitivity in Criminal Justice Experiments" Reassessing the Relationship between Sample Size and Statistical Power." In M. Tonry and N. Morris (eds.), *Crime and Justice,* Vol. 17, pp. 337–89. Chicago: University of Chicago Press.

Weisburd, D. A. and L. Green (1995) "Measuring Immediate Spatial Displacement: Methodological Issues and Problems." In D. Weisburd and J. E. Eck (eds.), *Crime and Place: Crime Prevention Studies,* Vol. 4, [1995.] Monsey, NY: Criminal Justice Press.

Zimring, F. (1978) "Policy Experiments in General Deterrence, 1970–75." In A. Blumstein, J. Cohen, and D. Nagin (eds.), *Deterrence and Incapacitation: Estimating the Effects of Criminal Sanctions on Crime Rates,* pp. 140–73. Washington, DC: National Academy of Sciences.

11

✴

Police Use
of Deadly Force

Research and Reform
JAMES J. FYFE

Police use of deadly force first became a major public issue in the 1960s when many urban riots were precipitated by police killings of citizens. Since then, departments have made significant reforms in their policies regarding the use of deadly force, and the U.S. Supreme Court in Tennessee v. Garner *(1985) voided the rule existing in about half the states that allowed the use of deadly force to apprehend unarmed, nonviolent, fleeing felony suspects. James Fyfe examines the factors that seem to distinguish the extensive use of deadly force in some departments.*

When police officers fire their guns, the immediate consequences of their decisions are realized at the rate of 750 feet per second and are beyond reversal by any level of official review. As most police recruits learn in the academy, the cop on the street . . . carries in his holster more power than has been granted the Chief Justice of the Supreme Court. When used injudiciously, this power has led to riot and additional death, civil and criminal litigation against police and their employers, and the ousters of police chiefs, elected officials, and entire city administrations. Even when used with great restraint, police deadly force has created polarization, suspicion, and distrust on the part of those who need the police most.

· · ·

Source: From James J. Fyfe, "Police Use of Deadly Force: Research and Reform," *Justice Quarterly* 5 (June 1988), pp. 165–166, 168–170, 171–174, 180–189, 199–205. Some footnotes and references deleted. Reprinted with Permission of the Academy of Criminal Justice Sciences.

LEGAL AND ADMINISTRATIVE
CONTROLS ON DEADLY FORCE

. . . The President's Commission on Law Enforcement and Administration of Justice looked carefully at police–community relations. In the report of its Task Force on the Police—which, in my view, remains the single most significant and most influential contribution to American police policy and practice to date— the commission made clear its dismay at the virtual absence of administrative policies to guide police officers' decisions to use deadly force (President's Commission 1967:189–190). In a report to the commission, Police Task Force chair Samuel Chapman cited the full text of one unnamed police department's policy on use of firearms as an illustration of the need for direction in this most critical matter of police discretion:

> Never take me out in anger; never put me back in disgrace (Chapman 1967).

Chapman also saw to it that the final report of the task force included a model administration policy on use of firearms (President's Commission 1967:188–189). This was not the first time he had championed this cause; in 1963 he and Thompson Crockett reported on a 1961 survey of seventy-one Michigan police departments serving populations of 10,000 or more. They found that

> 54 percent (27 of 50) of the agencies furnishing information had no written policies in effect to govern the use of firearms. These twenty-seven departments, which relied upon "oral policy," were asked to indicate the main points of oral instructions given to their officers regarding when to use firearms. Of the twenty-seven, only five departments mentioned such basic situations as self-defense and fleeing felons where firearms may be used. Thus, based on the reported practice in these Michigan cities, it would appear reasonable to regard with grave reservation that suitability of relying singularly upon "oral policy" (Chapman and Crockett 1963:42).

Further:

> "[W]hen to fire" is frequently trusted to the "judgment" or "discretion" of officers as individuals . . . (1963:41).

• • •

The Breadth of Law

In the absence of such policies, police shooting discretion generally was limited only by state criminal statutes or by case law defining justifiable homicide. These laws have several inadequacies. First, even the most restrictive state laws permit police to use their weapons in an extremely broad range of situations. Every state historically has permitted police officers to use deadly force to defend themselves or others against imminent death or serious physical harm, a provision that cannot be debated seriously. Indeed, except that generally they are obliged to attempt to retreat to safety before resorting to deadly force, American citizens enjoy the same justification for homicide. Because we ask the police to put their lives on the line in our behalf, it follows that they should enjoy this slight advantage over the rest of us.

Yet many states also have codified some variant of the common-law "fleeing felon" rule, which authorizes use of deadly force as a means of apprehending persons fleeing from suspected felonies. The Tennessee statute that eventually became the focus of *Tennessee v. Garner* (1985) illustrates the broadest category of such laws:

> *Resistance to Officer*—If after notice of the intention to arrest the [felony] defendant, he either flees or forcibly resists, the officer may use all the necessary means to effect the arrest (Tennessee Code Annotated sec. 40-7-108:55).

• • •

The manner in which felony suspects are pursued and apprehended has changed in important ways over the centuries. When the fleeing felon rule originated, those who typically pursued felons were ordinary male citizens who were obliged by law to respond to the *hue and cry* and to join in pursuit. Because they were usually armed only with clubs or knives, discharging their duty to arrest compelled them to overpower physically people who knew that arrest was likely to result in execution. These circumstances also are a far cry from more modern applications of the fleeing felon rule. The officer involved in *Garner,* for example, fired his fatal shot from the relative safety of 30 feet at the back of an unarmed, 5'4", 100-pound juvenile burglary suspect who, if apprehended alive, would likely have been sentenced to probation.

Debates about the merits of the *any* fleeing felon laws came to an abrupt end in 1985, when the Supreme Court ruled in *Garner* that the Tennessee statute, when applied against unarmed, nondangerous fleeing suspects, violated the Fourth Amendment's guarantees against unreasonable seizure. In his opinion for the majority, Justice White wrote that deadly force was a constitutional means of effecting arrest only when a felony "suspect threatens the officer with a weapon or there is probable cause to believe that he has committed a crime involving the infliction or threatened infliction of serious physical harm" (*Tennessee v. Garner,* 471 U.S. at 4). This decision affects the laws not only of the twenty-three states that followed the broad *any* fleeing felon rule; because Garner was a suspect in a nighttime residential burglary, it also affects the laws of several other states that included this offense under the limited category of offenses justifying deadly force for purposes of apprehension.

The Law as a Control on Professional Discretion

Although *Garner* moots some of the arguments about the great breadth of deadly force statutes, it does little to ameliorate a second and more general limitation of law in describing police shooting discretion: in no field of human endeavor does the criminal law alone define adequately the parameters of acceptable occupational behavior. In the course of their work, doctors, lawyers, psychologists, professors, soldiers, nursing home operators, truck drivers, government officials, and journalists can do many outrageous, unacceptable, and hurtful things without violating criminal law. In exchange for the monopolies on the activities performed by those in their crafts, the most highly developed of these professions keep their members' behavior in check by developing and enforcing codes of conduct that are both more specific and more restrictive than are criminal definitions. Who would submit to treatment by a surgeon whose choices in deciding how to deal with patients were limited only by the laws of homicide and assault?

Apply that logic to use of police firearms. Even post-*Garner,* no state law tells officers whether it is advisable to fire warning shots into the air on streets lined by high-rise buildings. The law provides no direction to officers who must decide quickly whether to shoot at people in moving vehicles and thereby risk turning them into speeding unguided missiles. The law related to police use of force, in short, is simply too vague to be regarded as a comprehensive set of operational guidelines.

RESISTANCE TO RULE MAKING
REGARDING DEADLY FORCE

Even so, many police administrators did not act on policy recommendations like Chapman's until their officers had become involved in shootings that (although noncriminal) generated community outcries and crises (Sherman 1983). Their sometimes vigorous resistance to change was rooted in many considerations. First, police authority to restrict shooting discretion more tightly than state law was uncertain. In 1971, for example, the Florida Attorney General issued a written opinion that administrative policies overriding the state's any fleeing felon law were legally impermissible (Florida Attorney General 1971:68–75); this narrow view of the separation of powers has been cast aside since in favor of more realistic interpretations of police chiefs' administrative prerogatives. In addition, apparently on the theory that jurors were unlikely to find police behavior unreasonable unless officers had violated their own departments' formal rules and policies, some police officials refrained from committing deadly force policies to paper. Time also has shown that this rather self-serving attempt to avoid accountability and liability was counterproductive: jurors don't need a piece of paper to tell them whether an individual officer acted reasonably, but typically they do find that a police department's failure to provide officers with such paper is inexcusable. Finally, many police officers feared that restrictive deadly force policies would endanger the public and the police; by removing whatever deterrent value inhered in the fleeing felon rule, such policies would result in an increase in crime and a decrease in police ability to apprehend fleeing criminals. Indeed, even when research suggested that this was not the case (Fyfe 1979), many police chiefs continued to regard restrictive deadly force policies as invitations to public accusations that they were "weak on crime" or had "handcuffed the police."

By now, however, the question of whether police should promulgate restrictive deadly force policies has been answered in the affirmative; at least among larger agencies, it is the rare department whose manual does not include such a policy. Social science research has played some part in easing police resistance to formulation of deadly force policy, and in the Supreme Court's *Garner* decision as well.

• • •

EXPLANATIONS OF VARIATIONS
IN POLICE HOMICIDE RATES

In attempts to explain why officers in some police departments are more likely than those in others to use deadly force and to kill, researchers generally have identified two sets of variables as salient. One is environmental and lies beyond the direct control of police administrators; the other is internal and is subject to control by police chiefs. The former category includes such variables as the level of violence among the constituencies of the police and the extent of lawful police authority to use deadly force. Included in the second category are such variables as general police operating philosophies and specific policies, both formal and unstated.

Environmental Explanations

Because police exposure to situations likely to precipitate shooting is presumably greatest where levels of general community violence are high, we would expect to find strong relationships between police homicide rates and measures of community violence and police contact with offenders. Perhaps the first researchers to explore such a hypothesis were Kania and Mackey (1977), who reported strong associations between the National Center for Health Statistics police homicide rates (however inaccurate) and rates of public homicide and violent crime across the states. In their intercity study, Sherman and Langworthy (1979) found the same kinds of associations between police homicide rates and such measures of potential police–citizen violence as gun density and rates of arrest for all offenses and for violent offenses. Finally, I (Fyfe 1980b) found strong associations between rates of shooting by onduty officers and rates of public homicide and arrests for violent crime across twenty police subjurisdictions within New York City.

There is a statistically significant association ($p = .002$) between the police homicide rates shown in Table 1 and the most easily derivable measure of public violence, the corresponding public homicide rates. As even a cursory examination of the table would suggest, however (is New Orleans really four times as violent as Washington, D.C., for example?), this measure accounts for only 13 percent of the variation in police homicide rates ($r = .37$; $r^2 = .13$).

The table also suggests that the second environmental factor, the law of police deadly force, is of little help in explaining variation in police homicide rates.

Table 1 Mean Annual Rate of Police Homicide per 1,000 Officers by Geographic Region and City, 1975–1983

	Rate per 1,000	Number		Rate per 1,000	Number
Northeast	1.39	480	Memphis	3.75	42
Boston	1.19	22	Miami	3.50	25
Buffalo	0.50	5	Nashville	3.28	28
Newark	1.90	22	New Orleans	6.80	91
New York	1.36	295	Norfolk	1.68	9
Philadelphia	1.66	116	Tampa	3.14	17
Pittsburgh	0.81	10	Washington	1.55	56
Rochester	1.78	10	West	2.85	751
North Central	2.24	628	Albuquerque	1.94	9
Akron	0.97	4	Austin	0.87	4
Chicago	1.71	197	Dallas	4.32	78
Cincinnati	1.88	17	Denver	2.26	28
Cleveland	2.59	44	El Paso	1.88	11
Columbus	2.94	28	Fort Worth	1.91	12
Detroit	3.33	143	Honolulu	0.37	5
Indianapolis	3.75	34	Houston	4.73	130
Kansas City	2.71	29	Long Beach	6.10	34
Milwaukee	0.86	16	Los Angeles	3.05	192
Minneapolis	1.62	11	Oakland	5.22	30
Omaha	2.42	12	Oklahoma City	4.79	30
St. Louis	3.61	64	Phoenix	1.84	27
St. Paul	0.42	2	Portland, OR	0.81	5
Toledo	1.86	11	Sacramento	0.44	2
Wichita	4.33	16	San Antonio	2.74	28
South	3.10	447	San Diego	2.87	32
Atlanta	3.28	37	San Francisco	1.40	22
Baltimore	1.82	53	San Jose	2.62	19
Birmingham	5.19	31	Seattle	1.86	17
Charlotte	1.31	7	Tucson	3.08	15
Jacksonville	7.17	61	Tulsa	3.54	21
Louisville	3.11	20	Totals	2.24	2,236

SOURCE: Derived from Kenneth Matulia, *A Balance of Forces,* 2d ed. (Gaithersburg, Md.: International Association of Chiefs of Police, 1985), pp. A–4, A–5.

If the law were operative here, one would not expect to find (for example) that officers in Long Beach (rate = 6.10) killed citizens twice as often as their colleagues across the city line in Los Angeles (rate = 3.05), or that the police homicide rate in Jacksonville (7.17) was twice as high as in the more notorious Miami (3.50).

Internal Organizational Explanations

Certainly the police reflect the violence of the environments in which they work, and the police are duty-bound to operate within the law. Yet the limits of the law have been discussed already, and it is apparent that other things also are at work here. More specifically, as Uelman (1973) suggested in his research on variations in shooting rates among fifty police departments in Los Angeles County, it is clear that such internal organizational variables as the philosophies, policies, and practices of individual police chiefs and supervisors account for a considerable amount of variation in police homicide rates. Uelman's conclusion has been buttressed by studies (Fyfe 1979; Gain 1971; Meyer 1980; Milton, Halleck, Lardner, and Abrecht 1977; Scharf and Binder 1983) that report, with varying degrees of rigor and certainty, that reductions in police shooting frequency and changes in police shooting patterns have followed implementation of restrictive administrative policies on deadly force and weapons use.

A Case in Point

Without detailed analysis of the context and content of police officials' utterances and policy statements, it is impossible in an essay of this type to sort out their effects in a manner that would satisfy methodological purists. Even so, the effect of police operating philosophy and policy on police deadly force has been most striking in Philadelphia. There the police commissioner in 1970 and 1971 was Frank Rizzo, the flamboyant hard-liner[1] who went on to serve as mayor from 1972 through 1979. In 1973, when the Pennsylvania legislature modified its deadly force statute to prohibit shooting at fleeing persons who were not suspected of "forcible felonies" (Pennsylvania Statutes Annotated 1973), the Philadelphia Police Department (PPD) abolished its former restrictive policy on deadly force on the grounds that the legislature had not defined "forcible felonies" adequately. From that point until Rizzo left office, PPD adopted an operating style in which police were effectively free do anything with their guns, as long as they did not use them to resolve their own personal disputes.[2]

Figure 1 suggests that some PPD officers took great advantage of this freedom. During 1972, the last full year in which PPD operated under a restrictive deadly force policy, the PPD homicide rate per 1,000 officers was 1.47 (with twelve deaths resulting); the rate jumped to 2.87 (twenty-three deaths) in 1973 and peaked at 3.52 (twenty-nine deaths) in 1974. In 1976, when the city was cooperating in a federal court request to develop means of ending abuse of citizens, the police homicide rate dipped briefly to 1.35. In 1977, after the Supreme Court dismissed the case that had resulted in this agreement, the rate doubled (deaths rose from eleven to twenty-one). In 1981, the first full year of a new restrictive deadly force policy,[3] the rate decreased to 0.80 and remained relatively low during the next two years. Overall, the PPD police homicide rates were 2.09 while Rizzo was police commissioner, 2.29 while he was mayor, and 1.05 after he was out of office (as compared to the annual PPD homicide rate of 0.61 over 1950–1960; see Robin 1963).

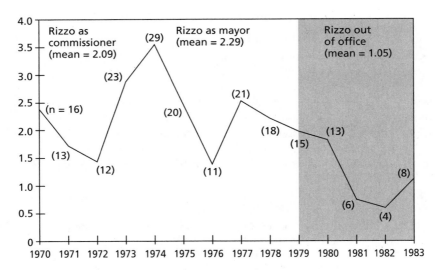

Figure 1 Fatal shootings per 1,000 police officers, Philadelphia, 1970–1983

SOURCE: Data for 1970–1978 from Philadelphia Police Department, Homicide Division, *Shooting Files*; 1979–1983 from Matulia (1985), p. A.5.

These are powerful numbers. Indeed, when I attempted to quantify Rizzo's influence (R) over PPD operations . . . I found that the extent of his authority was a strong predictor of the annual PPD police homicide rate ($r = .72$; $p = .002$), and that adding the public homicide rate to this equation added only marginally to predictive ability ($r = .26$; $R = .78$). In short—and except for the bizarre MOVE incident—knowing what Frank Rizzo was doing was far more valuable for estimating the PPD police homicide rate than were data on public homicides.

ELECTIVE AND NONELECTIVE SHOOTINGS

This analysis obviously suffers from the body count flaw; it includes only fatal shootings rather than all incidents of deadly force by PPD officers. Further, although I am convinced otherwise, many researchers will argue that my analysis of PPD homicides may have omitted some critical variable or set of variables. In addition, and if we assume for the moment that I am correct in asserting that Frank Rizzo was *the* critical variable in all Philadelphia police issues during the years in question, analysis of trends in police use of deadly force typically involves far more sophistication than when police or government administrators are as straightforward as Rizzo in espousing and executing their views.

In less extreme cases, examining in detail the circumstances of shootings is perhaps the most direct way to measure the relative effects of organizational and environmental variables on officers' use of deadly force. For these purposes it is useful to conceive of police shootings as incidents on a continuum that runs from *elective* situations, in which officers may decide to shoot or to refrain from shooting at no risk to themselves or to others, to *nonelective* situations, in which officers have no choice but to shoot or die (see Fyfe 1981c).

By these standards, Edward Garner's death—the shot at the back of the fleeing, unarmed, nonthreatening, property crime suspect who presents no apparent danger to anybody—was the prototypical elective shooting. Shootings such as this are influenced by internal police organizational variables; Garner and others in Memphis were shot in such circumstances because the police department encouraged or tolerated such action. Yet, as in the case of the Memphis Police Department in 1979, the police also can put an end to such shootings by simple administrative fiat (Memphis Police Department 1979). Shootings at the other end of the continuum are a different manner; no police department can direct officers to refrain from shooting when failure to do so may mean imminent death. Formal discretionary guidelines are of little relevance in such situations because, by any reasonable standard, the officers involved have only one choice.

Between these two extremes are more ambiguous police shootings that may be influenced to varying degrees by such variables as general organizational culture and the presence or absence of training in tactics. It is my experience, for example, that officers in some departments sometimes find themselves in harm's way because they respond to encouragement, both formal and from peers, to take charge of threatening situations quickly with as little assistance (and as little inconvenience to colleagues) as possible. In other departments, the operative norm encourages officers to use caution, to take cover, and to search for non-lethal means of resolving potential violence. These midrange shootings typically involve officers who, for whatever reasons, find themselves dangerously close to individuals who are armed with knives or other weapons, who attempt to run them down with vehicles, or who are determined to overpower them through mere physical force. Thus, in decreasing order of potential lethality, we can derive the following typology of police shootings, which will be useful in reexamining data already published elsewhere:

Gun assault: Citizen(s) armed with gun uses or attempts to use it against police.

Knife or other assault: Citizens(s) armed with cutting instrument or other weapon (for example, bat, chain, club, hammer, vehicle) uses or attempts to use it against police.

Physical assault: Citizen(s) attacks or attempts to attack police with fists, feet, or other purely physical means.

Unarmed, no assault: Unarmed citizen(s) makes no threat and attempts no attack on police or on any other person.

As inexact as this typology may be, it does allow for some assessment of the relative extent to which police shootings are influenced by environmental and internal organizational forces. One would expect, for example, that shootings by officers whose discretion is limited carefully would tend toward the nonelective end of this continuum, and that a great percentage of shootings by officers in less stringently regulated departments would be elective.

This said, we move to Table 2, which demonstrates great variation in the nature of reported shootings across Chicago, New York, and Philadelphia ($p <$ .0001). Even though the data included in the table are not absolutely compatible (my coding scheme for New York and Philadelphia includes accidental shootings and others that Geller and Karales [1981] treated separately, and that are described in note b of the table), it is clear that shootings occurred in significantly different circumstances in the places and times included in the table. About eight in ten of the shootings in Chicago and New York involved citizens who reportedly attacked officers with guns (Chicago = 62.1%; New York = 53.0%) or other weapons (Chicago = 15.3%; New York = 34.0%), but fewer than six in ten Philadelphia shootings (39% guns; 19.6% knives and other) fell into either of these two categories. At the other end of the continuum, the percentage of "unarmed, no-assault" incidents in New York City, which operated under an essentially "defense of life only" deadly force policy during much of the period studied (see Fyfe 1979), was considerably smaller than in either Chicago or Philadelphia (8.5% versus 20.9% and 24.9%, respectively), where police were given relatively more freedom to use their guns in elective situations. Therefore, not surprisingly, the rates presented on the table also indicate that the greatest discrepancies among these three police agencies' shooting experiences are found at the elective end of our continuum ("unarmed, no-assault" rates from New York, Philadelphia, and Chicago = 0.52, 2.94, and 1.36, respectively).

The rates in this table also illustrate the dangers of attempting to describe deadly force in terms of body counts. The three departments included in Table 2 do not appear to differ much in regard to deadly force resulting in fatalities (1971–1975 police homicide rates per 1,000 officers = 2.39 and 2.42 for New York and Philadelphia; 1974–1978 Chicago rate = 1.97). When incidents resulting in nonfatal wounds are added to these figures, however, the differences among these cities grow and change direction (rates = 6.09, 7.57, and 11.82 for New York, Chicago, and Philadelphia). In other words, Philadelphia police officers were only slightly more likely than New York or Chicago officers to shoot and kill citizens during the periods included in Table 2, but they were nearly twice as likely to shoot and kill *or wound* citizens. Further, because Chicago police apparently maintained records of missed shots only from 1975 through 1977 (Geller and Karales 1981:162) and because PPD did not do so at all during the period studied, there is no way to determine with any precision how great these discrepancies might have been if we had been able to include incidents in which officers' bullets failed to hit their targets.

Even so, there is reason to believe that the differences among these cities would be even more striking if such data were available. First, police departments that permit shooting in elective situations are likely to experience high percentages of missed shots. Just as nonelective shootings are extremely dangerous for the officers involved, they are also very dangerous for their opponents. It is far easier to hit someone who is standing 8 or 10 feet away with a shotgun

Table 2 Shooting Incident Types in New York City, Philadelphia, and Chicago

Shooting Type	New York 1971–1975[a]	Philadelphia 1971–1975[a]	Chicago 1974–1978[b]
Gun assault	53.0%	39.0%	62.1%
	(n = 481)	(n = 185)	(n = 264)
Rate[c]	3.20	4.60	4.02
Knife/other assault	34.0%	19.6%	15.3%
	(n = 308)	(n = 93)	(n = 65)
Rate	2.07	2.32	0.99
Physical assault	4.5%	16.5%	1.7%
	(n = 41)	(n = 78)	(n = 7)
Rate	0.28	1.95	0.11
Unarmed, no assault	8.5%	24.9%	20.9%
	(n = 77)	(n = 118)	(n = 89)
Rate	0.52	2.94	1.36
Totals	100.0%	100.0%	100.0%
	(n = 907)	(n = 474)	(n = 497)[d]
Rate	6.09	11.82	7.57

Chi-square = 216.45

p < .0001

[a]SOURCE: Fyfe (1988). Includes all reported incidents in which police officers shot and wounded or killed others.

[b]Derived from Geller and Karales (1981:103). Includes the number of persons shot rather than the number of incidents in which persons were shot. Excludes persons shot and wounded or killed for the following reasons:

Reason for shooting	n	Rate[c]
Not ascertained	6	0.09
Stray bullet	17	0.26
Mistaken identity	4	0.06
Accidental	52	0.79
Other intentional	7	0.11
Civilian appeared to display an unknown object without pointing it.	5	0.08
Civilian appeared to possess an unknown concealed object without pointing it.	7	0.11
Total	98	1.49

[c]Mean annual rate per 1,000 officers.

[d]Total number of incidents in which citizens were shot.

in his hands than someone who is running away in the dark (see, e.g., Horvath and Donahue 1982:87). Second, such departments also tend to experience high percentages of woundings in relation to fatalities. The four-to-one ratio of non-fatal to fatal wounds for Philadelphia did not result from any extraordinary humaneness on the part of PPD officers. It came about because an extraordinary percentage of the people shot at by the Philadelphia police were running targets; the officers fired at ranges so great that they were unable to hit the center body mass at which they were trained to shoot.

The data in my own work and in Geller and Karales's (1981) study support these assertions. The differences among police homicide rates for these cities are relatively small, but become more marked when nonfatal woundings are added to the equation. Finally, when the 1975–1977 data on all Chicago police shootings at citizens (n = 1,145; Geller and Karales 1981:162) are compared to the corresponding 1971–1975 data (n = 2,234; Fyfe 1978:390), the derived shooting rates per 1,000 officers differ greatly (Chicago = 29.07; New York = 14.09). It is difficult to imagine that inclusion of data from Philadelphia—where officers had by far the most liberal shooting license among these three cities—would not skew this contrast even further.

• • •

CONCLUSIONS

On balance, and even though the available data are skimpier than we would like, it appears that the frequency of police use of deadly force is influenced heavily by organizational philosophies, expectations, and policies; that levels of community violence are marginal predictors, useful chiefly when organizational variables may be held constant (as in studying a single police jurisdiction); and that variations in law play a role in determining frequency of deadly force only when administrators abdicate their responsibility to see that propriety is not limited only by statutory definitions of criminal assault and homicide.

For this last reason, *Tennessee* v. *Garner* probably is not as sweeping as many suspect. By the time this case was decided, virtually all major police departments had adopted their own administrative policies that were at least as restrictive as the *violent* felon rule propounded by the Supreme Court. In his decision for the majority, in fact, Justice White made repeated suggestions that the Court's holding was not a major intervention into police administrative prerogatives because most large police departments already were in compliance. Indeed, the fact that Memphis itself had abolished administratively the *any* fleeing felon rule five years before the case came to the Court weakened seriously the city attorney's oral argument that the *any* fleeing felon rule was a valuable adjunct to the effectiveness of law enforcement. Thus it is likely that the major effects of *Garner* will be (and have been) felt in smaller police jurisdictions where, as Neilsen (1983) suggests, administrative rule making related to deadly force has been less frequent.

Still, although *Garner* itself will not revolutionize American law enforcement, the process leading up to it has altered dramatically the police community's view of the whole deadly force issue. As recently as 1980, for example, attendees at the annual International Association of Chiefs of Police (IACP) meeting voted "by a 4-to-1 margin reaffirming [the association's] support of laws and policies permitting police to shoot fleeing felony suspects" (*St. Louis Post-Dispatch* 1980). In the same year, the International Union of Police Associations passed a resolution seeking to remove Patrick Murphy "as President of a private corporation known as the Police Foundation and to boycott any organization or foundation that supports the Police Foundation" because Murphy had criticized "police officers' use of weapons," "notoriously accused our nation's police officers as the immediate cause of the riots that took place in the 60's," indicated that four police officers who had been acquitted in a Miami beating death (a verdict that sparked Miami's Liberty City riot) had committed the beating of which they were accused, and had "further stated that a restrictive shooting policy not only reduces police shootings of civilians but does not result in any increased danger to police officers or a rise in crime" (International Union of Police Associations 1980).

By 1982, however, IACP had promulgated a model policy on police use of force that would permit shooting at fleeing felony suspects only when "freedom is reasonably believed to represent an *imminent* threat of grave bodily harm or death to the officer or other person(s)" (Matulia 1982:164; emphasis in original). In 1983 IACP joined in recommending that the Commission on Accreditation for Law Enforcement Agencies adopt its present strict *defense of life only* standard for deadly force policies (1983:1–2). In 1984 the Police Foundation's *amici curiae* brief against Tennessee and the Memphis Police Department in *Garner* was joined by "nine national and international associations of police and criminal justice professionals, the chiefs of police associations of two states, and thirty-one law enforcement chief executives" (Police Foundation 1984). Equally significant, and contrary to past practice in cases of substantial constitutional issues involving the police, no *amicus* briefs were filed on the other side of the case. In 1985, when *Garner* was decided, IACP's executive director hailed it as a great step forward. This remarkable turnaround and disavowal of tradition and professional dogma was stimulated in large measure by research findings that suggested that the value of broad police shooting authority was overrated; rarely have researchers had such an effect on criminal justice policies and practices.[4]

Research regarding the people involved in incidents of deadly force by police generally shows that blacks and other minorities are overrepresented at both ends of police guns. Explanations for these disparities vary, but at least by my interpretation they typically involve embarrassing realities over which police have little control. Black citizens are overrepresented in the most violent and most criminogenic neighborhoods; individual black officers, who are still underrepresented in American policing generally, are far more likely than individual white officers to draw the most hazardous police duties in those same neighborhoods. Until these realities are altered, we can expect continuing minority disproportion in deadly force statistics no matter how stringently police officers' discretion is controlled.

This probability, I think, illustrates the central theme that may be drawn from all the research on deadly force reviewed in this essay. Police officers and the people at whom they shoot are simply actors in a much larger play. When police officers' roles in this play are defined carefully by their administrators and when the officers have been trained well to perform those roles, their individual characteristics mean little; the young cop, the old cop, the male cop, the female cop, the white cop, and the black cop all know what is expected of them, and they do it. When such clear expectations are not provided, officers improvise, and often we give their performances bad reviews. Yet because we put them on the stage in the first place, we also should criticize ourselves for failing to ensure that they have been directed adequately. When black children's roles are defined so clearly by the conditions in which so many are raised, we should expect that some will end their lives at the wrong end of police guns. We should not blame the police for that; we should blame ourselves for creating the stages on which so many black lives are played out.

EDITOR'S POSTSCRIPT

What has been the impact of the Supreme Court's ruling in *Tennessee* v. *Garner* that the police may not use deadly force against a suspected fleeing, unarmed felon? In a 1990 study Fyfe and Walker found that only four of the thirty-one states affected by the *Garner* decision had made statutory changes to bring their laws in line with the Court's interpretation of the Fourth Amendment, yet the authors argue that police officers now know the rules and that *Garner* types of shootings are a thing of the past. From their research the authors draw the following conclusions (Fyfe 1991):

1. Statutes relating to deadly force are irrelevant to officers on the street. Like other professionals or craftsmen, police behavior is most directly affected by organizational and professional guidelines that place limits on their discretion.

2. Most likely changes have not been made in state laws because legislators are reluctant to build political records indicating that they have voted for restrictions that would appear to "handcuff" the police.

3. The decline in fleeing felon shootings is apparently the result of modifications to guidelines made by police administrators.

4. The post-*Garner* impact thus reinforces the belief that control of police street-level decisions is in the chief's office rather than in the legislature's, prosecutor's, or attorney general's chambers.

NOTES

1. Former Mayor Rizzo perhaps is best known for his advice that officers should "break their heads before they break yours." My favorite Rizzoism, however, dates from late 1979, when, in response to a question about a United States Justice Department suit against his administration and the Philadelphia Police Department, Rizzo commented on ABC-TV's *Nightline* that "when I became mayor, the Philadelphia Police Department had only one shotgun. Now we've got enough guns to invade Cuba and win."

2. Despite extensive review of PPD reports of all firearm discharges resulting in injury or death from 1970 through 1978, for example, I can find only two cases that re-

sulted in departmental discipline against officers who had fired their guns while on duty. In one case an officer shot and killed his wife in a police station during an apparent argument over the disposition of his paycheck; the other resulted in the two-day suspension of an officer who had fired unnecessary shots into the air.

3. The policy (Philadelphia Police Department 1980) was promulgated on April 2, 1980. It authorizes officers to shoot in defense of life and, when no alternative exists, to apprehend fleeing suspects who officers know are in possession of deadly weapons that they have used or threatened to use, or who have committed forcible felonies. Of

these last, PPD's position was as follows:

> Until forcible felony is defined by statute, the Police Department adopts the position that forcible felony includes the crimes of Murder, Voluntary Manslaughter, Rape, Robbery, Kidnapping, Involuntary Deviate Sexual Intercourse, Arson, Burglary of a Private Residence, Aggravated Assault Causing Serious Bodily Injury (Davis 1980).

4. This observation is tempered by the knowledge that increased governmental exposure to civil liability for failure to supervise police officers adequately has served also as a major stimulant to reform of deadly force policies and practices. Almost certainly, *Monell v. New York City Department of Social Services* (1978), in which the Supreme Court holds government entities liable when unreasonable policies and practices are proved to be the causes of constitutional violations suffered at the hands of individual agents, has had more effect on police operations than have any of the Court's more celebrated rulings related to criminal procedure.

REFERENCES

Chapman, S. G. (1967). *Police Firearms Use Policy.* Report to the President's Commission on Law Enforcement and Administration of Justice. Washington, D.C.: United States Government Printing Office.

Chapman, S. G., and T. S. Crockett (1963). "Gunsight Dilemma: Police Firearms Policy." *Police* 6:40–45.

Davis, A. J. (1980). Letter to Burton A. Rose of Peruto, Ryan, and Vitullo, counsel for the Philadelphia chapter of the Fraternal Order of Police, October 15.

Florida Attorney General (1971). *Annual Report.* In Herman Goldstein (ed.), *Policing a Free Society.* Cambridge, Mass.: Ballinger, p. 127.

Fyfe, J. J. (1978). "Shots Fired: An Analysis of New York City Police Firearms Discharge." Ph.D. dissertation, State University of New York at Albany. Ann Arbor: University Microfilms.

———— (1979). "Administrative Interventions on Police Shooting Discretion: An Empirical Examination." *Journal of Criminal Justice* 7:309–324.

———— (1980a). "Always Prepared: Police Off-Duty Guns." *Annals of the American Academy of Political and Social Science* 452:72–81.

———— (1980b). "Geographic Correlates of Police Shooting: A Microanalysis." *Journal of Research in Crime and Delinquency* 17:101–113

———— (1981a). "Observation on Police Deadly Force." *Crime and Delinquency* 27:376–389.

———— (1981b). "Race and Extreme Police-Citizen Violence." In R. L. McNeely and C. E. Pope (eds.), *Race, Crime, and Criminal Justice.* Beverly Hills: Sage, pp. 89–108.

———— (1981c). "Toward a Typology of Police Shootings." In J. J. Fyfe (ed.), *Contemporary Issues in Law Enforcement.* Beverly Hills: Sage, pp. 136–151.

———— (1981d). "Who Shoots? A Look at Officer Race and Police Shooting." *Journal of Police Science and Administration* 9:367–382.

———— (1982). "Blind Justice: Police Shootings in Memphis." *Journal of Criminal Law and Criminology* 73:707–722.

———— (1986). "Enforcement Workshop: The Supreme Court's New Rules for Police Use of Deadly Force." *Criminal Law Bulletin* 22:62–68.

———— (1988). "Police Shooting Environment and License." In J. E. Scott and T. Hirschi (eds.), *Controversial Issues in Crime and Justice.* Beverly Hills: Sage, pp. 79–94.

———— (1991). Communication to the editor.

Fyfe, J. J., and Jeffery T. Walker (1990). "*Garner* Plus Five Years: An Examination of Supreme Court Intervention into Police Discretion and Legislative

Prerogatives." *American Journal of Criminal Justice* 14:167–188.

Gain, C. (1971). "Discharge of Firearms Policy: Effecting Justice through Administrative Regulation." Unpublished statement, Oakland, Calif., December 23.

Geller, W. A., and K. J. Karales (1981). *Split-Second Decisions: Shootings of and by Chicago Police.* Chicago: Chicago Law Enforcement Study Group.

Horvath, F., and M. Donahue (1982). *Deadly Force: An Analysis of Shootings by Police in Michigan, 1976–1981.* East Lansing: Michigan State University.

Illinois Revised Statutes (1975). Chapter 38, Para. 2–8.

International Union of Police Associations (1980). *Resolution of July 15, 1980.* Washington, D.C.: mimeo.

Kania, R. R. E., and W. C. Mackey (1977). "Police Violence as a Function of Community Characteristics." *Criminology* 15:27–48.

Matulia, K. R. (1982). *A Balance of Forces.* Gaithersburg, Md.: International Association of Chiefs of Police.

———— (1985). *A Balance of Forces,* 2d ed. Gaithersburg, Md.: International Association of Chiefs of Police.

Memphis Police Department (1979). *General Order 95–79, Deadly Force Policy,* July 16.

Meyer, M. W. (1980). *Report to the Los Angeles Board of Police Commissioners on Police Use of Deadly Force in Los Angeles: Officer-Involved Shootings, Part IV.* Los Angeles: Los Angeles Board of Police Commissioners.

Milton, C., J. W. Halleck, J. Lardner, and G. L. Abrecht (1977). *Police Use of Deadly Force.* Washington, D.C.: Police Foundation.

Monell v. New York City Department of Social Services. (1978), 436 U.S. 658.

Nielsen, E. (1983). "Policy on the Police Use of Deadly Force: A Cross-National Analysis." *Journal of Police Science and Administration* 11:104–108.

Pennsylvania Statutes Annotated (1973).

Philadelphia Police Department (1980). *Directive* 10, April 2.

Police Foundation, Joined by Nine National and International Associations of Police and Criminal Justice Professionals, the Chiefs of Police Associations of Two States, and Thirty-One Law Enforcement Chief Executives (1984). *Amici Curiae Brief in Tennessee v. Garner.* United States Supreme Court 83-1035, 83-1070. Washington, D.C.: August 6.

President's Commission on Law Enforcement and Administration of Justice (1967). *Task Force Report: The Police.* Washington, D.C.: United States Government Printing Office.

Robin, G. (1963). "Justifiable Homicide by Police." *Journal of Criminal Law, Criminology and Police Science* (May/June): 225–231.

Scharf, P., and A. Binder (1983). *The Badge and the Bullet.* New York: Praeger.

Sherman, L. W. (1980). "Execution without Trial: Police Homicide and the Constitution." *Vanderbilt Law Review* 33:71–110.

———— (1983). "Reducing Police Gun Use: Critical Events, Administrative Policy and Organizational Change." In Maurice Punch (ed.), *The Management and Control of Police Organizations.* Cambridge, Mass.: M.I.T. Press, pp. 98–125.

Sherman, L. W., and R. Langworthy (1979). "Measuring Homicide by Police Officers." *Journal of Criminal Law and Criminology* 70:546–560.

St. Louis Post-Dispatch (1980). "The Police Chiefs on Deadly Force." Editorial, September 21:16.

Tennessee Code Annotated (1977).

Tennessee v. Garner (1985). 471 U.S. 1, 105 S. Ct. 1694, 85 L. Ed. 1.

Uelman, G. (1973). "Varieties of Public Policy: A Study of Police Policy Regarding the Use of Deadly Force in Los Angeles County." *Loyola of Los Angeles Law Review* 6:1–65.

PART III

Prosecution

For many years the radio serial *Mr. District Attorney* held audiences spellbound as its namesake sought "not only to prosecute to the limit of the law all persons accused of crime within this county, but to defend with equal vigor the rights and privileges of all its citizens." In real life, there are counterparts to the crusading fictional prosecutor. Over the years a number of political leaders at the national and state levels have come to prominence as fighting prosecutors. Many have based their campaigns for higher political office on reputations gained from widely publicized investigations or trials. The prosecutors' influence flows directly from their legal duties but must be understood within the context of the administrative and political environment of the system.

POWER OF THE PROSECUTOR

Prosecutors are powerful because they are concerned with all aspects of the criminal justice process. By contrast, other decision makers are involved in only certain segments of the process. From the time of arrest to the final disposition of a case, prosecutors can make a variety of decisions that will largely determine a defendant's fate. The prosecutor chooses the cases to be prosecuted, selects the charges that are to be brought into the courtroom, recommends the bail amount required for pretrial release, approves any negotiated agreements made with the defendant, and urges judges to impose particular sentences.

Throughout the justice process, prosecutors have links with the other actors in the system—police, defense attorneys, judges—and these relationships shape the prosecutor's decisions. Prosecutors may, for example, recommend bail amounts and sentences that demonstrate their understanding of and support for particular judges' preferences. In front of "tough" judges, prosecutors may make "tough" recommendations. However, they are likely to modify their arguments presented to judges who favor leniency or rehabilitation. Likewise, the other actors in the system may adjust their decisions and actions to solidify their relationships with the prosecutor. Police officers' investigation and arrest practices are likely to reflect their understanding of the prosecutor's priorities. Thus, prosecutors influence the decisions of others in the criminal justice process while also shaping their own actions to preserve and reinforce their relationships with police, defense attorneys, and judges.

Prosecutors gain additional power from the fact that their decisions and actions are confidential and hidden from public view. For example, a prosecutor and a defense attorney may strike a bargain outside the courtroom whereby the prosecutor reduces a charge in exchange for a guilty plea or drops a charge altogether if the defendant agrees to seek psychiatric help. In such instances the justice system reaches a decision about a case in a way that is nearly invisible to the public.

State laws do little to limit or guide prosecutors' decisions. Most laws describe the prosecutor's responsibility in such vague terms as "prosecuting all crimes and civil actions to which state or county may be party." Such laws do not instruct the prosecutor about which cases must be prosecuted and which cases can be dismissed. The prosecutor possesses significant discretion to make such decisions without direct interference from either the law or other actors in the justice system. When people attempt to challenge prosecutors' decisions as improper, judges generally reject such claims by demonstrating their acceptance of broad prosecutorial discretion as a legitimate, important component of the criminal justice process.

Because most local prosecutors are elected officials, their decisions may be responsive to changes in public opinion. When prosecutors feel that the community no longer considers that an act proscribed by law constitutes criminal behavior, they will probably refuse to prosecute or will expend every effort to convince the complainant that prosecution should be avoided. Thus, in some communities prostitution may be vigorously prosecuted while in others it is ignored while police and prosecutors focus on other crimes. The fact that about three-fourths of American prosecutors serve counties with populations of fewer than 100,000 accentuates the potential influence of public opinion. Local pressures may bear heavily on the single prosecution official in a community. Without the backing of public opinion, law enforcement and prosecution officers are powerless. Prosecutors develop policies that reflect community attitudes, especially with regard to victimless crimes such as marijuana smoking, petty gambling, and prostitution. A New York prosecutor has remarked, "We are pledged to the enforcement of the law, but we have to use our heads in the process."

PLEA BARGAINING

For the vast majority of cases, plea bargaining is the most important step in the criminal justice process. Very few cases go to trial; instead, a negotiated guilty plea developed through the interactions of prosecutors, defense lawyers, and judges determines what will finally happen to most criminal defendants. It is generally accepted that up to 90 percent of felony defendants in the United States plead guilty.

Thirty-five years ago, plea bargaining was not publicly acknowledged or discussed; it was the criminal justice system's "little secret." There were doubts about its constitutionality, and it clashed with the idealized image of the courtroom as a place where prosecutors and defense attorneys engaged in legal battles as the jury witnessed the emergence of "truth" amid the "smoke and noise" of courtroom "combat." Yet the quick and quiet resolution of cases through negotiated guilty pleas historically has been common. Indeed, scholars have documented that guilty pleas have been a primary means of finalizing criminal cases at least since the late 1800s. Scholars began to shed light on plea bargaining in the 1960s, and the U.S. Supreme Court openly acknowledged and endorsed the process in the 1970s.

Defendants have great incentives to plea-bargain because they can have their cases completed more quickly and they can participate in establishing a definite punishment rather than facing the uncertainty of a judge's discretionary sentencing decision after a trial. Moreover, in exchange for pleading guilty, the defendant is likely to receive less than the maximum punishment that might have been imposed after a trial. Prosecutors are not being "soft on crime" when they plea-bargain. Instead, they are gaining a relatively easy conviction, even in cases in which there may not have been enough evidence to convince a jury to convict the defendant. They also save time and resources by disposing of cases and recommending a punishment without the need for time-consuming trial preparations. Private defense attorneys also benefit from plea bargaining by saving the time involved in trial preparation, earning their fees quickly, and moving on to the next income-producing case. Likewise, plea bargaining helps public defenders cope with large and often-growing caseloads. Judges, too, avoid time-consuming trials and are spared the difficult prospect of determining what sentence to impose on the defendant. Instead, they frequently merely adopt the sentence recommended by the prosecutor in consultation with the defense attorney, provided the sentence fits within the range of sentences that the judge believes appropriate for a given crime and offender.

Neither the prosecutor nor the defense attorney is a free agent. Each must count on the cooperation of both defendants and judges. Attorneys often cite the difficulty they have convincing defendants that they should uphold their end of the bargain. Judges must cooperate in the agreement by sentencing the accused according to the prosecutor's recommendation. Although their role requires that they uphold the public interest, judges may be reluctant to interfere with a plea agreement in order to maintain future exchange relationships. Thus both the prosecutor and the defense attorney usually confer with the judge regarding the sentence to be imposed before agreeing on a plea. At the same time, however, the judicial role requires that judges hold in reserve their power to reject the agreement. Because uncertainty is one of the hazards of the organizational system, prosecutors and defense attorneys will evaluate each judicial decision as an indication of the judge's future behavior. If particular judges prove to be unpredictable in supporting a plea agreement, defense attorneys may be reluctant to readily reach agreements in subsequent cases.

LEGAL ISSUES IN PLEA BARGAINING

The constitutionality of plea bargaining has evolved over the last several decades. Questions concerning the voluntariness of the plea and the parties' obligation to uphold the agreement have forced the U.S. Supreme Court to confront these issues. In deciding these questions the justices have upheld the general constitutionality of the practice and have sought to ensure that due process rights have been upheld in developing and carrying out plea agreements.

The voluntariness of the defendant to plead guilty is a central concern. In *Boykin v. Alabama* (1969) the Court ruled that defendants must make an affirmative statement that the plea was made voluntarily before a judge may accept the plea. Trial judges are required to learn whether the defendant understands the consequences of an agreement to plead guilty and to ensure that pressures were not brought by either the prosecutor or the defense attorney to coerce the plea.

Can a trial court accept a guilty plea if the defendant's innocence is maintained? In *North Carolina v. Alford* (1970) the Court approved, in principle, a pleading of guilty by an innocent defendant for the purpose of obtaining a lesser sentence. Henry C. Alford was charged with first-degree murder, a capital offense. Although maintaining his innocence, Alford plea-bargained to second-degree murder, a charge for which the death penalty was not authorized. After receiving a thirty-year sentence, he complained to the Supreme Court that the plea had been coerced by the death penalty threat. He argued that he had never admitted his guilt throughout the proceedings. The Court disagreed, ruling that it was Alford's privilege to plead guilty to avoid a possible death penalty even though he continued to maintain his innocence. One result of this ruling is that courts in many parts of the country now routinely accept pleas based on the "Alford Doctrine," by which defendants plead guilty but say they are not guilty.

A second issue concerns fulfillment of the plea agreement. If the prosecutor has given a promise of leniency, it must be kept. In *Santobello v. New York* (1971), the Supreme Court ruled that "when a [guilty] plea rests in any significant degree on a promise or agreement of the prosecutor, so that it can be said to be part of the inducement or consideration, such promise must be fulfilled." That defendants must also keep their side of the bargain was decided by the Court in *Ricketts v. Adamson* (1987). Ricketts agreed to plead guilty and testify against a codefendant in exchange for a reduction of the charges from first- to second-degree murder. He carried out the bargain but refused to testify a second time when the codefendant appealed conviction (which was reversed). The prosecutor then withdrew the offer to reduce the charge. The Supreme Court upheld the recharging and said that Ricketts had to suffer the consequences of his voluntary choice not to testify at the codefendant's second trial.

May prosecutors threaten to penalize defendants who insist upon their right to a jury trial? Paul Hayes was indicted in Kentucky for forging an $88.50 check. The prosecutor offered to recommend a sentence of five years imprisonment if a guilty plea was entered, but said that if Hayes pleaded not guilty, he would be indicted under the state's habitual criminal act. If Hayes was then found guilty, a mandatory life sentence would result because he had two prior convictions. Hayes rejected the guilty plea, went to trial, and was sentenced to life imprisonment. On appeal, the U.S. Supreme Court ruled in *Bordenkircher v. Hayes* (1978) that in the "give and take" of plea bargaining, the prosecutor's conduct did not violate constitutional protections.

Plea bargaining, then, is no longer a secret of the courthouse. The Supreme Court has accepted the constitutionality of the practice and has emphasized the importance of protecting defendants' rights as cases are processed. Judges are increasingly discussing plea bargaining openly in their courts and admitting on the record that they are aware of plea negotiations. In many cases, judges have entered into plea discussions with respect to sentences in cases before them.

SUGGESTIONS FOR FURTHER READING

Heumann, Milton. *Plea Bargaining.* Chicago: University of Chicago Press, 1978. One of the first studies of how prosecutors, judges, and defense attorneys adapt to plea bargaining.

Humes, Edward. *Mean Justice: A Town's Terror, a Prosecutor's Power, a Betrayal of Innocence.* New York: Simon Schuster, 1999. An investigative reporter's examination of prosecutions in one California county in which apparently innocent people were sent to prison for crimes they did not commit.

McCoy, Candace. *Politics and Plea Bargaining.* Philadelphia: University of Pennsylvania Press, 1993. A study of California victims' rights legislation and its impact on plea bargaining.

Rowland, Judith. *The Ultimate Violation.* New York: Doubleday, 1985. A former San Diego district attorney describes her pioneering legal strategy to prosecute rapists.

Turow, Scott. *Presumed Innocent.* New York: Farrar, Straus, and Giroux, 1987. Fictional account of the indictment and trial of an urban prosecutor for the murder of a colleague. Excellent description of an urban court system.

1 2

✸

The Decision
to Prosecute

GEORGE F. COLE

The prosecuting attorney works within the context of an exchange system of clientele relationships that influence decision making. In this case study I explore the nature of these relationships and link politics to the allocation of justice.

This paper is based on an exploratory study of the Office of Prosecuting Attorney, King County (Seattle), Washington. The lack of social-scientific knowledge about the prosecutor dictated the choice of this approach. An open-ended interview was administered to one-third of the former deputy prosecutors who had worked in the office during the ten-year period 1955–1965. In addition, interviews were conducted with court employees, members of the bench, law-enforcement officials, and others having reputations for participation in legal decision making. Over fifty respondents were contacted during this phase. A final portion of the research placed the author in the role of observer in the prosecutor's office. This experience allowed for direct observation of all phases of the decision to prosecute so that the informal processes of the office could be noted. Discussions with the prosecutor's staff, judges, defendants' attorneys, and the police were held so that the interview data could be placed within an organizational context.

The primary goal of this investigation was to examine the role of the prosecuting attorney as an officer of the legal process within the context of the local

Source: From *Law and Society Review* 4 (February 1970): 313–343. Reprinted by permission of the Law and Society Association.

political system. The analysis is therefore based on two assumptions. First, that the legal process is best understood as a subsystem of the larger political system. Because of this choice, emphasis is placed upon the interaction and goals of the individuals involved in decision making. Second, and closely related to the first point, it is assumed that broadly conceived political considerations explained to a large extent "who gets or does not get—in what amount—and how, the good (justice) that is hopefully produced by the legal system."[1] By focusing upon the political and social linkages between these systems, it is expected that decision making in the prosecutor's office will be viewed as a principal ingredient in the authoritative allocation of values.

THE PROSECUTOR'S OFFICE
IN AN EXCHANGE SYSTEM

While observing the interrelated activities of the organizations in the legal process, one might ask, "Why do these agencies cooperate?" If the police refuse to transfer information to the prosecutor concerning the commission of a crime, what are the rewards or sanctions that might be brought against them? Is it possible that organizations maintain a form of "bureaucratic accounting" that, in a sense, keeps track of the resources allocated to an agency and the support returned? How are cues transmitted from one agency to another to influence decision making? These are some of the questions that must be asked when decisions are viewed as an output of an exchange system.

The major findings of this study are placed within the context of an exchange system.[2] This serves the heuristic purpose of focusing attention upon the linkages found between actors in the decision-making process. In place of the traditional assumptions that the agency is supported solely by statutory authority, this view recognizes that an organization has many clients with which it interacts and upon whom it is dependent for certain resources. As interdependent subunits of a system, then, the organization and its clients are engaged in a set of exchanges across their boundaries. These will involve a transfer of resources between the organizations that will affect the mutual achievement of goals.

The legal system may be viewed as a set of interorganizational exchange relationships analogous to what Long has called a community game.[3] The participants in the legal system (game) share a common territorial field and collaborate for different and particular ends. They interact on a continuing basis as their responsibilities demand contact with other participants in the process. Thus, the need for cooperation of other participants can have a bearing on the decision to prosecute. A decision not to prosecute a narcotics offender may be a move to pressure the U.S. Attorney's Office to cooperate on another case. It is obvious that bargaining occurs not only between the major actors in a case—the prosecutor and the defense attorney—but also between the clientele groups that are influential in structuring the actions of the prosecuting attorney.

Exchanges do not simply "sail" from one system to another but take place in an institutionalized setting that may be compared to a market. In the market, decisions are made between individuals who occupy boundary-spanning roles and who set the conditions under which the exchange will occur. In the legal system, this may merely mean that a representative of the parole board agrees to forward a recommendation to the prosecutor, or it could mean that there is extended bargaining between a deputy prosecutor and a defense attorney. In the study of the King County prosecutor's office, it was found that most decisions resulted from some type of exchange relationship. The deputies interacted almost constantly with the police and criminal lawyers; the prosecutor was more closely linked to exchange relations with the courts, community leaders, and the county commissioners.

THE PROSECUTOR'S CLIENTELE

In an exchange system, power is largely dependent upon the ability of an organization to create clientele relationships that will support and enhance the needs of the agency. For, although interdependence is characteristic of the legal system, competition with other public agencies for support also exists. Because organizations operate in an economy of scarcity, the organization must exist in a favorable power position in relation to its clientele. Reciprocal and unique claims are made by the organization and its clients. Thus, rather than being oriented toward only one public, an organization is beholden to several publics, some visible and others seen clearly only from the pinnacle of leadership. As Gore notes when these claims are "firmly anchored inside the organization and the lines drawn taut, the tensions between conflicting claims form a net serving as the institutional base for the organization."[4]

An indication of the stresses within the judicial system may be obtained by analyzing its outputs. It has been suggested that the administration of justice is a selective process in which only those cases that do not create strains in the organization will ultimately reach the courtroom.[5] As noted in Figure 1, the system operates so that only a small number of cases arrive for trial, the rest being disposed of through reduced charges, *nolle prosequi,* and guilty pleas.[6] Not indicated are those cases removed by the police and prosecutor prior to the filing of charges. As the focal organization in an exchange system, the office of the prosecuting attorney makes decisions that reflect the influence of its clientele. Because of the scarcity of resources, marketlike relationships, and the organizational needs of the system, prosecutorial decision making emphasizes the accommodations made to the needs of participants in the process.

Police

Although the prosecuting attorney has discretionary power to determine the disposition of cases, this power is limited by the fact that usually he is dependent upon the police for inputs to the system of cases and evidence. The prosecutor does not have the investigative resources necessary to exercise the kind of affirmative control over the types of cases that are brought to him. In this relationship, the prosecutor is not without countervailing power. His main check on the

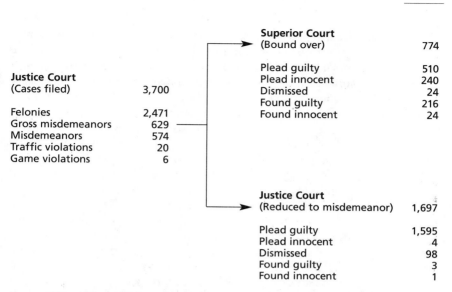

Figure 1 Disposition of Felony Cases, King County, 1964

police is his ability to return cases to them for further investigation and to refuse to approve arrest warrants. By maintaining cordial relations with the press, a prosecutor is often able to focus attention on the police when the public becomes aroused by incidents of crime. As the King County prosecutor emphasized, "That [investigation] is the job for the sheriff and police. It's their job to bring me the charges." As noted by many respondents, the police, in turn, are dependent upon the prosecutor to accept the output of their system; rejection of too many cases can have serious repercussions affecting the morale, discipline, and work load of the force.

A request for prosecution may be rejected for a number of reasons relating to questions of evidence. Not only must the prosecutor believe that the evidence will secure a conviction, but he must also be aware of community norms relating to the type of acts that should be prosecuted. King County deputy prosecutors noted that charges were never filed when a case involved attempted suicide or fornication. In other actions, the heinous nature of the crime, together with the expected public reaction, may force both the police and prosecutor to press for conviction when evidence is less than satisfactory. As one deputy noted, "In that case [murder and molestation of a six-year-old girl] there was nothing that we could do. As you know the press was on our back and every parent was concerned. Politically, the prosecutor had to seek information."

Factors other than those relating to evidence may require that the prosecutor refuse to accept a case from the police. First, the prosecuting attorney serves as a regulator of caseloads not only for his own office, but for the rest of the legal system. Constitutional and statutory time limits prevent him and the courts from building a backlog of untried cases. In King County, when the system reached the "overload point," there was a tendency to be more selective in choosing the cases to be accepted. A second reason for rejecting prosecution requests may stem from the fact that the prosecutor is thinking of his public exposure in the courtroom. He does not want to take forward cases that will place him in an embarrassing position. Finally, the prosecutor may return cases to check the quality of police work. As a former chief criminal deputy said, "You have to keep them on their toes, otherwise they get lazy. If they aren't doing their job, send the case back and then leak the situation to the newspapers." Rather than spend the resources necessary to find additional evidence, the police may dispose of a case by sending it back to the prosecutor on a lesser charge, implement the "copping out" machinery leading to a guilty plea, drop the case, or in some instances send it to the city prosecutor for action in municipal court.

In most instances, a deputy prosecutor and the police officer assigned to the case occupy the boundary-spanning roles in this exchange relationship. Prosecutors reported that after repeated contacts they got to know the policemen whom they could trust. As one female deputy commented, "There are some you can trust, others you have to watch because they are trying to get rid of cases on you." Deputies may be influenced by the police officer's attitude on a case. One officer noted to a prosecutor that he knew he had a weak case, but mumbled, "I didn't want to bring it up here, but that's what they [his superiors] wanted." As might be expected, the deputy turned down prosecution.

Sometimes the police perform the ritual of "shopping around," seeking to find a deputy prosecutor who, on the basis of past experience, is liable to be sympathetic to their view on a case. At one time, deputies were given complete authority to make the crucial decisions without coordinating their activities with other staff members. In this way the arresting officer would search the prosecutor's office to find a deputy he thought would be sympathetic to the police attitude. As a former deputy noted, "This meant that there were no departmental policies concerning the treatment to be accorded various types of cases. It pretty much depended upon the police and their luck in finding the deputy they wanted." Prosecutors are now instructed to ascertain from the police officer if he has seen another deputy on the case. Even under this more centralized system, it is still possible for the police to request a specific deputy or delay presentation of the case until the "correct" prosecutor is available. Often a prosecutor will gain a reputation for specializing in one type of case. This may mean that the police will assume he will get the case anyway, so they skirt the formal procedure and bring it to him directly.

An exchange relationship between a deputy prosecutor and a police officer may be influenced by the type of crime committed by the defendant. The prototype of a criminal is one who violates person and property. However, a large number of cases involve "crimes without victims." This term refers to those crimes generally involving violations of moral codes, where the general public is theoretically the complainant. In violations of laws against bookmaking, prostitution, and narcotics, neither actor in the transaction is interested in having an arrest made. Hence, vice control men must drum up their own business. Without a civilian complainant, victimless crimes give the police and prosecutor greater leeway in determining the charges to be filed.

One area of exchange involving a victimless crime is that of narcotics control. As Skolnick notes, "The major organizational requirement of narcotics policing is the presence of an informational system."[7] Without a network of informers, it is impossible to capture addicts and peddlers with evidence that can bring about convictions. One source of informers is among those arrested for narcotics violations. Through promises to reduce charges or even to *nolle pros.,* arrangements can be made so that the accused will return to the narcotics community and gather information for the police. Bargaining observed between the head of the narcotics squad of the Seattle police and the deputy prosecutor who specialized in drug cases involved the question of charges, promises, and the release of an arrested narcotics pusher.

In the course of postarrest questioning by the police, a well-known drug peddler intimated that he could provide evidence against a pharmacist suspected by the police of illegally selling narcotics. Not only did the police representative want to transfer the case to the friendlier hands of this deputy, but he also wanted to arrange for a reduction of charges and bail. The police officer believed that it was important that the accused be let out in such a way that the narcotics community would not realize that he had become an informer. He also wanted to be sure that the reduced charges would be processed so that the informer could be kept on the string, thus allowing the narcotics squad to maintain control over him. The deputy prosecutor, on the other hand, said that he wanted to make sure that procedures were followed so that the action would not bring discredit on his office. He also suggested that the narcotics squad "work a little harder" on a pending case as a means of returning the favor.

Courts

The ways used by the court to dispose of cases is a vital influence in the system. The court's actions affect pressures upon the prison, the conviction rate of the prosecutor, and the work of probation agencies. The judge's decisions act as clues to other parts of the system, indicating the type of action likely to be taken in future cases. As noted by a King County judge, "When the number of prisoners gets to the 'riot point,' the warden puts pressure on us to slow down the flow. This often means that men are let out on parole and the number of people given probation and suspended sentences increases." Under such conditions, it would be expected that the prosecutor would respond to the judge's actions by reducing the inputs to the court either by not preferring charges or by increasing the pressure for guilty pleas through bargaining. The adjustments of other parts of the system could be expected to follow. For instance, the police might sense the lack of interest of the prosecutor in accepting charges; hence they will send only airtight cases to him for indictment.

The influence of the court on the decision to prosecute is very real. The sentencing history of each judge gives the prosecutor, as well as other law-enforcement officials, an indication of the treatment a case may receive in a courtroom. The prosecutor's expectation as to whether the court will convict may limit his discretion over the decisions on whether to prosecute. "There is great concern as to whose court a case will be assigned. After Judge ———— threw out three cases in a row in which entrapment was involved, the police did not want us to take any cases to him." Since the prosecutor depends upon the plea-bargaining machinery to maintain the flow of cases from his office, the sentencing actions of judges must be predictable. If the defendant and his lawyer are to be influenced to accept a lesser charge or the promise of a lighter sentence in exchange for a plea of guilty, there must be some basis for belief that the judge will fulfill his part of the arrangement. Because judges are unable formally to announce their agreement with the details of the bargain, their past performance acts as a guide.

Within the limits imposed by law and the demands of the system, the prosecutor is able to regulate the flow of cases to the court. He may control the length of time between accusation and trial; hence he may hold cases until he has the evidence that will convict. Alternatively, he may seek repeated adjournment and continuances until the public's interest dies; problems such as witnesses becoming unavailable and similar difficulties make his request for dismissal of prosecution more justifiable. Further, he may determine the type of court to receive the case and the judge who will hear it. Many misdemeanors covered by state law are also violations of a city ordinance. It is a common practice for the prosecutor to send a misdemeanor case to the city prosecutor for processing in the municipal court when it is believed that a conviction may not be secured in justice court. As a deputy said, "If there is no case—send it over to the city court. Things are speedier, less formal, over there."

In the state of Washington, a person arrested on a felony charge must be given a preliminary hearing in a justice court within ten days. For the prosecutor, the preliminary hearing is an opportunity to evaluate the testimony of witnesses, assess the strength of the evidence, and try to predict the outcome of the case if it is sent to trial. On the basis of this evaluation, the prosecutor has several options: he may bind over the case for trial in superior court; he may reduce the charges to those of a misdemeanor for trial in justice court; or he may conclude that he has no case and drop the charges. The presiding judge of the Justice Courts of King County estimated that about 70 percent of the felonies are reduced to misdemeanors after the preliminary hearing.

Besides having some leeway in determining the type of court in which to file a case, the prosecutor also has some flexibility in selecting the judge to receive the case. Until recently the prosecutor could file a case with a specific judge. "The trouble was that Judge ———— was erratic and independent, [so] no one would file with him. The other judges objected that they were handling the entire work load, so a central filing system was devised." Under this procedure cases are assigned to the judges in rotation. However, as the chief criminal deputy noted, "The prosecutor can hold a case until the 'correct' judge comes up."

Defense Attorneys

With the increased specialization and institutionalization of the bar, it would seem that those individuals engaged in the practice of criminal law have been relegated, both by their profession and by the community, to a low status. The urban bar appears to be divided into three parts. First there is an inner circle, which handles the work of banks, utilities, and commercial concerns; second, another circle includes plaintiffs' lawyers representing interests opposed to those of the inner circle; and finally, an outer group scrapes out an existence by "haunting the courts in hope of picking up crumbs from the judicial table."[8] With the exception of a few highly proficient lawyers who have made a reputation by winning acquittal for their clients in difficult, highly publicized cases, most of the lawyers dealing with the King County prosecutor's office belong to this outer ring.

In this study, respondents were asked to identify those attorneys considered to be specialists in criminal law. Of the nearly 1,600 lawyers practicing in King County, only 8 can be placed in this category. Of this group, 6 were reported to enjoy the respect of the legal community, while the others were accused by many respondents of being involved in shady deals. A larger group of King County attorneys will accept criminal cases, but these lawyers do not consider themselves specialists. Several respondents noted that many lawyers, because of inexperience or age, were required to hang around the courthouse searching for clients. One Seattle attorney described the quality of legal talent available for criminal cases as "a few good criminal lawyers and a lot of young kids and old men. The good lawyers I can count on my fingers."

In a legal system where bargaining is a primary method of decision making, it is not surprising that criminal lawyers find it essential to maintain close personal ties with the prosecutor and his staff. Respondents were quite open in revealing their dependence upon this close relationship to pursue their careers successfully. The nature of criminal lawyer's work is such that his saleable product or service appears to be influence rather than technical proficiency in the law. Respondents hold the belief that clients are attracted partially on the basis of the attorney's reputation as a fixer, or as a shrewd bargainer.

There is a tendency for ex-deputy prosecutors in King County to enter the practice of criminal law. Because of his inside knowledge of the prosecutor's office and friendships made with court officials, the former deputy feels that he has an advantage over other criminal law practitioners. All of the former deputies interviewed said that they took criminal cases. Of the eight criminal law specialists, seven previously served as deputy prosecutors in King County and the other was once prosecuting attorney in a rural county.

Because of the financial problems of the criminal lawyer's practice, it is necessary that he handle cases on an assembly-line basis, hoping to make a living from a large number of small fees. Referring to a fellow lawyer, one attorney said, "You should see ———. He goes up there to Carroll's office with a whole fistful of cases. He trades on some, bargains on others, and never goes to court. It's amazing but it's the way he makes his living." There are incentives, therefore, to bargaining with the prosecutor and other decision makers. The primary aim of the attorney in such circumstances is to reach an accommodation so that the time-consuming formal proceedings need not be implemented. As a Seattle attorney noted, "I can't make money if I spend my time in a courtroom. I make mine on the telephone or in the prosecutor's office." One of the disturbing results of this arrangement is that instances were reported in which a bargain was reached between the attorney and deputy prosecutor on a "package deal." In this situation, an attorney's clients are treated as a group; the outcome of the bargaining is often an agreement whereby reduced charges will be achieved for some, in exchange for the unspoken assent by the lawyer that the prosecutor may proceed as he desires with the other cases. One member of the King County bar had developed this practice to such a fine art that a deputy prosecutor said, "When you saw him coming into the office, you knew that he would be pleading guilty." At one time this situation was so widespread that the "prisoners up in the jail had a rating list which graded the attorneys as either 'good guys' or 'sellouts.'"

The exchange relationship between the defense attorney and the prosecutor is based on their need for cooperation in the discharge of their responsibilities. Most criminal lawyers are interested primarily in the speedy solution of cases because of their precarious financial situation. Because they must protect their professional reputations with their colleagues, judicial personnel, and potential clientele, however, they are not completely free to bargain solely with this objective. As one attorney noted, "You can't afford to let it get out that you are selling out your cases."

The prosecutor is also interested in the speedy processing of cases. This can only be achieved if the formal processes are not implemented. Not only does the pressure of his caseload influence bargaining, but also the legal process, with its potential for delay and appeal, creates a degree of uncertainty that is not present in an exchange relationship with an attorney with whom you have dealt for a number of years. As the presiding judge of the Seattle District Court said, "Lawyers are helpful to the system. They are able to pull things together, work out a deal, keep the system moving."

Community Influentials

As part of the political system, the judicial process responds to the community environment. The King County study indicated that there are different levels of influence within the community and that some people had a greater interest in the politics of prosecution than others. First, the general public is able to have its values translated into policies followed by law-enforcement officers. The public's influence is particularly acute in those gray areas of the law where full enforcement is not expected. Statutes may be enacted by legislatures defining the outer limits of criminal conduct, but they do not necessarily mean that laws are to be fully enforced to these limits. There are some laws defining behavior that the community no longer considers criminal. It can be expected that a prosecutor's charging policies will reflect this attitude. He may not prosecute violations of laws regulating some forms of gambling, certain sexual practices, or violations of Sunday Blue Laws.

Because the general public is a potential threat to the prosecutor, staff members take measures to protect him from criticism. Respondents agreed that decision making occurs with the public in mind—"Will a course of action arouse antipathy toward the prosecutor rather than the accused?" Several deputies mentioned what they called the "aggravation level" of a crime. This is a recognition that the commission of certain crimes, within a specific context, will bring about a vocal public reaction. "If a little girl, walking home from the grocery store, is pulled into the bushes and indecent liberties taken, this is more disturbing to the public's conscience than a case where the father of the girl takes indecent liberties with her at home." The office of the King County prosecuting attorney has a policy requiring that deputies file all cases involving sexual molestation in which the police believe the girl's story is credible. The office also prefers charges in all negligent homicide cases where there is the least possibility of guilt. In such types of cases the public may respond to the emotional context of the case and demand prosecution. To cover the prosecutor from criticism, it is believed that the safest measure is to prosecute.

The bail system is also used to protect the prosecutor from criticism. Thus it is the policy to set bail at a high level with the expectation that the court will reduce the amount. "This looks good for Prosecutor Carroll. Takes the heat off of him, especially in morals cases. If the accused doesn't appear in court the prosecutor can't be blamed. The public gets upset when they know these types are out free." This is an example of exchange where one actor is shifting the responsibility and potential onus onto another. In turn, the court is under pressure from county jail officials to keep the prison population down.

A second community group having contact with the prosecutor is composed of those leaders who have a continuing or potential interest in the politics of prosecution. This group, analogous to the players in one of Long's community games, is linked to the prosecutor because his actions affect their success in playing another game. Hence community boosters want either a crackdown or a hands-off policy toward gambling, political leaders want the prosecutor to remember the interests of the party, and business leaders want policies that will not interfere with their own game.

Community leaders may receive special treatment by the prosecutor if they run afoul of the law. A policy of the King County office requires that cases involving prominent members of the community be referred immediately to the chief criminal deputy and the prosecutor for their disposition. As one deputy noted, "These cases can be pretty touchy. It's important that the boss knows immediately about this type of case so that he is not caught 'flat-footed' when asked about it by the press."

Pressure by an interest group was evidenced during a strike by drugstore employees in 1964. The striking unions urged Prosecutor Carroll to invoke a state law that requires the presence of a licensed pharmacist if the drugstore is open. Not only did union representatives meet with Carroll, but picket lines were set up outside the courthouse protesting his refusal to act. The prosecutor resisted the union's pressure tactics.

In recent years, the prosecutor's tolerance policy toward minor forms of gambling led to a number of conflicts with Seattle's mayor, the sheriff, and church organizations. After a decision was made to prohibit all forms of public gaming, the prosecutor was criticized by groups representing the tourist industry and such affected groups as the bartenders' union, which thought the decision would have an adverse economic effect. As Prosecutor Carroll said, "I am always getting pressures from different interests—business, the Chamber of Commerce, and labor. I have to try and maintain a balance between them." In exchange for these considerations, the prosecutor may gain prestige, political support, and admission into the leadership groups of the community.

SUMMARY

By viewing the King County Office of Prosecuting Attorney as the focal organization in an exchange system, data from this exploratory study suggests the marketlike relationships that exist between actors in the system. Because prosecution operates in an environment of scarce resources and because the decisions have potential political ramifications, a variety of officials influence the allocation of justice. The decision to prosecute is not made at one point, but rather the prosecuting attorney has a number of options he may employ during various stages of the proceedings. But the prosecutor is able to exercise his discretionary powers only within the network of exchange relationships. The police, court congestion, organizational strains, and community pressures are among the factors that influence prosecutorial behavior.

NOTES

1. James R. Klonoski and Robert I. Medelsohn, "The Allocation of Justice: A Political Analysis," *Journal of Public Law* 14 (May 1965): 323–342.

2. William M. Evan, "Toward a Theory of Inter-Organizational Relations," *Management Science* 11 (August 1965): 218–230.

3. Norton Long, *The Polity* (Chicago: Rand McNally, 1962), p. 142.

4. William J. Gore, *Administrative Decision-Making* (New York: John Wiley, 1964), p. 23.

5. William J. Chambliss, *Crime and the Legal Process* (New York: McGraw-Hill, 1969), p. 84.

6. The lack of reliable criminal statistics is well known. These data were gathered from a number of sources, including King County, "Annual Report of the Prosecuting Attorney," State of Washington, 1964.

7. Jerome L. Skolnick, *Justice Without Trial* (New York: John Wiley, 1966), p. 120.

8. Jack Ladinsky, "The Impact of Social Backgrounds of Lawyers on Law Practice and the Law," *Journal of Legal Education* 16 (1963): 128.

1 3

✪

Adapting to Plea Bargaining

Prosecutors

MILTON HEUMANN

Plea bargaining has been openly discussed only since the late 1960s. Before then, it was a widespread practice that was one of the secrets of criminal justice officials. In this analysis of the way new prosecutors adapt to plea bargaining, Milton Heumann shows how negotiated justice serves the needs of all participants in the process.

The new prosecutor shares many of the general expectations that his counterpart for the defense brings to the court. He expects factually and legally disputable issues, and the preliminary hearings and trials associated with these. If his expectations differ at all from the naive "Perry Mason" orientation, it is only to the extent that he anticipates greater success than the hapless Hamilton Burger of Perry Mason fame.

The new prosecutor's views about plea bargaining parallel those of the defense attorney. He views plea bargaining as an expedient employed in crowded urban courts by harried and/or poorly motivated prosecutors. He views the trial as "what the system is really about" and plea bargaining as a necessary evil dictated by case volume. The following exchange with a newly appointed prosecutor is illustrative.

> **Q:** Let's say they removed the effects of case pressure, provided you with more manpower. You wouldn't have that many cases. . . .

Source: Reprinted from *Plea Bargaining* by Milton Heumann by permission of the University of Chicago Press and the author. © 1978 by the University of Chicago Press.
Editor's note: This study is based on date from Connecticut, where, until a reorganization of the court system in July 1978, prosecution was conducted by state's attorneys in the supreme court and by prosecutors in the circuit court. Readers should understand that the powers of each office are essentially the same; only the workplace is different.

A: Then everybody should go to trial.

Q: Everybody should go to trial?

A: Yeah.

Q: Why?

A: Because supposedly if they're guilty they'll be found guilty. If they're not guilty they'll be found not guilty. That's the fairest way . . . judged by a group of your peers, supposedly.

Q: So you think that plea bargaining is a necessary evil?

A: Yeah.

Q: Would justice be better served if all cases went to trial?

A: That's the way it's supposed to be set up. Sure. Why wouldn't it?

Q: Would prosecutors be more satisfied?

A: Probably.

Q: If cases went to trial?

A: Sure.

Q: Why?

A: Because they could talk in front of twelve people and act like a lawyer. Right. Play the role.

It should be emphasized that these expectations and preferences of the new prosecutor are founded on the minimal law school preparation. . . . The newcomers simply do not know very much about the criminal justice system.

Unlike defense attorneys, however, the new prosecutor is likely to receive some form of structured assistance when he begins his job. The chief prosecutor or chief state's attorney may provide this aid, if the prosecutor's office is staffed by a number of prosecutors or state's attorneys—that is, if the newcomer is not the only assistant prosecutor—it is more common for the chief prosecutor to assign to one or more of his experienced assistants the responsibility for helping the newcomer adjust. Since the newcomer's actions reflect on the office as a whole, it is not surprising that this effort is made.

The assistance the newcomer receives can be described as a form of structured observation. For roughly two weeks, he accompanies an experienced prosecutor to court and to plea-bargaining sessions and observes him in action. The proximity of the veteran prosecutor—and his designation as the newcomer's mentor—facilitates communication between the two. The experienced prosecutor can readily explain or justify his actions, and the newcomer can ask any and all relevant questions. Certainly, this is a more structured form of assistance than defense attorneys receive.

However, new prosecutors still feel confused and overwhelmed during this initial period. Notwithstanding the assistance they receive, they are disoriented by the multitude of tasks performed by the prosecutor and by the environment in which he operates. This is particularly true in the circuit court, where the seemingly endless shuffling of files, the parade of defendants before the court and around the courtroom, the hurried, early-morning plea-bargaining sessions all come as a surprise to the new prosecutor.

Q: What were your initial impressions of the court during this "orientation period"?

A: The first time I came down here was a Monday morning at the arraignments. Let's face it, the majority of people here, you don't expect courts to be as crowded as they are. You don't expect thirty to thirty-five people to come out of the cell block who have been arrested over the weekend. It was . . . you sit in court the first few days, you didn't realize the court was run like this. All you see, you see Perry Mason on TV, or pictures of the Supreme Court, or you see six judges up there in a spotless courtroom, everyone well dressed, well manicured, and you come to court and find people coming in their everyday clothes, coming up drunk, some are high on drugs, it's . . . it's an experience to say the least.

Q: Could you describe your first days when you came down here? What are your recollections? Anything strike you as strange?

A: Just the volume of business and all the stuff the prosecutor had to do. For the first week or two, I went to court with guys who had been here. Just sat there and watched. What struck me was the amount of things he [the prosecutor] has to do in the courtroom. The prosecutor runs the courtroom. Although the judge is theoretically in charge, we're standing there plea bargaining and calling the cases at the same time and chewing gum and telling people to quiet down and setting bonds, and that's what amazed me. I never thought I would learn all the terms. What bothered me also was the paperwork. Not the Supreme Court decisions, not the *mens rea* or any of this other stuff, but the amount of junk that's in those files that you have to know. We never heard about this crap in law school.

As suggested in the second excerpt, the new prosecutor is also surprised by the relative insignificance of the judge. He observes that the prosecutor assumes—through plea bargaining—responsibility for the disposition of many cases. Contrary to his expectations of being an adversary in a dispute moderated by the judge, he finds that often the prosecutor performs the judge's function.

It is precisely this responsibility for resolving disputes that is most vexing to the new superior court state's attorney. Unlike his circuit court counterpart, he does not generally find hurried conferences, crowded courts, and so on. But he observes that, as in the circuit court, the state's attorney negotiates cases, and in the superior court far more serious issues and periods of incarceration are involved in these negotiations. For the novice state's attorney, the notion that he will in short order be responsible for resolving these disputes is particularly disturbing.

Q: What were your initial impressions of your job here [as a state's attorney]?

A: Well, I was frightened of the increased responsibility. I knew the stakes were high here. . . . I didn't really know what to expect, and I would say it took me a good deal of time to adapt here.

Q: Adapt in which way?

A: To the higher responsibilities. Here you're dealing with felonies, serious felonies all the way up to homicides, and I had never been involved in that particular type of situation. . . . I didn't believe that I was prepared to handle the type of job that I'd been hired to do. I looked around me and I saw the serious charges, the types of cases, and the experienced defense counsel on the one hand and the inexperience on my part on the other, and I was, well. . . .

Q: Did you study up on your own?

A: No more than. . . . Before I came over here I had done some research and made a few notes, et cetera, about the procedures. I think I was prepared from the book end of things to take the job, but, again, it was the practical aspects that you're not taught in law school and that you can only learn from experience that I didn't have, and that's what I was apprehensive about.

These first weeks in the court, then, serve to familiarize the newcomer with the general patterns of case resolution. He is not immediately thrust into the court but is able to spend some time simply observing the way matters are handled. The result, though, is to increase his anxiety. The confusion of the circuit court and the responsibilities of a state's attorney in the superior court were not anticipated. The newcomer expects to be able to prepare cases leisurely and to rely on the skills learned in law school. Yet he finds that his colleagues seem to have neither the time nor the inclination to operate in this fashion. As the informal period of orientation draws to a close, the newcomer has a better perspective on the way the system operates, but still is on very uneasy footing about how to proceed when the responsibility for the case is his alone. In short, he is somewhat disoriented by his orientation.

THE PROSECUTOR ON HIS OWN:
INITIAL FIRMNESS AND RESISTANCE
TO PLEA BARGAINING

Within a few weeks after starting his job, the prosecutor and the state's attorney are expected to handle cases on their own. Experienced personnel are still available for advice, and the newcomer is told that he can turn to them with his problems. But the cases are now the newcomer's, and, with one exception, he is under no obligation to ask anyone for anything.

The new prosecutor is confronted by a stream of defense attorneys asking for a particular plea bargain in a case. If the prosecutor agrees, his decision is irreversible. It would be a violation of all the unwritten folkways of the criminal court for either a defense attorney or a prosecutor to break his word. On the other hand, if the prosecutor does not plea bargain, offers nothing in exchange for a plea, he at least does not commit himself to an outcome that may eventually prove to be a poor decision on his part. However, a refusal to plea bargain also places him "out of step" with his colleagues and with the general expectation of experienced defense attorneys.

Like the new attorney, the new prosecutor is in no hurry to dispose of the case. He is (1) inclined toward an adversary resolution of the case through formal hearings and trial, (2) disinclined to plea bargain in general, and (3) unsure about what constitutes an appropriate plea bargain for a particular case. Yet he is faced with demands by defense attorneys to resolve the case through plea bargaining. The new defense attorney has the luxury of postponing his decision for any given case. He can seek the advice of others before committing himself to a particular plea bargain in a particular case. For the new prosecutor, this is more difficult, since he is immediately faced with the demands of a number of attorneys in a number of different cases.

When the new prosecutor begins to handle his own cases, then, he lacks confidence about how to proceed in his dealings with defense attorneys. He often masks his insecurity in this period with an outward air of firmness. He is convinced that he must appear confident and tough, lest experienced attorneys think they can take advantage of him.

Q: What happened during your first few days of handling cases on your own?

A: Well, as a prosecutor, first of all, people try to cater to you because they want you to do favors for them. If you let a lawyer run all over you, you are dead. I had criminal the first day, on a Monday, and I'm in there [in the room where cases are negotiated], and a guy comes in, and I was talking to some lawyer on his file, and he's just standing there. Then I was talking to a second guy, and he was about fourth or fifth. So he looked at me and says: "When the hell you going to get to me?" So I says: "You wait your fucking turn, I'll get to you when I'm ready. If you don't like it, get out." It's sad that you have to swear at people, but it's the only language they understand—especially lawyers. Lawyers are the most obstinate, arrogant, belligerent bastards you will ever meet. Believe me. They come into this court—first of all—and we are really the asshole of the judicial system [circuit court], and they come in here and don't really have any respect for you. They'll come in here and be nice to you, because they feel you'll give them a *nolle*. That's all. Lawyers do not respect this court. I don't know if I can blame them or not blame them. You can come in here and see the facilities here; you see how things are handled; you see how it's like a zoo pushing people in and out. . . . When they do come here, lawyers have two approaches. One, they try to soft-soap and kiss your ass if you give them a *nolle*. Two, they'll come in here and try to ride roughshod over you and try to push you to a corner. Like that lawyer that first day. I had to swear at him and show him I wasn't going to take shit, and that's that. The problem of dealing with lawyers is that you can't let them bullshit you. So, when I first started out I tried to be. . . . It's like the new kid on the block. He comes to a new neighborhood, and you've got to prove yourself. If you're a patsy, you're going to live with that as long as you're in court. If you let a couple of lawyers run over you, word will get around to go to ————, he's a pushover. Before you know it, they're running all over you. So you have to draw a line so they will respect you.

At first I was very tough because I didn't know what I was doing. In other words, you have to be very wary. These guys, some of them, have been practicing in this court for forty years. And they'll take you to the cleaners. You have to be pretty damn careful.

The new prosecutor couples this outward show of firmness toward attorneys with a fairly rigid plea-bargaining posture. His reluctance to offer incentives to the defendant for a plea or to reward the defendant who chooses to plead is, at this point in the prosecutor's career, as much a function of his lack of confidence as it is a reflection of his antipathy toward plea bargaining. During this very early stage he is simply afraid to make concessions. Experienced court personnel are well aware that new prosecutors adopt this rigid stance.

Q: Have you noticed any differences between new prosecutors and prosecutors that have been around a while?

A: Oh, yes. First of all, a new prosecutor is more likely to be less flexible in changing charges. He's afraid. He's cautious. He doesn't know his business. He doesn't know the liars. He can't tell when he's lying or exaggerating. He doesn't know all the ramifications. He doesn't know how tough it is sometimes to prove the case to juries. He hasn't got the experience, so that more likely than not he will be less flexible. He is also more easily fooled. [Circuit court judge]

I can only answer that question in a general way. It does seem to me that the old workhorses [experienced prosecutors] are more flexible than the young stallions. [Superior court judge]

Q: You were saying about the kids, the new prosecutors, the new state's attorneys. Are they kind of more hard-assed?

A: They tend to be more nervous. They tend to have a less well–defined idea of what they can do and what they can't do without being criticized. So, to the extent that they are more nervous, they tend to be more hard–assed. [Private criminal attorney]

Q: What about new prosecutors? Do they differ significantly from prosecutors who have been around a while?

A: Initially a new prosecutor is going to be reluctant to *nolle*, reluctant to give too good a deal because he is scared. He is afraid of being taken advantage of. And if you are talking about the circuit court, they've got the problem that they can't even talk it over with anybody. They've got a hundred fifty cases or whatever, and they make an offer or don't make an offer, that's it. Maybe at the end of the day they may get a chance to talk it over and say: "Gee, did I do the right thing?" The defense attorney, when the offer is made, has the opportunity to talk to somebody plus his client before making a decision. So I think it takes the prosecutor a longer time to come around and work under the system. [Legal aid attorney]

It is not difficult to understand why the new prosecutor is reluctant to plea bargain and why he appears rigid to court veterans. Set aside for the moment the prosecutor's personal preference for an adversary resolution and consider only the nature of the demands being made on him. Experienced attorneys want charges dropped, sentence recommendations, and *nolles*. They approach him with the standard argument about the wonderful personal traits of the defendant, the minor nature of the crime, the futility of incarceration, and so on. When the new prosecutor picks up the file, he finds that the defendant probably has an extensive prior criminal record and, often, that he has committed a crime that does not sound minor at all. Under the statute for the crime involved, it is likely that the defendant faces a substantial period of incarceration, yet in almost all circuit court cases and in many superior court cases, the attorneys are talking about a no-time disposition. What to the new prosecutor frequently seems like a serious matter is treated as a relatively inconsequential offense by defense attorneys. And, because the newcomer views the matter as serious, his resolve to remain firm—or, conversely, his insecurity about reducing charges—is reinforced.

Illustrations of this propensity for the new prosecutor or state's attorney to be "outraged" by the facts of the case, and to be disinclined to offer "sweet" deals, are plentiful. The following comments by two circuit court prosecutors and a superior court state's attorney, respectively, illustrate the extent to which the newcomer's appraisal of a case differed from that of the defense attorney and from that of his own colleagues.

Q: You used to go to ——— [chief prosecutor] for help on early cases. Were his recommendations out of line with what you thought should be done with the case?

A: Let's say a guy came in with a serious crime . . . a crime that I thought was serious at one time, anyway. Take fighting on ——— Avenue [a depressed area of Arborville]. He got twenty-five stitches in the head and is charged with aggravated assault. One guy got twenty-five stitches, the other fifteen. And the attorneys would want me to reduce it. I'd go and talk to ——— [chief prosecutor]. He'd say: "They both are drunk, they both got head wounds. Let them plead to breach of peace, and the judge will give them a money fine." Things like that I didn't feel right about doing, since, to me, right out of law school, middle class, you figure twenty-five stitches in the head, Jesus Christ.

Q: How did you learn what a case was worth?

A: What do you mean, what it's worth?

Q: In terms of plea bargaining. What the going rate. . . .

A: From the prosecutors and defense attorneys who would look at me dumbfounded when I would tell them that I would not reduce this charge. And then they would go running to my boss and he'd say, "Well, it's up to him." Some would even go running to the judge, screaming. One guy claimed surprise when I intended to go to trial for assault in second, which is a Class D felony. Two counts of that and two misdemeanor counts. It was set for jury trial. His witnesses were there. His experience in this court, he said, having handled two or three hundred cases, was that none has ever gone to trial. So he claimed surprise the day of trial. He just couldn't believe it.

Q: Were you in any way out of step with the way things were done here when you first began handling cases on your own?

A: In one respect I was. I evaluated a case by what I felt a proper recommendation should be, and my recommendations were almost always in terms of longer time. I found that the other guys in the office were breaking things down more than I expected. As a citizen, I couldn't be too complacent about an old lady getting knocked down, stuff like that. I thought more time should be recommended. I might think five to ten, six to twelve, while the other guys felt that three to seven was enough.

Implicit in these remarks are the seeds of an explanation for a prosecutor's gradually becoming more willing to plea bargain. One can hypothesize that as his experience with handling cases increases, he will feel less outraged by the crime, and thus will be more willing to work out a negotiated settlement. One assistant state's attorney likened his change in attitude to that of a nurse in an emergency room.

It's like nurses in emergency rooms. You get so used to armed robbery that you treat it as routine, not as morally upsetting. In the emergency room, the biggest emergency is treated as routine. And it's happening to me. The nature of the offense doesn't cause the reaction in me that it would cause in the average citizen. Maybe this is a good thing; maybe it isn't.

Though there is merit in this argument—prosecutors do become accustomed to crime—it is hardly a sufficient explanation of prosecutorial adaptation to plea bargaining. Other factors, often far more subtle, must be considered if we are to understand how and why the novice prosecutor becomes a seasoned plea bargainer.

LEARNING ABOUT PLEA BARGAINING

In the preceding sections I have portrayed the new prosecutor as being predisposed toward an adversary resolution of a case, uncertain about his responsibilities, rigid in his relations with defense attorneys, reluctant to drop charges and to plea bargain in cases that he considers serious, and anxious to try out the skills he learned in law school. This characterization of the newcomer contrasts sharply with that of the veteran prosecutor. [The veteran prosecutor takes] an active role in plea bargaining—urging, cajoling, and threatening the defense attorney to share in the benefits of a negotiated disposition. How is the veteran prosecutor to be reconciled with the new prosecutor . . . ?

The answer lies in what the prosecutor learns and is taught about plea bargaining. His education, like the defense attorney's, is not structured and systematic. Instead, he works his way through cases, testing the adversary and plea-bargaining approaches. He learns piecemeal the costs and benefits of these approaches, and only over a period of time does he develop an appreciation for the relative benefits of a negotiated disposition.

Rather than proceed with a sequential discussion of the newcomer's experience, I think it more profitable at this point to distill from his experiences those central concerns that best explain his adaptation to the plea-bargaining system. Some of the "flavor" of the adaptation process is sacrificed by the proceeding in this fashion, but in terms of clarity of presentation, I think it is a justifiable. Thus, I will discuss separately the considerations that move the prosecutor in the plea-bargaining direction, and later tie these together into an overall perspective on prosecutorial adaptation.

THE DEFENDANT'S FACTUAL
AND LEGAL GUILT

Prosecutors and state's attorneys learn that their roles primarily entail the processing of factually guilty defendants. Contrary to their expectations that problems of establishing factual guilt would be central to their job, they find that in most cases the evidence in the file is sufficient to conclude (and prove) that the defendant is factually guilty. For those cases where there is a substantial question as to factual guilt, the prosecutor has the power—and is inclined to exercise it—to *nolle* or dismiss the case. If he himself does not believe the defendant to be factually guilty, it is part of his formal responsibilities to filter the case out. But of the cases that remain after the initial screening, the prosecutor believes the majority of defendants to be factually guilty.

Furthermore, he finds that defense attorneys only infrequently contest the prosecutor's own conclusion that the defendant is guilty. In their initial approach to the prosecutor they may raise the possibility that the defendant is factually innocent, but in most subsequent discussions their advances focus on disposition and not on the problem of factual guilt. Thus, from the prosecutor's own reading of the file (after screening) and from the comments of his "adversary," he learns that he begins with the upper hand; more often than not, the factual guilt of the defendant is not really disputable.

Q: Are most of the defendants who come to this court guilty?

A: Yeah, or else we wouldn't have charged them. You know, that's something that people don't understand. Basically the people that are brought here are believed very definitely to be guilty or we wouldn't go on with the prosecution. We would *nolle* the case, and, you know, that is something, when people say, "Well, do you really believe. . . ." Yeah. I do. I really do, and if I didn't and we can clear them, then we *nolle* it, there's no question about it.

But most cases are good, solid cases, and in most of them the defendant is guilty. We have them cold-cocked. And they plead guilty because they are guilty . . . a guy might have been caught in a package store with bottles. Now, he wasn't there to warm his hands. The defendant may try some excuse, but they are guilty and they know they are guilty. And we'll give them a break when they plead guilty. I don't think we should throw away the key on the guy just because we got him cold-cocked. We've got good cases, we give them what we think the case is worth from our point of view, allowing the defendant's mitigating circumstances to enter.

Q: The fact that you're willing to offer a pretty good bargain in negotiations might lead a person to plead guilty even if he had a chance to beat it at trial. But if he was found guilty at the trial he might not get the same result?

A: That's possible, I mean, only the accused person knows whether or not he's committed the crime, and. . . . It's an amazing thing, where, on any number of occasions, you will sit down to negotiate with an accused's attorney . . . and you know [he will say]: "No, no, he's not guilty, he wants his trial." But then if he develops a weakness in the case, or points out a weakness to you, and then you come back and say: "Well, we'll take a suspended sentence and probation," suddenly he says, "Yes, I'm guilty." So it leads you to conclude that, well, all these people who are proclaiming innocence are really not innocent. They're just looking for the right disposition. Now, from my point of view, the ideal situation might be if the person is not guilty, that he pleads not guilty, and we'll give him his trial and let the jury decide. But most people who are in court don't want a trial. I'm not the person who seeks them out and says, "I will drop this charge" or "I will reduce this charge. I will reduce the amount of time you have to do." They come to us, so, you know, the conclusion I think is there that any reasonable person could draw, that these people are guilty, that they are just looking for the best disposition possible. Very few people ask for a speedy trial.

In addition to learning of the factual culpability of most defendants, the prosecutor also learns that defendants would be hard-pressed to raise legal challenges to the state's case. As was discussed earlier, most cases are simply barren of any contestable legal issue, and nothing in the prosecutor's file or the defense attorney's arguments leads the prosecutor to conclude otherwise.

The new prosecutor or state's attorney, then, learns that in most cases the problem of establishing the defendant's factual and legal guilt is nonexistent.

Typically, he begins with a very solid case, and, contrary to his expectations, he finds that few issues are in need of resolution at an adversary hearing or trial. The defendant's guilt is not generally problematic; it is conceded by the defense attorney. What remains problematic is the sentence the defendant will receive.

DISTINGUISHING AMONG THE GUILTY DEFENDANTS

Formally, the prosecutor has some powers that bear directly on sentence. He has the option to reduce or eliminate charges leveled against the defendant; the responsibility for the indictment is his, and his alone. Thus, if he *nolles* some of the charges against the defendant, he can reduce the maximum exposure the defendant faces or ensure that the defendant is sentenced only on a misdemeanor (if he *nolles* a felony), and so forth. Beyond these actions on charges, the formal powers of the prosecutor cease. The judge is responsible for sentencing. He is supposed to decide the conditions of probation, the length of incarceration, and so on. Notwithstanding this formal dichotomy of responsibility, prosecutors find that defense attorneys approach them about both charge and sentence reduction.

Since charge reduction bears on sentence reduction, it is only a small step for defense attorneys to inquire specifically about sentence; and, because there is often an interdependence between charge and sentence, prosecutors are compelled at least to listen to the attorney's arguments. Thus, the prosecutor finds attorneys parading before him asking for charge and sentence reduction, and, in a sense, he is obligated to hear them out.

It is one thing to say that prosecutors and state's attorneys must listen to defense attorneys' requests about disposition and another to say that they must cooperate with these attorneys. As already indicated, new prosecutors feel acutely uneasy about charge and sentence reduction. They have neither the confidence nor the inclination to usurp what they view as primarily the judge's responsibility. Furthermore, one would think that their resolve not to become involved in this area would be strengthened by their learning that most defendants are factually and legally guilty. Why should they discuss dispositions in cases in which they "hold all the cards"?

This query presupposes that prosecutors continue to conceive of themselves as adversaries, whose exclusive task is to establish the defendant's guilt or innocence. But what happens is that as prosecutors gain greater experience handling cases, they gradually develop certain standards for evaluating cases, standards that bear not just on the defendant's guilt or innocence but, more importantly, on the disposition of the defendant's case. These standards better explain prosecutorial behavior in negotiating dispositions than does the simple notion of establishing guilt or innocence.

Specifically prosecutors come to distinguish between serious and nonserious cases, and between cases in which they are looking for time and cases in which they are not looking for time. These standards or distinctions evolve after the prosecutor has processed a substantial number of factually and legally guilty defendants. They provide a means of sorting the raw material—the guilty defendants. Indeed, one can argue that the adversary component of the prosecutor's job is shifted from establishing guilt or innocence to determining the seriousness of the defendant's guilt and whether he should receive time. The guilt of the defendant is assumed, but the problem of disposition remains to be informally argued.

Prosecutors and state's attorneys draw sharp distinctions between serious and nonserious cases. In both instances, they assume the defendant guilty, but they are looking for different types of dispositions, dependent upon their classification of the case. If it is a nonserious matter, they are amenable to defense requests for a small fine in the circuit court, some short, suspended sentence, or some brief period of probation; similarly, in a nonserious superior court matter the state's attorney is willing to work out a combination suspended sentence and probation. The central concern with these nonserious cases is to dispose of them quickly. If the defense attorney requests some sort of no-time disposition that is dependent upon either a prosecutorial reduction of charges or a sentence recommendation, the prosecutor and state's attorney are likely to agree. They have no incentive to refuse the attorney's request, since the attorney's desire comports with what they are "looking for." The case is simply not worth the effort to press for greater penalty.

On the other hand, if the case is serious, the prosecutor and state's attorney are likely to be looking for time. The serious case cannot be quickly disposed of by a no-time alternative. These are cases in which we would expect more involved and lengthy plea-bargaining negotiations.

Whether the case is viewed as serious or nonserious depends on factors other than the formal charges the defendant faces. For example, these nonformal considerations might include the degree of harm done the victim, the amount of violence employed by the defendant, the defendant's prior record, the characteristics of the victim and defendant, the defendant's motive; all are somewhat independent of formal charge, and yet all weigh heavily in the prosecutor's judgment of the seriousness of the case. Defendants facing the same formal charges, then, may find that prosecutors sort their cases into different categories. Two defendants charged with robbery with violence may find that in one instance the state's attorney is willing to reduce the charge and recommend probation, while in the second case he is looking for a substantial period of incarceration. In the former case, the defendant may have simply brushed against the victim (still technically robbery with violence), whereas in the second, he may have dealt the victim a severe blow. Or possibly, the first defendant was a junkie supporting his habit, whereas the second was operating on the profit motive. These are, of course, imperfect illustrations, but the point is that the determination as to whether a case is serious or not serious only partially reflects the charges against the defendant. Often the determination is based on a standard that develops with experience in the court and operates, for the most part, independently of formal statutory penalties.

The following excerpts convey a sense of the serious/nonserious dichotomy and also support the argument that charge does not necessarily indicate seriousness.

Q: How did you learn what cases were worth?

A: You mean sentences.

Q: Yeah.

A: Well, that's a hit-or-miss kind of an experience. You take a first offender; any first offender in a nonviolent crime certainly is not going to jail for a nonviolent crime. And a second offender, well, it depends again on the type of crime, and maybe there should be some supervision, some probation. And a third time, you say, well now this is a guy who maybe you should treat a little more strictly. Now, a violent crime, I would treat differently. How did I learn to? I learned because there were a few other guys around with experience, and I got experience, and they had good judgments, workable approaches, and you pick it up like that. In other words, you watch others, you talk to others, you handle a lot of cases yourself.

Q: Does anybody, the public, put pressure on you to be tougher?

A: Not really.

Q: Wouldn't these sentences be pretty difficult for the public to understand?

A: Yeah, somewhat. . . . Sure, we are pretty easy on a lot of these cases except that. . . . We are tough on mugging and crimes by violence. Say an old lady is grabbed by a kid and knocked to the ground and her pocketbook taken as she is waiting for the bus. We'd be as tough as anybody on that one, whether you call it a breach of peace or a robbery. We'd be very tough. And in this case there would be a good likelihood of the first offender going to jail, whatever the charge we give him. The name of the charge isn't important. We'd have the facts regardless.

Q: So you think you have changed? You give away more than you used to?

A: I don't give away more. I think that I have reached the point where. . . . When I started I was trying to be too fair, if you want to say that, you know, to see that justice was done, and I was severe. But, you know, like ———— [head prosecutor] says, you need to look for justice tempered with mercy, you know, substantial justice, and that's what I do now. When I was new, a guy cut [knifed] someone he had to go to jail. But now I look for substantial justice—if two guys have been drinking and one guy got cut, I'm not giving anything away, but a fine, that's enough there.

Q: But you are easier now? I mean, you could look for time?

A: Look, if I get a guy that I feel belongs in jail, I try to sentence bargain and get him in jail. We had this one guy, ————. He was charged with breach of peace. We knew he had been selling drugs but we couldn't prove anything. He hits this girl in ————'s parking lot [large department store], and tried to take her purse. She screams and he runs.

This was a real son-of-a-bitch, been pimping for his own wife. On breach of peace I wanted the full year, and eventually got nine months. Cases like that I won't give an inch on. And the lawyer first wanted him to plead to suspended sentence and a money fine. I said this guy is a god-damned animal. Anybody who lets his wife screw and then gets proceeds from it, and deals in drugs . . . well, if you can catch the bastard on it, he belongs behind bars.

• • •

The second standard used by prosecutors and state's attorneys in processing factually and legally guilty defendants is the time/no-time distinction. There is an obvious relationship between the serious/nonserious standard and this one: in the serious case time is generally the goal; whereas in the nonserious case, a no-time disposition is satisfactory to the prosecutor. But this simple relationship does not always hold, and it is important for us to consider the exceptions.

In some serious cases, the prosecutor or state's attorney may not be looking for time. Generally, these are cases in which the prosecutor has a problem establishing either the factual or legal guilt of the defendant, and thus is willing to settle for a plea to the charge and offer a recommendation of a suspended sentence. The logic is simple: the prosecutor feels the defendant is guilty of the offense but fears that if he insists on time, the defense attorney will go to trial and uncover the factual or legal defects of the state's case. Thus, the prosecutor "sweetens the deal" to extract a guilty plea and to decrease the likelihood that the attorney will gamble on complete vindication.

Of the prosecutors I interviewed, a handful expressed disenchantment with plea bargaining. They felt that their associates were being too lenient, giving away too much in return for the defendant's plea. They argued that the prosecutor's office should stay firm and go to trial if necessary in order to obtain higher sentences. They were personally inclined to act this way: they "didn't like plea bargaining." But when pushed a bit, it became clear that their antipathy to plea bargaining was not without its exceptions. In the serious case with factual or legal defects they felt very strongly that plea bargaining was appropriate. The sentiments of such an "opponent" to plea bargaining are presented below.

Q: So you are saying that you only like some kinds of plea bargaining?

A: I like to negotiate cases where I have a problem with the case. I know the guy is guilty, but I have some legal problem, or unavailability of a witness that the defendant doesn't know about that will make it difficult for us to put the case on. I would have trouble with the case. Then it is in my interest to bargain; even in serious cases with these problems, it is in the best interests of the state to get the guy to plead, even if it's to a felony with suspended sentence.

Q: If there was no plea bargaining, then the state would lose out?

A: Yes, in cases like these. These would be cases that without plea bargaining we would have trouble convicting the defendant. But this has nothing to do with the defendant's guilt or innocence. Yet we might have to let him go. It is just to plea bargain in cases like this. It is fair to get the plea from the defendant, since he is guilty. Now, there is another situation; whereas in the first situation, I have no philosophical problems with plea bargaining. We may have a weak case factually. Maybe the case depends on one witness, and I have talked to the witness and realized how the witness would appear in court. Maybe the witness would be a flop when he testifies. If I feel the defendant is guilty, but the witness is really bad, then I know that we won't win the case at trial, that we won't win a big concession in plea bargaining. So I will evaluate the case, and I will be predisposed to talking about a more lenient disposition.

• • •

The other unexpected cross between the standards—nonserious case/looking for time—occurs in several types of situations. First, there is the case in which the defendant has a long history of nonserious offenses, and it is felt that a short period of incarceration will "teach him a lesson," or at least indicate that there are limits beyond which prosecutors cannot be pushed. Second, there is the situation where the prosecutor holds the defense attorney in disdain and is determined to teach the attorney a lesson. Thus, though the defendant's offense is nonserious, the prosecutor would generally be amenable to a no-time disposition, the prosecutor chooses to hold firm. It is precisely in those borderline cases that the prosecutor can be most successful in exercising sanctions against the uncooperative defense attorney. The formal penalties associated with the charges against the defendant give him ample sentencing range, and by refusing to agree to a no-time disposition, the costs to the defense attorney become great. The attorney is not able to meet his client's demands for no time, and yet he must be leery about trial, given the even greater exposure the defendant faces. These borderline decisions by prosecutors, then, are fertile grounds for exploring sanctions against defense attorneys. It is here that we can expect the cooperative defense attorney to benefit most, and the recalcitrant defense attorney to suffer the most. Relatedly, one can also expect prosecutors to be looking for time in nonserious offenses in which the defendant or his counsel insists on raising motions and going to trial. These adversary activities may be just enough to tip the prosecutor into looking for time.

In addition to its relationship to the serious/nonserious standard, the time/no-time standard bears on prosecutorial plea-bargaining behavior in another way. As prosecutors gain experience in the plea-bargaining system, they tend to stress "certainty of time" rather than "amount of time." This is to say that they become less concerned about extracting maximum penalties from defendants and more concerned with ensuring that in cases in which they are looking for time, the defendant actually receives some time. Obviously, there are limits to the prosecutor's largesse—in a serious case thirty days will not be considered sufficient time. But prosecutors are willing to consider periods of incarceration substantially shorter than the maximum sentence allowable for a particular crime. In return, though, prosecutors want a guarantee of sorts that the defendant will receive time. They want to decrease the likelihood that the defendant, by some means or other, will obtain a suspended sentence. Thus, they will "take" a fixed amount of time if the defendant agrees not to try to "pitch" for a lower sentence, or if the defendant pleads to a charge in which all participants know some time will be meted out by the judge. In the latter instance, the attorney may be free to "pitch," but court personnel know his effort is more a charade for the defendant than a realistic effort to obtain a no-time disposition. The following excerpts illustrate prosecutorial willingness to trade off years of time for certainty of time.

> I don't believe in giving away things. In fact ———— [a public defender] approached me; there's this kid ————, he has two robberies, one first degree, one second, and three minor cases. Now, this kid, I made out an affidavit myself for tampering with a witness. This kid is just n.g. ———— came to me and said, "We'll plead out, two to five." He'll go to state's prison. I agree to that—both these offenses are bindovers. These kids belong in jail. I'd rather take two to five here than bind them over to superior court and take a chance on what will happen there. At least my two to five will be a year and three-quarters in state's prison. The thing is, if I want to get a guy in jail for a year, I'll plea bargain with him, and I'll take six months if I can get it, because the guy belongs in jail, and if I can get him to jail for six months why should I fool around with that case, and maybe get a year if I am lucky? If I can put a guy away for six months I might be cheated out of six months, but at least the guy is doing six months in jail.
>
> What is a proper time? It never bothers me if we could have gotten seven years and instead we got five. In this case, there was no violence; minor stuff was stolen. We got time out of him. That is the important thing.
>
> **A:** It makes no difference to me really if a man does five to ten or four to eight. The important thing is he's off the street, not a menace to society for a period of time, and the year or two less is not going to make that great a difference. If you do get time, I think it's . . . you know, many prosecutors I know feel this way. They have achieved confinement, that's what they're here for.
>
> **Q:** Let's take another example. Yesterday an attorney walked in here when I was present on that gambling case. He asked you if it could be settled without time?
>
> **A:** And I said no. That ended the discussion.
>
> **Q:** What will he do now?
>
> **A:** He'll file certain motions that he really doesn't have to file. All the facts of our case were spelled out; he knows as much about our cases as he'll ever know. So his motions will just delay things. There'll come a point, though, when he'll have to face trial; and he'll come in to speak with

us, and ask if we still have the same position. We'll have the same position. We'll still be looking for one to three. His record goes back to 1923, he's served two or three terms for narcotics, and he's been fined five times for gambling. So we'd be looking for one to three and a fine. Even though he's in his sixties, he's been a criminal all his life, since 1923. . . .

Q: But if the attorney pushes and says, "Now look. He's an old guy. He's sixty-two years old, how about six months?"

A: I might be inclined to accept it because, again, confinement would be involved. I think our ends would be met. It would show his compadres that there's no longer any immunity for gambling, that there is confinement involved. So the end result would be achieved.

Justice Holmes, who is supposed to be the big sage in American jurisprudence, said it isn't the extent of the punishment but the certainty of it. This is my basic philosophy. If the guy faces twelve years in state's prison, I'm satisfied if on a plea of guilty he'll go to state's prison for two or three years.

The experienced prosecutor, then, looks beyond the defendant's guilt when evaluating a case. He learns—from a reading of the file and from the defense attorney's entreaties—that most defendants are factually and legally guilty and that he generally holds the upper hand. As he gains experience in processing these cases, he gradually begins to draw distinctions within this pool of guilty defendants. Some of the cases appear not to be serious, and the prosecutor becomes willing to go along with the defense attorney's request for no-time dispositions. The cases simply do not warrant a firmer prosecutorial posture. In serious cases, when he feels time is in order, he often finds defense attorneys in agreement on the need for some incarceration.

In a sense, the prosecutor redefines his professional goals. He learns that the statutes fail to distinguish adequately among guilty defendants, that they "sweep too broadly," and give short shrift to the specific facts of the offense, to the defendant's prior record, to the degree of contributory culpability of the victim, and so on. Possessing more information about the defendant than the judge does, the prosecutor—probably unconsciously—comes to believe that it is his professional responsibility to develop standards that distinguish among defendants and lead to "equitable" dispositions. Over time, the prosecutor comes to feel that if he does not develop these standards, if he does not make these professional judgments, no one else will.

The prosecutor seems almost to drift into plea bargaining. When he begins his job he observes that his colleagues plea bargain routinely and quickly finds that defense attorneys expect him to do the same. Independent of any rewards, sanctions, or pressures, he learns the strengths of his cases, and learns to distinguish the serious from the nonserious ones. After an initial period of reluctance to plea bargain at all (he is fearful of being taken advantage of by defense attorneys), the prosecutor finds that he is engaged almost unwittingly in daily decisions concerning the disposition of cases. His obligation to consider alternative charges paves the way for the defense attorney's advances; it is only a small jump to move to sentence discussions. And as he plea bargains more and more cases, the serious/nonserious and time/no-time standards begin to hold sway in his judgments. He feels confident about the disposition he is looking for, and if a satisfactory plea bargain in line with his goals can be negotiated, he comes to feel that there is little point to following a more formal adversary process. . . .

CASE PRESSURE
AND POTENTIAL BACKLOG

Though they may do so during the first few weeks, the newcomer's peers and superiors do not generally pressure him to move cases because of volume. Instead, he is thrust in the fray largely on his own and is allowed to work out his own style of case disposition. Contrary to the "conspiratorial perspective" of the adaptation process, he is not coerced to cooperate in processing "onerously large caseloads."

The newcomer's plea-bargaining behavior is conditioned by his reactions to particular cases he handles or learns about and not by caseload problems of the office. The chief prosecutor within the jurisdiction may worry about his court's volume and the speed with which cases are disposed, but he does not generally interfere with his assistant's decision about how to proceed in a case. The newcomer is left to learn about plea bargaining on his own, and for the reason already discussed, he learns and is taught the value of negotiating many of his cases. The absence of a direct relationship between prosecutor plea bargaining and case pressure is suggested in the following remarks.

Q: Is it case pressure that leads you to negotiate?

A: I don't believe it's the case pressure at all. In every court, whether there are five cases or one hundred cases, we should try to settle it. It's good for both sides. If I were a public defender, I'd try to settle all the cases for my guilty clients. By negotiating you are bound to do better. Now take this case. [He reviewed the facts of a case in which an elderly man was charged with raping a seven-year-old girl. The defendant claimed he could not remember what happened, that he was drunk, and that, though the girl might have been in the bed with him, he did not think he raped her.] I think I gave the defense attorney a fair deal. The relatives say she was raped, but the doctor couldn't conclusively establish that. I offered him a plea to a lesser charge, one dealing with advances toward minors, but excluding the sex act. If he takes it, he'll be able to walk away with time served [the defendant had not posted bail and had spent several months in jail]. It's the defendant's option though. He can go through trial if he wants, but if he makes that choice, the kid and her relatives will have to be dragged through the agonies of trial also. Then I would be disposed to look for a higher sentence for the defendant. So I think my offer is fair, and the offer has nothing to do with the volume of this court. It's the way I think the case—all things considered—should be resolved.

Q: You say the docket wasn't as crowded in 1966, and yet there was plea bargaining. If I had begun this interview by saying why is there plea bargaining here. . . .

A: I couldn't use the reason there's plea bargaining because there are a lot of cases. That's not so; that's not so at all. If we had only ten cases down for tomorrow and an attorney walked in and wanted to discuss a case with me, I'd sit down and discuss it with him. In effect, that's plea bargaining. Whether it's for the charge or for an agreed recommendation or reduction of the charge or what have you, it's still plea bargaining. It's part of the process that has been going on for quite a long time.

Q: And you say it's not because of the crowded docket, but if I gave you a list of reasons for why there was plea bargaining and asked you to pick the most important. . . .

A: I never really thought about the. . . . You talk about the necessity for plea bargaining, and you say, well, it's necessary, and one of the reasons is because we have a crowded docket, but even if we didn't we still would plea bargain.

Q: Why?

A: Well, it has been working throughout the years, and the way I look at it, it's beneficial to the defendant, it's beneficial to the court, and not just in saving time but in avoiding police officers coming to court, witnesses being subpoenaed in, and usually things can be discussed between prosecutors and defense counsel which won't be said in the open court and on the record. There are many times that the defense counsel will speak confidentially with the prosecutor about his client or about the facts or about the complainant or a number of things. So I don't know if I can justify plea bargaining other than by speaking of the necessity of plea bargaining. If there were only ten cases down for one day, it still would be something that would be done.

Maybe in places like New York they plea bargain because of case pressure. I don't know. But here it is different. We dispose of cases on the basis of what is fair to both sides. You can get a fair settlement by plea bargaining. If you don't try to settle a case quickly, it gets stale. In New York the volume probably is so bad that it becomes a matter of "getting rid of cases." In Connecticut, we have some pretty big dockets in some cities, but in other areas—here, for example—we don't have that kind of pressure. Sure, I feel some pressure, but you can't say that we negotiate our cases out to clear the docket. And you probably can't say that even about the big cities in Connecticut either.

Prosecutors, then, do not view their propensity to plea bargain as a direct outcome of case pressure. Instead, they speak of "mutually satisfactory outcomes," "fair dispositions," "reducing police overcharging," and so on. We need not here evaluate their claims in detail; what is important is that collectively their arguments militate against according case pressure the "top billing" it so often receives in the literature.

Another way to conceptualize the relationship between case pressure and plea bargaining is to introduce the notion of a "potential backlog." Some prosecutors maintain that if fewer cases were plea bargained, or if plea bargaining were eliminated, a backlog of cases to be disposed of would quickly clog their calendars. A potential backlog, then, lurks as a possibility in every jurisdiction. Even in a low-volume jurisdiction, one complex trial could back up cases for weeks, or even months. If all those delayed cases also had to be tried, the prosecutor feels he would face two not-so-enviable options. He could become further backlogged by trying as many of them as was feasible, or he could reduce his backlog by outright dismissal of cases. The following comments are typical of the potential backlog argument.

> **Q:** Some people have suggested that plea bargaining not be allowed in the court. All cases would go to trial before a judge or jury and. . . .
>
> **A:** Something like that would double, triple, and quadruple the backlog. Reduce that 90 percent of people pleading guilty, and even if you were to try a bare minimum of those cases, you quadruple your backlog. It's feasible.
>
> Well, right now we don't have a backlog. But if we were to try even 10 percent of our cases, take them to a jury, we'd be so backed up that we couldn't even move. We'd be very much in the position of. . . . Some traffic director in New York once said that there will come a time that there will be one car too many coming into New York and nobody will be able to move. Well, we can get ourselves into that kind of situation if we are going to go ahead and refuse to plea bargain even in the serious cases.

Though a potential backlog is an ever-present possibility, it should be stressed that most prosecutors develop this argument more as a prediction as to the outcome of a rule decreasing or eliminating plea bargaining than as an explanation for why they engage in plea bargaining. If plea bargaining were eliminated, a backlog would develop; but awareness of this outcome does not explain why they plea bargain.

Furthermore, prosecutors tend to view the very notion of eliminating plea bargaining as a fake issue, a straw-man proposition. It is simply inconceivable to them that plea bargaining could or would be eliminated. They maintain that no court system could try all of its cases, even if huge increases in personnel levels were made; trials consume more time than any realistic increase in personnel levels could manage. They were willing to speculate on the outcome of a rule proscribing plea bargaining, but the argument based on court backlog that they evoked was not a salient consideration in understanding their day-in, day-out plea-bargaining behavior.

It is, of course, impossible to refute with complete certainty an argument that prosecutors plea bargain because failure to do so would cause a backlog of unmanageable proportions to develop. However, the interviews indicate other more compelling ways to conceptualize prosecutorial adaptation to plea bargaining, and these do not depend on a potential backlog that always can be conjured up. Though the backlog may loom as a consequence of a failure to plea bargain, it—like its case pressure cousin—is neither a necessary nor sufficient explanatory vehicle for understanding the core aspects of prosecutorial plea-bargaining behavior.

A PERSPECTIVE
ON PROSECUTORIAL ADAPTATION

Perhaps the most important outcome of the prosecutor's adaptation is that he evidences a major shift in his own presumption about how to proceed with a case. As a newcomer, he feels it to be his responsibility to establish the defendant's guilt at trial, and he sees no need to justify a decision to go to trial. However, as he processes more and more cases, as he drifts into plea bargaining, and as he is taught the risks associated with trials, his own assumption about how to proceed with a case changes. He approaches every case with plea bargaining in mind, that is, he presumes that the case will be plea bargained. If it is a "nonserious" matter, he expects it to be quickly resolved; if it is "serious" he generally expects to negotiate time as part of the disposition. In both instances, he anticipates that the case will eventually be resolved by a negotiated disposition and not by a trial. When a plea bargain does not materialize, and the case goes to trial, the prosecutor feels compelled to justify his failure to reach an accord. He no longer is content to simply assert that it is the role of the prosecutor to establish the defendant's guilt at trial. This adversary component of the prosecutor's role has been replaced by a self-imposed burden to justify why he chose to go to trial, particularly if a certain conviction—and, for serious cases, a period of incarceration—could have been obtained by means of a negotiated disposition.

Relatedly, the prosecutor grows accustomed to the power he exercises in these plea-bargaining negotiations. As a newcomer, he argued that his job was to be an advocate for the state and that it was the judge's responsibility to sentence defendants. But, having in fact "sentenced" most of the defendants whose files he plea bargained, the distinction between prosecutor and judge becomes blurred in his own mind. Though he did not set out to usurp judicial prerogatives—indeed, he resisted efforts to engage him in the plea-bargaining process—he gradually comes to expect that he will exercise sentencing powers. There is no fixed point in time when he makes a calculated choice to become adjudicator as well as adversary. In a sense, it simply "happens"; the more cases he resolves (either by charge reduction or sentence recommendations), the greater the likelihood that he will lose sight of the distinction between the roles of judge and prosecutor.

PART IV

✵

Defense Attorneys

Defense attorneys have traditionally been caught between divergent conceptions of their positions. On the one hand, they are viewed as involved in a constant searching and creative questioning of official decisions at all stages of the justice process. On the other hand, they are seen as somehow "soiled" by their clients, engaged in shady practices to free clients from the rightful demands of the law. Although the television image of the defense attorney as seen on *The Practice* and *Law & Order* remains a hero, the public retains the more tarnished image.

THE ENVIRONMENT
OF CRIMINAL PRACTICE

Defense attorneys face special difficulties in their work. Much of the service they render involves preparing clients and their relatives for the likelihood of conviction and punishment. Although defense attorneys may have actual knowledge that their clients are guilty of a crime, they may become emotionally entangled as the only judicial actors who know the defendants as human beings and see them in the context of social environment and family ties.

Most defense lawyers interact continually with lower-class clients whose lives and problems are depressing. These lawyers may visit the jail at all hours of the day and night. Thus, the work setting of the criminal lawyer is far removed from the fancy offices and expensive restaurants that comprise the world of corporate attorneys.

Defense lawyers must also struggle with the fact that criminal practice does not pay well. Public defenders have relatively low salaries, and attorneys appointed to represent poor defendants are paid small sums. If privately retained attorneys do not demand payment from their clients at the start of the case, they may later find themselves trying to persuade the defendants' relatives to pay—since many convicted offenders have no incentive to pay for unsuccessful legal services while sitting in prison. In order to perform their jobs enthusiastically and derive satisfaction from their careers, defense attorneys must focus on goals other than money, such as their important role in protecting people's constitutional rights. However, that these attorneys are usually on the losing side of cases can make it especially difficult for them to feel like successful professionals.

Defense attorneys face additional pressures. If they mount a vigorous defense and gain an acquittal for their client, the community may blame them for using "technicalities" to keep a criminal on the streets. In addition, if they embarrass the prosecution in court, defense attorneys may harm their prospects for reaching cooperative plea agreements on behalf of future clients. Thus, criminal practice can impose significant financial, social, and psychological burdens. As a result, many attorneys get "burned out" after a few years and few criminal law specialists stay in the field past the age of fifty.

COUNSEL FOR INDIGENTS

Since the 1960s, the Supreme Court has interpreted the "right to counsel" in the Sixth Amendment of the Constitution as requiring that attorneys be provided for indigent defendants facing imprisonment—namely, those who are too poor to afford their own attorneys. The high court has also required that attorneys be provided early in the criminal justice process to protect suspects' rights during questioning and pretrial proceedings, such as preliminary hearings.

In the United States there are three basic methods of providing counsel to indigent defendants: (1) the *assigned counsel* system, by which a court appoints a private attorney to represent a particular accused; (2) the *contract counsel* system, by which an individual attorney, a nonprofit organization, or a private law firm contracts with a local government to provide legal services to indigent defendants for a specified dollar amount; and (3) *public defender* programs, established as public or private nonprofit organizations with full-time or part-time salaried staff. Let us look at these methods in turn.

Assigned Counsel

In the assigned counsel system, the court appoints a lawyer in private practice to represent an indigent defendant. This system is widely used in small cities and in rural areas, but even some urban areas with public defender systems follow the practice of assigning counsel in special circumstances, as when a case has multiple defendants and a conflict of interest might result if one were to be represented by a public lawyer.

Assigned counsel systems are organized on two bases: the ad hoc system and the coordinated system. In ad hoc assignment systems, private attorneys indicate to the judge that they are willing to take the cases of indigent defendants. When an indigent requires counsel the judge then either assigns lawyers in rotation from a prepared list or selects among attorneys who are known and present in the courtroom. In coordinated assignment systems a court administrator oversees the appointment of counsel.

Contract System

The contract system is used in a few rural counties, primarily in western states. In this system, the government contracts with an individual attorney, nonprofit association, or private law firm to handle all indigent cases. Some jurisdictions use public defenders for most cases but contract for services in multiple-defendant situations that might present conflicts of interest, in extraordinarily complex cases, or in cases that require more time than the government's salaried lawyers can provide.

Public Defender

The public defender is a twentieth-century response to the legal needs of the indigent. The concept started in Los Angeles County in 1914 when attorneys were first hired by government to work full-time in criminal defense. The most recent survey shows that public defender systems exist in 1,144 counties that cover more than 70 percent of the U.S. population. The public defender system is growing rapidly and is already the dominant form in most large cities, in populous counties, and in about twenty statewide, state-funded jurisdictions. Only two states, North Dakota and Maine, do not have public defenders.

The public defender system is often viewed as superior to the assigned counsel system because the attorneys are full-time specialists in criminal law. Because they are salaried government employees, public defenders, unlike appointed counsel and contract attorneys, do not sacrifice their clients' cases to protect their own financial interests.

Public defenders may have difficulty in gaining the trust and cooperation of their clients. Criminal defendants may assume that attorneys on the state payroll, even with the title "public defender," cannot possibly be devoted to protecting the defendants' rights and interests. A lack of cooperation may make it more difficult for the attorney to prepare the strongest possible arguments for use during hearings, plea negotiations, and trials.

Public defenders may also face burdensome caseloads. In New York City's public defender program, for example, Legal Aid lawyers may be responsible for as many as one hundred felony cases at any time. A public defender in Atlanta may be assigned as many as forty-five new cases *at a single arraignment*. Such heavy caseloads make it difficult for attorneys to be thoroughly familiar with each case.

Overburdened public defenders find it difficult to avoid processing cases by routine decisions. Decisions are made quickly and with minimal resources. One case may come to be viewed as very much like the next, and the process can become routine and repetitive. When the routine goes too far, no attorney looks closely at individual cases to see if there are special facts or other circumstances that would justify a more vigorous defense or other options.

DEFENSE COUNSEL IN THE SYSTEM

Most criminal lawyers in urban courts work in a difficult professional environment. They work very hard for small fees in unpleasant surroundings and are frequently not given respect by other lawyers or the public. Because plea bargaining is the primary method of deciding cases, defense attorneys believe they must maintain close personal ties with the police, prosecutor, judges, and other court officials. Critics point out that the defenders' independence is reduced by daily interactions with the same prosecutors and judges. There are risks that when the supposed adversaries become close friends from daily contact, the defense attorneys no longer fight vigorously on behalf of their clients.

At every step of the criminal justice process, from the first contact with the accused until final disposition of the case, defense attorneys depend upon decisions made by other judicial actors. Even seemingly minor activities such as visiting the defendant in jail, learning about the case against the defendant from the prosecutor, and setting bail can be difficult unless defense attorneys have the cooperation of others in the system. Thus defense attorneys may limit their activities in order to preserve their relationships with other courthouse actors.

For the criminal lawyer who depends on a large volume of petty cases from poor clients and assumes they are probably guilty of some offense, the incentives to bargain are strong. If the attorney is to gain appointments to handle additional cases, he or she must help to make sure that cases flow smoothly through the courthouse. This requires a cooperative relationship with judges, prosecutors, and others in the justice system.

In many cases there is evidence indicating the defendant's guilt that simply cannot be overcome by skilled lawyering. Thus good relationships can benefit the defendant by gaining plea agreements for a less-than-maximum sentence. At the same time, however, these relationships pose risks that if the defense attorney and prosecutor are too friendly then the defendant's case will not be presented in the best possible fashion in plea negotiations or trials.

Defense attorneys have been called "agent-mediators" because they frequently work to prepare the defendant for the likely outcome of the case—usually conviction. By mediating between the defendant and system through, for example, the encouragement of a guilty plea, the attorney helps to save time for the prosecutor and judge in obtaining a conviction and getting the case completed. In addition, appointed counsel and contract attorneys, in particular, may have a financial self-interest in getting the defendant to plead guilty quickly so that they can receive payment and move forward with their next case.

A more sympathetic view of defense attorneys labels them as "beleaguered dealers" who cut deals for defendants in a pressurized environment. While many of their actions assist in pushing cases through the courts, defense attorneys are under tremendous pressure to manage significant caseloads in a difficult court environment. From this perspective, their actions in encouraging clients to plead guilty result from the difficult aspects of their jobs rather than from self-interest.

SUGGESTIONS FOR FURTHER READING

Grisham, John. *A Time to Kill.* Tarrytown, NY: Wynwood, 1989. Contemporary novel of a vigilante killing and the significance of race in a small Southern courtroom.

Lewis, Anthony. *Gideon's Trumpet.* New York: Vintage, 1964. The classic case study of the case of *Gideon v. Wainwright.*

McIntyre, Lisa J. *The Public Defender: The Practice of Law in the Shadows of Repute.* Chicago: University of Chicago Press, 1987. A case study of the public defender's office in Cook County, Illinois.

Toobin, Jeffrey. *The Run of His Life: The People v. O. J. Simpson.* New York: Random House, 1996. A view of the "trial of the century" from the perspective of the defense and prosecution.

Tucker, John C. *May God Have Mercy.* New York, W.W. Norton, 1997. A former defense attorney turned writer investigates and reconstructs a murder case in which the defendant, who was ultimately executed for the crime, was represented by inexperienced defense attorneys.

1 4

✧

The Practice of Law as Confidence Game

Organization Co-Optation of a Profession

ABRAHAM S. BLUMBERG

Central to the adversary system is the defense attorney, who will engage the prosecution in a "fight" to ensure that the defendant's rights are protected and that the case is presented to the judge and jury in the best possible light. What happens when the professional environment of the criminal lawyer moderates the adversarial stance? Bargain justice occurs when it is believed to be in the best interests of both the prosecutor and the defense to avoid the courtroom confrontation. Abraham Blumberg argues that the defense attorney acts as a double agent, to get the defendant to plead guilty.

A recurring theme in the growing dialogue between sociology and law has been the great need for a joint effort of the two disciplines to illuminate urgent social and legal issues. Having uttered fervent public pronouncements in this vein, however, the respective practitioners often go their separate ways. Academic spokesmen for the legal profession are somewhat critical of sociologists of law because of what they perceive as the sociologist's preoccupation with the application of theory and methodology to the examination of legal phenomena, without regard to the solution of legal problems. Further, it is felt that "contemporary writing in the sociology of law . . . betrays the existence of painfully unsophisticated notions about the day-to-day operations of courts, legislatures, and law offices." Regardless of the merit of such criticism, scant attention—apart from explorations of the legal profession itself—has been given to

Source: From *Law and Society Review* 1 (June 1967): 15–39. Reprinted by permission of the Law and Society Association.

the sociological examination of legal institutions, or their supporting ideological assumptions. Thus, for example, very little sociological effort is expended to ascertain the validity and viability of important court decisions, which may rest on wholly erroneous assumptions about the contextual realities of social structure. A particular decision may rest upon a legally impeccable rationale; at the same time it may be rendered nugatory or self-defeating by contingencies imposed by aspects of social reality of which the lawmakers are themselves unaware.

Within this context, I wish to question the impact of three recent landmark decisions of the United States Supreme Court, each hailed as destined to effect profound changes in the future of criminal law administration and enforcement in America. The first of these, *Gideon v. Wainwright,* 372 U.S. 335 (1963), required states and localities henceforth to furnish counsel in the case of indigent persons charged with a felony. The *Gideon* ruling left several major issues unsettled, among them the vital question: What is the precise point in time at which a suspect is entitled to counsel? The answer came relatively quickly in *Escobedo v. Illinois,* 378 U.S. 478 (1964), which has aroused a storm of controversy. Danny Escobedo confessed to the murder of his brother-in-law after the police had refused to permit retained counsel to see him, although his lawyer was present in the station house and asked to confer with his client. In a 5 to 4 decision, the court asserted that counsel must be permitted when the process of police investigative efforts shifts from merely investigatory to that of accusatory: "when its focus is on the accused and its purpose is to elicit a confession—our adversary system begins to operate, and, under the circumstances here, the accused must be permitted to consult with his lawyer."

As a consequence, Escobedo's confession was rendered inadmissible. The decision triggered a national debate among police, district attorneys, judges, lawyers, and other law-enforcement officials, which continues unabated, as to the value and propriety of confessions in criminal cases. On June 13, 1966, the Supreme Court in a 5 to 4 decision underscored the principle enunciated in *Escobedo* in the case of *Miranda* v. *Arizona.* Police interrogation of any suspect in custody, without his consent, unless a defense attorney is present, is prohibited by the self-incrimination provision of the Fifth Amendment. Regardless of the relative merit of the various shades of opinion about the role of counsel in criminal cases, the issues generated thereby will be in part resolved as additional cases move toward decision in the Supreme Court in the near future. They are of peripheral interest and not of immediate concern in this paper. However, the *Gideon, Escobedo,* and *Miranda* cases pose interesting general questions. In all three decisions, the Supreme Court reiterates the traditional legal conception of a defense lawyer based on the ideological perception of a criminal case as an *adversary, combative* proceeding, in which counsel for the defense assiduously musters all the admittedly limited resources at his command to *defend* the accused. The fundamental question remains to be answered: Does the Supreme Court's conception of the role of counsel in a criminal case square with social reality?

The task of this paper is to furnish some preliminary evidence toward the illumination of that question. Little empirical understanding of the function of defense counsel exists; only some ideologically oriented generalizations and commitments. This paper is based upon observations made by the writer during many years of legal practice in the criminal courts of a large metropolitan area. No claim is made as to its methodological rigor, although it does reflect a conscious and sustained effort for participant observation.

· · ·

COURT STRUCTURE DEFINES ROLE OF DEFENSE LAWYER

The overwhelming majority of convictions in criminal cases (usually over 90 percent) are not the product of a combative, trial-by-jury process at all, but instead merely involve the sentencing of the individual after a negotiated, bargained-for plea of guilty has been entered. Although more recently the overzealous role of police and prosecutors in producing pretrial confessions and admissions has achieved a good deal of notoriety, scant attention has been paid to the organizational structure and personnel of the criminal court itself. Indeed, the extremely high conviction rate produced without the features of an adversary trial in our courts would tend to suggest that the "trial" becomes a perfunctory reiteration and validation of the pretrial interrogation and investigation.

The institutional setting of the court defines a role for the defense counsel in a criminal case radically different from the one traditionally depicted. Sociologists and others have focused their attention on the deprivations and social disabilities of such variables as race, ethnicity, and social class as being the source of an accused person's defeat in a criminal court. Largely overlooked is the variable of the court organization itself, which possesses a thrust, purpose, and direction of its own. It is grounded in pragmatic values, bureaucratic priorities, and administrative instruments. These exalt maximum production and the particularistic career designs of organizational incumbents, whose occupational and career commitments tend to generate a set of priorities. These priorities exert a higher claim than the stated ideological goals of "due process of law," and are often inconsistent with them.

Organizational goals and discipline impose a set of demands and conditions of practice on the respective professions in the criminal court to which they respond by abandoning their ideological and professional commitments to the accused client, in the service of these higher claims of the court organization. All court personnel, including the accused's own lawyer, tend to be co-opted to become agent-mediators who help the accused redefine his situation and restructure his perceptions concomitant with a plea of guilty.

Of all the occupational roles in the court, the only private individual who is officially recognized as having a special status and concomitant obligations is the lawyer. His legal status is that of "an officer of the court" and he is held to a standard of ethical performance and duty to his client as well as to the court. This obligation is thought to be far higher than expected of ordinary individuals occupying the various occupational statuses in the court community. However, lawyers, whether privately retained or of the legal-aid, public defender variety, have close and continuing relations with the prosecuting office and the court itself through discreet relations with the judges via their law secretaries or "confidential" assistants. Indeed, lines of communication, influence, and contact with those offices, as well as with the Office of the Clerk of the Court, the Probation Division, and the press, are essential to present and prospective requirements of criminal law practice. Similarly, the subtle involvement of the press and other mass media in the court's organizational network is not readily discernible to the casual observer. Accused persons come and go in the court system schema, but the structure and its occupational incumbents remain to carry on their respective career, occupational, and organizational enterprises. The individual stridencies, tensions, and conflicts a given accused person's case may present to all the participants are overcome, because the formal and informal relations of all the groups in the court setting require it. The probability of continued future relations and interaction must be preserved at all costs.

This is particularly true of the "lawyer regulars"—that is, those defense lawyers, who by virtue of their continuous appearances in behalf of defendants, tend to represent the bulk of a criminal court's nonindigent case work load, and those lawyers who are not "regulars," who appear almost casually in behalf of an occasional client. Some of the lawyer "regulars" are highly visible as one moves about the major urban centers of the nation; their offices line the back streets of the courthouses, at times sharing space with bondsmen. Their political "visibility" in terms of local clubhouse ties, reaching into the judge's chambers and the prosecutor's office, is also deemed essential to successful practitioners. Previous research has indicated that the "lawyer regulars" make no effort to conceal their dependence upon police, bondsmen, and jail personnel. Nor do they conceal the necessity for maintaining intimate relations with all levels of personnel in the court setting as a means of obtaining, maintaining, and building their practice. These informal relations are the *sine qua non* not only of retaining a practice but also in the negotiation of pleas and sentences.

The client, then, is a secondary figure in the court system as in certain other bureaucratic settings. He becomes a means to other ends of the organization's incumbents. He may present doubts, contingencies, and pressures which challenge existing informal arrangements or disrupt them; but these tend to be resolved in favor of the continuance of the organization and its relations as before. There is a greater community of interest among all the principal organizational structures and their incumbents than exists elsewhere in other settings. The accused's lawyer has far greater professional, economic, intellectual, and other ties to the various elements of the court system than he does to his own client. In short, the court is a closed community.

This is more than just the case of the usual "secrets" of bureaucracy which are fanatically defended from an outside view. Even all elements of the press are zealously determined to report on that which will not offend the board of judges, the prosecutor, and probation, legal-aid, or other officials, in return for privileges and courtesies granted in the past and to be granted in the future. Rather than any view of the matter in terms of some variation of a "conspiracy" hypothesis, the simple explanation is one of an ongoing system handling delicate tensions, managing the trauma produced by law enforcement and administration, and requiring almost pathological distrust of "outsiders" bordering on group paranoia.

The hostile attitude toward "outsiders" is in large measure engendered by a defensiveness itself produced by the inherent deficiencies of assembly-line justice, so characteristic of our major criminal courts. Intolerably large caseloads of defendants, which must be disposed of in an organizational context of limited resources and personnel, potentially subject the participants in the court community to harsh scrutiny from appellate courts and other public and private sources of condemnation. As a consequence, an almost irreconcilable conflict is posed in terms of intense pressures to process large numbers of cases, on the one hand, and the stringent ideological and legal requirements of "due process of law," on the other hand. A rather tenuous resolution of the dilemma has emerged in the shape of a large variety of bureaucratically ordained and controlled "work crimes," shortcuts, deviations, and outright rule violations adopted as court practice in order to meet production norms. Fearfully anticipating criticism on ethical as well as legal grounds, all the significant participants in the court's social structure are bound into an organized system of complicity. This consists of a work arrangement in which the patterned, covert, informal breaches and evasions of "due process" are institutionalized but are, nevertheless, denied to exist.

These institutionalized evasions will be found to occur to some degree in all criminal courts. Their nature, scope, and complexity are largely determined by the size of the court and the character of the community in which it is located— for example, whether it is a large, urban institution or a relatively small rural county court. In addition, idiosyncratic, local conditions may contribute to a unique flavor in the character and quality of the criminal law's administration in a particular community. However, in most instances a variety of stratagems are employed—some subtle, some crude, ineffectively disposing of what are often too-large caseloads. A wide variety of coercive devices are employed against an accused client, couched in a depersonalized, instrumental, bureaucratic version of due process of law, and which are in reality a perfunctory obeisance to the ideology of due process. These include some very explicit pressures which are exerted in some measure by all court personnel, including judges, to plead guilty and avoid trial. In many instances the sanction of a potentially harsh sentence is utilized as the visible alternative to pleading guilty, in the case of recalcitrants. Probation and psychiatric reports are "tailored" to organizational needs, or are at least responsive to the court organization's requirements for the refurbishment of a defendant's social biography, consonant with his new status. A resourceful judge can, through his subtle domination of the proceedings, impose his will on the final outcome of a trial. Stenographers and clerks, in their function as record keepers, are on occasion pressed into service in support of a judicial need to "rewrite" the record of a courtroom event. Bail practices are usually employed for purposes other than simply assuring a defendant's presence on the date of a hearing in connection with his case. Too often, the discretionary power as to bail is part of the arsenal of weapons available to collapse the resistance of an accused person. The foregoing is a most cursory examination of some of the more prominent "shortcuts" available to any court organization. There are numerous other procedural strategies constituting due process deviations, which tend to become the work-style artifacts of a court's personnel. Thus, only court "regulars" who are "bound in" are really accepted; others are treated routinely and in almost a coldly correct manner.

The defense attorneys, therefore, whether of the legal-aid, public defender variety or privately retained, although operating in terms of pressures specific to their respective role and organizational obligations, ultimately are concerned with strategies which tend to lead to a plea. It is the rational, impersonal elements involving economies of time, labor, expense, and a superior commitment of the defense counsel to these rationalistic values of maximum production of court organization that prevail in his relationship with a client. The lawyer "regulars" are frequently former staff members of the prosecutor's office and utilize the prestige, know-how, and contacts of their former affiliation as part of their stock-in-trade. Close and continuing relations between the lawyer "regular" and his former colleagues in the prosecutor's office generally overshadow the relationship between the regular and his client. The continuing colleagueship of supposedly adversary counsel rests on real professional and organizational needs of a *quid pro quo*, which goes beyond the limits of an accommodation or *modus vivendi* one might ordinarily expect under the circumstances of an otherwise seemingly adversary relationship. Indeed, the adversary features which are manifest are for the most part muted and exist even in their attenuated form largely for external consumption. The principals, lawyer and assistant district attorney, rely upon one another's cooperation for their continued professional existence, and so the bargaining between them tends usually to be "reasonable" rather than fierce.

FEE COLLECTION AND FIXING

The real key to understanding the role of defense counsel in a criminal case is to be found in the area of the fixing of the fee to be charged and its collection. The problem of fixing and collecting the fee tends to influence to a significant degree the criminal court process itself, and not just the relationship of the lawyer and his client. In essence, a lawyer–client "confidence game" is played. A true confidence game is unlike the case of the emperor's new clothes wherein that monarch's nakedness was a result of inordinate gullibility and credulity. In a genuine confidence game, the perpetrator manipulates the basic dishonesty of his partner, the victim or mark, toward his own (the confidence operator's) ends. Thus, "the victim of a con scheme must have some larceny in his heart."

Legal service lends itself particularly well to confidence games. Usually, a plumber will be able to demonstrate empirically that he has performed a service by clearing up the stuffed drain, repairing the leaky faucet or pipe—and therefore merits his fee. He has rendered, when summoned, a visible, tangible boon for his client in return for the requested fee. A physician, who has not performed some visible surgery or otherwise engaged in some readily discernible procedure in connection with a patient, may be deemed by the patient to have "done nothing" for him. As a consequence, medical practitioners may simply prescribe or administer by injection a placebo to overcome a patient's potential reluctance or dissatisfaction in paying a requested fee, "for nothing."

In the practice of law there is a special problem in this regard, no matter what the level of the practitioner or his place in the hierarchy of prestige. Much legal work is intangible either because it is simply a few words of advice, some preventive action, a telephone call, negotiation of some kind, a form filled out and filed, a hurried conference with another attorney or an official of a government agency, a letter or opinion written, or a countless variety of seemingly innocuous and even prosaic procedures and actions. These are the basic activities, apart from any possible court appearance, of almost all lawyers, at all levels of practice. Much of the activity is not in the nature of the exercise of the traditional, precise professional skills of the attorney such as library research and oral argument in connection with appellate briefs, court motions, trial work, drafting of opinions, memoranda, contracts, and other complex documents and agreements. Instead, much legal activity, whether it is at the lowest or highest "white shoe" law firm levels, is of the brokerage, agent, sales representative, lobbyist type of activity, in which the lawyer acts for someone else in pursuing the latter's interests and designs. The service is intangible.

The large-scale law firm may not speak as openly of their "contacts," their "fixing" abilities, as does the lower-level lawyer. They trade instead upon a facade of thick carpeting, walnut paneling, genteel low pressure, and superficialities of traditional legal professionalism. There are occasions when even the large firm is on the defensive in connection with the fees they charge because the services rendered or results obtained do not appear to merit the fee asked. Therefore, there is a recurrent problem in the legal profession in fixing the amount of fee and in justifying the basis for the requested fee.

Although the fee at times amounts to what the traffic and the conscience of the lawyer will bear, one further observation must be made with regard to the size of the fee and its collection. The defendant in a criminal case and the material gain he may have acquired during the course of his illicit activities are soon parted. Not infrequently the ill-gotten fruits of the various modes of larceny are sequestered by a defense lawyer in payment of his fee. Inexorably, the amount of the fee is a function of the dollar value of the crime committed and is frequently set with meticulous precision at a sum which bears an uncanny relationship to that of the net proceeds of the particular offense involved. On occasion, defendants have been known to commit additional offenses while at liberty on bail, in order to secure the requisite funds with which to meet their obligations for payment of legal fees. Defense lawyers condition even the most obtuse clients to recognize that there is a firm interconnection between fee payment and the zealous exercise of professional expertise, secret knowledge, and organizational "connections" in their behalf. Lawyers, therefore, seek to keep their clients in a proper state of tension, and to arouse in time the precise edge of anxiety which is calculated to encourage prompt fee payment. Consequently, the client attitude in the relationship between defense counsel and an accused is in many instances a precarious admixture of hostility, mistrust, dependence, and sycophancy. By keeping his client's anxieties aroused to the proper pitch, and establishing a seemingly causal relationship between a requested fee and the accused's ultimate extrication from his onerous difficulties, the lawyer will have established the necessary preliminary groundwork to assure a minimum of haggling over the fee and its eventual payment.

In varying degrees, as a consequence, all law practice involves a manipulation of the client and a stage management of the lawyer–client relationship so that at least an *appearance* of help and service will be forthcoming. This is accomplished in a variety of ways, often exercised in combination with each other. At the outset, the lawyer-professional employs with suitable variation a measure of sales puff which may range from an air of unbounding self-confidence, adequacy, and dominion over events, to that of complete arrogance. This will be supplemented by the affectation of a studied, faultless mode of personal attire. In the larger firms, the furnishings and office trappings will serve as the backdrop to help in impression management and client intimidation. In all firms, solo or large-scale, an access to secret knowledge and to the seats of power and influences is inferred, or presumed to a varying degree as the basic vendable commodity of the practitioners.

The lack of visible end product offers a special complication in the course of the professional life of the criminal court lawyer with respect to his fee and in his relations with his client. The plain fact is that an accused in a criminal case always "loses" even when he has been exonerated by an acquittal, discharge, or dismissal of his case. The hostility of an accused which follows as a consequence of his arrest, incarceration, possible loss of job, expense, and other traumas connected with his case is directed, by means of displacement, toward his lawyer. It is in this sense that it may be said that a criminal lawyer never really "wins" a case. The really satisfied client is rare, since in the very nature of the situation even an accused's vindication leaves him with some degree of dissatisfaction and hostility. It is this state of affairs that makes for a lawyer–client relationship in the criminal court which tends to be a somewhat exaggerated version of the usual lawyer–client confidence game.

At the outset, because there are great risks of nonpayment of the fee, due to the impecuniousness of his clients, and the fact that a man who is sentenced to jail may be a singularly unappreciative client, the criminal lawyer collects his fee *in advance*. Often, because the lawyer and the accused both have questionable designs of their own upon each other, the confidence game can be played. The criminal lawyer must serve three major functions, or stated another way, he must solve three problems. First, he must arrange for his fee; second, he must prepare and then, if necessary, "cool out" his client in case of defeat (a highly likely contingency); third, he must satisfy the court organization that he has performed adequately in the process of negotiating the plea, so as to preclude the possibility of any sort of embarrassing incident which may serve to invite "outside" scrutiny.

In assuring the attainment of one of his primary objectives, his fee, the criminal lawyer will very often enter into negotiations with the accused's kin, including collateral relatives. In many instances, the accused himself is unable to pay any sort of fee or anything more than a token fee. It then becomes important to involve as many of the accused's kin as possible in the situation. This is especially so if the attorney hopes to collect a significant part of a proposed substantial fee. It is not uncommon for several relatives to contribute toward the fee. The larger the group, the greater the possibility that the lawyer will collect a sizeable fee by getting contributions from each.

A fee for a felony case which ultimately results in a plea, rather than a trial, may ordinarily range anywhere from $550 to $1,500. Should the case go to trial, the fee will be proportionately larger, depending upon the length of the trial. But the larger the fee the lawyer wishes to exact, the more impressive his performance must be, in terms of his stage-managed image as personage of great influence and power in the court organization. Court personnel are keenly aware of the extent to which a lawyer's stock-in-trade involves the precarious stage management of an image which goes beyond the usual professional flamboyance, and for this reason alone the lawyer is "bound in" to the authority system of the court's organizational discipline. Therefore, to some extent, court personnel will aid the lawyer in the creation and maintenance of that impression. There is a tacit commitment to the lawyer by the court organization, apart from formal etiquette, to aid him in this. Such augmentation of the lawyer's stage-managed image as this affords is the partial basis for the *quid pro quo* which exists between the lawyer and the court organization. It tends to serve as the continuing basis for the higher loyalty of the lawyer to the organization; his relationship with his client, in contrast, is transient, ephemeral, and often superficial.

DEFENSE LAWYER AS DOUBLE AGENT

The lawyer has often been accused of stirring up unnecessary litigation, especially in the field of negligence. He is said to acquire a vested interest in a cause of action or claim which was initially his client's. The strong incentive of possible fee motivates the lawyer to promote litigation which would otherwise never have developed. However, the criminal lawyer develops a vested interest of an entirely different nature in his client's case: to limit its scope and duration rather than do battle. Only in this way can a case be "profitable." Thus, he enlists the aid of relatives not only to assure payment of his fee, but he will also rely on these persons to help him in his agent-mediator role of convincing the accused to plead guilty, and ultimately to help in "cooling out" the accused if necessary.

It is at this point that an accused-defendant may experience his first sense of "betrayal." While he had perhaps perceived the police and prosecutor to be adversaries, or possibly even the judge, the accused is wholly unprepared for his counsel's role performance as an agent-mediator. In the same vein, it is even less likely to occur to an accused that members of his own family or other kin may become agents, albeit at the behest and urging of other agents or mediators, acting on the principle that they are in reality helping an accused negotiate the best possible plea arrangement under the circumstances. Usually, it will be the lawyer who will activate next of kin in this role, his ostensible motive being to arrange for his fee. But soon latent and unstated motives will assert themselves with entreaties by counsel to the accused's next of kin to appeal to the accused to "help himself" by pleading. *Gemeinschaft* sentiments are to this extent exploited by a defense lawyer (or even at times by a district attorney) to achieve specific secular ends, that is, of concluding a particular matter with all possible dispatch.

The fee is often collected in stages, each installment usually payable prior to a necessary court appearance required during the course of an accused's career journey. At each stage, in his interviews and communications with the accused, or in addition, with members of his family, if they are helping with the fee payment, the lawyer employs an air of professional confidence and "inside-dopesterism" in order to assuage anxieties on all sides. He makes the necessary bland assurances, and in effect manipulates his client, who is usually willing to do and say the things, true or not, which will help his attorney extricate him. Since the dimensions of what he is essentially selling, organizational influence and expertise, are not technically and precisely measurable, the lawyer can make extravagant claims of influence and secret knowledge with impunity. Thus, lawyers frequently claim to have inside knowledge in connection with information in the hands of the district attorney, police, or probation officials or to have access to these functionaries. Factually, they often do, and need only to exaggerate the nature of their relationships with them to obtain the desired effective impression upon the client. But, as in the genuine confidence game, the victim who has participated is loath to do anything which will upset the lesser plea which his lawyer has "conned" him into accepting.

In effect, in his role as double agent, the criminal lawyer performs an extremely vital and delicate mission for the court organization and the accused. Both principals are anxious to terminate the litigation with a minimum of expense and damage to each other. There is no other personage or role incumbent in the total court structure more strategically located, who by training and in terms of his own requirements, is more ideally suited to do so than the lawyer. In recognition of this, judges will cooperate with attorneys in many important ways. For example, they will adjourn the case of an accused in jail awaiting plea or sentence if the attorney requests such action. While explicitly this may be done for some innocuous and seemingly valid reason, the tacit purpose is that pressure is being applied by the attorney for the collection of his fee, which he knows will probably not be forthcoming if the case is concluded. Judges are aware of this tactic on the part of lawyers, who, by requesting an adjournment, keep an accused incarcerated a while longer as a not too subtle method of dunning a client for payment. However, the judges will go along with this, on the ground that important ends are being served. Often, the only end served is to protect a lawyer's fee.

The judge will help an accused's lawyer in still another way. He will lend the official aura of his office and courtroom so that a lawyer can stage-manage an impression of an "all-out" performance for the accused in justification of his fee. The judge and other court personnel will serve as a backdrop for a scene charged with dramatic fire, in which the accused's lawyer makes a stirring appeal in his behalf; with a show of restrained passion, the lawyer will intone the virtues of the accused and recite the social deprivations which have reduced him to his present stage. The speech varies somewhat, depending on whether the accused has been convicted after trial or has pleaded guilty. In the main, however, the incongruity, superficiality, and ritualistic character of the total performance is underscored by a visibly impassive, almost bored reaction on the part of the judge and other members of the court retinue.

Afterward, there is a hearty exchange of pleasantries between the lawyer and district attorney, wholly out of context in terms of the supposed adversary nature of the preceding events. The fiery passion in defense of his client is gone, and the lawyers for both sides resume their offstage relations, chatting amiably and perhaps including the judge in their restrained banter. No other aspect of their visible conduct so effectively serves to put even a casual observer on notice that these individuals have claims upon each other. These seemingly innocuous actions are indicative of continuing organizational and informal relations, which, in their intricacy and depth, range far beyond any priorities or claims a particular defendant may have.

Criminal law practice is a unique form of private law practice since it really only appears to be private practice. Actually it is bureaucratic practice, because of the legal practitioner's enmeshment in the authority, discipline, and perspectives of the court organization. Private practice, supposedly, in a professional sense, involves the maintenance of an organized, disciplined body of knowledge and learning; the individual practitioners are imbued with a spirit of autonomy and service, the earning of a livelihood being incidental. In the sense that the lawyer in the criminal court serves as a double agent, serving higher organizational rather than professional ends, he may be deemed to be engaged in bureaucratic rather than private practice. To some extent the lawyer–client "confidence game," in addition to its other functions, serves to conceal this fact.

THE CLIENT'S PERCEPTION

The "cop-out" ceremony, in which the court process culminates, is not only invaluable for redefining the accused's perspectives of himself, but also in reiterating publicly in a formally structured ritual the accused person's guilt for the benefit of significant "others" who are observing. The accused not only is made to assert publicly his guilt of a specific crime, but also a complete recital of its details. He is further made to indicate that he is entering his plea of guilt freely, willingly, and voluntarily, and that he is not doing so because of any promises or in consideration of any commitments that may have been made to him by anyone. This last is intended as a blanket statement to shield the participants from any possible charges of "coercion" or undue influence that may have been exerted in violation of due process requirements. Its function is to preclude any later review by an appellate court on these grounds, and also to obviate any second thoughts an accused may develop in connection with his plea.

However, for the accused, the conception of self as a guilty person is in large measure a temporary role adaptation. His career socialization as an accused, if it is successful, eventuates in his acceptance and redefinition of himself as a guilty person. However, the transformation is ephemeral, in that he will, in private, quickly reassert his innocence. Of importance is that he accept his defeat, publicly proclaim it, and find some measure of pacification in it. Almost immediately after his plea, a defendant will generally be interviewed by a representative of the probation division in connection with a presentence report which is to be prepared. The very first question to be asked of him by the probation officer is: "Are you guilty of the crime to which you pleaded?" This is by way of double affirmation of the defendant's guilt. Should the defendant now begin to make bold assertions of his innocence, despite his plea of guilty, he will be asked to withdraw his plea and stand trial on the original charges. Such a threatened possibility is, in most instances, sufficient to cause an accused to let the plea stand and to request the probation officer to overlook his exclamations of innocence. Table 1 is a breakdown of the categorized responses of a random sample of male defendants in Metropolitan Court during 1962, 1963, and 1964 in connection with their statements during presentence probation interviews following their plea of guilty.

It would be well to observe at the outset that of the 724 defendants who pleaded guilty before trial, only 43 (5.94 percent) of the total group had confessed prior to their indictment. Thus, the ultimate judicial process was predicated upon evidence independent of any confession of the accused.

As the data indicate, only a relatively small number (95) out of the total number of defendants actually will even admit their guilt following the cop-out ceremony. However, even though they have affirmed their guilt, many of these defendants felt that they should have been able to negotiate a more favorable plea. The largest aggregate of defendants (373) were those who reasserted their "innocence" following their public profession of guilt during the cop-out ceremony. These defendants employed differential degrees of fervor, solemnity, and credibility, ranging from really mild, wavering assertions of innocence which were embroidered with a variety of stock explanations and rationalizations, to those of an adamant, "framed" nature. Thus, the "innocent" group, for the most part, were largely concerned with underscoring for their probation interviewer their essential "goodness" and "worthiness," despite their formal plea of guilty. Assertion of innocence at the postplea stage resurrects a more respectable and acceptable self-concept for the accused defendant who has pleaded guilty. A recital of the structural exigencies which precipitated his plea of guilt serves to embellish a newly proferred claim of innocence, which many defendants mistakenly feel will stand them in good stead at the time of sentence, or ultimately with probation or parole authorities.

Relatively few (33) maintained their innocence in terms of having been "framed" by some person or agent-mediator, although a larger number (86) indicated that they had been manipulated or conned by an agent-mediator to plead guilty, but as indicated, their assertions of innocence were relatively mild.

A rather substantial group (147) preferred to stress the pragmatic aspects of their plea of guilty. They would only perfunctorily assert their innocence and would in general refer to some adverse aspect of their situation which they believed tended to negatively affect their bargaining leverage, including in some instances a prior criminal record.

One group of defendants (92), while maintaining their innocence, simply employed some variation of a theme of following "the advice of counsel" as a covering response to explain their guilty plea in the light of their new affirmation of innocence.

Table 1 Defendant Responses as to Guilt or Innocence After Pleading Guilty (Years: 1962, 1963, 1964; *N* = 724)

Nature of Response		Number of Defendants
Innocent (manipulated)	"The lawyer, judge, police, or D.A. 'conned me'"	86
Innocent (pragmatic)	"Wanted to get it over with" "You can't beat the system" "They have you over a barrel when you have a record"	147
Innocent (advice of counsel)	"Followed my lawyer's advice"	92
Innocent (defiant)	"Framed"—Betrayed by "complainant," "police," "squealers," "lawyer," "friends," "wife," "girlfriend"	33
Innocent (adverse social data)	Blames probation officer or psychiatrist for "bad report," in cases where there was prepleading investigation	15
Guilty	"But I should have gotten a better deal" Blames lawyer, D.A., police, judge	74
Guilty	Won't say anything further	21
Fatalistic (doesn't press his "innocence," won't admit "guilt")	"I did it for convenience" "My lawyer told me it was only thing I could do" "I did it because it was the best way out"	248
No response		8
Total		724

The largest single group of defendants (248) were basically fatalistic. They often verbalized weak suggestions of their innocence in rather halting terms, wholly without conviction. By the same token, they would not admit guilt readily and were generally evasive as to guilt or innocence, preferring to stress aspects of their stoic submission in their decision to plead. This sizeable group of defendants appeared to perceive the total court process as being caught up in a monstrous organizational apparatus, in which the defendant's role expectancies were not clearly defined. Reluctant to offend anyone in authority, fearful that clear-cut statements on their part as to their guilt or innocence would be negatively construed, they adopted a stance of passivity, resignation, and acceptance. Interestingly, they would in most instances invoke their lawyer as being the one who crystallized the available alternatives for them and who was therefore the critical element in their decision-making process.

In order to determine which agent-mediator was most influential in altering the accused's perspectives as to his decision to plead or go to trial (regardless of the proposed basis of the plea), the same sample of defendants were asked to indicate the person who first suggested to them that they plead guilty. They were also asked to indicate which of the persons or officials who made such a suggestion was most influential in affecting their final decision to plead.

Table 2 indicates the breakdown of the responses to the two questions.

Table 2 Role of Agent-Mediators in Defendant's Guilty Plea

Person or Official	First Suggested Plea of Guilty	Influenced the Accused Most in His Final Decision to Plead
Judge	4	26
District attorney	67	116
Defense counsel	407	411
Probation officer	14	3
Psychiatrist	8	1
Wife	34	120
Friends and kin	21	14
Police	14	4
Fellow inmates	119	14
Others	28	5
No response	8	10
Total	724	724

It is popularly assumed that the police, through forced confessions, and the district attorney, employing still other pressures, are most instrumental in the inducement of an accused to plead guilty. As Table 2 indicates, it is actually the defendant's own counsel who is most effective in this role. Further, this phenomenon tends to reinforce the extremely rational nature of criminal law administration, for an organization could not rely upon the sort of idiosyncratic measures employed by the police to induce confessions and maintain its efficiency, high production, and overall rational-legal character. The defense counsel becomes the ideal agent-mediator since, as "officer of the court" and confidant of the accused and his kin, he lives astride both worlds and can serve the ends of the two as well as his own.

While an accused's wife, for example, may be influential in making him more amenable to a plea, her agent-mediator role has, nevertheless, usually been sparked and initiated by defense counsel. Further, although a number of first suggestions of a plea came from an accused's fellow jail inmates, he tended to rely largely on his counsel as an ultimate source of influence in his final decision. The defense counsel being a crucial figure in the total organizational scheme for constituting a new set of perspectives for the accused, the same sample of defendants was asked to indicate at which stage of their contact with counsel the suggestion of a plea was made. There are three basic kinds of defense counsel available in Metropolitan Court: legal-aid, privately retained counsel, and counsel assigned by the court (but may eventually be privately retained by the accused).

The overwhelming majority of accused persons, regardless of type of counsel, related a specific incident which indicated an urging or suggestion, either during the course of the first or second contact, that they plead guilty to a lesser charge if this could be arranged. Of all the agent-mediators, it is the lawyer who is most effective in manipulating an accused's perspectives, notwithstanding

**Table 3 Stage (Contact) at Which Each Type of Counsel Suggests
that Defendant Plead Guilty (N = 724)**

Contact	Privately Retained		Legal-Aid		Assigned		Total	
	N	%	N	%	N	%	N	%
First	66	35	237	49	28	60	331	46
Second	83	44	142	29	8	17	233	32
Third	29	15	63	13	4	9	96	13
Fourth or more	12	6	31	7	5	11	48	7
No response	0	0	14	3	2	4	16	2
Total	190	100	487	100[a]	47	101[a]	724	100

[a]Rounded percentage.

pressures that may have been previously applied by police, district attorney, judge, or any of the agent-mediators that may have been activated by them. Legal-aid and assigned counsel would apparently be more likely to suggest a possible plea at the point of initial interview as response to pressures of time. In the case of the assigned counsel, the strong possibility that there is no fee involved may be an added impetus to such a suggestion at the first contact.

In addition, there is some further evidence in Table 3 of the perfunctory, ministerial character of the system in Metropolitan Court and similar criminal courts. There is little real effort to individualize, and the lawyer's role as agent-mediator may be seen as unique in that he is in effect a double agent. Although, as "officer of the court" he mediates between the court organization and the defendant, his roles with respect to each are rent by conflicts of interest. Too often these must be resolved in favor of the organization which provides him with the means for his professional existence. Consequently, in order to reduce the strains and conflicts imposed in what is ultimately an overdemanding role obligation for him, the lawyer engages in the lawyer–client "confidence game" so as to structure more favorably an otherwise onerous role system.

CONCLUSION

Recent decisions of the Supreme Court, in the area of criminal law administration and defendants' rights, fail to take into account three crucial aspects of social structure which may tend to render the more libertarian rules as nugatory. The decisions overlook (1) the nature of courts as formal organization, (2) the relationship that the lawyer "regular" *actually* has with the court organization, and (3) the character of the lawyer–client relationship in the criminal court (the routine relationships, not those unusual ones that are described in "heroic" terms in novels, movies, and television).

Courts, like many other modern large-scale organizations, possess a monstrous appetite for the co-optation of entire professional groups as well as individuals. Almost all those who come within the ambit of organization authority find that their definitions, perceptions, and values have been refurbished, largely in terms favorable to the particular organization and its goals. As a result, recent Supreme Court decisions may have a long-range effect which is radically different from that intended or anticipated. The more libertarian rules will tend to produce the rather ironic end result of augmenting the *existing* organizational arrangements, enriching court organizations with more personnel and elaborate structure, which in turn will maximize organizational goals of "efficiency" and production. Thus, many defendants will find that courts will possess an even more sophisticated apparatus for processing them toward a guilty plea!

15

Indigent Defenders
Get the Job Done
and Done Well

ROGER A. HANSON
BRIAN J. OSTROM

Data from a nine-state trial court study show that the methods of providing counsel to indigents do not conform to the usual division of public defender, assigned counsel, and contract systems. The article also challenges the common assumption that attorneys for indigents are less successful in representing their clients than privately retained defense attorneys.

INTRODUCTION

It has been nearly thirty years [article originally published in 1989] since the U.S. Supreme Court in the case of *Gideon* v. *Wainwright* required that the states provide counsel for indigent defendants in criminal cases. Since that time the debate over whether indigent defenders are effective advocates or merely functionaries has continued unabated. Do attorneys paid by the state have the same skill, autonomy, and freedom to represent their clients as privately retained

Source: "Indigent Defenders Get the Job Done and Done Well" by Roger A. Hanson and Brian J. Ostrom. This article was developed under a grant from the State Justice Institute (SJI–89–05X–B–045) to the National Center for State Courts. Points of view are those of the authors and do not necessarily represent the official position of the State Justice Institute. Reprinted by permission.

attorneys? Serious doubts were expressed shortly after *Gideon* and continue to be echoed today. Moreover, current skeptics do not limit their judgments to backwater areas, as evidenced by the following view of McConville and Mirsky concerning New York City's appointed counsel arrangement:

> Against this background, the creation of an indigent defense system whose object is the mass disposal of criminal cases through guilty pleas, lesser pleas, and other non-trial dispositions should not be viewed as a heroic response to the needs of poor people by public-spirited individuals. Nor should it be viewed as a rational response to modern case pressure, as a product of the individual, or collective behavior of courtroom actors, or as the logical result of procedural and evidential complexity attendant upon a trial. Instead, the routine processing of defendants is exactly what the indigent defense system was designed to accomplish.[1]

The assertions that indigent defenders are inferior in training, limited advocates for their clients, and without sufficient resources accentuate the importance of understanding this area of legal policy. Are the critics correct or incorrect in their generalizations? Unfortunately, the answer is not obvious. There are several reasons for taking another look at this topic due to the inherent limitations in past research.

Prior studies have three deficiencies. First, many of the studies fail to go beyond the boundaries of a single court and thereby lack comparative perspective.[2] Second, cross-court studies tend not to incorporate large-, medium-, and small-sized communities.[3] This omission fails to control for the effects of population size, which generally are regarded as influential in shaping the delivery of public policy services. Third, none of the prior studies compare all of the basic types of defenders (for example, public defender, assigned counsel, and contract attorneys) to privately retained counsel.[4] As a result, available evaluations of indigent defense performance are incomplete.

The objective of this article is to describe the knowledge gained from an examination of felony case processing in nine state general jurisdiction trial courts and the role that indigent defenders play in their respective systems. The research was aimed at addressing a series of interrelated issues that are central to understanding the positive and negative effects that indigent defenders have both on court operations and on defendants. Do indigent defenders frustrate or promote the court's desire to dispose of cases expeditiously? How well do indigent defenders serve their clients? Do indigent defenders rush their clients to guilty pleas? When they go to trial, how frequently do they win?

The answers to these questions are drawn from the examination of felony case processing in the following nine diverse courts: (1) Wayne County (Detroit, Michigan) Circuit Court; (2) King County (Seattle, Washington) Superior Court; (3) Denver County (Colorado) District Court; (4) Norfolk (Virginia) Circuit Court; (5) Monterey County (Salinas, California) Superior Court; (6) Oxford County (South Paris, Maine) Superior Court; (7) Gila County (Globe, Arizona) Superior Court; (8) Island County (Coupeville, Washington) Superior Court; and (9) San Juan County (Friday Harbor, Washington) Superior Court.[5]

These courts were selected in order to gain a mixture of the basic categories of indigent defenders (public defender, assigned counsel, contract attorney) in large- and small-sized communities located in different parts of the country. They are not necessarily representative of all courts, but they do represent a broad spectrum along which many courts in the country are found.

Information was obtained from an examination of random samples of felony cases disposed of in 1987. As a result, this article provides a description of the courts in 1987 except where explicit references are made to other years. The analysis of case-level data was augmented with interviews with over 125 defense attorneys, prosecutors, judges, and court staff.

WHAT DO THE INDIGENT DEFENSE SYSTEMS LOOK LIKE?

Legal representation of indigent defendants is viewed commonly as fitting into one of three basic categories: (1) public defender, (2) assigned counsel, and (3) contract attorneys. Each category is assumed to have a particular organizational structure and a particular method of financing, and each is oriented toward achieving one or more of several different goals, such as efficiency, accountability, or effectiveness. Moreover, systems in each category are presumed to be alike (for example, all public defender offices are similar).

One or more of these three basic categories is represented in each of the nine courts. If the courts are classified according to the major provider of services, as shown in Table 1, then Seattle, Denver, and Monterey are public defender systems; Detroit, Norfolk, Oxford, and Island are assigned counsel systems; and Globe and San Juan are contract systems.

This configuration corresponds to the expected pattern of public defender offices existing primarily in large-sized communities and rarely, if at all, in small communities. The occurrence of assigned counsel systems in four of the nine courts is consistent with the national pattern of assigned counsel systems being the most frequent type of system. And the two contract systems in Globe and in San Juan fit the national estimate that this type of system exists in a minority of, usually small-sized, courts.[6]

Table 2 indicates the percent of felony dispositions in 1987 drawn from random samples of case files involving indigent defendants (represented by public defenders, assigned counsel, contract attorneys) and nonindigent defendants (represented by privately retained counsel) in each of the nine courts. Privately retained counsel represent 20 percent or more in five of the courts (Denver, Norfolk, Oxford, Island, and San Juan), and nearly that many in Globe (18 percent) and in Detroit (17.1 percent). Despite assertions to the contrary by some observers,[7] the evidence from the nine courts indicates that the private bar is not an endangered species, unless privately retained counsel are expected to handle a majority of the cases in order to be deemed viable.[8]

Table 1 Defense Representation—Structure and Institutional Issues

	Detroit	Seattle	Denver	Norfolk	Monterey	Globe	Oxford	San Juan and Island
Percent of all felony dispositions handled by indigent defenders	83%	88%	80%	71%	90%	82%	53%	SJ: 61% I: 66%
Type(s) of indigent defense structures	Assigned counsel, public defender	Three public defender firms on contract, assigned counsel	Public defender, assigned counsel, contract attorneys	Assigned counsel	Public defenders, contract attorneys, assigned counsel	Contract attorneys, assigned counsel	Assigned counsel	Contract attorneys, assigned counsel
Level of funding	County	County	State	State	County	County	State	County
Eligibility of attorneys for appointment	Certification by court; judge appoints to case at first appearance	Private assignment rare and handled informally	Pre-1990, no formal requirements and handled informally by judge at first appearance	Attorney requests to be added to list; no formal requirements	No formal requirements on rare occasions when individual attorney assigned	Not applicable	Informal by judge or clerk	SJ: N/A I: Must be approved by defender association
Average attorney tenure	3–6 years (LADA)	3–5 years	6–7 years	Not available	5–8 years	15–18 years	10–12 years	SJ: 3 years (1989) I: 3–8 years

Table 2 Percent of Felony Dispositions Handled by the Different Types of Defense Attorneys in the Courts

Types of Defense Attorneys	Detroit	Seattle	Denver	Norfolk	Monterey	Globe	Oxford	Island	San Juan
Public defender	18.4% (84)	86.8% (526)	74.6% (276)	0.0 (0)	72.8% (297)	0.0 (0)	0.0 (0)	0.0 (0)	0.0 (0)
Assigned counsel	64.6% (295)	1.2% (7)	5.4% (20)	71.1% (329)	3.7% (15)	0.0 (0)	52.9% (118)	65.6% (82)	0.0 (0)
Contract attorneys	0.0 (0)	0.0 (0)	0.0 (0)	0.0 (0)	13.5% (55)	82.4% (140)	0.0 (0)	0.0 (0)	61.3% (19)
Private counsel	17.1% (78)	12.0% (73)	20.0% (74)	28.9% (134)	10.0% (41)	17.6% (30)	47.1% (105)	34.4% (43)	38.7% (12)
Totals	100.1% (457)	100% (606)	100% (370)	100% (463)	100% (408)	100% (170)	100% (223)	100% (125)	100% (31)

These data also provide a background against which to reconsider the conventional wisdom that indigent defenders fall into three mutually exclusive categories (public defender, assigned counsel, and contract attorney). The experiences of the nine courts suggest that there is considerable flexibility in constructing indigent defense systems. For example, it is neither necessary nor true that the public defender's office must be the major provider of legal services, if it is to be used. Detroit's Legal Aid and Defender Association, which handles 25 percent of the appointments, is a counterexample to that proposition. Additionally, the types of indigent defense structures may be complementary rather than competitive, as commonly supposed. Monterey's use of all three types of indigent defenders illustrates this situation. Finally, the data from the nine courts do not support the inexorable law that says that a particular type of structure must exist in a particular size of community (for example, public defenders in a large-sized community). Again, Detroit, where the dominant category is assigned counsel, is a strong counterexample to that notion. The only linkage between the categories of indigent defenders and size is the absence of public defenders in the four small-sized communities. But even this remnant of the conventional wisdom unravels on closer examination. As noted below, Island County's system of assigned counsel exhibits several characteristics of a public defender office. A closer examination of the nine systems reveals interesting similarities and differences in the defense structures in greater detail.

Detroit's Indigent Defense System[9]

Detroit uses primarily assigned counsel for indigent defense. The assignments, however, are distributed between two major groups. Approximately 75 percent of the caseload is assigned by judges to individual private attorneys, with the remaining 25 percent going to the Legal Aid and Defender Association (LADA). LADA is essentially a public defender's office but without the usual publicly provided budget and management. It is a private, nonprofit defender organization that was established in 1968. The caseload division is the result of a 1972 Michigan Supreme Court ruling that mandated 25 percent of all criminal cases go to LADA. The director of LADA monitors this allocation very closely and ensures that it is met.

All indigent defenders, both assigned counsel and LADA attorneys, operate under the voucher system. The Wayne County payment system for assigned counsel underwent substantial change in 1988. Prior to July 1, 1988, attorneys were paid on an event-based schedule. They were paid separately for every court event (for example, each hearing, motion, trial day, and so forth) based upon the seriousness of the offense. Now attorneys are paid a fixed fee based on the statutory maximum penalty for the offense (ranging from a low of $475 for a twenty-four month maximum case to $1,400 for first-degree murder).

There are currently about 653 individual private attorneys on the assigned counsel list, with about ten new attorneys being added each month and an indeterminate number (less than ten) dropping off the roll or moving to a more occasional status. This total is composed of approximately 200 hard-core "regulars," who depend on the assigned counsel system for a substantial share of their clients and income, and about 450 "irregulars," who use the assigned counsel system to supplement their private (criminal and/or civil) practice.

There are nineteen defense attorneys (in addition to the director and deputy director) who work for the Legal Aid and Defender Association. Although LADA is often referred to as a public defender organization, its structure is closer to an assigned counsel/public defender hybrid. As with a public defender, the operation of LADA is overseen by an independent board, with no formal government connection, that chooses the office head and sets general policy. However, LADA attorneys generate fees in the same way as private assigned counsel (vouchers are submitted to the administrative office of the court and payments are calculated on the same scale), and this accounts for the vast majority of office funding. Finally, LADA attorneys have no overhead to pay and have access to good secretarial support and experienced in-house investigators. The average tenure of attorneys at LADA is three to six years.

Seattle's Indigent Defense System[10]

The provision of indigent defense services is overseen by the King County Office of Public Defense (OPD). The OPD contracts with three nonprofit public defender firms to provide the majority of defense representation for persons charged with felony offenses.[11] Each of the defender firms has its own board of directors and internal management structure. The oldest and largest of the three firms is The Defender Association (TDA). In 1990–1991, TDA was scheduled to handle approximately 41 percent of the felonies, 25 percent of the misdemeanors, 33 percent of the juvenile offender cases, 40 percent of the juvenile dependency cases, 100 percent of the involuntary commitments, and 43 percent of the cases in the Seattle municipal court.[12] The second largest firm is the Associated Counsel for the Accused (ACA), which was assigned 37 percent of the felonies, 50 percent of the misdemeanors, 22 percent of the juvenile offender cases, and 34 percent of the cases in the Seattle municipal court.[13] The third firm, the Society of Counsel Representing Accused Persons (SCRAP), was allocated 22 percent of the felonies, 25 percent of the misdemeanors, 33 percent of the juvenile offender cases, and 60 percent of the juvenile dependency cases.[14]

OPD is a division within the County Department of Human Services that provides management oversight of the indigent defense budget and services, and it assigns all indigent clients to the contracting public defender firms. OPD staff complete a two-page form during a defendant interview. It covers various aspects of the charged offense, whether an interpreter is needed, and the defendant's financial situation. Individuals are determined to be indigent if their total resources are less than 125 percent of the poverty line or if they are on public assistance.

OPD assigns each case to a particular defender firm the same day as indigency is determined. Notice of the case (defendant name, charge, and bail status) is delivered to the defender firm the following day. All payments to each defender firm are specified in the contract, except payments for aggravated homicide and complex fraud cases and conflicts appointments. The payment in these cases is based upon negotiation between OPD and the defender firm. The defense firms are paid monthly through OPD.[15]

Denver's Indigent Defense System[16]

A statewide public defender system has been in place in Colorado since the early 1970s. Organizationally, it is part of the judicial branch. It is responsible for all indigent representation except in conflict cases (in every court, an attorney may decline to accept appointment because it would conflict with the representation of defendants that were already being represented). There are eighteen regional trial offices with attorneys, two regional offices staffed only with support staff (paralegals and investigators), and an appellate division. The system is administered by a state public defender, a chief trial deputy, a chief deputy, and an administrative unit of five (three professionals). The public defender is appointed by an independent public defender commission established by the supreme court.

The Colorado public defender in Denver handles representation for the city and county of Denver. In 1987, the office had twenty-seven staff attorneys and eight contract attorneys. There were twenty-six staff attorneys in 1990. The appointment of counsel in felony cases generally takes place in the Denver County Court. Colorado uses federal guidelines for determining indigency, but the information that defendants give is not verified. Eligibility determination is done by the public defender.

The Denver office is unique in several ways. First, many public defenders begin their employment doing misdemeanor and juvenile casework there and then move to other locations in the state. Denver proper (as opposed to the surrounding counties) is decreasing in caseload, so the office is not expanding. Because it is easy to find private attorneys to do contract work, contract attorneys are used in Denver for county court work on misdemeanors at the rate of $2,025 per month. A similar use of contract attorneys elsewhere in the state is not typical.

The average tenure of public defenders in Denver was six to seven years, with the statewide average estimated at five years. Salaries of public defenders statewide are higher than those of prosecuting attorneys, but in Denver, the salaries start off even, with the public defenders losing ground as they go up. Attorneys who leave tend to go into solo practice, although some have gone to private firms, judgeships, and so forth.

Counsel are appointed by the court when the public defender must decline the representation of an indigent defendant. The assigned counsel attorneys indicate their areas of interest and expertise (for example, misdemeanors, lesser felonies, more serious felonies), and appointments are taken from the appropriate lists. The amount of reimbursement is determined by the judge, but since 1985, the state public defender administers the funds appropriated. Control over the conflict budget by the state public defender has created an incentive to minimize conflicts and to scrutinize requests by assigned counsel for payments. The state public defender is said to earn credit with the state legislature by returning unspent funds at the end of the year.

Norfolk's Indigent Defense System[17]

Representation of indigent defendants in the upper (circuit) court is provided by private attorneys who are appointed to individual cases. Appointments generally are made in lower (district) court; however, the circuit court appoints counsel for indigent defendants when the cases do not originate in the lower court.

Appointment of counsel is made from a list of attorneys that is maintained by the circuit court but is also used by the general district court. The list contains seventy-eight names. There is apparently no formal process for getting on the list: an individual writes to the court and sets forth whatever information is deemed relevant (for example, experience and references).

Compensation is by voucher. At the conclusion of the representation the attorney completes a form indicating the total of in-court (compensated at the rate of $60 per hour) and out-of-court ($40 per hour) time.

There were recent changes in how individuals received appointments. At one time, appointments were made from the list at the first appearance in the district court, with the attorney then being notified by mail that he or she had been appointed to a case. The approach had two shortcomings. First, the attorney was not present at the first appearance, thus missing an early opportunity to speak with the client. The attorney then had to arrange to see the client in jail or try to locate the individual in the community. Second, some attorneys contended that appointments were not being equitably made from the list.

To address both issues, the district court now assigns attorneys to specific court days. The designated attorney will be appointed to all new indigent cases that come before the court for first appearance on that day. With seventy-eight people on the list, an attorney will have a "duty day" about once every two and a half months. This system equalizes the number of appointments, or at least eliminates biased use of the list. A disadvantage, however, is that it treats the attorneys as fungible commodities and can result in inappropriate appointments when it is applied inflexibly by the court.

Monterey's Indigent Defense System[18]

Monterey's indigent defense services are provided primarily by the county public defender's office. Conflict cases are farmed out to a "consortium," which consists of six attorneys who contract with the county. Each consortium attorney handles a narrow range of cases and negotiates his own contract to provide those services. When neither the public defender's office nor a consortium attorney can be appointed, the court has a list of local attorneys on whom it can call.

The public defender's office has a staff of thirty-three individuals structured as follows: chief public defender, two assistant public defenders, eighteen deputy public defenders, seven secretaries, and five investigators. The office handles most of the indigent felony defendants. Felony cases are assigned to individual attorneys by the criminal division supervisor, taking work load and experience into account. Most of the new attorneys have worked in another public defender's office, usually in a metropolitan area. There is a low turnover rate, and those who have left have gone on to be judges or defenders in other jurisdictions or have gone into private practice. Training is primarily informal, by interoffice discussion, California Public Defender Association Briefs, bar courses, and communication with the bench.

The county contracts with six attorneys to provide indigent representation in conflict cases. Each attorney submits a monthly claim with a list of her or his active caseload to receive a monthly check from the county. The attorney must cover all expenses out of the contract (with the exception of investigative costs). The consortium attorneys tend to be experienced practitioners. All of them have been in practice for at least fifteen years. They include attorneys with prior experience in the public defender's office, including one of the former heads of the office.

When consortium attorneys are not able to take appointments, private attorneys are assigned. In 1987, there was no clear indication of what attorneys were eligible for these appointments, the process of how attorneys could be placed on the list was unspecified, and attorneys were not graded in a systematic way to handle different types of cases. More recently, the court has taken steps to formalize the assignment system by clarifying the criteria for appointment and what attorneys satisfy the criteria.

Globe's Indigent Defense System[19]

Gila County contracts with private lawyers for indigent services. From 1986 through 1989 three lawyers held contracts. A fourth attorney was added in 1990 to handle lesser felonies and juvenile dependency cases exclusively. Attorneys contract with the County Board of Supervisors, who fund indigent defense services. The system is not merely "low-bid," however, and the court plays a meaningful role in the process of awarding the contracts. Although the County Board of Supervisors issues a request for proposals, bids are returned to the judges of the court. Thereafter, applicants negotiate with the court before contracts are finalized. The system for assigning cases to each of the contract attorneys blends work load and geographic considerations. In theory, each contract attorney receives an equal number of new cases each year. One of the indigent defense attorneys practices almost exclusively in a remote community within the county (Payson-Pine), and the other attorneys occasionally practice there.

All of the attorneys have a private practice in addition to the Gila County contract. One attorney estimates that 60 percent of his work was indigent defense and 40 percent private practice. Another attorney supplements his Gila County practice with additional contract indigent defense work in an adjacent county, which compensates him on an hourly rather than flat-fee basis. All of the attorneys maintain an office in Gila County, except for the recently hired contract attorney, who handles the misdemeanors and less serious felony work.

The three attorneys who handle felony cases are veteran lawyers with more than fifteen years of experience in criminal practice, which includes forty to sixty felony cases each year. In Globe, the superiority of experience by indigent defense counsel over the deputy prosecuting attorneys is apparent and generally acknowledged. They go to trial infrequently, but they usually win when they do go.

Oxford's Indigent Defense System[20]

The state funds indigent defense in Maine, and Oxford County uses an assigned counsel system. Attorneys are appointed to a case by a judge from a list of available attorneys, with the assistance of the superior court clerk (in the instance of a direct indictment) and the chief deputy district court clerk (in the instance of a felony bind over). Attorneys who wish to be considered for assigned criminal cases inform the clerks of the respective courts who maintain the appointment lists. About twelve Oxford County lawyers accepted indigent criminal cases during the study period, with six of them receiving the majority of the appointments.

Although the state office manages the fiscal elements of the program, the local clerk of court processes the vouchers to get them approved by the judge and forwards them to the administrator in Portland. The state office reviews them and forwards them to Augusta for payment. Checks are written from the state capital in Augusta and mailed to the attorneys. Attorneys receive their checks four to ten weeks after submitting a voucher. The judges must approve vouchers submitted by counsel, and they may adjust the approved amount. The fee structure is set by the supreme court. No ceilings have been legislated for permissible attorney's fees, although the judge must approve the voucher. The judges have discretion to pay less than the full hourly rate.

Island's Indigent Defense System[21]

Island delivers indigent defense services through an assigned counsel system. In the 1970s an association of lawyers—Island County Defender's Association— was formed to certify lawyers for the service, to manage referrals and appointments, and to negotiate with the board of commissioners over fee schedules. The association maintained a governing board and employed a secretary to provide administrative services. The same secretary was hired later by the county commissioners as the full-time administrator of the indigent defense system. Through the association, the consortium of attorneys continued to speak to the county as a group, set standards for eligibility, and, in effect, controlled admission to the indigent defense practice. Thus, even though Island is classified as an assigned system, it has important elements characteristic of a public defender system.

The indigent defense administrator for the Island County Defender's Association runs a tight ship with lots of statistics, careful scrutiny of appointment documentation and the fees charged, review of defendant eligibility, and determination of partial ability to pay. She is responsible for quality control of services, fiscal control, and arrangement for promissory notes when clients have some ability to pay. There is an expectation that attorneys will meet with clients within forty-eight hours of admission to jail.

The assigned counsel system matches attorneys to case severity, with the more experienced attorneys getting the more serious cases. There are approximately twelve attorneys on the assigned counsel roster, all of whom have had several years of experience. Judges and other court personnel state that Island County's system appears to represent the values that should be present in a system of criminal defense—access to experienced attorneys who specialize in trial practice and criminal law and the opportunity for a "personal" relationship.

San Juan's Indigent Defense System

San Juan is an island community with no bridges to the mainland. Indigent defense service has been provided there since 1980 through a contract system. Before that time, defense was provided by an assigned counsel system, similar to Oxford County's. Most attorneys accepted appointments reluctantly, however. From 1979 to 1980, some local lawyers lobbied the county to revise the fee schedule upward; instead, a contract system was initiated by the county commissioners. Until recently, the contract was strictly on a low-bid criterion. The contract attorney assumed responsibility for all criminal, juvenile, and mental health cases, including all overhead. The court at the time was passive, under the theory that so long as there was a vehicle for appointment of counsel, the commissioners were free to fund the service in whatever manner they saw fit.

During the first year of the contract program, the contract attorney moved from the island to a mainland community, three hours distant by automobile and ferry. Thereafter, until 1990, a succession of three attorneys who did not live in the county held the contracts. One of these attorneys had previously been the deputy prosecutor responsible for criminal cases. Throughout this period there was general dissatisfaction with the contract service among the bar and criminal justice community, but no organized attempts to intervene with the commissioners were undertaken. Complaints generally had to do with the unavailability of the lawyer at critical times. Not only was the lawyer rarely available to clients immediately following arrest, but he also often would be late for, or entirely miss, scheduled court appearances. These proceedings would have to be rescheduled.

COMPARATIVE PERSPECTIVE

Indigent defense should be thought of in terms of a flexible system of interrelated elements rather than three mutually exclusive structures. There is no doubt that there are public defenders, assigned counsel, and contract attorneys and that the methods by which they receive appointments tend to be different. Looking at these systems in the nine courts, however, the following three lessons emerge.

First, there is no single organizational model of public defenders, assigned counsel, or contract attorneys. There are important variants within each of these three categories. Second, virtually all possible combinations of public defenders, assigned counsel, and contract attorneys are feasible. Courts have the opportunity to design the arrangements that meet their particular needs and circumstances. Third, indigent defense systems should not be assessed simply in terms of organizational structure and the assumed advantages of the preferred structure. Instead, the performance of a given structure should be measured in terms of how well the indigent defenders actually handle their cases. That topic is the subject of the next two sections.

TIMELINESS

The expeditious resolution of criminal cases is both a right guaranteed under the U.S. Constitution and a standard to which courts are held accountable. According to the Sixth Amendment, defendants are entitled to a speedy trial as well as the assistance of counsel. Consequently, indigent defenders have a fiduciary obligation to avoid unnecessary delays.

Timeliness is also a goal that the courts are expected to achieve. Both the American Bar Association (ABA) and the Conference of State Court Administrators (COSCA) have stipulated standards for courts. Specifically, the ABA states that all felony cases should take no longer than one year from the date of the arrest to be adjudicated. It is expected, moreover, that most cases should take considerably less than one year to reach final disposition. According to the ABA, 90 percent of all felony cases should be adjudicated within 120 days from the date of arrest and 98 percent should be adjudicated within 180 days from the date of arrest.

Length of Time from Arrest to Disposition

The indigent defenders consistently process the typical case in less time than privately retained attorneys, except in Island County. As shown in Table 3, the median number of days from the date of arrest to the date of adjudication for indigent defenders is less than it is for privately retained counsel in each of the eight other courts for all types of indigent defenders except for the small group of assigned counsel in Monterey. In Monterey, assigned counsel have a median number of days (115) that is longer than the time associated with privately retained counsel (eighty-nine days). However, both the public defenders (fifty-six days) and the contract attorneys (seventy-eight days), which are the primary and secondary providers of indigent defense in Monterey, are more timely than privately retained counsel (eighty-nine days).

Meeting the ABA Standard

The same pattern of positive performance by indigent defenders emerges when the ABA's standard of resolving 98 percent of felony cases within 180 days of the arrest data is used. Only San Juan meets the standard; in the other eight courts more than 2 percent of the felony cases are still open at 180 days. However, as shown in Table 4, the percentages of cases remaining open after 180 days is consistently less for the indigent defenders in all the courts except Globe. In Globe, 28.6 percent of the cases represented by contract attorneys remain open after 180 days, and 27.2 percent of the cases represented by privately retained attorneys remain open after 180 days from the date of arrest. Additionally, in Monterey, relatively more of the cases with privately retained counsel meet the ABA standard than do the cases with assigned counsel. However, the two larger groups of indigent defenders in Monterey (public defender and contract attorneys) approximate the standard more closely than do the privately retained attorneys.

Table 3 Typical Length of Time That Indigent Defenders and Privately Retained Counsel Take to Resolve Cases (Median Number of Days from Date of Arrest to Adjudication,[a] Felony Dispositions)

	Detroit	Seattle[b]	Denver	Norfolk	Monterey	Globe	Oxford	Island	San Juan
Public defender	79	75	151	—	56	—	—	—	—
Contract attorney	—	—	—	—	78	125	—	—	79
Assigned counsel	62	—	162	114	115	—	134	156	—
Privately retained counsel	102	101	167	184	89	141	215	131	88
All cases	71	85	156	126	63	129	161	146	83

[a]Adjudication is the entry of a dismissal, guilty plea, deferred adjudication, or diversion, or verdict.

[b]In Seattle, the indigent defense attorneys represented are from three public defender firms (The Defender Association [TDA]; Associated Counsel for the Accused [ACA]; Society of Counsel Representing Accused Persons [SCRAP]). The typical case processing time for each firm [is] as follows: TDA, 89 days; ACA, 77 days; SCRAP, 59 days.

Table 4 Percent of Felony Cases Unresolved after 180 Days from the Date of Arrest for Indigent Defenders and Privately Retained Counsel (ABA Standards Stipulate That 2 Percent or Less of the Cases Should Be Unresolved)

	Detroit	Seattle[a]	Denver	Norfolk	Monterey	Globe	Oxford	Island	San Juan
Public defender	16.7%	19.0%	43.8%	—	8.3%	—	—	—	—
Contract attorney	—	—	—	—	3.9%	28.6%	—	—	0%
Assigned counsel	11.9%	—	45.5%	20.9%	20.0%	—	42.4%	44.6%	—
Privately retained attorneys	21.8%	26.4%	45.6%	51.1%	11.5%	27.2%	60.0%	47.2%	9.1%
All cases	14.4%	21.1%	44.2%	29.7%	8.0%	28.3%	49.1%	45.6%	3.4%

[a]In Seattle, the indigent defense attorneys represented are from three public defender agencies (The Defender Association [TDA]; Associated Counsel for the Accused [ACA]; Society of Counsel Representing Accused Persons [SCRAP]). The percentages of unresolved cases after 180 days for the three firms are as follows: TDA, 23.0%; ACA, 17.6%; SCRAP, 16.3%.

The quantitative results, which indicate that indigent defenders do well in terms of timeliness, have profound implications. One implication is that the expeditious adjudication of cases reduces the demand for additional court appearances and the length of time that defendants spend in jail awaiting disposition of their cases. The assembling of all the participants in the legal process for court proceedings and the pretrial detention of defendants are undeniably costly. Hence, indigent defenders contribute to cost savings by their timeliness.

Second, the closer approximation by indigent defenders to established time standards presents a picture that diverges from the popular image. A common view of indigent defenders is that they are engaging in dilatory tactics in one case in order to meet deadlines in other cases. Simply stated, they are viewed as unable to schedule their work, to satisfy time requirements, and to live within budgetary constraints. That point of view is not supported by the data from the nine courts under study. In terms of approximating time standards, indigent defenders perform better than privately retained attorneys. What other public institutions can make the claim that they perform as well as (or better than) the private sector?

Third, the achievement of timeliness frames the issue of effective representation in a new light. Instead of engaging in a philosophical debate over whether timeliness is inherently good or bad, one can ask the empirical question, Are the gains in efficiency made at the expense of the defendants? Are the rights or interests of defendants sacrificed in some way? The achievement of timeliness needs to be viewed side by side with information on the outcomes for defendants. The tasks of presenting and interpreting the necessary information are the subject of the next section.

PERFORMANCE AND INDIGENT DEFENSE

There are two basic approaches to assessing indigent defenders in the literature. The first approach has what may be called an input orientation. Indigent defenders are expected to represent their clients by being adequately prepared— meeting with clients, contacting witnesses, conducting research, reviewing presentence investigation reports, and so forth. Hence, a body of guidelines has been formulated that identifies how effective representation is to be conducted and the resources required to facilitate advocacy.[22]

The second approach has what may be called an output orientation.[23] Indigent defenders are expected to represent their clients by achieving favorable outcomes, such as acquittals and dismissals, charge reductions, noncustodial sentences, and the shortest possible periods of incarceration in prison. In this approach, the performance of indigent defenders is determined by comparing them with privately retained counsel. Do indigent defenders achieve the same percentage of favorable outcomes for their clients as privately retained counsel? This comparison sets a very high standard of evaluation for indigent defenders. There are several factors that have very little to do with the relative capabilities of attorneys that make it more difficult for indigent than nonindigent defendants to gain favorable outcomes. First, indigent defendants are more likely to be detained than defendants who can afford an attorney. Second, indigent defendants are more likely to have prior records that will be influential at sentencing. Third, indigent defendants are thought to be less assertive of their rights than defendants who can afford to pay for attorneys.[24]

Both of these approaches have their role to play in assessing indigent defense counsel. The first approach is appropriate for examining work that individual attorneys put into specific cases, but it provides no assessment of what the attorney accomplishes. Certainly, an attorney may meet with the client, interview witnesses, research the law, but do none of these activities effectively. Because the second approach draws conclusions concerning the performance of attorneys, it is the preferred orientation.

Conviction Rates

A fundamental concern to criminal defendants is gaining an acquittal or a dismissal. With a conviction comes the imposition of penalties. One basic goal of the defense attorney is to minimize the possibility of criminal penalties. In terms of measuring this goal, the standard is that the lower the conviction rate for a given set of attorneys, the more successful they are in gaining favorable outcomes for their clients.

The data indicate that indigent defenders perform as well as privately retained counsel in meeting this standard under a wide range of conditions. The conviction rates of defendants represented by public defenders, contract attorneys, assigned counsel, and privately retained counsel, when all nine courts are combined, are strikingly similar. Public defenders have a rate of 84.4 percent, contract attorneys have a rate of 83.6 percent, assigned counsel have a rate of 85.3 percent, and privately retained counsel have a rate of 83.4 percent. There is no statistically significant difference (chi-square = 1.26, significance level = .77) among these rates.[25] Defendants are no worse off with one type of defense attorney than another, which means that defendants with privately retained counsel do no better, on average, than do indigent defendants with a publicly appointed attorney.

The similarity in the conviction rates among the different types of defense attorneys extends to cases that go to trial. Public defenders secured acquittal or dismissal in 23.2 percent of cases; contract attorneys, 28.6 percent; assigned counsel, 33.3 percent; and privately retained counsel, 25.6 percent. Thus indigent defenders are no less successful in gaining acquittals or dismissals for their clients than are privately retained counsel. There is no statistically significant relationship (chi-square = 2.74, significance level = .43) between the types of attorneys and the likelihood of conviction at trial.

These results raise an additional question. Are the conviction rates similar for different types of attorneys in both the large- and small-sized courts? This more refined question outstrips the available data to some extent. There are too few contract attorneys in either the large-sized or the small-sized courts to permit valid statistical testing. However, if all the indigent defenders are collapsed into one category, then this question can be addressed in terms of the conviction rates of publicly appointed attorneys versus privately retained counsel.

The data indicate that there is no linkage between the type of attorney and the likelihood of conviction either in the large-sized or in the small-sized courts. The conviction rates for publicly appointed and privately retained attorneys in the large courts (Detroit, Seattle, Denver, Norfolk, and Monterey) are 84.8 percent and 82 percent, respectively. In the small-sized courts (Oxford, Globe, Island, and San Juan), the parallel percentages are 84.1 and 86.3.[26] These are not statistically significant differences. Hence, within the limitations of the available data, the evidence indicates that indigent defenders do as well as privately retained counsel in terms of a fundamental criterion of performance. The likelihood of an indigent defendant being convicted is not influenced significantly by the fact that the defense attorney is publicly appointed.

Charge Reductions

From the perspective of the defendant and the defense attorney, any success is a victory. Given the fact that most defendants are convicted, one of the best outcomes that most defendants can realistically strive for is a reduction in the seriousness of charge. If the offense at conviction is a less serious offense than the offense with which the defendant was initially charged, this outcome is favorable to the defendant. The empirical question is, Do privately retained counsel have significantly different charge reduction rates from those of indigent defenders?

For the four types of defense attorneys, this question can be addressed only for the cases disposed of by guilty pleas, because the number of trials is limited for some categories of attorneys. The data reveal that there are significant differences in charge reduction rates among the categories of defense attorneys. The charge reduction rates for public defenders, contract attorneys, assigned counsel, and privately retained counsel are 25.7, 50.9, 26.4, and 31.9 percent, respectively. Contract attorneys do considerably better than the privately retained counsel, who do slightly better than the public defenders or the assigned counsel.[27] Hence, for cases involving guilty pleas, there are mixed results concerning the performance of indigent defenders. Some indigent defenders perform quite well whereas others perform less well than privately retained counsel.

If all indigent defenders are combined into one category, then the question of the linkage between type of attorney and charge reductions also can be examined for different-sized courts. From this perspective the size of the court produces opposite effects. In the large courts, privately retained attorneys gain more reductions (32 percent) than do publicly appointed counsel (26.3 percent). In the small-sized courts, privately retained counsel gain fewer reductions (28.7 percent) than do publicly appointed counsel (37.4 percent). Both sets of results are weak statistically, however.[28] In the large courts the correlation between the type of attorney and the likelihood of a charge reduction is very low (phi-square = .05). For the small-sized courts, the relationship is not statistically significant.[29] Hence, while the type of defense attorney may have some effect on charge reductions, the effect is negligible.

On the basis of these data, the performance of indigent defenders in gaining charge reductions is somewhat mixed. Contract attorneys do better than privately retained counsel, while public defenders and assigned counsel do less well.

This connection, however, is weak statistically (Cramer's $V = .15$). Similarly, publicly appointed counsel gain more charge reductions in small-sized courts and fewer charge reductions in large-sized courts than do privately retained counsel. These connections, while demonstrating opposite effects, are weak. Thus, overall, indigent defenders perform about as well as privately retained counsel in obtaining charge reductions.

Incarceration Rates

The potential advantage that privately retained counsel have over indigent defenders should be the greatest in determining whether a convicted defendant is incarcerated in jail or prison, sentenced to probation, given community service, or fined. The prior record of the defendant is likely to play a major role in this decision. Unfortunately, the collection of data on the defendant's prior record was beyond the scope of this research. If it is true that indigent defendants are more likely to have prior records than nonindigent defendants, this missing information means that the examination of incarceration rates, without controlling for the effects of prior record, is tipped somewhat in favor of privately retained counsel. Yet, despite this potential advantage, privately retained counsel are only slightly more successful in keeping their clients out of jail or prison.

The incarceration rates are lower for cases represented by privately retained counsel. Assigned counsel and privately retained counsel have approximately the same incarceration rates (60.3 versus 57.1). Public defenders (78.2) and contract attorneys (74.6) are less successful in keeping their clients out of penal institutions. However, the association between the four types of defense attorneys and the corresponding incarceration rates is only moderate (Cramer's $V = .20$).[30] This correlation means that privately retained attorneys are more likely to gain favorable outcomes for their clients, but this advantage is limited. A majority of the convicted defendants represented by every type of defense attorney are incarcerated. The size of the majority is greater for indigent defense attorneys, but nearly six of every ten defendants represented by privately retained counsel are incarcerated.

How indigent defenders and privately retained counsel compare is seen more clearly when all indigent defenders are grouped together. Felony defendants with publicly appointed counsel are incarcerated 72.4 percent of the time, while those who privately retain their attorneys end up in prison or jail 58.2 percent of the time. The correlation between these two types of defense attorneys and the in/out decision is a very weak one (phi-square = .12).[31] The slightly better performance by privately retained counsel, moreover, appears to be due to the effect of public defenders on the population of all indigent defenders. The use of a public defender appears to influence the higher incarceration rate among publicly appointed attorneys. The question thus arises, If public defenders are excluded from the analysis, then what do the results look like? The absence of public defenders occurs naturally when the courts are separated according to size. Whereas public defenders work in four of the five large courts, they are not present in any of the four small courts. The results of this analysis show that privately retained attorneys perform better than publicly appointed attorneys in both the large courts and the small courts.

In the large courts, privately retained attorneys perform better (50.5 percent of clients incarcerated) than publicly appointed counsel (71.5 percent of clients incarcerated). The difference in incarceration rates is statistically significant, but it is limited, as indicated by a weak correlation coefficient (phi-square = .17).[32] The underlying reason why the connection is weak rests on the fact that indigent defenders represented 83 percent of defendants and obtained 74 percent of the sentences involving some penalty other than incarceration. Privately retained counsel represented 17 percent of the defendants and obtained 26 percent of the sentences involving nonincarceration. Given that indigent defenders cannot choose their clients, and privately retained counsel do have some control over whom they represent, these differences are much smaller than expected. Moreover, in the small-sized courts, the differences are in favor of publicly appointed counsel, although the incarceration rates are not statistically different. The incarceration rate is 77.4 percent for privately retained counsel and 75.2 percent for publicly appointed counsel, which is in the opposite direction of the advantage that privately retained counsel are expected to enjoy.[33]

Thus, privately retained counsel perform somewhat better than indigent defenders on the basic in/out dimension. However, the greater likelihood that privately retained counsel keep their clients out of jail or prison is limited both in magnitude and in the scope of the effects. In the small-sized courts, privately retained counsel and publicly appointed attorneys perform at the same level. Given the assumption that indigent defendants are much less likely to win favorable outcomes because of their prior records, limited ties to the community, and other social circumstances, the limited degree of success by privately retained counsel falls short of that expectation. The results suggest that indigent defenders are able to overcome the potential liabilities of their clients to a very great extent.

CONCLUSION

How frequently do indigent defenders gain favorable outcomes for their clients? Are they more successful than, less successful than, or equally as successful as privately retained counsel in gaining favorable outcomes? The evidence gained from an examination of felony dispositions in the nine courts is that indigent defenders generally are as successful as privately retained counsel. The conviction rates, the charge reduction rates, and the incarceration rates for their clients are similar to the outcomes associated with privately retained counsel. These results raise a couple of issues for future consideration.

First, the results are helpful in identifying what aspects of performance are translatable into management information systems and what aspects warrant further research and development. The measurement of case outcomes seems sufficiently feasible and the results seem sufficiently meaningful to merit inclusion into the monitoring of indigent defense systems. Consequently, judges, policy makers, and others concerned with the quality of indigent defense representation should take the necessary steps to gather information on how well indigent defenders do in gaining favorable outcomes for their clients.

However, the measures of performance in this article do not speak to the issue of lawyer–client relations, especially the time that indigent defenders give to individual defendants. How frequently do they meet with clients? What is the average amount of time spent with clients? Previous research has indicated that the amount of time that indigent defenders spend with their clients makes a difference in client satisfaction. The more time that is spent, the more defendants are satisfied with their attorneys.

Satisfaction should not be confused with productive work. Indigent defenders know how to husband resources and to gain the most favorable outcomes for their clients expeditiously. However, satisfaction is part of performance and deserves further examination. Future research needs to be conducted on this topic in order to establish more precisely what amount and what kind of time indigent defenders should be expected to devote to meeting with their clients, within the constraints of their caseloads.[34]

Second, the results suggest that judges, policy makers, attorneys, and others are not required to choose between timeliness and performance. Evidence from the nine courts in this study indicate that both goals are possible to achieve. The fact that these goals are not necessarily in conflict means that the task confronting the courts is to organize an indigent defense system responsible to community needs and circumstances that achieves both goals. That task, which is neither easy nor obvious, is possible. However, the lesson to be learned is that courts have the opportunity to design a system where both timeliness and performance are attained.

NOTES

1. Michael McConville and Chester L. Mirsky, "Criminal Defense of the Poor in New York City," 15 *New York University Review of Law and Social Change* 881 (1986–1987). An underlying theme to McConville and Mirsky's work is that indigent defenders are coopted by the courthouse community. This theme is a traditional one in the literature. See, for example, David Sudnow, "Normal Crimes: A Sociological Feature of the Penal Code in a Public Defender Office," 12 *Social Problems* 253 (1965); Abraham S. Blumberg, "The Practice of Law Is a Confidence Game: Organizational Co-optation of a Profession," 1 *Law and Society Review* 15 (1967); Dennis R. Eckart and Robert V. Stover, "Public Defenders and Routinized Criminal Defense Processes," 51 *Journal of Urban Law* 665 (May 1974); J. P. Levine, "The Impact of 'Gideon': The Performance of Public and Private Defense Lawyers," 8 *Polity* 215 (1975); Suzzane E. Mounts and Richard

Wilson, "Systems for Providing Indigent Defense: An Introduction," 14 *New York University Review of Law and Social Change* 193 (1986).

2. See, for example, Lisa J. McIntyre, *The Public Defender: The Practice of Law in the Shadows of Repute* (Chicago: University of Chicago Press, 1987).

3. Some studies focus on very large communities. See, for example, Robert Hermann, Eric Single, and John Boston's study of New York, Los Angeles, and Washington, D.C., in *Counsel for the Poor: Criminal Defense in Urban America* (Lexington, Mass.: D. C. Heath, 1977). See also James Eisenstein and Herbert Jacob's study of Baltimore, Detroit, and Chicago in *Felony Justice: An Organizational Analysis of Criminal Courts* (Boston: Little, Brown, 1977). On the other hand, Peter Nardulli focuses exclusively on nine medium-sized communities (DuPage, Peoria, and St. Clair counties

in Illinois; Kalamazoo, Oakland, and Saginaw counties in Michigan; Dauphin, Erie, and Montgomery counties in Pennsylvania) in "Insider's Justice: Defense Attorneys and the Handling of Felony Cases," 77 *Journal of Criminal Law and Criminology* 379 (1986). Prior research with the broadest scope is a study of eight medium-sized and small-sized communities all located in Virginia by Larry J. Cohen, Patricia P. Semple, and Robert E. Crew, Jr., "Assigned Counsel versus Public Defender Systems in Virginia: A Comparison of Relative Benefits," in *The Defense Counsel,* edited by William F. McDonald (Newbury Park, Calif.: Sage Publications, 1983).

4. Some of the studies, in fact, do not compare indigent defenders with privately retained counsel. See, for example, McConville and Mirsky, "Criminal Defense of the Poor in New York City" (note 1). The lack of a comparison group poses severe methodological problems because evaluations require some form of comparison.

5. Hereafter the courts will be referred to by the names that they commonly are called in order to facilitate exposition. The names are Detroit, Seattle, Denver, Norfolk, Monterey, Oxford, Globe, Island, and San Juan.

6. Robert L. Spangenberg, Beverely Lee, Michael Batlaglia, Patricia Smith, and A. David Davis, *National Criminal Defense System Study: Final Report* (Washington, D.C.: U.S. Department of Justice, 1986).

7. Paul B. Wice, *Criminal Lawyers: An Endangered Species* (Newbury Park, Calif.: Sage Publications, 1978).

8. There are minor differences in the caseload composition of defense attorneys. All three basic categories of indigent defenders tend to have the same distribution of felony cases. Most of their cases involve burglary and theft offenses, followed by, in descending order of frequency, crimes against the person, drug sale and possession, and other types of felonies. The only difference between their caseloads and those of privately retained counsel lies in the fact that privately retained counsel have more crimes against the person than burglary and theft cases. However, this difference is not sharp.

9. The population of Wayne County was 2,164,300 in 1986. The city of Detroit accounted for just over one-half of the total county population (1,086,220), making it the sixth-largest city in the United States. The total population living within the city, however, has been in decline since the 1950s. Approximately 39 percent of the Wayne County population is identified as nonwhite. Per capita income is $10,681, with just over 14 percent of the population living below the poverty level. Wayne County's crime rate was 9,864 serious crimes per 100,000 population.

10. In 1988, the Seattle primary metropolitan area had a population of 1,862,000, with the city of Seattle accounting for just under one-third of the total (502,000). Seattle, the twenty-fourth-largest city in the country, experienced a growth in population of 1.7 percent from 1980 to 1988; just over 12 percent of its population is identified as nonwhite. Of the nine communities under examination, Seattle had the second-highest per capita income ($13,192) and the lowest percentage of individuals living below the poverty line (7.7 percent).

11. Several years ago, the Seattle City Council, members of the bar, and some indigent defendants questioned whether there was insufficient minority representation on the board of directors and in management positions at TDA, ACA, and SCRAP. The response, in addition to increasing the awareness of affirmative action in the three agencies, was to create a fourth firm with management by minority-group members, Northwest Defenders Association (NDA). NDA, which did not represent felony cases in 1990–1991, is not investigated in this study.

12. The Defender Association, an outgrowth of Seattle's Model City Program, was created in 1967 with a staff of five. In 1969, 166 individuals were employed at TDA, seventy-one of whom were attorneys. It was the only agency that provided indigent defense services for all case types: felony, misdemeanor, juvenile offender, juvenile dependency, and municipal court cases.

13. In 1987, ACA employed eighty-three individuals, fifty-five of whom were professional staff. The types of cases handled by ACA are felony, misdemeanor, juvenile offender, and Seattle municipal court cases.

The director of ACA values having a core of experienced attorneys (that is, four to six years), but he has reservations about "lifers." About 20 percent of the attorneys have five to seven years of experience, and most attorneys have about three years of experience.

14. In 1987, SCRAP employed 29.5 full-time equivalents, 18 of whom were professionals. Most attorneys are recent law school graduates. New attorneys start in juvenile offender or dependency and may work into felonies if they are interested. Most felony attorneys gain experience within the firm in other divisions, but there are some lateral hires of experienced felony lawyers. Felony attorneys are hired by an ad hoc, two-member hiring committee consisting of the felony supervisor and another felony lawyer. Tenure in the felony division was difficult to assess because the firm had been handling these cases for only about the last five years.

15. The defender firms have no funding in their own budgets for expert witnesses. Funds for experts are found in the superior court budget, and defenders obtain them through an order from the judge. The judge is able to sign off for up to $350. If a higher amount is requested, it goes to an audit committee for acceptance or rejection. Some of the attorneys who were interviewed were not aware of the procedure for obtaining an amount in excess of $350.

16. Denver is the largest city in the Rocky Mountain region. Its population of 505,000 in 1986 tended to be divided between a relatively affluent majority and a very poor minority. A most striking feature of Denver is its crime rate of 10,557 serious crimes per 100,000 population.

17. Norfolk, Virginia, is a core city declining in population, with limited growth due to the out-migration of both middle-income residents and some poor residents (through the demolition of housing projects). Racial minorities constitute 38.4 percent of the population, and about 21 percent live below the poverty level. Norfolk had a violent crime rate in 1985 of 6,561 per 100,000.

18. The population of Monterey County was 340,000 in 1986. Approximately 15 percent of the county's population is His-panic. In 1985, the per capita income was $10,420, with 11.4 percent of the population below the poverty level. Monterey County's crime rate was 5,419 serious crimes per 100,000 population.

19. Gila County is a large geographic area (4,752 square miles), approximately half the size of Rhode Island. It is located approximately 90 miles east of Phoenix in the state's copper mining region. It also includes a growing recreational and retirement community (Payson-Pine), although the Miami-Globe community is larger. Demographically, Gila County is a community of 37,000 persons, with 15 percent of the population identified as nonwhite (primarily Hispanic and American Indian, since the county is bordered on the east by two Indian reservations). The per capita income in 1985 was $7,399.

20. The population of Oxford County was 50,200 in 1986, approximately 4 percent of Maine's total population of 1,250,000. Oxford County is located in the southwestern mountain region of Maine. The basic industries in this area center around lumbering and paper production. The per capital income is $8,379, with just under 13 percent of the population living below the poverty level. Less than one-half of 1 percent of Oxford County is identified as nonwhite. The serious crime rate for Oxford was 1,781 index crimes per 100,000 population in 1985.

21. Island and San Juan counties are adjacent counties that consist only of islands. By Western United States standards they are very small in area (212 square miles for Island; 179 square miles for San Juan). Both counties are rural in character; however, a Naval Air Station in Island County gives Island a somewhat different flavor. Both counties have a low to virtually nonexistent minority population and high real estate values. The median value of homes in San Juan County is $87,300—the highest in the state and nearly one-third higher than the state median—and the median real estate value in Island County is nearly identical to the state median of $60,700. Crime rates are 2,278 and 2,843 per 100,000 population for Island and San Juan, respectively.

22. Roberta Rovner-Pieczenik, Alan Rapoport, and Martha Lane, *How Does*

Your Defender Office Rate? Self-Evaluation Manual for Public Defender Offices (Washington, D.C.: Government Publications Office, 1977), especially pages 38–43 concerning measures of "attorney competence." American Bar Association Project on Standards for Criminal Justice, *Standards Relating to the Prosecution Function and the Defense Function* (Washington, D.C.: American Bar Association, 1971), especially pages 225–228 concerning the "duty to investigate." William Genego, "Future of Effective Assistance of Counsel: Performance Standards and Complete Representation," 22 *American Criminal Law Review* 181 (Fall 1984). National Study Commission on Defense Services, *Guidelines for Legal Defense System in the United States* (Washington, D.C.: National Legal Aid and Defender Association, 1976), especially pages 428–447 on "ensuring effectiveness."

23. See, for example, Hermann, Single, and Boston, *Counsel for the Poor* (note 3); Joyce Sterling, "Retained Counsel Versus the Public Defender," in William F. McDonald, ed., *The Defense Counsel* (Newbury Park, Calif.: Sage Publications, 1983), pp. 68–76; David Willison, "The Effects of Counsel on the Severity of Criminal Sentences: A Statistical Assessment," 9 *Justice System Journal* 87 (1984).

24. Some scholars suggest that it is utopian to expect that indigent defenders will perform as well as privately retained counsel. Willison, "The Effects of the Severity of Criminal Sentences" (note 23), writes that indigent defenders will "fail to perform as successfully as privately retained counsel even if they are adequately funded and have workable caseloads so long as they continue to represent disadvantaged defendants facing serious criminal charges and possessing extensive criminal records" (88).

25. In this section, two basic statistical tests are applied to determine whether there is a connection between the different types of defense attorneys and performance and the strength of the connection. The first test is a test of significance. The test of significance indicates whether there is a systematic connection as opposed to a coincidental connection. The chi-square test is the particular test that is applied. This technique generates a number and a corresponding level of significance. The smaller the significance level, the less likely it is that the observed pattern could have happened by chance alone. In this article, the benchmark of .01 is used to determine when there are statistically significant differences (that is, results could have happened by chance alone only one time out of a hundred).

The second test is a test of association. If there is a systematic connection, how close is it? The test of association measures the strength of connection in terms of a correlation coefficient. The coefficient ranges in value from zero to one. Basically, the larger the value of the coefficient, the tighter the connection is between the different types of attorneys and various case outcomes. The phi-square and the Cramer's *V* correlations are the tests of association that are applied. Phi-square is appropriate for all two-by-two tables, and Cramer's *V* is appropriate for all the others. Finally, the rule of thumb is that coefficients below .20 are considered to be indications of weak connections between the types of attorneys and case outcomes, those from .21 to .40 are considered to indicate moderate connections, and coefficients from .41 to 1.0 are considered to indicate strong connections.

26. Large courts: chi-square = 1.91, significance level = .17, phi-square = .03. Small courts: chi-square = .46, significance level = .49, chi-square = .46.

27. The relatively high level of success among contract attorneys may be due to the unusually high level of experience, especially among the contract attorneys in Monterey and Globe.

28. Chi-square = 48.12, significance level = .0001, Cramer's *V* = .15.

29. Large courts: chi-square = 4.43, significance level = .04, phi-square = .05. Small courts: chi-square = .46, significance level = .49, phi-square = .03.

30. Chi-square = 87.79, significance level = .0001, Cramer's *V* = .20.

31. Chi-square = 36.00, significance level = .0001, phi-square = .12.

32. Chi-square = 55.00, significance level = .0001, phi-square = .17.

33. Chi-square $= .261$, significance level $= .01$, phi-square $= .03$.

34. Jonathan D. Casper, "Did You Have a Lawyer When You Went to Court? No. I Had a Public Defender," *Yale Review of Law and Social Action* 4–9 (Spring 1971). More generally, researchers have found that the felony defendant's degree of satisfaction with the outcome of the case is shaped by the procedural fairness of the process. Procedural fairness includes measures of the defendant's views of the defense attorney's, prosecutor's, and judge's behavior (for example, Did your lawyer listen to you? Did the prosecutor pay careful attention to your case? Did the judge try hard to find out if you were guilty or innocent?). See also Jonathan D. Casper, Tom Tyler, and Bonnie Fisher, "Procedural Justice in Felony Cases," 22 *Law and Society Review* 483 (1988).

PART V

Courts

Conditions in the lower criminal courts are shocking to observers. Most city courtrooms have little of the quiet dignity one expects to see when decisions concerning individual freedom and justice are being made. The scene is usually one of noise and confusion as attorneys, police, and prosecutors mill around conversing with one another and making bargains to keep the assembly line of the criminal justice process in operation. One might see a judge accepting guilty pleas and imposing sentences at a rapid pace, going through the litany of procedure like a bored priest. It is not surprising that visitors are shocked and that first offenders are confused by what they see.

The courts, like other parts of the justice system, function under conditions of mass production, congestion, and limited resources. Even in the courts, the interests of the organization and of the principal actors often take precedence over the claims of justice. The mass production of judicial decisions is accomplished because the street-level bureaucrats in the system work on the basis of three assumptions. The first is that only people for whom there is a high probability of guilt will be brought before the courts; doubtful cases will be filtered out of the system by the police and the prosecution. Second, the vast majority of defendants will plead guilty. In most urban courts less than 10 percent of defendants plead not guilty. Third, those charged with minor offenses will be processed quickly. This usually means that all the defendants will be called together before the bench, the citation will be read by the clerk, individual pleas will be taken by the judge, and sentences quickly pronounced.

It is tempting to believe that adding more judges and constructing new facilities will relieve courtroom overload, but other factors contribute to the situation—for example, poor management, the rise in the amount of crime, and the presence of lawyers. Some argue that the procedural requirements laid down by the U.S. Supreme Court have lengthened the processing time, yet observers point out that defendants are typically informed en masse of their rights by a droning bailiff. In addition, most defendants actually waive their right to a trial, and many do not even want the services of an attorney.

The problem of court congestion has become widely recognized during the past decade. Observers both inside and outside of government have deplored the fact that defendants in criminal cases often wait in jail for months before they come to trial. More important than conditions in the criminal courts are the filtering effect, the administrative determination of guilt, and the exchange relationships that characterize the system. As long as the system is able to function in accordance with the needs of the players, the additional judges and courtrooms demanded by reformers will not bring about a shift to due process values.

TO BE A JUDGE

More than any other person in the system, the judge is expected to embody justice, thereby ensuring that the right to due process is respected and that the defendant is treated fairly. We recognize that the prosecutor and the defense attorney each represent a particular side in a criminal case. By contrast, the judge's black robe and gavel symbolize the impartiality we expect from our courts. The judge is supposed to act both in and outside the courthouse according to a well-defined role designed to prevent involvement in anything that could tarnish the judiciary's reputation. We expect judges to make careful, consistent decisions that uphold the ideals of equal justice for all citizens.

This image of judges devoting themselves to careful deliberations and thoughtful decisions does not, in fact, reflect the daily reality for most American judges. Lower court judges can face significant caseloads that require them to quickly exercise discretion in the disposition and punishment of minor offenses with little supervision from any higher court. Although judges are popularly portrayed as being forced to decide complex legal issues, in reality their courtroom tasks are routine. Because of the unending flow of cases, they operate with assembly-line precision; many judges, like many workers, soon tire of the repetition.

In most cities, criminal court judges occupy the lowest rank in the judicial hierarchy. Lawyers and citizens alike fail to accord them the same respect and prestige enjoyed by judges in civil and appellate courts. As with other professions, the status of criminal trial judges may be linked to the status of the people whom they serve. Criminal court judges deal with the lowliest and most despised segment of society—criminal defendants—and the work is often conducted in the busiest, noisiest, and least attractive courtrooms. The never-ending flow of tragic stories, poor people, and substance abusers is a far cry from the solemn, wood-paneled, velvet-curtained marble temples that are more typical of higher courts. As a result, the possibility of moving to civil or appellate courts motivates many trial judges while they deal with the heavy caseloads and tough working conditions of the criminal court.

All judges are addressed as "Your Honor," and we must rise to our feet in deference whenever they enter or leave the courtroom. This respect and deference is not based on any certainty that each judge is highly qualified and fair. In fact, judges often are chosen for reasons that have very little to do with either their legal qualifications or their judicial manner. Instead, they may be chosen because of their political connections, friendships with influential officials, or financial contributions to political parties.

There is a strong reform movement to place men and women of quality on the bench. Reformers urge that judges be experienced experts in law. Many people believe that selection of judges on a nonpolitical basis will produce higher quality, more efficient, more independent, and consequently more impartial and fair members of the judiciary.

In opposition are those who argue that in a democracy the voters should elect the people charged with carrying out public policies, including judges. They contend that people chosen by their fellow citizens can better handle the steady stream of human problems confronting the judges of the nation.

THE COURTROOM: HOW IT FUNCTIONS

Although similar rules and processes are used in criminal cases throughout the nation, differences among courthouses are visible to anyone who has observed American courts. Some courts sentence offenders to longer terms than do others. In some jurisdictions, court delays and tough bail policies keep many of the accused in jail awaiting trial, while in other jurisdictions similar defendants gain pretrial release or have their cases resolved relatively quickly. Guilty pleas may make up 90 percent of dispositions in some communities but only 60 percent in others. How can we explain these differences among courts in various cities—differences which can exist even among different judges' courtrooms in the same city?

Social scientists have long recognized that culture of a community—its shared beliefs and attitudes—has a great influence on how its members behave. Culture implies shared beliefs about proper behavior. Sets of shared beliefs can span entire nations or exist within types of smaller communities. Within any community, large or small, the shared beliefs of its culture can exert a powerful influence over people's decisions and behavior.

Researchers have identified a *local legal culture*—values and norms shared by members of a particular court community (judges, attorneys, clerks, bailiffs, and others)—regarding the handling of cases and court officials' expected behavior in the judicial process. The local legal culture influences court operations in three ways.

First, shared values and expectations help participants distinguish between "our" court and other courts. Often a judge or prosecutor will proudly describe how "we" do the job differently and better than officials in the neighboring county or city.

Second, norms—the shared values and expectations—tell members of a court community how they should treat one another. For example, mounting a strong adversarial defense may be viewed as not in keeping with the norms of one court while it is the expected behavior in another.

Third, norms describe how cases *should* be processed. The best example of this situation is the *going rate,* the shared local view about the appropriate sentence given the offense, the defendant's prior record, and other characteristics. The local legal culture also includes attitudes about issues such as the appropriateness of judicial participation in plea negotiations, when continuances—lawyers' requests for delays in court proceedings—should be granted, and which defendants are eligible for representation by a public defender.

The differences among local legal cultures help to explain why court decisions are dissimilar even though the formal rules of criminal procedure are basically the same. For example, we often think of judges applying their discretion in determining sentences for convicted offenders. While judges' discretion can be an important factor in sentencing, the concept of the "going rate" helps to show us that sentences are normally the product of shared understandings among the prosecutor, defense attorney, and judge involved in the plea bargaining or trial for a particular case. In one courthouse, shared understandings may impose probation on the first-time thief, but in other locales, different shared values among lawyers and judges may send such first offenders to jail or prison for the same offense.

Informal rules and practices arise within particular settings, and "the way things are done" differs from place to place. As one might expect, the local legal culture of San Francisco inevitably differs from that of Burlington, Vermont, or Baltimore. The customs and traditions of each jurisdiction vary because local practices are influenced by factors such as size, politics, and demographics. Among these, differences between urban and rural areas are a major factor.

SENTENCING

Sentencing is often difficult, since it is not merely a matter of applying clear-cut principles to individual cases. In one case, a judge may decide to sentence a forger to prison as an example to others despite his being no threat to community safety and probably not in need of rehabilitative treatment. In another case, the judge may impose a light sentence on a youthful offender who, although he has committed a serious crime, may be a good risk for rehabilitation if he can be moved quickly back into society.

Legislatures establish the penal codes that set forth the sentences that judges may impose. These laws generally give judges wide powers of discretion with regard to sentencing. They may combine various forms of punishment to tailor the sanction to the offender. The judge may stipulate, for example, that the prison terms for two charges are to run either concurrently (at the same time) or consecutively (one after the other) or that all or part of the period of imprisonment may be suspended. In other situations, the offender may be given a combination of a suspended prison term, probation, and a fine. Judges may also suspend a sentence as long as the offender stays out of trouble, makes restitution, or seeks medical treatment. The judge may also delay imposing any sentence but retain power to set penalties at a later date if the offender misbehaves.

Within the discretion allowed by the penal code, various elements in the sentencing process influence the decisions of judges. These may include the administrative context of the court and the attitudes and values of the judges.

In the administrative context of the criminal courts, judges often do not have time to consider all the crucial elements of the offense and the special circumstances of the offender before imposing a sentence. Especially when the violation is minor, there is a tendency for judges to routinize decision making, announcing sentences to fit certain categories of crimes without paying much attention to the particular offender. Individuals convicted of minor offenses, and therefore possibly the most likely to be reformed, are frequently sentenced immediately after being found guilty or when they enter a guilty plea. If counsel requests a presentence report before imposition of sentence, the necessary delay may require that the defendant remain in jail—a price many are unwilling to pay.

That judges exhibit different sentencing tendencies is taken as a fact of life by the court community. These differences can be attributed to such factors as the conflicting goals of criminal justice; the differing backgrounds and social values of judges; and the influence of the local legal culture. Each of these factors influences a judge's exercise of discretion in sentencing offenders. In addition, a judge's perception of these factors can be dependent on his or her own attitudes toward the law, toward a particular crime, or toward a type of offender.

Who Gets the Harshest Punishment?

The prison population in most states contains a higher proportion of African Americans and Hispanic Americans than is found in the general population. In addition, poor people are more likely to be convicted of crimes than those with higher incomes. Is this situation a result of the prejudicial attitudes of judges, police officers, and prosecutors? Are poor people more liable to commit crimes that elicit a strong response from society? Are enforcement resources distributed so that certain groups are subject to closer scrutiny than other groups? Research on these and similar questions is inconclusive. Some studies have shown that members of racial minorities and the poor are treated more harshly by the system; other research has been unable to demonstrate a direct link between harshness of sentence and race or social class. These are a few of the questions that must be answered if we are to correct present inequities in the criminal justice system.

SUGGESTIONS FOR FURTHER READING

Eisenstein, James, Roy Flemming, and Peter Nardulli. *The Contours of Justice: Communities and Their Courts.* Pearson Education, Inc., 1988. A study of nine felony courts in three states. Emphasizes the impact of the local legal culture on court operations.

Eisenstein, James, and Herbert Jacob. *Felony Justice: An Organizational Analysis of Criminal Courts.* Boston: Little, Brown, 1977. Felony courts in three cities. Develops the concept of the courtroom workgroup and its impact on decision making.

Feeley, Malcolm M. *Court Reform on Trial.* New York: Basic Books, 1983. Study of court reform efforts such as diversion, speedy trial, bail reform, and sentencing reform. Notes the difficulties of bringing about change.

Gaylin, Willard. *The Killing of Bonnie Garland*. New York: Simon and Schuster, 1982. True story of the murder of a Yale student by her boyfriend and the reaction of the criminal justice system to the crime. Raises important questions about the goals of the criminal sanction and the role of the victim in the process.

Rosenberg, Gerald. *The Hollow Hope*. Chicago: University of Chicago Press, 1991. Explores the efficacy of courts as policy makers, how decisions influence implementation, and the ability of the courts to enact social change.

Satter, Robert. *Doing Justice: A Trial Judge at Work*. New York: Simon and Schuster, 1990. A judge's view of the cases that he faces daily and the factors that influence his decisions.

Wice, Paul. *Judges and Lawyers: The Human Side of Justice*. New York: Harper Collins, 1991. Provides detailed descriptions of the training, socialization, and work environments of lawyers and judges, including coverage of each profession's special pressures and ethical issues.

16

✦

The Criminal Court Community in Erie County, Pennsylvania

JAMES EISENSTEIN
ROY B. FLEMMING
PETER F. NARDULLI

The traditional picture of the courtroom emphasizes adversarial attitudes, but a more realistic picture might emphasize the interaction among the major actors within the normative context of the work group and the local legal culture. As you read about the criminal court community in Erie County, Pennsylvania, think about the impact of the local legal culture and the interpersonal relationships among the principal actors on decision making. How might the court in Erie County differ from that in your home community?

SIZE, COMPOSITION,
AND COMMUNICATION
IN THE COURT COMMUNITY

Erie's criminal court community displayed several features that reflected the characteristics of the county it served. We begin our description of the court community by looking at these characteristics.

People tended to stay in Erie County. In 1980, 90 percent of its population had lived there at least since 1975, the highest proportion among our nine

Source: From *The Contours of Justice: Communities and Their Courts,* by James Eisenstein et al., pp. 74–103. Copyright © 1988 by James Eisenstein, Roy B. Flemming and Peter F. Nardulli. Reprinted by permission of Pearson Education, Inc. Some footnotes deleted.

counties.[1] Among the five "standard metropolitan statistical areas" (SMSAs) in our nine counties, the Erie SMSA showed the lowest rate of migration into the area (10 percent) from 1975 to 1980. The low influx of newcomers meant that people tended to know each other. Despite its population of 280,000, the county, and especially the city and its suburbs, exhibited the familiarity and extensive network of social ties usually associated with small towns. One person told us:

> Erie's an interesting community in that there are a lot of people in this community who are related to one another. I mean with strings, and cousins and distant cousins—that's the problem. A lot of the marriages— I can think of several older Republican families, and their families have married. There are a lot of small (100 to 200) industrial firms that have been run by older Erie families. It's in the school board; it's in the government; it's just everywhere.

These patterns facilitated the development of another feature of small towns, a highly effective and extensive community grapevine. An attorney who had lived in Pittsburgh commented that

> you could go over into another segment of Pittsburgh and nobody would know you. Here, someone once said, if you break a window at 10th and State, by the time you hit 6th and State, it's in the morning newspaper. There are grapevines all over the place.

Like many newspapers serving smaller towns, Erie's morning and evening papers combined a conservative editorial policy with "community boosterism." Published by the same company, both papers' editorials called for harsher sentences, and the morning paper's managing editor was described as a "hard-line criminal justice man." Nevertheless, because the papers wanted to project an image of Erie as a nice community with few serious problems, they did not sensationalize crime, single out individuals for criticism, or engage in in-depth investigative reporting on the courts. A content analysis of the papers' coverage of crime found fewer and shorter articles about crime and the courts than in the other two Pennsylvania counties. Furthermore, the papers deliberately refrained from reporting an important feature of sentencing policy. One attorney told us that

> [E]verybody knows that prostitutes get six months or a year, and get out in ten days because the press doesn't follow it up. The press is there when the judge sentences them, but the press doesn't follow up, and the judge cuts them loose.

In fact, a prosecutor claimed that a reporter had written a story describing this practice, only to have it killed by his editors.

The newspapers' treatment of the courts probably also reflected the effects of social and business ties common in small communities. The head public defender's law firm and several of the judges had served as legal counsel to editors or publishers. Another attorney told us of his friendship with the editor: "We do things in charitable organizations together. It's a small town . . . everybody knows everybody."

The criminal court community reflected many of the characteristics of the larger community just described. Lawyers referred to the Erie County bar as "small," even though more than 300 lawyers practiced there. As one stated, "It's an easy place to get to know everybody." Furthermore, a relatively small group of people formed the core of the criminal court community. Three of the five judges heard most of the cases. Nine attorneys staffed the district attorney's office and fourteen the public defender's. Together, these twenty-eight people handled half the cases. A group of about fifty private attorneys joined the prosecutors and judges to handle the other half of the caseload. But just five of them represented about 40 percent of defendants with private counsel. Thus a core group of thirty-three people disposed of about 70 percent of the caseload.

Familiarity extended to other participants as well. One attorney summarized the results of his analysis of about 700 of his case files: "The same names appeared over and over again. . . . You see family names. . . . You'll get the father, the older brother, the younger brother, the sister, the mother." Another lawyer said that the judges, being political creatures, also knew many of the defendants. A third told us, "Basically, you see the same [police] officers. . . . There are a lot of detectives but there are only a few that do any work."

The Erie court community's small size and the familiarity of its members with one another undoubtedly contributed to the effectiveness of its grapevine.[2] . . . A public defender confirmed our suspicion about its effectiveness when we asked if there were *any* secrets in the county: "I'll tell you. Probably not very many. Because if you get around and know the people, you'll find out."

The grapevine, the court community's small size, and the familiarity of its members together provided the conditions for developing strong social ties that went beyond the courthouse. The description of an experienced defense attorney's ties to people in the district attorney's office illustrates these relationships:

> [One] is a personal friend of mine. He's over at my house; I'm over at his. A lot of those guys are personal friends. I have a corporation with another prosecutor. That's the thing that's unique about this county. Most of the lawyers—there's a couple of cliques—where everybody knows everybody else. After trial we go out and have dinner. . . . That's just the way we are.

Of course, criticism and conflict usually gave way to moderation and cooperation under such circumstances. One attorney explained, "Sometimes you have to be very careful whom you criticize in this town just because you never know who you're talking to." Mutual accommodation and working things out provided the principal formula for dealing with each other. A prosecutor explained,

> Detectives get along pretty well with defense attorneys, too. There's not a great deal of animosity. . . . The police get along with the DAs; the DAs get along with the defense attorneys.

A significant feature of Erie's court community was the ability to talk things over. This same prosecutor said that he shared a goal with public defenders, that if their client needed a break, they should "come see me." The ability to "talk about it" extended to judges: "I don't really have a problem walking in and seeing them at just about any time subject to their schedule," observed a prosecutor. A former public defender explained why Erie was a nice county in which to practice:

> It's a little bit looser than a lot of counties in Pennsylvania where the judges don't even want to talk to the lawyers. We have easy access to our judges.

And a full-time prosecutor, when asked what one needed to know to understand Erie's court, replied:

> My experience here has been that it's—I don't want to say that it's a family operation necessarily—but it's a fairly close interpersonal sort of operation, with some notable exceptions, like the public defender's office . . . in terms of the relationships, most of them are based on individual relationships with each other. Like given lawyers in this office and given probation officers on the third floor, or even given lawyers and judges.

He continued his description later:

> The judges' secretaries make a big difference too. . . . It's all part of the wheels, the wheels of the system. The court administrator is the same as you. You have to know how to handle him . . . he's our age, he worked on our campaign right along with us, he's a hell of a nice guy.

Thus, cooperating, "going along," and adhering to established ways of treating others and doing things received powerful support in Erie.

If social relationships encouraged cooperation, they also provided the means for punishing those who refused. A prosecutor explained how he would get a postponement in a trial's starting date if key witnesses were unavailable when the 180-day deadline was about to expire:

> So I'm gonna have to lean on the defense counsel to get a waiver of the 180-day rule. The judge will do it for me if necessary. He'll just lean on the defense counsel. This is a small town.

And a nonlawyer familiar with the court's operations explained that attorneys who violated widely accepted informal rules of behavior "suffered in some way down the line" in their dealings with the judges. Thus, the high degree of familiarity and interdependency characteristic of Erie's criminal court community heightened communication among its members and facilitated adherence to implicit rules. Personal rivalries and conflicts were there too, especially among the heads of the principal offices, but not extensively enough to threaten the prevailing mood of cooperation and accommodation.

GEOGRAPHY OF ERIE'S CRIMINAL COURT COMMUNITY

Where people worked subtly shaped the structure and dynamics of Erie's criminal court community. Here we explore the effects of the layout of the courthouse.

Public officials liked the façade of the old courthouse (built in 1852) so much that they built a new wing duplicating it in 1929. Behind these two buildings, traditional in appearance with marble columns and staircases, sat the newest addition, built in the 1970s. Here were housed county officials on the first floor, four of the five judges and the district attorney's office on the second, the public defender, probation department, and coffee room on the third, and the jail on the fourth.

These arrangements facilitated communication. A few steps led judges from their chambers to their courtroom or their brethren's quarters. The district attorney's cramped quarters forced frequent encounters among its staff, a pattern reinforced by the practice of gathering to work, meet, and shoot the breeze in the centrally located conference room. Any judge's chambers could be reached in thirty seconds. . . . The courthouse coffee room [was] a center for socializing, gossiping, and nourishing the grapevine. The presence of other county offices on the first floor guaranteed that the grapevine would carry information about everybody's activities. It was also a convenient shorthand in discussing relations between the court (the "second floor") and its source of funds (the "first floor").

· · ·

THE JUDGES

Unlike other enforcers of rules such as baseball umpires, judges find that their prestige, formal authority, and active participation place them at center stage in criminal courts. What kind of people are they? What attitudes, personality quirks, and decision patterns describe them? How do they get along with one another and with other members of the court community? These questions are a never-ending source of fascination and worry to other members of the court community. Though we can provide only brief answers, they will contribute much to understanding the criminal court community.

Five older, experienced "home-town boys" formed Erie's judiciary in 1980. One handled the juvenile docket; another devoted himself to probate. Only during trial terms did these two judges handle adult criminal cases, and then only by presiding over cases sent to them for trial. Our discussion consequently is focused on the three men who handled most of the criminal work load.

These three judges had served a total of thirty-five years. The youngest had already passed his sixtieth birthday and seventh year on the bench. The other two were sixty-four and sixty-seven, with thirteen and fifteen years' experience.

Each indicated they were Republicans, though one of the other two was a Democrat, and the last an independent. Born and raised in Erie County, all three won election as district attorney between 1964 and 1970. Their election campaigns for DA and judge familiarized them with the county and its people. Commenting on his experience in campaigning for judge, one concluded that:

> I think it is an advantage because you tend to have a better feeling for people, and I think you've got a better feeling for problems, people's problems, practical problems. . . . I think it's easier to understand how people get into a situation that has led to some difficulty that ended up in court.

Their attitudes toward criminal law were distinctly conservative. In an article in *Pennsylvania Law Journal,* one publicly criticized the Warren Court's criminal law decisions, especially those such as *Miranda* dealing with confessions, as tipping the balance too far in favor of defendants; he went on to chastise the Pennsylvania Supreme Court for adhering too strictly to such decisions. In an interview with us, an Erie judge expressed views that reflected the tone of the entire court on such issues:

> The criminal law has become so much more detailed and complex, and in my opinion a little nauseous, and I'm losing interest. I really am opposed to a lot of criminal law decisions in Pennsylvania. . . . Frankly, I think they're basically absurd. . . .

All three scored low on our measure of the extent to which they believed in the due process guarantees for criminal defendants (the "due process" scale). When the attitudes of all five judges as a group were compared to those of judges in the other counties, only one other county's judges (Dauphin) scored lower. Questions measuring "belief in punishment" showed Erie judges ranked fourth.

Long service together and ideological compatibility facilitated good relations and a sense of comradery among the judges, one of them saying,

> Three of us have been district attorneys . . . all of us have been defense attorneys for a longer period of time, so we're pretty familiar with criminal law. I mean, I think we think alike without even talking. . . . I could tell you what the president judge thinks about criminal law without even talking to him.

Personal relations among four of the five judges appeared congenial, even close. Referring to the president judge, one commented that "He's over here every day talking to me and we're very close friends." The four normally gathered for morning coffee in the coffee room, engaged in social banter, shared opinions, and discussed common problems. The fifth judge, however, did not share in this fellowship. Younger, stern and aloof in personality, and strong in his views, his operating style differed sharply from that of his colleagues. We heard stories of his conflicts with the president judge, praise for his willingness to work hard, and descriptions of his distant manner. Prosecutors and defense attorneys ranked him as the least responsive to them and least involved in trying to encourage guilty pleas in order to avoid a trial.

The chief judge, called the president judge in Pennsylvania, exercised strong leadership, though his influence varied from one area to another. One judge described these differences:

> I assure you, when he expresses an opinion about my schedule I take that as something more than just an expression of opinion. But if he tells me that he disagrees with a sentence I may have imposed, or a particular finding that I made, I don't pay much attention to it.

The president judge sought to control sentencing in one area by prohibiting acceptance of "Accelerated Rehabilitative Disposition" (ARD) in retail theft cases.[3] He failed, however, to achieve complete adherence. We witnessed his close friend grant ARD in a retail theft; the other criminal judge expressed to us his willingness to do so if a good argument for it were made out to him.

His sway in matters of scheduling was great. A court official familiar with the judges' interactions concluded:

> As far as a unified judicial policy, as far as judges affixing their signature to a particular document or scheduling or something like that, the president judge dominates that. He's pretty much autonomous from the rest of the judges. . . . They can offer comments and suggestions. . . . But he has the ultimate say. All the other judges recognize that whatever the president judge wants, the president judge usually gets.

The president judge's descriptions of his duties conformed to this view. Asked if he facilitated joint decisions or bore the responsibility for running the court and exerting strong leadership, he replied:

> I think we have a little bit of both. I think like the saying, "The buck stops here." Somebody has to make the ultimate decision. That's the way it is. In other words, you receive all the input you can or should get or need. But eventually you're gonna have to make the decision.

He backed up his position with expressed willingness to meet direct challenges to his authority. What would you do, we asked, if a judge consistently violated the prohibition against granting ARD in retail theft cases. "I talk to him and try to understand," he replied. But what if the judge persisted? "You'd have to report to the judicial review board . . . if there is an established policy, I think the judge should adhere to it."

Thus, the chief judge in Erie acted much like the president of the United States—exercising strong executive leadership. But like the president, his ability to get his way by persuasion surpassed his ability to command and order. Even in matters of scheduling, his control sometimes failed. When the juvenile court judge refused to hear adult trials because of a backlog in his own docket, the president judge backed down.

This description fails to convey adequately the personalities of the judges or the substantial differences among them. One judge earned a reputation, a prosecutor mentioned, as

> notorious for settling the case . . . leaning on the case or requiring a
> plea . . . in the conference before the trial, in the recesses during the trial,
> all the way through.

Prosecutors and defense attorneys ranked him very high in his "involvement" in determining how cases would be disposed and low in his "responsiveness" to the problems of attorneys. Another judge presented the opposite profile: reluctant to be directive in settling a case and highly responsive to attorneys' requests and needs. Nearly everyone commented on his reluctance to make decisions.

If the Erie criminal court system benefited from its judges' experience, it also paid a price in interest and vigor. Some lawyers in the community believed that time had begun to pass the judges by. Our interviews picked up the loss of vigor. "I'm sort of winding down," one judge told us. "I'm getting closer to when I think I'll retire." Asked what he found satisfying and unsatisfying about his work, another replied:

> Well, I read a lot and I enjoy studying, and I did originally enjoy studying
> and writing opinions. I'll admit it's getting a little tedious now, but at first I
> did. And I liked trial work at first. I liked all those things. Now I'm getting
> to the point where I'm thinking about retirement, to be frank with you.

The relations of Erie's judges with other significant figures in the courthouse presented a mixed picture. . . . The judges relied heavily on the probation department, routinely requiring a presentence report on convicted defendants from it before they imposed sentences. The chief probation officer enjoyed the judges' confidence, and had a crucial role in recommending which inmates in the overcrowded jail could be paroled to make room for a fresh recruit. But relations with the county executive and county council were strained. Products of Erie's old political system, the judges got on well with the old system's governing board, the three county commissioners. An individual who dealt with the new regime on behalf of the judges described the changes that came with the adoption of home rule in 1977:

> We're not dealing with three people any more. We're dealing with many
> more. . . . not only the county executive, but his director of finance, his
> personnel director, and his director of administration. . . . Not only that,
> but we have to deal with seven county councilmen, because everything
> has to go before them.

A judge lamented, "They don't understand the operations of the courts, and I think there is a sort of resentment there. They think the judges are high and mighty. . . ." The resentment was mutual. "They always try to cut us once they have satisfied the needs of the other people," observed a court administrator. A showdown over the judges' hiring of additional courtroom personnel and probation officers nearly occurred, and tension lingered. But the court's operations did not appear to be greatly threatened, and self-restraint avoided an all-out public battle. One judge, reminded that in Pennsylvania the court had the power to issue an order to the county for needed funds, remarked: "But you don't like to be dogmatic. You have to be a little bit politician to get along with people."

The "home-town," "old-style politician" character of the judges produced strong links between the judges and the larger community. They knew the county and its people well. Though they were somewhat isolated once on the bench, we got the impression that old ties and lines of communication did not disappear. A prosecutor intriguingly depicted the judges' informal contacts:

> **R:** There is an awful lot of hearsay about it. But my understanding of it is that it will break itself down generally into a contact from someone along the way. That's a contact in terms of "We'll take a look at this," or "Judge, what can you do about this?" or "Judge, what can you do about that?"
>
> **I:** Are these attorneys or political figures?
>
> **R:** Oh, anybody. Anybody. Political figures, people who you might not want to call political figures, people who worked in campaigns, that kind of thing.
>
> **I:** So the telephone lines are open?
>
> **R:** Yeah.
>
> **I:** And they pay attention to it?
>
> **R:** Oh sure. The chambers are open, and that's a very difficult thing to have to deal with.

However you interpret phrases like "the chambers are open" and "people who you might not want to call political figures," it is clear that major participants in the criminal process believed that the judges responded to outside influences on cases for reasons that went beyond facts and law.

PROSECUTOR'S OFFICE

Erie's prosecutors contrasted sharply with the judges in almost every characteristic. When the judges themselves were at equivalent stages in their careers, most members of the office had not been born. Five of its nine-member staff were thirty-one or younger, the oldest only forty-one, and the DA himself but thirty-two. As a group, these eight men and one woman had spent less than half their lives in Erie County; in fact, five indicated that they had moved to Erie for professional reasons. The judges counted three Republicans, one Democrat, and one independent; the prosecutors had two Republicans, six Democrats, and an independent. The DA, elected just a few months before our field research began, displayed a vigor, enthusiasm, and vision in his work that the judges did not. And if the judges stood as remnants of the old political order with strong ties to the community, the prosecutor came to office as an insurgent.

The story of the new DA's route to office illustrates how events and human values shape the life of a criminal court community. The highly regarded Democratic DA who hired him as a young assistant died suddenly in 1974. The judges appointed an experienced trial attorney in the office to replace him, and this individual, running as a Democrat, narrowly won a new term in 1975. Soon nearly everyone on the deceased DA's staff left, citing a litany of complaints about the new DA ("not giving a damn," "not bothering to delegate," "no organization," "no leadership"). The young assistant, who became a defense attorney after he quit, was increasingly dismayed at the deterioration of an office he felt had been a fine one. A combination of nostalgia and anger led him to challenge the incumbent's reelection in 1979.

Because both were Democrats, it meant a fight in the primary for the nomination. Anyone wise in the way of politics knows that challenging incumbents, especially in their own party's primary, usually results in failure. Established politicians counseled him to keep out; labor leaders refused to support him. Then the politically powerful mayor of Erie announced his support for a third candidate. But he stubbornly persisted, assembling a brain trust of politically experienced advisers, several of whom had also served with him in the deceased DA's office. They waged an aggressive campaign in the primary, criticizing the incumbent's loss of thirty-five cases for violating the speedy-trial rule, and hammering on the theme, "It's time to get tough." The incumbent suffered an astonishing defeat, receiving a paltry 10 percent of the vote. The results demonstrated how effective Erie's grapevine was in informing the community of the low regard in which he was allegedly held in the courthouse. Equally unusual was the insurgent's 20 percent margin of victory over the mayor's candidate.

The Republicans had a strong prospective candidate, the man who barely lost the DA's race in 1975. Personal problems, however, caused him to surprise everyone by declining to run, leaving the GOP with no candidate. The Democrats' insurgent candidate faced no opposition in the general election. Rebuffed by Democratic party and labor union leaders in the early stages of his campaign, bucked by the mayor of Erie, and not requiring anyone's assistance in the uncontested general election, he came to office with very few political obligations. Ironically, the new DA did face his potential GOP challenger, but in a different capacity. The Republican county executive fired the longtime incumbent Republican public defender and appointed him to the vacancy. The absence of organized, politically effective groups such as the American Civil Liberties Union, civil rights organizations, and even business groups capable of pressuring the office also contributed to the freedom enjoyed by the new DA. In fact, when asked what organizations or groups impinged on the office, office officials identified only the local rape crisis center.

Motivated by the desire to restore the office to what he believed to be its former competence and performance, and unencumbered by political debts, the new Erie district attorney came to office eager to make big changes. He began with a clear view of the potential his office offered, a view expressed when he was asked if the criminal court administrator could change the way in which cases were scheduled:

> He's not able to pull it off by himself. No. But the person who is, the guy who's got to be out on the point . . . is the district attorney—the combination lawyer, politician, administrator, social worker.

He started his initiatives before taking office, utilizing the general election campaign period to prepare an elaborate justification for increasing his budget. Initially rebuffed by the county executive, he finally prevailed by lobbying the county council to override the executive's veto of the increase. He consequently gained both an enhanced reputation for effectiveness and an additional $40,000.

The extra funds permitted basic restructuring of the office. Instead of five full-time assistants, he switched to three full-time and five half-time assistants. Only one attorney from the defeated incumbent's staff remained. His new full-time first assistant knew the criminal process well, because he had served as second assistant public defender. Two of the half-time assistants had also worked for the deceased DA, and a third had engaged in defense work for some time. The added half-timers gave the office some experienced "big guns" to handle the difficult cases and to help train the younger members of the staff who had never tried a case. The half-timers joined because of the new DA's leadership, not for the $12,000 salary. As one explained,

> I haven't been doing it for the money. It's a loss leader. It's a disaster. But it's fun. That's why you do it. That's why he has the staff that he has. It's an economic disaster, but you don't do everything for economic reasons in this world.

Several large changes in policy accompanied inauguration of the reinvigorated DA's office. And several of these flowed directly from the theme of the campaign. "It's time to get tough." The slogan reflected sentiment widely shared in the office, not merely campaign rhetoric. The office sought higher bail, especially in crimes of violence. "They oppose everything you do now," an experienced public defender complained. "You go in for a bond reduction and they oppose it, automatically." It became stingier in recommending lenient dispositions in less serious cases, including Accelerated Rehabilitative Disposition (ARD). The office's leadership felt the previous DA had agreed to plea bargains that reduced the seriousness of the charges "just for the sake of reduction." The new regime claimed it had stopped this practice, reducing charges only when the case was weak, a witness was missing, or the facts justified a lower charge. Finally, the office began writing what some referred to as "hate letters" to the probation department urging that its presentence reports to the judges recommend stiff sentences. Assistants also began appearing at sentencing to make their views known. A militant tenor about this practice arose from the interviews, as one assistant demonstrated:

> That's another thing that's happening that didn't happen before. The judges, under the old regime, were not asking the district attorney to comment at the time of sentence. They are now. We have a right to comment.

Despite widespread agreement among the staff on the need to "get tough," Erie's prosecutors did not appear from the interviews to be vindictive, "grind defendants into the dust" individuals. One administrator volunteered that he retained his belief in due process, and admitted he would find it difficult to sentence some defendants. As a group, Erie's prosecutors held less strong "belief in punishment" views and less negative attitudes toward "due process" than their counterparts in the other two Pennsylvania counties. They ranked seventh among the nine counties in "belief in punishment" and third in "regard for due process."

The leadership style of Erie's new district attorney flowed naturally from the composition of the office. Seven of the eight staff attorneys owed their appointments to the DA. Several part-timers helped plan election strategy, shared memories of the old office, and considered themselves close friends of his. The staff strongly approved of the changes in policy instituted. Its members also socialized in the evening. Both attorneys and secretaries, for instance, attended performances by a band in which one of the lawyers played. A spirit of comradery and pride seemed to prevail. One assistant enthusiastically remarked, "He's assembled a hell of a staff. And that's fun. It's always fun to be associated with competent people. It's interesting." Despite the youth of the office, it had much experience in the criminal process and a high degree of self-assurance, as one administrator's boast showed: "We know all the angles, we know the ropes, we know the way the system works."

These factors encouraged an informal, loose management style. No written rules or manual of office policies existed. No formal procedures for checking staff performance, such as auditing monthly disposition statistics for each attorney, were employed. The DA and the first assistant spent much time in the conference room: the proximity of the courtrooms made it easy to drop in on the inexperienced assistants' performances; the grapevine filled in any gaps. The DA gained familiarity with the cases by reviewing all new matters as they came into the office.

The half-timers were former colleagues older than the DA, precluding a traditional "boss–employee" relationship. The degree of supervision thus varied depending on the assistant's experience. The half-timers felt free to exercise discretion consistent with the DA's views, as the comments of one suggest:

> He knows me and I know him. If there is a question of policy, I would go and ask him. But generally, if a deal is to be made, I in my own discretion would make the deal, and I know he would accept it, just because I've been around. . . . I think we think alike, we act alike, and we have probably very similar attitudes on what law and order is and what justice is. . . . So consequently we really don't have any problems.

In fact, the DA did not always insist cases be handled as he would handle them, even when he became aware of such differences. An experienced assistant told us what happened when he discussed with his boss a plea bargain he had reached:

> He told me he disagreed with it. And I said, "Well, I think I have some pretty good reasons for doing it. . . ." He said, "Well, okay. I'm not going to overrule you. It's your decision."

Rookie assistants received closer scrutiny and direction, but typically through informal means. One, asked if his plea bargains were reviewed by the DA, explained:

> He does monitor that. Probably not on a formal basis as far as keeping a list. He very much stays in the conference room and just sort of sits here and sees what's going on, and asks, like, "Why did you do this?"

They often assisted veteran attorneys on difficult and important cases as part of their training. "Postmortems" in the conference room after trial were another way to give rookies feedback.

If internal office management and relations presented few problems and challenges, the same could not be said of external relations. The successful effort to obtain a budget increase was a significant though difficult victory in dealing with the county government. Like most members of criminal court communities everywhere, however, Erie's prosecutors felt county officials had little knowledge of or real interest in the operations of the criminal courts. The DA did not enjoy a close relationship with the Republican county executive, a political ally of the public defender. But he got on extremely well with the criminal court administrator, an employee of the judges who oversaw scheduling and other administrative matters pertaining to the criminal docket. In fact, everyone knew that the administrator participated actively in the DA's campaign. Good relations with the probation department also developed.

Interaction with several other organizations deserves brief mention. Relations with the news media seemed important to the office. One key office member, assessing the newspaper, strongly implied it favored the judges and the head public defender: "I've sensed that certain things will get printed and certain things won't get printed, and certain people get treated better in the media." The DA received better coverage from the broadcast media, appearing frequently on local television news programs. The office appreciated the cooperation the district justices showed, promptly forwarding copies of case documents after the preliminary hearing, but felt less happy about their refusal to toss out weak cases. Attitudes toward the police . . . varied from respect to disdain depending on the department.

Our description of the Erie DA's office would be incomplete without mentioning its desire to bring about a number of changes. It sought to enhance the office's investigative capabilities beyond the one county detective available, to institute a career criminal prosecution program, and to create a special unit to focus on consumer fraud, drug cases, and white-collar crime. The office's ambitious long-run agenda clashed with the bench's preferences. The judges engaged in almost no long-range planning. Major changes in the way things worked, indeed any changes, failed to excite them.

Our field research ended after the DA's first nine months, and so we could not assess his success in overcoming judicial apathy. His failure, however, to win the president judge's approval of a change in the structure of the criminal calendar demonstrated the need for judicial cooperation, and suggested the formidable obstacles to success that he faced.

PUBLIC DEFENDER'S OFFICE

If Erie's judges contrasted sharply with its prosecutors, the public defenders displayed many superficial similarities. The public defender himself had also assumed control recently. Though slightly larger, with thirteen attorneys (counting the head) handling adult criminal cases, the office's average age of thirty-three nearly matched that of the prosecutors. The staff also had three full-timers, including the first and second assistants, with the rest, including the head, part-timers. The new leader felt extensive changes needed to be made, and took steps to bring them about. He fired several people and encouraged others considered "deadwood" to retire. By June 1980, only two part-timers with the office when he took over in 1979 remained.

Despite these obvious similarities, however, major differences could be seen. All but three of the attorneys had lived in Erie County almost all their lives. Despite the head's status as a partisan Republican, the office had four Republicans, four Democrats, and five independents. Three women and two blacks worked there. The DA had one woman and no blacks. The PD's staff had much less experience in criminal law. The first assistant and the two holdover part-timers knew their way around criminal courts, though the first assistant won his knowledge in another state. But the other two full-timers were new both to the office and to criminal law, and five of the six other part-timers had served a year or less. The head PD owed his appointment to his political rather than legal activities. He practiced civil, not criminal, law, and had worked as a Washington lobbyist. Prominent in GOP politics, and narrowly defeated for DA in 1975, he played a central role in the county executive's campaign.

The office failed to achieve the esprit and social cohesion found in the prosecutor's office. The cramped third-floor offices provided space only for the full-timers. The others worked primarily from their private offices, appearing in the main office sporadically during trial terms. The PD called few staff meetings gathering everyone together. An assistant bothered by the lack of communication described several unsuccessful efforts to generate informal social get-togethers.

The head PD identified several long-range goals, including moving the main office out of the courthouse, establishing a student-intern program, and transforming the operation into a private corporation. Like the DA, he demonstrated considerable sophistication and political savvy in devising strategies to realize them. But he classified himself as a "short-run implementer" rather than a "long-range goal man."

Like nearly all supervisors we talked to in public defenders' offices, Erie's head PD believed his staff should be allowed wide autonomy in handling individual clients' cases.

> I am dealing with professionals and if they are good public defenders or good lawyers they have big egos. So that, to some extent, to get the best out of them, I have to take an equal or even a subordinate role in an individual case.

Some staff attorneys agreed that their discretion was not unduly limited. Asked what office policies influenced how he handled cases, one assistant public defender replied there were none. "And it's just like that person is a private client. I have complete latitude on the cases to do what I feel is in his best interest."

Several features of the office's relations outside the court community deserve mention. The head PD's relations with the county executive were very good, though no surprise given their close political ties. Like many aspects of life in other human communities, the effect of their ties on events, though powerful, was often quite subtle. For example, in January 1980, several assistant public defenders were, for various reasons, unavailable. Consistent with his desire to provide defendants with "continuous" representation by the same attorney, the head PD refused to reassign cases to other members of the office. The resulting disruption of the docket angered the rest of the court community, especially the judges. When we asked the public defender if his defiance of the judges might not lead to later trouble in the form of complaints from the judges to the county executive, he replied it would not be a problem due to the "independence" of the county executive from the president judge. Left unsaid was the fact that in such a dispute the public defender would win the county executive's support.

Like the prosecutor, the public defender received little pressure from the community. The private bar voiced few complaints about the office taking paying clients away from struggling attorneys, a situation the office attributed to its strict application of eligibility standards. The PD's law firm represented the newspapers, leading the prosecutors to claim that it received favorable coverage.

The office recognized the importance of district justices and probation officers, and sought to cultivate good relations with both. One policy the head PD pursued required cooperation by the district justices: disposition of minor charges at the preliminary-hearing stage. Erie's public defenders sounded a frequent refrain in discussing lower judges: "Some of the district judges are excellent; some are just dumb."

The lack of the same social cohesion and esprit found in the DA's office led to a less coherent "office view" among Erie's public defenders. The relative inexperience among its attorneys also made it difficult to summarize their attitudes neatly. We can, however, draw two useful conclusions. First, the office felt it did a very good job. An experienced assistant boasted:

> I think we give our clientele excellent service. I think we give the taxpayers a lot for their money. I think our services are really very effective, and are just as much—if not more—effective than private counsel.

The management orientation produced an emphasis on statistical measures of success. An office supervisor rattled off figures on performance in jury trials as proof of effectiveness:

> The public defender's staff had nine guilties, seven splits, nine not guilties, one hung, for twenty-six jury trials. The private bar had eleven guilties, five guilty of lesser offenses, seven not guilties. So we beat them in every category . . . we compare favorably with the private bar.

Several aspects of the head public defender's management style contrasted, though, with his expressed belief in autonomy. He believed strongly in "over-motioning," filing a whole series of pretrial motions as standard practice. Unlike the DA, he sought to implement and enforce this and other policies with formal written memos to the staff and a case file folder with places for the attorney to record every action taken. The data recorded there could then be used as a management tool. "I am not above evaluating lawyers and individual cases. That's one of the reasons I got this file-folder system," he informed us. He also differed from the DA in avoiding informal socializing with the staff: "It's fine when you're one or two years out of law school. But when you start fraternizing with people that you have to tell how to do things, it doesn't work." He used salary-increase allocations to reward some assistants, and gave no raises to others. Everyone knew he had fired several assistants. An individual who had served under the previous public defender summarized the changes as "a more formal and standardized basis now." Holdovers disliked his management style and some of the policies. One who quit complained: "Now it's kind of they're looking over your shoulder all the time. And when I've tried as many cases as I have, I don't need somebody looking over my shoulder."

Other stated policies contributed to the new regime's formal, strict tone. The office prohibited part-time assistants from representing paying criminal clients in their private practices, a common occurrence among part-time defenders in Montgomery County. It became stricter in applying criteria to determine eligibility of poor defendants for representation, and began keeping records of those turned down. It encouraged assistants to talk to defendants before preliminary hearings, tried to assign repeat clients to the attorney who handled the earlier case, and sought to provide a "continuous" or "vertical" defense (that is, have the same attorney represent the defendant from the initial stages to final disposition or sentencing). High turnover in the months just before our field research began, however, made such continuous assignment extremely difficult.

The head PD's management style thus contrasted with the DA's in his desire to establish and monitor compliance with formal policies, in his willingness to reward and punish assistants, in his rigidity, and in his lack of informality.

Did the PD succeed in running a tight ship and achieving conformity to his policies? The answer is complicated somewhat because assistants differed in their reaction to office policies. Acts that rankled old-timers as unnecessary interference were a perfectly acceptable and normal way of doing things for newcomers. A further complication arose from the head's spending relatively little time directly supervising the office. He remained uninvolved in day-to-day operations, and delegated much of the task of direct administration to the first assistant.

The first assistant employed a more informal and looser management style. He announced an open-door policy to assistants, especially the less experienced ones, and encouraged them to consult with him as equals in an atmosphere of low tension. He inserted memos in case files making suggestions to the trial attorney. "But," he told us, "I don't ever follow up to see if they do or not. It's none of my business." And he apparently failed to ensure that the head's wishes regarding "over-motioning" were met. One attorney said, "Each guy does as he sees fit—what he wants to do." The result was a public defender's office somewhat less tightly and formally run than the head sought, but also more formal and controlled than those in other counties.

Second, the office lacked a strong "defendant orientation" in the attitudes of its staff and its policies. Several assistants remarked that they could just as easily work for the prosecutor; one recent departee wanted to join the DA's staff. An assistant's answer to a question about his job's frustrations illustrated this attitude:

> Well, the frustration with being a public defender goes back to the fact that just basically our client is not what society is going to consider as an upstanding citizen by and large. . . . They don't really consider what they've done as wrong.

A recently departed assistant complained sentences were not harsh enough; another said he just got fed up with clients charged repeatedly with serious crimes lying each time about what happened. Public defenders in only one other county produced a higher mean on the "belief of punishment" measure, though they scored relatively high in "regard for due process." Finally, the office acquiesced in permitting defendants to accept a disposition entered in the records as "NPCOD," which stood for "Noll Pros (that is, dismissal by the prosecutor), Costs on Defendant." The office did not challenge the practice. And even though some defenders thought it was unfair for defendants to pay court costs when charges were dropped, they felt it was up to the defendant to accept or reject such a disposition.

ERIE'S PRIVATE DEFENSE BAR

In the first half of 1980, fifty different attorneys represented the 220 defendants who appeared on the arraignment docket in Erie's trial court. . . . Thirty-eight attorneys handled only one or two defendants. . . . Five men . . . handled the cases of ninety-one defendants, more than 40 percent of those privately represented. . . .

We found a few general characteristics of the defense bar. In the years just before our research began, several of the high-volume, established private defense attorneys began to cut back. Four of the five white male attorneys we spoke with had yet to reach their thirty-fifth birthdays. The gap in age between them and the fading group of old-timers interfered with the development of a cohesive defense bar, despite their familiarity with one another. One interviewee conveyed the tenor of relations among defense attorneys when he told us: "I'm not very active in the bar. I'm not crazy about most of them." . . . In 1980, only ten women practiced among the 300 lawyers in Erie; only the three assistant public defenders and an assistant prosecutor among them dealt with criminal matters. Except for several of the less active veteran specialists, the private defense bar enjoyed little status. Several had the reputation of benefiting their clients through, one prosecutor said, their "inexplicable access before certain judges" rather than through their legal ability. According to one judge, the top civil attorneys avoided criminal law.

Of course, the private defense bar had some communication and structure. As described earlier, a group of attorneys, including several currently handling criminal cases, joined in the effort to elect the new DA. They shared a common fate and interest. Several told us, for example, of widespread grumbling at the public defender's "slam" at the private bar when he hired an attorney from Pittsburgh to fill a vacancy.

. . .

SOCIAL AND WORKING RELATIONSHIPS
IN ERIE'S COURT COMMUNITY

For the most part, encounters between the people who formed Erie's criminal court community on the surface displayed courtesy, cordiality, and cooperation. This pattern seemed especially prevalent in personal relations between rank and file members of the DA's and the PD's offices. Referring to assistant prosecutors, a PD said:

> The average "belief in punishment" for prosecutors was higher than for public defenders. Erie's judges, in keeping with their conservative views, expressed attitudes closer to those of the prosecutors than the public defenders. Public defenders' "regard for due process" was positive, and the difference exceeded that seen for belief in punishment.
>
> They're nice guys, you know. They're professionally enjoyable and you can get them aside over a cup of coffee and quite frankly tell them that they're just full of crap and they'll just laugh about it.

A former assistant defender expressed a similar view.

> If you don't normally give the DA's office a rough time—by rough I mean by being unavailable or not around—you say, "Listen, I've got a real important civil matter this morning. Can I start it this afternoon?" They're going to accommodate you.

The stereotyped image of the friendly way of life in small communities, the avoidance of conflict in favor of cooperation, and the unwillingness to offend, held true much of the time.

Under the surface in most small towns, college faculties, workers in fast-food restaurants, and most other places where people gather, we find another pattern, with personality clashes, disagreements, grudges, and lack of cooperation. Erie's criminal court was no exception. Relationships between a few prosecutors and public defenders were less friendly. But more significantly, relations between the principal personalities in the community displayed considerable tension, criticism, and dislike. It would be impossible (and tedious) to describe these conflicts in full detail, but we will briefly summarize the crucial characteristics of relations among the leading members of the criminal court community to convey this feature of Erie's court community.

The judges' cohesiveness, mutual friendship, long joint service, and strong leadership from the president judge produced a common outlook toward the DA and PD. They mentioned improvement in prosecutors' performances since the new DA took office, describing them as "better prepared," "more on the ball," "aggressive," "intelligent and scholarly." Nevertheless, all opposed his call for a change in the calendar, blaming the office for its failure to use the full two weeks of existing trial terms.

The judges expressed very different opinions about the public defender's office. "I'm not satisfied with the public defender," one judge revealed. "I think it's pathetic." He regarded its attorneys as "very inexperienced" and "incompetent." Resentment lingered over the office's failure to reassign the cases of PDs unable to work during the January trial term. The president judge demonstrated his lack of confidence by taking over himself the job of deciding which private attorneys would represent homicide defendants, a task formerly delegated to the PD. The PD wanted to reacquire this power, but the president judge refused.

Members of the prosecutor's office shared the judges' assessment of the public defender's office. Said one:

> It's really a sin what's happened up there in the last year. . . . They don't have a single experienced trial attorney on the staff. . . . He's picking real bad people. In consequence of doing that he's really destroying the reputation of the office that was good for a long time.

Another reported the common belief that the PD's appointment resulted from the return of a political debt.

> There may be some merit to it because he doesn't have any trial experience, doesn't have any criminal law experience, and doesn't have any administrative experience.

An experienced assistant summarized the office's view:

> As a generalization, by and large we don't particularly care for the public defender's office. We don't like the way they handle their office. We don't think it's administered well and we just don't think too much of how they handle their clients.

Part of the explanation for this tension and dislike can be attributed to the relationship between the heads of the two offices. Though they professed mutual friendship, their assertions lacked credibility. In fact, one complained to us that the other had lied a lot to him. The opinions expressed by their staffs reflected the tension between them. A member of the PD's staff observed that the "political stuff" between them was both messy and petty, and that they were "at each other all the time." A counterpart in the DA's office expressed views that revealed their rivalry. "There is bad blood between [the DA] and [the PD]. The

[PD] is a political creature." Relations between assistants in administrative positions in the two offices showed similar tension. Prosecutors voiced other criticisms, such as, "they wait too long, or wait till the last minute to do much of their work."

The PD's office mirrored the DA's views in its assessment. An administrator charged the DA's office with lack of respect, failure to do its homework, and poor performance in trials. The public defenders considered a supervisor in the DA's office to be a poor trial attorney and a rigid, unreasonable administrator. They felt the DA's office had "gone overboard" in getting tough, refusing to plea bargain when it should have, backing out on tentative agreements, and generally being "inflexible," "unyielding," and "unbending."

We alluded to the attitudes of the prosecutor's office toward the judges. They blamed the early end of trial terms not on themselves, but on the pressures exerted by the judges to settle cases in order to avoid trials. Seven of the prosecutors we interviewed indicated in one way or another that they regarded the bench as a whole, and the two judges close to retirement in particular, as lazy. Immediately after stating that the aloof judge was "the only worker on the court," a prosecutor interjected:

> while the other ones are—classic example—today: President judge is out to lunch at 11:15, back at 2:00, gone at 3:30, a month's vacation right during the middle of a court term.

They resented the president judge's refusal to alter the calendar. The one judge labeled "the only worker" received praise for his sentences. But the others' sentences appeared "very lenient" to the DA's office, especially the standard 11.5- to 23-month county jail sentences that frequently resulted in the defendant's release in a few days.

The public defenders said little about the judges. They neglected to complain about the harshness of sentences, an indirect expression of their apparent satisfaction. They shared the prosecutor's judgment that only one judge worked hard, that another was slow in making decisions, and that a third lacked much knowledge of criminal law. But administrators knew the judges did not think well of the office, telling us they got the idea the judges were displeased. This recognition, however, brought forth no efforts to modify the practices that aroused criticism.

AGE AND GENERATIONS
IN ERIE'S COURT COMMUNITY

Differences in the ages of judges, prosecutors, and public defenders in Erie and the prominence of "cohorts" were striking. . . . Data on the average age of judges (60.4 years) compared to those of prosecutors and public defenders (33.1 years and 32.9 years, respectively) confirms the size of Erie's generation gap. Only Kalamazoo's judges had a higher average age. Only Saginaw's judges had a higher average of years of service on the bench (12.8 versus Erie's 12.0). The ages of prosecutors and public defenders differed little from those in other counties. . . . Erie's prosecutors were a little older than the average for all nine counties, and its public defenders about a year younger.

Comparing the differences in age of the judge, prosecutor, and either the PD or private counsel who handled each defendant's case provides a clearer picture of Erie's generation gap. Judges averaged more than 30 years older than prosecutors and 28.6 years older than defense attorneys, a larger gap than in seven of the eight other counties. In fact, the gap in three counties was only about half as great, about 15 years.

STRUCTURE OF INFLUENCE

In Erie, the judges set the tone and rhythm of the criminal court. The president judge believed in exercising strong leadership, and he enjoyed the support and friendship of a cohesive group of three of the four other judges. The general policies of Erie's newspapers, and their relationship with the president judge in particular, insulated the judges from criticism. The county's long tradition of strong president judges reinforced his status. One important attorney in the community minced no words in describing his control: "This is a county, historically, that has had under-the-thumb kind of rule from the president judge, from the incumbent as well as his predecessors." One subtle indication of his stature appeared in a prosecutor's response to a question about how the county officials on the first floor reacted when the judges came down from the second to request their budget:

> Well, the judges don't come down for their budget. I think that's a classic illustration of how it works. The second floor doesn't go down to see the first floor. The first floor comes up.

It was clear that his power had entered its final stages as retirement loomed. But his ability to prevail on issues like the structure of the calendar remained. Though the prosecutor began making speeches calling for change, he acknowledged that if the president judge were to call him in and ask him to stop, he would have to comply.

The public defender exerted little influence within the court community. He lost the duty of assigning attorneys to homicide cases, had an inexperienced staff, and was regarded by judges, prosecutors, and the private bar as inexperienced in criminal work and highly political. Only his strong ties to the county executive provided him with significant support. The new district attorney enjoyed a good reputation among the private bar and the judges. Though he established an ambitious agenda for change, only the initiatives that could be implemented within his own office succeeded in the early months of his tenure. The impending retirement of two judges, his vigor, and his access to the broadcast media augured well for a rise in the DA's influence. At the time of our research, however, the president judge still dominated Erie's criminal court community. As one important community member said, "It's a one-horse county. It always has been."

SUMMARY

. . . The small size and extensive familiarity of the [Erie criminal] court community, which reflected characteristics of the county generally, contributed to the development of an effective grapevine, and to a tradition of informality and accommodation in interpersonal relations. The proximity of major participants in the courthouse facilitated informal interaction and exchange of information.

The principal characteristics of each of the three major sponsoring organizations—the judges, prosecutors, and public defenders—are described in some detail. For each, we look at the age and experience of its members, the content of policies and internal management styles, the degree of cohesion, the structure of attitudes, and the nature of relations with the newspapers, lower-court judges, and others. Comparing attitudes, we found both judges and prosecutors adhering more strongly to a belief in punishment than public defenders did; the judges were surprisingly negative in their regard for due process.

We found tension in relations between the public defender's office on the one hand, and judges and prosecutors on the other. The prosecutors criticized the judges for their lack of hard work, their leniency, and their unwillingness to change the calendar. Continuing a long tradition in Erie county, the judges, and the president judge in particular, exerted the most influence over the operations of the court community.

NOTES

1. *Editor's note:* The nine counties studied by the authors were Erie, Dauphin, and Montgomery counties, Pennsylvania; Kalamazoo, Oakland, and Saginaw counties, Michigan; and DuPage, Peoria, and St. Clair counties, Illinois.

2. *Editor's note:* The "grapevine" is the informal social and communication network found in organizations. It serves the function of providing court community members with information useful in the performance of their jobs. A public defender in Erie told the authors:

   I don't know how it is in other counties, but in this county the courthouse is just

the fastest grapevine I've ever seen. If I fire a secretary at 9 o'clock, the whole courthouse knows about it by 9:30.

3. Prosecutors could propose to the court that offenders without a serious prior criminal record arrested for a minor offense could be placed on ARD. Prosecution was deferred, and if the defendant fulfilled the conditions set forth, such as attending classes and avoiding subsequent arrest, the case was dropped and the defendant had no conviction added to his or her record.

1 7

✦

The Process Is the Punishment

Handling Cases in a Lower Criminal Court

MALCOLM M. FEELEY

Many observers of the lower criminal courts are struck by the fact that the sentences seem to be so lenient. Malcolm Feeley's study of the Court of Common Pleas, New Haven, Connecticut, shows that the punishment given out by the judge is not the only cost imposed by the criminal justice system.

This article develops the argument that in the lower criminal courts the process itself is the primary punishment. I identify the costs involved in the pretrial process and examine the ways they affect the organization, as well as the way a defendant will proceed on his journey through the court. This examination should help explain why lower courts do not fit their popular image, and why cases are processed so quickly in the Court of Common Pleas, New Haven, Connecticut.

INTRODUCTION

The first set of factors I examine deals with the consequences of pretrial detention and the problems of securing pretrial release. The second explores the costs of securing an attorney. There are obvious financial outlays involved in retaining a private attorney, but there are also hidden costs associated with obtaining free counsel. A third set of factors deals with the problem of continuances. While delay often benefits the defendant, its importance for the defendant is often exaggerated, and it is crucial to distinguish defendant-induced delay from continuances which are arranged for the convenience of the court.

By themselves these costs may appear to be minor or even trivial in a process formally structured to focus on the crucial questions of adjudication and sentencing. However, in the aggregate, and in comparison with the actual consequences of adjudication and sentencing, they often loom large in the eyes of the criminally accused, and emerge as central concerns in getting through the criminal justice system.

These pretrial costs account for a number of puzzling phenomena: why so many people waive their right to free appointed counsel; why so many people do not show up for court at all; and why people choose the available adversarial options so infrequently. Furthermore, pretrial costs are part of the reason why pretrial diversion programs designed to *benefit* defendants and provide alternatives to standard adjudication do not receive a more enthusiastic response. The accused often perceive these programs as cumbersome processes which simply increase their contact with the system.

The relative importance of the pretrial process hinges on one important set of considerations. Students of the criminal courts often overlook what many criminologists and students of social class do not, that the fear of arrest and conviction does not loom as large in the eyes of many people brought into court as it does in the eyes of middle-class researchers. While I did not systematically interview a sample of defendants, I had informal and often extended discussions with dozens of defendants who were waiting for their cases to be called, and I watched still more discuss their cases with attorneys and prosecutors. While there were obvious and numerous exceptions, I was nevertheless struck by the frequent lack of concern about the stigma of conviction and by the more practical and far more immediate concerns about what the sentence would be and how quickly they could get out of court.

There are several reasons for this. First, many arrestees already have criminal records, so that whatever stigma does attach to a conviction is already eroded, if not destroyed.[1] Second, many arrestees, particularly young ones, are part of a subculture which spurns conventional values and for which arrest and conviction may even function as a celebratory ritual, reinforcing their own values and identity. In fact, they may even perceive it as part of the process of coming of age.[2] Third, lower-class people tend to be more *present*-oriented than middle-class people, and for obvious reasons.[3] Many defendants are faced with an immediate concern for returning to work or their children, and these concerns often take precedence over the desire to avoid the *remote* consequences that a (or another) conviction might bring. This *relative* lack of concern about conviction is reinforced by the type of employment opportunities available to lower-class defendants. If an employee is reliable, it may make little difference whether or not he pleads guilty to a minor charge emerging from a "Saturday night escapade." Indeed, an employer is not likely to find out about the incident unless his employee has to arrange to miss work in order to appear in court.

Table 1 Release Detention Rates

Condition Immediately Prior to Disposition	N	%
Released on Citation	244	16%
Released on PTA	565	36
Released on Bond	567	37
(Subtotal released)	(1376)	(89%)
Detained	166	11
TOTAL	1542	100%

If the stigma of the criminal sanction is not viewed as a significant sanction, the concrete costs of the pretrial process take on great significance. When this occurs, the process itself becomes the punishment.

PRETRIAL RELEASE: AN OVERVIEW

A quick reading of relevant Connecticut statutes, case law, and administrative directives conveys the impression that the state has an unswerving commitment to prompt pretrial release. There is an elaborate multi-layered system for decision and review, there are a variety of pretrial release alternatives, and assurance of appearance at trial is the sole criterion for establishing release conditions.

The police are empowered to make the initial release decision and can either release a suspect at the site of the arrest or take him to the central booking facility. Once the suspect is booked, police retain the power to establish release conditions, and they may release suspects on a written promise to appear (PTA) or on bond, which they set. If they do not release the arrestee, at this point, the police are then required to notify a bail commissioner who in turn is supposed to "promptly conduct [an] interview and investigation as he deems necessary to reach an independent decision." If after this the accused is still not released, then the bail commissioner "shall set forth his reasons . . . in writing."[4] The accused has a third opportunity to seek release at arraignment and all subsequent appearances, at which time he can request the judge to consider a bond reduction or release on PTA.

This liberal release policy is reflected in practice as well. Table 1 indicates that 89 percent of those arrested were released prior to the disposition of their cases, and that 52 percent of them were released on nonfinancial conditions, by police field citation or PTA. Thirty-seven percent were released on bond, and only 11 percent were detained until disposition. Although the proportion of arrestees released pending trial is typically regarded as the most important measure of a jurisdiction's "liberality," it is far from a complete picture. Two additional questions must be answered. First, at what point in the process do people secure release? To identify as "released" only those who were free at the time their cases were disposed of is to overlook those who were held in detention for a while before eventually securing release. And if a person is released on bail, at what price was freedom purchased?

Table 2 Length of Time in Pretrial Detention

Length of Time	N	%
none	244	17%
0–3 hours	624	43
4–7 hours	82	6
8–12 hours	92	6
13–24 hours	308	21
2 days	31	2
3 days	10	1
4–7 days	12	1
8–20 days	18	1
over 20 days	17	1
	1438	99%*

*Rounding error.

Length of Time in Pretrial Custody

Table 2 provides a breakdown of the length of time defendants in my sample were in custody before being released. Seventeen percent were released almost immediately on police citations. A much larger group—43 percent—was released within three hours after being taken to the "lockup," and a third group was released within a period of thirteen to twenty-four hours after arrest. Many of the people in this group were released in court the morning after their arrest, at which time they were able to secure reductions in the amount of bond or contact a bondsman or family member to post bond; some pleaded guilty and were discharged from custody. However, 6 percent of the sample remained in pretrial custody for a period of two days or longer, and a small number were held three weeks or more.

• • •

Other arrestees secure delayed release because the lockup facility becomes overcrowded. On Saturday evenings police may "weed out" the lockup by granting PTA's to Friday evening's arrestees in order to make room for new arrivals. Women are housed in a separate facility in another location and are generally more likely to be released earlier on lower bond.

• • •

PRETRIAL RELEASE: PROCESS

The Role of the Police

Although most students of the pretrial process focus on judicial bail setting at arraignment, their observations may often miss the mark, since in many jurisdictions—including New Haven—the bulk of the pretrial release decisions is made by other people before the accused is ever presented in court. In New Haven it is not the judge or the bail commissioner who dominates the release process, but rather the police. They are responsible not only for arresting and charging suspects, but also for releasing them before a trial. A number of observers have commented that Connecticut in general, and New Haven in particular, has liberal policies on pretrial release. They attribute these to the multi-layered system of decision and review, and the existence of bail commissioners. But in fact one cannot attribute these practices directly to this elaborate system. In fact, they probably have more to do with the intuitive judgments of the initial decision makers, the police.

Unless a suspect is released on a field citation at the site of an arrest, the arresting officer takes him to the central booking facility. After the booking, the officer is required by departmental order to complete a detailed bail interview form which seeks information about the arrestee's ties to the community and other factors on which the release decision is to be based. The form also provides a space for reasons if the arrestee should not be released. Rarely is there anything that might be characterized as an "interview." Only occasionally is the bail interview form completed in detail, and whatever information it does record is likely to have been filled in *after* a release decision has already been made. While different officers have different practices, most of them require little more than the accused's name, address, and the charges being pressed before making a decision to release on PTA or a small bond.

If the charges are more serious, or if the arrestee has a prior record of arrests or failure to appear (and well over 50 percent do), then the officer may insist on a bond. In setting its amount, he often consults a "bail schedule." This document, prepared by the Judicial Department and adopted by a resolution of all Circuit Court judges in 1967, specifies a monetary amount for each type of charge, and provides for "discounts," depending upon the accused's ties to the community.

Although officers setting the conditions of release must complete a section of the bail interview form which calls for a statement of reasons if an arrestee is not released immediately, this section is rarely filled out. In my review of over 100 bail interview forms for people who were *not* immediately released, only a handful—15 or so—had this section completed. Only occasionally did they specify that the arrestee was a "poor risk" because he had no local address, or because he had a record of failures to appear. Most of the reasons related instead to the police officer's perception of the arrestee's condition, which was often characterized as "abusive," "threatening," or "wants to return to the incident," reasons which encouraged them to favor immediate situational justice or specific deterrence.

These officers are often in a dilemma. They are agents of the community, expected to enforce the law and make arrests. But then they must immediately turn around and release those very people whom they have just apprehended and arrested. It is not surprising that the tensions produced by these conflicting roles place a strain in the formal rules these people are charged with applying, and that they have taken advantage of the lax enforcement of the law to pursue their own conceptions of rough justice. Occasionally they use this detention power arbitrarily to administer their own system of punishment. Often they fear that an arrestee will return to a fight if he is released, so that they purposefully set bail beyond the arrestee's means in order to detain him until they think he has calmed down. The statutes on release make no provision for this latter concern, and the police can pursue it only by ignoring the literal letter of the law. But in bending the law in this "reasonable" direction, the door is opened for justifications to bend it for other, less benign reasons. Police may impose situational sanctions on arrestees whom they think deserve to "sit in jail for a time" because the courts will just "let them out."

• • •

SECURING AN ATTORNEY

A person accused of a criminal offense must decide whether or not to obtain an attorney. This seemingly simple choice in fact involves a complex set of decisions: whether or not to get a lawyer; and who to get, a public defender or a private attorney; if a private attorney, then which one? The decision is confusing and costly in terms of both time and money.

Private Counsel

Unless an arrestee has had prior experience with a particular lawyer and has been satisfied, he is confused about what to do, whom to call, if anyone, how much it will cost him, and whether the amount is reasonable. He is overly suspicious and afraid of being taken advantage of. Some arrestees will call an attorney with whose name he or his friends are familiar. Others may turn to other inmates or their captors—the police—for advice, or perhaps to a bondsman. Still others, fearful of the expense, decide to do without representation.

If the arrestee telephones an attorney from the lockup, the attorney is likely to ask him a few questions about the charges, then ask to speak to the police officer in charge or contact a bail commissioner in an effort to get the bond lowered to an amount the arrestee can make. After this he may contact a bondsman. If the arrestee secures his release before arraignment, the case is scheduled for a week or two later, and in the interim the attorney will arrange an appointment with his caller. If the arrestee is not released, the attorney will try to meet his prospective client just before arraignment in order to argue for bail reduction and afterward hold a brief conference to discuss financial terms and the case.

It is important that an attorney assess his would-be client's ability to pay early on; once he has begun to represent a defendant, he is bound by the canon of ethics to continue his representation until disposition. While it is possible to withdraw later from the case, it can be awkward and embarrassing. Most attorneys can relate instances of being "taken" by clients, and the result is a rather hardnosed approach to fees, even among the more liberal "client-oriented" attorneys who are frequently young, not well-established, and in particular need of the income.

Fees and billing practices vary widely from attorney to attorney and from case to case. Most private attorneys expect an initial retainer based on their own assessment of the "worth of the case." As one private attorney observed:

> I want to get enough at the outset, so that if I don't get any more out of the case, I won't get burned. This amount varies. For instance, I told a guy it would cost a minimum of five hundred to take his case—it was a messy child-molesting thing—and perhaps more, but that I wanted five hundred dollars to begin with. He later called and said he could come up with three hundred, and I said I would take it. So now, even if he can't pay, I won't get burned too badly. . . . I suppose as I pick up business, I'll have to get tougher on this, but now I need the business and will take the chances. On a routine breach [of peace], or disorderly [conduct], I might very well take fifty dollars.

Although most attorneys bill clients based on the amount of time they spend—or say they spend—on a case (and all things being equal, they feel that the type of charge provides a rough indication of this), they also adjust this amount according to their assessment of their client's ability to pay. Some attorneys are critical of such billing practices, but those who use them claim that they allow the better-off to subsidize the less fortunate.

Some attorneys have experimented with a flat fee for a case, which in one small firm is $300 for a case in the lower court and $1,000 for a case in upper court. But this means that those people whose cases are disposed of quickly after only one or two court appearances pay an extremely high per hour or per appearance cost, while those whose cases require considerable research, investigation, court appearances, or a trial get a real bargain.

• • •

Public Defenders

In order to obtain a public defender a person must be poor. There are rather rigid guidelines for eligibility, but they are not strictly adhered to, and in fact most arrestees who apply for a PD routinely obtain one. There are several reasons for this. Perhaps most important is the prevailing belief among prosecutors, public defenders, and most judges that the formal guidelines are overly restrictive, and that by denying a person *free* counsel they are in effect denying him *any* counsel. As a consequence they may overlook an income ceiling or an obvious undervaluing of personal assets. Although some judges occasionally suggest it, few in fact seriously expect an applicant to sell his five-year-old automobile in order to raise an attorney's fee.

A second reason is the drive for administrative efficiency. The application form requires detailed information about the applicant's financial condition, and to verify all of it would require more effort than the PD is willing to extend in most cases. The PD's staff finds it far easier to take the partial information at face value and recommend assignment of a PD knowing that errors will be made. They justified this by arguing that it might permit a few more people to have a

PD than deserve one, but at least it does not exclude those who do. In addition, PDs are reluctant to question or challenge ambiguous or inconsistent answers about income and assets, feeling that to do so would create an atmosphere of suspicion and hostility, and undercut their ability to gain the full confidence of their clients.

But it can still be difficult to obtain an attorney. In court, the prosecutor's first question to an unrepresented defendant is: "Do you want to get your own attorney, apply for a public defender, or get your case over with today?" The very way the question is phrased encourages people *not* to seek counsel, and suggests preferential treatment if they plead guilty immediately. If someone asks for a PD, then he is shunted off for an interview to determine his eligibility, and the interview itself can become a humiliating experience.

• • •

In light of the consistently lenient sentences and the casual way in which so many cases linger on, it is understandable why many defendants do not obtain attorneys—public or private—at all, and when they do, why so many of them desire little more than a quick and perfunctory meeting with their attorneys.

CONTINUANCES

Although defendants usually want to get their cases over with as quickly as possible, they are not always successful. The court has its own pace, which is often at odds with the defendant's self-interest. Defense attorneys and prosecutors usually turn (or return) their attentions to a case on the morning it is scheduled on the calendar, and if they are not able to resolve any differences before the calendar call, they will agree to a (or another) continuance. Problems which impede the resolution of a case can vary considerably, and a great many continuations stem from confusion and carelessness. A defense attorney may have overcommitted himself on that day, or in a more difficult case be unwilling to spend a few additional moments to track down a full-time prosecutor. Occasionally a defendant may appear in court only to find that his case is not on the calendar. Or the defense attorney may forget to show up. A court-ordered report such as a laboratory report on drugs may not have been completed, or a defendant's file may simply be lost. Whatever the reasons for delay, it may be two or three hours after the defendant has first taken his seat in the gallery before he is informed that his case will be continued. Rarely is this decision made in consultation with him or even with an appreciation of the problems it might involve for him. Unable to comprehend the details of court operations, most defendants are overwhelmed by the details of the processes. Rarely can they distinguish reasonable from unreasonable, careful from careless decisions, and they are left with generalized discontent and haunting suspicions.

But delay is not always the result of bumbling, and it is often a highly effective defense strategy. As one attorney observed:

We can make life difficult for the prosecutors by filing a lot of motions. . . .
So when I push a legalistic line I am not expecting to have a complicated
legal discourse; rather it's part of my ammunition to secure my objectives.
They know I'm serious and that I'll spend a lot of time to pursue it. I'll
wear them down that way.

Motions may be filed one at a time, so that a case may be strung out over a long
period. Strategic delay can also be secured by pleading not guilty and asking for
a trial by jury. This request automatically provides a several-week (and at times
a several-month) continuance, during which period the complainant may calm
down or restitution can be arranged.

Because delay can be and often is an effective defense strategy, it can also be
used successfully by a defense attorney to justify his own carelessness or actions
performed for the sake of convenience. While public defenders may use it to
cope with a pressing caseload, private attorneys may use it to boost their own
fees or insure payment. In any case, all but the most knowledgeable of defendants will be unable to identify the *real* reasons for delay.

FAILURE TO APPEAR

The Causes of Nonappearance

For many arrestees the central question is not how to maneuver to reduce the
chances of conviction, a harsh sentence, or the number of court appearances, but
whether to show up in court at all. This consideration is not restricted to a small
handful of "absconders" or would-be absconders; it concerns large numbers of
arrestees. Roughly one-third of those in my sample missed one or more of their
scheduled court appearances, and a substantial number (one person in five) never
did return to court even after they received repeated letters of warning. While
a number of these people had their cases terminated by a court action which
called for a "bond forfeiture with no further action," about one in every eight
or nine cases was never formally resolved by the court in any way, and are filed
as outstanding, closed only if and when the accused is arrested on other unrelated charges. Most of those who fail to appear (FTA) are charged with minor
misdemeanors, but the problem is by no means restricted to them. A third of the
FTAs were charged with the most serious class of misdemeanors, and fully 20
percent of them were charged with felonies. Both in terms of absolute numbers
and the seriousness of the charges, failures to appear present a serious and continuing problem for the court.

• • •

Like other efforts, mine to identify predictors of appearance/nonappearance
focused on characteristics of *individual* defendants. Yet the discussion above suggests that the label FTA itself is problematic because it depends in part on
whether a bondsman is present in court to secure a continuance and whether a

prosecutor is willing to make accommodations for those who step out of the courtroom momentarily. Furthermore, by focusing on the *personal* characteristics of the defendant we overlook the importance of *organizational features* in the court which may encourage nonappearance. People without attorneys may *show up* in court with the same frequency as those with attorneys, but because their cases are not called until late in the day some of them give up and go home, either because they are bored and irritated or because they think a recess is an adjournment. My observations of the court lead me to believe that nonappearance is more likely to be accounted for in terms of how well defendants understand the operations of the court (for example, are they in the correct courtroom?), how much respect they have for the court, how seriously they take the proceedings, how aware they are of their scheduled court appearances, and what they believe the consequences will be if they fail to appear. In other words, the *interaction between the court organization and the accused* is likely to provide the best explanation for appearance or nonappearance.

PRETRIAL DIVERSION

One way for an accused person to reduce the chances of conviction and post-conviction penalty is to make an advance effort to "rehabilitate" himself. There are a variety of ways in which the accused can demonstrate this effort to the court. . . . One way is the Pretrial Diversion Program sponsored by the New Haven Pretrial Services Council. Representatives of this program approach new arrestees who meet its initial eligibility criteria, and offer them an opportunity to participate in its in-house group counseling program or to take advantage of its job placement services. If those who are accepted faithfully participate in these activities for a period of ninety days, then the program will recommend to the prosecutor that the charges be nolled.

Despite the seeming benefits which flow from this program, very few of the eligible arrestees take advantage of it. Estimates constructed from my sample indicated that over three-quarters of all arrestees met the program's *initial* eligibility requirements, but of the 800 eligibles for whom data were available, only 19, or 2.3 percent of them, actually participated in the diversion program. Officials of the diversion program attempt to account for these low numbers by pointing to the prosecutor's discretion to veto prospective participants who are otherwise eligible and interested. While these factors certainly limit the program's size, there is another much more important reason for its limited effectiveness: arrestees consider participation in the program itself a penalty that is much more severe than the one they think they will receive if they do *not* participate.

One evaluation of the program attempted to estimate what might have happened to the program's participants if they had not been "diverted." Identifying a control group and tracing its path through the court, the researchers found that one-fifth to one-third of the "control group" obtained nolles or dismissals; most of them pleaded guilty and received a small fine of $10 to $20. *None* of them went to jail. In short, they concluded tentatively, those people who are eligible but decline to enter the diversion program are not likely to be treated harshly by the court.

In contrast, people who do participate in the program must agree to participate in regularly scheduled meetings for a three-month period with no definite assurances that their cases will be nolled afterward. It is not surprising, then, that so many people pass up the diversion program.

• • •

CONCLUSION: THE AGGREGATED EFFECTS
OF THE PRETRIAL PROCESS

The figures on pretrial costs presented in the preceding discussion are rough estimates and should not be interpreted as facts. Because they suggest comparisons between groups and costs which are themselves quite different, they must also be interpreted with caution. Still, these figures point to the inescapable conclusion that the costs of lower court—the tangible, direct, and immediate penalties extracted from those accused of minor criminal offenses—are not those factors which have received the greatest attention from legal scholars, social scientists, or indeed court officials. Liberal legal theory directs attention to formal outcomes, to the conditions giving rise to the application of the criminal sanction at adjudication and sentence. Much social science research has followed this lead, searching for the causes of sanctioning at these stages. But this emphasis produces a distorted vision of the process and the sanctions it dispenses. The real punishment for many people is the pretrial process itself; that is why criminally accused invoke so few of the adversarial options available to them.

This inverted system of justice dramatizes the dilemma of lower courts. Expanded procedures designed to improve the criminal process are not invoked because they might be counterproductive. Efforts to slow the process down and make it truly deliberative might lead to still harsher treatment of defendants and still more time loss for complainants and victims. Devices designed to control official discretion do not perform their expected functions (the failure to litigate bail is a clear case-in-point). And whereas rapid and perfunctory practices foster error and caprice, they do reduce pretrial costs and in the aggregate may render rough justice.

In light of the pretrial costs and the actual penalties meted out in the lower court, one is tempted to scoff at the formal theory which so ineffectively governs official behavior in the lower court and to dismiss it as unworkable and overly elegant—as proceduralism run amok—for the types of petty problems presented to the court. Would not simple summary justice with a minimum of procedures provide a more appropriate and workable set of standards? Perhaps the police court magistrate meting out immediate kadi-like justice without reliance on defense counsel—but also without the need for bail, repeated court appearances, and the like—might be more satisfactory. Or perhaps community-based courts might be more adept at ferreting out the underlying causes of conflict and providing ameliorating responses.

In a great many cases these alternatives might work more effectively; yet the impulse for formality, even with its manifest shortcomings, cannot be so quickly dismissed. While lower courts sentence very few people to terms in jail, in theory almost all of those appearing before them face a slim possibility of incarceration. While creating a record of petty criminal offenses may not significantly affect the future of most people who find themselves before the bench, it can have a long-lasting and unpredictable impact on some. Citizenship can be placed in jeopardy, careers destroyed, aspirations dampened, delinquent propensities reinforced. Such problems may be few in number, but they do occur. And it is impossible to tell in advance which cases may precipitate these more serious consequences, since the specific impact of a record may not make itself felt until much later in life.

As long as conviction for petty criminal offenses carries the possibility of a jail sentence or of jeopardizing one's future, the ideal of a formal, adversarial process will remain strong and attractive even to those who acknowledge that the process itself is the punishment for most people. However, there may be some alternatives which both facilitate the rapid handling of petty cases and protect the interests of the accused.

NOTES

1. Over half the arrestees in my sample had a record of prior arrests by the New Haven police, and a large proportion of them had records of conviction. These figures are probably drastically low, however, since local authorities do not systematically obtain records from other jurisdictions, either within or outside the state.

2. Discussions of arrest and conviction frequently assume that arrestees have a great fear of the stigma of a conviction and will go to great lengths to avoid being formally labeled as criminals. But my observations are consistent with the findings of many criminologists who have studied juvenile delinquency and concluded that the disproportionate rate of criminal conduct by young lower-class males stems from a subculture which promotes such activity as a social mechanism for becoming a male adult. Rather than being a brand of inferiority for many lower- and working-class youths, arrest and conviction often reinforce the values of their subculture and can even enhance their status among their peers. This has been noted time and again in the literature on juvenile courts, but altogether overlooked and ignored in "adult" courts. See Walter B. Miller, "Lower Class Culture as a Generating Milieu of Gang Delinquency," *Journal of Social Issues* 14 (1958): 5–19, and Albert K. Cohen, *Delinquent Boys: The Culture of the Gang* (New York: Free Press, 1955). Also see Edwin H. Sutherland and Donald Cressey, *Principles of Criminology,* 7th ed. (Philadelphia: J. B. Lippincott, 1966), pp. 183–199, and Richard Quinney, *The Social Reality of Crime* (Boston: Little, Brown, 1970), pp. 207–276.

3. See Edward Banfield, *The Unheavenly City* (Boston: Little, Brown, 1971), pp. 45–56; and Edward Banfield and James Q. Wilson, "Public Regardingness as a Value Premise in Voting Behavior," *American Political Science Review* 58 (1964): 876–887.

4. Connecticut General Statute 54–63 (C) (A).

1 8

✪

Race and Sentencing

SAMUEL WALKER
CASSIA SPOHN
MIRIAM DELONE

Questions about racial bias in the sentencing process have been a major concern for decades. The authors argue that clear and convincing evidence exists that there is racial disparity in sentencing. They then provide three possible explanations for such bias.

Although charges of racial discrimination have been leveled at all stages of the criminal justice process, much of the harshest criticism has focused on judges' sentencing decisions. Critics of the sentencing process contend that crimes by African Americans and Hispanics are punished more harshly than similar crimes by equally culpable whites. Other scholars challenge this assertion. They contend that the harsher sentences imposed on racial minorities reflect their disproportionate involvement in serious crime, as well as other "legally relevant" factors that judges consider in determining the appropriate sentence.

Underlying this controversy are questions concerning discretion in sentencing. To be fair, a sentencing scheme must allow the judge or jury discretion to shape sentences to fit individuals and their crimes. The judge or jury must be free to consider all *relevant* aggravating and mitigating circumstances. To be consistent, on the other hand, a sentencing scheme requires the even-handed application of objective standards. The judge or jury must take only relevant

Source: Samuel Walker, Cassia Spohn, and Miriam DeLone, *The Color of Justice* (Belmont, Calif.: Wadsworth, 1996), pp. 151–175. Reprinted with permission. Some references deleted.

considerations into account and must be precluded from determining sentence severity based on prejudice or whim.

Critics of the sentencing process argue that judges and juries exercise their discretion inappropriately. While acknowledging that some degree of sentence disparity is to be expected in a system that attempts to individualize punishment, these critics suggest that there is *unwarranted* disparity in the sentences imposed on offenders convicted of similar crimes. More to the point, they assert that judges impose harsher sentences on African American and Hispanic offenders than on white offenders.

Other scholars contend that judges' sentencing decisions are not racially biased. They argue that disparity in sentencing is due to legitimate differences among individual cases and that racial disparities disappear once these differences are taken into consideration. These scholars believe, in other words, that judges' sentencing decisions are both fair and consistent.

RACIAL DISPARITY IN SENTENCING

There is clear and convincing evidence of racial *disparity* in sentencing. This evidence is of two types. The first is derived from national statistics on prison admissions and prison populations. These statistics reveal that the incarceration rate for African Americans is much higher than the rate for whites. On a typical day in 1990, for example, 1,860 of every 100,000 African Americans (but only 289 of every 100,000 white Americans) were in jail or prison.[1]

The second type of evidence of racial disparity in sentencing comes from studies of judges' sentencing decisions. These studies reveal that African American defendants are more likely than whites to be sentenced to prison; those who are sentenced to prison receive longer terms than whites. Consider the following statistics:

> Among offenders convicted of felonies in California in 1980, 44 percent of the African Americans, 37 percent of the Hispanics, and 33 percent of the whites were sentenced to prison.[2]

> Among offenders convicted of violent felonies in Detroit, 79 percent of the African Americans but only 58 percent of the whites were sentenced to prison.[3]

> The average prison sentence imposed on African American offenders convicted of felonies in Minnesota was 4.84 years; the average sentence for white offenders was 3.48 years.[4]

> Over 72 percent of the African Americans convicted of sexually assaulting whites in an Ohio county were sentenced to prison, compared to only 54.1 percent of the whites convicted of sexually assaulting whites and 39.3 percent of the African Americans convicted of sexually assaulting other African Americans.[5]

Three Explanations for Racial Disparities in Sentencing

Although these statistics indicate that African Americans receive more punitive sentences than whites, they do not tell us *why* this occurs. We suggest that there are at least three possible explanations. These explanations are discussed below and are diagrammed in Figure 1.

First, the differences in sentence severity could be due to the fact that African Americans commit more serious crimes and have more serious prior criminal records than whites. Studies of sentencing decisions consistently have demonstrated the importance of these two factors. Offenders who are convicted of more severe offenses, who use a weapon to commit the crime, or who seriously injure the victim receive harsher sentences, as do offenders who have prior felony convictions. The harsher sentences imposed on African Americans, then, might reflect the influence of these legitimate legal factors rather than the effect of racial prejudice on the part of judges.

The differences also could result from economic discrimination. Poor defendants are not as likely as middle- or upper-class defendants to have a private attorney or be released prior to trial. Both of these factors are related to sentence severity. Defendants represented by private attorneys or released prior to trial receive more lenient sentences. Since African American defendants are more likely than white defendants to be poor, economic discrimination amounts to *indirect* racial discrimination.

Finally, the differences could be because of overt or *direct* racial discrimination on the part of judges. They could be due to the fact that judges take the race of the offender into account in determining the appropriate sentence. This implies that judges who are confronted with African American and white offenders convicted of similar crimes and with similar prior criminal records impose harsher sentences on African Americans than on whites. It implies that judges, the majority of whom are white, stereotype African American offenders as more violent, more culpable, and less amenable to rehabilitation than white offenders.

EMPIRICAL RESEARCH ON RACE AND SENTENCING

Researchers have conducted dozens of studies to determine which of these explanations is more correct. Studies conducted from the 1930s through the 1960s often concluded that racial disparities in sentencing were due to racial discrimination. But in his review of these studies, Hagan found that most were methodologically unsound.[6] Many of them employed inadequate controls for crime seriousness and prior record or used simplistic statistical techniques. These methodological problems called their conclusions into question.

More recent and methodologically rigorous studies have produced conflicting findings regarding the effect of race on sentencing. Although a number of

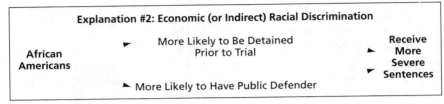

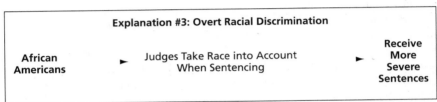

Figure 1 Three Explanations for Racial Disparity in Sentencing

studies have found that African Americans are sentenced more harshly than whites,[7] others have found either that there are no significant racial differences[8] or that African Americans are sentenced more *leniently* than whites.[9] These inconsistent findings have led researchers to conclude that the contemporary sentencing process, while not racially neutral, is not characterized by "a widespread systematic pattern of discrimination."[10]

A comprehensive review of the studies . . . is beyond the scope of this [article]. Instead, we describe in detail the results of three recent studies: one found that African Americans received more punitive sentences than whites, one found no racial differences, and one found that African Americans received more lenient sentences than whites for some types of offenses.

Discriminatory Sentencing in "Metro City"

A number of methodologically sound studies have concluded that African American offenders are sentenced more harshly than whites. Spohn et al.,[11] for example, analyzed the effect of race on the sentences imposed on males convicted of felonies in "Metro City," a large urban jurisdiction in the northeastern United States, from 1968 to 1980. They controlled for the race of the offender and other legal and extralegal variables that affect judges' sentencing decisions: the conviction charge, the defendant's prior criminal record, the type of attorney representing the defendant, the amount of bail, whether the defendant was detained or released prior to trial, and whether the defendant was convicted of the most serious charge.

The authors found that, even after the control variables were considered, the incarceration rate for African Americans was five percentage points higher than the rate for whites: 29 percent of the convicted African Americans and 24 percent of the convicted whites were sentenced to prison. Further analysis led them to conclude that judges in Metro City discriminated against African Americans in "borderline cases"—that is, in cases in which the judge could impose either a short prison sentence or a long probation sentence. In these types of cases, "the judge selected the probation option for whites more than blacks, the prison option for blacks more than whites."[12]

The authors also found evidence of economic discrimination. African American defendants were more likely than whites to be detained prior to trial, and those who were detained were more likely than those who were released to be incarcerated. African American defendants also were more likely than whites to be represented by a public defender, and those represented by public defenders were more likely than those represented by private attorneys to be sentenced to prison. The authors concluded, "Since blacks are more likely than whites to be poor, this type of discrimination affects blacks more than whites. It can, therefore, be seen as a possible source of indirect racial discrimination."[13]

As shown in Figure 2, this study found evidence of both direct and indirect discrimination against African American criminal defendants in Metro City. Although the authors concede that a five-percentage-point difference between African Americans and whites in the rate of incarceration might be perceived as "trivial," they argue that it is not. "Even though race accounts for 'only' four percent of the variation . . . in the decision to incarcerate, the tremendous difference between being confined and being free makes it a difference which is both substantial and disturbing."[14]

Racial Equity in Sentencing in California

The study described above concludes that African American offenders received harsher sentences than whites. Several methodologically rigorous studies reach a different conclusion. A study of the sentences imposed on male offenders convicted of a variety of felonies in California in 1980, for example, revealed that race did not affect sentence severity once controls for legally relevant variables were taken into consideration.[15]

Klein, Turner, and Petersilia compared the probability of incarceration and the mean prison sentence for African American, Hispanic, and white offenders. When they examined the overall incarceration rate for each group (without controlling for type of crime or prior record), they found substantial racial disparity: 44 percent of the African Americans, 37 percent of the Hispanics, and only 33 percent of the whites were sentenced to prison.[16] They also discovered, however, that the three groups were convicted of different types of crimes and that racial minorities were more likely than whites to have multiple conviction counts, to have used violence in the current offense, and to have extensive prior records.

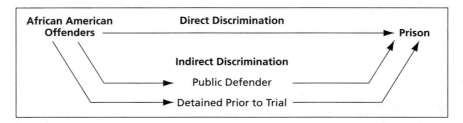

Figure 2 Direct and Indirect Racial Discrimination in "Metro City"

When the authors controlled for these factors, as well as a number of other offender and case characteristics, they found that race did not affect the incarceration rate. For each type of crime, the judge's decision to sentence an offender to prison was based primarily on the number of conviction counts; the defendant's prior record; the defendant's age; and whether the defendant used a weapon to commit the crime, had a history of drug or alcohol addiction, insisted on a trial, was detained prior to trial, and was not represented by a private attorney.[17]

The authors also discovered that knowing the defendant's race did not improve their ability to predict whether the defendant would be sentenced to prison. In fact, they found that they could use the offender and case characteristics (excluding race) to predict with 80 percent accuracy which offenders would be sentenced to prison and which would not. Adding offender race to the prediction equation did not improve the accuracy of these predictions by even one percentage point.[18]

Klein and his colleagues then analyzed the effect of race on the length of the prison term. Once again, they found that race did not influence sentence length and that including race in the model did not improve their ability to predict the length of the prison term.[19]

The authors of this study attributed their finding that "defendant race is not related to the sentence imposed"[20] in part to the passage of the California Determinate Sentencing Act (DSA). Enacted in 1977, this law established a short, middle, and long term for each offense and instructed judges to impose the middle term unless there were aggravating or mitigating circumstances. According to Klein et al., "The act does appear to contribute to racial equity in sentencing."[21]

More Lenient Sentences for Nonwhite Drug Offenders

Although most studies of the effect of race on sentencing have concluded either that African Americans are sentenced more harshly than whites or that there are no differences in the sentences imposed on offenders in the two racial groups, a handful of studies has shown that African Americans receive more lenient sentences than whites. Typically, as Kleck has noted,[22] these findings are "overlooked" or "downplayed" by criminal justice researchers, who characterize the findings as "anomalies."

Peterson and Hagan suggest that findings of more lenient treatment of African American offenders should not necessarily be seen as anomalies. These researchers assert that "the role of race is more variable and more complicated than previously acknowledged" and that "both differential severity and leniency are possible."[23] They note, for example, that African Americans who victimize whites might be sentenced more harshly but that African Americans who victimize other African Americans might be sentenced more leniently.

Peterson and Hagan suggest that race-related perceptions of victims and offenders might similarly affect the sentences imposed on individuals convicted of *victimless* crimes. More to the point, they state that minority drug users, at least during some time periods, might be typed or characterized as victims rather than as villains and that this distinction might result in more lenient sentences for minorities. If judges view minority youth as innocent targets of big-time dealers or professional traffickers, in other words, they might be reluctant to impose severe sentences on minority drug users. The authors also assert that leniency would be reserved for minority drug *users;* they argue that "on those rare occasions when nonwhites do rise to the position of big dealers, the predicted leniency should . . . disappear."[24]

To test these predictions, Peterson and Hagan examined the sentences imposed on drug offenders convicted in the Southern Federal District Court of New York from 1963 through 1976. They found that nonwhite drug *users* were sentenced more leniently than white drug users but that nonwhite drug *dealers* received substantially longer prison sentences than white dealers. Nonwhite drug users were significantly less likely than white users to be sentenced to prison; moreover, those nonwhites who were sentenced to prison received sentences that were, on the average, about six and one-half months shorter than the sentences received by whites.[25] In contrast, the average sentence imposed on nonwhite big dealers was nineteen months longer than the sentence imposed on white dealers.[26]

Peterson and Hagan conclude that researchers should not "treat the meaning of race as a constant."[27] They assert that it is overly simplistic to expect all African American offenders to be sentenced more harshly than all white offenders. Rather, "there are patterns of advantage and disadvantage that only contextualized analyses can reveal."[28]

Explanations for Contradictory Findings

As illustrated by the three studies described earlier, research on the effect of race on sentencing has produced conflicting results. Some of these studies support the discrimination thesis, while others do not. Indeed, some studies conclude that racial minorities are sentenced more leniently than whites.

Hawkins suggests that these inconsistent findings may result from an oversimplification of conflict theory, the principal theoretical model used in studies of race and criminal punishment.[29]

Most researchers simply test the hypothesis that racial minorities will be sentenced more harshly than whites. They assume, either explicitly or implicitly, that racial minorities will receive more severe sentences than whites regardless of the nature of the crime, the race of the victim, or the relationship between the victim and the offender.

Conflict theory, however, "does not support a simplistic expectation of greater punishment for blacks than whites under all circumstances."[30] Rather, conflict theorists argue that "the probability that criminal sanctions will be applied varies according to the extent to which the behaviors of the powerless conflict with the interests of the power segments."[31]

Crimes that threaten the power of the dominant class will therefore produce harsher penalties for African Americans who commit those crimes. Crimes that pose relatively little threat to the system of white authority, on the other hand, will not necessarily result in more severe sanctions for African Americans. According to this view, African Americans who murder, rape, or rob whites will receive harsher sentences, while African Americans who victimize members of their own race will be treated more leniently. As Peterson and Hagan note:

> When black offenders assault or kill black victims, the devalued status of the black victims and the paternalistic attitudes of white authorities can justify lenient treatment. . . . When blacks violate white victims, the high sexual property value attached to the white victims and the racial fears of authorities can justify severe treatment.[32]

Criminal justice scholars have proposed revising the conflict perspective on race and sentencing to account for the possibility of interaction between defendant race and other predictors of sentence severity. Hawkins,[33] for example, argues for the development of a more comprehensive conflict theory that embodies race-of-victim and type-of-crime effects. Similarly, Peterson and Hagan argue for research "that takes context-specific conceptions of race into account."[34]

Researchers examining the links between race and sentence severity have begun to heed these suggestions. They have started to conduct research designed to identify the circumstances under which African Americans will be sentenced more harshly than whites. In support of Hawkins's recommendations, their findings suggest that both the race of the victim and the seriousness of the crime are important factors.

In the sections that follow, we compare the treatment of interracial and intraracial crimes. We focus primarily on the crime of sexual assault. We also summarize the findings of research examining the effect of race on sentencing for different types of crimes.

DIFFERENTIAL TREATMENT
OF INTER- AND INTRARACIAL CRIME

There is compelling historical evidence that interracial and intraracial crimes were treated differently. Gunnar Myrdal's examination of the southern court system in the 1930s, for example, revealed that African Americans who victimized whites received the harshest punishment, while African Americans who victimized other African Americans were often "acquitted or given a ridiculously mild sentence."[35] Myrdal also noted that "it is quite common for a white criminal to be set free if his crime was against a Negro."[36]

These patterns are particularly pronounced for the crime of sexual assault. As Brownmiller notes, "No single event ticks off America's political schizophrenia with greater certainty than the case of a black man accused of raping a white woman."[37] Evidence of this attitude can be found in pre–Civil War statutes that prescribed different penalties for African American and white men convicted of sexual assault.

• • •

Differential treatment of interracial and intraracial sexual assaults continued even after passage of the Fourteenth Amendment, which outlawed the types of explicit statutory racial discrimination discussed earlier. In the first half of this century, African American men accused of, or even suspected of, sexually assaulting white women often faced white lynch mobs bent on vengeance.

African American men who escaped the mob's wrath were almost certain to be convicted. Those who were convicted were guaranteed a harsh sentence. Many, in fact, were sentenced to death; 405 of the 453 men executed for rape in the United States were African Americans.[38] According to Brownmiller, "Heavier sentences imposed on blacks for raping white women is an incontestable historic fact."[39] As we will show, it is not simply a historic fact; research conducted during the past two decades illustrates that judges continue to impose harsher sentences on African American men convicted of raping white women.

Offender–Victim Race and Sentences for Sexual Assault

Researchers analyzing the impact of race on sentencing for sexual assault have argued that focusing on only the race of the defendant and ignoring the race of the victim will produce misleading conclusions about the overall effect of race on sentencing. More to the point, they contend that researchers may incorrectly conclude that race does not affect sentence severity if only the race of the defendant is taken into consideration.

LaFree[40] examined the impact of offender–victim race on the disposition of sexual assault cases in Indianapolis. He found that African American men who assaulted white women were more likely than other offenders to be sentenced to prison. They also received longer prison sentences than any other offenders.

LaFree concludes that his results highlight the importance of examining the racial composition of the offender–victim pair. Because the law was applied *most* harshly to African Americans charged with raping white women but *least* harshly to African Americans charged with raping African American women, simply examining the overall disposition of cases with African American defendants would have produced misleading results.

Walsh[41] reached a similar conclusion. When he examined the sentences imposed on offenders convicted of sexual assault in a metropolitan Ohio county, he found that neither the offender's race nor the victim's race influenced the length of the sentence. In addition, the incarceration rate for white defendants was *higher* than the rate for African American defendants.

Further analysis, however, revealed that African Americans convicted of assaulting whites received more severe sentences than those convicted of assaulting members of their own race. This was true for those who assaulted acquaintances as well as those who assaulted strangers. As Walsh notes, "The leniency extended to blacks who sexually assault blacks provides a rather strong indication of disregard for minority victims of sexual assault."[42]

Spohn's[43] study of sentences imposed on defendants convicted of violent felonies in Detroit highlights the importance of testing a model incorporating both race-of-victim and type-of-crime effects. When the author examined the sentences imposed on all felony defendants, she found that offender–victim race did not affect the length of the sentence at all and did not influence the incarceration rate in the predicted way. The difference in the incarceration rates for black-on-black and black-on-white crimes was only two percentage points and was not statistically significant.

When she analyzed the effect of offender–victim race on sentence severity *separately* for the various types of crimes, on the other hand, Spohn found that offender–victim race did influence judges' sentencing decisions in sexual assault and murder cases. African Americans who sexually assaulted whites faced a greater risk of incarceration than either African Americans who sexually assaulted African Americans, or whites who sexually assaulted whites. Similarly, African Americans who murdered whites received longer sentences than did offenders in the other two categories. For these two crimes, then, the author found discrimination based on the race of the offender *and* the race of the victim.

The results of these studies demonstrate that criminal punishment is contingent upon the race of the victim as well as the race of the offender. They demonstrate that *"the meaning of race varies, and that, despite simplistic interpretations of conflict theory, both differential severity and leniency are possible."*[44] The harshest penalties will be imposed on African Americans who victimize whites, the most lenient penalties on African Americans who victimize other African Americans.

THE EFFECT OF RACE ON SENTENCING
FOR VARIOUS TYPES OF CRIMES

The importance of "rethinking the conflict perspective on race and criminal punishment"[45] is also demonstrated by the results of studies examining the effect of race on sentence severity for various types of crimes. Some researchers, building on Kalven and Zeisel's "liberation hypothesis,"[46] assert that African Americans will be sentenced more harshly than whites only in less serious cases.

The liberation hypothesis suggests that jurors deviate from their fact-finding mission in cases in which the evidence against the defendant is weak or contradictory. Jurors' doubts about the evidence, in other words, liberate them from the constraints imposed by the law and free them to consider their own sentiments or values. When Kalven and Zeisel examined jurors' verdicts in rape cases, for example, they found that jurors' beliefs about the victim's behavior were much more likely to influence their verdicts if the victim was raped by an unarmed acquaintance than if the victim was raped by a stranger armed with a gun or a knife.

The liberation hypothesis suggests that in more serious cases, the appropriate sentence is strongly determined by the seriousness of the crime and by the defendant's prior criminal record. In these types of cases, judges have relatively little discretion and thus few opportunities to consider legally irrelevant factors such as race. In less serious cases, on the other hand, the appropriate sentence is not clearly indicated by the features of the crime or the defendant's criminal record, which leaves judges more disposed to bring extralegal factors to bear on the sentencing decision.

Consider, for example, a case of sexual assault in which the offender, who has a prior conviction for armed robbery, raped a stranger at gunpoint. In this case a severe sentence is clearly called for; all defendants who fall into this category, regardless of their race or the race of their victims, will be sentenced to prison for close to the maximum term.

The appropriate sentence for a first-time offender who assaults an acquaintance with a weapon other than a gun, on the other hand, is not necessarily obvious. Some defendants who fall into this category will be incarcerated; others will not. This situation opens the door for judges to consider the race of the defendant and/or the race of the victim in determining the appropriate sentence.

Spohn and Cederblom used data on defendants convicted of violent felonies in Detroit to test the hypothesis that racial discrimination in sentencing is confined to less serious criminal cases.[47] Although they acknowledge that all of the cases included in their data file are by definition "serious cases," they argue that some are more serious than others; murder, rape, and robbery are more serious than assault; crimes in which the defendant used a gun are more serious than those in which the defendant did not use a gun; and crimes in which the defendant had a prior felony conviction are more serious than those in which the defendant did not have prior convictions.

As shown in Table 1, which summarizes the results of their analysis of the likelihood of incarceration (controlling for other variables linked to sentence severity), the authors found convincing support for their hypothesis. With only one exception, race had a significant effect on the decision to incarcerate only in less serious cases. African Americans convicted of assault were incarcerated at a higher rate than whites convicted of assault; there were no racial differences for the three more serious offenses. Similarly, race affected the likelihood of incarceration for defendants with no violent felony convictions but not for those with a prior conviction, for defendants who victimized acquaintances but not for those who victimized strangers, and for defendants who did not use a gun to commit the crime but not for those who did use a gun.

Spohn and Cederblom conclude that their results provide support for Kalven and Zeisel's liberation hypothesis, at least with respect to the decision to incarcerate. They also contend that their findings offer important insights into judges' sentencing decisions.

> When the crime is serious and the evidence strong, judges' sentencing decisions are determined primarily by factors of explicit legal relevance—the seriousness of the conviction charge, the number of conviction charges, the nature of the defendant's prior criminal record, and so on. Sentencing

Table 1 The Effect of Race on the Likelihood of Incarceration for Various Types of Cases in Detroit

	Effect of Race on Incarceration Statistically Significant?
Most serious conviction charge	
Murder	No
Robbery	No
Rape	No
Other sex offenses	No
Assault	Yes
Prior criminal record	
Violent felony conviction	No
No violent felony conviction	Yes
Relationship between offender and victim	
Strangers	No
Acquaintances	Yes
Use of a weapon	
Offender used a gun	No
Offender did not use a gun	Yes
Injury to victim	
Offender injured victim	Yes
Offender did not injure victim	Yes

SOURCE: Adapted from Cassia Spohn and Jerry Cederblom, "Race and Disparities in Sentencing: A Test of the Liberation Hypothesis," *Justice Quarterly* 8 (1991): 305–327.

decisions in less serious cases, on the other hand, reflect the influence of extralegal as well as legal factors.[48]

These results demonstrate that the criteria used by judges to determine the appropriate sentence will vary depending on the nature of the crime and the defendant's prior criminal record. More to the point, they illustrate that *the effect of race on sentence severity will vary.* Judges impose harsher sentences on African Americans than on whites under some circumstances and for some types of crime; they impose similar sentences under other circumstances and for other kinds of crime. The fact that race does not affect sentence severity for all cases, in other words, does not mean that judges do not discriminate in any cases.

CONCLUSION

Despite dozens of studies investigating the relationship between defendant race and sentence severity, a definitive answer to the question "Are racial minorities sentenced more harshly than whites?" remains elusive. Although a number of studies have uncovered evidence of racial discrimination in sentencing, others have found either that there are no significant racial differences or that blacks are sentenced more leniently than whites.

The failure of research to produce uniform findings of racial discrimination in sentencing has led to conflicting conclusions. Some researchers assert that racial discrimination in sentencing has declined over time and that the predictive power of race, once relevant legal factors are taken into account, is quite low. Other researchers claim that discrimination has not declined or disappeared but simply has become more subtle and difficult to detect. These researchers argue that discrimination against racial minorities is not universal but rather is confined to certain types of cases, certain types of settings, and certain types of defendants. We assert that the latter explanation is more convincing. We suggest that while the sentencing process in most jurisdictions today is not characterized by overt or systematic racism, racial discrimination in sentencing has not been eliminated. We argue that sentencing decisions in the 1990s reflect *contextual discrimination.* Judges in some jurisdictions continue to impose harsher sentences on African American defendants who murder or rape whites and more lenient sentences on African Americans who victimize other African Americans. Judges in some jurisdictions continue to impose racially biased sentences in less serious cases; in these "borderline cases," African Americans get prison, while whites get probation. Judges, in other words, continue to take race into account, either explicitly or implicitly, when determining the appropriate sentence.

It thus appears that while flagrant racism in sentencing has been eliminated, equality under the law has not been achieved. In the 1990s, whites who commit crimes against African Americans are not beyond the reach of the criminal justice system, African Americans suspected of crimes against whites do not receive "justice" at the hands of white lynching mobs, and African Americans who victimize other African Americans are not immune from punishment. Despite these significant changes, inequities persist. Racial minorities who find themselves in the arms of the law continue to suffer discrimination in sentencing.

NOTES

1. Louis W. Jankowski, *Correctional Populations in the United States, 1990* (Washington, D.C.: Department of Justice, Bureau of Justice Statistics, 1992).

2. Stephen Klein, Joan Petersilia, and Susan Turner, "Race and Imprisonment Decisions in California," *Science* 247 (1990): 812–816.

3. Cassia Spohn and Jerry Cederblom, "Race and Disparities in Sentencing: A Test of the Liberation Hypothesis," *Justice Quarterly* 8 (1991): 305–327.

4. Terance D. Miethe and Charles A. Moore, "Racial Differences in Criminal Processing: The Consequences of Model Selection on Conclusions About Differential Treatment," *Sociological Quarterly* 27 (1986): 217–237.

5. Anthony Walsh, "The Sexual Stratification Hypothesis and Sexual Assault in Light of the Changing Conceptions of Race," *Criminology* 25 (1987): 153–173.

6. John Hagan, "Extra-Legal Attributes and Criminal Sentencing: An Assessment of a Sociological Viewpoint," *Law & Society Review* 8 (1974): 357–383.

7. Joan Petersilia, *Racial Disparities in the Criminal Justice System* (Santa Monica, CA: Rand, 1983); Cassia Spohn, John Gruhl, and Susan Welch, "The Effect of Race on Sentencing: A Re-Examination of an Unsettled Question," *Law & Society Review* 16 (1981–82): 71–88; and Marjorie S. Zatz, "Race, Ethnicity, and Determinate Sentencing: A New Dimension to an Old Controversy," *Criminology* 22 (1984): 147–171.

8. Klein et al., "Race and Imprisonment Decisions."

9. Ilene Nagel Bernstein, William R. Kelly, and Patricia A. Doyle, "Societal Reaction to Deviants: The Case of Criminal Defendants," *American Sociological Review* 42 (1977): 743–795; James L. Gibson, "Race as a Determinant of Criminal Sentences: A Methodological Critique and a Case Study," *Law & Society Review* 12 (1978): 455–478; and Martin A. Levin, "Urban Politics and Policy Outcomes: The Criminal Courts," in *Criminal Justice: Law and Politics,* ed. George F. Cole (Belmont, CA: Wadsworth, 1988).

10. Alfred Blumstein, Jacqueline Cohen, Susan E. Martin, and Michael Tonry, *Research on Sentencing: The Search for Reform,* Vol. 1 (Washington, D.C.: National Academy Press, 1983), p. 93.

11. Spohn et al., "The Effect of Race on Sentencing."

12. Ibid., p. 85.

13. Ibid.

14. Ibid., p. 86.

15. Stephen P. Klein, Susan Turner, and Joan Petersilia, *Racial Equality in Sentencing* (Santa Monica, CA: Rand, 1988).

16. Ibid., p. 5.

17. Ibid., p. 7.

18. Ibid., p. 6.

19. Ibid., p. 10.

20. Ibid., p. 11.

21. Ibid.

22. Gary Kleck, "Racial Discrimination in Criminal Sentencing: A Critical Evaluation of the Evidence with Additional Evidence on the Death Penalty," *American Sociological Review* 46 (1981): 783–804.

23. Ruth D. Peterson and John Hagan, "Changing Conceptions of Race: Towards an Account of Anomalous Findings of Sentencing Research," *American Sociological Review* 49 (1984): 56–70.

24. Ibid., p. 66.

25. Ibid., p. 64.

26. Ibid., p. 67.

27. Ibid., p. 67.

28. Ibid., p. 69.

29. Darnell F. Hawkins, "Beyond Anomalies: Rethinking the Conflict Perspective on Race and Criminal Punishment," *Social Forces* 65 (1987): 719–745.

30. Ibid., p. 724.

31. Richard Quinney, *The Social Reality of Crime* (Boston: Little, Brown, 1970), p. 18.

32. Peterson and Hagan, "Changing Conceptions of Race," p. 57.

33. Hawkins, "Beyond Anomalies."

34. Peterson and Hagan, "Changing Conceptions of Race," p. 69.

35. Gunnar Myrdal, *An American Dilemma: The Negro Problem and Modern Democracy* (New York: Harper, 1944), p. 551.

36. Ibid., p. 553.

37. Susan Brownmiller, *Against Our Will: Men, Women and Rape* (New York: Bantam Books, 1975).

38. Marvin E. Wolfgang and Marc Reidel, "Race, Judicial Discretion and the Death Penalty," *Annals of the American Academy* 407 (1973): 119–133; Marvin E. Wolfgang and Marc Reidel, "Rape, Race and the Death Penalty in Georgia," *American Journal of Orthopsychiatry* 45 (1975): 658–668.

39. Brownmiller, *Against Our Will,* p. 237.

40. Gary D. LaFree, *Rape and Criminal Justice: The Social Construction of Sexual Assault* (Belmont, CA: Wadsworth, 1989).

41. Anthony Walsh, "The Sexual Stratification Hypothesis and Sexual Assault in Light of the Changing Conceptions of Race," *Criminology* 25 (1987): 153–173.

42. Ibid., p. 167.

43. Cassia Spohn, "Crime and the Social Control of Blacks: Offender/Victim Race and the Sentencing of Violent Offenders," in *Inequality, Crime and Social Control,* ed. George S. Bridges and Martha A. Myers (Boulder, CO: Westview, 1994).

44. Peterson and Hagan, "Changing Conceptions of Race," p. 67.

45. Ibid., p. 67.

46. Harry Kalven, Jr., and Hans Zeisel, *The American Jury* (Boston: Little, Brown, 1966).

47. Spohn and Cederblom, "Race and Disparities in Sentencing."

48. Ibid., p. 323.

1 9

✣

Maintaining the Myth of Individualized Justice

Probation Presentence Reports

JOHN ROSECRANCE

The presentence investigation has been justified so that judges can individualize sentences to fit the particular circumstances of the offender as well as the offense. In many states probation officers are required to submit presentence reports prior to sentencing in all felony cases. But what is the function of these reports in a system where plea bargaining is so dominant? Is justice really individualized, or are sentence recommendations actually influenced by the administrative context of the system?

The Justice Department estimates that over 1 million probation presentence reports are submitted annually to criminal courts in the United States. The role of probation officers in the presentence process traditionally has been considered important. After examining criminal courts in the United States, a panel of investigators concluded: "Probation officers are attached to most modern felony courts: presentence reports containing their recommendations are commonly provided and these recommendations are usually followed" (Blumstein, Martin, and Holt 1983). Judges view presentence reports as an integral part of sentencing, calling them "the best guide to intelligent sentencing" (Murrah 1963: 67) and "one of the most important developments in criminal law during the twentieth century" (Hogarth 1971: 246).

Source: From John Rosecrance, "Maintaining the Myth of Individualized Justice: Probation Presentence Reports," *Justice Quarterly* 5 (June 1988), pp. 235–256. Footnotes and some references deleted. Reprinted with permission of the Academy of Criminal Justice Sciences.

Researchers agree that a strong correlation exists between probation recommendations (contained in presentence reports) and judicial sentencing. In a seminal study of judicial decision making, Carter and Wilkins (1967) found 95 percent agreement between probation recommendations and sentence disposition when the officer recommended probation and 88 percent agreement when the officer opposed probation. Hagan (1975), after controlling for related variables, reported a direct correlation of .72 between probation recommendation and sentencing. Walsh (1985) found a similar correlation of .807.

Although there is no controversy about the correlation between probation recommendation and judicial outcome, scholars disagree as to the actual influence of probation officers in the sentencing process. That is, there is no consensus regarding the importance of the presentence investigator in influencing sentencing outcomes. On the one hand, Myers (1979: 538) contends that the "important role played by probation officer recommendation argues for greater theoretical and empirical attention to these officers." Walsh (1985: 303) concludes that "judges lean heavily on the professional advice of probation." On the other hand, Kingsnorth and Rizzo (1979) report that probation recommendations have been supplanted by plea bargaining and that the probation officer is "largely superfluous." Hagan, Hewitt, and Alwin (1979), after reporting a direct correlation between recommendation and sentence, contend that the "influence of the probation officer in the presentence process is subordinate to that of the prosecutor" and that probation involvement is "often ceremonial."

My research builds on the latter perspective and suggests that probation presentence reports do not influence judicial sentencing significantly but serve to maintain the myth that criminal courts dispense individualized justice. On the basis on an analysis of probation practices in California, I will demonstrate that the presentence report, long considered an instrument for the promotion of individualized sentencing by the court, actually de-emphasizes individual characteristics and affirms the primacy of instant offense and prior criminal record as sentencing determinants. The present study was concerned with probation in California; whether its findings can be applied to other jurisdictions is not known. California's probation system is the nation's largest, however, and the experiences of that system could prove instructive to other jurisdictions.

In many California counties (as in other jurisdictions throughout the United States) crowded court calendars, determinate sentencing guidelines, and increasingly conservative philosophies have made it difficult for judges to consider individual offenders' characteristics thoroughly. Thus judges, working in tandem with district attorneys, emphasize the legal variables of offense and criminal record at sentencing. Probation officers function as employees of the court; generally they respond to judicial cues and emphasize similar variables in their presentence investigations. The probation officers' relationship to the court is ancillary; their status in relation to judges and other attorneys is subordinate. This does not mean that probation officers are completely passive; individual styles and personal philosophies influence their reports. Idiosyncratic approaches, however, usually are reserved for a few special cases. The vast majority of "normal" (Sudnow 1965) cases are handled in a manner that follows relatively uniform patterns.

Hughes's (1958) work provides a useful perspective for understanding the relationship between probation officers' status and their presentence duties. According to Hughes, occupational duties within institutions often serve to maintain symbiotic status relationships as those in higher-status positions pass on lesser duties to subordinates. Other researchers (Blumberg 1967; Neubauer 1974; Rosecrance 1985) have demonstrated that although judges may give lip service to the significance of presentence investigations, they remain suspicious of the probation officers' lack of legal training and the hearsay nature of the reports. Walker (1985) maintains that in highly visible cases judges tend to disregard the probation reports entirely. Thus the judiciary, by delegating the collection of routine information to probation officers, reaffirms its authority and legitimacy. In this context, the responsibility for compiling presentence reports can be considered a "dirty-work" assignment that is devalued by the judiciary. Judges expect probation officers to submit noncontroversial reports that provide a facade of information, accompanied by bottom-line recommendations that do not deviate significantly from a consideration of offense and prior record. The research findings in this paper will show how probation officers work to achieve this goal.

In view of the large number of presentence reports submitted, it is surprising that so little information about the presentence investigation process is available. The factors used in arriving at a sentencing recommendation, the decision to include certain information, and the methods used in collecting data have not been described. The world of presentence investigators has not been explored by social science researchers. We lack research about the officers who prepare presentence reports, and hardly understand how they think and feel about those reports. The organizational dynamics and the status positions that influence presentence investigators have not been identified prominently. In this article I intend to place probation officers' actions within a framework that will increase the existing knowledge of the presentence process. My research is informed by fifteen years of experience as a probation officer, during which time I submitted hundreds of presentence reports.

Although numerous studies of probation practices have been conducted, an ethnographic perspective rarely has been included in this body of research, particularly in regard to research dealing with presentence investigations. Although questionnaire techniques, survey data, and decision-making experiments have provided some information about presentence reports, qualitative data, which often are available only through an insider's perspective, are notably lacking. The subtle strategies and informal practices used routinely in preparing presentence reports often are hidden from outside researchers.

The research findings emphasize the importance of *typing* in the compilation of public documents (presentence reports). In this paper "typing" refers to "the process by which one person (the agent) arrives at a private definition of another (the target)." A related activity, *designating,* occurs when "the typing agent reveals his attributions of the target to others." In the case of presentence investigations, private typings become designations when they are made part of an official court report. I will show that presentence recommendations are developed through a typing process in which individual offenders are subsumed into general dispositional categories. This process is influenced largely by probation officers' perceptions of factors that judicial figures consider appropriate; probation officers are aware that the ultimate purpose of their reports is to please the court. These perceptions are based on prior experience and are reinforced through judicial feedback.

METHODS

The major sources of data used in this study were drawn from interviews with probation officers. Prior experience facilitated my ability to interpret the data. Interviews were conducted in two three-week periods during 1984 and 1985 in two medium-sized California counties. Both jurisdictions were governed by state determinate sentencing policies; in each, the district attorney's office remained active during sentencing and generally offered specific recommendations. I did not conduct a random sample but tried instead to interview all those who compiled adult presentence reports. In the two counties in question, officers who compiled presentence reports did not supervise defendants.

Not all presentence writers agreed to talk with me; they cited busy schedules, lack of interest, or fear that I was a spy for the administration. Even so, I was able to interview thirty-seven presentence investigators, approximately 75 percent of the total number of such employees in the two counties. The officers interviewed included eight women and twenty-nine men with a median age of 38.5 years, whose probation experience ranged from one year to twenty-seven years. Their educational background generally included a bachelor's degree in a liberal arts subject (four had degrees in criminal justice, one in social work). Typically the officers regarded probation work as a "job" rather than a profession. With only a few exceptions, they did not read professional journals or attend probation association conventions.

The respondents generally were supportive of my research and frequently commented that probation work had never been described adequately. My status as a former probation officer enhanced the interview process greatly. Because I could identify with their experiences, officers were candid, and I was able to collect qualitative data that reflected accurately the participants' perspectives. During the interviews I attempted to discover how probation officers conducted their presentence investigations. I wanted to know when a sentencing recommendation was decided, to ascertain which variables influenced a sentencing recommendation decision, and to learn how probation officers defined their role in the sentencing process.

Although the interviews were informal, I asked each of the probation officers the following questions:

1. What steps do you take in compiling a presentence report?
2. What is the first thing you do upon receiving a referral?
3. What do you learn from interviews with the defendant?
4. Which part of the process (in your opinion) is the most important?

5. Who reads your reports?

6. Which part of the report do the judges feel is most important?

7. How do your reports influence the judge?

8. What feedback do you get from the judge, the district attorney, the defense attorney, the defendant, your supervisor?

In addition to interviewing probation officers, I questioned six probation supervisors and seven judges on their views about how presentence reports were conducted.

$\cdots$

FINDINGS

In the great majority of presentence investigations, the variables of present offense and prior criminal record determine the probation officer's final sentencing recommendations. The influence of these variables is so dominant that other considerations have minimal influence on probation recommendations. The chief rationale for this approach is "That's the way the judges want it." There are other styles of investigation; some officers attempt to consider factors in the defendant's social history, to reserve sentencing judgment until their investigation is complete, or to interject personal opinions. Elsewhere (Rosecrance 1987), I have developed a typology of presentence investigators that describes individual styles; these types include self-explanatory categories such as hard-liners, bleeding-heart liberals, and team players as well as mossbacks (those who are merely putting in their time) and mavericks (those who strive continually for independence).

All types of probation officers, however, seek to develop credibility with the court. Such reputation building is similar to that reported by McCleary (1978) in his study of parole officers. In order to develop rapport with the court, probation officers must submit reports that facilitate a smooth work flow. Probation officers assume that in the great majority of cases they can accomplish this goal by emphasizing offense and criminal record. Once the officers have established reputations as "producers," they have "earned" the right to some degree of discretion in their reporting. One investigation officer described this process succinctly: "When you've paid your dues, you're allowed some slack." Such discretion, however, is limited to a minority of cases, and in these "deviant" cases probation officers frequently allow social variables to influence their recommendation. In one report an experienced officer recommended probation for a convicted felon with a long prior record because the defendant's father agreed to pay for an intensive drug treatment program. In another case a probation officer decided that a first-time shoplifter had a "very bad attitude" and therefore recommended a stiff jail sentence rather than probation. Although these variations from normal procedure are interesting and important, they should not detract from our examination of an investigation process that is used in most cases.

On the basis of the research data, I found that the following patterns occur with sufficient regularity to be considered "typical." After considering offense and criminal record, probation officers place defendants into categories that represent the eventual court recommendation. This typing process occurs early in the course of presentence inquiry; the balance of the investigation is used to reaffirm the private typings that later will become official designations. In order to clarify the decision-making processes used by probation officers, I will delineate the three stages in a presentence investigation: (1) typing the defendant, (2) gathering further information, and (3) filing the report.

Typing the Defendant

A presentence investigation is initiated when the court orders the probation department to prepare a report of a criminal defendant. Usually the initial court referral contains such information as police reports, charges against the defendant, court proceedings, plea-bargaining agreements (if any), offenses in which the defendant has pleaded or has been found guilty, and the defendant's prior criminal record. Probation officers regard such information as relatively unambiguous and as part of the "official" record. The comment of a presentence investigator reflects the probation officer's perspective on the court referral:

> I consider the information in the court referral hard data. It tells me what I need to know about a case, without a lot of bullshit. I mean the guy has pled guilty to a certain offense—he can't get out of that. He has such and such a prior record—there's no changing that. So much of the stuff we put in these reports is subjective and open to interpretation. It's good to have some solid information.

Armed with information in the court referral, probation officers begin to type the defendants assigned for presentence investigation. Defendants are classified into general types based on possible sentence recommendations: a probation officer's statement indicates that this process begins early in a presentence investigation.

> Bottom line: it's the sentence recommendation that's important. That's what the judges and everybody wants to see. I start thinking about the recommendation as soon as I pick up the court referral. Why wait? The basic facts aren't going to change. Oh, I know some POs will tell you they weigh all the facts before coming up with a recommendation. But that's propaganda—we all start thinking recommendation right from the get-go.

At this stage in the investigation the factors known to probation officers are mainly legally relevant variables. The defendant's unique characteristics and special circumstances generally are unknown at this time. Although probation officers may know the offender's age, sex, and race, the relationship of these variables to the case is not yet apparent.

These initial typings are private definitions based on the officer's experience and knowledge of the court system. On occasion, officers discuss the case informally with their colleagues or supervisors when they are not sure of a particular typing. Until the report is complete, their typing remains a private designation. In most cases the probation officers type defendants by considering the known and relatively irrefutable variables of offense and prior record. Probation officers are convinced that judges and district attorneys are most concerned with that part of their reports. I heard the following comment (or versions thereof) on many occasions: "Judges read the offense section, glance at the prior record, and then flip to the back and see what we recommend." Officers indicated that during informal discussions with judges it was made clear that offense and prior record are the determinants of sentencing in most cases. In some instances judges consider extralegal variables, but the officers indicated that this occurs only in "unusual" cases with "special" circumstances. One such case involved a probation grant for a woman who killed her husband after she had been a victim of spouse battering.

Probation investigators are in regular contact with district attorneys and frequently discuss their investigations with them. In addition, district attorneys seem to have no compunction about calling the probation administration to complain about what they consider an inappropriate recommendation. Investigators agreed unanimously that district attorneys typically dismiss a defendant's social history as "immaterial" and want probation officers to stick to the legal facts.

Using offense and prior record as criteria, probation officers place defendants into dispositional (based on recommendation) types. In describing these types I have retained the terms used by probation officers themselves in the typing process. The following typology is community- (rather than researcher-) designated: (1) deal case, (2) diversion case, (3) joint case, (4) probation case with some jail time, (5) straight probation case. Within each of these dispositional types, probation officers designate the severity of punishment by labeling the case either lightweight or heavy-duty.

A designation of "lightweight" means that the defendant will be accorded some measure of leniency because the offense was minor, because the offender had no prior criminal record, or because the criminal activity (regardless of the penal code violation) was relatively innocuous. Heavy-duty cases receive more severe penalties because the offense, the offender, or the circumstances of the offense are deemed particularly serious. Diversion and straight-probation types generally are considered lightweight, while the majority of joint cases are considered heavy-duty. Cases involving personal violence invariably are designated as heavy-duty. Most misdemeanor cases in which the defendant has no prior criminal record or a relatively minor record are termed lightweight. If the defendant has an extensive criminal record, however, even misdemeanor cases can call for stiff penalties; therefore, such cases are considered heavy-duty. Certain felony cases can be regarded as lightweight if there was no violence, if the victim's loss was minimal, or if the defendant had no prior convictions. On occasion, even an offense like armed robbery can be considered lightweight. The following example (taken from an actual report) is one such instance: a first-time offender with a simulated gun held up a Seven-Eleven store and then returned to the scene, gave back the money, and asked the store employees to call the police.

The typings are general recommendations; specifics such as terms and conditions of probation or diversion and length of incarceration are worked out later in the investigation. The following discussion will clarify some of the criteria for arriving at a typing.

Deal cases involve situations in which a plea bargain exists. In California, many plea bargains specify specific sentencing stipulations; probation officers rarely recommend dispositions contrary to those stipulated in plea-bargaining agreements. Although probation officers allegedly are free to recommend a sentence different from that contained in the plea bargain, they have learned that such an action is unrealistic (and often counterproductive to their own interests) because judges inevitably uphold the primacy of sentence agreements. The following observation represents the probation officers' view of plea-bargaining deals.

> It's stupid to try and bust a deal. What's the percentage? Who needs the hassle? The judge always honors the deal—after all, he was part of it. Everyone, including the defendant, has already agreed. It's all nice and neat, all wrapped up. We are supposed to rubber-stamp the package—and we do. Everyone is better off that way.

Diversion cases typically involve relatively minor offenses committed by those with no prior record and are considered "a snap" by probation officers. In most cases, those referred for diversion have been screened already by the district attorney's office; the probation investigator merely agrees that they are eligible and therefore should be granted diversionary relief (and eventual dismissal of charges). In rare instances when there has been an oversight and the defendant is ineligible (because of prior criminal convictions), the probation officer informs the court, and criminal proceedings are resumed. Either situation involves minimal decision making by probation officers about what disposition to recommend. Presentence investigators approach diversion cases in a perfunctory, almost mechanical manner.

The last three typings generally refer to cases in which the sentencing recommendations are ambiguous and some decision making is required of probation officers. These types represent the major consequences of criminal sentencing: incarceration and/or probation. Those categorized as joint (prison) cases are denied probation; instead the investigator recommends an appropriate prison sentence. In certain instances the nature of the offense (for example, rape, murder, or arson) renders defendants legally ineligible for probation. In other situations, the defendants' prior record (especially felony convictions) makes it impossible to grant probation. In many cases the length of prison sentences has been set by legal statute and can be increased or decreased only marginally (depending on the aggravating or mitigating circumstances of the case).

In California, the majority of defendants sentenced to prison receive a middle term (between minimum and maximum); the length of time varies with the offense. Those cases that fall outside the middle term usually do so for reasons related to the offense (for example, using a weapon) or to the criminal record (prior felony convictions, or, conversely, no prior criminal record). Those typed originally as joint cases are treated differently from other probation applicants: concerns with rehabilitation or with the defendant's life situation are no longer relevant, and proper punishment becomes the focal point of inquiry. This perspective was described as follows by a probation officer respondent: "Once I know so-and-so is a heavy-duty joint case I don't think in terms of rehabilitation or social planning. It becomes a matter of how long to salt the sucker away, and that's covered by the code."

For those who are typed as probation cases, the issue for the investigator becomes whether to recommend some time in jail as a condition of probation. This decision is made with reference to whether the case is lightweight or heavy-duty. Straight probation usually is reserved for those convicted of relatively innocuous offenses or for those without a prior criminal record (first-timers). Some probation officers admitted candidly that all things being equal, middle-class defendants are more likely than other social classes to receive straight probation. The split sentence (probation and jail time) has become popular and is a consideration in most misdemeanor and felony cases, especially when the defendant has a prior criminal record. In addition, there is a feeling that drug offenders should receive a jail sentence as part of probation to deter them from future drug use.

Once a probation officer has decided that "some jail time is in order," the ultimate recommendation includes that condition. Although the actual amount of time frequently is determined late in the case, the probation officer's opinion that a jail sentence should be imposed remains constant. The following comment typifies the sentiments of probation officers whom I have observed and also illustrates the imprecision of recommending a period of time in custody:

> It's not hard to figure out who needs some jail. The referral sheet can tell you that. What's hard to know is exactly how much time. Ninety days or six months—who knows what's fair? We put down some number but it is usually an arbitrary figure. No one has come up with a chart that correlates rehabilitation with jail time.

Compiling Further Information

Once an initial typing has been completed, the next investigative stage involves collecting further information about the defendant. During this stage most of the data to be collected consists of extralegal considerations. The defendant is interviewed and his or her social history is delineated. Probation officers frequently contact collateral sources such as school officials, victims, doctors, counselors, and relatives to learn more about the defendant's individual circumstances. This aspect of the presentence investigation involves considerable time and effort on the part of probation officers. Such information is gathered primarily to legitimate earlier probation officer typings or to satisfy judicial requirements; recommendations seldom are changed during this stage. A similar pattern was described by a presentence investigator:

> Interviewing these defendants and working up a social history takes time. In most cases it's really unnecessary since I've already decided what I am going to do. We all know that a recommendation is governed by the offense and prior record. All the rest is just stuffing to fill out the court report, to make the judge look like he's got all the facts.

Presentence interviews with defendants (a required part of the investigation) frequently are routine interactions that were described by a probation officer as "anticlimactic." These interviews invariably are conducted in settings familiar to probation officers, such as jail interviewing rooms or probation department offices. Because the participants lack trust in each other, discussions rarely are candid and open. Probation officers are afraid of being conned or manipulated because they assume that defendants "will say anything to save themselves." Defendants are trying to present themselves in a favorable light and are wary of divulging any information that might be used against them.

It is assumed implicitly in the interview process that probation officers act as interrogators and defendants as respondents. Because presentence investigators select the questions, they control the course of the interview and elicit the kind of responses that serve to substantiate their original defendant typings. A probationer described his presentence interview to me as follows:

> I knew what the PO wanted me to say. She had me pegged as a nice middle-class kid who had fallen in with a bad crowd. So that's how I came off. I was contrite, a real boy scout who had learned his lesson. What an acting job! I figured if I didn't act up I'd get probation.

A probation officer related how she conducted presentence interviews:

> I'm always in charge during the interviews. I know what questions to ask in order to fill out my report. The defendants respond just about the way I expect them to. They hardly ever surprise me.

On occasion, prospective probationers refuse to go along with structured presentence interviews. Some offenders either attempt to control the interview or are openly hostile to probation officers. Defendants who try to dominate interviews often can be dissuaded by reminders such as "I don't think you really appreciate the seriousness of your situation" or "I'm the one who asks the questions here." Some defendants, however, show blatant disrespect for the court process by flaunting a disregard for possible sanctions.

Most probation officers have interviewed some defendants who simply don't seem to care what happens to them. A defendant once informed an investigation officer: "I don't give a fuck what you motherfuckers try and do to me. I'm going to do what I fuckin' well please. Take your probation and stick it." Another defendant told her probation officer: "I'm going to shoot up every chance I get. I need my fix more than I need probation." Probation officers categorize belligerent defendants and those unwilling to "play the probation game" as dangerous or irrational. Frequently in these situations the investigator's initial typing is no longer valid, and probation either will be denied or will be structured stringently. Most interviews, however, proceed in a predictable manner as probation officers collect information that will be included in the section of the report termed "defendant's statement."

Although some defendants submit written comments, most of their statements actually are formulated by the probation officer. In a sociological sense, the defendant's statement can be considered an "account." While conducting presentence interviews, probation officers typically attempt to shape the defendant's account to fit their own preconceived typing. Many probation officers believe that the defendant's attitude toward the offense and toward the future prospects for leading a law-abiding life are the most important parts of the statement. In most presentence investigations the probation investigator identifies and interprets the defendant's subjective attitudes and then incorporates them into the report. Using this procedure, probation officers look for and can report attitudes that "logically fit" with their final sentencing recommendation.

Defendants who have been typed as prison cases typically are portrayed as holding socially unacceptable attitudes about their criminal actions and unrealistic or negative attitudes about future prospects for living an upright life. Conversely, those who have been typed as probation material are described as having acceptable attitudes, such as contriteness about the present offense and optimism about their ability to lead a crime-free life. The structuring of accounts about defendant attitudes was described by a presentence investigator in the following manner:

> When POs talk about the defendant's attitude we really mean how that attitude relates to the case. Naturally I'm not going to write about what a wonderful attitude the guy has—how sincere he seems—and then recommend sending him to the joint. That wouldn't make sense. The judges want consistency. If a guy has a shitty attitude but is going to get probation anyway, there's no percentage in playing up his probation problem.

In most cases the presentence interview is the only contact between the investigating officer and the defendant. The brevity of this contact and the lack of postreport interaction foster a legalistic perspective. Investigators are concerned mainly with "getting the case through court" rather than with special problems related to supervising probationers on a long-term basis. One-time-only interviews rarely allow probation officers to become emotionally involved with their cases; the personal and individual aspects of the defendant's personality generally are not manifested during a half-hour presentence interview. For many probation officers the emotional distance from offenders is one of the benefits of working in presentence units. Such an opinion was expressed by an investigation officer: "I really like the one-shot-only part of this job. I don't have time to get caught up with the clients. I can deal with facts and not worry about individual personalities."

The probation officer has wide discretion in the type of collateral information that is collected from sources other than the defendant or the official record. Although a defendant's social history must be sketched in the presentence report, the supplementation of that history is left to individual investigators. There are few established guidelines for the investigating officer to follow, except that the psychiatric or psychological reports should be submitted when there is compelling evidence that the offender is mentally disturbed. Informal guidelines, however, specify that in misdemeanor cases reports should be shorter and more concise than in felony cases. The officers indicated that reports for municipal court (all misdemeanor cases) should range from four to six pages in length, while superior court reports (felony cases) were expected to be six to nine pages long. In controversial cases (to which only the most experienced officers are assigned) presentence reports are expected to be longer and to include considerable social data. Reports in these cases have been as long as thirty pages.

Although probation officers learn what general types of information to include through experience and feedback from judges and supervisors, they are allowed considerable leeway in deciding exactly what to put in their reports (outside of the offense and prior-record sections). Because investigators decide what collateral sources are germane to the case, they tend to include information that will reflect favorably on their sentencing recommendation. In this context the observation of one probation officer is understandable: "I pick from the mass of possible sources just which ones to put in the report. Do you think I'm going to pick people who make my recommendation look weak? No way!"

Filing the Report

The final stage in the investigation includes dictating the report, having it approved by a probation supervisor, and appearing in court. All three of these activities serve to reinforce the importance of prior record and offense in sentencing recommendations. At the time of dictation, probation officers determine what to include in the report and how to phrase their remarks. For the first time in the investigation, they receive formal feedback from official sources. Presentence reports are read by three groups important to the probation officers: probation supervisors, district attorneys, and judges. Probation officers recognize that for varying reasons, all these groups emphasize the legally relevant variables of offense and prior criminal record when considering an appropriate sentencing recommendation. Such considerations reaffirm the probation officer's initial private typing.

A probation investigator described this process:

> After I've talked to the defendants I think maybe some of them deserve to get special consideration. But then I remember who's going to look at the reports. My supervisor, the DA, the judge; they don't care about all the personal details. When all is said and done, what's really important to them is the offense and the defendant's prior record. I know that stuff from the start. It makes me wonder why we have to jack ourselves around to do long reports.

Probation officers assume that their credibility as presentence investigators will be enhanced if their sentencing recommendations meet with the approval of probation supervisors, district attorneys, and judges. On the other hand, officers whose recommendations are consistently "out of line" are subject to censure or transfer, or they find themselves engaged in "running battles" with court officials. During the last stage of the investigation probation officers must consider how to ensure that their reports will go through court without "undue personal hassle." Most investigation officers have learned that presentence recommendations based on a consideration of prior record and offense can achieve that goal.

Although occupational self-interest is an important component in deciding how to conduct a presentence investigation, other factors are also involved. Many probation officers agree with the idea of using legally relevant variables as determinants of recommendations. These officers embrace the retributive value of this concept and see it as an equitable method for framing their investigation.

Other officers reported that probation officers' discretion had been "short-circuited" by determinate sentencing guidelines and that they were reduced to "merely going through the motions" in conducting their investigations. Still other officers view the use of legal variables to structure recommendations as an acceptable bureaucratic shortcut to compensate partially for large case assignments. One probation officer stated, "If the department wants us to keep pumping out presentence reports we can't consider social factors—we just don't have time." Although probation officers are influenced by various dynamics, there seems little doubt that in California, the social history that once was considered the "heart and soul" of presentence probation reports has been largely devalued.

SUMMARY AND CONCLUSIONS

In this study I provide a description and an analysis of the processes used by probation investigators in preparing presentence reports. The research findings based on interview data indicate that probation officers tend to de-emphasize individual defendants' characteristics and that their probation recommendations are not influenced directly by factors such as sex, age, race, socioeconomic status, or work record. Instead, probation officers emphasize the variables of instant offense and prior criminal record. The finding that offense and prior record are the main considerations of probation officers with regard to sentence recommendations agrees with a substantial body of research.

My particular contribution has been to supply the ethnographic observations and the data that explain this phenomenon. I have identified the process whereby offense and prior record come to occupy the central role in decision making by probation officers. This identification underscores the significance of private typings in determining official designations. An analysis of probation practices suggests that the function of the presentence investigation is more ceremonial than instrumental.

I show that early in the investigation probation officers, using offense and prior record as guidelines, classify defendants into types; when the typing process is complete, probation officers essentially have decided on the sentence recommendation that will be recorded later in their official designation. The subsequent course of investigations is determined largely by this initial private typing. Further data collection is influenced by a sentence recommendation that already has been firmly established. This finding answers affirmatively the research question posed by Carter (1967: 211):

> Do probation officers, after "deciding" on a recommendation early in the presentence investigation, seek further information which justifies the decision, rather than information which might lead to modification or rejection of that recommendation?

The type of information and observation contained in the final presentence report is generated to support the original recommendation decision. Probation officers do not regard defendant typings as tentative hypotheses to be disproved through inquiry but rather as firm conclusions to be justified in the body of the report.

Although the presentence interview has been considered an important part of the investigation, I demonstrate that it does not significantly alter probation officers' perceptions. In most cases probation officers dominate presentence interviews; interaction between the participants is guarded. The nature of interviews between defendants and probation officers is important in itself; further research is needed to identify the dynamics that prevail in these interactions.

Attitudes attributed to defendants often are structured by probation officers to reaffirm the recommendation already formulated. The defendant's social history, long considered an integral part of the presentence report, in reality has little bearing on sentencing considerations. In most cases the presentence is no longer a vehicle for social inquiry but rather a typing process that considers mainly the defendant's prior criminal record and the seriousness of the criminal offense. Private attorneys in growing numbers have become disenchanted with the quality of probation investigations and have commissioned presentence probation reports privately. At present, however, such a practice is generally available only for wealthy defendants.

The presentence process that I have described is used in the great majority of cases: it is the "normal" procedure. Even so, probation officers are not entirely passive actors in this process. On occasion they will give serious consideration to social variables in arriving at a sentencing recommendation. In special circumstances officers will allow individual defendants' characteristics to influence their report. In addition, probation officers who have developed credibility with the court are allowed some discretion in compiling presentence reports. This discretion is not unlimited, however; it is based on a prior record of producing reports that meet the court's approval, and is contingent on continuing to do so. A presentence writer said, "You can only afford to go to bar for defendants in a few select cases; if you try to do it too much, you get a reputation as being 'out of step.'" This research raises the issue of probation officers' autonomy. Although I depict presentence investigators as having limited autonomy, other researchers contend that probation officers have considerable leeway in recommendation. This contradictory evidence can be explained in large part by the type of sentencing structure, the professionalism of probation workers, and the role of the district attorney at sentencing. Walsh's study (1985), for example, which views probation officers as important actors in the presentence process, was conducted in a jurisdiction with indeterminate sentencing, where the probation officers demonstrated a high degree of professionalism and the prosecutors "rarely made sentencing recommendations." A very different situation existed in the California counties that I studied: determinate sentencing was enforced, probation officers were not organized professionally, and the district attorneys routinely made specific court recommendations. It seems apparent that probation officers' autonomy must be considered with reference to judicial jurisdiction.

In view of the primacy of offense and prior record in sentencing considerations, the efficacy of current presentence investigation practices is doubtful. It seems ineffective and wasteful to continue to collect a mass of social data of uncertain relevance. Yet an analysis of courtroom culture suggests that the pre-sentence investigation helps maintain judicial mythology as well as probation of-ficer legitimacy. Although judges generally do not have the time or the inclination to consider individual variables thoroughly, the performance of a presentence in-vestigation perpetuates the myth of individualized sentences. Including a presen-tence report in the court file gives the appearance of individualization without influencing sentencing practices significantly.

Even in a state like California, where determinate sentencing allegedly has replaced individualized justice, the judicial system feels obligated to maintain the appearance of individualization. After observing the court system in California for several years, I am convinced that a major reason for maintaining such a prac-tice is to make it easier for criminal defendants to accept their sentences. The presentence report allows defendants to feel that their case at least has received a considered decision. One judge admitted candidly that the "real purpose" of the presentence investigation was to convince defendants that they were not getting "the fast shuffle." He observed further that if defendants were sentenced with-out such investigations, many would complain and would file "endless appeals" over what seems to them a hasty sentencing decision. Even though judges typ-ically consider only offense and prior record in a sentencing decision, they want defendants to believe that their cases are being judged individually. The presen-tence investigation allows this assumption to be maintained. In addition, some judges use the probation officer's report as an excuse for a particular type of sentence. In some instances they deny responsibility for the sentence, implying that their "hands were tied" by the recommendation. Thus judges are taken "off the hook" for meting out an unpopular sentence. Further research is needed to substantiate the significance of these latent functions of the presen-tence investigation.

The presentence report is a major component in the legitimacy of the pro-bation movement; several factors support the probation officers' stake in main-taining their role in these investigations. Historically, probation has been wedded to the concept of individualized treatment. In theory, the presentence report is suited ideally to reporting on defendants' individual circumstances. From a historical perspective this ideal has always been more symbolic than substantive, but if the legitimacy of the presentence report is questioned, so then is the entire purpose of probation.

Regardless of its usefulness (or lack of usefulness), it is doubtful that pro-bation officials would consider the diminution or abolition of presentence re-ports. The number of probation workers assigned to presentence investigations is substantial, and their numbers represent an obvious source of bureaucratic power. Conducting presentence investigations allows probation officers to re-main visible with the court and the public. The media often report on con-troversial probation cases, and presentence writers generally have more contact and more association with judges than do others in the probation department.

As ancillary court workers, probation officers are assigned the dirty work of collecting largely irrelevant data on offenders. Investigation officers have learned that emphasizing offense and prior record in their reports will enhance relationships with judges and district attorneys, as well as improving their occupational standing within probation departments. Thus the presentence investigation serves to maintain the court's claim of individualized concern while preserving the probation officer's role, although a subordinate role, in the court system.

The myth of individualization serves various functions, but it also raises serious questions. In an era of severe budget restrictions, should scarce resources be allocated to compiling predictable presentence reports of dubious value? If social variables are considered only in a few cases, should courts continue routinely to require presentence reports in all felony matters (as is the practice in California)? In summary, we should address the issue of whether the criminal justice system can afford the ceremony of a probation presentence investigation.

REFERENCES

Blumberg, Abraham (1967). *Criminal Justice.* Chicago: Quadrangle.

Blumstein, Alfred J., S. Martin, and N. Holt (1983). *Research on Sentencing: The Search for Reform.* Washington, D.C.: National Academy Press.

Carter, Robert M. (1967)."The Presentence Report and the Decision-Making Process." *Journal of Research in Crime and Delinquency* 4:203–11.

Carter, Robert M., and Leslie T. Wilkins (1967). "Some Factors in Sentencing Policy." *Journal of Criminal Law, Criminology, and Police Science* 58:503–14.

Hagan, John (1975). "The Social and Legal Construction of Criminal Justice: A Study of the Presentence Process." *Social Problems* 22:620–37.

Hagan, John, John Hewitt, and Duane Alwin (1979). "Ceremonial Justice: Crime and Punishment in a Loosely Coupled System." *Social Forces* 58:506–25.

Hogarth, John (1971). *Sentencing As a Human Process.* Toronto: University of Toronto Press.

Hughes, Everett C. (1958). *Men and Their Work.* New York: Free Press.

Kingsnorth, Rodney, and Louis Rizzo (1979). "Decision-Making in the Criminal Courts: Continuities and Discontinuities." *Criminology* 17:3–14.

McCleary, Richard (1978). *Dangerous Men.* Beverly Hills, Calif.: Sage.

Murrah, A. (1963). "Prison or Probation?" In B. Kay and C. Vedder (eds.), *Probation and Parole.* Springfield, Ill.: Charles C Thomas, pp. 63–78.

Myers, Martha A. (1979). "Offended Parties and Official Reactions: Victims and the Sentencing of Criminal Defendants." *Sociological Quarterly* 20:529–46.

Neubauer, David (1974). *Criminal Justice in Middle America.* Morristown, N.J.: General Learning.

Rosecrance, John (1985). "The Probation Officers' Search for Credibility: Ball Park Recommendations." *Crime and Delinquency* 31:539–54.

——— (1987). "A Typology of Presentence Probation Investigators." *International Journal of Offender Therapy and Comparative Criminology* 31:163–77.

Sudnow, David (1965). "Normal Crimes: Sociological Features of the Penal Code." *Social Problems* 12:255–76.

Walker, Samuel (1985). *Sense and Nonsense about Crime.* Monterey, Calif.: Brooks/Cole.

Walsh, Anthony (1985). "The Role of the Probation Officer in the Sentencing Process." *Criminal Justice and Behavior* 12:289–303.

2 0

❊

Does the Public Support
the Death Penalty?

MARK COSTANZO

Although public opinion polls show high support for the death penalty and about three hundred new death sentences are imposed each year, the number of executions remains low. Mark Costanzo points to surveys that show the public is about evenly split when respondents are asked to choose between life imprisonment without parole and death. Does this mean that Americans are ambivalent about carrying out the punishment? What does it say about capital punishment in the next decade?

Americans are devoted to the death penalty, or at least that's what we're told by the mass media. Nearly every article or news report on the topic proclaims that the penalty of death enjoys overwhelming public support. And, of course, these report are true: When asked questions such as "Are you in favor of the death penalty for persons convicted of murder?" more than 70 percent of Americans declare their support. Apparently, those who believe that capital punishment should be abolished have lost the battle for the hearts and minds of the American public.

The belief in broad, solid public support has consequences. Those who are entrusted to make decisions about the value of the death penalty often justify their decisions by proclaiming that they are carrying out the will of the people. Public opinion on the death penalty not only affects the actions of political candidates and office holders, it also affects the Supreme Court's judgments

Source: Mark Costanzo, *Just Revenge* (New York: St. Martin's Press, 1997), pp. 113–128.
Copyright © 1997 by Bedford/St. Martin's. Reprinted with permission.

concerning what does and does not constitute cruel and unusual punishment. Thus, it is vital to understand the dynamics of public opinion on this issue.

In 1972, when the United States Supreme Court ruled that our system of deciding who should live and who should die was unconstitutionally arbitrary and discriminatory, the justices looked to community standards for guidance. As Justice Powell explained:

> Members of this Court have recognized the dynamic nature of the prohibition against cruel and unusual punishments. The final meaning was not set in 1791. Rather, . . . the words of the Amendment are not precise, and their scope is not static. The Amendment must draw its meaning from the evolving standards of decency that mark the progress of a maturing society.[1]

Some justices relied on public-opinion surveys to assess prevailing standards of decency. Other justices looked to another source of information about community standards: the frequency with which juries handed out sentences of death. This data caused some justices to conclude that the death penalty violated the moral standards of the time.

> The objective indicator of society's view of an unusually severe punishment is what society does with it, and today society will inflict death upon only a small sample of the eligible criminals. [Juries]. . . . have been able to bring themselves to vote for death in a mere 100 or so cases among the thousands tried each year where the punishment is available. . . . At the very least, I must conclude that contemporary society views this punishment with substantial doubt.[2]

While the Supreme Court continues to pay some attention to public attitudes, its analyses of these attitudes tend to be cursory, quick to reconcile inconsistent data, and disinterested in underlying dynamics. Justices are facile in their ability to use the very same data to argue contradictory positions. At least for now, the Court has decided that capital punishment does not violate community standards.

But perhaps the justices, the politicians, the pundits, and the media have misread the public-opinion surveys. It may be, as one observer put it, that support for capital punishment is "a mile wide and an inch deep." Only a deeper analysis of the opinion data can reveal whether support for the death penalty is fragile or solid, shallow or deep, ephemeral or enduring.

WHAT THE SURVEYS TELL US

The Gallup Organization began surveying public opinion on the death penalty in December 1936, after unprecedented levels of public attention were directed toward the execution of Bruno Hauptmann, the alleged murdered of the Lindbergh baby. At that time, 61 percent of those questioned indicated support for the death penalty and 39 percent indicated opposition (a "no opinion" category was not included). In recent times, the standard question asked is, Do you favor or oppose the death penalty for persons convicted of murder? The pattern of responses to this question has oscillated wildly over the past sixty years. The percentage of Americans favoring capital punishment declined through the 1950s and early 1960s. Support fell to its nadir in 1966, when only 42 percent favored the death penalty, and it peaked in 1988, when 79 percent of Americans expressed support. For the past decade the overall level of support has hovered near 70 percent.[3]

Some demographic characteristics are systematically related to attitudes toward capital punishment. Differences have been found for the categories of race, income, gender, and political orientation. On average, whites favor the death penalty by a margin of about 20 percent over blacks. Blacks are more likely than whites to indicate opposition to the death penalty by a margin of about 17 percent, and about 4 percent more blacks than whites express "no opinion." When respondents are partitioned into three income categories—top, middle, and bottom—those in the top income category are 14 percent more likely than people in the bottom category to support the death penalty. More males than females support the death penalty (by about 9 percentage points), and females are more likely to indicate opposition by a margin of 4 percent. Political orientation also makes a difference. At present, Americans of all political persuasions favor the death penalty, though Republicans favor it more strongly. Support is also stronger among people living in the South and the West, and among suburbanites. In sum, the people most likely to support the death penalty are middle-to-upper class, conservative, white, male, and suburban. Although this is not the group most likely to be victimized by violent criminals, it is the group most likely to be disturbed and angered to social upheaval and change.[4]

Despite the broad appeal of capital punishment, there is considerable softness to public support. There is a rather high percentage of undecideds, and public opinion has been highly unstable over time. Pollsters at the Gallup Organization have observed "the trend of public opinion on capital punishment is among the most valuable in Gallup annals."[5] And there are other signs of weakness in support for the death penalty. The public has grave doubts about whether the death penalty is fairly applied—45 percent of Americans believe that a black person is more likely than a white person to receive the death penalty for the same crime, and 60 percent believe that poor people are more likely to be sentenced to death than wealthy people.[6] Unfortunately, too many surveys have used a superficial one-question approach, and there is considerable ambiguity in the nature of the question that has typically been asked. The meaning of general support or opposition is difficult to unravel because a host of crucial questions are left unanswered by most surveys. For example, Why do people support executions? Are supporters well informed about how the death penalty works? Are they aware of alternatives to capital punishment? Is there evidence of support for these alternatives?

The meaning of responses to a single survey question is uncertain. When people say that they support capital punishment, we do not know whether they mean that they favor executions for *every person* convicted of murder, we do not know if support extends to *all types* of murder (e.g., both aggravated and nonaggravated), and we do not know the *intensity* of support or opposition. Opinions expressed in response to a general survey question may indicate mild, unstable preferences or deeply held convictions. Although there have been efforts to probe more deeply into these attitudes, it is important to remember that most discussions of public opinion begin and end with a description of general levels of support or opposition.

Some surveys have asked people to indicate reasons for their support or opposition. Those who favor capital punishment give the following reasons: "a life for a life" (50 percent), deterrence (13 percent), elimination of the possibility of future violence by the offender (19 percent), and the cost of keeping the convicted person in prison for life (13 percent). Opponents of capital punishment cite the following reasons for their position: It is wrong to take a life (41 percent), punishment should be left to God (17 percent), people can be wrongly convicted (11 percent), executions do not deter (7 percent), and there is always the possibility of rehabilitation (6 percent).[7] The high cost of life imprisonment has gained the most as a reason cited for support of the death penalty, despite compelling evidence that the high cost of the death penalty should be a reason for opposition. And though deterrence is often cited as a basis for support, there is persuasive evidence that executions stimulate rather than deter murder.

THE DYNAMICS OF PUBLIC OPINION

There have been other shifts. For instance, among those who favor capital punishment, support for executing juveniles has surged. Thirty-five years ago, only 24 percent of the public believed that juveniles should receive the death penalty. By the late 1990s, 72 percent expressed a willingness to send adolescents to the execution chamber. For many Americans, the face of violent crime is the face of a teenager. Whereas official criminal statistics indicate that juveniles are responsible for only 13 percent of violent crimes, Americans estimate that juveniles are responsible for 43 percent.[8] The most dramatic shift has been the fading of deterrence as a justification and the ascendance of retribution. Twenty years ago most people claimed to support the death penalty because of a belief in deterrence. Since 1981, simple retribution has overtaken deterrence as the most common justification offered by supporters of the death penalty. The move away from deterrence and toward revenge as a reason for support could be due to an awareness of research indicating no deterrent effect. But that seems somewhat unlikely given the lack of public awareness of other research findings. It seems more likely that retribution was the real motive all along, and it has simply become more socially acceptable to admit to retribution as a reason for supporting executions.

For supporters of capital punishment, there is another benefit to the shift away from deterrence or any other pragmatic justification for capital punishment. If it is socially acceptable to support the death penalty for the sake of revenge—or some sanitized version of revenge like "a life for a life" or "retribution" or "killers deserve to die"—then no further argument is necessary. There is no need to consider evidence on deterrence or cost or discrimination. Evidence is irrelevant. Support is a matter of moral conviction. Unsettling facts about how the death penalty actually works in practice can be ignored, and one's critical capacities can be switched off.

Some researchers have found that support is substantially eroded when people are given information about the death penalty, while others have found that only people with weak to moderate preferences are persuaded by factual information that contradicts their beliefs.[9] People who are strong supporters of the death penalty are much less likely to be swayed by factual information. This general pattern holds for a variety of attitudes about important social issues; people whose opinions are extreme or rooted in strong emotions manage to remain unconvinced by even the most compelling evidence.

Soaring levels of public support are not grounded in factual knowledge about how the death penalty is administered. Most Americans are poorly informed about such issues as deterrence, the financial costs of capital punishment, discriminatory imposition of the death penalty, and the probability of wrongful conviction. If support is based on emotion instead of reason, then asking people to endorse one or more reasons for support or opposition may not be especially informative. Some researchers have even found that people responding to surveys simply endorse every reason that supports their position. That is, people who support the death penalty are likely to express a belief in deterrence, revenge, or any other justification offered them. Still, the belief in revenge is the factor that most clearly differentiates supporters from opponents. When given information challenging the effectiveness of the death penalty, those who believe most strongly in retribution show the least attitude change.

The percentage of people favoring capital punishment drops precipitously when concrete rather than abstract questions are asked. When presented with summaries of three aggravated murder cases, less than 15 percent of respondents said that they would vote for the death penalty. And only a small minority of people who favor the death penalty would be willing to take an active role in its administration by being part of a jury that sentences a defendant in a capital trial or by helping to carry out an execution.[10] Actual imposition of a death sentence in a specific case is not something that even strong supporters of capital punishment take lightly. Consistent with these findings is the fact that real capital juries—which must be comprised of people who are willing to consider the death penalty seriously—return death sentences in only about a third of capital murder trials.

The unwillingness of jurors to impose the sentence of death has been interpreted as an indicator of a deep ambivalence about the penalty. As Justice William Brennan explained:

> When an unusually severe punishment is authorized for wide-scale application but not, because of society's refusal, inflicted save in a few instances, the inference is compelling that there is a deep-seated reluctance

to inflict it. Indeed, the likelihood is great that the punishment is tolerated only because of its disuse.[11]

The striking disparity between abstract approval for the death penalty and jurors' reluctance to impose it in actual cases was dramatically illustrated in the case of Susan Smith. In the summer of 1995, a jury in South Carolina sentenced Smith to life imprisonment for the murder of her two young sons, Michael, age three, and Alex, age fourteen months. On an October night, Susan Smith served a pizza dinner to her sons and, like any good mother, strapped her boys into their protective car seats before going for a drive. She drove to John Long Lake, got out of her car, shut the door, and let the car roll into the dark water of the lake. A videotaped reenactment of the event suggested that the car took about six minutes to sink beneath the surface of the water. After claiming for nine days that an African-American carjacker had driven off with her children, Smith confessed to committing the horrible crime.

In many ways, Smith's crime was among the worst of those eligible for the death penalty: It was a double murder, both victims were helpless children, and, perhaps worst of all, the killer was the very person the children relied on for love and protection. The murder was apparently calculated, not an impulsive act in the heat of passion. If anyone deserved the death penalty, surely Smith did. Yet, despite the monstrous nature of the crime, the same jury that had convicted her in less than three hours just as swiftly decided to spare her life. As one juror put it, "We all felt like Susan was a really disturbed person. Giving her the death penalty wouldn't serve justice."[12] As with many capital cases, a majority of the public disagreed with the sentence. In this highly publicized case, the public heard much of the testimony and arguments made in the courtroom. Apparently, this information did weaken public support for executing Susan Smith. However, even after hearing about Smith's sordid life—which included the suicide of a father and repeated sexual molestation at the hands of her stepfather—a sizable majority of the public (63 percent) still said that Smith should be executed. Only 28 percent agreed with the sentence recommended by the jury.[13]

In one critical respect, jurors in the Smith case were like most jurors in capital cases. They heard unsettling details of the tragic, twisted life of the defendant. They heard about family tragedies, physical and sexual abuse, poverty and neglect. And like most jurors, they found a reason to show compassion. Although jurors express abstract support for the death penalty, most will choose to spare the particular defendant they are called upon to judge. It is much easier to support an execution in the abstract, much easier to demand executions from a safe distance.

WHAT DRIVES PUBLIC SUPPORT?

In one sense, the passionate debate over capital punishment is curious: Executions have a direct effect on only a minuscule percentage of the American public. Very few Americans are murderers, victims of murderers, or friends and family of either group. Also, opinions about the death penalty are in the main not formed on the basis of a careful and systematic examination of relevant data. Most people know very little about our system of capital punishment. Any attempt to understand the basis of expressed support for capital punishment must take these peculiar facts into account.

One straightforward explanation is that public support for capital punishment is propelled by the rate—or, more precisely, the perceived rate—of violent crime in America. This explanation fits the data nicely: The trend line for support of the death penalty shadows the trend line for violent crime. Support dropped during a period when violent crime was relatively low (i.e., the mid-fifties to late sixties), then rose from 1968 to the early eighties as the violent crime rate pressed upwards. The year 1968 is notable because in local and national elections, street crime and law and order became major campaign themes. Since the mid-eighties, support has stabilized along with the rate of violent crime.[14] By proclaiming support for capital punishment, citizens are able to give expression to their anger and frustration about the rising tide of violence. With apparently little headway being made against violent criminals, the public is willing to go farther to crack down on crime. At least in the abstract, the death penalty seems decisive and final.

Some researchers argue that support for the death penalty is best understood as a symbolic attitude. According to this view, one's attitude toward the death penalty is a matter of self-definition. The purpose is to express support for stronger methods of crime control and to express frustration with the apparent impotence of our criminal justice system. Symbolic attitudes are part of an underlying ideology and are "tightly bound up with deeply held convictions concerning the proper organization of society."[15]

Significantly, declarations of support for the death penalty rest on emotion rather than reason. They are a means of venting anger, a demand that decisive action be taken against violent criminals, a desperate attempt to reassert social order. Support for capital punishment may give voice to both the desire for protection and the desire for revenge.

SUPPORT FOR ALTERNATIVE PUNISHMENTS

Usually, voters or elected officials choose between two or more alternatives. Yet, until quite recently, most surveys failed to ask about alternative punishments. Conspicuously absent from most surveys are questions about reasonable alternative punishments such as life imprisonment without the possibility of parole (the alternative sentence in most states). Perhaps Americans are receptive to such alternatives. Maybe they would even prefer them. By asking people to choose between alternatives, it is possible to strip away some of the symbolism that accompanies the death penalty and uncover what people want in concrete, practical terms. Beginning in the late 1980s and continuing in the 1990s, a series of statewide and national surveys began to ask people to choose among punishments for murderers. This simple innovation exposed deep ambivalence about use of the death penalty.

It turns out that support for capital punishment plunges when alternatives are presented. Public opinion is about evenly split when respondents are simply asked to choose between life imprisonment without the possibility of parole (LWOP) and the death penalty. That is, more than 20 percent of those who would have expressed support for capital punishment switch to LWOP when given the chance. Here are the percentages of the public endorsing LWOP as compared to the percentages still supporting the death penalty in several states: Arkansas, 49 percent versus 45 percent; Georgia, 44 percent versus 46 percent; Indiana, 45 percent versus 40 percent; Kansas, 47 percent versus 49 percent; Kentucky, 46 percent versus 36 percent; Massachusetts, 54 percent versus 38 percent; and Oklahoma, 49 percent versus 48 percent.[16] These findings have two interesting implications: Support is much weaker than commonly supposed, and it appears that most Americans wrongly believe that persons convicted of capital murder are eligible for parole in most states. That is, people don't believe that life imprisonment means that convicted murderers will never be released from prison. In one recent study, only 4 percent of Americans believed that a life sentence meant that murderers actually spent the rest of their lives in prison. When respondents were asked to estimate the length of a life sentence, the overall average was 15.6 years.[17] In surveys conducted in New York, Nebraska, Kansas, and Massachusetts, the median estimate was 10 to 14 years. In most states with the death penalty, the *only* alternative punishment under current law is LWOP. But few Americans realize this. It appears that the public strongly favors the death penalty only when the alternative is a prison term that allows for parole.

Concern about the possibility of parole is a pivotal consideration for a very important segment of the public: the jurors who must actually decide whether a defendant should be sentenced to life imprisonment or death. In post-sentencing interviews, most jurors expressed the belief that, for the defendant they judged, the actual sentence would be more lenient than the one they voted for. Specifically, jurors who voted for life imprisonment believed that the defendant would eventually be paroled, and members of juries that voted for death believed that the execution would never occur. Here are some representative quotes from members of four juries:[18]

- "Because of our system, the way our system is now, life imprisonment doesn't mean life imprisonment. That was a very definite factor in deciding for the death penalty."

- "Most of the people that voted for the death sentence said, Who are you kidding. . . . Why don't you just vote for the death sentence? We know he's not going to get it. . . . We can sit here and vote for the death sentence—it doesn't mean that we're going to kill him."

- "I was convinced of it and I still am. . . . He's going to get out if you give him life imprisonment—he's going to get out. We all knew that. We talked about that. If I don't vote to kill this guy, then he's going to get out.

The only way I can guarantee that he will stay in prison is to vote the death penalty."

- "If he got life imprisonment and got out in ten years or fifteen years for good behavior and goes out and does it again, how could we live with that?"

This basic finding—that jurors vastly underestimate the sentences that will be served by murderers spared the death penalty—has now been replicated with hundreds of jurors.[19] Juries that render a death verdict often do so because they believe it is the only way to guarantee that the murderer will remain in prison for the rest of his life.

Like the general public, jurors find LWOP appealing for a variety of reasons. It offers a good compromise between the death penalty and life in prison with parole, it achieves the goal of protecting society while avoiding the burden of responsibility for ordering the defendant's death, and it bypasses the costly and unpredictable process of appeals. Unfortunately, most judges refuse to reassure jurors that a defendant will never be released from prison if he is sentenced to LWOP. This practice may result in more death sentences, because juries often assume that a life sentence includes parole.

The comments of jurors echo the concerns of the American public. Americans doubt both the certainty of life imprisonment and the certainty of the death penalty. More generally, most citizens express a deep distrust of the criminal justice system and its capacity to deal effectively with violent criminals. The option of LWOP allows citizens and jurors to punish murderers severely and to protect society permanently. At the same time, LWOP frees jurors from the burden of having to decide whether someone should be sent to the execution chamber.

Roughly half of the American public prefers LWOP, while half prefers the death penalty. But there is another alternative to capital punishment, one that garners the support of a clear majority of Americans: life without the possibility of parole plus restitution (LWOP+R). LWOP+R includes a requirement that all or part of what the convicted murderer earns from prison labor goes into a victims' support fund or is paid to the murder victim's survivors. In every state where LWOP+R has been offered as an alternative to the death penalty, a majority of survey respondents said they'd prefer it: 62 percent in Arkansas, 51 percent in Georgia, 62 percent in Indiana, 66 percent in Kansas, 62 percent in New York, 49 percent in Florida, 67 percent in California, 64 percent in Nebraska, 59 percent in Virginia, 67 percent in Massachusetts, and 51 percent in Georgia.[20] Averaging across states, 75.1 percent of the American public say that they favor capital punishment for convicted murderers when the only choice is between support or opposition. But the average level of support plunges to 43.1 percent when people are asked whether they prefer LWOP or the death penalty, and support drops even farther, to 31.6 percent, when people are asked whether they prefer LWOP+R or the death penalty.

Recent surveys demonstrate that support for the death penalty is neither as deep nor as stable as most general surveys seem to indicate. The widely cited "overwhelming support" for the death penalty may be something of an epiphenomenon, visible only in response to a general survey question about abstract support or opposition.

The death penalty attracts public support because it is a symbol of severe punishment for murderers. But when we look beneath the surface, it appears that Americans are ready to consider or even embrace other harsh punishments for murderers. As the data on support for LWOP show, many people who declare support for the death penalty are simply saying that they want to make sure murderers are never allowed to walk the streets again. Many people see the death penalty as their only guarantee. Support for LWOP+R reveals that goals such as protection of society and restitution to victims may be as important as revenge and punishment. Indeed, the survey data indicate that the requirement of restitution is especially appealing. Of course, symbolism is also at work in the desire to make the murderer provide restitution for his or her crimes. Clearly, no amount of restitution can begin to compensate for the terrible agony caused by the death of a loved one, and in any case, prison wages are extremely low. What seems crucial to support for LWOP+R is that the focus is on permanently protecting society and making the criminal pay. The prisoner would never again be permitted to lead a normal life, and he (or in rare case, she) would at least be giving something back to the society he damaged.

One of the oldest debates in criminal justice has to do with striking the ideal balance among several important goals: rehabilitation of the criminal, punishment, revenge, protecting society from criminals, and restitution to victims and society at large. But which of these goals should receive the highest priority? For less serious crimes, most people would endorse a policy that emphasizes restitution over punishment; a vandal could be made to paint over graffiti, or a petty thief might be made to pay for the stolen goods. But what about the most serious crimes? Clearly, the response to murder must favor punishment and the protection of society.

The public is receptive to the alternative punishments of LWOP and LWOP+R because these alternatives offer important benefits. First, both avoid the unfair application of the death penalty that most people find troubling. More than three-quarters of Americans believe that the death penalty is arbitrary and unfair, and more than half say that they are "not personally comfortable with" or have "moral doubts" about the death penalty. Because of these concerns and doubts, most Americans would prefer LWOP+R. Clearly, this does not mean that Americans are willing to retreat from harsh punishment. Indeed, a second reason for support of LWOP or LWOP+R is that both are severe forms of punishment: Murderers will endure the hardships of prison for the rest of their lives. Third, both alternatives offer an ironclad guarantee that vicious murderers will never again walk outside prison walls. Finally, in the case of LWOP+R, the added requirement that convicted murderers work in prison for the benefit of society enhances its appeal. Restitution forces prisoners to pay for part of the cost of their own incarceration; it offers a vehicle for acknowledging the murder victim, and, in the optimal case, it forces prisoners to act responsibly and allows for repentance. And, although most Americans don't know it, LWOP+R is far less costly than capital punishment.

In pushing for executions and the expansion of the death penalty, politicians often declare that they are carrying out the will of the people. But the will of the people may be different from what politicians usually suppose. While citizens are not filling the streets to scream for abolition of the death penalty, the public is clearly receptive to meaningful alternative punishments. What is necessary now is for our duly elected leaders to show the courage to propose alternative punishments and to engage the public in a discussion of the real costs and illusory benefits of capital punishment. There is no doubt that violence in America is a serious problem or that murderers deserve severe punishment. But the problem is made more serious by the use of the death penalty. By abandoning the failed policy of killing murderers, we could expand public discourse and focus on the prevention of crime instead of the craving for revenge.

NOTES

1. *Furman v. Georgia,* 408 U.S. 238 (1972), p. 429 (Powell, dissenting).

2. *Furman v. Georgia,* p. 299 (Brennan, dissenting).

3. Ellsworth, P. C., and Gross, S. R. (1994). "Hardening of the Attitudes: Americans' Views on the Death Penalty." *Journal of Social Issues,* vol. 50, pp. 19–52.

4. Bohm, R. M. (1991). "American Death Penalty Opinion, 1936–1986: A Critical Examination of the Gallup Polls." In R. M. Bohm (ed.), *The Death Penalty in America: Current Research.* Cincinnati: Anderson. Also see Fox, J. A., Radelet, M. L., and Bonsteel, J. L. (1991). "Death Penalty Opinion in the Post-Furman Years." *New York University Review of Law and Social Change,* vol. 28, pp. 499–528.

5. Gallup, G. H. (1987). *The Gallup Poll: Public Opinion, 1986.* Wilmington, Del.: Scholarly Resources, p. 57.

6. Gallup, A., and Newport, F. (1991, June). "Death Penalty Support Remains Strong." *The Gallup Poll Monthly,* 309, pp. 40–45.

7. Gallup and Newport (1991).

8. Moore, D. W. (September, 1994). "Majority Advocate Death Penalty for Teenage Killers." *The Gallup Monthly,* pp. 2–6.

9. Bohm, R. M., and Aveni, A. F. (1985). "Knowledge About the Death Penalty: A Test of the Marshall Hypothesis." Paper presented at the annual meeting of the American Society of Criminology, San Diego, California; Ellsworth, P. C., and Ross, L. (1983). "Public Opinion and Capital Punishment: A Close Examination of the Views of Abolitionists and Retentionists." *Crime and Delinquency,* 29, pp. 116–169.

10. Ellsworth and Ross (1983); Bohm (1991).

11. *Furman v. Georgia* (1972), p. 299 (Brennan, concurring).

12. Morganthau, T. (August 7, 1995). "Condemned to Life." *Newsweek,* p. 23.

13. Morganthau (1995).

14. Page, B. I., and Shapiro, R. Y. (1992) *The Rational Public.* Chicago: University of Chicago Press.

15. Ellsworth and Ross (1983), p. 168.

16. Bowers, W. J., Vandiver, M., and Dugan, P. H. (1994). "A New Look at Public Opinion on Capital Punishment: What Citizens and Legislators Prefer." *American Journal of Criminal Law,* vol. 22, pp. 77–150.

17. Dieter, R. C. (1993). *Sentencing for Life: Americans Embrace Alternatives to the Death Penalty.* Washington, D.C.: The Death Penalty Information Center.

18. All of these quotes from jurors are taken from Costanzo, M., and Costanzo, S. (1994). "The Death Penalty: Public Opinions, Legal Decisions, and Juror

Perspectives." In M. Costanzo and S. Oskamp (eds.), *Violence and the Law.* Thousand Oaks, Calif.: Sage, pp. 246–271.

19. Bowers, W. J. (1993). "Capital Punishment and Contemporary Values: People's Misgivings and the Court's Misperceptions." *Law and Society Review,* 27, pp. 157–176.

20. Bowers, Vandiver, and Dugan (1994).

PART VI

✪

Corrections

Prison comes to mind when most people think of corrections. This is understandable given the history of corrections, the folklore, films, and songs about prison life, and the fact that incarceration is the most visible aspect of the process. Many of us have seen the looming walls, barbed-wire fences, and searchlights of a prison. The prison is also brought to our attention by the media whenever there is inmate unrest or an escape. And it is the prison that legislators and politicians speak about when they debate changes in the penal code or appropriations for corrections.

For students of criminal justice, it should be no surprise that less than one-third of offenders under supervision are in prisons and jails. Most offenders are punished in the community through probation, intermediate sanctions, and parole. Thus corrections refers to the great number of programs, services, facilities, and organizations responsible for the management of people accused or convicted of criminal offenses. Besides prisons and jails, corrections includes probation, halfway houses, education and work release, boot camps, parole supervision, counseling, and community service. Many of these alternatives to incarceration rely on advances in technology such as electronic anklets, video surveillance, or global positioning systems, as well as more invasive measures, such as regular urine and blood testing. Correctional programs operate in Salvation Army hostels, in forest camps, along roadsides, in medical clinics, and in urban storefronts.

Corrections is authorized by all levels of government, administered by both public and private organizations, costing over $30 billion per year. Corrections supervises almost six million adults and juveniles. Supervision is carried out by more than five hundred thousand administrators, psychologists, officers, counselors, social workers, and others. An astounding 2.7 percent of U.S. adults (1 of every 21 men and 1 out of every 100 women) is incarcerated, on probation, or on parole. This is particularly alarming when we realize that 1 of every 6 African-American adult males and 1 of 3 African-American young adult males (aged 18–34) are under some form of correctional supervision.

COMMUNITY CORRECTIONS

Since the early nineteenth century, supervision in the community has been recognized as an appropriate punishment for some offenders. Although probation had been developed in the 1840s and was widely used by the 1920s, incarceration remained the usual sentence for serious crimes until the 1960s. At that time, with a new emphasis on community corrections, judges sentenced increased numbers of offenders to sanctions carried out in the community. As a result, incarceration rates fell as probation was viewed as the "punishment of choice" for most first-time offenders.

However, as Americans wearied of crime in the 1980s, legislatures passed tough sentencing laws and stipulated that incarceration should be the new priority punishment. By 1990 criminal justice scholars recognized that many imprisoned offenders, if properly supervised, could be punished more cheaply in the community. At the same time, probation was clearly inappropriate for offenders whose crimes were serious and who could not be effectively supervised by officers with large caseloads. What was needed was a set of intermediate sanctions, less restrictive of freedom than prison but more restrictive than probation, such as intensive probation supervision, home confinement, monetary sanctions, and boot camps.

In coming years community corrections can be expected to play a much greater role in the criminal justice system. The number of offenders supervised in the community is likely to increase as states try to deal with the high costs of incarceration. With incarceration rates at record highs, probation and intermediate sanctions appear to many criminal justice experts to be less expensive and just as effective as prison.

GOVERNING A SOCIETY OF CAPTIVES

The prison differs from almost every other institution or organization in modern society. Not only are its physical features different, but also it is a place where a group of persons devotes itself to managing a group of captives. Prisoners are required to live according to the rules of their keepers, and their movements are sharply restricted. Unlike managers of other government agencies, prison managers

- Cannot select their clients
- Have little or no control over the release of their clients
- Must deal with clients who are there against their will
- Must rely on clients to do most of the work in the daily operation of the institution and to do so by coercion and without fair compensation for their work
- Must depend on the maintenance of satisfactory relationships between clients and staff

With these unique characteristics, how should a prison be run? What rules should guide administrators? As we can see from the description above, wardens and other key personnel are asked to perform a difficult order, one that requires skilled and dedicated managers.

The correctional literature points to four factors that make the governing of prisons different from the administration of other public institutions: (1) the defects of total power; (2) the limited rewards and punishments that can be used by officials; (3) the exchange relations between correctional officers and inmates; and (4) the strength of inmate leadership.

The Defects of Total Power

Imagine a prison society comprised of hostile and uncooperative captives ruled by force, in which prisoners could be legally isolated from one another, physically abused until they cooperate, and put under continuous surveillance. Theoretically, such a society is possible. In reality, however, correctional officers have limited power, because many prisoners have little to lose by misbehaving and unarmed officers have only limited ability to force compliance with rules. Perhaps more important is the fact that forcing people to carry out complex tasks is basically inefficient. Prison efficiency is further diminished by the realities of the usual ratio of one officer to forty inmates and the potential danger of the situation.

Rewards and Punishments

Because there are few permissible situations for the use of physical coercion, corrections officials must gain compliance and maintain control through the use of limited rewards and punishments. For example, privileges such as good time allocations, choice job assignments, and favorable parole reports may be offered in exchange for obedience. The reward system is defective, however, because most privileges are given to the inmate at the start of the sentence and are taken away only if rules are broken. Few additional rewards can be granted for progress or exceptional behavior, although a desired work assignment or transfer to the honor cell block will induce some prisoners to maintain good behavior. One problem is that the punishments for breaking the rules do not represent a great departure from the prisoner's usual status. Because they are already deprived of many freedoms and valued goods—heterosexual relations, money, choice of clothing, and so on—inmates have little else left to lose. The punishment of not being allowed to attend a recreational period may not carry much weight. Moreover there are legal limitations on what types of punishments can be imposed.

Gaining Cooperation: Exchange Relationships

One way that correctional officers obtain inmates' cooperation is through exchange relationships. Although the formal rules require a social distance between officers and inmates, physical closeness makes them aware that each is dependent on the other. The officers need the cooperation of the prisoners so that they will look good to their superiors, and the inmates depend on the guards to relax the rules or occasionally look the other way.

Correctional officers must be careful not to pay too high a price for the cooperation of their charges. Officers who establish sub-rosa relationships can be manipulated by prisoners into smuggling contraband or committing other illegal acts. Officers are under pressure to work effectively with prisoners and may be blackmailed into doing illegitimate favors in return for cooperation.

Inmate Leadership

Some officials also try to use inmate leaders to exercise control over convicts. Inmate leaders have been "tested" over time so that they are neither pushed around by other inmates nor distrusted as stool pigeons. Because staff can also rely on them, inmate leaders serve as the essential communications link between staff and inmates. By being able to acquire inside information and access to higher officials, inmate leaders command the respect of other prisoners and are granted special privileges by officials. In turn, they distribute these benefits to other prisoners, thus bolstering their own influence within the society. In practice, however, prison administrators of earlier eras were more successful at using inmate leaders to maintain order than are today's administrators. In most of today's institutions, prisoners are divided by race, ethnicity, age, and gang affiliation, so that no single leadership structure exists.

The Challenge of Governing Prisons

The factors of total power, rewards and punishments, co-optation, and inmate leadership exist in every prison and must be managed. How they are managed greatly influences the quality of prison life. Among many correctional administrators and officers is the belief that "the cons run the joint." Instead, successful wardens have made their prisons "work" by the application of management principles within the context of their own style of leadership. Prisons can be governed, violence can be minimized, and services can be provided if correctional executives and wardens exhibit leadership appropriate to the task. Governing prisons is an extraordinary challenge, but it can be and has been successfully accomplished.

SUGGESTIONS FOR FURTHER READING

Byrne, James M., Arthur J. Lurigio, and Joan Petersilia. *Smart Sentencing: The Emergence of Intermediate Sanctions.* Newbury Park, Calif.: Sage, 1992. A collection of papers exploring various issues in the design and implementation of intermediate sanctions programs.

Clear, Todd R., and George F. Cole. *American Corrections,* 5th ed., Belmont,

Calif.: Wadsworth, 2000. A comprehensive look at the corrections system.

DiIulio, John J., Jr. *Governing Prisons.* New York: Free Press, 1987. A critique of the sociological perspective on inmate society. DiIulio argues that governance by correctional officers is the key to the maintenance of good prisons and jails.

Earley, Pete. *The Hot House: Life inside Leavenworth Prison.* New York: Bantam Books, 1992. An eyewitness account of daily life in the United States Penitentiary in Leavenworth, Kansas, written by the first journalist given unlimited access to a maximum security institution of the Federal Bureau of Prisons.

Garland, David. *Punishment and Modern Society.* Chicago: University of Chicago Press, 1990. Argues against punishment purely as a function of crime control.

Johnson, Robert. *Deathwork: A Study of the Modern Execution Process.* Pacific Grove, Calif.: Brooks/Cole 1990. First-person account detailing the execution process, including the death watch team, warden, condemned prisoner, and official witness.

Morris, Norval, and Michael Tonry. *Between Prison and Probation: Intermediate Punishments in a Rational Sentencing System.* New York: Oxford University Press, 1990. Urges development of a range of intermediate punishments that can be used to sanction offenders more severely than probation but less severely than incarceration.

Rothman, David J. *The Discovery of the Asylum: Social Order and Disorder in the New Republic.* Boston: Little, Brown, 1971. A history of the invention of the penitentiary. Rothman shows the links among the ideology of the 1830s, assumptions concerning corrections, and design of institutions.

Sheehan, Susan. *A Prison and a Prisoner.* Boston: Houghton Mifflin, 1978. A fascinating description of life in Green Haven Prison and the way one prisoner "makes it" through "swagging," "hustling," and "doing time." Contains an excellent discussion of the inmate economy.

Simon, Jonathon. *Poor Discipline: Parole and the Social Control of the Underclass.* Chicago: University of Chicago Press, 1993. Explores the use of parole to control poor and disadvantaged members of society.

21

✦

Between Prison
and Probation

Toward a Comprehensive
Punishment System

NORVAL MORRIS
MICHAEL TONRY

With record-high incarceration rates and overwhelming probation caseloads, Morris and Tonry argue for the need for intermediate punishments. These sanctions can be used in the community to punish offenders who do not require the restrictions of prison as well as offenders who require more restrictions than those imposed by probation.

There [are now] more than 1,000,000 Americans aged 18 and over in prison and jail, and more than 2,500,000 on parole or probation. If one adds those on bail or released awaiting trial or appeal and those serving other punishments such as community service orders, the grand total under the control of the criminal justice system exceeds four million, nearly 2 percent of the nation's adult population.

The pressure of these numbers on insufficient and mostly old penal institutions and on sparsely staffed probation offices has sharpened interest in all punishments lying between the prison and the jail at one end and insufficiently supervised probation at the other—there is general agreement about the need to develop and expand "intermediate punishments" but the path to that end is far from clear.

There are two main lines of argument. First, it is submitted that there has been a failure in this country to develop and institutionalize a range of punishments

Source: Norval Morris and Michael Tonry, *Between Prison and Probation* (New York: Oxford University Press, 1990): pp. 9–33. Copyright © 1990 by Oxford University Press, Inc. Used by permission of Oxford University Press, Inc.

lying between incarceration and probation. That argument can stand alone and would support an expansion of intermediate punishments without considering any questions of sentencing processes. The selection between those properly committed to prison and those sentenced to intermediate punishments cannot be based *alone* on the gravity of their crimes or the lengths of their criminal records, nor can the choice between probation and an intermediate punishment.

The second line of argument takes the matter further: for certain categories of offenders now in prison, some though not all could better be sentenced to intermediate punishments, and for certain categories of offenders now on probation, some though not all could be better subjected to more intensive controls in the community than probation now provides.

The first argument is obvious enough and does not deny the conventional wisdom; indeed, such is the extent of current experimentation with intermediate punishments that the ground is fertile and the time precisely right for their growth. The second argument will meet with more opposition since it seems to contradict the intuitive sense that like cases should be treated alike, that crimes of equal severity committed by criminals with equal criminal records should be punished identically. We regard this position as an erroneous application of principles of "just desert." A comprehensive and just sentencing system requires principled "interchangeability" of punishment of "like" cases, some going to prison, some receiving an intermediate punishment. Similarly, there must be principled interchangeability of punishment of like cases, with some being put on probation while others receive the more intensive control or qualitatively different experience of an intermediate punishment.

• • •

[The following is a bare statement of our recommendations:]

- Intermediate punishments should be applied to many criminals now in prison and jail and to many criminals now sentenced to probation or a suspended sentence.

- Intermediate punishments must be rigorously enforced; they should not, as is too often the present case, be ordered absent adequate enforcement resources.

- Breaches of conditions of intermediate punishments must be taken seriously by the supervising authority and, in appropriate cases, by the sentencing judge, if these punishments are to become credible sanctions.

- The fine should be greatly expanded, in amount and in frequency, both as a punishment standing alone and as part of a punishment package. Fines must be adjusted to the offender's financial capacity (to be achieved by a system of "day fines") and must be collected; this requires innovative assessment and enforcement arrangements, since at present fines are set too low, do not sufficiently match the means of the offender, and are too often not collected.

- The use of community service orders, standing alone or as part of a punishment package, should be greatly increased. Such punishments are applicable to the indigent and to the wealthy; they have much to contribute provided, as for other intermediate punishments, they are vigorously super-vised and enforced.

- Intensive probation is a mechanism by which reality can be brought to all intermediate punishments. Allied to house arrest, treatment orders, residential conditions up to house arrest, buttressed by electronic monitoring where appropriate, and paid for by fees for service by the offender where that is realistic, intensive supervision has the capacity both to control offenders in the community and to facilitate their growth to crime-free lives.

- Current sentencing reforms, both proposals and developments, devote in-adequate attention to intermediate punishments. Sentencing guidelines, legislative or voluntary, shaped by a sentencing commission or by a court system, must provide better guidance to the judiciary in the use of inter-mediate punishments if a comprehensive sentencing system is to be devel-oped. In particular:
  1. there is a range of offense–offender relationships in which incarcerative and intermediate punishments are equally applicable;
  2. there is a range of offense–offender relationships in which intermediate punishments and lesser community-based controls are equally applicable;
  3. the sentencing judge requires adequate information about the offender and his financial and personal circumstances to decide on the applicabil-ity to each convicted offender of a fine, of a community service order, of a treatment or residential order, of intensive supervision, or of a split sentence involving incarceration and an intermediate punishment— or a mixture of several of these punishments;
  4. the judge should retain ultimate responsibility for the decision on the "back-up" sentence, that is, on what should be done if the conditions of an intermediate punishment are not adhered to.

- As intermediate punishments become part of a comprehensive sentencing system, their efficacy must be critically evaluated so that, in time, an effec-tive treatment classification may emerge.

THE OVERUSE OF IMPRISONMENT
AND PROBATION

The figures again: 1,000,000 in prison and jail, over 2,500,000 on probation. How many of these would be better subjected to intermediate punishments cannot be precisely calculated but that the number is large can be confidently affirmed.

Who among the sentenced offenders now in prison or jail need not be there? One way to get at this question is to define the criteria that justify incarceration and then to ask how many in prison and jail do not meet those criteria.

Some years ago, one of us argued in *The Future of Imprisonment* that prison is an appropriate punishment only when one or more of the following three con-ditions is fulfilled:

- Any lesser punishment would depreciate the seriousness of the crime or crimes committed.
- Imprisonment is necessary for deterrence, general or special.
- Other less restrictive sanctions have been frequently or recently applied to this offender.

We hope it is not stubborn persistence in error that leads us to reaffirm allegiance to those propositions. They track ideas offered by the American Law Institute's *Model Penal Code* and by the American Bar Association's *Standards for Criminal Justice*. Both of these organizations and many other commentators on sentencing have expressed a preference for parsimony in incarceration with a presumption against that punishment unless it be necessary for one or more of these three purposes: to affirm the gravity of the crime, to deter the criminal and others who are like-minded, or because other sanctions have proved insufficient.

Judged by these criteria there are many in prison and jail who need not be there, who are at a shallow end of severity of crime and have criminal records that do not trigger any one of these selecting criteria. How many is a matter of guesswork. Prison wardens differ in their estimates, but it is common to hear talk of 10 to 15 percent. And there are other straws in the wind of this assessment.

In practice, there is another reason, and an increasingly popular reason, why convicted criminals are imprisoned. The sentencing judge may be skeptical that imprisoning a given criminal is necessary to reaffirm any behavioral standards, may doubt that it will have either a general or special deterrent effect, and may doubt that imprisonment will prove any more effective, whatever its purposes, than any other punishment. But this, at least, the judge knows: an offender who is in prison will not be committing any crimes against other than the prison community. Incapacitation plays an increasing role in the sentencing decision and may in considerable part account for the present overcrowding of penal institutions.

Incapacitation is a function of risk-assessment. This becomes clear when "caps" are put on prison populations or on jail populations by court orders pursuant to Eighth Amendment suits. Those running the prisons or jails have frequently had to arrange, and have arranged, early release programs, freeing many who otherwise would be in prison or jail. Wisely they select for such release the lower-risk offenders, those who seem most likely to avoid crime, at least during the remainder of the period to which they had been sentenced. This, of course, is exactly what parole boards do, particularly when they are guided by parole prediction tables such as the "salient factor score" developed for the federal parole system. There are many now in prison who have a low likelihood of future criminality, particularly if that prediction is confined to crimes of personal violence.

In the broad sense, then, there are certainly prisoners who in terms of risk to society or other punitive purpose need not serve the prison terms now imposed. Within that group a number need never have been so sentenced had there existed a sufficient range of intermediate punishments to provide community protection from them.

Even more certainly, of the more than 2 million convicted offenders now sentenced to probation there are many who should be under closer supervision than ordinary probation provides and also many who by fines or by community service should make larger amends for their crimes than ordinary probation now provides. It would be misleading to suggest with any attempt at precision what that number might be, since it is in large part a function of what community-based treatment and control resources are available. But when one finds caseloads of 200 and more per probation officer in some of our cities, it is clear both that probation is often a merely token sanction providing scant community protection and that the number of probationers meriting middle-range intermediate punishment is large.

We have, in short, created a punishment system that is polarized and ill-adapted to the gradations of severity of crime and magnitude of future threat that are the grist of the mill of our criminal courts. Between overcrowded prisons and even more overcrowded probation, there is a near-vacuum of appropriate and enforced middle-range punishments. . . . Unless and until such intermediate punishments are developed and institutionalized, there can be no comprehensive punishment system suited to the realities of crime and criminals in this country.

THE UNDERUSE
OF INTERMEDIATE PUNISHMENTS

At last, there is an experiment with a day-fine system in this country, decades after it became entrenched in many European punishment systems. At last, federal fines have been raised to realistic levels, decades after the threats of white-collar crime and organized crime were understood. Some countries now treat the fine as their main punishment for quite serious crime; such a thought is brushed aside in the United States, a country otherwise dedicated to the power of the economic incentive. Why not, then, let the fine serve as a powerful penal disincentive rather than a mere adjunct to other punishments?

The reasons for the neglect of the fine as a weapon against other than minor crime are not clear. That the fine is an insufficiently used punishment is, however, clear beyond argument. It is seen as ineffective against the wealthy and inapplicable to the poor. Far too often, when a fine is imposed it is not collected, and this holds true in federal as well as state and local courts.

All that is now affirmed is that a system of fines graduated to the severity of the crime and the capacity of the criminal to pay, if imposed and collected, is an essential part of a comprehensive punishment system. The knowledge base exists to develop and implement such a system. Widespread experimentation has taken place in this country with various methods of assessing, imposing, and collecting fines and other countries have moved toward implementing such systems.

Unlike the other intermediate punishments we shall consider, the development of an effective system of fines could be achieved cheaply, without the development of any large-scale enforcement mechanisms. This is one area of the criminal justice system to which the private sector can make a significant contribution—and to its own profit. Private financial institutions are good at collecting debts; the courts are not.

All who have studied criminal punishments in this country, be they from the bleeding-hearted left or the lantern-jawed right, lament the state of the fine. There is less unanimity concerning the underuse of the other punishments in the middle range between prison and probation, but in our view the cases are equally strong.

The community service order is analogous to the fine, clearly applicable to the indigent, for whom a fine may be inappropriate, but also suited, either alone or as an adjunct to other punishments, to many who can and should pay fines. Later we tell the story of experimentation with this punishment in this country and abroad; for the time being all that is being suggested is that one important way in which the criminal can make amends to the community he has wronged—make a contribution to it given that he has inflicted injury on it—is by providing some form of community service that is needed and that otherwise would not be provided. In the destroyed inner-city areas there is much need for rehabilitation of otherwise unusable housing; there is unlimited work to be done to preserve our heritage of natural resources; our hospitals and all our community services stand in need of assistance—it seems obvious that there is ample opportunity here for some offenders, as part of their punishment or as their punishment, to give of their labor and skills to our benefit and possibly also to theirs.

Intermediate punishments encompass a wide diversity of community-based treatments and controls of the convicted offender, ranging from house arrest, to halfway houses, to intensive probation with conditions of treatment or control vigorously enforced and, if appropriate, backed up by the emerging technology of electronic and telephonic monitoring. . . . The probation order has become the punishment of choice for a wide swath of crimes. Like prison, inadequately supplied with the resources to fulfill its mission, probation has been overwhelmed by numbers. But, this reality apart, it has come to be realized that many offenders require closer supervision than the usual probation order provides. Hence the development of these more intensive controls, combining elements of police supervision and casework assistance. . . . For some criminals, as a punishment standing alone, for others, as part of a larger punishment package, community-based punishments stand in urgent need of further development as a necessary and integral part of a comprehensive punishment system.

THE ENFORCEMENT
OF INTERMEDIATE PUNISHMENTS

As we surveyed experimentation with intermediate punishments, one pattern emerged which may go far to explain their small role in punishment policy and practice: an enthusiastic reformer, a judge as in the origins of the community service order, or an agency as in much experimentation with intensive supervision

probation, seeks and finds funds to launch an experimental program of intermediate punishments. It "works well": the early enthusiasm of a new initiative leads
the sentencing court and the community in which it is established to be satisfied
with its observed results. It does not have a high failure rate; it is hard to know,
however, whether the failure rate would have been higher or lower if some other
punishment had been imposed on the same offenders. There is always the possibility that the new initiative skimmed the least threatening offenders from the
pool of convicted offenders possibly suited to this new punishment; at any event,
those who launch it and those who are subject to it feel [good] about it. It is
written up in some popular literature and often featured on local or national television, usually with excessive claims of success. Then the task of building it into
the larger punishment system in the city or state where it was established begins—and usually ends. The enthusiasm of the early reformers dissipates; they
move on to other pastures. The other punishment agencies, prison and probation, are not excited by this new competition for their clientele, even though
they recognize their overload. Bureaucratic inertia dominates. The "reform" is
allowed quietly to die.

We draw two morals from this oft repeated experience. First, the designers
and administrators of new initiatives must face and overcome daunting organizational, political, financial, and bureaucratic problems if new programs are to be
institutionalized and their promised benefits achieved. Second, and more important for our purposes here, the development of a comprehensive punishment
system requires the dedication of appreciable resources of men and women,
money and materials, to the implementation and enforcement of a range of intermediate punishments if we are to move beyond experimentation.

· · ·

It may be true that, in the long run, a punishment system making appropriate use of a range of punishments from probation through the middle range of
punishments and on to imprisonment may be less expensive than one that relies
excessively on prison; but that will be true, if at all, in the very long run. Community-based controls are labor intensive if they are to be effective. If the convicted offender is to be supervised effectively, with or without the assistance of
electronic or similar monitoring, with or without, for example, regular drug
testing, supervising officers cannot carry a large caseload. The "alternatives to
imprisonment" movement sailed under false colors when it claimed immediate
savings; prison budgets decline only when substantial numbers are taken out of
the prison so that a prison or a wing of a prison may be closed—and that does
not seem an immediate likelihood in most American jurisdictions.

And there is another aspect of reality that is not usually stressed by those who
advocate this type of development of our punishment system: the intermediate
punishment must be rigorously enforced, it must be "backed up" by enforcement
mechanisms that take seriously indeed any breach of the conditions of the community-based sanction. This does not mean, for example, that the addict who
once relapses in a treatment program must by that fact and without more be incarcerated; but it does mean that this relapse must be taken seriously and that there
is a real possibility of the imposition of a prison term because of the relapse.

If a fine is imposed, adjusted to the criminal's financial circumstances and potential, and time given to pay if necessary, it is of the first importance that an effective and determined enforcement machinery be in place. It seems unnecessary to make such a point, but the record of failure to collect fines in the federal system, and similar experience in state and local fining practice, compel such a stressing of the obvious.

Here too the law must keep its promises. The promise of intermediate punishments demands for its fulfillment resources adequate to their support and sufficient for their determined enforcement.

SENTENCING TO INTERMEDIATE PUNISHMENTS

Concerns for justice and fairness in sentencing will lead, in time, probably within 25 years, to the creation in most American states of comprehensive systems of structured sentencing discretion that encompass a continuum of punishments from probation to imprisonment, with many intermediate punishments ranged between. These systems may take the form of the sentencing guidelines now in place in Minnesota, Washington, and elsewhere, or they may take some other form, but they will all provide for interchangeability of punishments for like-situated offenders. They will establish ranges of interchangeable punishments, bounded by considerations of desert, that are presumed to be applicable to the cases governed by each range, subject to the right of the judge to impose some other sentence if he provides written reasons for so doing; the adequacy and appropriateness of those reasons will be subject to review by appellate courts that will consult a body of case law, a common law of sentencing, for guidance.

These predictions may seem millenarian, but they are the foreseeable extension of developments and practices that are already in place. Anyone who in 1970 predicted the radical changes in American sentencing practices that have taken place since that date would have seemed even more romantic than we do now. The developments that underlay the past two decades of evolution in American sentencing practices will continue to shape reform for decades to come in the directions that we have identified. . . .

In 1970 the indeterminate sentencing systems in the United States, federal and state, had continued virtually unchanged from at least 1930 and looked much the same everywhere. Premised at least in theory on commitment to the values of individualized sentencing and rehabilitative correctional programs, indeterminate sentencing systems gave officials wide-ranging discretion and freedom from external controls over their decisions. Criminal statutes and common law doctrines defined the elements of crimes. Statutes established maximum terms of probation and imprisonment, and maximum amounts of fines, that could be imposed. Occasionally, but rarely, the statutes established mandatory minimum prison terms for persons convicted of particular crimes. Prosecutors had complete control over charging and plea bargaining. Judges had little-fettered discretion to "individualize punishment" in deciding who received probation and who was sentenced to jail or prison, and, for those to be confined, to set minimum or maximum terms, and sometimes both. Parole boards, subject only to statutory provisions on parole eligibility, generally when a third of the maximum term had been served, decided who was released from prison prior to the expiration of their terms, when, and under what conditions.

None of these decisions—charging and plea bargaining, sentencing, paroling—was governed by legal or administrative decision rules and only rarely did these decisions raise issues cognizable in the appellate courts. Well-established doctrines based on notions of separation of powers and deference to administrative expertise led appellate courts to refuse to review prosecutorial and parole decisions on the substantive merits. Equivalent notions of comity between judges and deference to the better information of the trial judge caused appellate courts to accord extreme deference to the discretionary sentencing decisions of the trial judge.

When courts did consider appeals from parole and prosecutorial decisions, which was uncommon before 1970, the cases generally involved procedural issues. When appellate courts considered sentence appeals in the few states where such appeals were allowed, few sentences were overturned and they tended to be such gross departures from standard practice that the appeals courts felt comfortable concluding that they constituted an "abuse of discretion" or that they "offended the conscience."

In effect, prosecutors, judges, and parole boards were accountable for their decisions in individual cases only to their political constituencies and their consciences. Few would have guessed in 1970 that nearly every facet of indeterminate sentencing in theory and in practice would be decisively repudiated within a decade.

• • •

The theoretical attacks were most influentially advanced by Francis Allen in his 1964 book, *The Borderland of Criminal Justice,* and in 1974 by Norval Morris in *The Future of Imprisonment.* Their arguments had two major elements. First, from an ethical perspective, it is simply wrong to take or extend the state's criminal law powers over individuals for, ostensibly, their own good, especially in light of pessimistic findings on the correctional systems' abilities to rehabilitate offenders. Second, from a psychological perspective, it defies common experience to imagine that coerced participation in treatment programs will often facilitate personal growth and change. Generally, self-improvement is voluntary; coupling participation in treatment programs with a likelihood of earlier release motivated prisoners to participate, but often it did not motivate them to change.

Taken together, these critiques greatly undermined indeterminate sentencing and the practices and institutions that went with it. It is not easy to defend a major set of social institutions that are portrayed as based on unsound empirical, ethical, and psychological premises, as characterized by racial and class bias, by arbitrariness, by lawlessness, and by unfairness, and as conspicuously ineffective at achieving the larger social purposes of reducing crime and rehabilitating offenders—and few tried.

Hence American sentencing institutions and practices underwent more extensive and more radical changes between 1975 and 1985 than in any other decade in our history. Most of the changes attempted to structure or eliminate the discretionary decisions exercised by public officials. Although new initiatives affecting decision making by judges and prosecutors were not uncommon, it was the parole boards, the institutions that in theory based their decisions on rehabilitative predictions and assessments, that experienced the most drastic changes.

• • •

Many of the sentencing innovations since the midseventies have not achieved their proponents' aims. Mandatory sentencing laws, for example, had at best a modest short-term deterrent effect on the crimes they affect and usually produced very little change in sentencing practices. For serious crimes, the one- or two-year minimum sentence usually prescribed was generally less than would normally be imposed even without a mandatory sentencing law. For less serious offenses and offenders, lawyers and judges could usually devise a method for circumventing the mandatory sentence when its imposition seemed to them unduly harsh.

Voluntary guidelines for sentencing fared little better. Voluntary guidelines were voluntary in two senses; their development by judges was self-initiated and not in furtherance of a statutory directive, and whether and to what extent judges followed them was entirely in the hands of each individual judge. In most jurisdictions, voluntary guidelines seem to have had little effect on sentencing. Although courts in more than 40 states established voluntary guidelines between 1975 and 1980, in most places they were soon abandoned or soon became dead letters.

Statutory determinate sentencing laws did somewhat better and in some states, notably North Carolina and California, they seem to have reduced sentencing disparities and made sentencing somewhat more predictable. In other states, however, like Illinois and Indiana, the new laws offered no meaningful constraints on judicial discretion and proved to be no improvement on the indeterminate sentencing systems they replaced.

Parole guidelines in some jurisdictions, such as Minnesota and the federal system, accomplished much of what their creators had in mind. Consistently applied, they made release dates more predictable and served to even out disparities in the lengths of prison sentences meted out by judges. Their major shortcoming from a reform perspective was that they affect only those offenders who are sent to prison and accordingly have no effect whatever on the question of who is sentenced to prison or on what happens to those who are not imprisoned.

The sentencing reform initiative of the future is the combination of the sentencing commission and presumptive sentencing guidelines that Judge Frankel first proposed in 1972 as a solution to the lawlessness that he decried, that Minnesota first implemented in 1980, and that other jurisdictions have elaborated as the years have passed. Presumptive sentencing guidelines establish presumptions that govern judges' decisions whether to imprison an offender and, if so, for how long. The judge may conclude that special circumstances justify some other sentence or, in other words, that the presumption should be rejected. If so, the judge must explain his reasoning and its adequacy is subject to review by appeal of sentence to a higher court. Careful evaluations of the experience in Minnesota and later Washington showed that presumptive sentencing guidelines could reduce sentencing disparities, reduce differences in sentencing patterns associated with race, increase consistency in sentencing statewide, and make sentencing much more predictable, so that state sentencing policies could be related in a meaningful way to the availability of prison beds and other correctional resources.

Presumptive sentencing guidelines appear to be a way to address most of the major critiques of indeterminate sentencing. They reduce disparities and the potential for decisions based on invidious considerations of race and class. They provide decision rules to guide the sentencing choices judges make. Judges are made accountable because they must comply with the guidelines' presumptions or give reasons for doing something else. Sentence appeals become meaningful because appellate judges have some basis for assessing the correctness of the trial judge's decisions and the reasons that are invoked to justify them.

The wisdom of Judge Frankel's proposal, and the core of the sentencing commission idea, was its combination of the sentencing commission, sentencing guidelines, and appellate sentence review. All three elements were crucial. The creation of an administrative agency responsible for formulation of sentencing policy provided an institution much better situated than any legislature to accumulate specialized expertise to develop comprehensive sentencing policies and sufficiently removed from the glare of day-to-day legislative politics to approach these often controversial matters in a principled and thoughtful way. The resulting sentencing guidelines for the first time provided an instrument for the expression of finely tuned standards for exercise of the punitive powers of the state, and their presumptive character required that judges give reasons for their decisions to depart from the guidelines' presumptions. Those reasons, in turn, for the first time in this country provided the material for development of principled appellate review of sentences. . . .

A comprehensive sentencing system must provide guidance to judges in choosing among all available sentencing options, including probation, prison, and all the intermediate punishments that fall between them in severity and intrusiveness. . . . There is, however, one threshold that must be crossed before such a system becomes a viable possibility—the prison or probation, something or nothing, simplicities of too much present thought must be rejected.

• • •

Here we simply set out the components of a comprehensive sentencing system.

1. The principle of interchangeability of punishments must be recognized.
2. The "in/out" line must be erased to eliminate the false dichotomous prison–or–nothing simplicities.

3. In place of a two-part in-or-out sentencing grid, there should be at least four graded categories of punishment presumptions: "out," "out unless . . . ," "in unless . . . ," and "in."

4. Within the governing purposes *of* sentencing established by policymakers, the guidelines should permit the judge to look to the applicable purposes of punishment to be served *at* sentencing in choosing among the available interchangeable punishments.

5. The principle of interchangeability should be recognized for all crimes for which the presumptive prison sentence (for those cases where the applicable purposes at sentencing will best be served by incarceration) is two years or less.

6. The system should provide guidance for all sentencing decisions for all felonies and misdemeanors.

7. The choice among interchangeable punishments is for the judge to make, not the offender.

The preceding list does not address all of the issues our proposals raise. For example, it does not explain how the exchange rates between different punishments are to be determined or calculated, or how judges are to know what the governing purposes are *at* sentencing. We discuss such problems later. We believe, however, that they are simpler than at first appears and that their apparent difficulty results mainly from their novelty.

Our mission is to explain how in principle and in practice a comprehensive sentencing system, which incorporates a rich variety of intermediate punishments linked to one another and to probation and prison by a principle of interchangeability, can be established and implemented. Before we turn to that fuller explication and justification, a critical issue of justice as fairness must be mentioned and its implications noted.

Fitting intermediate punishments into a principled sentencing system has proved to be the Achilles heel of both sentencing reform proposals and practice. The central reason for this is (somewhat unexpectedly given the general human capacity to tolerate the sufferings of others with a degree of equanimity) a sense of unfairness when it is suggested that two equally undeserving criminals should be treated differently—since differently here means that one will be treated more leniently than the other.

The conceptual keystone of the argument is that a developed punishment theory requires recognition that precise equivalency of punishment between equally undeserving criminals in the distribution of punishments is in practice unattainable and is in theory undesirable. We argue that all that can be achieved is a rough equivalence of punishment that will allow room for the principled distribution of punishments on utilitarian grounds, unfettered by the miserable aim of making suffering equally painful. . . .

The first consequence is that it now becomes possible to move appreciable numbers who otherwise would be sentenced to prison into community-based intermediate punishments, having a roughly equivalent punitive bite but serving both the community and the criminal better than the prison term. It also becomes possible to move appreciable numbers who otherwise would be sentenced to token probationary supervision into intermediate punishments that exercise larger controls over them and provide us with larger social protection from their criminality. The advantages are obvious; it is a liberating idea—but it has its problems, theoretical and practical.

First, the theoretical problem. If appropriate guidance is to be given the sentencing judge under such a system of punishment, some "exchange rates" between punishments to achieve this rough equivalence must be stated in advance. There exist a few fledgling efforts to state these exchange rates; we believe that a principled system of punishment can be defined in which rough equivalence of punitive bite and identity of process in relation to stated purposes of punishment provide the necessary guidance to the judge and also give both the appearance and the reality of fairness to the community and to the convicted offender.

Among the practical problems that accompany such a purposive introduction of intermediate punishments into the body of a punishment system, none is more troublesome than its impact on existing class and race biases.

At present black adult males per hundred thousand are more than seven times as likely to be in prison as white adult males. The reasons for this are deeply rooted in history, social structure, and social attitudes; but it also seems clear that the criminal justice systems of this country—federal, state, and local—make some contribution to this sad result. Are we really proposing the introduction of a punishment system that by its expansion of intermediate punishments will make this racial skewing worse? At first blush it would appear so.

Take two addict-criminals convicted of selling relatively small amounts of cocaine on a number of separate occasions. Each has once before been convicted of illegal possession of marijuana. Each is aged 20. Criminal A is in college, the son of a loving and supportive middle-class family, living in a district where space is available in drug treatment programs. Criminal B has never met his putative father, lives in a high-rise apartment in a slum area with his mother and his two much younger siblings, welfare being their major financial support. The waiting list at the available drug treatment center is long, the waiting time three months.

You know the pigmentation of the two hypothetical but far from unreal criminals.

Are we really suggesting that Criminal B serve a jail or prison term with the hope that thereafter he can be fitted into a drug treatment program, while Criminal A should pay a substantial fine, be under intensive probationary supervision with a condition of regular attendance at a drug treatment program where he is tested regularly to ensure that he is drug-free, and be subjected possibly to house arrest in the evenings and weekends—electronically monitored if that be necessary? This will, of course, be the likely result. Is it unprincipled? We think not.

The criminal justice system lacks both resources and capacity to take on the task of rectification of social inequalities of race or class. It will do well if it does not exacerbate them. To insist that Criminal A go to jail or prison because resources are lacking to deal sensibly with Criminal B is to pay excessive tribute to an illusory ideal of equality. That is not the way equality of opportunity and equality of punitive pain is to be achieved; it is to be achieved by efforts to provide within the criminal justice system for Criminal B what exists for Criminal A, and to intercede by means other than the criminal justice system to eradicate the inequalities that generate the present discrimination.

The comprehensive punishment system we propose will, we believe, in the longer run reduce the impact of race and class on sentencing practice. The more clearly the exchange rates between punishments and the purposes each is to serve can be articulated in advance, the more possible it will be to reduce race and class biases in the selection of sanctions. Strong racial and class prejudices, conscious and less perceived, already drive sentencing practice; the substitution of purposive principles framed independently of race and class but necessarily having race and class correlates will make matters better, not worse.

2 2

❂

Further Exploration of the Flight from Discretion

The Role of Risk/Need Instruments in Probation Supervision Decisions

ANNE L. SCHNEIDER
LAURIE ERVIN
ZOANN SNYDER-JOY

Quantitative decision models increasingly are replacing human judgment and discretion in criminal justice decision making. Risk and need assessment instruments are increasingly used for decisions about the proper level of supervision in probation and parole situations. What are the implications of these tools for community corrections?

INTRODUCTION

Decision making in the public sector has undergone extraordinary changes in the past several decades. While most decisions in public agencies were once based on case-by-case analysis, judgment, intuition, experience, patronage, and other personal or political considerations, decisions in the modern

Source: Anne L. Schneider, Laurie Ervin, and Zoann Snyder-Joy, "Further Exploration of the Flight from Discretion: The Role of Risk/Need Instruments in Probation Supervision Decisions," *Journal of Criminal Justice,* Vol. 24, No. 2, 1996, pp. 109–121. Some references deleted.

personal or political considerations, decisions in the modern agency often are guided or determined by tests, quantitative criteria, or formal multivariate statistical decision models. Discretionary decision making has been widely criticized as being arbitrary, unfair, race or gender biased, too dependent on political power arrangements or social stereotyping, and ineffective in achieving policy goals. . . .

The attempt to control or eliminate discretion through reliance on quantitative decision models also has been criticized, however, and viewed as part of an inevitable and detrimental scientification of administration and politics.

Formal decision models have been used in criminal justice to guide decisions regarding diversion, sentencing, bail, parole, intensity of probation supervision, and treatment modality. . . . In spite of the enormous increase in reliance on scientific decision aids, very little is known about how these instruments have been implemented, how they are actually used, and how they are viewed by those whose discretion is being curtailed.

The research reported here is a study of how a statistical decision system (the Wisconsin risk/need instruments) was implemented in the Oklahoma Probation and Parole Department, as well as a study of probation officers' perceptions of this innovation. Data are drawn from historical records, in-depth interviews, and a structured survey of probation officers throughout the state.

THEORY AND APPROACH

Two perspectives have dominated the debate about the use of technical and scientific analysis in administrative decision making. Some view the primary problems in administration as human irrationality, politics, and organizational dynamics that preclude achievement of the instrumental goals of policy. From this perspective, quantitative risk/need instruments that have been adequately validated and properly implemented should produce an improvement in agency performance.

Critics, however, place more confidence in human judgment and discretion guided by professional norms. . . . Decentralized organizations, combined with grass roots learning models of organizational behavior are viewed as superior to rule oriented hierarchies and to scientific or pseudoscientific decision-making systems. The scientification of bureaucracy and government, from this point of view, is simply a mechanism for avoiding accountability and eschewing responsibility for policy failures. Better decisions would be made in more flexible, professionally oriented settings where service deliverers and clients come face to face and negotiate the conditions of their encounter. If quantitative decision models are used at all, they would be flexible guidelines easily overridden by the better judgment of the case worker. If the agency prohibited discretionary decisions, case workers would develop other schemes to bypass the advice from the instruments and rely on their own judgment.

Another much less explored possibility turns away from the issue of whether quantitative decision models or discretionary judgment is most effective, and examines the role and function of such decision models within the highly politicized, ideologically divisive, and critical environment within which probation officers carry out their responsibilities.

Anticipated Advantages of Formal Decision Models

Formal models usually are thought to be more consistent and uniform than discretionary decisions and are generally believed to predict risks and needs more accurately than human decision makers. . . . Risk/need estimates are expected to improve efficiency by enabling agencies to concentrate resources on those persons with the greatest probability of failure. . . . Proponents emphasize the fallibility of human judgment, abuse of discretion, and the politicization of administration, any of which could produce errors in decisions. . . . From the perspective of those who believe that increasing reliance on scientific analysis will improve policy and administration, the introduction of quantitative decision aids is a sign of progress and is expected to have the potential for increasing public safety by reducing recidivism rates, reducing costs, and increasing accountability.

Proponents of quantitative decision models draw heavily on the experimental research carried out on human decision making, which almost always finds that formal decision models outperform human judgment. . . . Dawes (1975), for example, has shown that formal models predicted graduate student success better than university professors, even when the models incorporated exactly the variables that the professors said were important, and when the models used the exact weights the professors claimed they were using.

A second reason for expecting formal decision models to outperform human judgment in criminal justice lies in the political and social nature of decision making within this policy context. Decisions by persons in public life have implications beyond those for which the decisions putatively are intended. When risky decisions are involved and outcomes are highly uncertain, it is reasonable to expect public officials to deviate from the presumably rational decision in the direction of increased protection against political or administrative criticism. Thus, probation officers may be inclined to overclassify cases and assess the risk at higher levels than is needed, thereby providing greater intensity of supervision, . . . higher costs, and less efficiency.

The Limitations of Formal Decision Models

A number of criticisms have been advanced about the widespread adoption of quantitative decision models. From a technical perspective, concern has been expressed when decision models have been adopted by jurisdictions without sufficient validation of their predictive validity, . . . or when they are used for purposes other than those for which they were developed.

The presumed effectiveness of these instruments in increasing uniformity, effectiveness, or efficiency may be undermined by implementation problems, including the reluctance of professionals to permit quantitative prediction systems to replace their professional judgments. Almost nothing is known about whether the formal decision models are as objective as they appear, as the initial assignment of points to each of the attributes on some of the instruments may involve a measure of subjectivity. It is possible that those who score the attributes used in the decision system are able to produce the classification they subjectively determined was most appropriate. Formal decision models have been suspected of introducing race, ethnicity, or gender bias into decision outcomes, much in the same manner as discretionary decision systems, due to the intercorrelation of certain risk and need variables with the personal characteristics of the individual. . . .

Critics of formal decision models defend discretionary decisions on the grounds that there is not a system of rules or scientific aids that can anticipate all of the possible contingencies and variances in human behavior that will actually be encountered. . . .These models also cannot adequately handle complex decision situations characterized by multiple definitions of "good decisions," particularly when these vary widely in their predictors (such as the different variables that might produce fairness v. recidivism). Reliance on a limited set of variables with questionable validity to predict only one of many different desirable outcomes may introduce errors in decisions for which no one can be held accountable.

Critics also note that the proliferation of quantitative decision aids within criminal justice is an indication of the increasing scientification of administration that has occurred in virtually all areas of administration within the United States. Such trends are seen as inevitable in advanced, modern societies, but many scholars view them with alarm. Haberman (1975), for example, argues that governments faced with declining performance and increasing expectations from citizens will seek to define most problems as technical ones, and will seek to convince the public that they are searching for technically correct solutions rather than acknowledging the structural basis of the problems. Stone (1993) argues that "clinical reason" eliminates discourse and creates new elites thereby thwarting democratic participatory decisions. Thus, governments increasingly are not held accountable for policy failures, and the public is increasingly excluded from meaningful discourse about public issues.

Purpose of the Study

The purpose of this study is to fill some of the gaps in the literature regarding the implementation of risk/need instruments and perceptions about the value of such instruments, using data from probation and parole officers in the Oklahoma Department of Corrections (DOC). The first part of the study traces the evolution of parole and probation decision making regarding the intensity of supervision through six distinctive decision-making models over a fifteen-year time period. This historical analysis provides insight on how decisions about the appropriate level of supervision actually were made as well as the rationales for changes as they occurred. The specific characteristics of the Wisconsin risk/need instruments changed in intriguing ways during this time period, and there was considerable experimentation with different approaches, including experimentation with the Iowa risk/need instruments.

The second part of the study taps the attitudes, perceptions, and expectations about the risk/need instruments held by those persons whose discretion was being limited through their use. Probation and parole officers were asked about the usefulness of the instruments to probation/parole officers, to supervisors, to the system, and whether they believed the instruments actually were capable of making better decisions than they would have made relying on their discretion. They were asked why they used them at all and whether or how they manipulated them. The underlying themes for this part of the study were drawn from ideas about the role of expertise in administration and were intended to examine whether case workers will "buy into" the notion of scientific rationality as the superior decision model or whether they will resist the imposition of scientific rationality and find ways to avoid the loss of their professional judgment. The study tapped into the various ways that administrative systems may induce people to believe in scientific rationality, such as an ideology that scientific instruments can make better decisions and are more professional, or more specific tools, such as explicit positive and negative incentives for complying with the levels of supervision dictated by the instruments.

The third part of the study turns to a correlation analysis to assess the nature of relationships between confidence in the value of risk/need instruments and beliefs about one's own effectiveness and job satisfaction. Predictors of higher and lower levels of confidence in the risk/need instruments also were examined.

Methodology and Data

Data for the study were drawn from several sources. Much of the information for the fifteen-year history was drawn from a compilation of articles and memoranda edited by Robin Berry (1988) of the Department of Corrections. This information was supplemented with in-depth interviews and a focus group discussion involving a nonrandom sample of six persons from the Oklahoma Department of Corrections. The group included two senior probation officers who worked in the central office, a district supervisor with fifteen years of experience as a probation officer, a case supervisor with twelve years as a probation officer, a team supervisor with ten years of experience, and one additional probation officer. After the focus group discussion was complete, these persons were interviewed individually. The in-depth interviews and focus group discussion were used to gather qualitative information, identify issues regarding the risk/need instrument, obtain insights that would help interpret the survey results, and to sensitize the researchers to the nuances of language and meanings of the probation and parole officers who would be involved in the survey. After the qualitative information had been obtained, a questionnaire was constructed and sent to all probation and parole officers in the state (N = 296), with 179 (60 percent) responding. A letter from the Department of Corrections was sent in advance explaining the study and ensuring employees that they could participate in the study anonymously. The surveys were returned directly to the researchers, and telephone follow-ups were used to encourage additional participation. The questionnaires were used for the quantitative parts of the study.

The average age of the respondents was thirty-five years, the average length of employment was 5.5 years. Most of the respondents were men (63 percent), most were Caucasian (83 percent), and all had at least a bachelor's degree.

HISTORICAL CONTEXT

During the fifteen-year time period covered by the study, Oklahoma used six different decision-making systems for determining the level of supervision that should be given to persons serving sentences of probation or parole under the supervision of the State Department of Corrections (DOC) (Berry, 1988).

The Committee System

Before 1976, there was no formal assessment of risks or needs and no formal assignment of cases to levels of supervision intensity. The system was based on judgment and discretion, with both in the hands of the probation and parole officers and their supervisors. The gradual replacement of individual judgment with more structured decisions began in 1976 when decision making shifted to a three-person committee of probation and parole officers along with their supervisors. These individuals assessed the risks and needs of each person referred to probation and parole and assigned them to one of three different levels of supervision intensity: Level I (maximum supervision), Level II (moderate), or Level III (minimum supervision). These classification decisions were based on subjective assessments without benefit of formal decision aids (Collins, 1988). Two other levels of supervision (Levels IV and V) were specified, but both dealt with persons who could not be kept under direct supervision, such as mental commitments or absconders.

As was to be true until 1984, the contrast in required supervision intensity was surprisingly small. Levels I and II both required one contact per month, with the contact being out-of-the-office for Level I and in-office for Level II. Level III required one contact every ninety days (Berry, 1988). Other contacts were encouraged. Interviews with the six respondents from the nonrandom sample indicated there may not have been much actual difference in the amount of supervision probation officers provided to clients, or there may have been substantial differentiation that was not related to the point system.

Adoption of the Wisconsin Instruments

The committee system was abandoned in 1981, reportedly on the grounds that it was arbitrary and inconsistent (Berry, 1988), and the Wisconsin Client Classification instruments were adopted to replace the committee decision systems. The major impetus for shifting to a structured decision system was to gain accreditation from the American Correctional Association (ACA). Collins (1988) reported that the instrument adopted was the original Wisconsin instrument, although the scoring system used in it differs form the Wisconsin instruments studied by Wright, Clear, and Dickson (1984). There was no validation of the instrument in Oklahoma or on cases drawn from Oklahoma files.

Berry's (1988) historical account says that there were three major goals proposed for the shift to an objective client classification system: (a) to maintain the current level of client misbehavior (arrests, new convictions, technical violations); (b) to improve resource utilization; and (c) to minimize client involvement in formal supervision and minimize client contact with officers. The official statement of purpose was:

> A sound classification system is the most effective means to accomplish effective utilization of resources in probation and parole supervision efforts. The classification system must ensure service delivery in accordance with the needs of the client and safety of the community. The goal of our classification system is having clients progress to the point that services are no longer needed and our efforts may be redirected to those in need. (Berry, 1988)

The Assessment of Client Risk used ten variables, seven of which were verifiable items in the file: number of address changes, employment, age at first conviction, prior periods of supervision, prior revocations, prior felony convictions, and prior convictions for any offense. Three subjective factors were scored by the officials: alcohol use, drug use, and attitude. Alcohol and drug use were assessed in terms of no problem, moderate problem, or serious problem. Interestingly, serious alcohol problems were scored more heavily (4) than serious drug problems (2). Attitudes were scored from 0 to 5, using response categories of whether the person was "motivated to change" or "rationalizes behavior; negative, not motivated to change." The maximum score ws unlimited, as the instrument counted all prior convictions toward the total. In fact, prior convictions could entirely dominate the scoring on this instrument. The second instrument, Assessment of Client Needs, was considerably more subjective and incorporated variables ranging from employment and financial management to sexual behavior.

Pilot Test of the Wisconsin System

A pilot test of Oklahoma's version of the Wisconsin instruments was conducted in 1981 by the Department of Corrections (Collins, 1988), in which two-thirds of the probation officers in each of the seven districts in the state were randomly selected to begin using the new risk classification instrument. Others continued with the committee approach. Officers participating in the experiment reclassified all clients on their case load.

Reanalysis of the 1,600 cases (see Table 1) showed a substantial difference in the proportion classified at each level. The Wisconsin classification system assessed only 3.9 percent of the cases as needing Level I supervision (the maximum level), compared with 11.3 percent of the cases assessed by the committee. The contrast at Level III is even more stark, as 75 percent of the cases were classified as Level III by the Wisconsin system, compared with 28 percent by the committee system. This finding is not entirely unexpected, given the contention that probation officers will overclassify as a strategy to protect them from political or agency criticism if a person on their case load reoffends. It is a completely different result than that found by Sigler and Williams (1994) whose study compared officers' classifications with those of four different screening instruments. In that study, the probation officer classifications put far fewer people into the maximum category (6 percent) than three of the instruments, which ranged

Table 1 Classification Decisions: Comparison of Committee Decisions and Formal Decision Model in Oklahoma

Classification Decisions	Supervision		
	Level I (Maximum) %	Level II (Moderate) %	Level III (Minimum) %
Committee	11	60	28
Wisconsin model	4	21	75

Note: Data are recalculations from Collins (1988: 11).

from 33 to 38 percent in the maximum category. The difference between the findings could reflect different political or agency contexts. As will be explained more fully below, the Oklahoma system was expected to be used to help determine statewide allocation of resources, so that allocations would not be based solely on the number of persons on probation, but also on the intensity of supervision that would be needed. This could provide an agency incentive to overclassify as a means of enhancing the agency budget.

Experimentation with the Iowa Instruments

In 1985, three districts were asked to test the Iowa risk instrument. The Iowa instrument initially was developed for parole release decisions. It did not contain a need assessment (although Oklahoma incorporated a need instrument in its implementation), and it relied almost exclusively on information about the number and type of prior offenses. In comparison with the Wisconsin instruments, the Iowa protocol was more sophisticated, complex, and time consuming to complete. It also required considerably more data and training. Respondents in the study reported that the instrument was less intuitively understandable, as well, because it is almost impossible to determine from a casual inspection how the various attributes were being weighted and combined to produce the final level of risk.

The Iowa instrument was used for about eighteen months and then dropped due to general dissatisfaction. Department of Corrections officials enumerated some of the problems: it required data that often were available, it was being used in a manner different than that for which it was developed, staff did not trust the results, and it was time consuming and confusing to complete.

Changes in the Wisconsin System

The Wisconsin system was changed repeatedly during its use in Oklahoma. In 1984, there was an expansion in the number of levels from three to five, a change in the points assigned to the specific categories within the reassessment risk/need instruments, and an increase in the contrast among levels in the intensity of supervision. Maximum supervision cases (Level I) were changed to require two face-to-face contacts per month; Level II cases required one contact per month, and Level III cases were to have one contact every three months. Level IV, a new classification, was for persons assessed as low risk and low need who had been under supervision for at least six months. Contacts were to occur only as needed, and the client was expected only to submit a written monthly report. Level V was for clients on early termination, and the level of supervision was not specified.

More changes were made in the Wisconsin instrument in 1987: changes in the classification categories, changes in the intensity of supervision, changes in the items on the risk/need instruments, and changes in the points. Three face-to-face contacts were now required for the Level I cases, two for the Level II, one for the Level III, one per every three months for Level IV cases, and only a mail in report for persons classified as Level V.

Generally, the Oklahoma adaptation of the Wisconsin model can be characterized as a relatively flexible, somewhat judgmental, constantly changing yet highly structured decision system. In the early years, it prescribed very little differences in the level of supervision, but permitted probation officers to use heavier supervision for whichever cases they believed needed it. Over time, considerably greater differentiation was incorporated into the system, so that offenders in the maximum supervision category (Level I) received far more intensive supervision than those in the minimum category (Level V), and there was considerably less discretion available to officers to determine on the basis of their own judgment which offenders should receive heavier supervision.

ATTITUDES ABOUT THE RISK/NEED INSTRUMENTS

Qualitative Information

The qualitative data obtained from the six DOC officials through in-depth interviews and the focus group indicated considerable ambivalence about the purposes of the instruments and whether they were being used effectively. The respondents said the risk/need instruments were supposed to help probation officers understand the factors that make a person more likely to commit crimes, and to ensure that the officers carefully reviewed the person's file to determine their scores on these factors. As one person pointed out, the forms made it easy for a supervisor to determine whether the probation officer had studied the file.

The six officials agreed that the instruments were supposed to be used to ensure uniformity in allocating resources. Probation officers would know how much time they needed to spend on a case; supervisors would know how to allocate cases across officers to ensure equitable case loads; and state level officials would have a better idea how state-wide resource allocations should be distributed to take into account not only the number of persons on probation, but also the intensity of supervision needed. The officials, however, did not believe that these goals were being met because there were too many overrides and too much discretion in the way the instruments were being scored. One person noted:

> It [the scoring] is not uniform among districts. Some have more people in lower classifications; some in higher. This is a sign that the instrument has been manipulated. That is one of the dangers. Some districts override more than others, perhaps because they are more law-enforcement oriented. (Hatley, 1989)

Another doubted that probation officers actually were paying attention to the level of supervision that the instrument said should be used:

> As for classifying people of different levels of supervision, it is doing that; but I don't think it is meeting any of the purposes I've described. Most officers (I may be over generalizing) prefer the client to report in a routine way, and gives the officer contact with clients each month, even if they are on Level III or Level IV. It is easier for the officer to keep track of them if they report in every month. On 90 day supervision, for example, you lose track of them and then have to track them down. The instrument was designed to improve allocation of resources, but I don't think it is accomplishing those ends. (Hatley, 1989)

The persons in the focus group talked about the role of the instrument in holding probation officers accountable and ensuring that they were doing their job. One pointed out that "the instrument is the only measurement tool we have to judge an officer's performance. It is a quantitative measurement of how to maintain a case load. One of the effects is that the emphasis has shifted to quantity rather than quality time. Rather than concentrating on how many you need to see, you should be making a difference in their lives. Because of the instrument, more emphasis is placed on number of visits rather than quality of visits" (Hatley, 1989).

The instrument provided a specific record of how many contacts were to occur, and whether they were to occur in the probation officer's office or in the field. These were monitored monthly for compliance by the probation officer. Under a more discretionary system, there was no way to determine how often a contact was supposed to be made, as this was a discretionary decision by the officer; therefore, there was no way to determine whether the officer was meeting with the client as often as needed.

Assessments were not totally negative, however. When asked what would happen if the instruments were suddenly abandoned, one person said:

> If your clients are obnoxious, as most of the high risk clients are, you don't want to see them as often. But if you have the instrument reminding you that you have to see them, then you'll do it more often than you would otherwise be inclined to. If I didn't have the instrument, and a full case load, then those are the people I would not see. (Hatley, 1989)

Another said that abandoning the instruments would result in more clients being seen at the higher and medium levels, especially in the high crime areas of the state:

In our district we see the clients more often to hold them more account-able. It is better to err by giving too much supervision than to give too little and get burned by it later. This protects the officer and community. We have to oversupervise in this district. (Hatley, 1989)

Another said:

I think we need some sort of structure. I am one of the few people left who used the unstructured approach. Judgment, however, was too subjec-tive, appearances are a poor judge. Some of the areas on the instrument are good predictors. You need to combine the instrument with discretion. (Hatley, 1989)

The discussion of overrides indicated that most were upward—moving an offender into a higher level of supervision. The strategy for getting an offender into a less intensive supervision did not rely on overrides but on ignoring prob-lems on the need instrument, or underestimating risk in some of the judg-mental categories, so that the number of points would be low enough to ensure a lower classification. According to one of the probation officers, this was a way to organize a case load and ensure that you did not have too many high risk cases:

Officers can manipulate the system by scoring the instrument however they want to. There are instructions about scoring, but I'm not sure if there is attention paid here or anywhere else as far as whether the forms are correct. (Hatley, 1989)

One of the reasons there were not more overrides is that these were a hassle:

They [overrides] are not common, really, because they are a hassle. You have to talk to your supervisor. You never override to a lower level, al-ways to a higher. Frequently an officer may feel a client's risk should be overridden but to avoid the hassle will see the client more often and leave the instrument showing a lower risk assignment. Overrides increase super-vision. (Hatley, 1989)

The quantitative system was implemented without any officer input, as a strategy to help ensure ACA accreditation. Training was limited:

There really wasn't any officer input at all. Some people went out and got trained; then came back and trained us. At that time, case loads were high. We didn't have much money or resources, so they pushed it as a way for the officer to reduce the case load. The instrument was supposed to make case load management easier. A lot of officers at that time re-sented the instrument for attempting to quantify human behavior. The of-ficers felt they had a good feel for which clients were going to be bad and good. Some officers, early on, figured out that if they could get their clients to the lowest possible assessment, [requiring contact only every three months], and then see them once per month, they'd be heroes for seeing their clients more often than they were required to. (Hatley, 1989)

The Survey of Probation Officers

Attitudes toward the instruments from probation officers around the state were generally negative or neutral (Table 2). Slightly more than one-third (37 percent) believed that the risk/need instruments were appropriate for making decisions about the level of supervision, and less than one-half (47 percent) believed they were a helpful tool. Strong majorities of 76 percent and 61 percent believed the officers should have more discretion in selecting the level of supervision and that the officer's knowledge is better than the instruments.

On the various ways that the instruments were supposed to be useful, only one-fourth to one-third generally occurred with their presumed value. Twenty-six percent said the instruments were useful in identifying high risk offenders; 37 percent said they were useful in providing initial insight into the offender or in helping the officers allocate their time among different cases. More than one-half agreed that the instruments help ensure that high risk cases get more intensive supervision. Generally, less than one-half of the respondents believed that the instruments were useful in any of the specific tasks of the probation officer.

The instruments were not judged much better in terms of their usefulness to supervisors or to the system. More than one-half said that they were useful in providing uniformity of supervision state-wide, but most disagreed with assertions that the instruments helped supervisors evaluate probation officers, helped supervisors allocate case loads, and they emphatically rejected the notion that the instruments reduced the costs of probation and parole.

Less than a majority believed the instruments were useful in justifying the supervision level to the public or legislature, but they strongly rejected the notion that reliance on quantitative decision aids protected the employee from blame if an offender committed another offense while on supervision.

The survey posed questions regarding four different reasons for why the officers completed the instruments and used them in their decision making: (a) trust in expertise (i.e., they believe the instruments are scientific and are willing to yield their subjective judgment to it); (b) professionalism (i.e., professional norms work in favor of relying on the instruments); (c) positive incentives; and (d) expectations of supervisors within the hierarchical system of control, including negative evaluations.

Respondents strongly rejected the notion that the instruments reflect expertise. When asked whether the officer's knowledge is more accurate than the instrument, only 15 percent disagreed. Only 13 percent agreed with the statement that experienced officers find the instruments make better decisions than they would. Professionalism also was not viewed as the reason for using them, as only 20 percent agreed with the statement that they would use the instruments even if they were not required because it is the professional thing to do. About one-third said that positive rewards were provided for properly completing the instruments; while 83 percent said that negative evaluations were given for failure to complete the instruments positively and 78 percent said that supervisors look more favorably on those who properly complete the instruments.

Table 2 Perceptions of the Risk/Need Instruments

Item	Agree %	Neutral %	Disagree %
Are the risk/need instruments useful?			
The risk/need instruments are appropriate for making decisions about the level of supervision	37	31	33
The instruments are a helpful tool for the probation officer	47	26	28
Officers should have more discretion in selecting the level of supervision	76	18	6
The officer's knowledge is more accurate than the instrument	61	24	15
Instruments are useful to probation officers			
In identifying high risk offenders	26	29	45
In providing initial insight into the offender	37	31	31
In helping officer manage case load (i.e., allocate their time)	37	29	33
In making sure high risk cases get intensive supervision	53	23	24
In assisting the offender to get assistance needed for success	24	31	45
Instruments are useful to supervisors and the system			
In providing uniformity of supervision state wide	57	23	20
In helping supervisors evaluate probation officers	21	22	48
In reducing costs of probation and parole	10	27	63
The instruments are useful in protecting the employee from blame	19	18	63
They are useful in justifying the supervision level to the public or legislature	49	27	24
Reasons for using the risk/need instruments			
Research has shown these instruments to be effective	24	44	32
The instruments are more accurate than a subjective evaluation of an offender	27	31	42
The officer's knowledge is more accurate than the instrument	13	26	53
Experienced officers find it makes better decisions than they would	13	29	53
Using the instruments is the professional thing to do	20	26	42
Positive rewards are provided for properly completing the instruments	31	26	42
Negative evaluations are given for failure to properly complete the instruments	83	12	4
Supervisors look more favorably on those who properly complete the instruments	78	15	6
The system would be better off without the risk/need instruments	23	25	52

Several questions probed for information about whether the officers manipulated the point system and the ways in which this occurred (Table 3). One type of manipulation reported during the open-ended interviews was to ignore serious needs of the offender and not record his or her problems accurately in order to obtain a lower supervision level and lessen work load. Only 12 percent said that this happens often or always, but 42 percent said it happens sometimes (Table 3). The qualitative portion of the study also revealed the contention that officers score the instruments incorrectly in order to manage their case load within the time frame they have available—that is, they underestimate the level of supervision needed to ensure that they can actually provide the level called for in their case load. Only 22 percent said this happens often or always, and 36 percent said it happens sometimes. About the same results were obtained from a question about whether officers scored the instruments incorrectly to justify the level of supervision they believed was appropriate. Another type of manipulation reported during the qualitative phase was to ignore the classification level when it suggested a less intensive level of supervision and simply see the offender more often, rather than seek an override from the supervisor. This manipulation was noted as a way to let the officer exercise independent judgment without calling this to the attention of the supervisor. Fourteen percent said that this happens often or always, and 32 percent said it happens sometimes.

Two questions probed the extent of media and political influence. Fifty-three percent of the respondents indicated that media and public opinion seldom influenced the level of supervision, compared with 32 percent who said it happened sometimes and 14 percent who said it often or always influenced the level of supervision. The political agenda of the sheriff or district attorney was rejected as a factor influencing their decisions in scoring or using the instrument by 75 percent of the respondents, although 20 percent said it influenced them sometimes and 5 percent said it often or always was a factor in determining the levels assigned to probationers.

One of the paradoxes of the study is that, in spite of the generally negative views of the instruments, when asked whether the system would be better off without the risk/need instruments, only 23 percent agreed, 25 percent were neutral, and 52 percent disagreed.

Correlates of Belief in the Usefulness of the Instruments

The final part of the analysis probed for possible causes and consequences of perceptions that the risk/need instruments were useful. For this analysis, a thirteen-item scale of usefulness was constructed from the questions on the instrument. The specific items include all of those shown in the usefulness section of Table 2, except for the item on whether the instruments were useful in justifying the level of supervision to the public and legislature, which had a negative correlation with several of the other items. Cronbach's alpha was .93 for the thirteen-item usefulness scale.

It was expected that some correlation would be found between the background characteristics of the respondents and confidence in the instrument, particularly the contention that younger and less experienced officers would find the instruments more useful; however, there were no relationships of this type. The level of education, gender, age, and years of experience did not correlate with positive attitudes about the instruments. It also was expected that persons who had received more training would find them more useful, but there were

Table 3 Extent of Manipulation and Outside Influence

	Never/Seldom %	Sometimes %	Often/Always %
Problems are ignored and not recorded properly to lessen work load	46	42	12
Officers score the instruments incorrectly to manage their case loads	41	36	22
When officers believe an override is needed, they just see the client more often rather than getting an override	44	32	14
Do media and public opinions influence level of supervision?	53	32	14
Does the political agenda of the district attorney or sheriff influence the level assignments?	75	20	5

no relationships here, either. Small but statistically significant correlations were found for three variables, however. These included those who believed that their level of training was adequate ($r = .15$, $s = .04$), those who were familiar with research on risk/need instruments ($r = .12$, $s = .10$), and those who were aware of local research that had been done to validate the instruments ($r = .18$, $s = .01$).

Two additional scales were developed to measure the respondents' perceptions of how effective they were in their jobs and their satisfaction with the job. The effectiveness scale was constructed from three five-point agree/disagree questions regarding the extent to which the probation officer believed he or she was: (a) effective in rehabilitating offenders, (b) effective in preventing recidivism, and (c) effective in contributing to a reduction in the crime rate. Cronbach's alpha was .78. The job satisfaction scale was constructed from nine agree/disagree items (using a five-point scale) pertaining to whether they like their duties, are satisfied with their job assignment, would not be interested in another job, enjoy their work, like their job better than the average person, are enthusiastic about their job, have a strong sense of accomplishment, have an opportunity to use their skills and abilities, and find the work interesting and challenging. Cronbach's alpha for this scale was .91. A correlation was not observed between the perceptions of the instrument's usefulness and the nine-point scale of job satisfaction.

There was a strong relationship between beliefs that the risk/need instruments were useful and the probation officers' perceptions of effectiveness ($r = .42$, $s = .001$). This study's interpretation of this finding is that the risk/need instruments serve a particular purpose—perhaps not the one intended, but, instead, one that enables probation officers to believe in the risk/need instruments as the product of a rational, scientific society that will enable them to be effective in their work. The risk/need instruments rationalize the work and grant renewed confidence that they can make a difference in the lives of persons who have violated the law.

CONCLUSIONS

The optimistic vision of increased rationality, professionalism, and efficiency in probation supervision decisions that would accompany the introduction of quantitative risk/need instruments was not borne out in the Oklahoma experiment. The paradox, however, was that even though most persons involved in this study recognized the limitations of the instruments and acknowledged that they were not being used as intended and were not having the effects that were promised, they were reluctant to abandon them. In practice, the use of the risk/need instruments mirrored the findings reported by Simon (1993:4) that "the risks and needs score was a constructive compromise that lent the aura of statistical prediction to the process without really taking away any power from the local case-by-case system or even accurately mirroring past experience."

More than just a constructive compromise, however, the findings from this study suggest that the risk/need instruments lend perceptual rationality and legitimation to the work carried out by probation officers. These instruments fit the model of a scientific profession and the style of decision making that modern correctional systems should adopt. Persons who believed in the instruments—in their logic, rationality, consistancy with values—believed they were personally more effective in rehabilitating offenders, reducing recidivism, and reducing the crime rate.

REFERENCES

Berry R., ed. (1988). *Department of Corrections Division of Probation and Parole, assessment history since 1976.* Oklahoma City, OK: Oklahoma Department of Corrections.

Collins, D. (1988). Analysis of the Wisconsin assessment of client risk as implemented in Oklahoma. In *Department of Corrections Division of Probation and Parole, assessment history since 1976,* ed. R. Berry. Oklahoma City, OK: Oklahoma Department of Corrections.

Dawes, R. (1975). Case by case vs. rule-generated procedures for the allocation of scarce resources. In *Human judgement and decision processes in applied settings,* eds. M. Kaplan and S. Schwartz. New York: Academic Press.

Habermas, J. (1975). *Legitimation crisis.* Translated by T. McCarthy, Boston: Beacon Press.

Hatley, E. (1989). Interviews with Oklahoma Correctional Personnel, Oklahoma City, Oklahoma.

Sigler, R., and Williams, J. J. (1994). A study of the outcomes of probation officers and risk-screening instruments classifications. *Journal of Criminal Justice* 22:495–502.

Simon, J. (1993). *Poor discipline.* Chicago: University of Chicago Press.

Stone, D. (1993). Clinical authority in the construction of citizenship. In *Public policy and democracy,* eds. H. Ingram and S. R. Smith, Washington, DC: Brookings.

Wright, K., Clear, T., and Dickson, P. (1984). Universal applicability of probation risk-assessment instruments: A critique. *Criminology* 22:113–34.

2 3

✪

The Society of Captives

The Defects of Total Power

GRESHAM M. SYKES

*In theory, prisons are organized in an authoritarian manner. In such a "society of captives,"
one might assume that guards have only to give orders and inmates will follow them. Because
the guards have a monopoly on the legal means of enforcing rules, many people believe that
there should be no question about how the prison is run. In reality, however, the relationship
between the guards and the prisoners is based on a more fragile foundation. As this article
shows, there are limitations on the ability of correctional officers to use total power.*

"For the needs of mass administration today," said Max Weber, "bureaucratic administration is completely indispensable. The choice is between bureaucracy and dilettantism in the field of administration."[1]
To the officials of the New Jersey State Prison the choice is clear, as it is clear to
the custodians of all maximum security prisons in the United States today. They
are organized into a bureaucratic administrative staff—characterized by limited
and specific rules, well-defined areas of competence and responsibility, impersonal
standards of performance and promotion, and so on—which is similar in many respects to that of any modern, large-scale enterprise; and it is this staff which must
see to the effective execution of the prison's routine procedures.

Source: Selection from Gresham M. Sykes, *The Society of Captives: A Study of a Maximum
Security Prison* (copyright © 1958 by Princeton University Press: Princeton Paperback,
1971), pp. 40–first 2 paragraphs p. 53. Reprinted by permission of Princeton University
Press. Portions of this article concerning the corruption of the guards' authority are to
be found in Gresham M. Sykes, *Crime and Society* (New York: Random House, 1956).
Reprinted by permission of Random House, Inc.

Of the approximately 300 employees of the New Jersey State Prison, more than two-thirds are directly concerned with the supervision and control of the inmate population. These form the so-called custodian force which is broken into three eight-hour shifts, each shift being arranged in a typical pyramid of authority. The day shift, however—on duty from 6:20 A.M. to 2:20 P.M.—is by far the largest. As in many organizations, the rhythm of life in the prison quickens with daybreak and trails off in the afternoon, and the period of greatest activity requires the largest number of administrative personnel.

In the bottom ranks are the wing guards, the tower guards, the guards assigned to the shops, and those with a miscellany of duties such as the guardianship of the receiving gate or the garage. Immediately above these men are a number of sergeants and lieutenants, and these in turn are responsible to the warden and his assistants.

The most striking fact about this bureaucracy of custodians is its unparalleled position of power—in formal terms, at least—vis-à-vis the body of men which it rules and from which it is supposed to extract compliance. The officials, after all, possess a monopoly on the legitimate means of coercion (or, as one prisoner has phrased it succinctly, "They have the guns and we don't"); and the officials can call on the armed might of the police and the National Guard in case of an overwhelming emergency. The twenty-four-hour surveillance of the custodians represents the ultimate watchfulness, and presumably noncompliance on the part of the inmates need not go long unchecked. The rulers of this society of captives nominally hold in their hands the sole right of granting rewards and inflicting punishments and it would seem that no prisoner could afford to ignore their demands for conformity. Centers of opposition in the inmate population—in the form of men recognized as leaders by fellow prisoners—can be neutralized through the use of solitary confinement or exile to other state institutions. The custodians have the right not only to issue and administer the orders and regulations which are to guide the life of the prisoner, but also the right to detail, try, and punish any individual accused of disobedience—a merging of legislative, executive, and judicial functions which has long been regarded as the earmark of complete domination. The officials of the prison, in short, appear to be the possessors of almost infinite power within their realm; and, at least on the surface, the bureaucratic staff should experience no great difficulty in converting their rules and regulations—their blueprint for behavior—into a reality.

It is true, of course, that the power position of the custodial bureaucracy is not truly infinite. The objectives which the officials pursue are not completely of their own choosing and the means which they can use to achieve their objectives are far from limitless. The custodians are not total despots, able to exercise power at whim, and thus they lack the essential mark of infinite power, the unchallenged right of being capricious in their rule. It is this last which distinguishes terror from government, infinite power from almost infinite power, and the distinction is an important one. Neither by right nor by intention are the officials of the New Jersey State Prison free from a system of norms and laws which curb their actions. But within these limitations the bureaucracy of the prison is organized around a grant of power which is without an equal in American society; and if the rulers of any social system could secure compliance with their rules and regulations—however sullen or unwilling—it might be expected that the officials of the maximum security prison would be able to do so.

When we examine the New Jersey State Prison, however, we find that this expectation is not borne out in actuality. Indeed, the glaring conclusion is that despite the guns and the surveillance, the searches and the precautions of the custodians, the actual behavior of the inmate population differs markedly from that which is called for by official commands and decrees. Violence, fraud, theft, aberrant sexual behavior—all are commonplace occurrences in the daily round of institutional existence in spite of the fact that the maximum security prison is conceived of by society as the ultimate weapon for the control of the criminal and his deviant actions. Far from being omnipotent rulers who have crushed all signs of rebellion against their regime, the custodians are engaged in a continuous struggle to maintain order—and it is a struggle in which the custodians frequently fail. Offenses committed by one inmate against another occur often, as do offenses committed by inmates against the officials and their rules. And the number of undetected offenses is, by universal agreement of both officials and inmates, far larger than the number of offenses which are discovered.

Some hint of the custodial bureaucracy's skirmishes with the population of prisoners is provided by the records of the disciplinary court which has the task of adjudicating charges brought by guards against their captives for offenses taking place within the walls. The following is a typical listing for a one-week period:

Charge	Disposition
1. Insolence and swearing while being interrogated	1. Continue in segregation
2. Threatening an inmate	2. Drop from job
3. Attempting to smuggle roll of tape into institution	3. 1 day in segregation with restricted diet
4. Possession of contraband	4. 30 days loss of privileges
5. Possession of pair of dice	5. 2 days in segregation with restricted diet
6. Insolence	6. Reprimand
7. Out of place	7. Drop from job. Refer to classification committee for reclassification
8. Possession of homemade knife, metal, and emery paper	8. 5 days in segregation with restricted diet
9. Suspicion of gambling or receiving bets	9. Drop from job and change Wing assignment
10. Out of place	10. 15 days loss of privileges
11. Possession of contraband	11. Reprimand
12. Creating disturbance in Wing	12. Continue in segregation
13. Swearing at an officer	13. Reprimand

14. Out of place	14. 15 days loss of privileges
15. Out of place	15. 15 days loss of privileges

Even more revealing, however, than this brief and somewhat enigmatic record are the so-called charge slips in which the guard is supposed to write out the derelictions of the prisoner in some detail. In the New Jersey State Prison, charge slips form an administrative residue of past conflicts between captors and captives and the following accounts are a fair sample:

This inmate threatened an officer's life. When I informed this inmate he was to stay in to see the Chief Deputy on his charge he told me if he did not go to the yard I would get a shiv in my back.
Signed: Officer A _____

Inmate X cursing an officer. In mess hall inmate refused to put excess bread back on tray. Then he threw the tray on the floor. In the Center, inmate cursed both Officer Y and myself.   Signed: Officer B _____

This inmate has been condemning everyone about him for going to work. The Center gave orders for him to go to work this A.M. which he refused to do. While searching his cell I found drawings of picks and locks.   Signed: Officer C _____

Fighting. As this inmate came to 1 Wing entrance to go to yard this A.M. he struck inmate G in the face.   Signed: Officer D _____

Having fermented beverage in his cell. Found while inmate was in yard.
Signed: Officer E _____

Attempting to instigate wing disturbance. When I asked him why he discarded [sic] my order to quiet down he said he was going to talk any time he wanted to and _____ me and do whatever I wanted in regards to it.   Signed: Officer F _____

Possession of home-made shiv sharpened to razor edge on his person and possession of 2 more shivs in cell. When inmate was sent to 4 Wing officer H found 3″ steel blade in pocket. I ordered Officer M to search his cell and he found 2 more shivs in process of being sharpened.
Signed: Officer G _____

Insolence. Inmate objected to my looking at papers he was carrying in pockets while going to the yard. He snatched them violently from my hand and gave me some very abusive talk. This man told me to _____ myself, and raised his hands as if to strike me. I grabbed him by the shirt and took him to the Center.   Signed: Officer H _____

Assault with knife on Inmate K. During Idle Men's mess at approximately 11:10 A.M. this man assaulted Inmate K with a home-made knife. Inmate K was receiving his rations at the counter when Inmate B rushed up to him and plunged a knife in his chest, arm, and back. I grappled with him and with the assistance of Officers S and V, we disarmed the inmate and took him to the Center. Inmate K was immediately taken to the hospital.   Signed: Officer I _____

Sodomy. Found inmate W in cell with no clothing on and inmate Z on top of him with no clothing. Inmate W told me he was going to lie like a _____ _____ _____ to get out of it.   Signed: Officer J _____

Attempted escape on night of 4/15/53. This inmate along with inmates L and T succeeded in getting on roof of 6 Wing and having home-made bombs in their possession.   Signed: Officer K _____

Fighting and possession of home-made shiv. Struck first blow to Inmate P. He struck blow with a roll of black rubber rolled up in his fist. He then produced a knife made out of wire tied to a toothbrush.
     Signed: Officer L _____

Refusing medication prescribed by Doctor W. Said "What do you think I am, a damn fool, taking that _____ for a headache, give it to the doctor."   Signed: Officer M _____

Inmate loitering on tier. There is a clique of several men who lock on top tier, who ignore rule of returning directly to their cells and attempt to hang out on the tier in a group.   Signed: Officer N _____

It is hardly surprising that when the guards at the New Jersey State Prison were asked what topics should be of first importance in a proposed in-service training program, 98 percent picked "what to do in event of trouble." The critical issue for the moment, however, is that the dominant position of the custodial staff is more fiction than reality, if we think of domination as something more than the outward forms and symbols of power. If power is viewed as the probability that orders and regulations will be obeyed by a given group of individuals, as Max Weber has suggested, the New Jersey State Prison is perhaps more notable for the doubtfulness of obedience than its certainty. The weekly records of the disciplinary court and charge slips provide an admittedly poor index of offenses or acts of noncompliance committed within the walls, for these form only a small, visible segment of an iceberg whose greatest bulk lies beneath the surface of official recognition. The public is periodically made aware of the officials' battle to enforce their regime within the prison, commonly in the form of allegations in the newspapers concerning homosexuality, illegal use of drugs, assaults, and so on. But the ebb and flow of public attention given to these matters does not match the constancy of these problems for the prison officials who are all too well aware that "incidents"—the very thing they try to minimize—are not isolated or rare events but are instead a commonplace. The number of "incidents" in the New Jersey State Prison is probably no greater than that to be found in most maximum security institutions in the United States and may, indeed, be smaller, although it is difficult to make comparisons. In any event, it seems clear that the custodians are bound to their captives in a relationship of conflict rather than compelled acquiescence, despite the custodians' theoretical supremacy, and we now need to see why this should be so.

In our examination of the forces which undermine the power position of the New Jersey State Prison's custodial bureaucracy, the most important fact is, perhaps, that the power of the custodians is not based on authority.

Now power based on authority is actually a complex social relationship in which an individual or a group of individuals is recognized as possessing a right to issue commands or regulations and those who receive these commands or regulations feel compelled to obey by a sense of duty. In its pure form, then, or as an ideal type, power based on authority has two essential elements: a rightful or legitimate effort to exercise control on the one hand and an inner, moral compulsion to obey, by those who are to be controlled, on the other. In reality, of course, the recognition of the legitimacy of efforts to exercise control may be qualified or partial and the sense of duty, as a motive for compliance, may be mixed with motives of fear or self-interest. But it is possible for theoretical purposes to think of power based on authority in its pure form and to use this as a baseline in describing the empirical case.

It is the second element of authority—the sense of duty as a motive for compliance—which supplies the secret strength of most social organizations. Orders and rules can be issued with the expectation that they will be obeyed without the necessity of demonstrating in each case that compliance will advance the subordinate's interests. Obedience or conformity springs from an internalized morality which transcends the personal feelings of the individual; the fact that an order or a rule is an order or a rule becomes the basis for modifying one's behavior, rather than a rational calculation of the advantages which might be gained.

In the prison, however, it is precisely this sense of duty which is lacking in the general inmate population. The regime of the custodians is expressed as a mass of commands and regulations passing down a hierarchy of power. In general, these efforts at control are regarded as legitimate by individuals in the hierarchy, and individuals tend to respond because they feel they "should," down to the level of the guard in the cell block, the industrial shop, or the recreation yard. But now these commands and regulations must jump a gap which separates the captors from the captives. And it is at this point that a sense of duty tends to disappear, and with it goes that easily won obedience which many organizations take for granted in the naïveté of their unrecognized strength. In the prison, power must be based on something other than internalized morality, and the custodians find themselves confronting men who must be forced, bribed, or cajoled into compliance. This is not to say that inmates feel that the efforts of prison officials to exercise control are wrongful or illegitimate; in general, prisoners do not feel that the prison officials have usurped positions of power which are not rightfully theirs, nor do prisoners feel that the orders and regulations which descend upon them from above represent an illegal extension of their rulers' grant of government. Rather, the noteworthy fact about the social system of the New Jersey State Prison is that the bond between recognition of the legitimacy of control and the sense of duty has been torn apart. In these terms the social system of the prison is very similar to a *Gebietsverband,* a territorial group living under a regime imposed by a ruling few. Like a province which has been conquered by force of arms, the community of prisoners has come to accept the validity of the regime constructed by their rulers but the subjugation is not complete. Whether he sees himself as caught by his own stupidity, the workings of chance, his inability to "fix" the case, or the superior skill of the police, the

criminal in prison seldom denies the legitimacy of confinement.[2] At the same
time, the recognition of the legitimacy of society's surrogates and their body of
rules is not accompanied by an internalized obligation to obey and the prisoner
thus accepts the fact of his captivity at one level and rejects it at another. If for
no other reason, then, the custodial institution is valuable for a theory of human
behavior because it makes us realize that men need not be motivated to conform
to a regime which they define as rightful. It is in this apparent contradiction that
we can see the first flaw in the custodial bureaucracy's assumed supremacy.

Since the officials of prison possess a monopoly on the means of coercion, as we
have pointed out earlier, it might be thought that the inmate population could
simply be forced into conformity and that the lack of an inner moral compulsion to obey on the part of the inmates could be ignored. Yet the combination
of a bureaucratic staff—that most modern, rational form of mobilizing effort to
exercise control—and the use of physical violence—that most ancient device to
channel man's conduct—must strike us as an anomaly and with good reason.
The use of force is actually grossly inefficient as a means for securing obedience,
particularly when those who are to be controlled are called on to perform a task
of any complexity. A blow with a club may check an immediate revolt, it is true,
but it cannot assure effective performance on a punch-press. A "come along," a
straitjacket, or a pair of handcuffs may serve to curb one rebellious prisoner in a
crisis, but they will be of little aid in moving more than 1,200 inmates through
the mess hall in a routine and orderly fashion. Furthermore, the custodians are
well aware that violence once unleashed is not easily brought to heel and it is
this awareness that lies behind the standing order that no guard should ever strike
an inmate with his hand—he should always use a nightstick. This rule is not an
open invitation to brutality but an attempt to set a high threshold on the use of
force in order to eliminate the casual cuffing which might explode into extensive and violent retaliation. Similarly, guards are under orders to throw their
nightsticks over the wall if they are on duty in the recreation yard when a riot
develops. A guard without weapons, it is argued, is safer than a guard who tries
to hold on to his symbol of office, for a mass of rebellious inmates may find a
single nightstick a goad rather than a restraint and the guard may find himself
beaten to death with his own means of compelling order.

In short, the ability of the officials to physically coerce their captives into the
paths of compliance is something of an illusion as far as the day-to-day activities
of the prison are concerned and may be of doubtful value in moments of crisis.
Intrinsically inefficient as a method of making men carry out a complex task, diminished in effectiveness by the realities of the guard–inmate ratio,[3] and always
accompanied by the danger of touching off further violence, the use of physical
force by the custodians has many limitations as a basis on which to found the
routine operation of the prison. Coercive tactics may have some utility in checking blatant disobedience—if only a few men disobey. But if the great mass of
criminals in prison are to be brought into the habit of conformity, it must be on
other grounds. Unable to count on a sense of duty to motivate their captives to
obey and unable to depend on the direct and immediate use of violence to

ensure a step-by-step submission to the rules, the custodians must fall back on a system of rewards and punishments.

Now if men are to be controlled by the use of rewards and punishments—by promises and threats—at least one point is patent: The rewards and punishments dangled in front of the individual must indeed be rewards and punishments from the point of view of the individual who is to be controlled. It is precisely on this point, however, that the custodians' system of rewards and punishments founders. In our discussion of the problems encountered in securing conscientious performance at work, we suggested that both the penalties and the incentives available to the officials were inadequate. This is also largely true, at a more general level, with regard to rewards and punishments for securing compliance with the wishes of the custodians in all areas of prison life.

In the first place, the punishments which the officials can inflict—for theft, assaults, escape attempts, gambling, insolence, homosexuality, and all the other deviations from the pattern of behavior called for by the regime of the custodians—do not represent a profound difference from the prisoners' usual status. It may be that when men are chronically deprived of liberty, material goods and services, recreational opportunities, and so on, the few pleasures that are granted take on a new importance and the threat of their withdrawal is a more powerful motive for conformity than those of us in the free community can realize. To be locked up in the solitary-confinement wing, that prison within a prison; to move from the monotonous, often badly prepared meals in the mess hall to a diet of bread and water; to be dropped from a dull, unsatisfying job and forced to remain in idleness—all, perhaps, may mean the difference between an existence which can be borne, painful though it may be, and one which cannot. But the officials of the New Jersey State Prison are dangerously close to the point where the stock of legitimate punishments has been exhausted and it would appear that for many prisoners the few punishments which are left have lost their potency. To this we must couple the important fact that such punishments as the custodians can inflict may lead to an increased prestige for the punished inmate in the eyes of his fellow prisoners. He may become a hero, a martyr, a man who has confronted his captors and dared them to do their worst. In the dialectics of the inmate population, punishments and rewards have, then, been reversed and the control measures of the officials may support disobedience rather than decrease it.

In the second place, the system of rewards and punishments in the prison is defective because the reward side of the picture has been largely stripped away. Mail and visiting privileges, recreational privileges, the supply of personal possessions—all are given to the inmate at the time of his arrival in one fixed sum. Even the so-called good time—the portion of the prisoner's sentence deducted for good behavior—is automatically subtracted from the prisoner's sentence when he begins his period of imprisonment. Thus the officials have placed themselves in the peculiar position of granting the prisoner all available benefits or rewards at the time of his entrance into the system. The prisoner, then, finds himself unable to win any significant gains by means of compliance, for there are no gains left to be won.

From the viewpoint of the officials, of course, the privileges of the prison social system are regarded as rewards, as something to be achieved. That is to say, the custodians hold that recreation, access to the inmate store, good time, or visits from individuals in the free community are conditional upon conformity or good behavior. But the evidence suggests that from the viewpoint of the inmates the variety of benefits granted by the custodians is not defined as something to be earned but as an inalienable right—as the just due of the inmate which should not turn on the question of obedience or disobedience within the walls. After all, the inmate population claims these benefits have belonged to the prisoner from the time when he first came to the institution.

In short, the New Jersey State Prison makes an initial grant of all its rewards and then threatens to withdraw them if the prisoner does not conform. It does not start the prisoner from scratch and promise to grant its available rewards one by one as the prisoner proves himself through continued submission to the institutional regulations. As a result a subtle alchemy is set in motion whereby the inmates cease to see the rewards of the system as rewards, that is, as benefits contingent upon performance; instead, rewards are apt to be defined as obligations. Whatever justification might be offered for such a policy, it would appear to have a number of drawbacks as a method of motivating prisoners to fall into the posture of obedience. In effect, rewards and punishments of the officials have been collapsed into one and the prisoner moves in a world where there is no hope of progress but only the possibility of further punishments. Since the prisoner is already suffering from most of the punishments permitted by society, the threat of imposing those few remaining is all too likely to be a gesture of futility.

Unable to depend on that inner moral compulsion or sense of duty which eases the problem of control in most social organizations, acutely aware that brute force is inadequate, and lacking an effective system of legitimate rewards and punishments which might induce prisoners to conform to institutional regulations on the grounds of self-interest, the custodians of the New Jersey State Prison are considerably weakened in their attempts to impose their regime on their captive population. The result, in fact, is, as we have already indicated, a good deal of deviant behavior or noncompliance in a social system where the rulers at first glance seem to possess almost infinite power.

Yet systems of power may be defective for reasons other than the fact that those who are ruled do not feel the need to obey the orders and regulations descending on them from above. Systems of power may also fail because those who are supposed to rule are unwilling to do so. The unissued order, the deliberately ignored disobedience, the duty left unperformed—these are cracks in the monolith just as surely as are acts of defiance in the subject population. The "corruption" of the rulers may be far less dramatic than the insurrection of the ruled, for power unexercised is seldom as visible as power which is challenged, but the system of power still falters.

Now the official in the lowest ranks of the custodial bureaucracy—the guard in the cell block, the industrial shop, or the recreation yard—is the pivotal figure on which the custodial bureaucracy turns. It is he who must supervise and control the inmate population in concrete and detailed terms. It is he who must see to the translation of the custodial regime from blueprint to reality and engage in the specific battles for conformity. Counting prisoners, periodically reporting to the center of communications, signing passes, checking groups of inmates as they come and go, searching for contraband or signs of attempts to escape—these make up the minutiae of his eight-hour shift. In addition, he is supposed to be alert for violations of the prison rules which fall outside his routine sphere of surveillance. Not only must he detect and report deviant behavior after it occurs; he must curb deviant behavior before it arises as well, as when he is called on to prevent a minor quarrel among prisoners from flaring into a more dangerous situation. And he must make sure that the inmates in his charge perform their assigned tasks with a reasonable degree of efficiency.

The expected role of the guard, then, is a complicated compound of policeman and foreman, of cadi [judge], counselor, and boss all rolled into one. But as the guard goes about his duties, piling one day on top of another (and the guard too, in a certain sense, is serving time in confinement), we find that the system of power in the prison is defective not only because the means of motivating the inmates to conform are largely lacking but also because the guard is frequently reluctant to enforce the full range of the institution's regulations. The guard frequently fails to report infractions of the rules which have occurred before his eyes. The guard often transmits forbidden information to inmates, such as plans for searching particular cells in a surprise raid for contraband. The guard often neglects elementary security requirements and on numerous occasions he will be found joining his prisoners in outspoken criticisms of the warden and his assistants. In short, the guard frequently shows evidence of having been "corrupted" by the captive criminals over whom he stands in theoretical dominance. This failure within the ranks of the rulers is seldom to be attributed to outright bribery—bribery, indeed, is usually unnecessary, for far more effective influences are at work to bridge the gap supposedly separating captors and captives.

In the first place, the guard is in close and intimate association with his prisoners throughout the course of the working day. He can remain aloof only with great difficulty, for he possesses few of those devices which normally serve to maintain social distance between the rulers and the ruled. He cannot withdraw physically in symbolic affirmation of his superior position; he has no intermediaries to bear the brunt of resentment springing from orders which are disliked; and he cannot fall back on a dignity adhering to his office—he is a *hack* or a *screw* in the eyes of those he controls and an unwelcome display of officiousness evokes that great destroyer of unquestioned power, the ribald humor of the dispossessed.

There are many pressures in American culture to "be nice," to be a "good Joe," and the guard in the maximum security prison is not immune. The guard is constantly exposed to a sort of moral blackmail in which the first sign of condemnations, estrangement, or rigid adherence to the rules is countered by the inmates with the threat of ridicule or hostility. And in this complex interplay, the guard does not always start from a position of determined opposition to "being friendly." He holds an intermediate post in a bureaucratic structure between top prison officials—his captains, lieutenants, and sergeants—and the prisoners in his charge. Like many such figures, the guard is caught in a conflict of loyalties. He often has reason to resent the actions of his superior officers—the reprimands, the lack of ready appreciation, the incomprehensible order—and in the inmates he finds willing sympathizers. They, too, claim to suffer from the unreasonable irritants of power. Furthermore, the guard in many cases is marked by a basic ambivalence toward the criminals under his supervision and control. It is true that the inmates of the prison have been condemned by society through the agency of the courts, but some of these prisoners must be viewed as a success in terms of a worldly system of values which accords high prestige to wealth and influence even though they may have been won by devious means; and the poorly paid guard may be gratified to associate with a famous racketeer. Moreover, this ambivalence in the guard's attitudes toward the criminals nominally under his thumb may be based on something more than a sub-rosa respect for the notorious. There may also be a discrepancy between the judgments of society and the guard's own opinions as far as the "criminality" of the prisoner is concerned. It is difficult to define the man convicted of deserting his wife, gambling, or embezzlement as a desperate criminal to be suppressed at all costs, and the crimes of even the most serious offenders lose their significance with the passage of time. In the eyes of the custodian, the inmate tends to become a man in prison rather than a criminal in prison, and the relationship between captor and captive is subtly transformed in the process.

In the second place, the guard's position as a strict enforcer of the rules is undermined by the fact that he finds it almost impossible to avoid the claims of reciprocity. To a large extent the guard is dependent on inmates for the satisfactory performance of his duties; and like many individuals in positions of power, the guard is evaluated in terms of the conduct of the men he controls. A troublesome, noisy, dirty cell block reflects on the guard's ability to "handle" prisoners and this ability forms an important component of the merit rating which is used as the basis for pay raises and promotions. As we have pointed out above, a guard cannot rely on the direct application of force to achieve compliance nor can he easily depend on threats of punishment. And if the guard does insist on constantly using the last few negative sanctions available to the institution—if the guard turns in charge slip after charge slip for every violation of the rules which he encounters—he becomes burdensome to the top officials of the prison bureaucratic staff who realize only too well that their apparent dominance rests on some degree of cooperation. A system of power which can enforce its rules only by bringing its formal machinery of accusation, trial, and punishment into play at every turn will soon be lost in a haze of pettifogging detail.

The guard, then, is under pressure to achieve a smoothly running tour of duty not with the stick but with the carrot, but here again his legitimate stock is limited. Facing demands from above that he achieve compliance and stalemated from below, he finds that one of the most meaningful rewards he can offer is to ignore certain offenses or make sure that he never places himself in a position where he will discover them. Thus the guard—backed by all the power of the state, close to armed men who will run to his aid, and aware that any prisoner who disobeys him can be punished if he presses charges against him—often discovers that his best path of action is to make "deals" or "trades" with the captives in his power. In effect, the guard buys compliance or obedience in certain areas at the cost of tolerating disobedience elsewhere.

Aside from winning compliance "where it counts" in the course of the normal day, the guard has another favor to be secured from the inmates which makes him willing to forgo strict enforcement of all prison regulations. Many custodial institutions have experienced a riot in which the tables are turned momentarily and the captives hold sway over their quondam captors; and the rebellions of 1952 loom large in the memories of the officials of the New Jersey State Prison. The guard knows that he may some day be a hostage and that his life may turn on a settling of old accounts. A fund of goodwill becomes a valuable form of insurance and this fund is almost sure to be lacking if he has continually played the part of a martinet. In the folklore of the prison, there are enough tales about strict guards who have had the misfortune of being captured and savagely beaten during a riot to raise doubts about the wisdom of demanding complete conformity.

In the third place, the theoretical dominance of the guard is undermined in actuality by the innocuous encroachment of the prisoner on the guard's duties. Making out reports, checking cells at the periodic count, locking and unlocking doors—in short, all the minor chores which the guard is called on to perform—may gradually be transferred into the hands of inmates whom the guard has come to trust. The cell block runner, formally assigned the tasks of delivering mail, housekeeping duties, and so on, is of particular importance in this respect. Inmates in this position function in a manner analogous to that of the company clerk in the armed forces and like such figures they may wield power and influence far beyond the nominal definition of their role. For reasons of indifference, laziness, or naïveté, the guard may find that much of the power which he is supposed to exercise has slipped from his grasp.

Now power, like a person's virtue, once lost is hard to regain. The measures to rectify an established pattern of abdication need to be much more severe than those required to stop the first steps in the transfer of control from the guard to his prisoner. A guard assigned to a cell block in which a large portion of power has been shifted in the past from the officials to the inmates is faced with the weight of precedent; it requires a good deal of moral courage on his part to withstand the aggressive tactics of prisoners who fiercely defend the patterns of corruption established by custom. And if the guard himself has allowed his control to be subverted, he may find that any attempts to undo his error are checked by a threat from the inmate to send a *snitch-kite*—an anonymous note—to the guard's superior officers explaining his past derelictions in detail. This simple form of blackmail may be quite sufficient to maintain the relationships established by friendship, reciprocity, or encroachment.

It is apparent, then, that the power of the custodians is defective, not simply in the sense that the ruled are rebellious, but also in the sense that the rulers are reluctant. We must attach a new meaning to Lord Acton's aphorism that power tends to corrupt and absolute power corrupts absolutely. The custodians of the New Jersey State Prison, far from being converted into brutal tyrants, are under strong pressure to compromise with their captives, for it is a paradox that they can ensure their dominance only by allowing it to be corrupted. Only by tolerating violations of "minor" rules and regulations can the guard secure compliance in the "major" areas of the custodial regime. Ill-equipped to maintain the social distance which in theory separates the world of the officials and the world of the inmates, their suspicions eroded by long familiarity, the custodians are led into a *modus vivendi* with their captives which bears little resemblance to the stereotypical picture of guards and their prisoners.

The fact that the officials of the prison experience serious difficulties in imposing their regime on the society of prisoners is sometimes attributed to inadequacies of the custodial staff's personnel. These inadequacies, it is claimed, are in turn due to the fact that more than 50 percent of the guards are temporary employees who have not passed a Civil Service examination. In 1952, for example, a month and a half before the disturbances which dramatically underlined some of the problems of the officials, the deputy commissioner of the Department of Institutions and Agencies made the following points in a report concerning the temporary officers of the New Jersey State Prison's custodian force:

1. Because they are not interested in the prison service as a career, the temporary officers tend to have a high turnover as they are quick to resign to accept more remunerative employment.

2. Because they are inexperienced, they are not able to foresee or forestall disciplinary infractions, the on-coming symptoms of which the more experienced officer would detect and take appropriate preventive measures against.

3. Because they are not trained as the regular officers, they do not have the self-confidence that comes with the physical training and defensive measures which are part of the regular officers' pre-service training and, therefore, it is not uncommon for them to be somewhat timid and inclined to permit the prisoner to take advantage of them.

4. Because many of them are beyond the age limit or cannot meet the physical requirements for regular employment as established by Civil Service, they cannot look forward to a permanent career and are therefore less interested in the welfare of the institution than their brother officers.

5. Finally, because of the short period of employment, they do not recognize the individual prisoners who are most likely to incite trouble or commit serious infractions, and they are at a disadvantage in dealing with the large groups which congregate in the cellblocks, the mess hall, the auditorium, and the yard.

The fact that the job of the guard is often depressing, dangerous, and possesses relatively low prestige adds further difficulties. There is also little doubt that the high turnover rate carries numerous evils in its train, as the comments of the deputy commissioner have indicated. Yet even if higher salaries could counterbalance the many dissatisfying features of the guard's job—to a point where the custodial force consisted of men with long service rather than a group of transients—there remains a question of whether or not the problems of administration in the New Jersey State Prison would be eased to a significant extent. This, of course, is heresy from the viewpoint of those who trace the failure of social organizations to the personal failings of the individuals who man social organizational structure. Perhaps, indeed, there is some comfort in the idea that if the budget of the prison were larger, if higher salaries could be paid to entice "better" personnel within the walls, if guards could be persuaded to remain for longer periods, then the many difficulties of the prison bureaucracy would disappear. From this point of view, the problems of the custodial institution are rooted in the niggardliness of the free community and the consequent inadequacies of the institution's personnel rather than flaws in the social system of the prison itself. But to suppose that higher salaries are an answer to the plight of the custodian is to suppose, first, that there are men who by reason of their particular skills and personal characteristics are better qualified to serve as guards if they could be recruited; and second, that experience and training within the institution itself will better prepare the guard for his role, if greater financial rewards could convince him to make a career of his prison employment. Both of these suppositions, however, are open to some doubt. There are few jobs in the free community which are comparable to that of the guard in the maximum security prison and which, presumably, could equip the guard-to-be with the needed skills. If the job requirements of the guard's position are not technical skills, but turn on matters of character such as courage, honesty, and so on, there is no assurance that men with these traits will flock to the prison if the salary of the guard is increased. And while higher salaries may decrease the turnover rate—thus making an in-service training program feasible and providing a custodial force with greater experience—it is not certain if such a change can lead to marked improvement. A brief period of schooling can familiarize the new guard with the routines of the institution, but to prepare the guard for the realities of his assigned role with lectures and discussions is quite another matter. And it seems entirely possible that prolonged experience in the prison may enmesh the guard deeper and deeper in patterns of compromise and misplaced trust rather than sharpening his drive toward a rigorous enforcement of institutional regulations.

We are not arguing, of course, that the quality of the personnel in the prison is irrelevant to the successful performance of the bureaucracy's task, nor are we arguing that it would be impossible to improve the quality of the personnel by increasing salaries. We are arguing, however, that the problems of the custodians far transcend the size of the guard's paycheck or the length of his employment and that better personnel is at best a palliative rather than a final cure. It is true, of course, that it is difficult to unravel the characteristics of a social organization from the characteristics of the individuals who are its members, but there seems to be little reason to believe that a different crop of guards in the New Jersey State Prison would exhibit an outstanding increase in efficiency in trying to impose the regime of the custodians on the population of prisoners. *The lack of a sense of duty among those who are held captive, the obvious fallacies of coercion, the pathetic collection of rewards and punishments to induce compliance, the strong pressures toward the corruption of the guard in the form of friendship, reciprocity, and the transfer of duties into the hands of trusted inmates—all are structural defects in the prison's system of power rather than individual inadequacies.*

The question of whether these defects are inevitable in the custodial institution—or in any system of total power—must be deferred. For the moment it is enough to point out that in the New Jersey State Prison the custodians are unable or unwilling to prevent their captives from committing numerous violations of the rules which make up the theoretical blueprint for behavior and this failure is not a temporary, personal aberration but a built-in feature of the prison social system. It is only by understanding this fact that we can understand the world of the prisoners, since so many significant aspects of inmate behavior—such as coercion of fellow prisoners, fraud, gambling, homosexuality, sharing stolen supplies, and so on—are in clear contravention to institutional regulations. It is the nature of this world which must now claim our attention.

NOTES

1. Max Weber, *The Theory of Social and Economic Organization,* ed. Talcott Parsons (New York: Oxford University Press, 1947), p. 337.

2. This statement requires two qualifications. First, a number of inmates steadfastly maintain that they are innocent of the crime with which they are charged. It is the illegitimacy of their particular case, however, rather than the illegitimacy of confinement in general, which moves them to protest. Second, some of the more sophisticated prisoners argue that the conditions of imprisonment are wrong, although perhaps not illegitimate or illegal, on the grounds that reformation should be the major aim of imprisonment and the officials are not working hard enough in this direction.

3. Since each shift is reduced in size by vacations, regular days off, sickness, and so on, even the day shift—the largest of the three—can usually muster no more than ninety guards to confront the population of more than 1,200 prisoners. The fact that they are so heavily outnumbered is not lost on the officials.

2 4

✦

Well-Governed Prisons
Are Possible

JOHN J. DiIULIO, JR.

Political scientist John DiIulio challenges the view of Sykes and other sociologists that prisons should be analyzed from the perspective of the inmate society. He argues that because of the dominance of the view that "the cons run the joint," the importance of good management has been neglected.

Although a disputatious lot, public management scholars tend to agree strongly (if implicitly) on one thing: public management matters. They share a belief ("faith" might be a better word) that how public organizations are managed has a significant bearing on how, and how well, those organizations perform. They assume that how public executives, managers, and line workers behave affects significantly what and how much their organizations produce in the way of public safety, health, education, environmental protection, national security, and so on. This assumption undergirds every public administration text and many books and articles on the organization of the White House, Congress, and the lesser bodies that form each institution.

Source: "Well-Governed Prisons Are Possible," by John J. DiIulio, Jr.
Author's Note: Portions of this article have been adapted from my previously published works, including "Recovering the Public Management Variable: Lessons from Schools, Prisons, and Armies," *Public Administration Review* (March/April 1989): 127–133; *No Escape: The Future of American Corrections* (New York: Basic Books, 1991), Chap. 1; and "Understanding Prisons: The New Old Penology," *Law and Social Inquiry* 16 (Winter 1991): 65–86.

For example, many studies now suggest that student performance on standardized tests and other measures of educational attainment is largely a function of school management, which is defined in terms of such hard-to-measure factors as how teachers structure their classes, how principals lead their teachers, and how superintendents coordinate their principals. In popular and scholarly discourse, these works are often lumped together and called the "effective-schools" literature.[1] This literature deepens one's faith in the efficacy of the public management variable. Broadly stated, if society's goal is to make students literate and social, then it matters greatly how the schools are managed. The studies indicate that simply paying teachers more, "tinkering" with testing devices, or "fiddling" with pupil-to-teacher ratios does not work.

WELL-GOVERNED PRISONS

No literature is available on prisons that parallels the "effective-schools" literature. Most of the research on prisons has been done by sociologists and focuses heavily on the social order of the cell blocks.[2] The "ineffective-prisons" literature might be the most fitting label for the past five decades of research on prisons.

Most works on prisons by sociologists and penologists embody grave doubts about the efficacy of prison management. Indeed, most of this literature suggests that prison managers can do virtually nothing to improve conditions behind bars: if prisons develop a distinctive social system along racial and ethnic lines, reinforced by an informal but powerful distribution of authority, then policy makers can do little more than take notice, while prison managers must compromise their formal authority. To the extent that any of these studies relate prison management practices to the quality of life behind bars, the results are maddening: prisons that are managed in a tight, authoritarian fashion are plagued by disorder and inadequate programs; prisons that are managed in a loose "participative" fashion are equally troubled; and "mixed" cell block management regimes do no better.

But general faith in the efficacy of public management, the existence of numerous (through admittedly laughable) "prison administrator" textbooks and former wardens' "how-to" memoirs, and a few quite recent empirical studies of prison management conspire to challenge this perplexing view of these "barbed-wire bureaucracies."

My *Governing Prisons: A Comparative Study of Correctional Management* reports on three years of exploratory research on prison management in the Texas, Michigan, and California departments of corrections.[3] In sum, that book analyzed intersystem, intrasystem, and historical variations in the quality of life, which were measured in terms of three criteria: order (rates of individual and collective violence and other forms of misconduct), amenity (availability of clean cells, decent food, and so on), and service (availability of work opportunities, educational programs, and so forth).

Using the simplest sort of approach and having weighed the possibility of problems in the data, I found no evidence that levels of order, amenity, and service varied directly with any of these factors: a "better class" of inmates; greater per capita spending; lower levels of crowding; lower inmate-to-staff ratios; greater officer training; more modern plant and equipment; more elaborate systems to sensitize official decision makers to the views (especially the grievances) of inmates; more elaborate systems to improve inmate–staff and inmate–inmate race relations (including the existence of a more racially "representative" officer force); and a more routine use of repressive measures, including official and quasi-official beatings of "troublemakers," by officers or by designated inmate "trustees."

All roads, it seemed, led to the conclusion that the quality of prison life depended mainly on the quality of prison management. This conclusion was teased from a close analysis of the history, politics, penological credo, and administration of each system and was bolstered by two natural experiments in the data. To simplify greatly, prison organizations that were led strongly by a stable team of like-minded executives, structured in a paramilitary, security-driven bureaucratic fashion, and coordinated proactively in conjunction with the demands of relevant outside actors (including key legislators, community activists, judges, and overseers) had higher levels of order, amenity, and service than prison organizations that were managed in other ways, *even when* the former institutions were more crowded, spent less per capita, had higher inmate–staff ratios, and so on. The research supported this conclusion: *"The only findings of this study that, to me at least, seem indisputable, is that . . . prison management matters."*[4]

Other recent studies are part of what might be termed the emerging "well-governed prisons" literature. Bert Useem, analyzing major prison riots in the United States between 1971 and 1986, provides ample evidence that the riots were due mainly to a breakdown in security procedures—the daily routine of numbering, counting, frisking, locking, contraband control, and cell searches that is the heart of administration in most prisons.[5] The main determinants of prison riots are obvious and proximate factors relating to the quality of prison management. Crowding, underfunding, court intervention, festering inmate–staff or inmate–inmate racial animosities, and other widely cited causes of prison disorders may make riots more likely, but only failed security management makes them "inevitable."[6] In short, how prisons are managed may increase or decrease the probability of an inmate living out his term in a safe, lawful environment.

Similarly, my *Principled Agents: The Cultural Bases of Behavior in a Federal Government Bureaucracy* shows how efficacious prison management can be.[7] The Federal Bureau of Prisons is recognized far and wide as one of the nation's most successful correctional agencies. Almost without exception, its prisons have been safe and humane; they have improved every decade since the agency came into being. There are two popular but false explanations for the bureau's success relative to state prison systems. The first explanation is that the bureau has always gotten "a better class of criminals." Historically, however, the bureau has never held only white-collar offenders: in mid-1988, for example, 46 percent of its prisoners had a history of violence; and each year the states transfer many of their "too-hard-to-handle" inmates to "the Feds." The second explanation is that the bureau's annual per-inmate expenditures far exceed the states'; in fact, historically the agency has spent almost exactly at the national median. Furthermore, like many states systems, the bureau has had overcrowding, poorly designed cell houses, staff shortages, and other problems that adversely affect the quality of prison life. But the bureau has met these challenges better, and with greater consistency, than any other correctional agency in the land.

The reason: bureau management. In sum, unlike most state prison systems, the bureau has had stable and talented executive leadership (only four directors in its first fifty-seven years of existence); a progressive inmate classification system; an elaborate system of audits, transfers, and other internal "checks and balances"; a positive, closely knit organizational culture; and many other positive features. State and local agencies that have copied bureau management practices have improved. For example, recent analysis of intrasystem differences in the New York City system documents the comparative strengths of "unit management," a form of correctional administration pioneered by the bureau in which security staff and noncustodial personnel are given responsibility for a wing of an institution and trained to work cohesively.[8] In these and other recent studies, prison management emerges as the crucial variable in determining the quality of life behind bars.

GENERAL PRINCIPLES OF GOOD CORRECTIONAL LEADERSHIP

Successful correctional leaders differ in many ways, from their own penological credos to their personal styles. However, in certain crucial aspects, they and the organization they lead are the same.

One important trait shared by successful correctional leaders is devotion to building or maintaining an organizational culture. James Q. Wilson has defined *organizational culture* as "a persistent, patterned way of thinking about the central tasks of and human relationships within an organization. Culture is to organization what personality is to an individual. Like human culture generally, it is passed on from one generation to the next."[9] As Wilson has observed, unlike students of business administration, students of public administration have not puzzled much over "creating the right organizational culture," and little is known about how government executives "define tasks and motivate workers to perform those tasks."[10]

While the literature of public administration includes nothing of note about the relationship between correctional leadership and organizational culture, certain interlocking patterns are clear. In *No Escape: The Future of American Corrections,* I identified six general principles of good leadership drawn from my observations of correctional managers in both state and national agencies.[11] Let us examine these principles closely.

1. *The successful leaders focus, and inspire their subordinates to focus, on results rather than process, on performance rather than procedures, on ends rather than means.* Managers are rewarded (or not) according to whether the cell blocks are clean, the inmates safe, the classes orderly, the industry productive, the staff turnover rate low, the escape rate zero, and so on. A warden who fails to deliver these goods cannot excuse himself by reciting budget woes, crowding problems, red tape, too many "heavies," or anything else.

    Some of the successful correctional leaders have concentrated more or less exclusively on results, but all of them have stressed results in accordance with their sense of the organization's mission and primary objectives. But in each case, a clear mission statement existed and the institutions were organized and managed around it.

2. *Organizational culture is custodial at core.* Doctors, nurses, secretaries, counselors, accountants, and other nonuniformed institutional staff are trained to think as correctional officers first, and the primary responsibility of every employee is to protect the inmates and to keep them from escaping. Leaders have made institutional safety and security their top priority and have worked hard to see to it that the organization's formal and informal (peer group) incentive structure mirrored this emphasis.

    In the Federal Bureau of Prisons, for example, all staff members have undergone the same basic training. They have been required to take target practice and are expected to join shoulders with uniformed officers in the event of a major disturbance. The spectacle of middle-aged secretaries in skirts toting guns on the perimeter of a prison amazed (and distressed) some on-site observers of the 1987 hostage incident at the bureau's Atlanta Penitentiary—but it was an example of the kind of management that has made the bureau a close-knit family organization with high esprit de corps and little of the workaday tension between treatment and custodial personnel that has harmed other corrections agencies. Similarly, a Michigan prisons research analyst was amused when he telephoned his counterpart in the Texas Department of Corrections and was told that the fellow was out hunting down escapees. Such practices accounted for the once-healthy staff morale and good relations among Texas prison workers at all levels.

    As Wilson points out, public organizations that have strong management and a concomitantly strong sense of mission sometimes suffer from resistance to needed administrative changes, slowness in adapting to new political circumstances, and other problems.[12] The net effect, however, is almost always positive, and correctional organizations that have been led in ways that promote a strong custodial culture have everywhere been more safe and humane than those that have not.

3. *Leaders of successful institutions follow the MBWA principle: management by walking around.* "Walking" George Beto, director of the Texas Department of Corrections from 1962 to 1972, takes the prize for this approach to management, but his successful peers come in as close seconds.

New Jersey's William Fauver, for example, began his practice of "feet-on" leadership when he was the warden of Trenton State Prison. As he later recalled: "When I first came to Trenton, a warden walking around without a bodyguard was unheard of. I felt it was necessary—a symbolic thing that says you're in charge." He has continued this practice as commissioner, making regular visits (not "tours" or "inspections") to each of his facilities.

The same has been true for other successful leaders. None are strangers to the cell blocks; each knows the facilities almost as well as he knows his own home, and he is always on the scene (often in the center of things) when major trouble erupts. MBWA keeps correctional managers from becoming hostages to (often distorted or incomplete) reports from the field and helps them escape the iron bars of paperwork. Moreover, it gives the staff greater personal respect for their chief and also enhances his reputation among the inmates.

In prison and jail settings, one's personal reputation is crucial: inmates who lie about their criminal exploits or "punk out" when challenged physically by their peers are not respected; and officers who are easily intimidated, break their word, or do not act in a "firm but fair" manner are not taken seriously. Everyone "looks through" the uniform to the person inside it. Of senior officers who have weak personal reputations, one often hears comments such as "He's just a paper captain," or "His bars aren't for real," or (from inmates), "He's Major No-Balls."

Correctional leaders who have not practiced MBWA have not made a reputation; instead, staff and inmates have made one for them. In most cases, the reputation they fastened to the director was not flattering ("removed," "chickenshit," "out of touch," "head up his ass," and so on). Leaders who have practiced MBWA have not always done so successfully, but most have.

4. *Successful leaders make significant alliances with key politicians, judges, journalists, reformers, and other outsiders with the ability to affect the organization's fiscal health, statutory authority, and public image.* Among the strategies employed by successful correctional leaders are throwing parties for key outsiders (in some cases at the executive's personal expense), responding quickly and cordially to legislative inquiries for information, lecturing in public, attending conferences, freely granting interviews, publishing articles and essays, and developing good personal relationships with top officials in other law-enforcement agencies—or, when that failed, creating interagency procedures to "force" and routinize cooperation.

Above all else, important outsiders are invited into the facilities to see for themselves what conditions are like and how things operate. Often, events are staged; for example, an inmate college graduation ceremony. Just as often, however, the outsiders (including judges) are invited to take a long, hard look at what is going on. Sometimes they like what they see; other times they do not. In some instances, the resultant political fallout, press coverage, and public attention is favorable; in other cases, it causes fresh headaches for the director and his staff.

But successful correctional leaders follow a policy of openness and alliance building, and in the long run they are better than leaders who do not. Leaders who try to keep the outsiders out, or who simply ignore them, are more likely to wind up fired, burned out, or forced to resign, even when their institutions do not fare as badly as those of other systems where leaders are more open.

Successful leaders take it as axiomatic that the general public can neither know nor care enough about correctional staff (or the unpopular people they supervise) to furnish anything like sturdy political support for their institutions. Instead, they have made such broad appeals only one component, and by no means the largest one, of the strategy for handling outside "coaches, customers, and critics."[13] They consciously manage their agency's external relations with as much zeal as they have managed their cell blocks.

5. *Successful leaders rarely innovate, but their innovations are far-reaching and the reasons for them are made known in advance to both inmates and staff.* Changes are made slowly, allowing staff and inmates plenty of time to learn the new ways and "get on board." For the most part, the innovations address a current or potential problem that most of those who live and work in the facilities already acknowledge as serious. As often as not, the innovations represent a fundamentally new way of achieving an old mission, rather than being a new mission itself. And in most cases, the old practices are abolished without any implication that they (and hence those who followed and believed in them) failed or were misguided: rather, they are presented as necessary or unavoidable responses to changed circumstances and "sold" to inmates and staff accordingly.

Correctional line staff are notoriously sensitive to what their leaders "do for the inmates" versus "what they do for us." Signs of appreciation, tangible and symbolic, for the public service that line staff perform tend to be few and to come from within the organization. As one warden stated, at times it is almost as though there were a sibling rivalry between inmates and line officers. Thus, to give inmates a new athletic facility without making a commensurate gesture toward line staff, or to enhance inmates' eligibility for college and vocational courses without improving (or at least attempting to improve) the educational benefits of staff, can erode staff loyalty to "the brass," harm labor–management relations in other areas, and cost a director much of whatever personal and professional capital with line workers he may have accumulated over the years. Thus, many "innovations" in correctional settings are in actuality attempts to correct this sort of real or perceived imbalance.

6. *Successful leaders are in office long enough to understand and, as necessary, to modify the organization's internal operations and external relations.* Most correctional leaders who are successful serve for at least six consecutive years in one

position; some, for over a decade. With respect to length of service, there have been four kinds of correctional leaders, which I classify (with shameless alliteration) as flies, fatalists, foot soldiers, and founders.

Over the past two decades, corrections officers have served an average of only three years before quitting, getting fired, or moving on to another agency; several have stayed in office less than a year. These flies of summer have either come and gone unnoticed or have attempted to reform the agency in one fell swoop. The former flies are inconsequential; the latter buzzed loudly and were a nuisance until they were swatted down by reality.

The fatalists served similarly brief terms that began and ended with their complaining about the futility of incarceration and the hopelessness of institutional reform. Often, they had little or no previous experience managing correctional institutions. In some cases, they were talented and energetic people who convinced key decision makers that their institutions were beyond repair; several brought about deinstitutionalization schemes of one sort or another. Whatever the results of these schemes (usually the results have been poor to mixed), the fatalists did nothing to achieve institutional reform but did succeed in abolishing some institutions.

Compared to the flies and most of the fatalists, the foot soldiers served long terms. Whether they inherited their job from a fly, a fatalist, or a founder, they worked in the trenches to make whatever incremental improvements they could, usually in a pragmatic spirit unleavened by a commitment to any particular penological theory. When what they inherited was good, they tried to preserve as much of it as they could and to consolidate new administrative measures around old routines. W. J. Estelle in Texas, Steve Bablitch in Wisconsin, and Orville Pung in Minnesota would rank among the foot soldiers.

The founders were those who created an agency or reorganized it in major and positive ways. Generally, like directors James V. Bennett and Norman A. Carlson of the Federal Bureau of Prisons, and New Jersey's William Fauver and William Lecke, they served long terms.

Not every leader who served a long term has done good things organizationally. And some leaders are hard to classify meaningfully. But the record suggests that foot soldiers and founders are a boon to the quality of institutional life; indeed, if I were forced to choose between one mediocre leader for ten years and a succession of four talented ones over the same period, I would probably entrust the institutions to the former.

SUMMARY

Throughout the nineteenth century and the early part of the twentieth, studies of prisons focused more on the administrators than on the inmates. Prison governance was the central and abiding focus of these studies. To permit prisoners to associate freely was to abandon them to criminal mischief and corruption and to raise the likelihood of criminal disorders behind bars.

Beginning in the 1940s with the publication of research by sociologists, there was a shift in focus from sympathy for the work of prison administrators to sympathy for prison inmates. Whereas the "old penology" maintained that prisons must be governed strictly by duly appointed officials, the "new penology" maintained that prisons must be governed by the prisoners themselves.

In the 1960s the prison population became increasingly black and Hispanic. In a spate of studies, a second generation of new penologists documented the rise of a younger, more aggressive, more politicized breed of convict chieftains. These new inmate leaders were far less willing and able to get other inmates to go along with even the most basic wishes of the administration. Prison populations became fractionalized along racial and ethnic lines. The pliable con-boss was succeeded by the inflexible prison gang leader. The society of captives, it seemed, was about to run out of control.

The old penology, of course, had a cure for this virus of inmate dominance: namely, rigorous internal controls, rule enforcement, and the atomization of the "prison community." And in the few corrections agencies where old penologists remained at the helm, that is precisely the medicine they administered.

To old penologists, prison administrators were admirable public servants, inmate associations behind the walls were to be restricted and minimized, and any form of inmate self-government was considered a nightmare. To new penologists, prison administrators were damnable ogres, prisoners were responsible souls, and complete inmate self-government was a pleasant dream. By the mid-1980s, the new penologists' dream had come true in many places, but with precisely the ill consequences that the old penologists would have predicted.

Publication in 1987 of *Governing Prisons* gave rise to what has been called the "new old penology," a shift of attention from the society of captives to the government of keepers.[14] In that book I presented empirical evidence and arguments that tight administrative control was often more conducive to decent prison conditions (and possibly rehabilitation) than loose administrative control; highlighted the moral and practical sophistry of inmate self-government schemes; and otherwise restored some, though by no means all, of the claims of the old penology. This approach to understanding prisons pushes administrators back to the bar of attention, is inclined to treat them at least as sympathetically as it treats their charges, and attempts to translate empirically grounded research on prisoner behavior into ideas about how to manage toward more safe and humane conditions behind bars.

The "new old penology" posits as central that, other things being equal, correctional leaders who follow the precepts discussed above produce more in the way of safe and humane conditions behind bars than leaders who do not. It is time to stop treating correctional management as an impossible job. And it is long past time to stop offering lame sociological excuses for real failures of administration. What Sykes called the "society of captives" can be governed well or ill.

NOTES

1. Edward B. Fiske, "New Look at Effective Schools," *New York Times,* April 15, 1984, Section 12.

2. Major works in this large literature include Donald Clemmer, *The Prison Community* (New York: Holt, Rinehart & Winston, 1940); Gresham M. Sykes, *The Society of Captives: A Study of a Maximum Security Prison* (Princeton: Princeton University Press, 1958); Donald R. Cressey (ed.), *The Prison: Studies in Institutional Organization and Change* (New York: Holt, Rinehart & Winston, 1961); John Irwin, *The Felon* (Englewood Cliffs, N.J.: Prentice-Hall, 1970); John Irwin, *Prisons in Turmoil* (Boston: Little, Brown, 1980).

3. John J. DiIulio, Jr., *Governing Prisons: A Comparative Study of Correctional Management* (New York: Free Press, 1987).

4. Ibid., p. 256.

5. Bert Useem, *States of Siege: U.S. Prison Riots, 1971–1986* (New York: Oxford University Press, 1988).

6. Contrary to much of the "ineffective-prisons" literature, Useem's carefully documented work provides no support for the theory that security-driven management and prison violence vary inversely. The idea that the more prison authorities do to control inmates, the more inmates will run out of control is intriguing, counterintuitive, and wholly without empirical evidence to support it. For a discussion of this theory, see DiIulio, *Governing Prisons,* pp. 22–23, and Useem, *supra.*

7. John J. DiIulio, Jr., *Principled Agents: The Cultural Bases of Behavior in a Federal Government Bureaucracy,* Journal of Public Administration Research and Theory (July 1994): 4.

8. John J. DiIulio, Jr., *Interim Report on Corrections in New York City* (New York: New York City Board of Corrections, September 10, 1987); and Richard J. Koehler, Memo to First Deputy Mayor Stanley Brezenoff, New York City Department of Corrections, April 19, 1988.

9. James Q. Wilson, *Bureaucracy: What Government Agencies Do and Why They Do It* (New York: Basic Books, 1989), p. 91.

10. Ibid.

11. John J. DiIulio, Jr., *No Escape: The Future of American Corrections* (New York: Basic Books, 1991), Chap. 1.

12. Wilson, *Bureaucracy.*

13. This alliterative phrase is from Richard A. McGee, *Prisons and Politics* (Lexington, Mass.: Lexington Books, 1981). McGee directed the California penal system for several decades.

14. The term was coined by Bert Useem in "Correctional Management: How to Govern Our 'Cities,'" *Corrections Today* (February 1990): 88.

2 5

✦

What Works?
Questions and Answers
about Prison Reform

ROBERT MARTINSON

Publicaiton of this article in 1974 framed the debate about rehabilitation as a correctional goal. This recidivism-based research was much cited by practitioners and policy makers alike, as the reason for shifting to determinate sentences and for limiting discretionary release on parole. While Martinson fought to correct what he felt was a misinterpretation of this influential work, it is credited with reducing the role of treatment programs.

• • •

One of the problems in the constant debate over "prison reform" is that we have been able to draw very little on any systematic empirical knowledge about the success or failure that we have met when we *have* tried to rehabilitate offenders, with various treatments and in various institutional and non-institutional settings. The field of penology has produced a voluminous research literature on this subject, but until recently there has been no comprehensive review of this literature and no attempt to bring its findings to bear, in a useful way, on the general question of "What works?" My purpose in this essay is to sketch an answer to that question.

Source: Robert Martinson, "What Works? Questions and Answers about Prison Reform," *The Public Interest,* No. 35 (1974), pp. 22–54. Reprinted with permission of the author from *The Public Interest,*© 1974 by National Affairs, Inc. Footnotes and references have been deleted.

THE TRAVAILS OF A STUDY

...

What we set out to do in this study was fairly simple, though it turned into a massive task. First we undertook a six-month search of the literature for any available reports published in the English language on attempts at rehabilitation that had been made in our corrections systems and those of other countries from 1945 through 1967. We then picked from that literature all those studies whose findings were interpretable—that is, whose design and execution met the conventional standards of social science research. Our criteria were rigorous but hardly esoteric: A study had to be an evaluation of a treatment method, it had to employ an independent measure of the improvement secured by that method, and it had to use some control group, some untreated individuals with whom the treated ones could be compared. We excluded studies only for methodological reasons: They presented insufficient data, they were only preliminary, they presented only a summary of findings, their results were confounded by extraneous factors, they used unreliable measures, one could not understand their descriptions of the treatment in question, they drew spurious conclusions from their data, their samples were undescribed or too small or provided no true comparability between treated and untreated groups, or they had used inappropriate statistical tests and did not provide enough information for the reader to recompute the data. Using these standards, we drew from the total number of studies 231 acceptable ones, which we not only analyzed ourselves but summarized in detail so that a reader of our analysis would be able to compare it with his independent conclusions.

These treatment studies use various measures of offender improvement: recidivism rates (that is, the rates at which offenders return to crime), adjustment to prison life, vocational success, educational achievement, personality and attitude change, and general adjustment to the outside community. We included all of these in our study, but in these pages I will deal only with the effects of rehabilitative treatment on recidivism, the phenomenon which reflects most directly how well our present treatment programs are performing the task of rehabilitation. The use of even this one measure brings with it enough methodological complications to make a clear reporting of the findings most difficult. The groups that are studied, for instance, are exceedingly disparate, so that it is hard to tell whether what "works" for one kind of offender also works for others. In addition, there has been little attempt to replicate studies; therefore one cannot be certain how stable and reliable the various findings are. Just as important, when the various studies use the term "recidivism rate," they may in fact be talking about somewhat different measures of offender behavior—i.e., "failure" measures such as arrest rates or parole violation rates, or "success" measures such as favorable discharge from parole or probation. And not all of these measures correlate very highly with one another. These difficulties will become apparent again and again in the course of this discussion.

With these caveats, it is possible to give a rather bald summary of our findings: *With few and isolated exceptions, the rehabilitative efforts that have been reported so far have had no appreciable effect on recidivism.* Studies that have been done since our survey was completed do not present any major grounds for altering that original conclusion. What follows is an attempt to answer the questions and challenges that might be posed to such an unqualified statement.

EDUCATION AND VOCATIONAL TRAINING

1. *Isn't it true that a correctional facility running a truly rehabilitative program—one that prepares inmates for life on the outside through education and vocational training—will turn out more successful individuals than will a prison which merely leaves its inmates to rot?*

If this is true, the fact remains that there is very little empirical evidence to support it. Skill development and educational programs are in fact quite common in correctional facilities, and one might begin by examining their effects on young males, those who might be thought most amenable to such efforts. A study by New York State (1964) found that for young males as a whole, the degree of success achieved in the regular prison academic education program, as measured by changes in grade achievement levels, made no significant difference in recidivism rates. The only exception was the relative improvement, compared with the sample as a whole, that greater progress made in the top seven per cent of the participating population—those who had high I.Q.'s, had made good records in previous schooling, and who also made good records of academic progress in the institution. And a study by Glaser (1964) found that while it was true that, when one controlled for sentence length, more attendance in regular prison academic programs slightly decreased the subsequent chances of parole violation, this improvement was not large enough to outweigh the associated disadvantage for the "long-attenders": Those who attended prison school the longest also turned out to be those who were in prison the longest. Presumably, those getting the most education were also the worst parole risks in the first place.

• • •

In sum, many of these studies of young males are extremely hard to interpret because of flaws in research design. But it can safely be said that they provide us with no clear evidence that education or skill development programs have been successful.

TRAINING ADULT INMATES

When one turns to adult male inmates, as opposed to young ones, the results are even more discouraging. There have been six studies of this type; three of them report that their programs, which ranged from academic to prison work experience, produced no significant differences in recidivism rates, and one—by Glaser (1964)—is almost impossible to interpret because of the risk differentials of the prisoners participating in the various programs.

Two studies—by Schur (1948) and by Saden (1962)—*do* report a positive difference from skill development programs. In one of them, the Saden study, it is questionable whether the experimental and control groups were truly comparable. But what is more interesting is that both these "positive" studies dealt with inmates incarcerated prior to or during World War II. Perhaps the rise in our educational standards as a whole since then has lessened the differences that prison education or training can make. The only other interesting possibility emerges from a study by Gearhart (1967). His study was one of those that reported vocational education to be non-significant in affecting recidivism rates. He did note, however, that when a trainee succeeded in finding a job related to his area of training, he had a slightly higher chance of becoming a successful parolee. It is possible, then, that skill development programs fail because what they teach bears so little relationship to an offender's subsequent life outside the prison.

One other study of adults, this one with fairly clear implications, has been performed with women rather than men. An experimental group of institutionalized women in Milwaukee was given an extremely comprehensive special education program, accompanied by group counseling. Their training was both academic and practical; it included reading, writing, spelling, business filing, child care, and grooming. Kettering (1965) found that the program made no difference in the women's rates of recidivism.

Two things should be noted about these studies. One is the difficulty of interpreting them as a whole. The disparity in the programs that were tried, in the populations that were affected, and in the institutional settings that surrounded these projects makes it hard to be sure that one is observing the same category of treatment in each case. But the second point is that despite this difficulty, one can be reasonably sure that, so far, educational and vocational programs have not worked. We don't know why they have failed. We don't know whether the programs themselves are flawed, or whether they are incapable of overcoming the effects of prison life in general. The difficulty may be that they lack applicability to the world the inmate will face outside of prison. Or perhaps the type of educational and skill improvement they produce simply doesn't have very much to do with an individual's propensity to commit crime. What we do know is that, to date, education and skill development have not reduced recidivism by rehabilitating criminals.

THE EFFECTS
OF INDIVIDUAL COUNSELING

2. *But when we speak of a rehabilitative prison, aren't we referring to more than education and skill development alone? Isn't what's needed some way of counseling inmates, or helping them with the deeper problems that have caused their maladjustment?*

This, too, is a reasonable hypothesis; but when one examines the programs of this type that have been tried, it's hard to find any more grounds for enthusiasm than we found with skill development and education. One method that's been tried—though so far, there have been acceptable reports only of its application to young offenders—has been individual psychotherapy. For young males, we found seven such reported studies. One study, by Guttman (1963) at the Nelles School, found such treatment to be ineffective in reducing recidivism rates; another, by Rudoff (1960), found it unrelated to *institutional* violation rates, which were themselves related to parole success. It must be pointed out that Rudoff used only this indirect measure of association, and the study therefore cannot rule out the possibility of a treatment effect. A third, also by Guttman (1963) but at another institution, found that such treatment was actually related to a slightly *higher* parole violation rate; and a study by Adams (1959b and 1961b) also found a lack of improvement in parole revocation and first suspension rates.

• • •

There have been two studies of the effects of individual psychotherapy on young incarcerated *female* offenders, and both of them (Adams, 1959; Adams, 1961) report no significant effects from the therapy. But one of the Adams studies (1959) does contain a suggestive, although not clearly interpretable, finding: If this individual therapy was administered by a psychiatrist or a psychologist, the resulting parole suspension rate was almost two-and-a-half times *higher* than if it was administered by a social worker without this specialized training.

There has also been a much smaller number of studies of two other types of individual therapy: counseling, which is directed towards a prisoner's gaining new insight into his own problems, and casework, which aims at helping a prisoner cope with his more pragmatic immediate needs. These types of therapy both rely heavily on the empathetic relationship that is to be developed between the professional and the client. It was noted above that the Adams study (1961b) of therapy administered to girls, referred to in the discussion of individual psychotherapy, found that social workers seemed better at the job than psychologists or psychiatrists. This difference seems to suggest a favorable outlook for these alternative forms of individual therapy. But other studies of such therapy have produced ambiguous results. Bernsten (1961) reported a Danish experiment that showed that socio-psychological counseling combined with comprehensive welfare measures—job and residence placement, clothing, union and health insurance membership, and financial aid—produced an improvement among some short-term male offenders, though not those in either the highest-risk or the lowest-risk categories. On the other hand, Hood, in Britain (1966), reported generally non-significant results with a program of counseling for young males. (Interestingly enough, this experiment *did* point to a mechanism capable of changing recidivism rates. When boys were released from institutional care and entered the army directly, "poor risk" boys among both experimentals *and* controls did better than expected. "Good risks" did worse.)

So these foreign data are sparse and not in agreement; the American data are just as sparse. The only American study which provides a direct measure of the effects of individual counseling—a study of California's Intensive Treatment Program (California, 1958), which was "psychodynamically" oriented—found no improvement in recidivism rates.

• • •

GROUP COUNSELING

Group counseling has indeed been tried in correctional institutions, both with and without specifically psychotherapeutic orientation. There has been one study of "pragmatic," problem-oriented counseling on *young* institutionalized males, by Seckel (1965). This type of counseling had no significant effect. For adult males, there have been three such studies of the "pragmatic" and "insight" methods. Two (Kassebaum, 1971; Harrison, 1964) report no long-lasting significant effects. (One of these two did report a real but short-term effect that wore off as the program became institutionalized and as offenders were at liberty longer.) The third study of adults, by Shelley (1961), dealt with a "pragmatic" casework program, directed towards the educational and vocational needs of institutionalized young adult males in a Michigan prison camp. The treatment lasted for six months and at the end of that time Shelley found an improvement in attitudes; the possession of "good" attitudes was independently found by Shelley to correlate with parole success. Unfortunately, though, Shelley was not able to measure the *direct* impact of the counseling on recidivism rates. His two separate correlations are suggestive, but they fall short of being able to tell us that it really is the counseling that has a direct effect on recidivism.

With regard to more professional group *psychotherapy,* the reports are also conflicting. We have two studies of group psychotherapy on young males. One, by Parsons (1966), says that this treatment did in fact reduce recidivism. The improved recidivism rate stems from the improved performance only of those who were clinically judged to have been "successfully" treated; still, the overall result of the treatment was to improve recidivism rates for the experimental group as a whole. On the other hand, a study by Craft (1964) of young males designated "psychopaths," comparing "self-government" group psychotherapy with "authoritarian" individual counseling, found that the "group therapy" boys afterwards committed *twice* as many new offenses as the individually treated ones. Perhaps some forms of group psychotherapy work for some types of offenders but not others; a reader must draw his own conclusions, on the basis of sparse evidence.

With regard to young females, the results are just as equivocal. Adams, in his study of females (1959a), found that there was no improvement to be gained from treating girls by group rather than individual methods. A study by Taylor of borstal (reformatory) girls in New Zealand (1967) found a similar lack of any great improvement for group therapy as opposed to individual therapy or even to no therapy at all. But the Taylor study does offer one real, positive finding: When the "group therapy" girls *did* commit new offenses, these offenses were less serious than the ones for which they had originally been incarcerated.

• • •

As with the question of skill development, it is hard to summarize these results. The programs administered were various; the groups to which they were administered varied not only by sex but by age as well; there were also variations in the length of time for which the programs were carried on, the frequency of contact during that time, and the period for which the subjects were followed up. Still, one must say that the burden of the evidence is not encouraging. These programs seem to work best when they are new, when their subjects are amenable to treatment in the first place, and when the counselors are not only trained people but "good" people as well. Such findings, which would not be much of a surprise to a student of organization or personality, are hardly encouraging for a policy planner, who must adopt measures that are generally applicable, that are capable of being successfully institutionalized, and that must rely for personnel on something other than the exceptional individual.

TRANSFORMING THE INSTITUTIONAL ENVIRONMENT

3. *But maybe the reason these counseling programs don't seem to work is not that they are ineffective* per se, *but that the institutional environment outside the program is unwholesome enough to undo any good work that the counseling does. Isn't a truly successful rehabilitative institution the one where the inmate's whole environment is directed towards true correction rather than towards custody or punishment?*

This argument has not only been made, it has been embodied in several institutional programs that go by the name of "milieu therapy." They are designed to make every element of the inmate's environment a part of his treatment, to reduce the distinctions between the custodial staff and the treatment staff, to create a supportive, non–authoritarian, and non–regimented atmosphere, and to enlist peer influence in the formation of constructive values. These programs are especially hard to summarize because of their variety; they differ, for example, in how "supportive" or "permissive" they are designed to be, in the extent to which they are combined with other treatment methods such as individual therapy, group counseling, or skill development, and in how completely the program is able to control all the relevant aspects of the institutional environment.

One might well begin with two studies that have been done of institutionalized adults, in regular prisons, who have been subjected to such treatment; this is the category whose results are the most clearly discouraging. One study of such a program, by Robison (1967), found that the therapy did seem to reduce recidivism after one year. After two years, however, this effect disappeared, and the treated convicts did no better than the untreated. Another study, by Kassebaum, Ward, and Wilner (1971), dealt with a program which had been able to effect an exceptionally extensive and experimentally rigorous transformation of the institutional environment. This sophisticated study had a follow–up period of 36 months, and it found that the program had no significant effect on parole failure or success rates.

The results of the studies of youth are more equivocal. As for young females, one study by Adams (1966) of such a program found that it had no significant effect on recidivism; another study, by Goldberg and Adams (1964), found that such a program *did* have a positive effect. This effect declined when the program began to deal with girls who were judged beforehand to be worse risks.

As for young males, the studies may conveniently be divided into those dealing with juveniles (under 16) and those dealing with youths. There have been five studies of milieu therapy administered to juveniles. Two of them—by Laulicht (1962) and by Jesness (1965)—report clearly that the program in question either had no significant effect or had a short-term effect that wore off with passing time. Jesness does report that when his experimental juveniles did commit new offenses, the offenses were less serious than those committed by controls. A third study of juveniles, by McCord (1953) at the Wiltwych School, reports mixed results. Using two measures of performance, a "success" rate and a "failure" rate, McCord found that his experimental group achieved both less failure *and* less success than the controls did. There have been two positive reports on milieu therapy programs for male juveniles; both of them have come out of the Highfields program, the milieu therapy experiment which has become the most famous and widely quoted example of "success" via this method. A group of boys was confined for a relatively short time to the unrestrictive, supportive environment of Highfields; and at a follow-up of six months, Freeman (1956) found that the group did indeed show a lower recidivism rate (as measured by parole revocation) than a similar group spending a longer time in the regular reformatory. McCorkle (1958) also reported positive findings from Highfields. But in fact, the McCorkle data show, this improvement was not so clear: The Highfields boys had lower recidivism rates at 12 and 36 months in the follow-up period, but not at 24 and 60 months. The length of follow-up, these data remind us, may have large implications for a study's conclusions. But more important were other flaws in the Highfields experiment: The populations were not fully comparable (they differed according to risk level and time of admission); different organizations—the probation agency for the Highfields boys, the parole agency for the others—were making the revocation decisions for each group; more of the Highfields boys were discharged early from supervision, and thus removed from any risk of revocation. In short, not even from the celebrated Highfields case may we take clear assurance that milieu therapy works.

In the case of male youths, as opposed to male juveniles, the findings are just as equivocal, and hardly more encouraging. One such study by Empey (1966) in a residential context did not produce significant results. A study by Seckel (1967) described California's Fremont Program, in which institutionalized youths participated in a combination of therapy, work projects, field trips, and community meetings. Seckel found that the youths subjected to this treatment committed *more* violations of law than did their non-treated counterparts.

• • •

So the youth in these milieu therapy programs at least do no worse than their counterparts in regular institutions and the special programs may cost less. One may therefore be encouraged—not on grounds of rehabilitation but on grounds of cost-effectiveness.

WHAT ABOUT MEDICAL TREATMENT?

4. *Isn't there anything you can do in an institutional setting that will reduce recidivism, for instance, through strictly medical treatment?*

A number of studies deal with the results of efforts to change the behavior of offenders through drugs and surgery. As for surgery, the one experimental study of a plastic surgery program—by Mandell (1967)—had negative results. For non-addicts who received plastic surgery, Mandall purported to find improvement in performance on parole; but when one reanalyzes his data, it appears that surgery alone did not in fact make a significant difference.

One type of surgery does seem to be highly successful in reducing recidivism. A twenty-year Danish study of sex offenders, by Stuerup (1960), found that while those who had been treated with hormones and therapy continued to commit both sex crimes (29.6 per cent of them did so) and non-sex crimes (21.0 per cent), those who had been castrated had rates of only 3.5 per cent (not, interestingly enough, a rate of zero; where there's a will, apparently there's a way) and 9.2 per cent. One hopes that the policy implications of this study will be found to be distinctly limited.

As for drugs, the major report on such a program—involving tranquilization—was made by Adams (1961b). The tranquilizers were administered to male and female institutionalized youths. With boys, there was only a slight improvement in their subsequent behavior; this improvement disappeared within a year. With girls, the tranquilization produced worse results than when the girls were given no treatment at all.

THE EFFECTS OF SENTENCING

5. *Well, at least it may be possible to manipulate certain gross features of the existing, conventional prison system—such as length of sentence and degree of security—in order to affect these recidivism rates. Isn't this the case?*

At this point, it's still impossible to say that this is the case. As for the degree of security in an institution, Glaser's (1964) work reported that, for both youth and adults, a less restrictive "custody grading" in American federal prisons was related to success on parole; but this is hardly surprising, since those assigned to more restrictive custody are likely to be worse risks in the first place. More to the point, an American study by Fox (1950) discovered that for "older youths" who were deemed to be good risks for the future, a minimum security institution produced better results than a maximum security one. On the other hand, the data we have on youths under 16—from a study by McClintock (1961), done in Great Britain—indicate that so-called Borstals, in which boys are totally confined, are more effective than a less restrictive regime of partial physical custody. In short, we know very little about the recidivism effects of various degrees of security in existing institutions; and our problems in finding out will be compounded by the probability that these effects will vary widely according to the particular *type* of offender that we're dealing with.

The same problems of mixed results and lack of comparable populations have plagued attempts to study the effects of sentence length. A number of studies— by Narloch (1959), by Bernsten (1965), and by the State of California (1956)— suggest that those who are released earlier from institutions than their scheduled parole date, or those who serve short sentences of under three months rather than longer sentences of eight months or more, either do better on parole or at least do no worse. The implication here is quite clear and important: Even if early releases and short sentences produce no improvement in recidivism rates, one could at least maintain the same rates while lowering the cost of maintaining the offender and lessening his own burden of imprisonment. Of course, this implication carries with it its concomitant danger: the danger that though shorter sentences cause no worsening of the recidivism rate, they may increase the total amount of crime in the community by increasing the absolute number of potential recidivists at large.

• • •

More important, the effect of sentence length seems to vary widely according to type of offender. In a British study (1963), for instance, Hammond found that for a group of "hard-core recidivists," shortening the sentence caused no improvement in the recidivism rate. In Denmark, Bernsten (1965) discovered a similar phenomenon: That the beneficial effect of three-month sentences as against eight-month ones disappeared in the case of these "hard-core recidivists." Garrity found another such distinction in his 1956 study. He divided his offenders into three categories: "pro-social," "anti-social," and "manipulative." "Pro-social" offenders he found to have low recidivism rates regardless of the length of their sentence; "anti-social" offenders did better with short sentences; the "manipulative" did better with long ones. Two studies from Britain made yet another division of the offender population, and found yet other variations. One (Great Britain, 1964) found that previous offenders—but not first offenders— did better with *longer* sentences, while the other (Cambridge, 1951) found the *reverse* to be true with juveniles.

To add to the problem of interpretation, these studies deal not only with different types and categorizations of offenders but with different types of institutions as well. No more than in the case of institution type can we say that length of sentence has a clear relationship to recidivism.

DECARCERATING THE CONVICT

6. *All of this seems to suggest that there's not much we know how to do to rehabilitate an offender when he's in an institution. Doesn't this lead to the clear possibility that the way to rehabilitate offenders is to deal with them* outside *an institutional setting?*

This is indeed an important possibility, and it is suggested by other pieces of information as well. For instance, Miner (1967) reported on a milieu therapy program in Massachusetts called Outward Bound. It took youths 15½ and over; it was oriented toward the development of skills in the out-of-doors and conducted in a wilderness atmosphere very different from that of most existing institutions. The culmination of the 26-day program was a final 24 hours in which each youth had to survive alone in the wilderness. And Miner found that the program did indeed work in reducing recidivism rates.

But by and large, when one takes the programs that have been administered in institutions and applies them in a non-institutional setting, the results do not grow to encouraging proportions. With casework and individual counseling in the community, for instance, there have been three studies; they dealt with counseling methods from psycho-social and vocational counseling to "operant conditioning," in which an offender was rewarded first simply for coming to counseling sessions and then, gradually, for performing other types of approved acts. Two of them report that the community-counseled offenders did no better than their institutional controls, while the third notes that although community counseling produced fewer arrests per person, it did not ultimately reduce the offender's chance of returning to a reformatory.

• • •

PSYCHOTHERAPY
IN COMMUNITY SETTINGS

There is some indication that individual psychotherapy may "work" in a community setting. Massimo (1963) reported on one such program, using what might be termed a "pragmatic" psychotherapeutic approach, including "insight" therapy and a focus on vocational problems. The program was marked by its small size and by its use of therapists who were personally enthusiastic about the project; Massimo found that there was indeed a decline in recidivism rate. Adamson (1956), on the other hand, found no significant difference produced by another program of individual therapy (though he did note that arrest rates among the experimental boys declined with what he called "intensity of treatment"). And Schwitzgebel (1963, 1964), studying other, different kinds of therapy programs, found that the programs *did* produce improvements in the attitudes of his boys—but, unfortunately, not in their rates of recidivism.

And with *group* therapy administered in the community, we find yet another set of equivocal results. The results from studies of pragmatic group counseling are only mildly optimistic. Adams (1965) did report that a form of group therapy, "guided group interaction," when administered to juvenile gangs, did somewhat reduce the percentage that were to be found in custody six years later. On the other hand, in a study of juveniles, Adams (1964) found that while such a program did reduce the number of contacts that an experimental youth had with police, it made no ultimate difference in the detention rate. And the attitudes of the counseled youth showed no improvement. Finally, when O'Brien

(1961) examined a community-based program of group psychotherapy, he found not only that the program produced no improvement in the recidivism rate, but that the experimental boys actually did worse than their controls on a series of psychological tests.

PROBATION OR PAROLE VERSUS PRISON

But by far the most extensive and important work that has been done on the effect of community-based treatments had been done in the areas of probation and parole. This work sets out to answer the question of whether it makes any difference how you supervise and treat an offender once he has been released from prison or has come under state surveillance in lieu of prison. This is the work that has provided the main basis to date for the claim that we do indeed have the means at our disposal for rehabilitating the offender or at least de-carcerating him safely.

One group of these studies has compared the use of probation with other dispositions for offenders; these provide some slight evidence that, at least under some circumstances, probation may make an offender's future chances better than if he had been sent to prison. Or, at least, probation may not worsen those chances. A British study, by Wilkins (1958), reported that when probation was granted more frequently, recidivism rates among probationers did not increase significantly. And another such study by the state of Michigan in 1963 reported that an expansion in the use of probation actually improved recidivism rates—though there are serious problems of comparability in the groups and systems that were studied.

• • •

Quite a large group of studies deals not with probation as compared to other dispositions, but instead with the type of treatment that an offender receives once he is *on* probation or parole. These are the studies that have provided the most encouraging reports on rehabilitative treatment and that have also raised the most serious questions about the nature of the research that has been going on in the corrections field.

Five of these studies have dealt with youthful probationers from 13 to 18 who were assigned to probation officers with small caseloads or provided with other ways of receiving more intensive supervision (Adams, 1966—two reports; Fiestman, 1966; Kawaguchi, 1967; Pilnick, 1967). These studies report that, by and large, intensive supervision does work—that the specially treated youngsters do better according to some measure of recidivism. Yet these studies left some important questions unanswered. For instance, was this improved performance a function merely of the number of contacts a youngster had with his probation officer? Did it also depend on the length of time in treatment? Or was it the quality of supervision that was making the difference, rather than the quantity?

INTENSIVE SUPERVISION:
THE WARREN STUDIES

The widely reported Warren studies (1966a, 1966b, 1967) in California constitute an extremely ambitious attempt to answer these questions. In this project, a control group of youths, drawn from a pool of candidates ready for first admission to a California Youth Authority institution, was assigned to regular detention, usually for eight to nine months, and then released to regular supervision. The experimental group received considerably more elaborate treatment. They were released directly to probation status and assigned to 12-man caseloads. To decide what special treatment was appropriate within these caseloads, the youths were divided according to their "interpersonal maturity level classification," by use of a scale developed by Grant and Grant. And each level dictated its own special type of therapy.

• • •

"Success" in this experiment was defined as favorable discharge by the Youth Authority; "failure" was unfavorable discharge, revocation, or recommitment by a court. Warren reported an encouraging finding: Among all but one of the "subtypes," the experimentals had a significantly lower failure rate than the controls. The experiment did have certain problems: The experimentals might have been performing better because of the enthusiasm of the staff and the attention lavished on them; none of the controls had been *directly* released to their regular supervision programs instead of being detained first; and it was impossible to separate the effects of the experimentals' small caseloads from their specially designed treatments, since no experimental youths had been assigned to a small caseload with "inappropriate" treatment, or with no treatment at all. Still, none of these problems were serious enough to vitiate the encouraging prospect that this finding presented for successful treatment of probationers.

This encouraging finding was, however, accompanied by a rather more disturbing clue. As has been mentioned before, the experimental subjects, when measured, had a lower *failure* rate than the controls. But the experimentals also had a lower *success* rate. That is, fewer of the experimentals as compared with the controls had been judged to have successfully completed their program of supervision and to be suitable for favorable release. When my colleagues and I undertook a rather laborious reanalysis of the Warren data, it became clear why this discrepancy had appeared. It turned out that fewer experimentals were "successful" because the experimentals were actually committing more offenses than their controls. The reason that the experimentals' relatively large number of offenses was not being reflected in their failure rates was simply that the experimentals' probation officers were using a more lenient revocation policy. In other words, the controls had a higher failure rate because the controls were being revoked for less serious offenses.

So it seems that what Warren was reporting in her "failure" rates was not merely the treatment effect of her small caseloads and special programs. Instead, what Warren was finding was not so much a change in the behavior of the experimental youths as a change in the behavior of the experimental *probation officers,* who knew the "special" status of their charges and who had evidently decided to revoke probation status at a lower than normal rate. The experimentals continued to commit offenses; what was different was that when they committed these offenses, they were permitted to remain on probation,

The experimenters claimed that this low revocation policy, and the greater number of offenses committed by the special treatment youth, were *not* an indication that these youth were behaving specially badly and that policy makers were simply letting them get away with it. Instead, it was claimed, the higher reported offense rate was primarily an artifact of the more intense surveillance that the experimental youth received. But the data show that this is not a sufficient explanation of the low failure rate among experimental youth; the difference in "tolerance" of offenses between experimental officials and control officials was much greater than the difference in the rates at which these two systems detected youths committing new offenses. Needless to say, this reinterpretation of the data presents a much bleaker picture of the possibilities of intensive supervision with special treatment.

"TREATMENT EFFECTS" VS. "POLICY EFFECTS"

This same problem of experimenter bias may also be present in the predecessors of the Warren study, the ones which had also found positive results from intensive supervision on probation; indeed, this disturbing question can be raised about many of the previously discussed reports of positive "treatment effects."

This possibility of a "policy effect" rather than a "treatment effect" applies, for instance, to the previously discussed studies of the effects of intensive supervision on juvenile and youthful probationers. These were the studies, it will be recalled, which found lower recidivism rates for the intensively supervised.

• • •

One must conclude that the "benefits" of intensive supervision for youthful offenders may stem not so much from a "treatment" effect as from a "policy" effect—that such supervision, so far as we now know, results not in rehabilitation but in a decision to look the other way when an offense is committed. But there is one major modification to be added to this conclusion. Johnson performed a further measurement (1962b) in his parole experiment: He rated all the supervising agents according to the "adequacy" of the supervision they gave. And he found that an "adequate" agent, whether he was working in a small *or* a large caseload, produced a relative improvement in his charges. The converse was not true: An *in*adequate agent was more likely to produce youthful "failures" when he was given a *small* caseload to supervise. One can't much help a "good" agent, it seems, by reducing his caseload size; such reduction can only do further harm to those youths who fall into the hands of "bad" agents.

So with youthful offenders, Johnson found, intensive supervision does not seem to provide the rehabilitative benefits claimed for it; the only such benefits may flow not from intensive supervision itself but from contact with one of the "good people" who are frequently in such short supply.

INTENSIVE SUPERVISION OF ADULTS

The results are similarly ambiguous when one applies this intensive supervision to adult offenders. There have been several studies of the effects of intensive supervision on adult parolees. Some of these are hard to interpret because of problems of comparability between experimental and control groups (general risk ratings, for instance, or distribution of narcotics offenders, or policy changes that took place between various phases of the experiments), but two of them (California, 1966; Stanton, 1964) do not seem to give evidence of the benefits of intensive supervision. By far the most extensive work, though, on the effects of intensive supervision of adult parolees has been a series of studies of California's Special Intensive Parole Unit (SIPU), a 10-year-long experiment designed to test the treatment possibilities of various special parole programs. Three of the four "phases" of this experiment produced "negative results." The first phase tested the effect of a reduced caseload size; no lasting effect was found. The second phase slightly increased the size of the small caseloads and provided for a longer time in treatment; again there was no evidence of a treatment effect. In the fourth phase, caseload sizes and time in treatment were again varied, and treatments were simultaneously varied in a sophisticated way according to personality characteristics of the parolees; once again, significant results did not appear.

The only phase of this experiment for which positive results were reported was Phase Three. Here, it was indeed found that a smaller caseload improved one's chances of parole success. There is, however, an important caveat that attaches to this finding: When my colleagues and I divided the whole population of subjects into two groups—those receiving supervision in the North of the state and those in the South—we found that the "improvement" of the experimentals' success rates was taking place primarily in the North. The North differed from the South in one important aspect: Its agents practiced a policy of returning both "experimental" and "control" violators to prison at relatively high rates. And it was the North that produced the higher success rate among its experimentals. So this improvement in experimentals' performance was taking place only when accompanied by a "realistic threat" of severe sanctions.

• • •

THE EFFECTS OF COMMUNITY TREATMENT

In sum, even in the case of treatment programs administered outside penal institutions, we simply cannot say that this treatment in itself has an appreciable effect on offender behavior. On the other hand, there is one encouraging set of findings that emerges from these studies. For from many of them there flows the strong suggestion that even if we can't "treat" offenders so as to make them do better, a great many of the programs designed to rehabilitate them at least did not make them do *worse*. And if these programs did not show the advantages of actually rehabilitating, some of them did have the advantage of being less onerous to the offender himself without seeming to pose increased danger to the community. And some of these programs—especially those involving less restrictive custody, minimal supervision, and early release—simply cost fewer dollars to administer. The information on the dollar costs of these programs is just beginning to be developed but the implication is clear: *that if we can't do more for (and to) offenders, at least we can safely do less.*

There is, however, one important caveat even to this note of optimism: In order to calculate the true costs of these programs, one must in each case include not only their administrative cost but also the cost of maintaining in the community an offender population increased in size. This population might well not be committing new offenses at any greater rate; but the offender population might, under some of these plans, be larger in absolute *numbers*. So the total number of offenses committed might rise, and our chances of victimization might therefore rise too. We need to be able to make a judgment about the size and probable duration of this effect; as of now, we simply do not know.

DOES NOTHING WORK?

7. *Do all of these studies lead us irrevocably to the conclusion that nothing works, that we haven't the faintest clue about how to rehabilitate offenders and reduce recidivism? And if so, what shall we do?*

We tried to exclude from our survey those studies which were so poorly done that they simply could not be interpreted. But despite our efforts, a pattern has run through much of this discussion—of studies which "found" effects without making any truly rigorous attempt to exclude competing hypotheses, of extraneous factors permitted to intrude upon the measurements, of recidivism measures which are not all measuring the same thing, of "follow-up" periods which vary enormously and rarely extend beyond the period of legal supervision, of experiments never replicated, of "system effects" not taken into account, of categories drawn up without any theory to guide the enterprise. It is just possible that some of our treatment programs *are* working to some extent, but that our research is so bad that it is incapable of telling.

Having entered this very serious caveat, I am bound to say that these data, involving over two hundred studies and hundreds of thousands of individuals as they do, are the best available and give us very little reason to hope that we have in fact found a sure way of reducing recidivism through rehabilitation. This is not to say that we found no instances of success or partial success; it is only to say that these instances have been isolated, producing no clear pattern to indicate the efficacy of any particular method of treatment. And neither is this to say that factors *outside* the realm of rehabilitation may not be working to reduce recidivism—factors such as the tendency for recidivism to be lower in offenders over the age of 30; it is only to say that such factors seem to have little connection with any of the treatment methods now at our disposal.

From this probability, one may draw any of several conclusions. It may be simply that our programs aren't yet good enough—that the education we provide to inmates is still poor education, that the therapy we administer is not administered skillfully enough, that our intensive supervision and counseling do not yet provide enough personal support for the offenders who are subjected to them. If one wishes to believe this, then what our correctional system needs is simply a more full-hearted commitment to the strategy of treatment.

It may be, on the other hand, that there is a more radical flaw in our present strategies—that education at its best, or that psychotherapy at its best, cannot overcome, or even appreciably reduce, the powerful tendency for offenders to continue in criminal behavior. Our present treatment programs are based on a theory of crime as a "disease"—that is to say, as something foreign and abnormal in the individual which can presumably be cured. This theory may well be flawed, in that it overlooks—indeed, denies—both the normality of crime in society and the personal normality of a very large proportion of offenders, criminals who are merely responding to the facts and conditions of our society.

This opposing theory of "crime as a social phenomenon" directs our attention away from a "rehabilitative" strategy, away from the notion that we may best insure public safety through a series of "treatments" to be imposed forcibly on convicted offenders. These treatments have on occasion become, and have the potential for becoming, so draconian as to offend the moral order of a democratic society; and the theory of crime as a social phenomenon suggests that such treatments may not be only offensive but ineffective as well. This theory points, instead, to decarceration for low-risk offenders—and, presumably, to keeping high-risk offenders in prisons which are nothing more (and aim to be nothing more) than custodial institutions.

But this approach has its own problems. To begin with, there is the moral dimension of crime and punishment. Many low-risk offenders have committed serious crimes (murder, sometimes) and even if one is reasonably sure they will never commit another crime, it violates our sense of justice that they should experience no significant retribution for their actions. A middle-class banker who kills his adulterous wife in a moment of passion is a "low-risk" criminal; a juvenile delinquent in the ghetto who commits armed robbery has, statistically, a much higher probability of committing another crime. Are we going to put the first on probation and sentence the latter to a long term in prison?

Besides, one cannot ignore the fact that the punishment of offenders is the major means we have for *deterring* incipient offenders. We know almost nothing about the "deterrent effect," largely because "treatment" theories have so dominated our research, and "deterrence" theories have been relegated to the status of a historical curiosity. Since we have almost no idea of the deterrent functions that our present system performs or that future strategies might be made to perform, it is possible that there is indeed something that works—that to some extent is working right now in front of our noses, and that might be made to work better—something that deters rather than cures, something that does not so much reform convicted offenders as prevent criminal behavior in the first place. But whether that is the case and, if it is, what strategies will be found to make our deterrence system work better than it does now, are questions we will not be able to answer with data until a new family of studies has been brought into existence. As we begin to learn the facts, we will be in a better position than we are now to judge to what degree the prison has become an anachronism and can be replaced by more effective means of social control.

PART VII

❂

Policy Perspectives

C rime and the administration of justice have been prominent on the public policy agenda since the mid–1960s. During this period, Congress has created and abolished the Law Enforcement Assistance Administration (LEAA), two presidential commissions have made extensive suggestions for reform, and billions of dollars have been spent in attempts to reduce crime and improve the justice system. Initially, an air of certainty about the causes of crime and the way to reform criminals characterized official and scholarly statements on the problem. Like the bulk of policy research, rationality and scientific reasoning drove research agendas in criminal justice. But only during the past few years have the true dimensions of crime and the potential for dealing with it been viewed with a new realism, in part because humans confound true scientific approaches and limit possibilities for authentic experimentation. As James Q. Wilson, a leading exponent of this realistic stance, stated, our efforts to understand and curb the rise in crime have been frustrated by "our optimistic and unrealistic assumptions about human nature." This view is a far cry from the previously prevalent belief that crime, like poverty, could be ended if only there were enough money to apply the techniques of the social and behavioral sciences to the "root causes"—poor housing, unemployment, and racial prejudice.

In the past quarter century, research has provided a glimmer of hope for those who believe that the social sciences have the analytical tools to understand crime and to contribute to formation of public policies to deal with it. This research appears to be more systematic, to be based on empirical findings, and to challenge much of the "conventional wisdom" about crime, criminal behavior, and the administration of justice. There is a new appreciation of the complex dimensions of criminal behavior and of the fact that the law-enforcement function is only one role of the police. The courts are increasingly viewed as organizations composed of small groups, and it is recognized that rehabilitative techniques have had a low success rate. In addition, the dominant approach has been that criminal justice is a system.

Research should be the essential activity on which public policies are built. If government decisions were not influenced by politics, one might be able to show how the findings of social scientists could be directly applied to solving a public problem. Ideally, policies should reflect state-of-the-art research, the best of our expert wisdom. Yet public decisions arise from a complicated confluence of public and legislative recognition of a problem, well-defined and measured solutions in the policy realm, and negotiation in the political arena. The latter may well include considerations like types of interest groups, the balance of power between congressional and executive branches, and the national mood. Thus, solutions discussed by experts usually have little relation to the operational plans that emerge from the policy process.

We know that Americans feel strongly about crime, and feel it is deserving of governmental attention. With equal certainty, we know that Americans remain strong in their feelings about the preservation of individual liberty and self-governance. Although Americans are fearful of crime, and want action to address it, what remains unclear is precisely what action the polis would condone. Increases in press coverage of focusing events such as the tragedy of Columbine, O. J. Simpson, and the Oklahoma City bombing help prioritize crime as a top public concern, but political communication research tells us that the media can only tell us what to think about, not what to think. Thus, Americans' real policy preferences toward crime control remain unclear. Debate over criminal justice policies may be daily noted in the press, in legislative assemblies, and in private conversations. Should the police be allowed to detain suspects without bail? Should sentences emphasize incapacitation or rehabilitation? Should efforts be undertaken to improve neighborhoods that breed crime? Should the War on Drugs be continued?

Discussions of these and similar questions get to basic questions about crime and justice policies in a democracy. During the past quarter of a century one can detect a shift in public opinion and policy direction. Until the mid-1970s the recommendations of the 1967 report of the President's Commission on Law Enforcement and Administration of Justice seemed to hold sway at both the federal and state levels of government. The commission declared that crime was caused essentially by disorganization in American society; that agencies engaged in enforcement, adjudication, and corrections lacked sufficient resources; and that rehabilitation had been insufficiently emphasized in the treatment of offenders. The writers of the report recommend eliminating social conditions that bring about crime, doing away with social and racial injustices in order to achieve the ideals of the American ethic, and reintegrating those who commit crime into their communities.

The middle of the 1970s saw a shift in criminal justice policies that mirrored the ascendance of conservative political leaders. Since that time the conservative critique of the liberal policies of the 1960s has been constant. The critique gained credence during the 1970s in part because research cast doubt on many previous policies. Debate about "what works" sparked a reconsideration of the role of rehabilitative programs. Committees of the National Academy of Sciences recommended that greater weight be given to policies of incarceration and deterrence.

Questions were raised about the dangers posed by the practice of allowing bail to repeat offenders, the prosecution of career criminals, lengths of incarcerative sentences, and the broader efforts to reduce crime through social reform.

The election of Ronald Reagan in 1980 consolidated the shift in crime control policies. Actions taken during the Reagan, Bush, and Clinton administrations, and copied in most states, placed greater emphasis upon increasing resources for police and prosecutors, raising sentence lengths, increasing the use of incarceration, tightening the insanity defense, and abolishing parole release. These policies are expected to continue during the current administration.

Now that we have experienced almost twenty years of harsher crime control policies, have they made a difference? Some will point to the leveling off of the crime rate during the mid-1970s and argue that the tougher policies have worked. Opponents point to the doubling of the incarcerative population during the past decade as proof that these policies have failed. Is another shift in crime and justice policies in the offing? Will the costs of the War on Drugs and increased use of prison cause taxpayers to raise questions about the future of these policies? Will concerned citizens again call for policies that emphasize justice over crime control?

SUGGESTIONS FOR FURTHER READING

Horney, Julie, and Cassia Spohn. "Rape Law Reform and Instrumental Change in Six Urban Jurisdictions," 25 *Law and Society Review* 117 (1991). Characterizes rape reform law as symbolic, and recommends monitoring implementation and enforcement of these laws.

Rossi, Peter H., and Richard A. Berk. *Just Punishments: Federal Guidelines and Public Views Compared.* New York: Aldine de Gruyter, 1997. Examines agreement between public perceptions of crime seriousness, and policies for sentencing of convicted offenders set forth by the United States Sentencing Commission.

Sampson, Robert, and John Laub. *Crime in the Making: Pathways and Turning Points Through Life.* Cambridge, Mass.: Harvard University Press, 1993.

2 6

✪

Legalization Madness

JAMES A. INCIARDI
CHRISTINE A. SAUM

It has been said that the War on Drugs has succeeded only in filling of prisons. Frustrations with this policy have led many to advocate legalization and treating drug use as a public health problem. The authors of this title take an opposing view on this important policy issue.

Frustrated by the government's apparent inability to reduce the supply of illegal drugs on the streets of America, and disquieted by media accounts of innocents victimized by drug-related violence, some policy makers are convinced that the "war on drugs" has failed. In an attempt to find a better solution to the "drug crisis" or, at the very least, to try an alternative strategy, they have proposed legalizing drugs.

They argue that, if marijuana, cocaine, heroin, and other drugs were legalized, several positive things would probably occur: (1) drug prices would fall; (2) users would obtain their drugs at low, government-regulated prices, and they would no longer be forced to resort to crime in order to support their habits; (3) levels of drug-related crime, and particularly violent crime, would significantly decline, resulting in less crowded courts, jails, and prisons (this would allow law-enforcement personnel to focus their energies on the "real criminals" in society); and (4) drug production, distribution, and sale would no longer be controlled

Source: James A. Inciardi and Christine A. Saum, "Legalization Madness," *The Public Interest,* No. 123 (Spring 1996), pp. 72–82. Reprinted with permission of the author from *The Public Interest,* © 1996 by National Affairs, Inc.

by organized crime, and thus such criminal syndicates as the Colombian cocaine "cartels," the Jamaican "posses," and the various "mafias" around the country and the world would be decapitalized, and the violence associated with drug distribution rivalries would be eliminated.

By contrast, the anti-legalization camp argues that violent crime would not necessarily decline in a legalized drug market. In fact, there are three reasons why it might actually increase. First, removing the criminal sanctions against the possession and distribution of illegal drugs would make them more available and attractive and, hence, would create large numbers of new users. Second, an increase in use would lead to a greater number of dysfunctional addicts who could not support themselves, their habits, or their lifestyles through legitimate means. Hence crime would be their only alternative. Third, more users would mean more of the violence associated with the ingestion of drugs.

These divergent points of view tend to persist because the relationships between drugs and crime are quite complex and because the possible outcomes of a legalized drug market are based primarily on speculation. However, it is possible, from a careful review of the existing empirical literature on drugs and violence, to make some educated inferences.

CONSIDERING "LEGALIZATION"

Yet much depends upon what we mean by "legalizing drugs." Would all currently illicit drugs be legalized or would the experiment be limited to just certain ones? True legalization would be akin to selling such drugs as heroin and cocaine on the open market, much like alcohol and tobacco, with a few age-related restrictions. In contrast, there are "medicalization" and "decriminalization" alternatives. Medicalization approaches are of many types, but, in essence, they would allow users to obtain prescriptions for some, or all, currently illegal substances. Decriminalization removes the criminal penalties associated with the possession of small amounts of illegal drugs for personal use, while leaving intact the sanctions for trafficking, distribution, and sale.

But what about crack-cocaine? A quick review of the literature reveals that the legalizers, the decriminalizers, and the medicalizers avoid talking about this particular form of cocaine. Perhaps they do not want to legalize crack out of fear of the drug itself, or of public outrage. Arnold S. Trebach, a professor of law at American University and president of the Drug Policy Foundation, is one of the very few who argues for the full legalization of all drugs, including crack. He explains, however, that most are reluctant to discuss the legalization of crack-cocaine because, "it is a very dangerous drug. . . . I know that for many people the very thought of making crack legal destroys any inclination they might have had for even thinking about drug-law reform."

There is a related concern associated with the legalization of cocaine. Because crack is easily manufactured from powder cocaine (just add water and baking soda and cook on a stove or in a microwave), many drug-policy reformers hold that no form of cocaine should be legalized. But this weakens the argument that legalization will reduce drug-related violence; for much of this violence would appear to be in the cocaine- and crack-distribution markets.

To better understand the complex relationship between drugs and violence, we will discuss the data in the context of three models developed by Paul J. Goldstein of the University of Illinois at Chicago. They are the "psychopharmacological," "economically compulsive," and "systemic" explanations of violence. The first model holds, correctly in our view, that some individuals may become excitable, irrational, and even violent due to the ingestion of specific drugs. In contrast, taking a more economic approach to the behavior of drug users, the second holds that some drug users engage in violent crime mainly for the sake of supporting their drug use. The third model maintains that drug-related violent crime is simply the result of the drug market under a regime of illegality.

PSYCHOPHARMACOLOGICAL VIOLENCE

The case for legalization rests in part upon the faulty assumption that drugs themselves do not cause violence; rather, so goes the argument, violence is the result of depriving drug addicts of drugs or of the "criminal" trafficking in drugs. But, as researcher Barry Spunt points out, "Users of drugs do get violent when they get high."

Research has documented that chronic users of amphetamines, methamphetamine, and cocaine in particular tend to exhibit hostile and aggressive behaviors. Psychopharmacological violence can also be a product of what is known as "cocaine psychosis." As dose and duration of cocaine use increase, the development of cocaine-related psychopathology is not uncommon. Cocaine psychosis is generally preceded by a transitional period characterized by increased suspiciousness, compulsive behavior, fault finding, and eventually paranoia. When the psychotic state is reached, individuals may experience visual, as well as auditory, hallucinations, with persecutory voices commonly heard. Many believe that they are being followed by police or that family, friends, and others are plotting against them.

Moreover, everyday events are sometimes misinterpreted by cocaine users in ways that support delusional beliefs. When coupled with the irritability and hyperactivity that cocaine tends to generate in almost all of its users, the cocaine-induced paranoia may lead to violent behavior as a means of "self-defense" against imagined persecutors. The violence associated with cocaine psychosis is a common feature in many crack houses across the United States. Violence may also result from the irritability associated with drug-withdrawal syndromes. In addition, some users ingest drugs before committing crimes to both loosen inhibitions and bolster their resolve to break the law.

Acts of violence may result from either periodic or chronic use of a drug. For example, in a study of drug use and psychopathy among Baltimore City jail inmates, researchers at the University of Baltimore reported that cocaine use was related to irritability, resentment, hostility, and assault. They concluded that these indicators of aggression may be a function of drug effects rather than of a predisposition to these behaviors. Similarly, Barry Spunt and his colleagues at National Development and Research Institutes (NDRI) in New York City found that of 269 convicted murderers incarcerated in New York State prisons, 45 percent were high at the time of the offense. Three in 10 believed that the homicide was related to their drug use, challenging conventional beliefs that violence only infrequently occurs as a result of drug consumption.

Even marijuana, which pro-legalizers consider harmless, may have a connection with violence and crime. Spunt and his colleagues attempted to determine the role of marijuana in the crimes of the homicide offenders they interviewed in the New York State prisons. One-third of those who had ever used marijuana had smoked the drug in the 24-hour period prior to the homicide. Moreover, 31 percent of those who considered themselves to be "high" at the time of committing murder felt that the homicide and marijuana were related. William Blount of the University of South Florida interviewed abused women in prisons and shelters for battered women located throughout Florida. He and his colleagues found that 24 percent of those who killed their abusers were marijuana users while only 8 percent of those who did not kill their abusers smoked marijuana.

AND ALCOHOL ABUSE

A point that needs emphasizing is that alcohol, because it is legal, accessible, and inexpensive, is linked to violence to a far greater extent than any illegal drug. For example, in the study just cited, it was found that an impressive 64 percent of those women who eventually killed their abusers were alcohol users (44 percent of those who did not kill their abusers were alcohol users). Indeed, the extent to which alcohol is responsible for violent crimes in comparison with other drugs is apparent from the statistics. For example, Carolyn Block and her colleagues at the Criminal Justice Information Authority in Chicago found that, between 1982 and 1989, the use of alcohol by offenders or victims in local homicides ranged from 18 percent to 32 percent.

Alcohol has, in fact, been consistently linked to homicide. Spunt and his colleagues interviewed 268 homicide offenders incarcerated in New York State correctional facilities to determine the role of alcohol in their crimes: Thirty-one percent of the respondents reported being drunk at the time of the crime and 19 percent believed that the homicide was related to their drinking. More generally, Douglass Murdoch of Quebec's McGill University found that in some 9,000 criminal cases drawn from a multinational sample, 62 percent of violent offenders were drinking shortly before, or at the time of, the offense.

It appears that alcohol reduces the inhibitory control of threat, making it more likely that a person will exhibit violent behaviors normally suppressed by fear. In turn, this reduction of inhibition heightens the probability that intoxicated persons will perpetrate, or become victims of, aggressive behavior.

When analyzing the psychopharmacological model of drugs and violence, most of the discussions focus on the offender and the role of drugs in causing or facilitating crime. But what about the victims? Are the victims of drug- and alcohol-related homicides simply casualties of someone else's substance abuse? In addressing these questions, the data demonstrates that victims are likely to be drug users as well. For example, in an analysis of the 4,298 homicides that occurred in New York City during 1990 and 1991, Kenneth Tardiff of Cornell University Medical College found that the victims of these offenses were 10 to 50 times more likely to be cocaine users than were members of the general population. Of the white female victims, 60 percent in the 25- to 34-year age group had cocaine in their systems; for black females, the figure was 72 percent. Tardiff speculated that the classic symptoms of cocaine use—irritability, paranoia, aggressiveness—may have instigated the violence. In another study of cocaine users in New York City, female high-volume users were found to be victims of violence far more frequently than low-volume and nonusers of cocaine. Studies in numerous other cities and countries have yielded the same general findings—that a great many of the victims of homicide and other forms of violence are drinkers and drug users themselves.

ECONOMICALLY COMPULSIVE VIOLENCE

Supporters of the economically compulsive model of violence argue that in a legalized market, the prices of "expensive drugs" would decline to more affordable levels, and hence, predatory crimes would become unnecessary. This argument is based on several specious assumptions. First, it assumes that there is empirical support for what has been referred to as the "enslavement theory of addiction." Second, it assumes that people addicted to drugs commit crimes only for the purpose of supporting their habits. Third, it assumes that, in a legalized market, users could obtain as much of the drugs as they wanted whenever they wanted. Finally, it assumes that, if drugs are inexpensive, they will be affordable, and thus crime would be unnecessary.

With respect to the first premise, there has been for the better part of this century a concerted belief among many in the drug-policy field that addicts commit crimes because they are "enslaved" to drugs, and further that, because of the high price of heroin, cocaine, and other illicit chemicals on the black market, users are forced to commit crimes in order to support their drug habits. However, there is no solid empirical evidence to support this contention. From the 1920s through the end of the 1960s, hundreds of studies of the relationship between crime and addiction were conducted. Invariably, when one analysis would support the posture of "enslavement theory," the next would affirm the view that addicts were criminals first and that their drug use was but one more manifestation of their deviant lifestyles. In retrospect, the difficulty lay in the ways that many of the studies had been conducted. Biases and deficiencies in research designs and sampling had rendered their findings of little value.

Studies since the mid 1970s of active drug users on the streets of New York, Miami, Baltimore, and elsewhere have demonstrated that the "enslavement theory" has little basis in reality. All of these studies of the criminal careers of drug users have convincingly documented that, while drug use tends to intensify and perpetuate criminal behavior, it usually does not initiate criminal careers. In fact, the evidence suggests that among the majority of street drug users who are involved in crime, their criminal careers are well established prior to the onset of either narcotics or cocaine use. As such, it would appear that the "inference of causality"—that the high price of drugs on the black market itself causes crime—is simply false.

Looking at the second premise, a variety of studies show that addicts commit crimes for reasons other than supporting their drug habit. They do so also for daily living expenses. For example, researchers at the Center for Drug and Alcohol Studies at the University of Delaware who studied crack users on the streets of Miami found that, of the active addicts interviewed, 85 percent of the male and 70 percent of the female interviewees paid for portions of their living expenses through street crime. In fact, one-half of the men and one-fourth of the women paid for 90 percent or more of their living expenses through crime. And, not surprisingly, 96 percent of the men and 99 percent of the women had not held a legal job in the 90-day period before being interviewed for the study.

With respect to the third premise, that in a legalized market users could obtain as much of the drugs as they wanted whenever they wanted, only speculation is possible. More than likely, however, there would be some sort of regulation, and hence black markets for drugs would persist for those whose addictions were beyond the medicalized or legalized allotments. In a decriminalized market, levels of drug-related violence would likely either remain unchanged or increase (if drug use increased).

As for the last premise, that cheap drugs preclude the need to commit crimes to obtain them, the evidence emphatically suggests that this is not the case. Consider crack-cocaine: Although crack "rocks" are available on the illegal market for as little as two dollars in some locales, users are still involved in crime-driven endeavors to support their addictions. For example, researchers Norman S. Miller and Mark S. Gold surveyed 200 consecutive callers to the 1-800-COCAINE hotline who considered themselves to have a problem with crack. They found that, despite the low cost of crack, 63 percent of daily users and 40 percent of non-daily users spent more than $200 per week on the drug. Similarly, interviews conducted by NDRI researchers in New York City with almost 400 drug users contacted in the streets, jails, and treatment programs revealed that almost one-half of them spent over $1,000 a month on crack. The study also documented that crack users—despite the low cost of their drug of choice—spent more money on drugs than did users of heroin, powder cocaine, marijuana, and alcohol.

SYSTEMIC VIOLENCE

It is the supposed systemic violence associated with trafficking in cocaine and crack in America's inner cities that has recently received the attention of drug-policy critics interested in legalizing drugs. Certainly it might appear that, if heroin and cocaine were legal substances, systemic drug-related violence would decline. However, there are two very important questions in this regard: First, is drug-related violence more often psychopharmacological or systemic? Second, is the great bulk of systemic violence related to the distribution of crack? If most of the drug-related violence is psychopharmacological in nature, and if systemic violence is typically related to crack—the drug generally excluded from consideration when legalization is recommended—then legalizing drugs would probably *not* reduce violent crime.

Regarding the first question, several recent studies conducted in New York City tend to contradict, or at least not support, the notion that legalizing drugs would reduce violent, systemic-related crime. For example, Paul J. Goldstein's ethnographic studies of male and female drug users during the late 1980s found that cocaine-related violence was more often psychopharmacological than systemic. Similarly, Kenneth Tardiff's study of 4,298 New York City homicides found that 31 percent of the victims had used cocaine in the 24-hour period prior to their deaths. One of the conclusions of the study was that the homicides were not necessarily related to drug dealing. In all likelihood, as victims of homicide, the cocaine users may have provoked violence through their irritability, paranoid thinking, and verbal or physical aggression—all of which are among the psychopharmacological effects of cocaine.

Regarding the second question, the illegal drug most associated with systemic violence is crack-cocaine. Of all illicit drugs, crack is the one now responsible for the most homicides. In a study done in New York City in 1988 by Goldstein and his colleagues, crack was found to be connected with 32 percent of all homicides and 60 percent of all drug-related homicides. Furthermore, although there is evidence that crack sellers are more violent than other drug sellers, this violence is not confined to the drug-selling context—violence potentials appear to precede involvement in selling.

Thus, though crack has been blamed for increasing violence in the marketplace, this violence actually stems from the psychopharmacological consequences of crack use. Ansley Hamid, a professor of anthropology at the John Jay College of Criminal Justice in New York, reasons that increases in crack-related violence are due to the deterioration of informal and formal social controls throughout communities that have been destabilized by economic processes and political decisions. If this is the case, does anyone really believe that we can improve these complex social problems through the simple act of legalizing drugs?

DON'T JUST SAY NO

The issue of whether or not legalization would create a multitude of new users also needs to be addressed. It has been shown that many people do not use drugs simply because drugs are illegal. As Mark A. R. Kleiman, author of *Against Excess: Drug Policy for Results,* recently put it: "Illegality by itself tends to suppress consumption, independent of its effect on price, both because some consumers are reluctant to disobey the law and because illegal products are harder to find and less reliable as to quality and labeling than legal ones."

Although there is no way of accurately estimating how many new users there would be if drugs were legalized, there would probably be many. To begin with, there is the historical example of Prohibition. During Prohibition, there was a decrease of 20 percent to 50 percent in the number of alcoholics. These estimates were calculated based on a decline in cirrhosis and other alcohol-related deaths; after Prohibition ended, both of these indicators increased.

Currently, relatively few people are steady users of drugs. The University of Michigan's *Monitoring the Future* study reported in 1995 that only two-tenths of 1 percent of high-school seniors are daily users of either hallucinogens, cocaine, heroin, sedatives, or inhalants. It is the addicts who overwhelmingly consume the bulk of the drug supply—80 percent of all alcohol and almost 100 percent of all heroin. In other words, there are significantly large numbers of non-users who have yet to even try drugs, leg alone use them regularly. Of those who begin to use drugs "recreationally," researchers estimate that approximately 10 percent go on to serious, heavy, chronic, compulsive use. Herbert Kleber, the former deputy director of the Office of National Drug Control Policy, recently estimated that cocaine legalization might multiply the number of addicts form the current 2 million to between 18 and 50 million (which are the estimated numbers of problem drinkers and nicotine addicts).

This suggests that drug prohibition seems to be having some very positive effects and that legalizing drugs would not necessarily have a depressant effect on violent crime. With legalization, violent crime would likely escalate; or perhaps some types of systematic violence would decline at the expense of greatly increasing the overall rate of violent crime. Moreover, legalizing drugs would likely increase physical illnesses and compound any existing psychiatric problems among users and their family members. And finally, legalizing drugs would not eliminate the effects of unemployment, inadequate housing, deficient job skills, economic worries, and physical abuse that typically contribute to the use of drugs.

2 7

✪

Crime-Fighting
and Urban Renewal

ELI LEHRER

What is the relationship between poverty and crime? Does crime develop from the conditions of poverty, inadequate housing, and unemployment, or is it crime that creates neighborhoods of poverty? This is a key question for the fashioning of crime policies in urban areas.

For most of the past 35 years, convention wisdom has held that poverty causes crime. "Warring on poverty, inadequate housing, and unemployment is warring on crime," wrote the members of the 1967 Presidential Commission on Law Enforcement and the Administration of Criminal Justice. In college sociology courses, such thinking still dominates discourse: Steven R. Donzinger's *The Real War on Crime,* an influential book published in 1996, concludes that "a program to reduce poverty levels . . . will reduce levels of crime and violence and make the country safer." In 1999, a widely publicized report from the Milton S. Eisenhower Foundation came to much the same conclusion, arguing that well-run social programs for everyone, from at-risk youth to recently released prisoners, would mitigate the effects of poverty and, thus, reduce crime.

Yet a substantial body of criminological research over the past 20 years suggests that the relationship between poverty and crime runs counter to conventional wisdom. Social scientists such as John J. DiIulio, Jr., James Q. Wilson, Wesley Skogan, Leo Schuerman, and Solomon Korbin have shown that, in fact,

Source: Eli Lehrer, "Crime-Fighting and Urban Renewal," *The Public Interest,* No. 141 (Fall 2000), pp. 91–103. Reprinted with permission of the author from *The Public Interest,* © 2000 by National Affairs, Inc. Eli Lehrer is a visiting fellow at the Heritage Foundation, a Washington, D.C.–based public policy research institute. He can be reached by e-mail at elirl@msn.com.

poverty and neighborhood degradation often result from crime—not the other way around. Skogan, a Northwestern University criminologist who has studied what happens to places where crime and disorder increase, describe a scene of utter desolation: "These areas are no longer recognizable as neighborhoods."

I spent several months traveling to low-income areas around the country to investigate whether reductions in crime led to neighborhood renewal. My first-hand experience only reaffirmed the new thinking on poverty and crime: In short, when crime drops drastically, low-income neighborhoods come back to life. Commercial strips blossom with new businesses, housing improves, streets become safe at night, mediating institutions become stronger, and disorder vanishes from public spaces. Thus warring on crime is the best way to remedy a wide variety of social ills, and America's success in reducing crime ranks with welfare reform as the greatest *social policy* triumph of the 1990s.

CUTTING THE CRIME TAX

Today, for the first time in a generation, police and low-income communities are winning the war on crime. When final statistics come out later this year, the FBI will announce that crimes such as murder, rape, robbery, aggravated assault, burglary, larceny, motor vehicle theft, and arson fell over one-third between 1990 and 1999, due largely to improvements in a few large cities like New York. Nevertheless, the late 1990s saw declines in every type of city and in every major category of crime. Between 1994 and 1998, only 29 of the 205 American cities with 1999 populations over 100,000 for which comparable data are available saw their crime rates rise. The preliminary data for 1999 paint an even more positive picture. In 1999, there would have been nearly 8,000 additional murders, about 20,000 additional rapes, and over 200,000 additional armed attacks had crime not fallen. Criminals would have committed more than 3 million additional crimes during 1999 alone and over 18 million more during the decade.

Many economists think of crime as a tax on urban life. In this regard, it proves particularly cruel; the "crime tax" actually charges the poor a *higher* rate than the wealthy. The Bureau of Justice Statistics' National Crime Victimization Survey shows just how much crime hurts the poorest Americans. For the 30 million or so Americans living in households earning less than $15,000 a year, crime represents a horrific fact of daily life. Compared to the middle class, the poor fall victim to nearly six times as many rapes, more than twice as many robberies, almost double the number of aggravated assaults, and half again more acts of theft. Crime is, in short, an inversely progressive tax.

NINE NEIGHBORHOODS

To study the effects of crime reduction on civil society, I visited nine different neighborhoods in the cities of New York, Los Angeles, Boston, Garden Grove, California, and Providence, Rhode Island. I included New York and Los Angeles because they are the country's two largest cities and have reduced crime significantly. (Between 1994 and 1999, New York reduced crime nearly 45 percent; Los Angeles about 41 percent.) I selected the other three cities because they have reduced crime more than the average for cities similar in size and character. (Providence's reductions actually fall below the national average but are larger than those in most other small-center cities in the Northeast.) In the selected areas, which represented a range of low-income neighborhoods, overall reductions in neighborhood-level crime ranged from about a third to over 70 percent. Because precise neighborhood-level population counts aren't available, crime rates are all approximations. In most cases, crime fell as quickly or almost as quickly in neighborhoods adjoining those that I visited. For the most part, that is, police did not simply move crime from one neighborhood to another.

I made three stops in Boston. The Four Corners, Dorchester neighborhood is synonymous with the name of Reverend Eugene Rivers, who decided to work there in the early 1980s because it was so troubled. Between 1990 and 1999, serious crime rates have dropped nearly 70 percent for the mostly African-American neighborhood of about 28,000. Boston's Hyde Square, Jamaica Plain neighborhood once qualified as a war zone, but its 12,000 residents saw crime fall about 50 percent between 1990 and 1999. Boston's Upham's Corner, Dorchester neighborhood of 24,000 residents has also seen crime fall over 50 percent since 1990.

I made three stops in California, two in Garden Grove and one in Los Angeles. Garden Grove's Stewart Drive neighborhood was out of control by the early 1990s. Crime rates in this ethnically mixed neighborhood dropped by half for the area's 2,100 or so residents between 1995 and 1998. In 1983, the *Los Angeles Times* called Garden Grove's Buena-Clinton neighborhood "Orange County's Worse Slum." Yet crime has fallen around 50 percent. In the late 1980s, the residents of Yucca Corridor in Los Angeles often slept on the floor to avoid gunshots from rival gangs. Today, the neighborhood of about 8,500, just steps away from the tawdry glitz of Hollywood Boulevard, has a new park, scores of new community activities, and much improved housing. Crime rates fell over 40 percent between 1994 and 1999.

In Providence, Rhode Island, serious crime in the Armory District has fallen nearly 60 percent since 1989. Investment by the Armory Revival Company, a private, profitable concern with revenues that averaged about $7 million a year in the late 1990s, has transformed the neighborhood from a collection of burned-out hulks into a vibrant area of about 4,500.

New York's Alphabet City, a Lower-East Side Manhattan neighborhood, hit bottom when Ed Koch's administration sent in SWAT-team–like anti-drug forces under the mostly ineffective Operation Pressure Point in the late 1980s. Since then, the crime-fighting efforts of Rudy Giuliani and a series of new investments have slowly transformed Alphabet City from an open-air heroin market and campground for the homeless to a gentrifying area full of nightspots and boutiques. Crime has decreased about 65 percent since 1990 for the neighborhood's 70,000 residents.

By the early 1980s, The Bronx's Hunt's Point was one of New York's most desolate neighborhoods. The infamous Fort Apache police station sat on a plot of land where rampant arson had reduced several acres to prairie. Today, the once barren area around the Fort Apache contains prosperous looking single-family homes, and vacancies have nearly vanished along the Southern Boulevard commercial strip. Official crime rates fell a bit over 30 percent between 1990 and 1998 for the area's 50,000 residents. But neighborhood leaders point out that Hunt's Point experienced significant population growth in the 1990s, so safety has probably increased more than statistics indicate. After a population crash in the late 1970s, the area grew faster than any other in New York during the late 1980s, and fast growth continued in the 1990s.

REDUCING CRIME PAYS

All of these neighborhoods consist overwhelmingly of people with low-to-moderate incomes: Poverty rates range between 20 and 55 percent, and a majority of students at local schools qualify for free or reduced-price lunches. Alphabet City, Hyde Square, and the Armory District—all well-located neighborhoods endowed with good housing stock and parks—have begun to see a sizable influx of young professionals and families, but remain mostly low-income by local standards.

For people living at the bottom of the economic ladder, commercial opportunities are quite limited. For such individuals, the improvements in the consumer economy stimulated by reductions in crime tend to make an enormous difference. When crime drops, the prospects of stores large enough to attract customers who don't live within walking distance improve. But since many neighborhood stores sell liquor and thrive when people fear leaving the few blocks they know best, such businesses see fewer positive effects. Shopping strips, however, benefit from a longer shopping day, reductions in merchants' fears, increased competition, and an influx of new types of business.

Through the 1970s and 1980s, crime degraded inner-city shopping strips throughout the nation. A 1999 Initiative for a Competitive Inner City/*Inc. Magazine* study found that nearly half of inner-city entrepreneurs believed perceptions of crime kept business out of the inner city, while around a quarter cited crime itself as a major consideration. (These results are understated: Most of those surveyed provide business-to-business services or manufacture low-value industrial components and, thus, don't handle products susceptible to theft.) Academic, government, and business researchers have found that inner-city residents leave their neighborhoods for more than half of all purchases—a conclusion that affirmed reams of previous research. If crime falls, in other words, profit-seeking businesses will fill the void that exists in inner cities.

Consider what has happened in neighborhoods with fast-falling crime rates: Upham's Corner Main Street Inc. says the commercial vacancy rate has fallen from nearly 40 percent to 16 percent since 1995. (Main Street programs, which exist in nearly every Boston neighborhood, perform the same promotion and retention functions as business-improvement districts but get most of their revenue from the city government rather than a local tax assessment.) Just as important, short-term vacancies tend to fill more quickly.

Hunt's Point's Southern Boulevard-area shopping strip had a high vacancy rate (and several nearby vacant lots) during the early 1980s. Walking along the street, longtime resident and business owner Ray Colon stops frequently to point out a store that sat vacant for years as the neighborhood declined. Today, only a few storefronts lack tenants, and business leaders say they tend to rent quickly.

In the Hyde/Jackson Square commercial area—which covers a slightly larger area than Hyde Square proper—almost no vacancies exist, and a new supermarket and strip mall have greatly increased total commercial space. In Alphabet City, once desolate streetscapes have blossomed with boutiques and bistros, and the city has sold most of its (almost always abandoned) properties along Avenues A, B, C, and D to private developers. In Yucca Corridor, a strip mall that provided a hangout for homeless people and gang members has shut down to make way for a new community center. A new motel and a high-end boutique have opened up in recent years, and a large new drugstore opened in the spring of 2000.

Commercial streets have become safer and more pleasant in every neighborhood studied, and the business environment improves when falling crime rates extend the useful shopping day. As Mark Culliton, the director of the Upham's Corner Main Street, points out: "Certain kinds of businesses believed that they couldn't thrive along this strip where people would only shop in the daytime." Since 1994, the percentage of area residents who felt afraid to shop in the Upham's Corner area has declined by more than half. "If it had remained an open-air drug market, we simply couldn't have expanded," says Linda Heidinger, owner of a gift shop in Alphabet City. "In December when it's dark all the time, people aren't going to do Christmas shopping here when they can do it somewhere where they feel safer," she says.

Falling crime rates also mitigate entrepreneurs' fears. Nearly every merchant interviewed who operated through a period of high crime tells a story of being held up at gunpoint and feeling helpless against shoplifting. "[Getting held up] at gunpoint was a constant fear," says Hyde Square children's clothing store owner Tony Barros. "It was a fact of being a small businessman in this neighborhood." As James K. Stewart noted in *Policy Review,* the high cost of insurance and security systems can prevent businesses from ever opening in crime-ridden area.

At the same time, retail strips become more attractive to new categories of business when crime falls. "We had one drugstore but it wasn't enough; now that the area looks more attractive, we're bringing in a second one," says Culliton of Upham's Corner Main Street. New drugstores also opened in Hunt's Point and Yucca. In Upham's Corner, several new eateries have emerged. In Hyde Square, a new Stop & Shop provides competition for the *bodegas* that were once the only place to buy food.

Another effect of crime reduction is that law-abiding residents regain control of commercial sidewalks and other public places. Certain kinds of businesses, particularly liquor stores and bars, are often driven out, along with the criminal types they serve. "One of the liquor stores we bought out [to build a community center] was, simply put, a detriment," says Roxana Tynan, a community organizer in Los Angeles. In Buena-Clinton, a strip mall anchored by a crime-ridden bar fell to make room for a new factory producing beverage dispensers for recreational vehicles. With the exception of Alphabet City, where nightlife has produced a commercial renaissance, community leaders and investors all say that reducing the number of liquor stores, bars, and similar businesses plays a key role in cutting crime. And when crime declines, merchants become more amenable to efforts to make streets pleasant. "I would never have wanted it when we had all the crime," says Barros, motioning towards a small plaza with benches and a decorative sign.

With the improved atmosphere comes more competition—a boon for consumers, if not for individual businesses. For example, Barros, the Hyde Square clothier, says that his business remains below the $17,000-gross-sales-a-week level that he maintained when junkies taunted his customers. Of 23 retailers interviewed who worked through a period of high crime, not one said that falling crime rates played a key role in improving profits. On balance, however, falling crime rates serve to integrate inner-city shopping strips into the mainstream economy. Existing business owners do not always benefit, but the overall economy, residents, and shopping strips all thrive when crime goes down.

HOME IMPROVEMENT

Large reductions in crime also improve housing. Throughout the 1970s and 1980s, many buildings in the neighborhoods studied were destroyed. But reducing crime enables landlords to get returns high enough to stimulate increased investment in housing. In New York's Alphabet City and Hunt's Point, there has been several hundred million dollars in new housing construction and remodeling since the early 1980s. Investment in Hunt's Point by the two largest non-profits, Banana Kelly and SEBCO, created over $600 million in new or remodeled housing during the 1980s and 1990s, while Alphabet City saw the drug-addicted squatters immortalized in the musical *Rent* evicted from its buildings as profit-making developers entered in large numbers.

Boston's Four Corners currently has $22 million worth of new residential construction in progress, with another $30 million or so in advanced planning stages. Upham's Corner has benefited from over $120 million in total new investment during the 1990s, slightly more private sector than public sector. In Hyde Square, requests for rehab permits have more than doubled since 1990, and several sizeable new buildings have gone up. Armory Revival has poured nearly $10 million into Armory District construction and remodeling since it began operations. In Yucca, at least $5 million went toward refurbishment and redesign of dilapidated buildings. Units damaged during the 1994 Northridge earthquake were also quickly replaced. (Previous earthquake damage was repaired much more slowly. Legal action by tenants' groups forced some landlords to perform basic repairs, while efforts to clean up other buildings continue. Requests for rehab permits also increased greatly.

In Garden Grove, California, Buena-Clinton has seen over $20 million in investment since the early 1980s—about half of it private (most of the money was spent in the early to mid 1980s, so the improvements would cost far more today).

In 1983, all but three buildings in the area were substandard; today, almost none are. Stewart Drive, the smallest and newest neighborhood studied, benefited from $20 million in investment—almost all of it through tax-exempt bonds.

Developers point out that the relationship between housing improvement and crime reduction is quite complex. On one hand, working, law-abiding tenants won't move into neighborhoods where crime rates are horrific. On the other hand, the first stages of remodeling tend to bring in "pioneers" who brave high crime in return for freshly remodeled living spaces. Housing investment in the neighborhoods I visited began before the drop in crime, but without the improved environment the new investments could not have been sustained. Edward Kuo, through his company Golden Remco, remodeled apartments in Buena-Clinton before crime began to fall, but saw them trashed. "Banks found out that we knew how to handle money and they made us a sort of Community Reinvestment Act poster child," says Armory Revival general partner Le Baron Preston, "[but] if everything had gotten destroyed . . . eventually, the money would have dried up." Capoccia says that he can do more projects when crime goes down. "I would still want to invest if crime weren't down, but many of these large investments just wouldn't happen," he says. Kuo says that he might have give up if the police had not been able to reduce crime.

Although bad landlords do not disappear when crime goes down, their numbers decrease significantly because falling crime rates create hope for the future. Studies by numerous social scientists have established a link between housing values, the physical state of a neighborhood, and crime. When a landlord's property values drop significantly, burning a building to collect insurance often becomes one of the few ways to get a return on his investment. In addition, when crime drives rents low enough that a landlord's mortgage payments become greater than what he can collect in rent, overcrowding tends to increase. Filling a building to twice its legal capacity can yield enough revenue to pay a mortgage while still keeping rents low enough so that those who can't live elsewhere can afford them. Even landlords who are too ethical to violate the law will do only the legal minimum amount of upkeep if they feel that stable or even rising rents will not cover investment.

CIVIL SOCIETY'S REBIRTH

In neighborhoods around the country, community organizations provide more services when crime falls. Safer neighborhoods enable residents to spend more time participating in community activities and allow community activists to focus on issues other than crime. In addition, people with middle-class values find their position strengthened when crime rates fall.

Less crime means safer evening hours and, as a result, more time for activities ranging from summer camps to sewing classes. Representatives of community organizations in neighborhoods with significant declines in crime all said that they now offer more activities in the evenings. In Hunt's Point, the Casita Maria settlement house, which closed at 7:00 P.M. most nights before crime rates began to fall, now stays open until 1:00 A.M. on weeknights. "It used to be that we couldn't fill a lot of programs in the winter because people were just too scared," says Casita Maria director Martha Rivera. "Today, we have waiting lists for ESL classes, basketball leagues, sewing classes, whatever." Rivera estimates that enrollment in the center's programs has more than coubled since New York City's crime rate began its steep decline in 1992.

In Garden Grove, the Boys and Girls Club and landlord Golden Remco have begun to offer classes in Buena-Clinton (virtually no community programs existed before), while the landlord-sponsored "Uth Force" tutoring program has increased high-school graduation rates along Stewart Drive. "As best as we know, not a single Hispanic kid in the neighborhood graduated from high school until five years ago," says neighborhood leader and property owner Vincent Vander Burgh. The numbers tell the story of Uth Force's success. In 1996, two area students finished high school; five did in 1997 and eight in 1998; 14 finished in 1999, and about the same number graduated in 2000. When the program first started, however, even getting students into the homework center proved a considerable challenge: Nobody wanted to come out at night. Now, Golden Remco's homework help center in Buena-Clinton stays open late nearly every school night—something manager Betty Chu says would have been impossible 15 years ago. Likewise, Buena-Clinton has gained a roller-hockey rink on the site of an apartment building once ruled by drug lords.

In Yucca, an area that had almost no community organizations five years ago, citizens now offer an almost bewildering array of activities ranging from ESL classes to parenting seminars. "It was so much easier to organize when safety wasn't always the number one concern," explains Tynan the community organizer. A new park has appeared where drug houses once stood, and a temporary community center now provides a daily hub for activities ranging from youth soccer leagues in the area's new park to language classes. A permanent facility will open in 2001.

Reducing crime also gives neighborhood activists more time to pay attention to their community's social needs. In its days as the Four Corners Public Safety Action Project, the Greater Four Corners Action Coalition dealt only with crime. Now the Coalition does everything from providing summer programs for children to attracting developers. "If you're worrying about crime all the time then you can't really do much else," explains director Marvin Martin. Other community leaders echoed Martin's sentiments. "Once you've gotten crime down a little, you can move organizing efforts on to other topics—like city services, voter registration, parks, housing," says Jeanne DuBois, Executive Director of the Dorchester Bay Economic Development Corporation in Upham's Corner. In Dorchester, voter registration has boomed, while Reverend Eugene Rivers's organization has more than tripled the number of people it serves in Four Corners. Across town, the Hyde Square Task Force deals with about 150 youths a year through new summer camps and educational programs. When crime declines, government officials also have more time. "Five years ago, nearly all of our priorities would have had something to do with crime," says John Robert, the Community Board District Manager for the Hunt's Point area. "Now we can focus on parks."

Reducing crime also improves the credibility of the values of decency and hard work, and reduces the influence of what sociologist Elijah Anderson calls the "Code of the Street." As Anderson explains in his 1999 book by that name:

> Simply living in [a crime-ridden, downtrodden neighborhood] places young people at special risk of falling victim to aggressive behavior . . . street culture has evolved into a "code of the street" which amounts to informal rules governing interpersonal behavior, particularly violence.

As Anderson explains, even those who accept "decent" middle-class values need to know the Code of the Street in a neighborhood where violence represents a fact of daily life. In his book *Disorder and Decline,* Northwestern University's Wesley Skogan comes to much the same conclusion based on extensive research in Chicago and elsewhere: "Disorder," he writes, "fosters withdrawal, inhibits cooperation between neighbors and discourages people from making efforts to protect themselves and their community."

When crime declines, however, community leaders and, more importantly, ordinary residents, feel far more free to assert their values. "A lot of it was a matter of getting into a strong enough position," says Eugene Rivers, who spearheaded Boston's area-wide 10 Point Coalition of black churches. "It sometimes seemed like we were only making a little bit of progress but, eventually, the walls began to come down." Mark Van Noppen tells a similar story about Armory Revival's work. "At first, we would always have to put up with these street punks and almost had to go to war with them," he says. "After a while, things changed." Ordinary residents also feel better. "When you have lots of people trashing their homes and doing drugs, it's hard to think that you'll have any place to work from," says Providence's Anne Hill. "Once you reach a certain point, it's a lot easier to take good care of your neighborhood."

A CONSERVATIVE SOCIAL POLICY

At least since the 1960s, a great many social scientists have thought that alleviating poverty will alleviate crime. In the early twenty-first century, this thesis stands on shaky ground. Some social programs, particularly those that work with children and inculcate moral values, probably do help reduce crime. But the latest wave of evidence shows that the best way to restore communities and lessen poverty is to reduce crime itself, not the supposed "root causes" of crime. The best-conceived and best-funded programs, public or private, will do little good in a dangerous environment. Alternatively, when falling crime rates bring commercial strips back to life, improve housing, help residents feel safe at night, and strengthen a community's stabilizing moral forces, it becomes possible to integrate even the most troubled areas into the American mainstream. So far the evidence looks good, and it is fair to say that crime-reduction ranks with welfare reform as the greatest social policy triumph of the past decade.

2 8

✸

Putting Justice Back into Criminal Justice

Notes for a Liberal Criminal Justice Policy

SAMUEL WALKER
GEORGE F. COLE

The 1967 report of the President's Commission on Law Enforcement and Administration of Justice recommended crime policies that attacked the causes of crime, that rehabilitated offenders, and that upheld civil rights. Many of these ideas have been criticized by conservatives as not effectively dealing with crime control. Samuel Walker and George Cole argue that the policies of the past three decades have not reduced crime and that liberal policies are more likely to achieve justice.

INTRODUCTION

The principal thrust of criminal justice policy for the last thirty years has been the effort to enhance crime control: to arrest, prosecute, convict, and punish more offenders—or at least those who are guilty of serious crimes. There has been an increase in the number of actions that are criminalized; the War on Drugs serves as a prime example. That effort, which should be seen as a vast social experiment, has failed. We do not control crime any more effectively now than we did before, and have strained our correctional system well beyond its capacity. The time has come for a new direction in criminal justice policy. It is time to focus less on the tool of the law and reintroduce justice back into criminal justice.

Source: "Putting Justice Back into Criminal Justice: Notes for a Liberal Criminal Justice Policy," by Samuel Walker and George F. Cole, 2001.

The conservative domination of criminal justice policy is the result of several forces. Persistently high crime rates have produced deep public frustration about crime and about efficacy of the criminal justice system, and the perceived leniency of judges. Fear of crime, moreover, is inextricably bound up with issues of race—as evidenced by the Willie Horton issue in the 1988 presidential election. The 1990s gave us the debate over disparate punishments for powder versus crack cocaine, and in the twenty-first century we are still grappling with racial profiling and police brutality, as evidenced by the L.A. riots in the wake of Rodney King, and the Cincinnati riots in 2001. Evidence of the conservative mood on crime policy is everywhere. The philosophy of rehabilitation has been abandoned in favor of a new interest in punishment, retribution, incapacitation, and deterrence. But beyond punishing a broader range of crimes for a longer time, we are also turning to forms of punishment that are particularly liberty invasive— detaining people past their sentence if they are still designated as dangerous, or requiring compulsory medication for sex offenders if they are "potentially" violent. There has been particular interest in identifying and punishing the so-called career criminal or high-rate offender.[1] In its zeal to combat drugs, Congress and state legislatures have imposed long mandatory minimum sentences for drug offenders. The number of people incarcerated has skyrocketed 300 percent.[2] And, since the death penalty was reinstituted in 1977, more than seven hundred individuals have been executed and by 2001 more than thirty-seven hundred were on death rows.[3]

The Supreme Court has followed the popular mood as expressed in national elections. The present Court has a razor-thin conservative majority. Unlike the Warren court in the 1960s, the Court today is willing to side with the asserted claims of law-enforcement officials. It has sanctioned drunk driving checkpoints, a public safety exception to the *Miranda* warning, and a good faith exception to the exclusionary rule, has dramatically limited the use of habeas corpus as an avenue of relief for convicted offenders, has allowed the use of pretextual traffic stops by police officers, and has held schools liable for student-on-student harassment.

This, at any rate, is the conventional wisdom about national crime policy over the past thirty years. Upon closer inspection, however, the matter is a lot more complex. Change in the criminal justice system has not been completely dominated by a conservative agenda. There have been a number of very important changes that reflect the traditional liberal values of due process and equal protection. A surprising number of reforms have in fact achieved their stated goals.[4] These successes form the building blocks for a new direction in national criminal justice policy.

TWO DEADLY MYTHS ABOUT
CRIMINAL JUSTICE POLICY

Creating a liberal criminal justice policy has to begin by demolishing two prevalent myths about national crime policy.

The first is that liberal reforms don't work. While many reforms reflecting liberal social values did prove to be failures, others have succeeded and represent significant improvements in criminal justice policy. The second myth is that conservative "get-tough" crime-fighting policies do work. There is no evidence to support this belief. We can view the past twenty years as a vast social experiment in which conservative crime policies have been tried and found wanting.

THE FOUNDATIONS OF A LIBERAL CRIMINAL JUSTICE POLICY

A liberal criminal justice policy begins with a renewed commitment to the traditional liberal values of fairness and equality. These values are embodied in the constitutional principles of due process, equal protection of the law, and protection against cruel and unusual punishment. In many, but not always all, cases, liberal values are consistent with civil libertarian principles. The criminal justice system has two basic goals: to control crime and ensure justice. The time has come to put a renewed emphasis on justice for people who are the victims of discrimination at the hands of the system.

A renewed commitment to a national policy based on liberal values does not mean that every proposal cloaked in the garb of justice and fairness is a good idea. Good intentions alone do not make for good crime policy. Some of the well-intentioned reforms of the 1960s did fail. And we now see that the noble goals inherent in determinate sentencing have resulted in net-widening, particularly for those already disenfranchised. Nor does a commitment to liberal values mean that criminal behavior is excused. Wrongdoing should be punished. There is nothing inconsistent between liberal values and punishing those people found guilty of a serious crime. Liberal values, however, do require that use of the most serious penalties be carefully limited and tailored to the crime involved.

The second key element in a liberal criminal justice policy is a sober appreciation of the limits of the criminal justice system. We should not ask it to do things it cannot do. Criminal justice officials need to learn how to "just say no." When the public and elected officials ask it to do things that are beyond its power, responsible officials have a professional and social obligation to explain why they cannot. Already, for example, some police chiefs have been willing to publicly say that more arrests will not solve the nation's drug problem. The evidence on the limits of some of the more popular crime control programs is explored in detail later in this essay.[5]

The third element of a liberal approach to crime would be to direct public attention to the social problems that underly criminal behavior. This point flows inexorably from a recognition of the limits of the criminal process. The problems the criminal justice system is asked to handle (murder, robbery) are the end product of larger forces, which in turn are influenced by social policies related to employment, housing, race relations, transportation, social welfare, and so on.

The limits of the criminal justice system are best symbolized by the police officer called for the third time to a domestic disturbance. The people involved have a lot of problems: unemployment, alcohol abuse, psychological problems, and so on. The officer cannot solve those problems. At best, he or she can do a professional job of resolving the immediate dispute. Policies based on liberal values should attempt to enhance that professionalism. But the ultimate solution to this particular domestic incident lies elsewhere, outside the justice system.

The Myth of Liberal Failure

The conservative mood that began in the mid-1970s and reached its peak with the election of Ronald Reagan as president in 1980 was based in part on a reaction against liberal social programs of the 1960s. According to the conventional wisdom, those policies failed. With respect to criminal justice policy, that indictment is partly true. But it is also true that we know many liberal reforms in criminal justice were tempered in the compromises that are characteristic of the legislative process. Our large-scale omnibus crime bills of the 1990s illustrate how difficult it is to maintain the integrity or spirit of the research idea or philosophy. The task of policy analysis at the moment is to sort out the failures and the successes.

The proper point of reference for this analysis is the 1967 report of the president's crime commission, *The Challenge of Crime in a Free Society*.[6] The commission's recommendations had two broad thrusts. The first was that more money needed to be spent on criminal justice. The administration of justice would be substantially improved by hiring more police, raising their salaries, subsidizing their education, expanding their training, developing more sophisticated communications technology, expanding pretrial services for arrestees, creating more community-based treatment programs for convicted offenders, funding research, and so on. This approach was consistent with liberal social policy generally: investing in programs to deal with social problems (for example, the so-called War on Poverty). Furthermore, the commission recommended that the federal government undertake, for the first time, comprehensive assistance to state and local criminal justice agencies.

In many respects, this goal was achieved. Spending on criminal justice did increase substantially. The federal government did initiate a comprehensive program of financial assistance. Whether or not all this spending improved the administration of justice, however, is another question altogether. Much of the increase in spending has been a result of inflation and rising crime rates. It is not clear that the spending has improved either the crime control effectiveness of the system or the quality of justice.

The second general element of the crime commission's recommendations was a general belief in rehabilitation. This consisted of several different parts. The first was the optimistic belief that criminal offenders would be rehabilitated (or corrected, or treated, or resocialized) into productive law-abiding lives. The second element was the belief that this could be more effectively achieved in a community-based setting. There was a strong anti-institutional current in the commission's recommendations. Diversion was better than prosecution; probation was better than imprisonment; parole was better than long imprisonment.

It is the commitment to rehabilitation that has been the target of the strongest reaction over the past twenty years. The concept of rehabilitation fell into

disrepute and is, today, the object of much derision. The reaction against rehabilitation was summed up by Robert Martinson's survey of correctional treatment programs. Asking the basic question, "What works?" he found that few
programs could persuasively demonstrate their effectiveness.[7] Although he did
find that some programs were more effective than alternatives, the public translated his findings into the conclusion that "nothing works."

The idea that nothing works has, on occasion, been inflated into a general
indictment of criminal justice reform, particularly reforms reflecting liberal values. Some analysts argue that well-intentioned reforms backfire and aggravate
the problem they set out to correct.[8] Other analysts argue that reforms are simply negated by the informal resistance of criminal justice officials.[9]

The most extreme versions of the nothing-works argument arise from the
literature on correctional programs. Martinson's report seemed to indict all rehabilitation programs. One widely cited example of failure is the so-called "net-
widening" phenomenon. Some evaluations indicated that programs designed to
divert offenders from the criminal justice system actually brought more people
under some form of official control.

With respect to the issue of rehabilitation, the critics have a good point. Few
correctional treatment programs have persuasively demonstrated that a convicted
offender is less likely to recidivate because he or she received a particular kind of
"treatment" as opposed to a conventional form of punishment or treatment.
Thus, the prisoner who participated in group therapy sessions is no less likely to
recidivate than the offender who did his time in prison and was released at the
same time; intensive parole supervision is no more successful than normal supervision. The list could be extended.

The Hidden Successes of Criminal Justice Reform

Not all of the crime commission's recommendations failed, however. A number
of them have had considerable vitality and are responsible for significant improvements in the administration of justice. Nearly all are consistent with liberal
values. The most important of these goals are (1) the control of discretion,
(2) the reduction of official misconduct, and (3) equal employment opportunity.
In addition, there is a new goal, (4) community renewal, which is an indirect result of the crime commission's work.

Controlling Discretion

Perhaps the most important recommendation made by the crime commission was
one that did not receive much attention at the time: the control of discretion by
criminal justice officials. In fact, it is largely hidden in the commission's report,
buried among innumerable other recommendations. It was most explicit with respect to the police, where the commission recommended that "police departments should develop and enunciate policies that give police personnel specific
guidance for the common situations requiring exercise of police discretion."[10] It
also recommended that departments develop "a comprehensive regulation" on

officer use of firearms.[11] With respect to plea bargaining, the commission recommended the "establishment of explicit policies for the dismissal or informal disposition" of cases,[12] along with a written record for guilty pleas (pp. 337–338). Correctional agencies, meanwhile, were advised to adopt "explicit standards and administrative procedures" for decisions affecting prisoners.[13]

The commission's recommendations were part of a broader recognition of the phenomenon of discretion. The pioneering field research by the American Bar Foundation has identified discretion as one of the key elements of a new paradigm of the administration of justice. This paradigm was embodied in the now-famous flowchart of the criminal justice system. It not only provided a graphic representation of the "system" but also focused attention on the many decision points in the system.

In the intervening years, the control of discretion has become one of the central issues in criminal justice policy. Every decision point in the system has been subject to new controls. The police department SOP (Standard Operating Procedure) manual has become a large document and the principal instrument of contemporary police management. Bail decisions have been subject to controls by several different types of bail reform. Prosecutors' decisions to charge and to accept guilty pleas have been subject to both legislative and administrative controls. Sentencing, through mandatory provisions and sentencing guidelines have been instituted to limit discretion. Prisoners' rights litigation produced an intricate network of controls over correctional decisions, particularly disciplinary actions against inmates.

There are several notable examples of positive gains resulting from new controls over discretion. Restrictive deadly force policies have reduced the number of citizens shot and killed by the police. This has been accomplished without endangering police officers or contributing to an increase in the crime rate. Even more important, Lawrence W. Sherman's and Ellen G. Cohn's data indicates that the limits on shootings have reduced the racial disparity in persons shot and killed, from about 6:1 to 3:1.[14] Given the urgent nature of the race issue in American society, this reduction in police shootings is extremely important.

There are also new police department policies attempting to control officer discretion with respect to domestic violence and high-speed pursuits. It is still too early, however, to say whether these policies have had a significant effect on routine police practices.

Other attempts at discretion control have also produced some modest gains. The bail reform movement of the 1960s, which sought to guide bail-setting decision of judges, did reduce the number of pretrial detainees in many cities, thereby reducing discrimination against defendants because of their economic status. Some analysts, however, suggest that this reduction might have occurred even without the benefit of "reform." There is also some evidence that administrative controls over plea negotiations, in the form of written standards about dismissals and charge reductions, have resulted in greater consistency in case disposition.

The results of attempting to control judicial sentencing discretion through sentencing guidelines are even more dramatic. The greatest success appears to have occurred in Minnesota, where formal guidelines have significantly limited the use of imprisonment and have reduced, although not eliminated, racial and economic disparities in sentencing.[15] Minnesota has the lowest imprisonment rate in the entire country. Moreover, it maintained a very low rate through the 1980s and 1990s while other states were drastically increasing their prison populations. As will be discussed below, limiting the use of imprisonment yields additional benefits in terms of maintaining humane conditions within prisons.

These successes represent building blocks for a more comprehensive effort to control discretion. One of the principal items on the agenda of a liberal criminal justice policy should be to continue the effort to control discretion for the purpose of reducing and eliminating racial and economic injustice. Formal controls over discretionary decision making should be extended to those decision points that remain free of controls. The most important of all is the arrest decision. Apart from the new policies on domestic violence, the decision of the police officer to take a suspect into custody is unregulated. A second extremely important area involves the complex relationship between the various decisions that constitute plea bargaining and sentencing.

Reducing Official Misconduct

A second major goal should be the elimination or reduction of official misconduct. The control of discretion is one means of achieving this goal, although there are several other means as well.

In the 1960s the most important attacks on official misconduct came through Supreme Court decisions. The exclusionary rule (*Mapp v. Ohio*) was essentially an attempt to eliminate illegal searches and seizures. The *Miranda* warning was an attempt to eliminate or reduce coercive interrogations. The *Gault* decision imposed some minimal standards of due process in juvenile court proceedings. The many prisoners' rights decisions have reduced some of the more barbaric practices in prisons.

One of the most important corollary effects of these Supreme Court decisions was a transformation of the working environment of policing. A study of narcotics detectives in Chicago found that court decisions had forced significant improvements in training and supervision. At the same time, a new generation of officers had come to accept the principles underlying court decisions protecting individual rights. Many stated that formal, externally imposed limits on police powers were a necessary means of controlling police conduct.[16]

Another important area of police misconduct involves the unjustified use of physical force and abusive language directed at citizens. The crime commission recommended that police departments create a formal process for handling citizen complaints. As a part of that, it also recommended that every department have a separate internal-affairs unit. To a large extent these recommendations have been fulfilled. Formal complaint procedures are now standard items in virtually all big-city departments. Despite this progress, the problem of police misconduct continues—as the killing of Amadou Diallo by New York City officers, the indictment of forth-three officers in Cleveland for cocaine dealing, and corruption of Los Angeles officers assigned to the Ramparts area clearly indicate.

However, the number of fatal shootings is down since the 1970s, and grotesque incidents of physical brutality are rather than common events. Most observers believe that with the exception of certain departments, police behavior has in fact improved in most cities and counties over the past thirty years.[17]

Public attention has now focused on the effectiveness of police disciplinary procedures. The belief that they are inadequate has led to the creation of some form of civilian oversight procedures in about 80 percent of the police departments in the fifty largest cities.[18]

One of the most important consequences of the Rodney King incident in Los Angeles has been the new focus on the phenomenon of the "problem-prone" officer. Investigations in Los Angeles, Kansas City, Boston, Houston, and elsewhere have consistently found that a small percentage of officers are involved in a disproportionate number of citizen complaints.[19]

The U.S. Civil Rights Commission identified this problem in 1981 and recommended that police departments create "early-warning systems" to identify these officers and take appropriate remedial steps.[20] Apparently, no department followed this recommendation. In the wake of the Rodney King incident, however, several police departments have begun to address the problem. A liberal criminal justice program would emphasize the reduction of police misconduct through the development of "early-warning" procedures in all police departments.

A major part of a liberal criminal justice program would be to continue the movement to instill respect for legal principles in criminal justice agencies and to encourage the growth of self-regulation. One form of self-regulation is accreditation. Litigation against police misconduct led to the creation of the Commission on Accreditation for Law Enforcement Agencies, which by 1998 accredited more than 460 agencies. Administrative rule making—controls over deadly force, handling of domestic violence, and high-speed pursuits—may be the most promising avenue for controlling police behavior in the immediate future.

Another significant area of official misconduct involves the abuse of prison inmates: physical brutality, prolonged sentences to solitary confinement, absence of due process in disciplinary procedures, and the violation of other individual rights such as access to reading material, visits, mail, and so forth. The crime commission called for "explicit standards and administrative procedures" regarding decisions affecting prisoners, but it did not give the matter a great deal of attention.[21] The commission's report was published before the modern prisoners' rights movement began. Since then, litigation based on constitutional principles has created a vast body of prisoners' rights, including physical facilities, services and programs, and the rights and privileges of inmates.

This litigation has had a far-reaching impact on American prisons. Many of the grossest abuses have been eliminated. Formal disciplinary procedures have been established. Also, litigation stimulated the correctional accreditation movement, which has resulted in the development of minimum standards for institutions. As is the case with the police, these developments represent a step in the direction of self-regulation and a transformation of the working environment of institutions. This is an important and overdue development that a liberal criminal justice program would continue to foster.

Many of the gains of the prisoners' rights movement began to be eroded in the 1980s, however. The dramatic increase in prison populations resulted in severe overcrowding, which, in turn, aggravated tensions among inmates, overloaded prison programs, and made routine supervision and discipline far more difficult.

The key to maintaining humane conditions in prisons—and in the process reducing both misconduct by officials and violence by inmates—is to limit the use of imprisonment. The state of Minnesota has shown that this can be done. The use of sentencing guidelines to control judicial discretion is a viable technique for limiting imprisonment. By limiting prison populations, states will be able to maintain humane conditions inside prisons within the constraints of limited state budgets.

Providing Equal Employment Opportunity

The crime commission also recommended the hiring of more racial minorities and women in policing. The commission produced devastating data on the underrepresentation of African-Americans (then referred to as Negroes) in big-city police departments. They represented 38 percent of the population of Atlanta but only 9.3 percent of the police force; 23 percent of the population of Oakland but only 2.3 percent of the police; 29 percent of the population of Detroit but only 3.9 percent of the police force.[22] Significantly, the employment of Hispanic Americans was not even mentioned.

In the intervening thirty-five years, there has been considerable progress in minority employment. Nationally, the percentage of African Americans as sworn officers has increased from 6.5 percent in 1973 to about 12 percent in 1997. Hispanics represented about 7 percent of all sworn officers in municipal departments in 1997.[23] In some departments African-American and Hispanic officers are now the majority. Several departments approach the theoretical ideal where the percentage of minority officers on the force equals the presence of minorities in the community.

Increased racial-minority employment has furthered several important goals. Most important, it represents a commitment to the principle of equality. In the process it has created real employment opportunities for thousands of people of color. It also has some positive impact on police–community relations. A more diverse police force does not appear to be an all-white occupying army. Diversity also alters the police subculture such that, today, national organizations representing African-American officers offer a different point of view on such issues as civilian review and police brutality. Together with the growing number of female officers, minority officers have shattered the once-homogeneous police subculture.

At the same time, however, increased minority employment has not fulfilled all the objectives of reformers. The impact on police–community relations is indirect at best. Studies of police behavior have found no significant differences between white and black officers. Thus, minority employment does not automatically translate into improved police work.

With respect to women in policing, there has been a revolution in social policy since the mid-1960s. At that time, women represented an estimated

1 percent of all sworn officers and were relegated to second–class status in police work: excluded from patrol work and restricted to juvenile, clerical, or other
peripheral tasks. In some departments they were barred from promotion to the
highest ranks as a matter of official policy. The *Task Force Report* (but not the
main report) delicately raised the question of recruiting more women officers
and assigning them to patrol duty.[24]

Following the crime commission's recommendation, the Police Foundation
conducted an experiment on women on patrol in 1973. This was followed by
similar experiments. Evaluations of these experiments reached consistent conclusions: despite minor differences, women officers performed just as well as
male officers in routine patrol duty. The formal barriers to female recruitment
quickly fell, in large part because of federal civil rights laws. The presence of
women in policing increased to about 10 percent of all sworn officers by 1996.
Informal barriers to employment, however, have remained.[25]

As has been the case with racial–minority employment, the addition of female officers has enhanced the principle of equality, provided real job opportunities for many women, and diversified the police subculture. At the same time,
the addition of female officers has not fulfilled all reform expectations. The performance of female officers is essentially the same as male officers; thus, they are
not fundamentally better able to mediate disputes. This notion rested on an in-
verse sexist stereotype of women as more verbal and nurturing than men.

There has also been progress in terms of the employment of women in other
parts of the criminal justice system. The enrollment of women in law schools has
increased substantially, and more women are securing jobs as prosecutors and defense attorneys, as well as election and appointment as judges. Women are also
being employed as correctional officers in male institutions.

The increase in racial–minority and female employment in criminal justice
represents a good beginning. But it is only a beginning. In every occupation category, both groups remain underrepresented. Even more ominous has been the
hostility of the Supreme Court to affirmative action. The studies of employment
in policing all conclude that affirmative action plans have been critical to increased racial–minority and female employment. Recent court decisions threaten
to remove this remedy and undermine progress to date. A liberal criminal justice program would reaffirm the commitment to equal employment opportunity
in all aspects of the criminal justice system.

Stimulating Community Renewal

Another important goal of a liberal criminal justice program is community renewal. Specifically, this refers to programs that criminal justice agencies might
undertake to help communities resist the downward spiral of deterioration. This
goal rests on the recognition that the criminal justice system cannot, by itself,
control crime. It is a last–resort mechanism that comes into play only when all
other instruments of social control have failed.

Some of the most creative thinking in policing over the past decade argues
that the police might play a vital role in community renewal. This idea has been

given the label "community policing." The essence of community policing is that the police should de-emphasize traditional crime fighting in favor of attention to long-range problem solving and attention to small signs of disorder in the community.

Community policing is an indirect result of the crime commission's work. First, the commission's *Task Force Report: The Police* was the first full statement of the idea that the police have a diverse and complex role, with only a small part of their work being devoted to crime fighting.[26] This point was reinforced by the field studies of policing sponsored by the commission.[27] Subsequent studies found that increased patrol presence did not reduce crime[28] and that faster response time did not result in more arrests. All of this research demolished the "crime fighter" image of the police role.

Drawing upon this accumulated research, first Herman Goldstein and then James Q. Wilson and George Kelling sketched out new models of policing. Wilson and Kelling argued that the capacity of the police to control crimes was very limited and that, instead, they should concentrate on the less serious problems of disorder (which they identified by the metaphor of "broken windows").[29] This was designed to accomplish two things. First, it would enhance feelings of community safety. Second, it would help to arrest the process of community deterioration at an early stage and, thus, help prevent neighborhoods from sinking into serious crime. Wilson and Kelling's "Broken Windows" article was enormously influential and, more than anything else, launched the community policing movement.

Herman Goldstein, meanwhile, had already developed the concept of "problem-oriented policing."[30] He argued that the police should disaggregate the different aspects of their role and develop strategies to address particular ones. Problem-oriented policing is really a planning process. It does not tell the police what to do; it tells them only how to approach their mission in a different fashion. Community policing, at least as defined by Wilson and Kelling, did have a specific content. By de-emphasizing crime fighting, however, both approaches involved a very different conception of the police role.

In *Fixing Broken Windows,* a book written in response to the Wilson and Kelling article, George L. Kelling and Catherine Coles call for strategies to restore order and reduce crime in public spaces.[31] They point to many American cities where the police are paying greater attention to "quality-of-life crimes"—by arresting subway fare-beaters, rousting loiterers and panhandlers from parks, and aggressively dealing with those obstructing sidewalks, harassing, and soliciting. By handling these "little crimes," they argue that the police not only reduce disorder and fear but their actions help to stem deterioration of the community.

By the 1990s, community policing and problem-oriented policing had, together, become a national movement. Many, if not most, police departments claimed to be engaged in one or the other. Community policing received a major boost with the 1994 Violent Crime Control Act, which provided $8 billion to hire 100,000 additional police officers. The program is administered by the Office of Community Oriented Police Services (COPS), which requires that departments develop a community policing plan in order to receive the federal funds for additional officers.[32]

The jury is still out on community policing. There is the danger that it will be destroyed by its own early success. It has quickly become a fad, in some cases nothing more than a rhetorical phrase with no content. As was the case with team policing thirty years ago, many departments are jumping on the bandwagon with no planning. In some instances, community policing has become a trendy label for putting more police on the streets in response to community fears about crime. Even under the best of circumstances—assuming careful planning, training, and supervision—there are serious limits to what community policing could accomplish in the way of community renewal. The key word here is *renewal*. Taking Wilson and Kelling at their word, the police might be able to help communities resist the downward spiral of deterioration. That, however, assumes the existence of a viable community. Yet in the most crime-ridden neighborhoods today, no such community exists. One of the main characteristics of economically devastated neighborhoods is the absence of the institutions and informal networks that make up a "community." Indeed, one could argue that drug gangs thrive because they fill that void, providing identity, protection, work, and income. In this respect, community policing has been oversold.

Nonetheless, community policing represents a bold concept of the police role. It recognizes that the police cannot, by themselves, control crime, but that they might be able to help communities renew themselves and resist the forces that lead to high levels of crime.

The blunt fact is that the police cannot create a community where one does not exist. No amount of creative community policing can hope to overcome the devastating effect of massive unemployment and declining job opportunities—the conditions that affect today's inner cities. The real solution to the crime problem lies outside the realm of criminal justice policy: in the realm of economic policy and job creation. This conclusion is not based on liberal sentimentality about the "roots" of crime; it reflects a sober assessment of what the criminal justice system can and cannot do.

THE FAILURE OF TOUGH CRIME CONTROL

For the past thirty years, national criminal justice policy has been dominated by a conservative "get tough with crime" approach. This represents a far longer period than the heyday of 1960s liberalism. We can now look back and evaluate it as we would any other social experiment.

Contrary to public opinion and the claims of politicians, rates for many crimes have dropped since the early 1980s. The National Crime Victimization Surveys have shown that the greatest declines are in property crimes, but crimes of violence have also dropped, especially since 1993.[33] These declines, however, can be attributed largely to demographic changes, particularly the aging of the baby boom generation, fewer users of crack cocaine, and the positive economic climate of the 1990s. There is little evidence that the "tough on crime policies" of the past quarter century have had much impact on the crime problem.[34]

What is evident is that the conservative experiment has been costly. Operating the criminal justice system costs taxpayers more than $100 billion a year. A major portion of these resources could be diverted to the underlying causes of criminal behavior—poor housing, unemployment, and racial injustice. Another price of the tough crime control policies has been an erosion of civil rights and liberties—especially for racial and ethnic minorities. Tough incarceration policies have devastated poor communities. With large numbers of young males in prison, families live in poverty, and children grow up without guidance from their fathers and older brothers.

It is now the conventional wisdom, even among conservatives, that traditional police crime control efforts will not reduce crime. Adding more patrol officers, increasing response time, and adding more detectives will not produce either fewer crimes or more arrests. The evidence is also overwhelming on the long-standing controversy over the exclusionary rule. Studies have convincingly found that the rule affects a tiny percentage of criminal cases at best.

With respect to bail, the federal government and many states have adopted some form of preventive detention that is designed to allow judges to deny bail to allegedly dangerous offenders. The Supreme Court upheld the federal law in 1987. The impact of preventive detention on crime has been negligible. Prior studies indicated that serious crime by persons on pretrial release was confined to a small percentage of defendants and that it was impossible to identify exactly which ones they were. Evaluations of the federal preventive detention law have found little change in the total percentage of defendants being held before trial. Judges have always practiced a covert form of preventive detention. The new procedures have yielded no gain.[35]

With respect to the disposition of criminal cases, studies have persuasively demonstrated that plea bargaining is not a loophole by which dangerous people beat the system. Persons who have committed a serious crime against a stranger, who have a prior criminal record, and against whom there is solid evidence are charged with the top offense, convicted of that offense, and sentenced to prison. "Career criminal" prosecution programs have produced no net gain in the imprisonment of dangerous criminals because those people were being treated fairly harshly under normal conditions.[36]

With respect to sentencing, there has been an enormous increase in imprisonment. The prison population more than tripled between 1980 and 2000. With more than two million behind bars, the size of the United States prison population is second only to that of Russia. This growth has largely resulted from changes to sentencing statutes that emphasize retribution and incapacitation through policies or mandatory minimums, "three strikes," "truth in sentencing," and restrictions on parole release. Community corrections, initially conceptualized as an alternative to incarceration, are now being used to extend sentences. Split sentences are not replacing lengthy sentences, they are being used in addition to them.

Trends with respect to drug offenses dramatize the failure of the conservative experiment even further. In every state and the federal system, the most dramatic change has been the increase in the number of incarcerated drug offenders. Yet there is no evidence that this has curbed the drug problem through either incapacitation or deterrence. Indeed Governor Johnson (New Mexico), a Republican, has brought the decriminalization of drugs to the table at the National Governor's meetings, where he is promoting both a fiscal examination of the failure of our drug strategy, and a public health cost analysis reacting to the violence that this war escalates. In fact, the problem of drug gangs and gang-related violence worsened in the early 1990s—after more than fifteen years of increasing use of imprisonment. The much-publicized idea of selective incapacitation had no effect on policy, in large part because normal prosecution and sentencing were already highly selective.

Nor has the revival of the death penalty had any discernible effect on crime. The sudden upsurge in murders in the early 1990s, almost all of them related to inner-city drug gang activity, occurred after a yearly average of more than twenty people were executed in the mid-1980s. Only at the end of the century were a few politicians, such as Governor George Ryan of Illinois, willing to raise questions about the possibility that innocent people have been executed.

In short, the conservative criminal justice program of "getting tough" with crime has failed in all of its manifestations.

CONCLUSION

A sound criminal justice policy begins with a sober respect for the limits of what can be accomplished through the criminal justice system.

The first principle is that criminal justice agencies—police, courts, prisons—cannot make significant changes in the level of criminal behavior. This is where much of the liberal thinking of the 1960s went wrong. It assumed that the right kind of programs—diversion of minor offenders, community-based treatment programs, and the like—would affect the lives of offenders: resocializing them into law-abiding lives. There is no reason to believe that today. By the same token, it should be noted that many of the popular conservative crime control programs of the past thirty years assume an ability to change people's behavior. To cite one example: the concept of deterrence assumes that by raising the cost of crime, potential offenders will choose not to offend. Altering criminal justice programs, in short, has little effect on criminal behavior.

The crime commission also assumed that pouring more money into the justice system—for more personnel, better equipment, better training, more research—would enhance the crime control capacity of the system. There is no support for that assumption either.

This is not to say that many of the crime commission's proposals were entirely wrong. More money, resources, and research may not reduce crime but it can help to improve the *quality* of justice. And that is an important goal. By the same token, community-based programs for convicted offenders may not rehabilitate them, but they may well be cheaper and more humane forms of punishment.

If our capacity to affect the behavior of criminals and potential criminals is very limited, we can control the behavior of criminal justice officials. The evidence indicates that we can control their discretion, we can reduce misconduct, and we can eliminate employment discrimination. These goals, which reflect the liberal values of fairness and equality, are the proper goals of a national criminal justice policy.

NOTES

1. Alfred Blumstein et al., *Criminal Careers and "Career Criminals"* (Washington, D.C.: National Academy Press, 1986).

2. U.S. Department of Justice, Bureau of Justice Statistics, *Bulletin* (August, 2000).

3. NAACP Legal Defense and Educational Fund, *Death Row USA* (Winter, 2001).

4. A full discussion of these developments is in Samuel Walker, *Taming the System: The Control of Discretion in Criminal Justice, 1950–1990* (New York: Oxford University Press, 1993).

5. The limits of the "get-tough" approach are examined in Samuel Walker, *Sense and Nonsense about Crime and Drugs: A Policy Guide,* 5th ed. (Belmont, Calif.: Wadsworth, 2001).

6. U.S. President's Commission on Law Enforcement and Administration of Justice, *The Challenge of Crime in a Free Society* (Washington, D.C.: Government Printing Office, 1967).

7. Robert Martinson, "What Works? Questions and Answers about Prison Reform," *Public Interest* 35 (Spring, 1974): 22–54.

8. Eugene Doleschal, "The Dangers of Criminal Justice Reform," *Criminal Justice Abstracts* 14 (March, 1982): 133–152.

9. Malcolm Feeley, *Court Reform on Trial* (New York: Basic Books, 1983).

10. President's Commission, *The Challenge of Crime,* p. 104.

11. Ibid., p. 119.

12. Ibid., p. 134.

13. Ibid., pp. 181–182.

14. Lawrence W. Sherman and Ellen G. Cohn, *Citizens Killed by Big City Police, 1970–1984* (Washington, D.C.: Crime Control Institute, 1986).

15. Terance D. Miethe and Charles A. Moore, "Socioeconomic Disparities under Determinate Sentencing Systems: A Comparison of Preguideline and Post-guideline Practices in Minnesota," *Criminology* 23 (May, 1985): 337–363. Minnesota Sentencing Guidelines Commission, *Guidelines and Commentary,* rev. ed. (St. Paul: August, 1981).

16. "The Exclusionary Rule and Deterrence: An Empirical Study of Chicago Narcotics Officers," *University of Chicago Law Review* 54 (1987): 1016–1069.

17. Samuel Walker, *Police Accountability: The Role of Citizen Oversight* (Belmont, Calif.: Wadsworth, 2001), p.45.

18. Ibid., p. 40.

19. Ibid., p. 110.

20. Samuel Walker, *The Police in America,* 3d ed. (New York: McGraw-Hill, 1999), p. 285.

21. President's Commission, *The Challenge of Crime,* pp. 181–182.

22. President's Commission, *Task Force Report: The Police* (Washington, D.C.: Government Printing Office, 1967), p. 168.

23. U.S. Department of Justice, Bureau of Justice Statistics, *Executive Summary: Local Police Departments, 1997* (October, 1999).

24. President's Commission, *Task Force Report: The Police,* p. 125.

25. U.S. Department of Justice, Bureau of Justice Statistics, *Fiscal Year 1996: At a Glance* (Washington, D.C.: Government Printing Office, 1996), p. 25.

26. President's Commission, *Task Force Report: The Police.*

27. Albert Reiss, *The Police and the Public* (New Haven, Conn.: Yale University Press, 1971).

28. George Kelling et al., *The Kansas City Preventive Patrol Experiment* (Washington, D.C.: The Police Foundation, 1974).

29, James Q. Wilson and George L. Kelling, "Broken Windows: The Police and Neighborhood Safety," *Atlantic Monthly* 249 (March, 1982): 29–38.

30. Herman Goldstein, "Improving Policing: A Problem-Oriented Approach," *Crime and Delinquency* 25 (1979): 236–258; Herman Goldstein, *Problem-Oriented Policing* (New York: McGraw-Hill, 1990).

31. George L. Kelling and Catherine M. Coles, *Fixing Broken Windows: Restoring and Reducing Crime in our Communities* (New York: Free Press, 1996).

32. U.S. Office of Community Oriented Policing Services, *COPS Office Report* (Washington, D.C.: Government Printing Office, 1997).

33. U.S. Department of Justice, Bureau of Justice Statistics, *National Crime Victimization Survey* (August, 2000).

34. *The Crime Drop in America,* ed. Alfred Blumstein and Joel Wallman (New York: Cambridge University Press, 2000).

35. Lynn Zimmer, "Proactive Policing against Street-Level Drug Trafficking," *American Journal of Police* IX (1990, No. 1), 43–74.

36. Eleanor Chelimsky and Judith H. Dahmann, *National Evaluation of the Career Criminal Program: Final Report* (McLean, Va.: Mitre Corp., 1979).